Just what you nee NOW!

ThomsonNOW™ for Corey, Corey, and Callanan's *Issues and Ethics in the Helping Professions,* Seventh Edition with Personalized Learning Plan

A dynamic, online study system that helps students improve their understanding

Designed by students for students, ***ThomsonNOW for Corey, Corey, and Callanan's Issues and Ethics in the Helping Professions,*** **Seventh Edition featuring the Personalized Learning Plan** is an online suite of services and resources providing you with the choices and tools you need to become an effective counselor. ThomsonNOW is your source for results NOW!

Pre-Tests, Post-Tests, and Personalized Learning Plans that help you get more from your study time

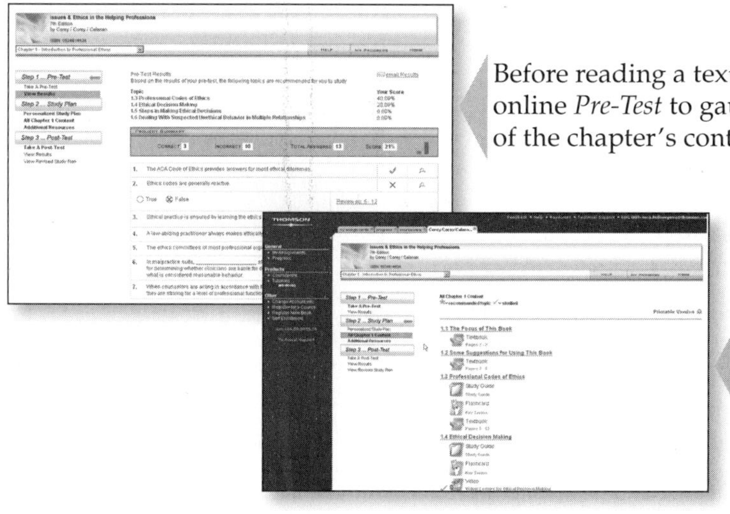

Before reading a text chapter, you can take an online *Pre-Test* to gauge your understanding of the chapter's contents.

ThomsonNOW then provides a *Personalized Learning Plan*—unique to you—based on the results of your automatically graded *Pre-Test.*

More exciting features of ThomsonNOW

Through text pages, web links, video clips, and more, this *Personalized Learning Plan* lets you focus your efforts on the content and concepts that are essential to your success in the course.

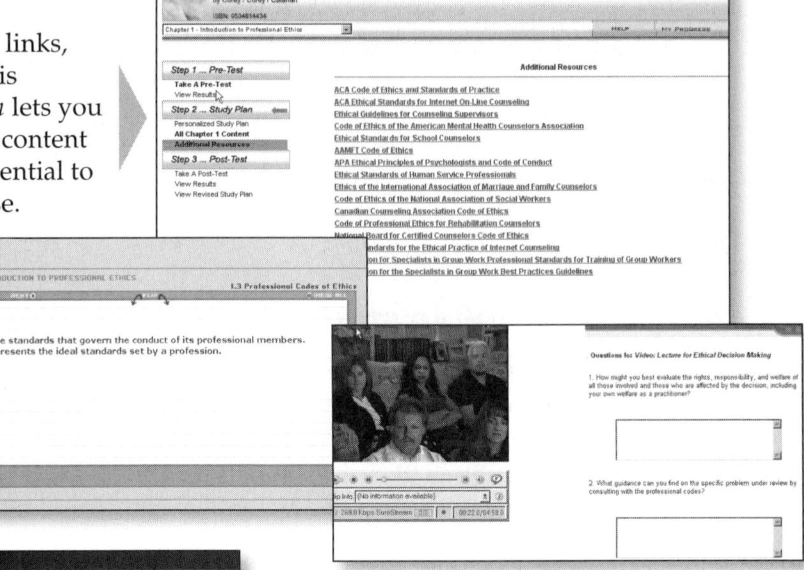

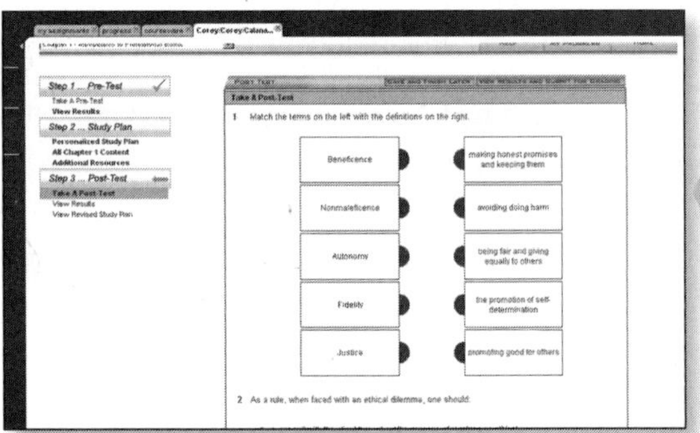

After working through the *Personalized Learning Plans*, you then complete a follow-up *Post-Test* to assess how well you've mastered the material.

Integrated video case study activities

Additional resources, including video clips, over seventy case studies, and interactive flash cards, provide further opportunities for exploration, discussion, and study. A key component of the *Personalized Learning Plan*, the engaging video clips feature the Coreys facilitating role-play scenarios that you can watch, respond to, and reflect on.

If an access card came with this book, you can start using many of these resources right away by following the directions on the card. If it did not, visit ***http://www.thomsonedu.com*** *to learn how you can gain access!*

SEVENTH EDITION

Issues and Ethics in the Helping Professions

Gerald Corey
California State University, Fullerton
Diplomate in Counseling Psychology,
American Board of Professional Psychology

Marianne Schneider Corey
Private Practice/Consulting

Patrick Callanan
Private Practice

Australia • Canada • Mexico • Singapore • Spain • United Kingdom • United States

Counseling Editor: *Marquita Flemming*
Assistant Editor: *Jennifer Walsh*
Editorial Assistant: *Christine Northup*
Technology Project Manager: *Inna Fedoseyeva*
Marketing Manager: *Caroline Concilla*
Marketing Assistant: *Rebecca Weisman*
Marketing Communications Manager: *Tami Strang*
Project Manager, Editorial Production: *Rita Jaramillo*
Creative Director: *Rob Hugel*
Art Director: *Vernon Boes*
Print Buyer: *Doreen Suruki*
Permissions Editor: *Stephanie Lee, Bob Kauser*
Production Service: *Ben Kolstad, International Typesetting and Composition*
Text Designer: *Cheryl Carrington*
Copy Editor: *Kay Mikel*
Cover Designer: *Cheryl Carrington*
Cover Printer: *Phoenix Color Corp-MD*
Compositor: *International Typesetting and Composition*
Printer: *Courier-Stoughton*

Printed in the United States of America

2 3 4 5 6 7 09 08 07 06

Library of Congress Control Number: 2005931722

ISBN-13: 978-0-534-61443-0
ISBN-10: 0-534-61443-4

Thomson Higher Education
10 Davis Drive
Belmont, CA 94002-3098
USA

For more information about our products, contact us at:
Thomson Learning Academic Resource Center
1-800-423-0563

For permission to use material from this text or product, submit a request online at
http://www.thomsonrights.com.

Any additional questions about permissions can be submitted by e-mail to
thomsonrights@thomson.com.

Dedicated to
the friends, colleagues, clients, and
students who helped us to see and appreciate the complexities
and subtleties of ethical thinking and practice

Gerald Corey is Professor Emeritus of Human Services at California State University at Fullerton. He received his doctorate in counseling from the University of Southern California. He is a Diplomate in Counseling Psychology, American Board of Professional Psychology; a licensed psychologist; a National Certified Counselor; a Fellow of the American Psychological Association (Counseling Psychology); a Fellow of the American Counseling Association; and a Fellow of the Association for Specialists in Group Work (ASGW). Jerry received the ASGW's Eminent Career Award in 2001 and the Outstanding Professor of the Year Award from California State University at Fullerton in 1991. He teaches both undergraduate and graduate courses in group counseling, as well as courses in experiential groups, the theory and practice of counseling, and professional ethics. He is the author or co-author of 15 textbooks in counseling currently in print, along with numerous journal articles. His book, *Theory and Practice of Counseling and Psychotherapy*, has been translated into Arabic, Indonesian, Portuguese, Korean, Chinese and Turkish. *Theory and Practice of Group Counseling* has been translated into Chinese, Korean, Spanish and Russian. *Issues and Ethics in the Helping Professions* has recently been translated into Chinese and Japanese.

Along with Marianne Schneider Corey, Jerry often presents workshops in group counseling. In the past 25 years the Coreys have conducted group counseling training workshops for mental health professionals at many universities in the United States as well as in Mexico, China, Germany, Belgium, Scotland, Canada, Korea, and Ireland. In his leisure time, Jerry likes to travel, hike and bicycle in the mountains, and drive his 1931 Model A Ford.

Recent publications by Jerry Corey, all with Thomson Brooks/Cole, include:

- *Becoming a Helper,* Fifth Edition (2007, with Marianne Schneider Corey)

About the Authors

- *Groups: Process and Practice,* Seventh Edition (2006, with Marianne Schneider Corey)
- *I Never Knew I Had a Choice*, Eighth Edition (2006, with Marianne Schneider Corey)
- *Theory and Practice of Counseling and Psychotherapy*, Seventh Edition (and *Manual*) (2005)
- *Case Approach to Counseling and Psychotherapy*, Sixth Edition (2005)
- *Theory and Practice of Group Counseling*, Sixth Edition, (and *Manual*) (2004)
- *Group Techniques*, Third Edition (2004, with Marianne Schneider Corey, Patrick Callanan, and J. Michael Russell)
- *Clinical Supervision in the Helping Professions: A Practical Guide* (2003, with Robert Haynes and Patrice Moulton).
- *The Art of Integrative Counseling* (2001)

Jerry is co-author, with his daughters Cindy Corey and Heidi Jo Corey, of an orientation-to-college book entitled *Living and Learning* (1997), published by Wadsworth. He is also co-author (with Barbara Herlihy) of *Boundary Issues in Counseling: Multiple Roles and Responsibilities,* Second Edition (2006) and *ACA Ethical Standards Casebook*, Sixth Edition (2006), both published by the American Counseling Association.

He has also made three CD-ROM and DVD programs on various aspects of counseling practice: (1) *CD-ROM for Integrative Counseling* (2005, with Robert Haynes); (2) *Groups in Action: Evolution and Challenges, DVD and Workbook* (2006, with Marianne Schneider Corey and Robert Haynes); and (3) *Ethics in Action* CD-ROM (2003, with Marianne Schneider Corey and Robert Haynes). All of these educational programs are available through Thomson Brooks/Cole.

Marianne Schneider Corey is a licensed marriage and family therapist in California and is a National Certified Counselor. She received her master's degree in marriage, family, and child counseling from Chapman College. She is a Fellow of the Association for Specialists in Group Work and was the recipient of this organization's Eminent Career Award in 2001. She also holds memberships in the American Counseling Association; the Association for Spiritual, Ethical, and Religious Values in Counseling; the Association for Counselor Education and Supervision (both national and regional); and the Association for Specialists in Group Work.

Marianne has been actively involved in leading groups for different populations, providing training and supervision workshops in group process, and co-facilitating training groups for group counselors and residential workshops in personal growth. She sees groups as the most effective format in which to work with clients and finds it the most rewarding for her personally. With her husband, Jerry, Marianne has conducted training workshops, continuing education seminars, and personal-growth groups in Germany, Ireland, Belgium, Mexico, China, and Korea, as well as regularly doing these workshops in the United States. In her free time, Marianne enjoys traveling, reading, visiting with friends, and hiking.

Marianne has co-authored several articles in group work, as well as the following books with Thomson Brooks/Cole:

- *Becoming a Helper*, Fifth Edition (2007, with Gerald Corey)
- *Groups: Process and Practice*, Seventh Edition (2006, with Gerald Corey)
- *I Never Knew I Had a Choice*, Eighth Edition (2006, with Gerald Corey)
- *Group Techniques* (2004, with Gerald Corey, Patrick Callanan, and Michael Russell)

Marianne has also made two educational CD-ROM and DVD/workbook programs: (1) *Groups in Action: Evolution and Challenges, DVD and Workbook* (2006, with Gerald Corey and Robert Haynes), and (2) *Ethics in Action* CD-ROM (2003, with Gerald Corey and Robert Haynes). Several of Marianne's co-authored books have been translated into other languages. *Becoming a Helper* has been translated into Korean and Japanese; *Group Techniques* has been translated into Portuguese, Korean, and Japanese; *Issues and Ethics in the Helping Professions* has been translated into Japanese and Chinese; *Groups: Process and Practice* has been translated into Polish, Chinese, and Korean; and *I Never Knew I Had a Choice* has been translated into Chinese.

Marianne and Jerry have been married since 1964. They have two adult daughters, Heidi and Cindy. Marianne grew up in Germany and has kept in close contact with her family there.

Patrick Callanan is a licensed marriage and family therapist in private practice in Santa Ana, California. In 1973 he graduated with a bachelor's degree in Human Services from California State University at Fullerton, and he received his master's degree in professional psychology from United States International University in 1976. He has had a private practice for more than 20 years, working with individuals, couples, families, and groups.

Patrick is on the part-time faculty of the Human Services Program at California State University at Fullerton, where he regularly teaches an internship course. He also offers his time each year to the university to assist in training and supervising group leaders and co-teaches a graduate course on ethical and professional issues in counseling. Along with Marianne Schneider Corey and Gerald Corey, he received an Award for Contributions to the Field of Professional Ethics by the Association for Spiritual, Ethical, and Religious Values in Counseling in 1986.

Patrick co-authored *Group Techniques,* Third Edition (2004), which as been translated into Portuguese, Korean, and Japanese. In his free time, Patrick enjoys reading, walking fast, and playing golf. Each year he returns for a stay in his home town in Ireland.

Contents

Preface

Issues and Ethics in the Helping Professions is written for both graduate and undergraduate students in the helping professions. This book is suitable for courses in counseling, human services, couples and family therapy, counseling and clinical psychology, and social work. It can be used as a core textbook in courses such as practicum, fieldwork, internship, and ethical and professional issues or as a supplementary text in courses dealing with skills or theory. Because the issues we discuss are likely to be encountered throughout one's professional career, we have tried to use language and concepts that will be meaningful both to students doing their fieldwork and to professionals interested in keep abreast of developments in ethical, professional, and legal matters pertaining to therapeutic practice.

In this book, we want to involve you, our readers, in learning to deal with the ethical and professional issues that most affect the actual practice of counseling and related helping professions. We ask the following questions of helping professionals: How do your values and life experiences affect the therapeutic process? What are the rights and responsibilities of both the client and the counselor? How can you determine your level of competence? How can you provide quality services for culturally diverse populations? What major ethical issues might you encounter in couples and family therapy? in group work? in community agencies? in private practice? Our goal is both to provide a body of information and to teach you a process of thinking about and resolving the basic issues you will face throughout your career. For most of the issues we raise, we present various viewpoints to stimulate discussion and reflection. We also present our views and personal commentaries, when appropriate, and challenge you to formulate your own position.

The ethics codes of various professional organizations offer some guidance for practice. However, these guidelines leave many questions unanswered. We believe that as a student or a professional you will ultimately struggle with the issues of responsible practice, deciding how accepted ethical principles apply in the specific cases you encounter.

We have tried to make this book a personal one that will involve you in an active and meaningful way. To this end we provide many opportunities for you to respond to our discussions. Each chapter begins with a self-inventory designed to help you focus on the key topics to be discussed in the chapter. Within the chapters we frequently ask you to think about how the issues apply to you. Open-ended cases and situations are presented to stimulate thought and discussion. We also cite related literature when exploring ethical, legal, and professional issues. This book combines the advantages of both the textbook and a workbook. Instructors will find an abundance of material and suggested activities, surely more than can be covered in a single course.

An *Instructor's Resource Manual* is available that contains chapter outlines, suggestions for teaching an ethics course, test items, additional exercises and activities, InfoTrac® College Edition online resources, a list of transparency masters, and study guide questions. An electronic version of the *Instructor's Resource Manual* is available for all platforms.

New to this edition is an online resource known as ThomsonNOW, which is available to students who are using *Issues and Ethics in the Helping Professions*. ThomsonNOW is a Web-based, intelligent study system that saves students time by providing a complete package of diagnostic quizzes, a personalized study plan, integrated multimedia elements, and learning modules. These include pre- and posttests, cases for discussion and analysis, glossary of key terms, video clips depicting key ethical issues, a study guide for each chapter, links to websites, and other supplementary features.

The codes of ethics of the various helping professions are discussed in Chapter 1, and they are available in a booklet titled *Codes of Ethics for the Helping Professions*, which can be packaged with the text for a nominal price.

An integrated learning package entitled *Ethics in Action* CD-ROM is available to enhance the seventh edition of *Issues and Ethics in the Helping Professions*. The *Ethics in Action* CD-ROM is designed to bring to life the ethical issues and dilemmas counselors often encounter and to provide ample opportunity for discussion, self-exploration, and problem solving of these issues and dilemmas. The vignettes on the CD-ROM are based on a weekend workshop co-led by Marianne Schneider Corey and Gerald Corey for a group of counseling students, which included challenging questions and lively discussion, role plays to bring the issues to life, and comments from the students and the Coreys. Additional material on the CD-ROM is designed to provide a self-study guide for students who are also reading this book. This educational program is divided into three segments: ethical decision making, values and the helping relationship, and boundary issues and multiple relationships in counseling. At the end of several chapters in this book are suggested activities and guidelines for integrating the CD-ROM with this textbook.

What's New in the Seventh Edition of *Issues and Ethics*

New to this edition, we have boldfaced key terms in the chapters and defined the terms in the text itself to help students study and review the material. We have also updated and expanded the InfoTrac® College Edition entries at the end of each chapter. For the seventh edition, each chapter has been carefully examined. Students may not realize how much has changed from edition to edition. The following chapter-by-chapter list of highlights outlines what has been added, updated, expanded, and revised for the seventh edition. We urge students to purchase this new edition rather than making do with an older edition. The most current research and thinking is reflected in this seventh edition.

Chapter 1 Introduction to Professional Ethics

- Updated material on the recently revised ethics codes of APA (2002) and ACA (2005)
- Sample standards added throughout the book from the Canadian Counselling Association, the Canadian Psychological Association, the Canadian Association of Social Workers, the American Psychiatric Association, the Feminist Therapy Institute, and the Commission on Rehabilitation Counselor Certification
- New material on the purpose of codes of ethics
- Inclusion of cultural consideration in the steps in ethical decision making
- New section on dealing with suspected unethical behavior of colleagues

Chapter 2 The Counselor as a Person and as a Professional

- Revised section on personal problems and conflicts of counselors
- New discussion of experiential learning aimed at self-understanding
- Updated discussion of the role of personal therapy in training programs
- Addition of a recent study to answer the question, "What is the value of psychotherapy when it is applied to the remediation of therapy trainees?"
- New material on the hazards of the helping professions
- Expanded discussion of self-care for professionals
- Expanded discussions of counselor impairment and maintaining vitality

Chapter 3 Values and the Helping Relationship

- Revised section on value conflicts regarding sexual attitudes
- An extensively revised section on value conflicts pertaining to abortion
- Expanded and updated section on the role of spirituality and religion in counseling
- Revised and updated section on end-of-life decisions

Chapter 4 Multicultural Perspectives and Diversity Issues

- New guidelines on multicultural education, training, research, practice, and organizational change for psychologists
- Revised section on ethics codes from a diversity perspective
- Revised and expanded section on issues pertaining to sexual orientation
- New material on matching client and counselor and on multicultural competence

Chapter 5 Client Rights and Counselor Responsibilities

- Revised section on informed consent
- Addition of a detailed sample informed consent document for therapy with children and adolescents
- Updated and expanded discussion of record keeping
- Revised section dealing with online counseling
- Updated and expanded treatment of risk management

Chapter 6 Confidentiality: Ethical and Legal Issues

- Recent codes of ethics on confidentiality and privileged communication
- New section on the implications of HIPAA for mental health providers
- New section on the school counselor's role in prevention of violence in schools
- Additional material on the duty to warn and protect
- New section on protecting children, the elderly, and dependent adults from harm

Chapter 7 Managing Boundaries and Multiple Relationships

- Revised section on multiple relationships in perspective
- New section on factors to consider before entering into a nonsexual dual relationship
- New section on managing multiple relationships in rural practice
- Updated discussion of bartering and receiving gifts
- Revised section on social relationships with clients
- Updated treatment of sexual relationships with both current clients and former clients

Chapter 8 Professional Competence and Training

- New discussion of psychological fitness in selecting counselor trainees
- Discussion of when a therapist is ready to practice independently
- New section on evaluating knowledge, skills, and personal functioning
- New section on the gatekeeper role of faculty in promoting competence
- New material on the responsibility of professional organizations in identifying standards for evaluating students
- New section on dismissing students for nonacademic reasons
- New section on court cases pertaining to dismissing students from a program

Chapter 9 Issues in Supervision and Consultation

- New material on the supervisee's bill of rights
- Recent research dealing with impaired supervisees
- New material on risk management practices for supervisors
- New section on issues in supervision for school counselors
- New section on spiritual issues in supervision

- Revised discussion of multiple relationships in supervision
- Revised section on ethical issues in consultation

Chapter 10 Issues in Theory, Practice, and Research

- Greatly revised and expanded section on assessment and diagnosis
- New section on theoretical orientations and perspectives on assessment and diagnosis
- New section on empirically supported treatments and evidence-based practice
- Addition of recent research on psychotherapy process and outcomes

Chapter 11 Ethical Issues in Couples and Family Therapy

- Addition of relevant standards from the International Association of Marriage and Family Counselors
- New information on why couples seek marital therapy
- Revised section on confidentiality in couples and family therapy

Chapter 12 Ethical Issues in Group Work

- Updated research on outcomes of group counseling
- Updated research on training and supervision of group leaders
- New material on group supervision with group counselors
- Revised and expanded section on diversity issues in training group leaders
- Updated discussion of confidentiality and online group work

Chapter 13 Ethical Issues in Community Work

- Updated and expanded discussion of the community mental health perspective
- Discussion of how to build on the strengths within a community
- New section on the implications of ethics codes for practice in the community
- Revised discussion of the tasks of community counseling
- Increased emphasis on addressing the needs of underserved communities and the delivery of services in nontraditional settings
- Examples of five therapists who are making a difference in the community

Acknowledgments

We would like to thank the book's reviewers for their helpful suggestions: Louis Jenkins, Loma Linda University; Maureen Kenny, Florida International University; Sarah Leverett-Main, Eastern Washington University; Donald MacDonald, Seattle Pacific University; Margaret Miller, Boise State University; Michelle Muratori, Center for Talented Youth, Johns Hopkins University; Beverly Palmer, California State University, Dominguez Hills; Terrence Patterson, University of San Francisco; Elizabeth Pomeroy, University of Texas at Austin; and M. Carolyn Thomas, Auburn University Montgomery.

We appreciate the feedback from the following people on selected chapters in this edition, based on their areas of expertise. For Chapters 1, 5, and 6: Mary Hermann, Mississippi State University; and Rahn Minagawa, Forensic Psych Consultants, San Diego. For Chapter 9: A. Michael Dougherty, Western Carolina University. For Chapter 10: James Bitter, East Tennessee State University; Frank Dattilio, Harvard Medical School and University of Pennsylvania School of Medicine; Robert Haynes, Borderline Productions; Allen Ivey, University of Massachusetts; Arnold Lazarus, Rutgers University; Michael Nystul, New Mexico State University; Michael Russell, California State University, Fullerton; William Wheeler, Mississippi College; Robert Wubbolding, Center for Reality Therapy, Cincinnati. For Chapter 13 on ethical issues in community work, our thanks to John Doyle, California State University at Fullerton; Larry Golan, Los Angeles County Children and Family Services; Mark Homan, Pima Community College, Tucson, Arizona; John Mooradian, Michigan State University; Deb Padgett, University of Wisconsin; and Rick Thompson, Austin Community College.

These individuals provided initial input as pre-revision reviewers: Jeff Ashby, Georgia State University; Rachell Anderson, University of Illinois at Springfield; Steven Berman, University of Central Florida; Joseph Bertinetti, University of Nebraska at Omaha; Richard Boettcher, Ohio State University; Brandon Hunt, Pennsylvania State University; Ken Johnson, Amberton University; Larry Kontosh, Florida Atlantic University; and Daniel Yazak, Montana State University.

The members of the Thomson Brooks/Cole team continue to offer support for all our projects. It is a delight to work with a dedicated staff of professionals who go out of their way to give their best. These people include Marquita Flemming, editor of counseling and human services; Christine Northup, editorial assistant, who monitored the review process; Caroline Concilla, marketing manager; and Rita Jaramillo, project manager. We thank Ben Kolstad of International Typesetting and Composition, who coordinated the production of this book, and Kay Mikel, the manuscript editor of this edition, whose exceptional editorial talents continue to keep this book reader friendly. We appreciate the careful work that Madeleine Clark did in preparing the index. Their efforts and dedication certainly contribute to the quality of this edition.

Gerald Corey
Marianne Schneider Corey
Patrick Callanan

The Focus of This Book

Working both independently and together, the three of us have, over the years, confronted a variety of professional and ethical issues that do not have clear-cut solutions. Conversations with students and colleagues show us that others struggle similarly. Exchanging ideas helps us clarify our positions on these issues. We are convinced that students in the helping professions need to anticipate and be prepared for these kinds of problems before their first internship, and certainly before they begin practicing.

We have discovered that many of the issues relevant to beginning professionals resurface and take on different meanings at various stages of professional development. This book will help both experienced practitioners and students about to embark on their professional careers. We have tried to avoid dispensing prescriptions or providing simple solutions to complex problems. Our main purpose is to establish a basis for formulating your own ethical guidelines within the broad limits of professional codes and divergent theoretical positions. We raise what we consider to be central issues, present a range of views on these issues, discuss our position, and provide you with many opportunities to refine your own thinking and actively develop your position.

As you read this book, it will be apparent that we have certain biases and viewpoints about ethical behavior. We hope you will see these stances as our points of view rather than the correct points of view. We try to keep our viewpoints open to revision. We state our position on issues not to sway you to adopt our view but to challenge you to develop your own position.

In the end, you are responsible for your own ethical practice; however, be wary of choosing any set of ethical views merely because it "feels right" to you. Codes of ethics provide general standards, but these are not sufficiently explicit to deal with every situation. It is often difficult to interpret ethics codes, and opinions differ over how to apply them in specific cases. Consequently, you will encounter many situations that demand the exercise of sound judgment to further the best interests of your clients. In all cases the welfare of the client

Introduction to Professional Ethics

demands that you become familiar with the guiding principles of the ethics codes and the accepted standards of practice. In the end, always err in favor of the long-term benefits of your clients.

The various mental health professions have developed codes of ethics that are binding on their members. As a professional, you are expected to know the ethics code of your specialty and to be aware of the consequences of practicing in ways that are not sanctioned by your professional organization. In addition, responsible practice requires that you use informed, sound, and responsible judgment. It is essential that you demonstrate a willingness to consult with colleagues, to keep yourself up to date through reading and continuing education, and to continually attend to your behavior.

Be prepared to reexamine many of the issues discussed here throughout your professional life. Even if you resolve some of these issues at the initial stage of your development as a counselor, these topics are likely to take on new dimensions as you gain experience. Minor questions may become major concerns as you progress in your profession. Many students burden themselves with the expectation that they should resolve all possible issues before they begin to practice. However, the definition and refinement of such concerns is an ongoing evolutionary process that requires an open and self-critical attitude. Our goal is to give you a flexible framework and a direction for working through ethical dilemmas. Your challenge is to be able to find and justify your own answers to the questions we raise here.

Some Suggestions for Using This Book

In this book we cover the central professional and ethical issues you are likely to encounter in your work. We aim to stimulate your thinking on these issues.

We frequently imagine ourselves in conversations with our students. We often state our own thinking and offer a commentary on how we arrived at the positions we hold. We think it is important to reveal our biases, convictions, and attitudes. On many issues we present a range of viewpoints. Give attention to integrating your own thoughts and experiences with the positions we explore. In this way you will absorb information, deepen your understanding, and develop an ethical way of thinking.

We offer several specific suggestions for getting the most from this book and from your course. Many of these ideas come from students who have been in our classes. In general, you will get from this book and course whatever you are willing to invest of yourself, so it is important to clarify your goals and to think about ways of becoming actively involved. Here are some suggestions that can help you become an active learner.

- *Be prepared.* You can best prepare yourself to become active in your class by spending time reading and thinking about the questions we pose. Completing the exercises and responding to the questions and open-ended cases will help you focus on where you stand on controversial issues.
- *Examine your expectations.* Students often have unrealistic expectations of themselves. You may think you should have solutions to all problems before you begin to work with people. If you have limited experience in counseling clients, you can think about situations in which friends sought your help and how you dealt with them. You can also reflect on the times when you were experiencing conflicts and needed someone to help you gain clarity. In this way you may be able to relate the material to events in your own life.
- *Complete the self-assessment survey.* The multiple-choice survey at the end of this chapter is designed to help you discover your attitudes concerning most of the issues we deal with in the book. Take this inventory before you read the book to determine where you stand on these issues at this time. We also suggest that you take the inventory again after you complete the book. You can then compare your responses to see what changes, if any, have occurred in your thinking.
- *Identify your viewpoint by reviewing the self-inventories.* Each chapter begins with an inventory designed to encourage reflection on the issues to be explored in the chapter. You can bring your responses to class and discuss your views with those of fellow students. You can retake the inventory after you finish reading the chapter to see if your views have changed.
- *Think about the examples, cases, and questions.* Many examples in this book are drawn from actual counseling practice in various settings with different types of clients. We ask you to consider how you might have worked with a given client or what you might have done in a particular counseling situation. Think about these questions and briefly respond to them as you read each chapter.
- *Do the end-of-chapter suggested activities.* Each chapter ends with suggested activities intended to help you integrate and apply what you have learned. These exercises challenge you to be active both in class and on your own, and they give you a chance to apply your ideas about the issues to various situations.
- *Explore the InfoTrac College Edition resources.* This vast online library of current articles enables you to expand your reading in areas of particular interest to you. Use this resource as questions arise throughout the course.

Try to involve yourself personally in thinking about the issues we raise. Focus on the questions, cases, and activities that have the most meaning for you at this time, and remain open to new issues as they assume importance for you. Formulate your own personal ethical perspective on the issues in this book. As you become actively involved in your ethics course, you will discover additional ways to look at the process of ethical decision making.

Professional Codes of Ethics

Various professional organizations (counseling, social work, psychiatry, psychology, marriage and family therapy) have established codes of ethics that provide broad guidelines for mental health practitioners. These national professional organizations have similarities, and they also have differences. In addition, national certification boards, other professional associations, specialty areas within the counseling profession, and state regulatory boards all have their own ethics or professional practice documents. Specialty guidelines are available to cover areas not adequately addressed by the general ethics codes. For example, the American Psychological Association has the following specialty guidelines:

- Guidelines for providers of psychological services to ethnic, linguistic, and culturally diverse populations (APA, 1993)
- Guidelines for psychotherapy with lesbian, gay, and bisexual clients (APA, 2000)
- Guidelines on multicultural education, training, research, practice, and organizational change for psychologists (APA, 2003a)
- Record keeping guidelines (Committee on Professional Practice and Standards, Board of Professional Affairs, 1993)

You will find many resources to help you understand the issues underlying the ethical decisions you will be making in your professional life.

Using Codes of Ethics

Become familiar with the ethics codes of your specialization, but know that there are challenges in the application of these codes in your practice. The ethics codes offered by most professional organizations are broad and general rather than precise and specific. Your own ethical awareness and problem-solving skills will determine how you translate these general guidelines into professional behavior. As Welfel (2006) indicates, codes of ethics are not cookbooks for responsible professional behavior. Indeed, they offer unmistakably clear guidance for only a few problems. In short, ethics codes are necessary, but not sufficient, for exercising ethical responsibility. It is essential that you be aware of the limitations of such codes (see Herlihy & Corey, 2006a; Herlihy & Remley, 1995; Ibrahim & Arredondo, 1990; Mabe & Rollin, 1986; Mappes, Robb, &

Codes of Ethics

Each major mental health professional organization has its own code of ethics, and we strongly recommend that you obtain a copy of the ethics code of the profession you are planning to enter and familiarize yourself with their basic standards for ethical practice. Pleading ignorance of the specifics of the ethics code of one's profession is not an excuse when engaging in unethical behavior. Ethics codes do not provide specific answers to the ethical dilemmas you will encounter, but they do offer general guidance.

The ethics codes listed here are reproduced in a supplement to this textbook titled *Codes of Ethics for the Helping Professions* (2007), which is free when ordered as a bundle with this textbook. Alternatively, you may obtain particular codes of ethics by contacting the organizations directly.

1. *Code of Ethics,* American Counseling Association (ACA, 2005)
2. "Ethical Principles of Psychologists and Code of Conduct," American Psychological Association (APA, 2002)
3. *Code of Ethics,* National Association of Social Workers (NASW, 1999)
4. *AAMFT Code of Ethics,* American Association for Marriage and Family Therapy (AAMFT, 2001)
5. "Ethical Standards of the National Organization for Human Services," National Organization for Human Services (NOHS, 2000)
6. *Code of Professional Ethics for Rehabilitation Counselors,* Commission on Rehabilitation Counselor Certification (CRCC, 2001)
7. *CCA Code of Ethics,* Canadian Counselling Association (CCA, 1999)
8. *Code of Ethics,* Canadian Association of Social Workers (CASW, 1994)
9. *Canadian Code of Ethics for Psychologists,* Canadian Psychological Association (CPA, 2000).
10. *Ethical Standards for School Counselors,* American School Counselor Association (ASCA, 2004)
11. "Ethical Code for the International Association of Marriage and Family Counselors," (IAMFC, 2002)
12. *Code of Ethics of the American Mental Health Counselors Association,* American Mental Health Counselors Association (AMHCA, 2000)
13. "Ethical Guidelines for Counseling Supervisors," Association for Counselor Education and Supervision (ACES, 1995)
14. *Feminist Therapy Code of Ethics,* Feminist Therapy Institute (FTI, 2000)
15. *The Principles of Medical Ethics With Annotations Especially Applicable to Psychiatry,* American Psychiatric Association (2001).

Engels, 1985; Pope & Vasquez, 1998). Here are some limitations and problems you might encounter as you strive to be ethically responsible:

- Some issues cannot be handled solely by relying on ethics codes.
- Some codes lack clarity and precision, which makes assessment difficult.
- Simply learning the ethics codes and casebooks will not necessarily make for ethical practice.
- Consumers of counseling services may not have the knowledge or experience to determine whether a therapist is practicing ethically.
- Conflicts sometimes emerge within ethics codes as well as among various organizations' codes.
- Practitioners who belong to multiple professional associations, are licensed by their state, and hold national certifications may be responsible to practice

within the framework of numerous codes of ethics, yet these codes may not be uniform.

- Ethics codes tend to be reactive rather than proactive.
- A practitioner's personal values may conflict with a specific standard within an ethics code.
- Codes may conflict with institutional policies and practices.
- Ethics codes need to be understood within a cultural framework; therefore, they must be adapted to specific cultures.
- Codes may not align with state laws or regulations regarding reporting requirements.
- Because of the diverse viewpoints within any professional organization, not all members will agree with all proposed ideas.

In the *Code of Ethics* of the National Association of Social Workers (1999) the limits of the code are succinctly described:

> A code of ethics cannot guarantee ethical behavior. Moreover, a code of ethics cannot resolve all ethical issues or disputes, or capture the richness and complexity involved in striving to make responsible choices within a moral community. Rather a code of ethics sets forth values, ethical principles and ethical standards to which professionals aspire and by which their actions can be judged. (Purpose of NASW Code of Ethics.)

The code of ethics for the Canadian Counselling Association (1999) makes it clear that professionals are challenged to make sound decisions based on their own values:

> Although a Code of Ethics is essential to the maintenance of ethical integrity and accountability, it cannot be a substitute for the active process of ethical decision-making. Members increasingly confront challenging ethical demands and dilemmas in a complex and dynamic society to which a simple and direct application of this code may not be possible. Also, reasonable differences of opinion can and do exist among members with respect to how ethical principles and values should be rank-ordered when they are in conflict. Therefore, members must develop the ability and the courage to exercise a high level of ethical judgment. (Preamble.)

It is clear that ethics codes are not intended to be blueprints that remove all need for judgment and ethical reasoning. Pope and Vasquez (1998) maintain that formal ethical principles can never be substituted for an active, deliberative, and creative approach to meeting ethical responsibilities. They remind us that ethics codes cannot be applied in a rote manner, mainly because each client's situation is unique and calls for a different solution. Handelsman, Gottlieb, and Knapp (2005) remind us that becoming an ethical practitioner is a more complex process than simply following a set of rules. They contend that "ethics is the study of right and wrong but is often taught as the study of wrong. Many ethics courses are devoted to laws, disciplinary codes, and risk management strategies and do not focus on best practices" (p. 59). From our perspective, practitioners face the challenge of making ethical decisions and ultimately taking responsibility for the outcomes. This process takes time, and it should include consultation.

Herlihy and Corey (2006a) suggest that codes of ethics fulfill three objectives. The first objective is to educate professionals about sound ethical conduct. Reading and reflecting on the standards can help practitioners expand their awareness and clarify their values in dealing with the challenges of their work. Second, ethical standards provide a mechanism for professional accountability. Practitioners are obliged not only to monitor their own behavior but also to encourage ethical conduct in their colleagues. One of the best ways for practitioners to guard the welfare of their clients or students and to protect themselves from malpractice suits is to practice within the spirit of the ethics codes. Third, codes of ethics serve as catalysts for improving practice. When practitioners must interpret and apply the codes in their own practices, the questions raised help to clarify their positions on dilemmas that do not have simple or absolute answers. You can imagine the chaos if people were to practice without guidelines so that the resolution of ethical dilemmas rested solely with the individual clinician.

We must never forget that the primary purpose of a code of ethics is to safeguard the welfare of clients by providing what is in their best interest. Ethics codes are also designed to safeguard the public and to guide professionals in their work so that they can provide the best service possible. The community standard (what professionals *actually* do) is generally less rigorous than the ethical standard (what professionals *should* do). It is important to be knowledgeable of what others in your local area and subspecialties are doing in their practices.

Bersoff (2003a) makes a distinction between the ideal and realistic purpose of a code of ethics. Ideally, ethics codes provide guidance in resolving moral problems encountered by members of the profession. Bersoff writes:

> Realistically, however, what a code of ethics does is validate the most recent views of a majority of professionals empowered by their colleagues to make decisions about ethical issues. Thus, a code of ethics is, inevitably, anachronistic, conservative, ethnocentric, and the product of political compromise. But recognition of that reality should not inhibit the creation of a document that fully realizes and expresses fundamental moral principles. (p. 1)

At this point, what do you think it takes to be an ethical professional? Is it primarily knowing and following the ethics code of your profession? What else might it take to be an ethical practitioner? You may find that you answer differently in different situations.

Ethics Codes and the Law

Ethical issues in the mental health professions are regulated by both laws and professional codes. These guidelines, however, seldom provide clear-cut answers to situational problems. The Committee on Professional Practice and Standards (2003) differentiates between ethics and law as follows: **Ethics** pertains to the standards that govern the conduct of its professional members; **law** is the body of rules that govern the affairs of people within a community, state, or country. Laws define the minimum standards society will tolerate, which are enforced by government. An example of a minimum standard is the legal obligation mental health professionals have to report suspected child abuse. All of the codes of ethics state that practitioners must act in accordance with relevant federal and state statutes and government regulations. It is essential that practitioners be able to identify legal problems as they arise in their work because many of the situations they encounter that involve ethical and professional judgment will also have legal implications. In their discussion of counseling and the law, Rowley and MacDonald (2001) state: "Counselors must demonstrate ethical standards of the profession and abide by the law. This task is made challenging by the fact that the mental health and legal systems represent 2 different, sometimes conflicting cultures" (p. 422).

Counselors often have difficulty determining when they have a legal problem, or what to do with a legal issue once it has been identified. Remley and Herlihy (2005) recommend a way to determine when a legal issue is involved. They suggest assessing the situation to determine if any of the following apply: (a) legal proceedings have been initiated, (b) lawyers are involved, or (c) the practitioner is in danger of having a complaint filed against him or her for misconduct. They advise that in those situations involving legal matters, it is important to consult a lawyer in determining which course of action to take.

Crawford (1999) points out that counselors do not have to be lawyers to practice with a lawful perspective. As is the case with ethical dilemmas, Crawford tells us not to expect simple solutions to every legal problem. One of the reviewers of this book, Mary Hermann, an attorney and counselor educator, teaches a course in legal and ethical issues in counseling. She finds that her students get frustrated because they want concrete answers to legal problems. She tells us that most of the time even legal scholars can only speculate about the answers to these questions. Stating this reality immediately helps to get students thinking about their options and making the best choices they can make under the circumstances rather than searching for some mythical "right answer" to a legal issue (personal communication, March 10, 2005).

Lacking a definitive answer of what is legal or illegal, some professionals increasingly limit their options of ways to work with clients for fear of a possible lawsuit. This raises a potential ethical issue of delivering less than effective services, especially if this narrowing of available options to clients is not clearly expressed during the initial interview.

Laws and ethics codes tend to emerge from what has occurred rather than from anticipating what may occur. It is neither wise nor ethical to limit your behavior to merely obeying statutes and following ethical standards. It is very important that you acquire this ethical sense at the beginning of your professional program. Remember that the basic purpose of practicing ethically is to further the welfare of your clients.

At times there may be conflicts between the law and ethical principles, and in these cases the values of the counselor come into play. Conflict between ethics codes and the law may arise in areas such as advertising, confidentiality, and clients' rights of access to their own files. The Committee on Professional Practice and Standards (2003) suggests that if obeying one's professional code of ethics would result in disobeying the law, it is essential to seek legal advice.

A licensed mental health professional might also contact his or her state licensing board for consultation. On this point, the National Association of Social Workers (1999) guideline is clear:

> When such conflicts occur, social workers must make a responsible effort to resolve the conflict in a manner that is consistent with the values, principles, and standards expressed in this *Code*. If a reasonable resolution of this conflict does not appear possible, social workers should seek proper consultation before making a decision. (Purpose of NASW Code of Ethics.)

One example of a potential conflict between legal and ethical standards involves counseling minors. This is especially true as it pertains to counseling children or adolescents in school settings. Counselors may be committed to following ethical standards in maintaining the confidentiality of the sessions with a minor, yet at times parents may have a legal right to information that is disclosed in these sessions. Counselors will often struggle between doing what they believe to be ethically appropriate for their client and their legal responsibilities to parents. This subject is addressed more fully in Chapter 5.

Another example of a potential conflict between legal and ethical standards pertains to breaking confidentiality of a client who is HIV-positive by informing a third party of his or her condition. The American Counseling Association's *Code of Ethics* (2005) standard regarding contagious, life-threatening diseases suggests that practitioners *may* be justified in reporting to an identifiable third party, *under certain circumstances*. Generally, there is no legal imperative to do so at this time, but Utah's state statute seems to extend counselors' duty to warn to include a client's possible transmission of communicable diseases (Glosoff, Herlihy, & Spence, 2000). Practitioners may act in ways they deem to be ethical only to find that they have broken a legal standard. For example, in California the ACA standard regarding reporting a health risk could conflict with state law, placing the individual who divulges this confidential information at risk for fines, civil penalties, incarceration, and loss of license (Rahn Minagawa, forensic psychologist, personal communication, August 14, 2003). This topic is explored in more detail in Chapter 6.

In cases of conflict between ethics and the law, the American Psychological Association's (2002) ethics code indicates that psychologists should seek to resolve the conflict in a way that complies with the law and at the same time most nearly conforms to the code. If the conflict is not resolvable by such means, psychologists may adhere to the requirements of the law or other governing legal authority. The *Code of Professional Ethics for Rehabilitation Counselors* (CRCC, 2001) addresses legal standards and ethical practice in this way:

> a. Rehabilitation counselors will obey the laws and statutes of the legal jurisdiction in which they practice unless there is a conflict with the Code, in which case they should seek immediate consultation and advice.
>
> b. Rehabilitation counselors will be familiar with and observe the legal limitations of the services they offer to clients. They will discuss these limitations as well as all benefits available to clients they serve in order to facilitate open, honest communication and avoid unrealistic expectations. (D.2.)

In ethical dilemmas involving legal issues, seek advice from legal counsel and discuss the issues with colleagues familiar with the law (Remley, 1996). In those cases where neither the law nor an ethics code resolves an issue, therapists are advised to consider other professional and community standards and their own conscience as well.

Evolution of Ethics Codes

Codes of ethics are established by professional groups for the purpose of protecting consumers, providing guidelines for practitioners, and clarifying the professional stance of the organizations. As such, these codes do not convey ultimate truth, nor do they provide readymade answers for the ethical dilemmas practitioners must face. These codes undergo periodic revisions. For instance, the most recent revisions of both the ACA's (2005) and the APA's (2002) ethics codes represented a 10-year period between revised versions of their codes. In the preamble to the Canadian Counselling Association *Code of Ethics* (CCA, 1999) is this statement: "This Code is not a static document, but will need revisions over time because of the continuing development of ethical knowledge and the emergence of consensus on challenging ethical issues."

In addition to codes of ethics, some professional organizations also provide casebooks, which interpret and explain various ethical standards contained with the code. Three examples are *A Guide to the 2002 Revision of the American Psychological Association's Ethics Code* (Knapp & VandeCreek, 2003a), *Ethical Standards in Social Work: A Review of the NASW Code of Ethics* (Reamer, 1998), and *ACA Ethical Standards Casebook* (Herlihy & Corey, 2006a). However useful these casebooks may be, they can never replace the informed judgment and goodwill of the individual counselor. They are tools that must be used in making difficult decisions in complex situations. We emphasize again the need for a level of ethical functioning higher than merely following the letter of the law or the code. For instance, you might avoid a lawsuit or professional censure by ignoring cultural diversity, but many of your ethnically diverse clients could suffer from your insensitive professional behavior.

Walden, Herlihy, and Ashton (2003) surveyed ACA Ethics Committee chairs in addressing the evolution of ethics codes. One trend emerging as a future issue in the field of counseling ethics relates to cultural considerations and a continued emphasis on the role of diversity in counseling practice. The ethics chairs surveyed predicted the development of a culturally competent code of ethics, increased globalization of counseling, and health care models that take into account the place of diversity in counseling. Other emerging issues that were perceived as necessary to consider in revising ethics codes included the influence of technology on counseling and proactively addressing the impaired professional. Walden and her colleagues concluded that it is important that codes of ethics be evolving documents that are responsive to the needs of counselors, the clients they serve, and society in general.

Professional Monitoring of Practice

Most professional organizations have ethics committees, elected or delegated bodies that oversee the conduct of members of the organization. The main purposes of these ethics committees are to educate the association's membership about ethics codes and to protect the public from unethical practices. As a rule, these committees meet regularly to process formal complaints against individual members of the professional organization.

When necessary, counselors must explain to clients how to lodge an ethical complaint. When a complaint is lodged against a member, the committee launches an investigation and deliberates on the case. Eventually, a disposition is reached. The complaint may be dismissed, specific charges within the complaint may be dismissed, or the committee may find that ethical standards have been violated and impose sanctions. Generally, possible sanctions include a reprimand; probation or suspension for a specified period of time; a recommendation that the member be allowed to resign from the organization; a recommendation that the member be expelled; or a recommendation that a specific course of remedial action be taken, such as obtaining ongoing supervision or personal therapy.

Expulsion or suspension of a member is a major sanction. Members have the right to appeal the committee's decision, and once the appeals process has been completed or the deadline for appeal has passed, the sanctions of suspension and expulsion are published in writing in the journal of the professional organization. Practitioners who are expelled from the association may also face the loss of their license or certificate to practice, but only if the state board conducts an independent investigation. Cases that result in expulsion are often serious enough to involve law enforcement and criminal charges. Many cases also result in civil court proceedings, which are usually published in the local press.

Ethical Decision Making

Some Key Terms

Although values and ethics are frequently used interchangeably, the two terms are not identical. **Values** pertain to beliefs and attitudes that provide direction to everyday living, whereas ethics pertain to the beliefs we hold about what constitutes right conduct. Ethics are moral principles adopted by an individual or group to provide rules for right conduct. **Morality** is concerned with perspectives of right and proper conduct and involves an evaluation of actions on the basis of some broader cultural context or religious standard.

Ethics represents aspirational goals, or the maximum or ideal standards set by the profession, and they are enforced by professional associations, national certification boards, and government boards that regulate professions (Remley, 1996). Codes of ethics are conceptually broad in nature and generally subject to interpretation by practitioners. Although these minimum and maximum standards may differ, they are not necessarily in conflict.

Bersoff (1996) describes *ethical conduct* as the result of a combination of knowledge and a clear conception of the philosophical principles that underlie an ethics code. Ethical conduct leads you to respond with maturity, judgment, discretion, wisdom, and prudence.

Community standards (or *mores*) vary on an interdisciplinary, theoretical, and geographical basis. The standard for a counselor's social contact with clients may be different in a large urban area than in a rural area or between practitioners employing an analytic versus a behavioral approach. Community standards often become the ultimate *legal* criteria for determining whether practitioners are liable for damages because these standards define what is considered reasonable behavior when a case involving malpractice is litigated. Courts have consistently found that mental health care providers have a duty to exercise a reasonable degree of skill, knowledge, and care. **Reasonableness** is usually defined as the care that is ordinarily exercised by others practicing within that specialty in the professional community.

Professionalism has some relationship to ethical behavior, yet it is possible to act unprofessionally and still not act unethically. For instance, not returning a client's telephone calls promptly might be viewed as unprofessional, but it would probably not be considered unethical unless the client were in crisis.

Some situations cut across these concepts. For instance, sexual intimacy between counselors and clients is considered unethical, unprofessional, immoral, and illegal. Keep the differences in the meanings of these various concepts in mind as you read.

Levels of Ethical Practice

One way of conceptualizing professional ethics is to contrast mandatory ethics with aspirational ethics. **Mandatory ethics** describes a level of ethical functioning wherein counselors act in compliance with minimal standards, acknowledging the basic "musts" and "must nots." The focus is on behavioral rules. **Aspirational ethics** describes the highest standards of thinking and conduct professional counselors seek, and it requires that counselors do more than simply meet the letter of the ethics code. It entails an understanding of the spirit behind the code and the principles on which the code rests. Practitioners who comply at the first level, mandatory ethics, are generally safe from legal action or professional censure. Courts of law and state licensure boards now require minimal standards to which all mental health professionals will be held accountable. At the higher level of ethical functioning, aspirational ethics, practitioners go further and reflect on the effects their interventions may have on the welfare of their clients. In the most recent revision of the ACA's (2005) *Code of Ethics,* each section begins with an introduction, which sets the tone and addresses what counselors should aspire to with regard to ethical practice.

When the word **unethical** is used, people think of extreme violations of established codes. In reality, most violations of ethics probably happen quite inadvertently in clinical practice. The ethics codes of most professional organizations require practitioners to engage in self-monitoring and to take responsibility for misconduct. Welfel (2005) indicates that the professional literature focuses on preventing misconduct and on responding to serious ethical violations. However, the literature has not offered much guidance regarding minor infractions committed by professionals. Welfel states that by taking minor ethical violations seriously and by seeking honest ways to remediate such infractions, counselors can demonstrate their professionalism and personal commitment to benefiting those they serve.

Welfel's model progresses from awareness, through reflection, to a plan of action whereby counselors can ethically repair damage when they recognize they have violated ethics codes in minor ways. She emphasizes that the first step in recovering from an ethical violation is for the practitioner to recognize that he or she has acted in a way that is likely to be ethically problematic. If a practitioner is not aware of the subtle ways his or her behavior can adversely affect the client, such behavior can go unnoticed, and the clients will suffer. For instance, a professional who is struggling financially in her private practice may prolong the therapy of her clients and justify her actions on theoretical grounds. She is likely to ignore the fact that the prolongation of therapy is influenced by her financial situation.

Practitioners can easily find themselves in an ethical quagmire based on competing role expectations. The best way to maintain a clear ethical position is to focus on your clients' best interests. School counselors may be so focused on academic and scheduling issues that they do not reach out to the community and develop the network with other helping professionals needed to make productive referrals for families and students in crises. In school systems teachers and others sometimes label students and families as dysfunctional or unmotivated. The counselor needs to advocate and help others look for strengths and reframe limitations if progress is to be made. The counselor can be an ethical model in a system where ethics is not given much consideration.

Clients' needs are best met when practitioners monitor their own ethics. Ethical violations may go undetected because only the individual who committed the violation knows about it. Rather than just looking at others and proclaiming "That's unethical!" we encourage you to challenge your own thinking and apply guidelines to your behavior by asking yourself, "Is what I am doing in the best interests of my clients? Would the codes of my professional organization agree?"

Principle Ethics and Virtue Ethics

Several writers have developed models for ethical decision making (Cottone, 2001; Cottone & Claus, 2000; Cottone & Tarvydas, 2003; Forester-Miller & Davis, 1995; Frame & Williams, 2005; Hill, Glaser, & Harden, 1995; Jordan & Meara, 1990; Kitchener, 1984; Koocher & Keith-Spiegel, 1998; Meara, Schmidt, & Day, 1996; Paradise & Siegelwaks, 1982; Smith, McGuire, Abbott, & Blau, 1991; Stadler, 1986a; Tymchuk, 1981; Welfel, 2005, 2006). This section is based on an amalgamation of elements from these various models and our own views.

In a major article entitled "Principles and Virtues: A Foundation for Ethical Decisions, Policies, and Character," Meara, Schmidt, and Day (1996) differentiate between principle ethics and virtue ethics. **Principle ethics** is a set of obligations and a method that focuses on moral issues with the goals of (a) solving a particular dilemma or set of dilemmas and (b) establishing a framework to guide future ethical thinking and behavior. Principles typically focus on acts and choices, and they are used to facilitate the selection of socially and historically acceptable answers to the question "What shall I do?"

A thorough grounding in principle ethics opens the way for another important perspective, virtue ethics. **Virtue ethics** focuses on the character traits of the counselor and nonobligatory ideals to which professionals aspire rather than on solving specific ethical dilemmas. Simply stated, principle ethics asks "Is this situation unethical?" whereas virtue ethics asks "Am I doing what is best for my client?" Even in the absence of an ethical dilemma, virtue ethics compels the professional to be conscious of ethical behavior. Meara and her colleagues maintain that it is not a question of subscribing to one or the other form of ethics. Rather, professional counselors should strive to integrate virtue ethics and principle ethics to reach better ethical decisions and policies.

Some mental health practitioners concern themselves primarily with avoiding malpractice suits. They follow the law and ethics codes to stay out of trouble. Other professionals, although concerned with avoiding litigation, are first and foremost interested in doing what is best for their clients. These professionals would consider it unethical to use techniques that might not result in the greatest benefit to their clients or to use techniques in which they were not thoroughly trained, even though these techniques might not lead to a lawsuit. For example, a Gestalt therapist might refer a client to a cognitive-behavioral therapist because, in her opinion, the client is more suited to the latter approach. Although this therapist could legally and ethically justify seeing this client, it may be more "virtuous" to refer the client in this instance. As Jordan and Meara (1990) write, "The ideals of professional psychology must include conscientious decision making, but they also must include virtuous deciders, who emphasize not so much what is permitted as what is preferred" (p. 112).

Meara and colleagues (1996) identify four core virtues—prudence, integrity, respectfulness, and benevolence—that are appropriate for professionals to adhere to in making ethical decisions. They also describe five characteristics of virtuous professionals, which they see as being at the heart of virtue ethics.

- Virtuous agents are motivated to do what is right because they judge it to be right, not just because they feel obligated or fear the consequences.
- Virtuous agents rely on vision and discernment, which involve sensitivity, judgment, and understanding that leads to decisive action.
- Virtuous agents have compassion and are sensitive to the suffering of others. They are able to take actions to reduce their clients' pain.
- Virtuous agents are self-aware. They know how their assumptions, convictions, and biases are likely to affect their interactions with others.
- Virtuous agents are connected with and understand the mores of their community and the importance of community in moral decision making, policy

setting, and character development. They understand the ideals and expectations of their community.

Virtue ethics focuses on ideals rather than obligations and on the character of the professional rather than on the action itself. To meet the goals, ideals, and needs of the community being served, consider both principles and virtues because both are important elements in thinking through ethical concerns.

✓ **A Case Illustrating Virtue Ethics.** Your client, Kevin, is doing well in his counseling with you. Then he informs you that he has lost his job and will not be able to continue seeing you because of his inability to pay your fees. Here is how four different therapists handled a similar situation:

Therapist A: I'm sorry but I can't continue seeing you without payment. I'm giving you the name of a local community clinic that provides low-cost treatment.

Therapist B: I don't usually see people without payment, but I appreciate the difficulty you find yourself in through no fault of your own. I'll continue to see you, and you pay whatever portion of my fee you can afford. In addition I want you to seek out a community agency and do volunteer work in lieu of the full payment.

Therapist C: I suggest that you put therapy on hold until you can financially afford it.

Therapist D: I can't afford to see you without payment, but I am willing to suggest an alternative plan. Continue writing in your journal, and once a month I will see you for half an hour to discuss your journal. You pay what you can afford for these sessions. When your financial situation has been corrected, we can continue therapy as usual.

What are your reactions to the various therapists' responses? Which position appeals to you and why? Can you think of another response? Would you be willing to see a client without payment? Why or why not? Do you have concerns about the responses of any of these therapists?

In considering what you might do if you were the therapist in this case, reflect on the standards pertaining to **pro bono** (or free) **services** found in the ethics codes of NASW (1999), ACA (2005), and APA (2002). What these three codes have in common is the encouragement that practitioners contribute to society by devoting a portion of their professional time and skills to services for which there is no expectation of significant financial return.

Commentary. If you did not want to abandon your client, you could refer Kevin to an agency that would see him without a fee, assuming such a facility exists in your area. You could also see him as part of your pro bono services. Ethically you are obliged to provide the best quality of care; however, you may be part of a managed care system that limits the number of sessions and has a very limited focus of goals and treatment. Even though you want to do what is best for your client, you may be unable to provide pro bono care without creating other problems for yourself. In essence, there is no simple solution to this situation. It combines the therapist, the client, and the situation, all of which need to be considered in context.

Moral Principles to Guide Decision Making

Building on the work of others, especially Kitchener (1984), Meara and colleagues (1996) describe six basic moral principles that form the foundation of functioning at the highest ethical level as a professional: autonomy, nonmaleficence, beneficence, justice, fidelity, and veracity. Applying these ethical principles and the related ethical standards is not as simple as it may seem, especially when dealing with culturally diverse populations. (See Chapters 4 and 13 for more on this issue.) These moral principles involve a process of striving that is never fully complete. We illustrate each of these six basic moral principles by citing a specific ethical guideline from the ACA, APA, or NASW and by providing a brief discussion of the cultural implications of using each principle.

- **Autonomy** refers to the promotion of self-determination, or the freedom of clients to choose their own direction. Respect for autonomy entails acknowledging the right of another to choose and act in accordance with his or her wishes, and the professional behaves in a way that enables this right of another person. The ACA's (2005) introduction to Section A states it this way: "Counselors encourage client growth and development in ways that foster the interest and welfare of clients and promote formation of healthy relationships. Counselors actively attempt to understand the diverse cultural backgrounds of the clients they serve. Counselors also explore their own cultural identities and how these affect their values and beliefs about the counseling process."

The helping services are based on traditional Western values of individualism, independence, interdependence, self-determination, and making choices for oneself. It often appears as though Western cultures promote individualism above any other cultural value. However, many cultures follow a different path, stressing decisions with the welfare of the family and the community as a priority. As the ACA standard described here implies, ethical practice involves considering the influence of cultural variables in the counseling relationship.

We cannot apply a rigid yardstick of what is a value priority in any culture without exploring how a particular client views priorities. For instance, what are the implications of the principle of autonomy when it is applied to clients who do not place a high priority on the value of being autonomous? Does it constitute an imposition of values for counselors to steer clients toward autonomous behavior when such behavior could lead to problems with others in their family, community, or culture? What about promoting autonomy for those incapable of it (for example, dependent youths)?

- **Nonmaleficence** means avoiding doing harm, which includes refraining from actions that risk hurting clients. Professionals have a responsibility to avoid engaging in practices that cause harm or have the potential to result in harm. The APA (2002) principle states, "Psychologists strive to benefit those with whom they work and take care to do no harm."

What are the cultural implications of the principle of nonmaleficence? Traditional diagnostic practices can be inappropriate for certain cultural groups. For instance, a therapist may assign a diagnostic label to a client based on a pattern of behavior the therapist judges to be abnormal, such as inhibition of emotional expression, hesitation to confront, being cautious about self-disclosing, or not making direct eye contact while speaking. Yet these behaviors may be considered normal in certain cultures. Another example may be a school counselor who inappropriately labels a boy ADHD, which may color the perceptions of other staff members in a negative way so they pressure the parents to put the boy on medication. Practitioners need to develop cultural awareness and sensitivity in using assessment, diagnostic, and treatment procedures.

- **Beneficence** refers to promoting good for others. Ideally, counseling contributes to the growth and development of clients within their cultural context. Whatever practitioners do can be judged against this criterion. The following ACA (2005) guideline illustrates beneficence: "The primary responsibility of counselors is to respect the dignity and to promote the welfare of clients" (A.1.a.).

Consider the possible consequences if a therapist encourages a Vietnamese client to behave more assertively toward his father. The reality of this situation may be that the father would refuse to speak again to a son who confronted him. Even though counselors may be operating with good intentions and may think they are being beneficent, they may not always be doing what is in the best interest of the client. Is it possible for counselors to harm clients unintentionally by encouraging a course of action that has negative consequences? How can counselors know what is in the best interest of their clients? How can counselors determine whether their interventions will lead to growth and development in their clients?

- **Justice** means to be fair by giving equally to others. Everyone, regardless of age, sex, race, ethnicity, disability, socioeconomic status, cultural background, religion, or sexual orientation, is entitled to equal access to mental health services. An example might be a social worker making a home visit to a parent who cannot come to the school because of transportation or child care issues and poverty. NASW's (1999) guideline illustrates this principle:

> Social workers pursue social change, particularly with and on behalf of vulnerable and oppressed individuals and groups of people. Social workers' social change efforts are focused primarily on issues of poverty, unemployment, discrimination, and other forms of social injustice. These activities seek to promote sensitivity to and knowledge about oppression and cultural and ethnic diversity. Social workers strive to ensure access to needed information, services, and resources; equality of opportunity; and meaningful participation in decision making for all people. (Ethical Principles, Social Justice.)

Another illustration of the principle of justice can be found in the APA (2002) guideline: "Psychologists recognize that fairness and justice entitle all persons to access to and benefit from the contributions of psychology to equal quality in the processes, procedures, and services being conducted by psychologists." (Principle D.).

Traditional mental health services may not be just and fair to everyone in a culturally diverse society. If intervention strategies are not relevant to some segments of the population, justice is being violated. How can practitioners adapt the techniques they use to fit the needs of diverse populations? How can new helping strategies be developed that are consistent with the worldview of culturally different clients?

- **Fidelity** means that professionals make promises and keep these promises. This entails fulfilling one's responsibilities of trust in a relationship. ACA's (2005) code encourages counselors to inform clients about counseling and to be faithful in keeping commitments made to clients:

> Clients have the freedom to choose whether to enter into or remain in a counseling relationship and need adequate information about the counseling process and the counselor. Counselors have an obligation to review in writing and verbally with clients the rights and responsibilities of both the counselor and the client. Informed consent is an ongoing part of the counseling process, and counselors appropriately document discussions of informed consent throughout the counseling relationship. (A.2.a.)

Fidelity involves creating a trusting and therapeutic relationship whereby people can search for their own solutions. However, what about clients whose culture teaches them that counselors are experts who have the function of providing answers for clients' specific problem situations? What if a client expects the counselor to provide a solution to a particular problem? If the counselor does not meet the client's expectations, is trust being established?

- **Veracity** means truthfulness. Unless practitioners are truthful with their clients, the trust required to form a good working relationship will not develop, especially in working with culturally diverse client populations. The principle of veracity is found in APA's (2002) Principle C, which deals with integrity. "Psychologists seek to promote accuracy, honesty, and truthfulness in the science, teaching, and practice of psychology."

The six principles discussed here are a good place to start in determining the degree to which your practice is consistent with promoting the welfare of the clients you serve.

Steps in Making Ethical Decisions

When making ethical decisions, ask yourself these questions: "Which values do I rely on and why? How do my values affect my work with clients?" The National Association of Social Workers (1999) cautions that you must be aware of your clients' as well as your own personal values, cultural and religious beliefs, and practices when making ethical decisions. Acting responsibly implies recognizing any conflicts between personal and professional values and dealing with them effectively. The American Counseling Association's (2005) *Code of Ethics* states that when counselors encounter an ethical dilemma they are expected to carefully consider an ethical decision-making process. Although no one ethical decision-making model is most effective, counselors need to be familiar with at least one of these models, or some combination of models.

Ethical decision making is not a purely cognitive and linear process that follows clearly defined and predictable steps. Indeed, it is crucial to acknowledge that emotions play a part in how we make ethical decisions. As a practitioner, your feelings will likely influence how you interpret both your client's behavior and your own behavior. Furthermore, if you are uncomfortable with an ethical decision and do not adequately deal with this discomfort, it will certainly influence your future behavior with your client. An integral part of recognizing and working through an ethical concern is discussing your beliefs and values, motivations, feelings, and actions with a supervisor or a colleague.

In the process of making the best ethical decisions, it is also wise to involve your clients whenever possible. Because you are making decisions about what is best for the welfare of your clients, you should discuss with them the nature of the ethical dilemma that pertains to them. The **feminist model** for ethical decision making calls for maximum involvement of the client at every stage of the process, a strategy based on the feminist principle that power should be equalized in the therapeutic relationship (Hill, Glaser, & Harden, 1995).

Consulting with the client fully and appropriately is an essential step in ethical decision making, for doing so increases the chances of making the best possible decision. Hill and colleagues (1995) suggest that in most cases the therapist does well to seek the collaboration of the client, even though the therapist bears the sole responsibility for the ultimate decision. Hill and colleagues state that the following seven steps do not always occur in this order, and that certain steps may need to be repeated, but that this model is a blueprint for action:

1. Recognizing a problem
2. Defining the problem (collaboration with client is essential at this stage)
3. Developing solutions (with client)
4. Choosing a solution
5. Reviewing the process (with client) and rechoosing
6. Implementing and evaluating (with client)
7. Continuing reflection

Walden (2006) suggests that important therapeutic benefits can result from inclusion of the client in the ethical decision-making process, and she offers some strategies for accomplishing this goal at both the organizational and individual levels. When we make decisions about a client *for* the client rather than *with* the client, Walden maintains that we rob the client of power in the relationship. When we collaborate with clients, they are empowered. By soliciting the client's perspective, we stand a good chance of achieving better counseling results and the best resolution for any ethical questions that arise. Not only are there potential therapeutic benefits to be gained by including clients in dealing with ethical concerns, but such practices also imply functioning at the aspirational level. In fact, Walden questions whether it is truly possible to attain the aspirational level of ethical functioning *without* including the client's voice in ethical concerns. By adding the voice and the unique perspective of the consumers of professional services, we indicate to the public that we as a profession are genuinely interested in protecting the rights and welfare of those who make use of our services. Walden sees few risks in bringing the client into ethical matters, and there are many benefits to both the client and the professional.

The **social constructionist model** of ethical decision making shares some aspects with the feminist model but focuses primarily on the social aspects of decision making in counseling (Cottone, 2001). This model redefines the ethical decision-making process as an interactive rather than an individual or intrapsychic process and places the decision in the social context itself, not in the mind of the person making the decision. This approach involves negotiating, consensualizing, and when necessary, arbitrating.

Garcia, Cartwright, Winston, and Borzuchowska (2003) describe a **transcultural integrative model** of ethical decision making that addresses the need for including cultural factors in the process of resolving ethical dilemmas. They present their model in a step-by-step format that counselors can use in dealing with ethical dilemmas in a variety of settings and with different client populations. Frame and Williams (2005) have developed a model of ethical decision making from a multicultural perspective based on universalist philosophy. In this model cultural differences are recognized, yet common principles such as altruism, responsibility, justice, and caring that link cultures are emphasized.

Keeping in mind the feminist model of ethical decision making, Walden's (2006) views on including the client's voice in ethical concerns, a social constructionist approach to ethics, and a transcultural integrative model of ethical decision making, we present our approach to thinking through ethical dilemmas. Following these steps may help you think through ethical problems.

1. *Identify the problem or dilemma.* Gather all the information that sheds light on the situation. Clarify whether the conflict is ethical, legal, clinical, professional, or moral—or a combination of any or all of these. The first step toward resolving an ethical dilemma is recognizing that a problem exists and identifying its specific nature. Because most ethical dilemmas are complex, it is useful to look at the problem from many perspectives. Consultation with your client begins at this initial stage and continues throughout the process of working toward an ethical decision, as does the process of documenting your decisions and actions. Frame and Williams (2005) suggest reflecting on these questions to identify and define an ethical dilemma: "What is the crux of the dilemma? Who is involved? What are the stakes? What are my values? What cultural and historical factors are in play? What insights does my client have regarding the dilemma? How is the client affected by the various aspects of the problem? What are my insights about the problem?"

2. *Identify the potential issues involved.* After the information is collected, list and describe the critical issues and discard the irrelevant ones. Evaluate the rights, responsibilities, and welfare of all those who are affected by the situation. Consider the cultural context of the situation, including any relevant cultural dimensions of the client's situation. It is important to consider the context of power and also to assess acculturation and racial identity development of the client (Frame & Williams, 2005). Part of the process of making ethical decisions involves identifying and examining the ethical principles that are relevant in the situation. Consider the six basic moral principles of autonomy, nonmaleficence, beneficence, justice, fidelity, and veracity and apply them to the

situation, including those that may be in conflict. It may help to prioritize these ethical principles and think through ways in which they can support a resolution to the dilemma. Reasons can be presented that support various sides of a given issue, and different ethical principles may sometimes imply contradictory courses of action. When it is appropriate and to the degree that it is possible, involve your client in identifying potential issues in the situation.

3. *Review the relevant ethics codes.* Ask yourself whether the standards or principles of your professional organization offer a possible solution to the problem. Consider whether your own values and ethics are consistent with, or in conflict with, the relevant codes. If you are in disagreement with a particular standard, do you have a rationale to support your position? It is imperative to document this process to demonstrate your conscientious commitment to solving a dilemma.

4. *Know the applicable laws and regulations.* It is essential for you to keep up to date on relevant state and federal laws that might apply to ethical dilemmas. This is especially critical in matters of keeping or breaching confidentiality, reporting child or elder abuse, dealing with issues pertaining to danger to self or others, parental rights, record keeping, assessment, diagnosis, licensing statutes, and the grounds for malpractice. You can also seek guidance from your professional organization on any specific concern relating to an ethical or legal situation. In addition, be sure you understand the current rules and regulations of the agency or organization where you work.

5. *Obtain consultation.* At this point, it is generally helpful to consult with colleagues to obtain different perspectives on the problem. Do not limit the individuals with whom you consult to those who share your viewpoint. If there is a legal question, seek legal counsel. If the ethical dilemma involves working with a client from a different culture or who has a different worldview than yours, it is prudent to consult with a person who has expertise in this culture. After you present your assessment of the situation and your ideas of how you might proceed, ask for feedback on your analysis. Are there factors you are not considering? Have you thoroughly examined all of the ethical, clinical, and legal issues involved in the case? It is wise to document the nature of your consultation, including the suggestions provided by those with whom you consulted. In court cases a record of consultation illustrates that you have attempted to adhere to community standards by finding out what your colleagues in the community would do in the same situation. For example, in an investigation the "reasonable person" standard may be applied: "What would a professional in your community with 3 years' experience have done in your situation?"

6. *Consider possible and probable courses of action.* At this point, you are equipped to generate a variety of possible solutions to the dilemma (Frame & Williams, 2005), and brainstorming may be useful. By listing a wide variety of courses of action, you may identify a possibility that is unorthodox but useful. Of course, one alternative is that no action is required. As you think about the many possibilities for action, discuss these options with your client as well as with other professionals and document these discussions.

7. *Enumerate the consequences of various decisions.* Ponder the implications of each course of action for the client, for others who are related to the client, and for you as the counselor. Examine the probable outcomes of various actions, considering the potential risks and benefits of each approach. Again, collaboration with your client about consequences for him or her is most important, for doing this can lead to your client's empowerment. Consider using the six fundamental moral principles (autonomy, nonmaleficence, beneficence, justice, fidelity, and veracity) as a framework for evaluating the consequences of a given course of action.

8. *Decide on what appears to be the best course of action.* To make the best decision, carefully consider the information you have received from various sources. The more obvious the dilemma, the clearer is the course of action; the more subtle the dilemma, the more difficult the decision will be. After deciding, try not to second-guess your course of action. You may wonder if you have made the best decision in a given situation, or you may realize later that another action might have been more beneficial. Hindsight does not invalidate the decision you made based on the information you had at the time. Once you have made what you consider to be the best decision, evaluate your course of action by asking these questions (Frame & Williams, 2005): "How does my action fit with my profession's code of ethics? To what degree does the action taken consider the cultural values and experiences of the client? How have my own values been affirmed or challenged? How might others evaluate my action? What did I learn from dealing with this ethical dilemma?" Reflecting on your assessment of the situation and on the actions you have taken is essential if you are to learn from your experience. Review your notes and follow up to determine the outcomes and whether further action is needed. To obtain the most accurate picture, involve your client in this process.

The procedural steps we have listed here should not be thought of as a simple and linear way to reach a resolution on ethical matters. However, we have found that these steps stimulate self-reflection and encourage discussion with clients and colleagues. Using this process, we are confident that you will find a solution that is helpful for your client, your profession, and yourself.

Dealing With Suspected Unethical Behavior of Colleagues

In our classes and workshops the question has been raised, "What should I do when I suspect other mental health professionals or colleagues are engaging in questionable behavior?" You may wonder whether it is your place to judge the practices of other practitioners. Even if you are convinced that the situation involves clear ethical violations, you may be in doubt about the best way to deal with it. Should you first discuss the matter with the person? Assuming that you do and that the person becomes defensive, should you take any other action or simply drop the matter? When would a violation be serious enough

Ethics Codes

Unethical Behavior by Colleagues

American Psychological Association (2002)

When psychologists believe that there may have been an ethical violation by another psychologist, they attempt to resolve the issue by bringing it to the attention of that individual, if an informal resolution appears appropriate and the intervention does not violate any confidentiality rights that may be involved. (1.04.)

American Counseling Association (2005)

Counselors expect colleagues to adhere to the ACA Code of Ethics. When counselors possess knowledge that raises doubts as to whether another counselor is acting in an ethical manner, they take appropriate action. (H.2.a.)

When counselors believe that another counselor is violating or has violated an ethical standard, they attempt first to resolve the issue informally with the other counselor if feasible, providing that such action does not violate confidentiality rights that may be involved. (H.2.b.)

National Association of Social Workers (1999)

Social workers should take adequate measures to discourage, prevent, expose, and correct the unethical conduct of colleagues. (2.11.)

National Organization for Human Services (2000)

Human service professionals respond appropriately to unethical behavior of colleagues. Usually this means initially talking directly with the colleague and, if no resolution is forthcoming, reporting the colleague's behavior to supervisory or administrative staff and/or to the professional organization(s) to which the colleague belongs. (Statement 24.)

that you would feel obligated to bring it to the attention of an appropriate local, state, or national committee on professional ethics? Most professional organizations have specific ethical standards that clearly place the responsibility for confronting recognized violations squarely on members of their profession. Ignoring an ethical violation is considered to be a violation in itself (see the ethics code box titled Unethical Behavior by Colleagues).

Professionals have an obligation to deal with colleagues when they suspect unethical conduct—first by informally dealing with the person, and if that does not work, then by using more formal methods of addressing the situation. Generally, the best way to proceed when you have concerns about the behavior of colleagues is to tell them directly. Then, depending on the nature of the complaint and the outcome of the discussion, reporting a colleague to a professional board would be one of several options open to you.

It is sometimes easier to see the faults in others and to judge their behavior than to examine our own behavior. Make a commitment to continually reflect on what you are doing personally and professionally. Being your own judge is more realistic and more valuable than being someone else's judge.

Self-Assessment: An Inventory of Your Attitudes and Beliefs About Ethical and Professional Issues

This inventory surveys your thoughts on various professional and ethical issues in the helping professions. The inventory is designed to introduce you to issues and topics presented in this book and to stimulate your thoughts and interest. You may want to complete the inventory in more than one sitting, giving each question your full concentration.

This is not a traditional multiple-choice test in which you must select the "one right answer." Rather, it is a survey of your basic beliefs, attitudes, and values on specific topics related to the practice of therapy. For each question, write in the letter of the response that most clearly reflects your viewpoint at this time. In many cases the answers are not mutually exclusive, and you may choose more than one response if you wish. In addition, a blank line is included for each item so you can provide a response more suited to your thinking or qualify a chosen response.

Notice that there are two spaces before each item. Use the space on the left for your answer at the beginning of the course. At the end of the course, take this inventory again, placing your answer in the space on the right. Cover your initial answers so you won't be influenced by how you originally responded. Then you can see how your attitudes have changed as a result of your experience in this course.

We suggest that you bring the completed inventory to a class session to compare your views with those of others in the class. Such a comparison might stimulate debate and help the class understand the complexities in this kind of decision making. In choosing the issues you want to discuss in class, circle the items that you felt most strongly about. Ask others how they responded to these items in particular.

___ ___ 1. **Fees.** If I were working with a client who could no longer continue to pay my fees, I would most likely

a. see this person at no fee until his or her financial position changed.
b. give my client the name of a local community clinic that provides low-cost treatment.
c. suggest bartering of goods or services for therapy.
d. lower my fee to whatever the client could afford.
e. ______________________________

___ ___ 2. **Therapy for therapists.** For those who wish to become therapists, I believe personal psychotherapy

a. should be required for licensure.
b. is not an important factor in the ability to work with others.
c. should be encouraged but not required.
d. is needed only when the therapist has some form of psychological impairment.
e. ______________________________

___ ___ 3. **Therapist effectiveness.** To be an effective helper, I believe a therapist
- a. must like the client.
- b. must be free of any personal conflicts in the area in which the client is working.
- c. needs to have experienced the same problem as the client.
- d. needs to have experienced feelings similar to those being experienced by the client.
- e. ______________________

___ ___ 4. **Ethical decision making.** If I were faced with an ethical dilemma, the first step I would take would be to
- a. review the relevant ethics codes.
- b. consult with an attorney.
- c. identify the problem or dilemma.
- d. decide on what appears to be the best course of action.
- e. ______________________

___ ___ 5. **Being ethical.** For me, being an ethical practitioner *mainly* entails
- a. acting in compliance with mandatory ethical standards.
- b. reflecting on the effects my interventions are likely to have on the welfare of my clients.
- c. avoiding obvious violations of my profession's ethics codes.
- d. thinking about the legal implications of everything I do.
- e. ______________________

___ ___ 6. **Unethical supervisor.** If I was an intern and was convinced that my supervisor was encouraging trainees to participate in unethical behavior in an agency setting, I would
- a. first discuss the matter with the supervisor.
- b. report the supervisor to the director of the agency.
- c. ignore the situation for fear of negative consequences.
- d. report the situation to the ethics committee of the state professional association.
- e. ______________________

___ ___ 7. **Multicultural knowledge and skills.** Practitioners who work with culturally diverse groups without having multicultural knowledge and skills
- a. may be insensitive to their clients.
- b. may be guilty of unethical behavior.
- c. should realize the need for specialized training.
- d. may be acting illegally.
- e. ______________________

___ ___ 8. **Feelings toward clients.** If I had strong feelings, positive or negative, toward a client, I would most likely
- a. discuss the feelings with my client.
- b. keep my feelings to myself.
- c. discuss my feelings with a supervisor or colleague.
- d. accept my feelings unless they began to interfere with the counseling relationship.
- e. ______________________

___ ___ 9. **Being ready.** I won't be ready to counsel others until

a. my own life is free of problems.
b. I have experienced counseling as a client.
c. I feel confident and know that I will be effective.
d. I have developed the ability to examine my own life and relationships.
e. ______________________________

A ___ 10. **Client's feelings.** If a client expressed strong feelings of attraction or dislike for me, I would

a. help the client work through these feelings and understand them.
b. enjoy these feelings if they were positive.
c. refer my client if these feelings were negative.
d. direct the sessions into less emotional areas.
e. depends on whats in the best interest; can I maintain neutrality

___ ___ 11. **Dealing with diversity.** Practitioners who counsel clients whose sex, race, age, social class, or sexual orientation is different from their own

a. will most likely not understand these clients fully.
b. need to be sensitive to the differences between their clients and themselves.
c. can practice unethically if they ignore diversity factors.
d. will probably not be effective with such clients because of these differences.
e. ______________________________

A ___ 12. **Ethics versus law.** If I were faced with a counseling situation where it appeared that there was a conflict between an ethical and legal course to follow, I would

a. immediately consult with an attorney.
b. always choose the legal path first and foremost.
c. strive to do what I believed to be ethical, even if it meant challenging a law.
d. refer my client to another therapist.
e. ______________________________

___ ___ 13. **Values.** In terms of appreciating and understanding the value systems of clients who are culturally different from me,

a. I would not impose my cultural values on them.
b. I would encourage them to accept the values of the dominant culture for survival purposes.
c. I would attempt to modify my counseling procedures to fit their cultural values.
d. I would familiarize myself with the specific cultural values of my clients.
e. ______________________________

___ ___ 14. **Objectivity.** If a client came to me with a problem and I could see that I would not be objective because of my values, I would

a. accept the client because of the challenge to become more tolerant of diversity.

b. tell the client at the outset about my fears concerning our conflicting values.
c. refer the client to someone else.
d. attempt to understand my need to impose my values.
e. ______________________________

___ ___ 15. **End-of-life decisions.** With respect to a client's right to make his or her own end-of-life decisions, I would
a. always use the principle of a client's self-determination as the key in any dilemma of this sort.
b. tell my client what I would do if I were in this situation.
c. suggest that my client see a clergy person.
d. encourage my client to find meaning in life, regardless of his or her psychological and physical condition.
e. ______________________________

___ ___ 16. **When to refer.** I would tend to refer a client to another therapist
a. if I had a strong dislike for the client.
b. if I did not have much experience working with the kind of problem the client presented.
c. if I saw my own needs and problems getting in the way of helping the client.
d. if I had strong value differences with my client.
e. ______________________________

___ ___ 17. **Role of values.** My ethical position regarding the role of values in therapy is that, as a therapist, I should
a. never impose my values on a client.
b. expose my values, without imposing them on the client.
c. challenge my clients to find other ways of viewing their situation.
d. keep my values out of the counseling relationship.
e. ______________________________

___ ___ 18. **Sexual orientation.** If I were to counsel lesbian and gay clients, a major concern of mine would be
a. maintaining objectivity.
b. not knowing and understanding enough about their sexual orientation.
c. establishing a positive therapeutic relationship.
d. being limited by my own values.
e. ______________________________

X B ___ 19. **Unethical behavior.** Of the following, I consider the most unethical form of therapist behavior to be
a. promoting dependence in the client.
b. becoming sexually involved with a client.
c. breaking confidentiality without a good reason to do so.
d. accepting a client who has a problem that goes beyond my competence.
e. ______________________________

___ ___ 20. **Counseling friends.** Regarding the issue of counseling friends, I think that

a. it is seldom wise to accept a friend as a client.
b. it should be done rarely, and only if it is clear that the friendship will not interfere with the therapeutic relationship.
c. friendship and therapy should not be mixed.
d. it should be done only when it is acceptable to both the client and the counselor.
e. ______________________________

___ ___ 21. **Confidentiality.** Regarding confidentiality, I believe it is ethical to

a. break confidence when there is reason to believe a client may do serious harm to him- or herself.
b. break confidence when there is reason to believe that a client will do harm to someone else.
c. break confidence when the parents of a client ask for certain information.
d. inform the authorities when a client is breaking the law.
e. ______________________________

___ ___ 22. **Termination.** A therapist should terminate therapy with a client when

a. the client decides to do so.
b. the therapist judges that it is time to terminate.
c. it is clear that the client is not benefiting from the therapy.
d. the client reaches an impasse.
e. ______________________________

___ ___ 23. **Sex in therapy.** A sexual relationship between a *former* client and a therapist is

a. ethical if the client initiates it.
b. ethical only 5 years after termination of therapy. (legal after 2 years)
c. ethical only when client and therapist discuss the issue and agree to the relationship.
d. never ethical, regardless of the time that has elapsed.
e. ______________________________

___ ___ 24. **Touching.** Concerning the issue of physically touching a client, I think that touching

a. is unwise, because it could be misinterpreted by the client.
b. should be done only when the therapist genuinely thinks it would be appropriate.
c. is an important part of the therapeutic process.
d. is ethical when the client requests it.
e. of service to the clients therapy + when they consent

___ ___ 25. **Sex in supervision.** A clinical supervisor has initiated sexual relationships with former trainees (students). He maintains that because he no longer has any professional responsibility to them this practice is acceptable. In my view, this behavior is

a. clearly unethical, because he is using his position to initiate contacts with former students.

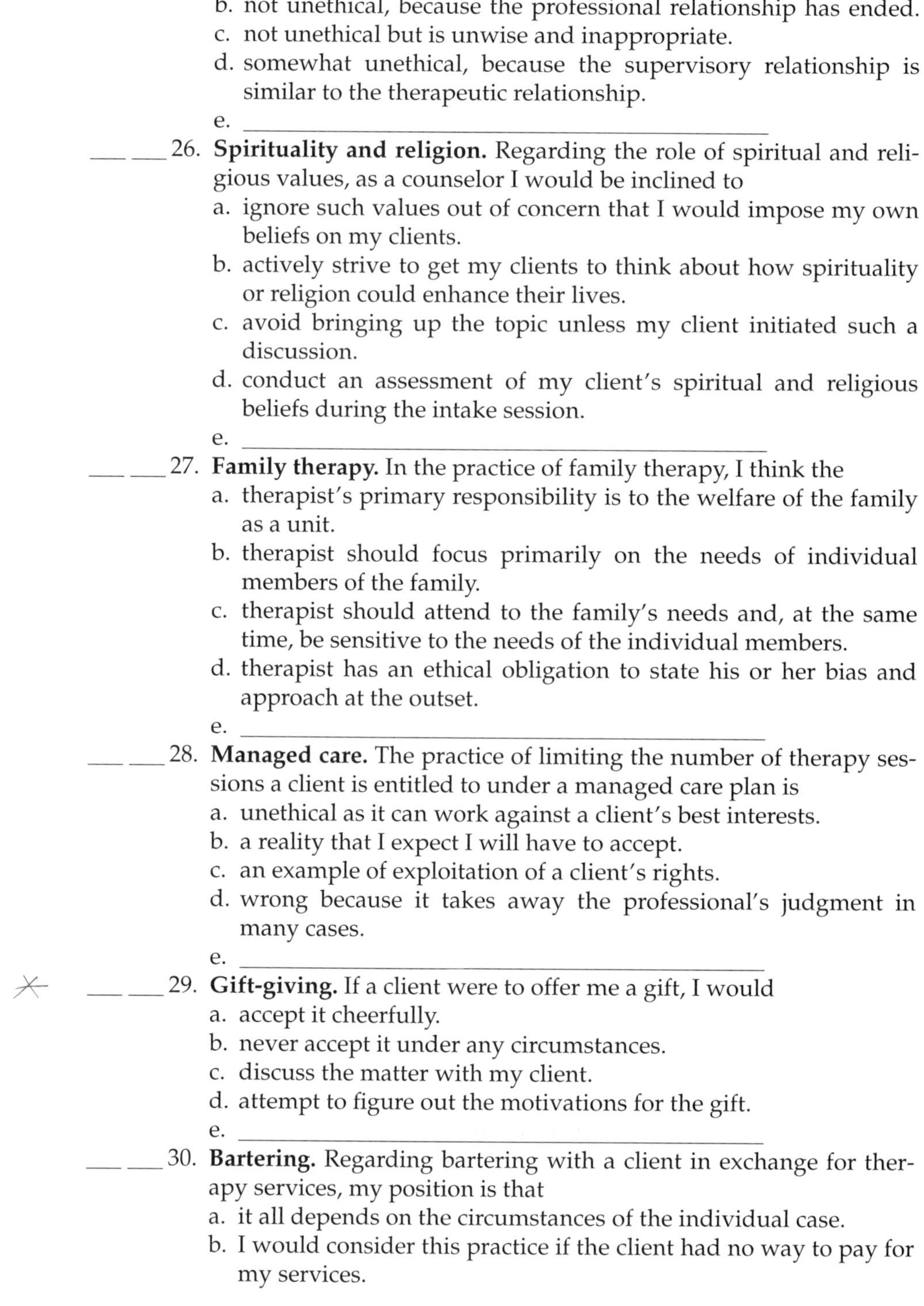

b. not unethical, because the professional relationship has ended.
c. not unethical but is unwise and inappropriate.
d. somewhat unethical, because the supervisory relationship is similar to the therapeutic relationship.
e. ______________________________

___ ___ 26. **Spirituality and religion.** Regarding the role of spiritual and religious values, as a counselor I would be inclined to
a. ignore such values out of concern that I would impose my own beliefs on my clients.
b. actively strive to get my clients to think about how spirituality or religion could enhance their lives.
c. avoid bringing up the topic unless my client initiated such a discussion.
d. conduct an assessment of my client's spiritual and religious beliefs during the intake session.
e. ______________________________

___ ___ 27. **Family therapy.** In the practice of family therapy, I think the
a. therapist's primary responsibility is to the welfare of the family as a unit.
b. therapist should focus primarily on the needs of individual members of the family.
c. therapist should attend to the family's needs and, at the same time, be sensitive to the needs of the individual members.
d. therapist has an ethical obligation to state his or her bias and approach at the outset.
e. ______________________________

___ ___ 28. **Managed care.** The practice of limiting the number of therapy sessions a client is entitled to under a managed care plan is
a. unethical as it can work against a client's best interests.
b. a reality that I expect I will have to accept.
c. an example of exploitation of a client's rights.
d. wrong because it takes away the professional's judgment in many cases.
e. ______________________________

___ ___ 29. **Gift-giving.** If a client were to offer me a gift, I would
a. accept it cheerfully.
b. never accept it under any circumstances.
c. discuss the matter with my client.
d. attempt to figure out the motivations for the gift.
e. ______________________________

___ ___ 30. **Bartering.** Regarding bartering with a client in exchange for therapy services, my position is that
a. it all depends on the circumstances of the individual case.
b. I would consider this practice if the client had no way to pay for my services.

c. the practice is unethical.
d. before agreeing to bartering I would always seek consultation.
e. ______________________________

___ ___ 31. **Diagnosis.** Concerning the role of diagnosis in counseling, I believe
a. diagnosis is essential for planning a treatment program.
b. diagnosis is counterproductive for therapy, because it is based on an external view of the client.
c. diagnosis can be harmful in that it tends to label people, who then are limited by the label.
d. the usefulness of diagnosis depends on the theoretical orientation and the kind of counseling a therapist does.
e. ______________________________

___ ___ 32. **Testing.** Concerning the place of testing in counseling, I think that tests
a. generally interfere with the counseling process.
b. can be valuable tools if they are used as adjuncts to counseling.
c. are essential for people who are seriously disturbed.
d. can be either used or abused in counseling.
e. ______________________________

___ ___ 33. **Risks of group therapy.** Regarding the issue of psychological risks associated with participation in group therapy, my position is that
a. clients should be informed at the outset of possible risks.
b. these risks should be minimized by careful screening.
c. this issue is exaggerated because there are very few real risks.
d. careful supervision will offset some of these risks.
e. ______________________________

___ ___ 34. **Internet counseling.** Regarding the practice of counseling via the Internet, I believe
a. the practice is fraught with ethical and legal problems.
b. this is a form of technology with real promise for many clients who would not, or could not, seek out face-to-face counseling.
c. it is limited to dealing with simple problems because of the inability to make an adequate assessment.
d. I would never provide Internet counseling without having some personal contact with the client.
e. ______________________________

___ ___ 35. **Inadequate supervision.** As an intern, if I thought my supervision was inadequate, I would
a. talk to my supervisor about it.
b. continue to work without complaining.
c. seek supervision elsewhere.
d. question the commitment of the agency toward me.
e. ______________________________

___ ___ 36. **Supervision.** My view of supervision is that it is
a. a place to find answers to difficult situations.
b. an opportunity to increase my clinical skills.
c. valuable to have when I reach an impasse with a client.
d. a way for me to learn about myself and to get insights into how I work with clients.
e. ____________________

___ ___ 37. **Addressing diversity.** In working with clients from different ethnic groups, it is most important to
a. be aware of the sociopolitical forces that have influenced them.
b. understand how language can be a barrier to effective multicultural counseling.
c. refer these clients to some professional who shares their ethnic and cultural background.
d. help these clients modify their views so that they will feel more accepted.
e. ____________________

___ ___ 38. **Diversity competence.** To be effective in counseling clients from a different culture, a counselor must
a. possess specific knowledge about the particular group he or she is counseling.
b. be able to accurately "read" nonverbal messages.
c. have had direct contact with this group.
d. treat these clients no differently from clients from his or her own cultural background.
e. ____________________

___ ___ 39. **Community responsibility.** Concerning the mental health professional's responsibility to the community, I believe
a. practitioners should educate the community concerning the nature of psychological services.
b. professionals should attempt to change patterns that need changing.
c. community involvement falls outside the proper scope of counseling.
d. practitioners should empower clients in the use of the resources available in the community.
e. ____________________

___ ___ 40. **Role in community.** If I were working as a practitioner in the community, the major role I would expect to play would be that of
a. a change agent.
b. an adviser.
c. an educator or a consultant.
d. an advocate.
e. ____________________

Chapter Summary

This introductory chapter focused on the foundations of creating an ethical sense and explored various perspectives on teaching the process of making ethical decisions. Professional codes of ethics are indeed essential for ethical practice, but merely knowing these codes is not enough. The challenge comes with learning how to think critically and knowing ways to apply general ethical principles to particular situations. We encourage you to become active in your education and training (see the box titled Internet Resources for information on joining a professional association). We also suggest that you try to keep an open mind about the issues you encounter during this time and throughout your professional career. An important part of this openness is a willingness to focus on yourself as a person and as a professional as well as on the questions that are more obviously related to your clients.

Suggested Activities

Note to the student. At the end of each chapter we have deliberately provided a range of activities for instructors and students to choose from. The questions and activities are intended to stimulate you to become an active learner. Our purpose is to invite you to personalize the material and develop your own positions on the issues we raise. We suggest that you choose those activities that you find the most challenging and meaningful.

1. As a practitioner, how will you determine what is ethical and what is unethical? How will you develop your guidelines for ethical practice? Make a list of behaviors that you judge to be unethical. After you have thought through this issue by yourself, you may want to explore your approach with fellow students.

Internet Resources

The following professional organizations provide helpful information on their websites about what each has to offer prospective members.

American Counseling Association (ACA)
Website: http://www.counseling.org
American Psychological Association (APA)
Website: http://www.apa.org
National Association of Social Workers (NASW)
Website: http://www.socialworkers.org
American Association for Marriage and Family Therapy (AAMFT)
Website: http://www.aamft.org
National Organization for Human Services (NOHS)
Website: http://www.nationalhumanservices.org

2. Take the self-assessment survey of your attitudes and beliefs about ethics in this chapter. Now circle the five items that you had the strongest reactions to or that you had the hardest time answering. Bring these items to class for discussion.

3. Look over the professional codes of ethics of one or more of the professional organizations. What are your impressions of each of these codes? To what degree do they provide you with the needed guidelines for ethical practice? What are the values of such codes? What limitations do you see in them? What do the various codes have in common?

Ethics in Action CD-ROM Exercises

The *Ethics in Action* CD-ROM and this text deal with the topic of ethical decision making—with emphasis on the eight steps in making ethical decisions. Other topics explored in the first part of the CD-ROM include the role of codes of ethics in making decisions and basic moral principles as they apply to resolving ethical dilemmas.

In Part 1 of the CD-ROM program, three role plays provide concrete examples of applying the steps in making ethical decisions described in this chapter. The role plays illustrate ethical dilemmas pertaining to teen pregnancy, interracial dating, and culture clash between client and counselor. After viewing each of these three vignettes, we strongly encourage you to complete the exercises that are a part of each role-play situation.

To make the fullest use of this integrated learning package, conduct small group discussions in class and engage in role-playing activities. Students can assume the role of counselor for the vignette and demonstrate how they would deal with the dilemma presented by the client. For those not using the CD-ROM, descriptive summaries of the vignettes are provided with these exercises to facilitate role plays and class discussions. We hope that the material in the CD-ROM, and in this text as well, will be a catalyst for students to try out alternative approaches to dealing with each ethical challenge presented.

InfoTrac® College Edition Resources

For additional readings, explore InfoTrac College Edition, our online library. Key words are listed in a form that enables the search engine to locate a wider range of articles in the online university library. Key words should be entered exactly as shown, including asterisks, "Wl," "W2," "AND," and other search engine tools. Go to http://www.infotrac-college.com and select these key word searches:

ethic* W4 model*
ethical community standard*
aspiration* N2 ethic*
mandat* W2 ethic*

community W1 standard* AND (psych????y OR psychotherapy OR couns*)
professionalism AND (psych????y OR psychotherapy OR couns*)
principle N2 ethic*
virtue N2 ethic* AND (psych????y OR psychotherapy OR couns*)
pro W1 bono AND (psych????y OR psychotherapy OR couns*) NOT lawyer* NOT law NOT legal
nonmaleficence AND (psych????y OR psychotherapy OR couns*) NOT medic*
beneficence AND (psych????y OR psychotherapy OR couns*) NOT medic*
social W1 construct* W1 model AND ethical decision making
feminist W1 model AND ethical decision making
transcultural integrative AND ethical decision-making model

Chapter 2

Pre-Chapter Self-Inventory

The pre-chapter self-inventories will help you identify and clarify your attitudes and beliefs about the issues to be explored in the chapter. Keep in mind that the "right" answer for you is the one that best expresses your thoughts at the time. We suggest that you complete the inventory before reading the chapter; then, after reading the chapter and discussing the material in class, complete the inventory again to see if your positions have changed in any way.

Directions: For each statement, indicate the response that most closely identifies your beliefs and attitudes. Use the following code:

5 = I *strongly agree* with this statement.
4 = I *agree* with this statement.
3 = I am *undecided* about this statement.
2 = I *disagree* with this statement.
1 = I *strongly disagree* with this statement.

_____1. Unless therapists have a high degree of self-awareness, there is a real possibility that they will use their clients to satisfy their own needs.

_____2. Before therapists begin to practice, they should be free of personal problems and conflicts.

_____3. Therapists should be required to undergo their own therapy before they are licensed to practice.

The Counselor as a Person and as a Professional

_____4. Mental health practitioners who satisfy personal needs through their work are behaving unethically.

_____5. Many in the helping professions face a high risk of burnout because of the demands of their job.

_____6. Clinicians who are self-aware are more likely to avoid experiencing overidentification with their clients.

_____7. Strong feelings about a client indicate that the practitioner needs further therapy.

_____8. Feelings of anxiety in a beginning counselor indicate unsuitability for the counseling profession.

_____9. A competent professional can work with any client.

____10. I fear that I will have difficulty challenging my clients.

____11. Ethics codes apply to the professional role behaviors of members, but it is difficult to distinguish between the personal and the professional.

____12. The person and the professional are often inseparable.

____13. Real therapy does not occur unless a transference relationship is developed.

____14. When therapists are not aware of their own needs, they may misuse their power in the therapeutic situation.

____15. An experienced and competent clinician has little need for either periodic or ongoing psychotherapy.

Introduction

A primary issue in the helping professions is the role of the counselor *as a person* in the therapeutic relationship. Because counselors are asking clients to look honestly at themselves and to choose how they want to change, counselors must be open to the same scrutiny. Counselors need to repeatedly ask themselves these questions: "What makes me think I am capable of helping anyone? What do I personally have to offer others who are struggling with their problems? Am I doing in my own life what I urge others to do?"

Counselors and psychotherapists acquire an extensive theoretical and practical knowledge as a basis for their practice, but they also bring their human qualities and life experiences to every therapeutic session. Professionals can be well versed in psychological theory and can learn diagnostic and interviewing skills and still be ineffective helpers. If counselors are to promote growth and change in their clients, they must be willing to promote growth in their own lives. This willingness to live in accordance with what they teach is what makes counselors "therapeutic persons." Mental health professionals without this focus will find it difficult to help clients make life-affirming choices. In addition, ethical problems can arise when therapists are unable to carry out this modeling role.

In this chapter we deal with some of the ways therapists' personal needs and problems can present ethical issues for the client-therapist relationship. It is difficult to talk about the counselor *as a professional* without considering personal qualities. Pipes, Holstein, and Aguirre (2005) point out that there is often a reciprocal and causal relationship between a practitioner's personal life and his or her professional behavior. For example, impairment is a debilitating intrusion of a personal difficulty into the professional realm. Likewise, feelings of pride in professional achievement can ameliorate old feelings of personal insecurity. Pipes and colleagues believe that the personal and the professional are often inseparable and point out that it can be difficult to distinguish between what is personal and what is professional. A clinician's beliefs, personal attributes, level of personal functioning, and ways of living inevitably influence the way he or she carries out a professional role, which to us is central to ethical practice. This point is emphasized in the APA's (2002) ethics code: "Psychologists strive to be aware of the possible effects of their own physical and mental health on their ability to help those with whom they work."

Some of the issues we address are specifically related to the counselor's professional identity. Although these professional issues are dealt with throughout this book, in this chapter we take up problems that are closely linked to the counselor's personal life: self-awareness, influence of counselor's personality traits, goals, needs, transference, countertransference, personal dynamics, job stress, impairment, the challenge to balance life roles, and the importance of self-care.

Self-Awareness and the Influence of the Therapist's Personality and Needs

Professionals who work intimately with others have a personal responsibility to be committed to awareness of their own life issues. Moreover, without a high level of self-awareness, mental health professionals will most likely obstruct the progress of their clients as the focus of therapy shifts from meeting the client's needs to meeting the needs of the therapist. Consequently, practitioners must be aware of their own needs, areas of "unfinished business," personal conflicts, defenses, and vulnerabilities and how these may interfere in their therapeutic work. In this section we consider two specific areas that we think you need to examine if you are going into one of the helping professions: personal needs and unresolved conflicts.

Motivations for Becoming a Counselor

Ask yourself these two critical questions: "What are my motivations for becoming a counselor?" and "What are my rewards for counseling others?" There are many answers to these questions. Therapists often experience excitement and a deep sense of satisfaction from being with people who are struggling to achieve self-understanding and who are willing to experience pain as they seek a healthier lifestyle. Some counselors appreciate the feeling of being part of this process of change. Still others are motivated to question their own lives as they work with their clients. In many ways therapeutic encounters serve as mirrors in which therapists can see their own lives reflected. As a result, therapy can become a catalyst for change in the therapist as well as in the client.

Of course, therapists *do* have their own personal needs, but these needs do not have to assume priority or get in the way of a client's growth. Therapists need to be aware of the possibility of working primarily to be appreciated by others instead of working toward the best interests of their clients. Therapeutic progress can be blocked if therapists use their clients, perhaps unconsciously, to fulfill their own needs.

Out of an exaggerated need to nurture others or to feel powerful, for example, professional helpers sometimes feel that they know how others should be. The tendency of a counselor to give advice and to direct another's life can be especially harmful because it encourages dependence on the part of clients and promotes a tendency for clients to look to others instead of themselves for answers. Therapists who need to feel powerful or important may begin to think that they are indispensable to their clients or, worse still, try to *make* themselves so.

The goals of therapy can also suffer when therapists with a strong need for approval focus on trying to win the acceptance, admiration, and even awe of their clients. Guy (2000) reminds us of the danger of depending on our clients as the main source for meeting our needs of admiration or belonging. When we are unaware of our needs and personal dynamics, we are likely to satisfy our own unmet needs or perhaps steer clients away from exploring conflicts that we ourselves fear. Because clients often feel a need to please their therapist, clients are easily drawn into taking care of their therapist's psychological needs.

Some therapists feel ill at ease if their clients fail to make immediate progress; consequently, they may push their clients to make premature decisions or may make decisions for them. The key is for therapists to avoid meeting their own needs at the expense of the client, which is articulated in the *Code of Professional Ethics for Rehabilitation Counselors* (CCRC, 2001):

> In the counseling relationship, rehabilitation counselors will be aware of the intimacy and responsibilities inherent in the counseling relationship, maintain respect for clients, and avoid actions that seek to meet their personal needs at the expense of clients. (A.4.)

As a way of understanding your needs and their possible influence on your work, ask yourself these questions:

- How will I know when I'm working for the client's benefit or working for my own benefit?
- Even though I have personal experiences with a problem a client is having, can I be objective enough to relate to this person professionally and ethically?
- How much do I depend on being appreciated by others in my own life? Am I able to appreciate myself, or do I depend primarily on sources outside of myself to confirm my worth?
- Am I getting my needs for nurturance, recognition, and support met from those who are significant in my life?
- Do I feel inadequate when clients don't make progress? If so, how could my attitude and feelings of inadequacy adversely affect my work with these clients?

With the exception of a crisis situation, therapists who tell clients what to do with their lives diminish the autonomy of their clients and invite increased dependence in the future. Examine your behavior to see if you are depending on your clients to fulfill your need for self-worth.

Personal Problems and Conflicts

Mental health professionals can and should be *aware* of their own biases, areas of denial, and unresolved problems and conflicts. Personal therapy may reduce the intensity connected with these problems, but it is probably a misconception to believe that such problems are ever fully resolved. Clearly, then, we are not implying that therapists should have resolved all their personal difficulties before they begin to counsel others. Indeed, such a requirement would eliminate most of us from the field. In fact, a counselor who rarely struggles or experiences anxiety may have real difficulty relating to a client who feels desperate or caught in a hopeless conflict. Most ethics codes address this issue, including this APA (2002) standard on the importance of recognizing personal problems and taking appropriate action:

> Psychologists refrain from initiating an activity when they know or should know that there is a substantial likelihood that their personal problems will prevent them from performing their work-related activities in a competent manner. (2.06.a.)

To illustrate, suppose you are experiencing anger and frustration in your own life. Your home life is tense, and you are wondering what to do. You may be caught between fears of loneliness and a desire to be on your own, or between your fear of and need for close relationships. Can you counsel others effectively while you are struggling with your own uncertainty?

The critical point is not *whether* you happen to be struggling with personal questions but *how* you are struggling with them. Do you recognize and try to deal with your problems, or do you invest a lot of energy in denying their existence? Do you find yourself generally blaming others for your problems? Are you willing to consult with a therapist, or do you tell yourself that you can handle it, even when it becomes obvious that you are not doing so very effectively? In short, can you do in your own life what you might challenge your clients to do?

If you are in denial of your own problems, you will be in a poor position to pay attention to the problems of your clients, especially if their problem areas are also problem areas for you. Suppose a client is trying to deal with feelings of hopelessness and despair. How can you explore these feelings if in your own life you are denying them? Or consider a client who wants to explore her feelings about her sexual orientation. Can you facilitate this exploration if you feel uncomfortable talking about sexual identity issues and do not want to deal with your discomfort? Can you stay with your client emotionally when she introduces her concerns?

Because you will have difficulty helping a client in an area that you are reluctant or fearful to deal with, pay attention to the kinds of issues that make you uncomfortable, not just with clients but in your personal life as well. Knowing that your discomfort will most probably impede your work with a client can supply the motivation for you to change and to realize that you also have an ethical responsibility to be available to your clients so that they can change.

The Case of Rollo. Rollo is an intern in a clinic specializing in the treatment of children from abusive homes. He came from a family where both parents abused alcohol. Rollo finds himself easily moved to tears as he works with the children. At times he becomes angry with the parents of these children, and he agonizes over the plight of the children. He devotes extra time beyond the scheduled activities. He finds it difficult to say "no" to his clients, and his personal life, as a result, suffers. It comes to the attention of his supervisor that Rollo frequently seems stressed and short-tempered with other staff members. In their supervision hour, Rollo claims that the agency is not doing enough for the children. He proceeds to tell his supervisor how much he is affected by them and how he is continually trying to come up with ways to help them. After listening to Rollo, his supervisor suggests that Rollo consider personal therapy to further explore the way in which he is affected by these children.

- Do you see anything unethical in Rollo's behavior? Is there a point where personal involvement can be counterproductive? How would you determine that?
- Does the supervisor have a responsibility to respond to the content of Rollo's complaint? Was suggesting personal therapy sufficient as an intervention?
- What possible conflicts are you aware of in your life that might get in your way of helping certain clients through their difficulties? If you are moved to tears by your clients, does that imply that you have unresolved conflicts? Does anger directed toward abusive parents mean that you have unresolved conflicts with your parents?

Personal Therapy for Counselors

Throughout this chapter we stress the importance of counselors' self-awareness. A closely related issue is whether those who wish to become counselors should themselves undergo psychotherapy, and whether continuing or periodic personal therapy is valuable for practicing professionals. Avail yourself of therapeutic experiences aimed at increasing your availability to your clients. There are many ways to accomplish this goal: individual therapy, group counseling, consultation with colleagues, continuing education (especially of an experiential nature), and reading. Other less formal avenues to personal and professional development are reflecting on and evaluating the meaning of your work and life, remaining open to the reactions of significant people in your life, traveling to experience different cultures, meditating, engaging in spiritual activities, enjoying physical exercise, spending time with friends and family, and most important, paying attention to the areas and situations that make you feel uncomfortable.

Experiential Learning Toward Self-Understanding

Experiential learning is a basic component of many counseling programs, providing students with the opportunity to share their values, life experiences, and personal concerns in a peer group. Many training programs in counselor education recognize the value of having students participate in personal-awareness groups with their peers. Such a group experience does not necessarily constitute group therapy; however, it can be therapeutic in that it provides students with a framework for understanding how they relate to others and can help them gain a deeper insight into their shared concerns. A group can be set up specifically for the exploration of personal concerns, or such exploration can be made an integral part of training and supervision groups. Whatever the format, students will benefit most if they are willing to focus on themselves personally and not merely on their clients. Beginning counselors tend to focus primarily on client dynamics, as do many supervisors and counselor educators. Being in a group affords students the opportunity to explore questions such as these: "How am I feeling about being a counselor? Do I like my relationships with my clients? What reactions are being evoked in me as I work with them?" By becoming personally invested in their own therapeutic process, students can use the training program as an opportunity for expanding their abilities to be helpful.

It is important for teachers and supervisors to clarify the fine line between training and therapy in the same way that fieldwork agencies must maintain the distinction between training and service. Although these areas overlap, it is clear that the emphasis for students needs to be on training in both academic and clinical settings, and it is the educator's and supervisor's responsibility to maintain that emphasis. The essential point is that students are informed at the outset of the program of any requirement for personal exploration and self-disclosure, and also that they be informed about the nature of courses that involve experiential learning. The informed consent process is especially important in cases where the instructor also functions in the role of the facilitator of a group experience. We discuss this topic at greater length in Chapters 7, 8, and 9.

✓ **The Case of a Required Therapeutic Group.** Miranda is a psychologist in private practice who is hired by the director of a graduate program in counseling psychology to lead an experiential group. She assumes that the students have been informed about this therapeutic group, and she is given the impression that the students are eagerly looking forward to it. When she encounters the students at the first class, however, she meets with resistance. They express resentment that they were not told that they would be expected to participate in a therapeutic group. Many of the students are attending out of fear that there will be negative consequences if they do not. They question the validity of their consent.

- If you were a student in this program, how might you have reacted?
- Is it ever ethical to mandate self-exploration experiences?
- If you were the director of the program, how would you handle the situation?
- The students knew from their orientation and the university's literature that this graduate program included some form of self-exploration. In your opinion, was this disclosure sufficient for ethical purposes?
- If you were Miranda, what would you do in this situation? How would you deal with the students' objections?

Personal Therapy During Training

Studies on Personal Therapy for Trainees. In a study conducted by Coster and Schwebel (1997), psychologists favored recommending personal therapy in general to all students but not requiring it unless it appeared to be professionally necessary. Schwebel and Coster (1998) report that requiring personal therapy for graduate students is overwhelmingly supported by administrators of programs in professional psychology. Dearing, Maddux, and Tangney (2005) emphasize the responsibility of faculty, supervisors, and mentors in educating trainees about appropriate pathways to self-care and prevention of impairment. They suggest that students are more likely to seek personal therapy when faculty convey favorable and supportive attitudes about students participating in therapy. It is apparent that more attention needs to be paid to the risk factors associated with problems such as compassion fatigue, distress, impairment, and self-care (Gilroy, Carroll, & Murra, 2002; Kramen-Kahn & Hansen, 1998; Schwebel & Coster, 1998; Skovholt, 2001). Gilroy and colleagues (2002) believe self-care, which may include personal therapy, is a moral imperative for mental health practitioners. They state that the current focus of training programs on clinical skills is not enough.

Personal therapy seems to be a necessary component for the growth of clinicians. However, few empirical studies in the literature focus on the benefits or liabilities of personal therapy (Gilroy et al., 2002). Dearing and colleagues (2005) indicate that confidentiality issues, general attitudes about therapy, and the importance of personal therapy for professional development were key predictors for trainees seeking their own therapy. They suggest that students consider the potential benefits, both personally and professionally, of psychotherapy during their training, including alleviation of personal distress, a means of gaining insight into being an effective therapist, and development of healthy and enduring self-care habits.

Holzman, Searight, and Hughes (1996) conducted a survey to investigate the experience of personal therapy among clinical psychology graduate students. Nearly 75% of the respondents reported receiving personal therapy at some point in their lives, most often during graduate school. Of those who had been in therapy prior to or during graduate school, 99% reported that they were still in therapy or would consider getting involved in therapy again. Among those receiving therapy, the average length of treatment was 1.5 years. Generally, they saw their experience in personal therapy as being positive, and they viewed this experience as important for practicing as a therapist. The vast majority of the sample entered treatment voluntarily rather than meeting a requirement of their graduate program. They perceived their therapy as providing them with valuable experiential learning that complemented their education and supervision as clinical psychologists.

This study sheds a positive light on the degree to which many graduate students seek therapy for personal enrichment and as a source of training. It challenges counselor education programs to work with therapy providers outside the program to offer psychological services to graduate students in their programs. Because of the ethical problems of counselor educators and supervisors providing therapy for their students and supervisees, faculty members have an obligation to become advocates for their students by identifying therapeutic resources students can afford. There are both practical and ethical reasons to prefer professionals external to a program (who are not part of a program and who do not have any evaluative role in the program) when providing psychological services for students. Practitioners from the community could be hired by a counselor-training program to conduct therapeutic groups, or students might take advantage of either individual or group counseling from a community agency, a college counseling center, or a private practitioner.

In a doctoral dissertation on the effects of personal counseling on the professional counselor in the delivery of clinical services, Newhouse-Session (2004) found that all 10 clinicians who participated in her qualitative study believed that personal therapy was beneficial, not only for them personally but in their delivery of services to their clinical practice as well. The results of her study revealed that personal therapy improved the clinician's awareness of areas of conflict and resolution of his or her own problems. Eight of the 10 clinicians in her study thought that personal counseling should be mandated for any person in the counseling profession, a sentiment echoed by Gilroy and colleagues (2002) for students. The participants in the study reported that their ability to be effective and to form a successful working alliance with clients was enhanced by keeping a check on their own past or current issues through personal counseling.

Reasons for Participating in Personal Psychotherapy. As a potential helper, we encourage you to experience your own therapy. First, it is helpful for you to know what the experience of being a client is really like. Therapy can help you take an honest look at your motivations in becoming a helper. Through therapy you can explore how your needs influence your actions, how you use power in your life, what your values are, and whether you have a need to tell others what to do.

When students are engaged in practicum, fieldwork, and internship experiences and the accompanying individual and group supervision sessions, the following issues may surface:

- A tendency to tell people what to do
- A desire to alleviate clients' pain
- A need for quick solutions
- A fear of making mistakes
- A desire to be recognized and appreciated
- A tendency to assume too much responsibility for client change
- A fear of doing harm, however inadvertently
- A tendency to deny or not recognize client issues that may relate to their own issues

As students begin to practice counseling, they sometimes become aware that they are taking on a professional role that resembles the one they played in their family. They may recognize a need to preserve peace by becoming caretakers. When students become aware of concerns such as these, therapy can provide a safe place to explore these personal issues.

Most of us have areas in our lives that are not developed and that limit our effectiveness, both as persons and as professionals. Trainees need to be aware of these areas and the ways in which they affect their professional work. Personal therapy is one way of understanding your dynamics and enhancing your effectiveness as a helper.

Psychotherapy for Remediation Purposes. What is the value of psychotherapy when it is applied to the remediation of the problems of psychology trainees? Elman and Forrest (2004) conducted interviews with the training directors of 14 doctoral programs regarding the use of personal therapy for remediation. Elman and Forrest point to the literature that shows a high frequency of recommending personal psychotherapy for remediation purposes during professional training. However, they add that there are limited empirical findings about its effectiveness and ethical concerns about the way personal therapy is sometimes used. A theme that emerged from a qualitative analysis of these exploratory interviews with training directors was balancing confidentiality of the trainee's therapy with accountability of training programs to protect future consumers.

Training programs have the challenge of providing developmentally appropriate educational experiences for trainees in a safe learning environment and at the same time protecting the public by graduating competent professionals. Another study (Vacha-Haase, Davenport, & Kerewsky, 2004) showed that although personal psychotherapy was often endorsed as a remediation measure for students with deficient interpersonal skills, the efficacy of this approach has not been well established empirically. In short, mandated psychotherapy is not always viewed as an effective intervention.

It is important for graduate programs to provide a safe context for training, and the rights and welfare of students must be considered. However, we believe counselor educators can go too far in the direction of protecting the rights of counselor trainees, for example, by refusing to require any form of self-exploratory experience as part of their program lest it invade the privacy of students. Although it is important to protect students' rights to privacy, we are also concerned about protecting the public. One way to ensure that the consumer will get the best help available is to prepare students both academically and personally for the challenges they will face when they become practitioners.

Ethical Issues in Requiring Personal Therapy. Professional organizations often provide guidelines regarding personal therapy for trainees or converting supervision sessions into therapy sessions for supervisees. Certain codes emphasize the right of students and trainees to make informed decisions about disclosing personal matters. For example, APA (2002) has the following standard on mandatory individual or group therapy:

> (a) When individual or group therapy is a program or course requirement, psychologists responsible for that program allow students in undergraduate and graduate programs the option of selecting such therapy from practitioners unaffiliated with the program.
>
> (b) Faculty who are or are likely to be responsible for evaluating students' academic performance do not themselves provide that therapy. (7.05.)

Although it is *not* appropriate for supervisors to function as therapists for their supervisees, good supervision is therapeutic in the sense that the supervisory process involves dealing with the supervisee's personal limitations and impairments so that clients are not harmed. Working with difficult clients often affects trainees in personal ways. It is a challenge for both trainees and experienced therapists to recognize and deal effectively with their countertransference. A study by Sumerel and Borders (1996) indicates that supervisors who are open to discussing personal issues with supervisees in an appropriate manner do not necessarily affect the supervisor-supervisee relationship negatively.

We believe it is appropriate for supervisors to encourage their supervisees to consider personal therapy with another professional as a route to becoming more effective both personally and professionally. A more detailed exploration of the multiple roles and responsibilities of supervisors, along with ethical issues in combining therapy with supervision, is included in Chapter 9. At this point, ask yourself these questions:

- What kind of self-exploration have I engaged in prior to or during my training?
- How open am I to examining my own personal characteristics that could be either strengths or limitations in my role as a counselor?
- At this time, what am I doing to work through personal problems?

Ongoing Therapy for Practitioners

Experienced practitioners can profit from a program that will challenge them to reexamine their beliefs and behaviors, especially as these pertain to their effectiveness in working with clients. Committed professionals engage in a lifelong self-examination as a means of remaining self-aware and genuine. Baker (2003) advocates personal psychotherapy as being beneficial to both trainees and experienced practitioners, contending that therapy serves different functions at different stages of life:

> As a young trainee, therapy in the service of deepening self-awareness is invaluable. Granting one's self the option to return to therapy as a seasoned therapist for further psychotherapy work is also potentially very beneficial, personally and professionally. . . . Therapy is also an appropriate means of addressing the major occupational hazard of consciously or unconsciously using the demands and involvements of work as a way to avoid dealing with our own personal issues. (pp. 84–85)

In a national survey of therapists as patients, Pope and Tabachnick (1994) found that of the 84% who had been in personal therapy only two individuals described it as unhelpful. Respondents mentioned three outcomes as the most beneficial: self-awareness or self-understanding, self-esteem or self-confidence, and improved skills as a therapist. The problem areas most often mentioned as being addressed in personal therapy were depression or general unhappiness, marriage or divorce, relationship concerns, self-esteem and self-confidence, anxiety, career, academics, and family-of-origin issues.

When practitioners have been found guilty of a violation, some licensing boards require therapy as a way for practitioners to recognize and monitor their countertransference. We think this provides a rationale for psychotherapy for both trainees and practitioners as a way of reducing or eliminating the potential negative consequences of practicing psychotherapy. Mahrer (2000) makes the case for mental health professionals to use psychotherapy "on oneself, for oneself, and by oneself":

> I find that there is almost always a huge hiatus between what most psychotherapists rely on and trust in their own personal lives and what they rely on and trust in their professional work with clients. It seems sensible that if therapists truly have faith in some of the methods they use in their professional work, they would use these methods on and for themselves in their personal lives. (p. 228)

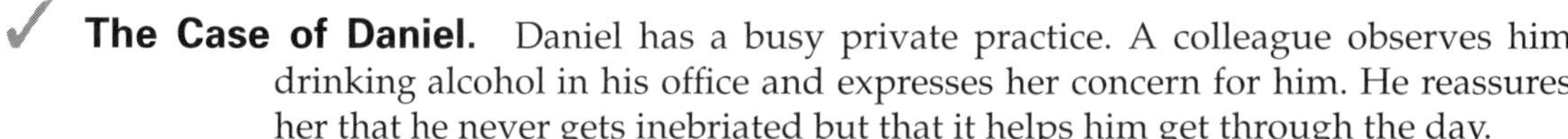

The Case of Daniel. Daniel has a busy private practice. A colleague observes him drinking alcohol in his office and expresses her concern for him. He reassures her that he never gets inebriated but that it helps him get through the day.

- Would you have a problem with Daniel's behavior?
- Does his assertion that "I never get inebriated" suffice to render the situation harmless?
- Is his method of stress reduction acceptable and ethical? Would you personally challenge Daniel in this situation, and how would you do it?
- As his colleague, do you have an ethical obligation to report the matter?

On an ongoing basis, therapists have to recognize and deal with their personal issues as they affect their clients. A high degree of self-awareness and a deep respect and concern for clients are safeguards. In the next section we explore ways in which transference and countertransference can facilitate or interfere with therapy.

Transference and Countertransference

Although the terms *transference* and *countertransference* derive from psychoanalytic theory, they are universally applicable to counseling and psychotherapy and refer to the client's general reactions to the therapist and to the therapist's reactions in response (Gelso & Carter, 1985). Conceptualizing transference and countertransference broadly, Gelso and Carter assume that these processes are universal and that they occur, to varying degrees, in most relationships. The therapeutic relationship can intensify the reactions of both client and therapist, and how practitioners handle both their own feelings and their clients' feelings will have a direct bearing on therapeutic outcomes. If these issues are not attended to, clients' progress will most likely be impeded. Therefore, this matter has implications from both an ethical and a clinical perspective.

Transference: The "Unreal" Relationship in Therapy

Transference is the process whereby clients project onto their therapists past feelings or attitudes they had toward significant people in their lives. Transference typically has its origins in early childhood and constitutes a repetition of past material. This causes a distortion in the way clients perceive and react to the therapist. The client's feelings are rooted in past relationships but those feelings are now directed toward the therapist. How the therapist handles this is crucial. If therapists are unaware of their own dynamics, they may miss important therapeutic issues when they should be challenging their clients to understand and resolve the feelings they are bringing into the present from their past.

Transference is not a catch-all concept intended to explain every feeling clients express toward a therapist. If a client expresses anger toward you, it may be justified. If a client expresses affection toward you, these feelings may be genuine; dismissing them as infantile fantasies can be a way of putting distance between yourself and your client. It is possible for therapists to err in either direction—being too quick to explain away negative feelings or too willing to accept positive feelings. To understand the real import of clients' expressions of feelings, therapists have to actively work at being open, vulnerable, and honest with themselves. Although ethical practice implies that therapists are aware of the possibility of transference, they also need to be aware of the potential of discounting the genuine reactions their clients have toward them.

Let's look at two brief, open-ended cases in which we ask you to imagine yourself as the therapist. How do you think you would respond to each client? What are your own reactions?

✓ **The Case of Shirley.** Your client, Shirley, seems extremely dependent on you for advice in making even minor decisions. It is clear that she does not trust herself and that she often tries to figure out what you might do in her place. She asks you personal questions about your marriage and your family life. She has elevated you to the position of someone who makes wise choices, and she is trying to emulate you. At other times she tells you that her decisions typically turn out to be poor ones. Consequently, when faced with a decision, she vacillates and becomes filled with self-doubt. Although she says she realizes that you cannot give her the answers, she keeps asking you what you think about her decisions.

- How would you deal with Shirley's behavior?
- How would you respond to her questions about your private life?
- If many of your clients expressed the same thoughts as Shirley, is there anything in your counseling style that you may need to examine?

✓ **The Case of Marisa.** Marisa tells you that she is disappointed in her counseling. She doesn't know if you really care about her. She would like to be more special to you, rather than "just another client."

- How would you deal with Marisa's expectations?
- Can you see a potential ethical issue in the manner in which you would respond to her?
- Would you tell her how she affected you? Why or why not?

Countertransference: Clinical Implications

So far we have focused on the transference feelings of clients toward their counselors, but counselors also have emotional reactions to their clients, some of which may involve their own projections. It is not possible to deal fully here with all the possible nuances of transference and countertransference. Instead, we will focus on improperly handling these reactions in the therapeutic relationship, a situation that directly pertains to ethical practice.

Countertransference can be considered, in the broad sense, as any projections by therapists that distort the way they perceive and react to a client. In other words, the therapist's reaction to the client is intensified by the therapist's own experience. Ethically, therapists are expected to identify and deal with their reactions through supervision or consultation so that "their problem" does not become the client's problem. There are also deeper issues, some of which may be unconscious, that evoke strong reactions to the client. It may be helpful to consider the countertransference material being stirred up as a way of interpreting subtle or unconscious messages from the client. The client might actually want an "aloof therapist" because of a fear that more difficult material would surface if the therapist was more approachable. If a therapist becomes frustrated with a client, it could be that this client, possibly unconsciously, wants progress to stop.

Countertransference can be either a constructive or a destructive element in the therapeutic relationship. A therapist's countertransference can illuminate some significant dynamics of a client. A client may actually be stimulating reactions in a therapist by the ways in which he or she makes the therapist into a key figure from the past. The fact that the client may have stimulated the countertransference in the therapist does not make this the client's problem. The key here is how the therapist responds. The therapist who recognizes these patterns can eventually help the client change old dysfunctional themes. Destructive countertransference occurs when a counselor's own needs or unresolved personal conflicts become entangled in the therapeutic relationship, obstructing or destroying a sense of objectivity. In this way, countertransference becomes an ethical issue, as is illustrated in the case that follows.

✓ **The Case of Lucia.** Lucia is a Latina counselor who has been seeing Thelma, who is also a Latina. Thelma's presenting problem was her depression related to an unhappy marriage. Her husband, an alcoholic, refuses to come to counseling with Thelma. She works full time in addition to caring for their three children. Lucia is aware that she is becoming increasingly irritated and impatient with her client's "passivity" and lack of willingness to take a strong stand with her husband. During one of the sessions, Lucia says to Thelma: "You are obviously depressed, yet you seem unwilling to take action to change your situation. You have been talking about the pain of your marriage for several months and tend to blame your husband for how you feel. You keep saying the same things, and nothing changes. Your husband refuses to seek treatment for himself or to cooperate with your therapy, yet you are not doing anything to change your life for the better." Lucia says this with a tinge of annoyance. Thelma seems to listen but does not respond. When Lucia reflects on this session she becomes aware that she has a tendency to be more impatient and harsh with female clients from her own culture, especially over the issue of passivity. She realizes that she has not invited Thelma to explore ways that her cultural background and socialization have influenced her decisions. In talking about this case with a supervisor, Lucia explores why she seems to be triggered by women like Thelma. She recognizes that she has a good deal of unfinished business with her mother, whom she experienced as extremely passive.

- If you were Lucia's supervisor, what would you most want to say to her?
- Both the therapist and the client share a similar cultural background. To what extent does that need to be explored?
- If you were Lucia's supervisor, would you suggest self-disclosure as a way to help her client? What kind of therapist disclosure might be useful? Can you see any drawbacks to therapist self-disclosure in this situation?
- Because of Lucia's recognition of her countertransference with passive women, would you suggest that she refer Thelma to another professional? Why or why not?
- What reactions do you have to the manner in which Lucia dealt with Thelma? Could any of Lucia's confrontation be viewed as therapeutic? What would make her confrontation nontherapeutic?
- Are there any ways that Lucia's recognition of her own struggles with her mother could actually facilitate her work with women like Thelma?
- What are the ethical dimensions in this case?

If you found yourself in a situation where your unresolved personal problems and countertransference reactions were interfering with your ability to work effectively with a particular client, what actions would you take?

Commentary. Regardless of how self-aware and insightful counselors are, the demands of practicing therapy are great. The emotionally intense relationships therapists develop with clients can be expected to tap into their own unresolved conflicts. Because countertransference may be a form of identification with the client, the counselor can easily get lost in the client's world and be of little therapeutic value. In the case of Lucia, the ethical course of action we would suggest would be for Lucia to involve herself in personal therapy to address some of her own unresolved issues. Supervision would enable her to monitor her reactions to certain behaviors of clients that remind her of aspects in herself that she struggles with.

If countertransference is recognized by counselors, they can seek supervision and perhaps their own therapy if their countertransference is pervasive. Ethical practice requires that practitioners remain alert to their emotional reactions to their clients, that they attempt to understand such reactions, and that they do not inflict harm because of their personal problems and conflicts.

✓ **The Case of Ruby.** Ruby is counseling Henry, who expresses extremely hostile feelings toward homosexuals and toward people who have contracted AIDS. Henry is not coming to counseling to work on his feelings about gay people; his primary goal is to work out his feelings of resentment over his wife, who left him. In one session he makes derogatory comments about gay people. He thinks they are all deviant and that it serves them right if they do get AIDS. Ruby's son is gay, and Henry's prejudice affects her emotionally. She is taken aback by her client's comments, and she finds that his views are getting in the way as she attempts to work with him. Her self-dialogue has taken the following turns:

- Maybe I should tell Henry how he is affecting me and let him know I have a son who is gay. If I don't, I am not sure I can continue to work with him.
- I think I will express my hurt and anger to a colleague, but I surely won't tell Henry how he is affecting me. Nor will I let him know I am having a hard time working with him.
- Henry's disclosures get in the way of my caring for him. Perhaps I should tell him I am bothered deeply by his prejudice but not let him know that I have a gay son.
- Because of my own countertransference, it may be best that I refer him without telling him the reason I am having trouble with him.
- Maybe I should just put my own feelings aside and try to work with him on reducing his prejudice and negative reactions toward gays.

Which of Ruby's possible approaches to Henry do you find yourself most in agreement with? If Ruby came to you as a colleague and wanted to talk about her reactions and the course she should take with Henry, what might you say to her? In reflecting on what you might tell her, consider these issues:

- Is it ethical for Ruby to work on a goal that her client has not brought up?
- To what degree would you encourage Ruby to be self-disclosing with Henry? What do you think she should reveal of herself to him? What do you think she should not disclose? Why?
- Is it ethical for Ruby to continue to see Henry without telling him how she is affected by him?

Countertransference: Ethical Implications

Countertransference can show itself in many ways, as has been described by Watkins (1985). Each example in the following list presents an ethical issue because the therapist's clinical work is obstructed by countertransference reactions:

1. *Being overprotective with a client* can reflect a therapist's deep fears. A counselor's unresolved conflicts can lead him or her to steer a client away from those areas that open up the therapist's own pain. Such counselors may treat those clients as fragile and infantile.

- Are you aware of reacting to certain types of people in overprotective ways? If so, what might this behavior reveal about you?
- Do you find that you are able to allow others to experience their pain, or do you have a tendency to want to take their pain away quickly?

2. *Treating clients in benign ways* may stem from a counselor's fear of their anger. To guard against this anger, the counselor creates a bland counseling atmosphere. This tactic results in exchanges that are superficial.

- Are you aware of how you typically react to anger expressed toward you?
- What might you do if you became aware that your exchanges are primarily superficial?

3. *Rejecting a client* may be based on the therapist's perception of the client as needy and dependent. Instead of moving toward the client to protect him or her, the counselor may move away from the client. The counselor remains cool and aloof and does not let the client get too close (Watkins, 1985).

- How do you react to unmotivated clients?
- Do you find yourself wanting to create distance from certain types of people?
- What can you learn about yourself by looking at those people whom you are likely to reject?

4. *Needing constant reinforcement and approval* can be a reflection of countertransference. Just as clients may develop an excessive need to please their therapists, therapists may have an inordinate need to be reassured of their effectiveness. When therapists do not see immediate positive results, they become discouraged and anxious.

- Do you need to have the approval of your clients? How willing are you to confront them even at the risk of being disliked?
- How effectively are you able to confront others in your own life? What does this behavior tell you about yourself as a therapist?

5. *Seeing yourself in your clients* can be another form of countertransference. This is not to say that feeling close to a client and identifying with that person's struggle is necessarily countertransference. However, beginning therapists often identify with clients' problems to the point that they lose their objectivity. Therapists may become so lost in the client's world that they are unable to distinguish their own feelings.

- Have you ever found yourself so much in sympathy with others that you could no longer be of help to them? What would you do if you felt this way about a client?
- From an awareness of your own dynamics, list some personal traits of clients that would be most likely to elicit overidentification on your part.

6. *Developing sexual or romantic feelings* toward a client can exploit the vulnerable position of the client. Seductive behavior on the part of a client can easily lead to the adoption of a seductive style by the therapist, particularly if the therapist is unaware of his or her own dynamics and motivations. It may be natural for therapists to be more drawn to some clients than to others, and these feelings do not necessarily mean that they cannot counsel these clients effectively. More important than the mere existence of such feelings is the manner in which therapists deal with them. The possibility that therapists' sexual

feelings and needs might interfere with their work is one important reason therapists should experience their own therapy when starting to practice and should consult other professionals when they encounter difficulty due to their feelings toward certain clients. Besides being unethical and countertherapeutic, it is also illegal in many states to sexually act out with clients, a topic that we discuss in detail in Chapter 7.

- What would you do if you experienced sexual feelings toward a client?
- How would you know whether your sexual attraction to a client was countertransference?
- What would you do if you found yourself more and more frequently being sexually attracted to your client?

7. *Giving advice* can easily happen with clients who seek immediate answers. The opportunity to give advice places therapists in a superior position, and they may delude themselves into thinking that they do have answers for their clients. Some therapists experience impatience with their clients' struggles toward autonomous decision making. Such counselors may engage in excessive self-disclosure, especially by telling their clients how they have solved a particular problem for themselves. In doing so, the focus of therapy shifts from the client's struggle to the needs of the counselor. Even if a client has asked for advice, there is every reason to question whose needs are being served when a therapist falls into advice giving.

- Do you ever find yourself giving advice? What do you think you gain from it? In what ways might the advice you give to clients represent advice that you could give yourself?
- Are there any times when advice is warranted? If so, when?

8. *Developing a social relationship with clients* may stem from countertransference, especially if it is acted on while therapy is taking place. Clients occasionally let their therapist know that they would like to develop a closer relationship than is possible in the limited environment of the office. They may, for instance, express a desire to get to know their therapist as "a regular person." Mixing personal and professional relationships often destroys the relationship and could lead to a lawsuit. This is a topic we examine in Chapter 7. Ask yourself these questions:

- If I establish social relationships with certain clients, will I be as inclined to confront them in therapy as I would be otherwise?
- Will my own needs for preserving these friendships interfere with my therapeutic activities and defeat the purpose of therapy?
- Will my client be able to return to therapy if we form a social relationship after termination?
- Am I sensitive to being called an "aloof professional," even though I may strive to be real and straightforward in the therapeutic situation?
- What do I know about myself that explains my need to form friendships with clients? Whose interests are being served?

Client Dependence

Clients frequently experience a period of dependence on counseling or on their counselor. This temporary dependence is not necessarily problematic. Others see the need to consult a professional as a sign of weakness. If these clients finally allow themselves to need others, their dependence does not necessarily mean that the therapist is unethical. An ethical issue does arise, however, when counselors *encourage* dependence on the part of their clients. They may do so for any number of reasons. Counselor interns need clients, and sometimes they may keep clients longer than is necessary because they need more clinical hours or will look bad if they "lose" a client. Some therapists in private practice might fail to challenge clients who show up and pay regularly, even though they appear to be getting nowhere. Therapists can foster dependence in their clients in subtle ways. When clients insist on answers, these counselors may readily tell them what to do. Dependent clients can begin to view their therapists as having better solutions; therapists who have a need to be perceived in this way collude with their clients in keeping them immature and dependent.

DiVerde-Nushawg and Walls (1998) conducted a study of the use of pagers by clinicians and noted countertransference aspects of this practice related to promoting client dependence. Some clinicians believe they should be available to take all messages from their clients, and they have every voice mail or answering machine message paged to them, whether they are at home or in session with another client. This behavior may be based on a need to appear competent, to have solutions to every problem, and to be perceived as being in great demand. These therapists may be using their professional role as a way to avoid facing their own problems. Misuse or overuse of pagers might reflect therapists' grandiosity of how essential they are to their clients' lives and to the solution of their problems. In essence, practitioners who think they must be available 24 hours a day for any reason are probably communicating to their clients that they are not able to function on their own without therapist direction. There are ethical implications involved for therapists who implicitly or explicitly promote between-session phone calls even when clients are not in a crisis. This practice may be meeting the therapist's needs more than the needs of the client.

Client dependence can be fostered in other ways as well. If therapists are inclined to offer quick solutions to clients' problems, they could be preventing clients' empowerment. With the growth of managed care in the United States as an alternative to traditional fee-for-service delivery systems, the client-counselor relationship is changing in many ways. In the relatively brief treatment and the restricted number of sessions allowed in most managed care plans, client dependence is often less of an issue than it might be with longer term therapy. However, even in short-term, problem-oriented therapy aimed at solutions, clients can still develop an unhealthy dependence on their therapist.

Like many other ethical issues discussed here, encouraging dependence in clients is often not clear-cut. To stimulate you to think of possible ways that you might foster dependence or independence in your clients, consider the following case.

The Case of Eduardo. Eduardo, a young counselor, encourages his clients to call him at home when they need to. He expects to be on call at all times. He frequently lets sessions run overtime, lends money to clients when they are destitute, and devotes many more hours to his job than are required. He says that he lives for his work and that it gives him a sense of being a valuable person. The more he can do for people, the better he feels. This is a significant aspect of his religious commitment.

- How might his style of counseling either help or hinder a client?
- Do you see any potential ethical issues in the way Eduardo treats his clients?
- In what ways could Eduardo's style be keeping his clients dependent on him?
- Can you identify with him in any ways? Do you see yourself as potentially needing your clients more than they need you?
- How would you include or exclude his religious commitment in evaluating the potential ethical issues of the case?

Delaying Termination as a Form of Client Dependence

Most professional codes have guidelines that call for termination whenever further therapy will not bring significant gains, but some therapists have difficulty letting go of their clients. They run the risk of unethical practice because of either financial or emotional needs. Obviously, termination cannot be mandated by ethics codes alone; it rests on the honesty of the therapist and the willingness to include the client in that process.

We agree with Kramer (1990) that, more than at any other phase of therapy, the ending demands that therapists examine and understand their own needs and feelings about endings. Kramer emphasizes the therapist's role in enabling clients to understand and accept the termination process: "A general philosophy that is respectful of patients and sees them as autonomous, proactive, and self-directive is essential if the therapist is to facilitate healthy, productive endings" (p. 3). In our view, the ultimate sign of an effective therapist is his or her ability to help clients reach a stage of self-determination wherein they no longer need a therapist.

Most of the ethics codes of the various professions state that practitioners should terminate services to clients when such services are no longer required, when it becomes reasonably clear that clients are not benefiting from therapy, or when the agency or institution limits do not allow provision of further counseling services. Apply the general spirit of these codes to these questions:

- How would you know when services are no longer required?
- What criteria would you use to determine whether your client is benefiting from therapy?
- What would you do if your client feels he or she is benefiting from therapy but you don't see any signs of progress?

- What would you do if you are convinced that your client is coming to you seeking friendship and not really for the purpose of changing?
- What are the ethical issues involved if your agency limits the number of sessions yet your client is clearly benefiting from counseling? What if termination is likely to result in harm to the client?

Imagine yourself as the therapist in the following two cases. Ask yourself what you would do, and why, if you were confronted with the problem described.

✓ **The Case of Jesse.** After five sessions your client, Jesse, asks: "Do you think I'm making any progress toward solving my problems? Do I seem any different to you now than I did 5 weeks ago?" Before you give him your impressions, you ask him to answer his own questions. He replies: "Well, I'm not sure whether coming here is doing that much good or not. I suppose I expected resolutions to my problems before now, but I still feel anxious and depressed much of the time. It feels good to come here, and I usually continue thinking about what we discussed after our sessions, but I'm not coming any closer to decisions. Sometimes I feel certain this is helping me, and at other times I wonder whether I'm just fooling myself."

- What criteria can you employ to help you and your client assess the value of counseling for him?
- Does the fact that Jesse continues to think about his session during the rest of the week indicate that he is probably getting something from counseling? Why or why not?

✓ **The Case of Enjolie.** Enjolie has been coming regularly to counseling for some time. When you ask her what she thinks she is getting from the counseling, she answers: "This is really helping. I like to talk and have somebody listen to me. I often feel like you are the only friend I have and the only one who really cares about me. I suppose I really don't do that much outside, and I know I'm not changing that much, but I feel good when I'm here."

- Is it ethical to continue the counseling if Enjolie's main goal seems to be the "purchase of friendship"? Why or why not?
- Would it be ethical to terminate Enjolie's therapy without exploring her need to see you?
- How ethical would it be for you to continue to see Enjolie if you were convinced that she wasn't changing?

Stress in the Counseling Profession

The Hazards of Helping

Counseling can be a hazardous profession, and its stresses stem from the nature of the work, from the professional role expectations of helpers, and from the individual dynamics of the practitioner. Mental health practitioners are typically not given enough warning about the hazards of the profession they are about to enter. Radeke and Mahoney (2000) offer some sound advice:

> Persons considering a career in psychotherapy should be informed that it will be likely to result in changes in their personal lives. Their development may be accelerated, their emotional life may be amplified, and they are likely to feel both stressed and satisfied by their work. (p. 82)

Many counselors in training look forward to a profession in which they can help others and, in return, feel a deep sense of self-satisfaction. They are not told that the commitment to self-exploration and to inspiring this search in clients can be fraught with difficulties. Effective practitioners use their own life experiences and personal reactions to help them understand their clients and as a method of working with them. As you will recall, the process of working therapeutically with people opens up personal themes in the therapist's life. The counselor, as a partner in the therapeutic journey, can be deeply affected by a client's pain. The activation of painful memories can resonate with the practitioner's own life experiences. Old pain can be stirred up and old wounds can be opened. Pain connects with pain. If these countertransference issues are not recognized, they can have ethical and painful implications for the therapist. Clinicians overburdened with stress cannot work effectively.

Graduate training programs in the helping professions need to prepare students for the disappointments they may encounter in the work they will eventually be doing. Students can be prepared for both the joys and the pains of their profession. It is good that they be informed about the hazards of the profession they are choosing. If students are not adequately prepared, they may be especially vulnerable to early disenchantment and burnout due to unrealistic expectations. There is an ethical mandate for training programs to design strategies to assist students in effectively dealing with job stress, in preventing burnout, and in emphasizing the role of self-care as a key factor in maintaining vitality.

Stress Caused by Being Overly Responsible

Many of the stressful client behaviors we discuss in this section could easily be understood as countertransference issues of the therapist. When therapists assume full responsibility for their clients' lack of progress, for instance, they are not helping clients to be responsible for their own therapy. Therapists should explore this situation with their clients. In this exploration they may discover together how assuming too much responsibility actually is a barrier to client empowerment.

Practitioners who have a tendency to readily accept full responsibility for their clients often experience their clients' stress as their own. It is important to recognize when this is happening. Some signs to look for are irritability and emotional exhaustion, feelings of isolation, abuse of alcohol or drugs, reduced personal effectiveness, indecisiveness, compulsive work patterns, drastic changes in behavior, and feedback from friends or partners. **Stress** is an event or a series of events that leads to strain, which often results in physical and psychological health problems. To assess the impact of stress on you both personally and professionally, reflect on these questions:

- To what degree are you able to recognize your problems?
- What steps are you willing to take in dealing with your problems?
- Do you practice strategies for managing stress, such as meditation, time management, and relaxation training?
- To what degree are you taking care of your personal needs in daily life?
- Are you able to recognize the symptoms warning you that you are in trouble?
- Do you listen to your family, friends, and colleagues when they tell you that stress seems to be getting the better of you?
- Are you willing to ask for help when you become aware that you are not effectively dealing with stress?

Although it is not realistic to expect to eliminate the strains of daily life, you can develop practical strategies to recognize and cope with stress that is having adverse effects on you.

Sources of Stress

Deutsch (1984) and Farber (1983b) found surprisingly similar results in their surveys of therapists' perceptions of stressful client behavior (see the box titled Most Stressful Client Behaviors for Therapists). In both studies therapists reported that clients' suicidal statements were the most stressful. Other sources of stress that therapists reported in the Deutsch (1984) study included these:

- Being unable to help distressed clients feel better
- Seeing more than the usual number of clients
- Not liking clients
- Having self-doubts about the value of therapy
- Having professional conflicts with colleagues
- Feeling isolated from other professionals
- Overidentifying with clients and failing to balance empathy with appropriate professional behavior

Most Stressful Client Behaviors for Therapists

Deutsch's (1984) Findings

1. Suicidal statements
2. Anger toward the therapist
3. Severely depressed clients
4. Apathy or lack of motivation
5. Client's premature termination

Farber's (1983a) Findings

1. Suicidal statements
2. Aggression and hostility
3. Premature termination
4. Agitated anxiety
5. Apathy and depression

- Being unable to leave client concerns behind when away from work
- Feeling sexual attraction to a client
- Not receiving expressions of gratitude from clients

Other writers have identified major sources of stress that frequently result in **burnout,** which can be defined as a state of physical, emotional, intellectual, and spiritual exhaustion characterized by feelings of helplessness and hopelessness. Kramen-Kahn and Hansen (1998) identify business aspects, economic uncertainty, professional conflicts, time pressures, sense of enormous responsibility, excessive workload, and caseload uncertainties as the most frequently endorsed occupational hazards of psychotherapists. According to Brown and O'Brien (1998), crisis intervention and other frontline mental health workers experience these sources of stress that often lead to burnout: lacking full involvement in the decision-making process related to work; feeling that their abilities are not being fully utilized on the job; being taxed by regulations, procedures, and paperwork; and being exposed to discomfort and dangers in their work setting. Sapienza and Bugental (2000) believe one of the main causes of burnout is the pressure of assuming the responsibility of solving the problems that clients bring to therapy. Lazarus (2000) views avarice and greed as the major stressors in a therapist's life. Striving to make more and more money often increases work-related pressures and emotional strain. Lazarus emphasizes how essential it is for professionals to replenish themselves. The challenge is to create a style of life that enables professionals to nourish themselves so that they can prevent distress and burnout.

Beside these sources of stress, we add the stresses associated with working in managed care and educational systems. For mental health professionals who deal with managed care, pressures revolve around getting a client's treatment approved, justifying needed treatment, quickly alleviating a client's problem, dealing with paperwork, and the anxiety of being put in an ethical dilemma when clients are denied clinically necessary further treatment. For school counselors, in addition to the expectation that they can immediately solve the behavioral problems of children, there is the added stress of dealing with the frustrations of the family, the teachers, and the administrators in the school system.

Practitioners who set exceptionally high personal goals and those with perfectionistic strivings related to helping others often report a high level of stress. Skovholt (2001) writes about the hazards of practice and points out that people tend to seek out helpers only when they are unable to solve their own problems or when their problems become too large to handle. Those in the helping professions may experience demoralizing hopelessness when confronted with what may appear to be a plethora of unsolvable problems.

In reading this section on the impact of stress on the practitioner, some readers may find the discussion discouraging. It is our contention that what is most problematic is failing to recognize inevitable stresses and, therefore, not giving ourselves the opportunity to resolve the difficulties created in and by our work so that we can continue to be effective.

Counselor Impairment

Unmanaged stress is a major cause of burnout and eventual impairment. Maslach and Leiter (1997) define burnout thusly: "Burnout is the index of the dislocation between what people are and what they have to do. It represents an erosion in values, dignity, spirit, and will—an erosion of the human soul" (p. 17). It is our belief that burnout comes at the end of a long process of what we refer to as "therapist decay." Based on our observations over the years, we have identified the following signs of therapist decay:

- An absence of boundaries with clients
- An excessive preoccupation with money and being successful
- Accepting clients beyond one's level of competence
- Poor health habits in the areas of nutrition and exercise
- The absence of camaraderie with friends and colleagues
- Living in isolated ways, both personally and professionally
- Failure to recognize how they are being affected by their clients' issues
- Being unwilling to avail themselves of personal therapy when experiencing personal distress

Impairment is the presence of an illness or severe psychological depletion that is likely to prevent a professional from being able to deliver effective services and results in consistently functioning below acceptable practice standards. A number of factors can negatively influence a counselor's effectiveness, both personally and professionally, including substance abuse, physical illness, and burnout. Impaired counselors are unable to effectively cope with stressful events and are unable to adequately carry out their professional duties, which raises both ethical and legal issues. Those therapists whose inner conflicts are consistently activated by client material may respond by distancing themselves rather than facilitating the growth of their clients.

Zur (1994) maintains that psychotherapists focus on the problems of others, yet they often fail to attend to their own needs and pay little attention to the effect their profession has on them. They sometimes avoid examining the effects of their work on their families. Zur believes that being a psychotherapist has both advantages and liabilities for one's family life. It takes a conscious effort for a therapist to minimize the liabilities and maximize the advantages. Therapists face the challenge of dealing with the negative aspects of their profession, such as emotional depletion, isolation, depression, and burnout. It is essential for therapists to let go of their professional role when they are at home, yet this is easier said than done at times.

Clearly, impaired counselors are not helping their clients. For example, the sexually exploitive behavior of counselors is a manifestation of impairment (Emerson & Markos, 1996). Counselors who become sexually involved with clients often show these personality characteristics:

- Fragile self-esteem
- Difficulty establishing intimacy in their personal lives

- Professional isolation
- A need to rescue clients
- A need for reassurance about one's attractiveness
- Substance abuse

Benningfield (1994) identifies other personal characteristics associated with impaired functioning. These signs include lack of empathy, loneliness, poor social skills, social isolation, discounting the possibility of harm to others, preoccupation with personal needs, justification of behavior, and denial of professional responsibility to clients and students. Because a common characteristic of impairment is denial, Herlihy (1996) points out that professional colleagues may need to confront the irresponsible behavior of an impaired counselor. Herlihy suggests confronting the impaired counselor with sensitivity and respect. Benningfield (1994) maintains that the responsibility for addressing the assessment, remediation, and prevention of professional impairment lies not just with the impaired practitioner, ethics committees, or licensing boards but also with colleagues.

Most therapists know that supervision, consultation, and therapy are useful resources for dealing with personal problems, but they may be hesitant to actually make use of these resources without the challenge from and encouragement of colleagues. Colleagues can play a critical role in helping impaired practitioners recognize their condition and take remedial action. However, as Benningfield (1994) points out, all therapists have an ethical responsibility to themselves, to their clients and students, and to their colleagues to monitor their own professional practice (see the ethics code box titled Professional Impairment). She suggests that therapists should engage in an ongoing process of self-assessment as a way to increase their awareness of problematic attitudinal and behavioral patterns that may lead to serious impairment. Here are some of the questions Benningfield offers for this self-assessment:

- Is my personal life satisfying and rewarding?
- To what degree am I taking care of myself, both physically and emotionally?
- Would I be willing for other therapists I respect to know about my professional conduct and decisions?
- Can I acknowledge and disclose my mistakes?
- Am I generally consistent in my practice?
- Do I think or fantasize about a relationship that goes beyond being a professional with some clients or students?

One of our reviewers observed that stress and burnout are occupational hazards in the school counseling context, which is focused on academics and teacher needs. Although school counselors have a multiplicity of demands on them, they often must function alone with little opportunity for their own supervision or for talking about how their work is affecting them personally. Time for a counselor's supervision is not built into the educational day.

What is the profession doing to address the difficulties of distressed and impaired practitioners? Barnett and Hillard (2001) conducted a survey of all 59 state and provincial psychological associations (SPPAs) to examine the

Ethics Codes

Professional Impairment

American Association for Marriage and Family Therapy (2001)

Marriage and family therapists seek appropriate professional assistance for their personal problems or conflicts that may impair work performance or clinical judgment. (3.3.)

National Association of Social Workers (1999)

Social workers whose personal problems, psychosocial distress, legal problems, substance abuse, or mental health difficulties interfere with their professional judgment and performance should immediately seek consultation and take appropriate remedial action by seeking professional help, making adjustments in workload, terminating practice, or taking any other steps necessary to protect clients and others. (4.05.b.)

American Psychological Association (2002)

When psychologists become aware of personal problems that may interfere with their performing work-related duties adequately, they take appropriate measures, such as obtaining professional consultation or assistance, and determine whether they should limit, suspend, or terminate their work-related duties. (2.06.b.)

American Counseling Association (2005)

Counselors are alert to the signs of impairment from their own physical, mental, or emotional problems and refrain from offering or providing professional services when such impairment is likely to harm a client or others. They seek assistance for problems that reach the level of professional impairment and, if necessary, they limit, suspend, or terminate their professional responsibilities, until such time it is determined that they may safely resume their work. (C.2.g.)

programs and resources available for impaired psychologists. Between 1998 and 1999, the findings of their survey indicate that 69% of all SPPAs (41 out of 59) reported that a colleague assistance program did not exist for distressed or impaired psychologists. Of these 41 SPPAs, 24% reported that they had a formal colleague assistance program available in the past. Some of the most common reasons given for discontinuing such a program included lack of use (70%), risk of liability too great (10%), and lack of volunteer support (10%). Furthermore, 61% of these 41 SPPAs reported that there were no plans to develop a program in the future, and 54% stated that a need for such resources was not perceived by the SPPA leadership. The authors of this survey indicate that the field of psychology has been slow to address issues of professional impairment, and they suggest that the profession of psychology may wish to emulate the lead of other healing professions that have effective means of preventing, identifying, and treating professional impairment. Barnett and Hillard write:

> Having an established and effective assistance program model from which to conceptualize would help the field of psychology to develop effective colleague assistance programs, as well as refine those programs that are already in existence. (p. 209)

We encourage you to reflect on the sources of stress in your life. What patterns do you see? How effectively are you managing stress? What steps can you take to recognize danger signals before you become an impaired practitioner? Would you ask for help from peers, colleagues, or supervisors? Would you seek personal therapy? Do you have a passion in your life for anything other than your work? Is there consistency between your personal life and your professional behavior? By developing a method of self-assessment for danger signs leading to impairment, you are taking important steps toward preventing problems for both yourself and your clients.

Maintaining Vitality

Sustaining the personal self is a serious ethical obligation. We agree with Skovholt (2001) that "maintaining oneself personally is necessary to function effectively in a professional role. By itself, this idea can help those in the caring fields feel less selfish when meeting the needs of the self" (p. 146). For Skovholt, **self-care** involves searching for positive life experiences that lead to zest, peace, excitement, and happiness. The demands of professional work cannot be met if practitioners are not engaged in self-care. Some ethics codes specifically address self-care, such as that of the Canadian Psychological Association (2000):

> Engage in self-care activities that help to avoid conditions (e.g., burnout, addictions) that could result in impaired judgment and interfere with their ability to benefit and not harm others. (II.12.)

Another example of the emphasis on self-care is the ethics code of the Canadian Association of Social Workers (1994):

> A social worker shall maintain an acceptable level of health and well-being in order to provide a competent level of service to a client. (3.4.)

Self-care is addressed in the *Feminist Therapy Code of Ethics* (Feminist Therapy Institute, 2000):

> A feminist therapist engages in self-care activities in an ongoing manner outside the work setting. She recognizes her own needs and vulnerabilities as well as the unique stresses inherent in this work. She demonstrates an ability to establish boundaries with the client that are healthy for both of them. She also is willing to self-nurture in appropriate and self-empowering ways. (IV.E.)

The topic of self-care for mental health professionals is receiving increased attention. For example, the American Psychological Association devoted considerable attention to self-care in an issue of *Monitor on Psychology* (July/August, 2002, Vol. 33, No. 7). This particular issue of the *Monitor* featured articles on a range of topics—from exercising and weight control to meditating and finding balance between work and family. Although professionals often have knowledge about self-care, the critical question is whether they actually apply what they know to their daily lives.

In *Caring for Ourselves: A Therapist's Guide to Personal and Professional Well-Being*, Baker (2003) emphasizes the importance of tending to mind, body, and spirit. This involves learning to pay attention to and be respectful of our needs, which is a lifelong task for therapists. Baker makes the point that for us to have enough to share with others in our personal and professional lives, we need to nourish ourselves. It will be difficult to maintain our vitality if we do not find ways to consistently tend to our whole being.

It is useful to conceptualize counselor vitality from the perspective of wellness, and several models of wellness can be applied to counseling practitioners. In a study on well-functioning, Coster and Schwebel (1997) surveyed experienced professional psychologists who identified factors that contributed to their ability to function well. The dimensions most often mentioned included self-awareness and monitoring; support from peers, spouses, friends, mentors, and colleagues; values; and a balanced life that allowed time for family and friends, not just work.

Myers, Sweeney, and Witmer (2000) define wellness as "a way of life oriented toward optimal health and well-being in which body, mind, and spirit are integrated by the individual to live more fully within the human and natural community" (p. 252). Myers and colleagues borrow from the Adlerian perspective and identify five life tasks on their wheel of wellness that are a basic part of healthy functioning. As we look briefly at each of these components, consider how you might benefit from balancing these life tasks more effectively.

- *Spirituality* is an awareness of a being or force or value that goes beyond the material dimension and gives a deep sense of wholeness or connectedness to the universe. Do you have a definition of spirituality? How do you find it reflected in the way you live and work?
- *Self-direction* involves a sense of mindfulness and intentionality in meeting major life tasks. A sense of worth, a healthy sense of control, realistic beliefs, emotional awareness and coping, problem solving and creativity, a sense of humor, good nutrition, exercise, gender identity, and cultural identity are all part of self-direction. How does each of these components play out in your life? Is self-direction important to you? Identify some ways you feel in control of your life and some ways that you do not.
- *Work and leisure* provide a sense of accomplishment. List your weekly activities. Do you have a balance between work and leisure? When you consider your family of origin, what did you learn about the role of work and leisure in life?
- *Friendship* incorporates all of one's social relationships that involve a connection with others. Do you have the kind of friends that you want? Are your friendships nourishing to you? Do you have time in your life to reach out to others without remuneration? Are you ever not a therapist?
- *Love* involves long-term, intimate, trusting, compassionate, and mutually committed relationships. Do you have a love relationship in your life? To what degree does that relationship refurbish you emotionally?

Preventing yourself from becoming an impaired professional requires that you become committed to promoting your own wellness from a holistic perspective. Perhaps the most basic way to retain your vitality as a person and as a professional is to realize that you have limitations and you cannot give and give without replenishing yourself. How do you replenish yourself? How much time do you devote to activities other than your work? And finally, do you have a good support system?

Mental health professionals often ignore the signs that they are becoming depleted. Simply recognizing that you cannot be a universal giver without getting something in return is not enough to keep you alive as a person and a professional. In writing about self-care, Lazarus (2000) points to the importance of nourishing ourselves both physically and emotionally. He suggests asking yourself these fundamental questions:

- What fun things can I do?
- What positive emotions can I generate?
- What sensory experiences can I enjoy?
- What empowering and pleasant mental images can I conjure up?
- What positive self-talk can I employ?
- Which amiable people can I associate with?
- What specific health-related activities can I engage in?

Self-care is not a luxury but an ethical mandate. You cannot provide nourishment to your clients if you don't nourish yourself. Skovholt (2001) notes that those in the helping professions are experts at one-way caring, and he warns of the dangers involved in this practice. Those who spend most of their professional time in caring for others need to acquire the art of caring for self by nurturing the emotional self, the financial self, the humorous self, the loving self, the nutritious self, the physical self, the playful self, the priority-setting self, the recreational self, the relaxation–stress reduction self, the solitary self, and the spiritual or religious self.

It is essential to create an action plan and make a commitment to carry out this plan. Learning to cope with personal and professional sources of stress generally involves making some fundamental changes in your lifestyle. It may be extremely helpful to get involved in postgraduate supervision or a peer-consultation group as a way to get feedback on your practice and the toll it may be taking on you. Take some time to ask yourself what basic changes, if any, you are willing to make in your behavior to promote your own wellness. Remember, this is routinely the question you ask your clients.

Chapter Summary

The life experiences, attitudes, and caring that we bring to our practice are crucial factors in establishing an effective therapeutic relationship. If we are unwilling to engage in self-exploration, it is likely that our fears, personal conflicts, and personal needs will interfere with our ability to be present for our clients. No amount of knowledge or technical skill can replace that component of helping.

Personal therapy during training and throughout therapists' professional careers can enhance the counselor's ability to focus on the needs and welfare of their clients. Therapists cannot take clients any further than they have taken themselves; therefore ongoing self-exploration is important. By focusing on your own personal development, you will be better equipped to deal with the range of transference reactions your clients are bound to have toward you. You will also be better able to detect potential countertransference on your part and have a basis for dealing with such reactions in a therapeutic manner. There is a potential for unethical behavior in mismanaging countertransference, and you may find that you need to review your personal concerns periodically throughout your career. This honest self-appraisal is an essential quality of effective helpers.

Stress and the inevitable burnout that typically results from inadequately dealing with chronic sources of stress also raise ethical questions. Therapists who are psychologically and physically exhausted can rarely help their clients. Mental health professionals who have numbed themselves to their own pain are ill equipped to deal with the pain of their clients. Impaired practitioners may do more harm than good for those who seek their assistance. There is no simple answer to the question of how to maintain your vitality, but you are ethically responsible for taking care of yourself both personally and professionally.

Suggested Activities

These activities and questions are designed to help you apply your learning. Many of them can be done alone or with another person; others are designed for discussion either with the whole class or in small groups. Select those that seem most significant to you and write on these issues in your journal.

1. In small groups, explore your reasons for going into a helping profession. What do you see yourself as being able to do for others?
2. In your journal or in small groups, explore these questions: To what degree might your personal needs get in the way of your work with clients? How can you recognize and meet your needs—which are a real part of you—without having them interfere with your work with others?
3. In small groups share your own concerns over becoming a counselor. What problems do you expect to face as a beginning counselor? What did you learn about yourself from a discussion of your concerns?
4. "Who has a right to counsel anybody?" In groups of three, take turns briefly stating the personal and professional qualities that you can offer people. Afterward, explore any self-doubts you have concerning your ability to counsel others.
5. Think of the type of client you might have the most difficulty working with. Then become this client in a role play with one other student. Have your partner attempt to counsel you. After you have had a chance to be the client, reverse roles and you become the counselor.

6. In small groups discuss any possible experiences you have had with burnout and what contributed to it. Discuss some possible causes of professional burnout and examine specific ways you would deal with this problem.

Ethics in Action CD-ROM Exercises

7. In video role play #2, Big Brother, the client (Richard) reports that his sister is dating an Asian man. Richard is angry and says that he is not going to let that happen. He adds that his sister is not going to mess with his family like that. The counselor (Nadine) asks Richard if he thinks his sister should live to make him happy. He says, "My sister is going to do what I say and that's just it!"

This vignette shows how a counselor's own unfinished personal issues can get in the way of counseling an upset client. Identify and discuss the ethical issues you see played out in this vignette. Reenact the role play by having several students take the role of counselor to show alternative perspectives.

InfoTrac® College Edition Resources

For additional readings, explore InfoTrac College Edition, our online library. Key words are listed in a form that enables the search engine to locate a wider range of articles in the online university library. Key words should be entered exactly as shown, including asterisks, "Wl," "W2," "AND," and other search engine tools. Go to http://www.infotrac-college.com and select these key word searches:

countertransference
transference AND (psych????y OR couns*) AND psychotherapy
counselor N4 stress
counselor* N4 impairment* OR therapist* N4 impairment*
mental N3 health N6 burnout

Pre-Chapter Self-Inventory

Directions: For each statement, indicate the response that most closely identifies your beliefs and attitudes. Use the following code:

5 = I *strongly agree* with this statement.
4 = I *agree* with this statement.
3 = I am *undecided* about this statement.
2 = I *disagree* with this statement.
1 = I *strongly disagree* with this statement.

4 1. It is both possible and desirable for counselors to remain neutral and keep their values from influencing clients.

2 2. In certain situations, counselors should influence clients to adopt values that in their opinion seem to be in the clients' best interests.

3 3. It is appropriate for counselors to express their values as long as they do not try to impose them on clients.

4 4. Counselors can challenge clients to make value judgments regarding their own behavior.

2 5. Before I can effectively counsel a person, I have to decide whether our life experiences and values are similar enough for me to understand that person.

Values and the Helping Relationship

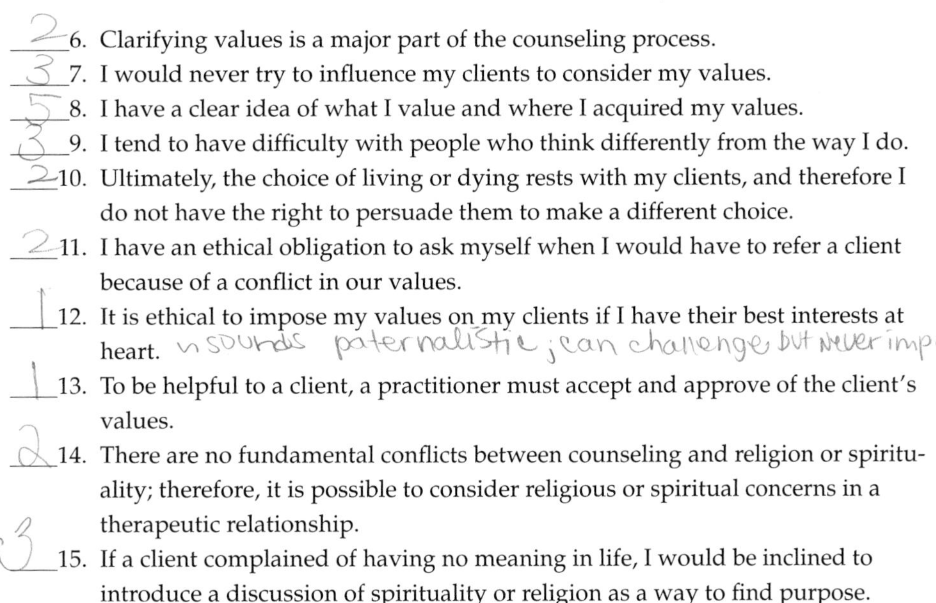

____ 6. Clarifying values is a major part of the counseling process.

____ 7. I would never try to influence my clients to consider my values.

____ 8. I have a clear idea of what I value and where I acquired my values.

____ 9. I tend to have difficulty with people who think differently from the way I do.

____ 10. Ultimately, the choice of living or dying rests with my clients, and therefore I do not have the right to persuade them to make a different choice.

____ 11. I have an ethical obligation to ask myself when I would have to refer a client because of a conflict in our values.

____ 12. It is ethical to impose my values on my clients if I have their best interests at heart.

____ 13. To be helpful to a client, a practitioner must accept and approve of the client's values.

____ 14. There are no fundamental conflicts between counseling and religion or spirituality; therefore, it is possible to consider religious or spiritual concerns in a therapeutic relationship.

____ 15. If a client complained of having no meaning in life, I would be inclined to introduce a discussion of spirituality or religion as a way to find purpose.

Introduction

The question of values permeates the therapeutic process. In this chapter we want to stimulate your thinking about your values and life experiences and the influence they will have on your counseling. We ask you to consider the possible impact of your values on your clients, the effect your clients' values will have on you, and the conflicts that may arise if you and your clients have different values.

Can therapists keep their values out of their counseling sessions? Richards, Rector, and Tjeltveit (1999) address this fundamental question of **value neutrality** by summarizing theoretical and research literature that discredits the notion that therapists can and should keep their values out of therapy. Research has shown that counselors' values influence every phase of the therapeutic process, including the theories of personality and therapeutic change employed, assessment strategies, therapy goals, identifying client problems that will be treated, choice of techniques, and evaluation of therapeutic outcomes. Clients are influenced by therapists' values and often adopt some of these values. According to Falender and Shafranske (2004), the assumption that psychotherapy is value neutral is no longer tenable. Therefore, clinicians need to take into consideration the role of personal influence in their practice.

In our view, it is neither possible nor desirable for counselors to be completely neutral in this respect. Although it is not the counselor's function to persuade clients to accept a certain value system, we do think it is crucial for counselors to be clear about their own values and how they influence their work with clients, perhaps even unconsciously.

Clarifying Your Values and Their Role in Your Work

When therapists expose their values, it is important that they clearly label them as their own. Then values can be discussed in an open and noncoercive way, which can assist clients in their exploration of their own values and the behavior that stems from these values. Clinicians may not agree with the values of their clients, but it is essential that they respect the rights of their clients to hold a different set of values. The way therapists deal with clients' values can raise ethical issues. Richards, Rector, and Tjeltveit (1999) do not think therapists should attempt to teach clients specific moral rules and values because doing so violates clients' diversity and prevents them from growing by making their own choices based on their values. Bergin (1991) writes, "It is vital to be open about values but not coercive, to be a competent professional and not a missionary for a particular belief, and at the same time to be honest enough to recognize how one's value commitments may not promote health" (p. 399). Bergin sees the core challenge as being able to use values to enhance the therapeutic process without abusing the therapist's power and exploiting the client's vulnerability.

Not everyone who practices counseling or psychotherapy would agree with these views. At one extreme are counselors who have definite, absolute value systems. They believe their task is to exert influence on their clients to adopt *better* values. Such counselors would direct their clients toward the attitudes and behaviors that *they* judge to be in their clients' best interests. At the other extreme are counselors who are so anxious to avoid influencing their clients that they make themselves invisible. They keep themselves and their values hidden so they will not contaminate their clients' process.

The *Canadian Code of Ethics for Psychologists* (CPA, 2000) recognizes that the personal values of therapists can affect the questions they ask, the assumptions they make, the methods they employ, and what they observe and fail to observe.

> Psychologists are not expected to be value-free or totally without self-interest in conducting their activities. However, they are expected to understand how their backgrounds, personal needs, and values interact with their activities, to be open and honest about the influence of such factors, and to be as objective and unbiased as possible under the circumstances. (Principle III.)

Holmes (1996) and Edwards and Bess (1998) clarify the concept of **therapeutic neutrality** in their writings. If you cannot accomplish this neutrality (objectivity), it is essential that you own this as your problem rather than the client's. Inform your client of the areas in which you think you cannot be neutral. We hope that there would be very few instances in which you would tell clients you could not work with them because of your conflict with their value system. Your task is not to approve or disapprove of your clients' values but to help them explore and clarify their beliefs and apply their values to solving their own problems. The only exception to this would be values and behavior that violate the law.

Counseling is not a form of indoctrination, nor is it the therapist's function to teach clients so-called proper behavior. It is unfortunate that some well-intentioned mental health professionals believe this is what they are supposed to be doing. We agree with Holmes (1996) in his contention that "when psychotherapy becomes certain of itself or its values, it ceases to be psychotherapy and becomes something akin to a proselytizing religion" (p. 272). We question the implication that counselors have a greater wisdom than their clients and can prescribe ways of being happier. This myth may be exaggerated by the radio and television psychologists who are seen as "doing counseling" by prescribing quick solutions to complex problems. No doubt, teaching is a part of counseling, and clients do learn in both direct and indirect ways from the opinions and examples of their therapists, but counseling is not synonymous with preaching, persuasion, or instruction.

However, neither do we favor the opposite extreme of trying so hard to be "objective" that counselors keep their personal reactions and values hidden from clients. In our opinion, clients demand a lot more involvement from therapists than mere reflection and clarification. Clients want and need to know where their therapist stands so they can test their own thinking. We believe clients are helped by this kind of honest involvement.

Practitioners will inevitably incorporate certain value orientations into their therapeutic approaches and methods. Goals are usually based on values and beliefs, and clients may adopt goals that the therapist thinks are beneficial. But if clients change the direction of their values without being aware of what they are doing, they are being deprived of self-determination (Brace, 1997). It may be appropriate at times for the therapist to do more than merely watch clients make "bad decisions" without interference. Bergin (1991) asserts that it is irresponsible for a therapist to fail to inform clients about alternatives: "We need to be honest and open about our views, collaborate with the client in setting goals that fit his or her needs, then step aside and allow the person to exercise autonomy and face consequences" (p. 397).

The following questions may help you to begin thinking about the role of your values in your work with clients:

- Do you think it is ever justified to influence a client's choice of values? If so, when and in what circumstances?
- Do you worry that openly discussing your values with certain clients might unduly influence their decision-making process?
- Is it possible for therapists to interact honestly with clients without making value judgments? Is it desirable for therapists to avoid making such judgments?
- If you were convinced that your client was making a "self-destructive decision," would you express your concerns, and if so, how would you do it?
- Do you think therapists are responsible for informing clients about a variety of value options?
- How are you affected when your clients adopt your beliefs and values?
- Can you remain true to yourself and at the same time allow your clients the freedom to select their own values, even if they differ from yours?
- How do you determine when a conflict between your values and those of your client necessitates a referral to another professional?
- Do you believe certain values are inherent in the therapeutic process? If so, what are these values?
- How does honestly exposing your clients to your viewpoint differ from subtly "guiding" them to accept your values?
- To what degree do you need to have had life experiences that are similar to those of your clients? What are some potential advantages and disadvantages in having similar life experiences with your client?

Because your values will significantly affect your work with clients, it is incumbent on you to clarify your assumptions, core beliefs, and values and the ways in which they enter the therapeutic process. For example, counselors who have "liberal" values may find themselves working with clients who have more traditional values. If these clinicians privately scoff at conventional values, can they truly respect clients who do not think as they do? Or if counselors have a strong commitment to values they rarely question, whether these values are conventional or unconventional, will they be inclined to promote these values at the expense of their clients' exploration of their own attitudes and beliefs? If counselors rarely reexamine their own values, it is unlikely that they will provide a climate in which clients can reexamine their values.

From time to time your values may present some difficulty for you in your work with clients. In the following sections we examine some sample cases and issues to help you clarify what you value and how your values might influence the goals of counseling and the interventions you make with your clients. As you read these examples, keep the following questions in mind:

- What is my position on this issue?
- Where did I develop my views?
- Are my values open to modification?
- Am I open to being challenged by others?
- Do I feel so deeply committed to some of my values that I might want my clients to accept them? Will I be closed to clients with a different set of values?
- When would I disclose my values to my clients? Why?
- How can I communicate my values without imposing those values on clients?
- Do my actions reveal that I respect the principle of clients' self-determination that is consistent with their culture?
- How are my own values and beliefs reflected in the manner in which I help my clients set their goals?

The Ethics of Imposing Your Values on Clients

Value imposition refers to counselors directly attempting to influence a client to adopt their own values, attitudes, beliefs, and behaviors. It is possible for counselors to impose their values either actively or passively. Counselors are cautioned about this kind of value imposition in their professional work in this ACA (2005) standard:

> *Personal Values*. Counselors are aware of their own values, attitudes, beliefs, and behaviors and avoid imposing values that are inconsistent with counseling goals. Counselors respect the diversity of clients, trainees, and research participants. (A.4.b.)

APA's ethics code (2002) provides an ethical mandate for respecting people's rights and dignity:

> Psychologists respect the dignity and worth of all people, and the rights of individuals to privacy, confidentiality, and self-determination. Psychologists are aware that special safeguards may be necessary to protect the rights and welfare of persons or communities whose vulnerabilities impair autonomous decision making. Psychologists are aware of and respect cultural, individual, and role differences, including those based on age, gender, gender identity, race, ethnicity, culture, national origin, religion, sexual orientation, disability, language, and socioeconomic status and consider these factors when working with members of such groups. Psychologists try to eliminate the effect on their work of biases based on those factors, and they do not knowingly participate in or condone activities of others based upon such prejudices. (Principle E.)

ASCA's (2004) code specifies that the school counselor "respects the student's values and beliefs and does not impose the counselor's personal values" (A.1.c.).

A national survey found a consensus among a representative group of mental health practitioners that basic values such as self-determination are important for clients to become mentally healthy and to guide and evaluate the course of psychotherapy (Jensen & Bergin, 1988). Other basic values include developing effective strategies for coping with stress; developing the ability to give and receive affection; increasing one's ability to be sensitive to the feelings of others; becoming able to practice self-control; having a sense of purpose for living; being open, honest, and genuine; finding satisfaction in one's work; having a sense of identity and self-worth; being skilled in interpersonal relationships; having deepened self-awareness and motivation for growth; and practicing good habits of physical health. These values were considered to be universal, and practitioners surveyed based their therapy on them.

It is now generally recognized that the therapeutic endeavor is a value-laden process and that all clinicians, to some degree, communicate their values to clients (Richards & Bergin, 1997). An abundance of evidence shows that therapy not only is value laden but that counselors and clients often have different value systems (Zinnbauer & Pargament, 2000). Some researchers have found evidence that clients tend to change in ways that are consistent with the values of their therapists, and clients often adopt the values of their counselors (Zinnbauer & Pargament, 2000). It will be difficult to avoid communicating your values to your clients, even if you do not explicitly share them. What you pay attention to during counseling sessions will direct what your clients choose to explore. The methods you use will provide them with clues as to what you value.

Your nonverbal behavior and body language also give clients indications of how you are being affected. If clients have a need for your approval, they may respond to these cues by acting in ways that they imagine will please you. Suppose, for example, that an unhappily married man surmised that you really thought he was wasting good years of his life in the marriage and he proceeded with a divorce mostly because of his perceptions of your beliefs. Although you may believe in not imposing your values on clients, the subtle messages you project can have a powerful influence. For example, a school counselor may communicate her disapproval of a teacher who has frequent classroom management issues. A student referred to this counselor may believe that the counselor supports the student's version of the classroom conflict.

Value Conflicts: To Refer or Not to Refer

Some counselors believe they can work with any client or with any problem. They may be convinced that being professional means being able to assist everyone. Others are so unsure of their abilities that they are quick to refer anyone who makes them feel uncomfortable. Somewhere between these extremes are the cases in which your values and those of your client clash to such an extent that you question your ability to be helpful.

Yarhouse and VanOrman (1999) assert that value conflicts between clients and therapists are inevitable. The challenge for therapists is to recognize when their values clash with a client's values to the extent that they are not able to function effectively. Merely having a conflict of values does not necessarily require a referral; it is possible to work through such conflicts successfully. In fact, we think of a referral as the last resort.

Before making a referral, explore your part of the difficulty through consultation. What barriers within you would prevent you from working with a client who has a different value system? Merely disagreeing with a client or not particularly liking what a client is proposing to do is not ethical grounds for a referral. When you recognize instances of such value conflicts, ask yourself this question: "Why is it necessary that there be congruence between my value system and that of my client?"

If you have sought consultation and exhausted all other possibilities and still feel that you are at an impasse, you may need to consider a referral. When a referral is decided upon, *how* it is done is crucial. Make it clear to the client that it is *your* problem and not the client's. It can be very burdensome to clients to be saddled with your disclosure of not being able to get beyond value differences. Clients may interpret this as a personal rejection and suffer harm as a result. To avoid such situations, disclose in writing from the outset any values you hold that might pose a challenge for you in working effectively with certain value systems of clients. In this way, clients can be empowered to decide whether they want to work with you from the beginning.

Consider the list of potential clients that follows and indicate whether you believe you could work with the client or would find this a challenge because of a conflict of value systems between you and the client. You may think it unlikely that you will encounter some of these situations in your counseling career, but you need to be mentally prepared to deal with them if and when they do arise. Use the following code:

A = I *could* work with this person.
B = I *would have difficulty* working with this person.
C = I *could not* work with this person.

_____ 1. A person with fundamentalist religious beliefs
_____ 2. A woman who says that if she could only turn her life to Christ she would find peace
_____ 3. A person who shows little conscience development, who is strictly interested in his or her own advancement, and who uses others to achieve personal aims
_____ 4. A gay or lesbian couple wanting to work on conflicts in their relationship
_____ 5. A man who wants to leave his wife and children for the sake of sexual adventures with other women
_____ 6. A woman who has decided to leave her husband and children to gain her independence but who wants to explore her fears of doing so
_____ 7. A woman who is seriously considering an abortion but wants help in making her decision
_____ 8. A teenager who is having unsafe sex and sees no problem with this behavior
_____ 9. A high school student who is sent to you by his parents because they suspect he is abusing drugs

_____ 10. A person who is very cerebral and is convinced that feelings should be kept to oneself

_____ 11. A man who believes the best way to discipline his children is through corporal punishment

_____ 12. An interracial couple coming for premarital counseling

_____ 13. A high school student who seeks counseling to discuss conflicts she is having with her adopted parent from a different culture

_____ 14. A high school student who thinks she may be lesbian and wants to explore this gender identification

_____ 15. A gay or lesbian couple wanting to adopt a child

_____ 16. A man who has found a way of cheating the system and getting more than his legal share of public assistance

_____ 17. A woman who comes with her husband for couples counseling while maintaining an extramarital affair

_____ 18. An interracial couple wanting to adopt a child and being faced with their respective parents' opposition to the adoption

_____ 19. A client from another culture who has values very different from your own

_____ 20. A mother who is intent on blaming the school for her son's behavior problems and constantly makes excuses for the child

Go back over the list, and pay particular attention to the items you marked "C." What is your difficulty in working with these people? In assessing the ethical ramifications of declining to work with certain clients, what are the potential risks and benefits of making a referral? If you decide not to make a referral, what are the possible risks and benefits to the client if you work with this person?

Values Conflicts Regarding Sexual Attitudes and Behavior

Mental health practitioners may be working with clients whose sexual values and behaviors differ sharply from their own. Ford and Hendrick's (2003) study was designed to assess therapists' sexual values for both themselves and their clients in the areas of premarital sex, casual sex, extramarital sex, open marriages, sexual orientation, and sex in adolescence and late adulthood. Ford and Henrick's study also addressed how therapists deal with value conflicts as they arise in therapy.

Although therapists have personal values about sexual practices, the study found that when therapists' beliefs conflict with those of clients, therapists appear to be able to avoid imposing their personal values on clients. However, 40% had to refer a client because of a value conflict. This research supports previous conclusions that the practice of therapy is not value free, particularly where sexual values are concerned. Respondents indicated that they valued the following: sex as an expression of love and commitment, fidelity and monogamy in marital relationships, and committed life partnerships. Therapists reported handling value conflicts by (a) referring clients (40%), (b) discussing the issues with their clients (25%), and (c) consulting with a colleague, supervisor, or peer

(18%). The respondents in this survey report that they are aware of their personal values and make efforts to keep their values from having a negative impact on their clients.

Examine your values with respect to sexual attitudes and behavior. Do you see them as being restrictive or permissive? Think about each of the following statements and mark "A" in the space provided if you mostly agree and "D" if you mostly disagree with the statement.

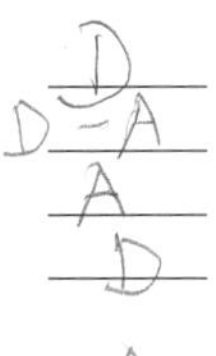

_____ 1. Sex belongs in marriage only.
_____ 2. Sex is most meaningful as an expression of love and commitment.
_____ 3. Recreational sex is healthy if it is consensual.
_____ 4. Sex with multiple partners is not okay without protection unless you know your partners well.
_____ 5. Safe sexual practices are essential throughout your life.
_____ 6. Extramarital sex is acceptable if you stay in a failed marriage for the sake of children.
_____ 7. Premarital sex promotes intimacy later in a relationship.
_____ 8. Same-gender sex is the right choice for some people.
_____ 9. Sex becomes less important as you grow older.
_____ 10. Adolescents should avoid becoming sexually intimate because they cannot deal with the consequences.

Can you counsel people who are experiencing conflict over their sexual choices if their values differ dramatically from your own? For example, if you have permissive attitudes about sexual behavior, will you be able to respect the conservative views of some of your clients? If you think their moral views are giving them difficulty, will you try to persuade your clients to adopt a more liberal view? How will you view the guilt clients may experience? Will you treat it as an undesirable emotion that they need to overcome? Conversely, if you have fairly strict sexual guidelines for your own life, will the more permissive attitudes of some of your clients be a problem for you? Can you respect the self-determination of clients who have sharply different sexual values from your views? Who has influenced your choices pertaining to sexual practices?

As you study the following case, reflect on how your sexual attitudes and values are likely to influence your interventions with Virginia and Tom.

The Case of Virginia and Tom. Virginia and Tom find themselves in a marital crisis when Virginia discovers that Tom has had several affairs during the course of their marriage. Tom agrees to see a marriage counselor. Tom says that he cannot see how his affairs necessarily got in the way of his relationship with his wife, especially since they were never meaningful. He believes that what is done is done and that it is pointless to dwell on past transgressions. He is upset over his wife's reaction to learning about his affairs. He says that he loves his wife and that he does not want to end the marriage. His involvements with other women were sexual in nature rather than committed love relationships. Virginia says that she would like to forgive her husband but that she finds it too painful to continue living with him knowing of his activities, even though they are in the past. She is not reassured by Tom's reactions to his past activities and that he might continue to rationalize these activities.

Counselor A. This counselor tells the couple at the initial session that from her experience extramarital affairs add many strains to a marriage, that people get hurt in such situations, and that affairs do pose some problems for couples seeking counseling. However, she adds that affairs sometimes actually have positive benefits for both the wife and the husband. She says that her policy is to let the couple find out for themselves what is acceptable to them. She accepts Virginia and Tom as clients and asks them to consider as many options as they can to resolve their difficulties.

- Is this counselor neutral or biased? Explain.
- Does this approach seem practical and realistic to you? Explain.

Counselor B. From the outset this counselor makes it clear that she sees affairs as disruptive in any marriage. She maintains that affairs are typically started because of a deep dissatisfaction within the marriage and are symptomatic of other real conflicts. The counselor says she can help Tom and Virginia discover these conflicts in couples therapy. She further says that she will not work with them unless Tom's affairs are truly in the past, because she is convinced that counseling will not work unless he is fully committed to doing what is needed to work on his relationship with Virginia.

- Is this counselor imposing her values?
- Is it appropriate for the counselor to openly state her conditions and values from the outset?
- To what degree do you agree or disagree with this counselor's thinking and approach?
- If, after working with them for a time, the counselor discovers that Tom has begun another affair, what do you think she should do and why?

Counselor C. This counselor views the affairs much as Tom does. She points out that the couple seems to have a basically sound marriage and suggests that with some individual counseling Virginia can learn to get past the affairs.

- With her viewpoint, is it ethical for this counselor to accept this couple for counseling? Should she suggest a referral to another professional? Explain.
- Should the counselor have given more attention to the obvious pain expressed by Virginia?
- Should the counselor have kept her values and attitudes to herself so that she would be less likely to influence this couple's decisions?

Value Conflicts Pertaining to Abortion

People's views about abortion are emotionally charged, and counselors may experience a value clash with their clients on this issue. The following discussion is largely taken from an article by Millner and Hanks (2002) titled "Induced Abortion: An Ethical Conundrum for Counselors." Induced abortion is one of the most controversial moral issues in American culture, yet little professional literature addresses abortion-related legal and ethical issues. In their article the authors (a) identify issues relevant to counselors regarding abortion, (b) examine how these issues relate to ethical principles, and (c) suggest practical ways in which counselors can resolve dilemmas involving clients' decisions.

Clients who are exploring abortion as an option often present a challenge to clinicians, both legally and ethically. From a legal perspective, mental health professionals are expected to exercise "reasonable care," and if they fail to do so, clients can take legal action against them for negligence. Counselors can be charged with negligence if they (a) do not act with skill and withhold relevant information or provide inaccurate information; (b) do not refer a client; or (c) make an inadequate referral. For example, a counselor who makes a referral that supports his or her values rather than one in keeping with the client's values is vulnerable to a lawsuit.

Millner and Hanks provide the following recommendations when making ethical decisions in cases involving a discussion of abortion.

1. Make a comprehensive examination of your own moral and ethical views on abortion. As a part of this critical examination, ask yourself these questions: "Under what circumstances, if any, would an abortion be justified? Is abortion warranted if the pregnancy is the result of rape or incest? If the mother's life or health is endangered, is abortion justified? To what degree would abortion be acceptable if the fetus was determined to be an unwanted gender? To what degree would abortion be a viable alternative to birth control measures? How are matters such as age of the mother, financial considerations, and marital status relevant considerations?" Self-examination within the context of a clinician's personal ethics and the application of the principles of autonomy, fidelity, justice, beneficence, and nonmaleficence are useful in helping counselors resolve dilemmas they encounter pertaining to abortion.

2. Determine when your own personal ethics would make it difficult for you to be objective and respectful of the client's autonomy. If possible, clinicians should decide in advance in what circumstances they might be inclined to misuse their influence to steer clients toward a decision that is consistent with their own values rather than in keeping with the client's values.

3. Be prepared to refer clients to other professionals when it is appropriate. Making a referral is often a complex matter. For instance, it may be easier to make a referral for a client who raises abortion as a consideration at the initial counseling session than to refer a long-standing client, which could raise an issue of client abandonment.

4. Become familiar with state and federal laws pertaining to abortions. This is especially true for school counselors who are dealing with minors. Laws, regulations, and policies vary widely; consult with an attorney when necessary.

5. Anticipate circumstances that would make it difficult for you to maintain a sense of objectivity because of a conflict between your values and those of the client. You cannot foresee every possible situation, but you can reflect on an ethical decision-making model you could apply to a range of cases. If you have

clarity on your personal values and ethics, you are in a good position to address the challenges of dealing with clients who are considering abortion.

We suggest that you familiarize yourself with the legal requirements in your state that impinge on your work with clients, especially if you are counseling minors who are considering an abortion. The matter of parental consent in working with minors varies from state to state. For example, in 1987 Alabama enacted the Parental Consent for Abortion Law, requiring physicians to have parental consent or a court waiver before performing an abortion on an unemancipated woman. Consider the situation of an unmarried young woman under the age of 18 who tells her school counselor that she is planning to get an abortion and does not want her parents to know about this. In Alabama this counselor is expected to show this law to the young woman (including the option of a court waiver of parental consent) and advise her that he or she is obliged to comply with this law, and not encourage any violation of it. In her discussion of abortion counseling, Stone (2002) concludes that school counselors can discuss the topic of abortion with a student if the school board has not adopted a policy forbidding such a discussion. Stone adds that counselors who impose their values on a minor student are not acting in an appropriate, professional, or reasonable manner.

In the following vignette, we present the case of Candy. In light of our previous discussion, what value conflicts, if any, might you face with Candy? What issues do you find most challenging, and how might you deal with them?

The Case of Candy. Candy is a 14-year-old student who is sent to you because of her problematic behavior in the classroom. Her parents have recently divorced, and Candy is having difficulty coping with the breakup. Eventually, she tells you that she is having sexual relations with her boyfriend without using any form of birth control.

- What are your reactions to Candy's sexual activity?
- Would you want to know the age of her boyfriend?
- If you sense that her behavior is an attempt to overcome her feelings of isolation, how might you deal with it?
- Would you try to persuade her to use birth control? Why or why not?
- Do you see any ethical or legal implications in the ways you responded to these questions?

You have been working with Candy for several sessions now, and she discovers that she is pregnant. Her boyfriend is 15 and declares that he is in no position to support her and a child. She has decided to have an abortion but feels anxious about following through with it. How would you respond? In the blanks put an "A" if you agree more than disagree with the statement, and put a "D" if you mainly disagree.

_____ 1. I would explore Candy's ambivalence relative to the abortion.

_____ 2. I would encourage Candy to consider other options, such as adoption, keeping the child as a single parent, or marrying.

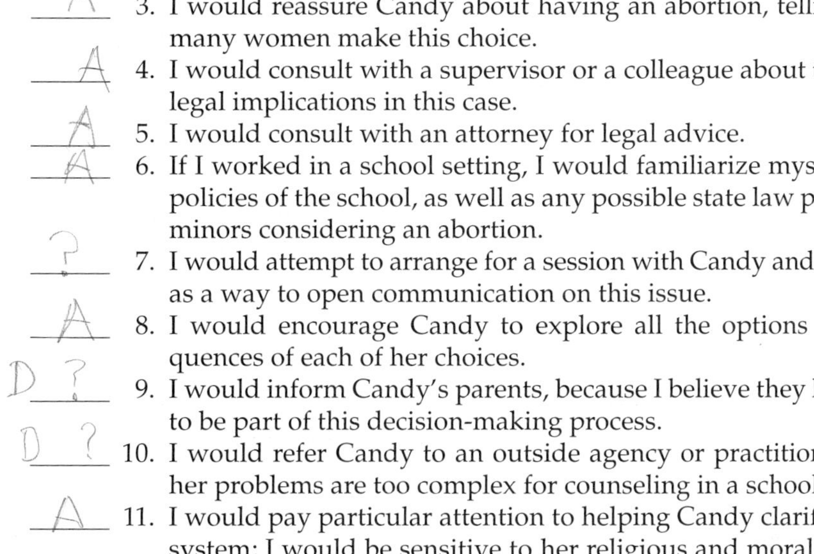

_____ 3. I would reassure Candy about having an abortion, telling her that many women make this choice.

_____ 4. I would consult with a supervisor or a colleague about the possible legal implications in this case.

_____ 5. I would consult with an attorney for legal advice.

_____ 6. If I worked in a school setting, I would familiarize myself with the policies of the school, as well as any possible state law pertaining to minors considering an abortion.

_____ 7. I would attempt to arrange for a session with Candy and her parents as a way to open communication on this issue.

_____ 8. I would encourage Candy to explore all the options and consequences of each of her choices.

_____ 9. I would inform Candy's parents, because I believe they have a right to be part of this decision-making process.

_____ 10. I would refer Candy to an outside agency or practitioner because her problems are too complex for counseling in a school setting.

_____ 11. I would pay particular attention to helping Candy clarify her value system; I would be sensitive to her religious and moral values and the possible implications of specific choices she might make.

_____ 12. I would refer Candy to another professional because of my opposition to abortion.

_____ 13. I would tell Candy that I am personally opposed to (or in favor of) abortion, that I want to remain her counselor during this difficult time, and that I will support whatever decision she makes for herself.

Commentary. Candy's case illustrates several complex problems. What do you do if you cannot be objective because of your personal views on abortion? Do you refer Candy to someone else? If you do, might she feel that you think less of her because of her decision? If you are firmly opposed to abortion, could you support Candy in her decision to have an abortion? Would you try to persuade her to have the baby because of your views on abortion? Which of your values are triggered by Candy's case, and how might these values either help or hinder you in working with her?

One possible course of action would be to tell Candy about your values and how you think they would influence your work with her. If you determine that you could not work effectively with her, explore your reasons for making this decision. Why is it crucial that her decision be compatible with your values? Do you necessarily have to approve of the decisions your clients make? Do you see a distinction between a counselor suggesting a course of action and helping a client make her own decision on the matter?

When the subject of abortion arises, some women may be reluctant to consider this option, either because of their value system or because of feelings of guilt, shame, and fear. Other women may feel ambivalent and may want to explore all of their options. How would you react to not being allowed to explore abortion as one option for your client? Do you think it is unethical to fail to discuss all of a client's options if this is her desire?

✓ **The Case of Marion.** Marion is a 15-year-old honors student. She discovered that she is pregnant and feels she would be better off dead than being a teenage mom. Marion was born to teenage parents, so she knows they will never allow her to have an abortion. Marion went to see the school counselor to talk about her situation. The counselor educated Marion on the different options she had in regard to her pregnancy. Marion stated that she wanted to abort her pregnancy. If her parents would not allow her to have an abortion, Marion said she would kill herself. With Marion's permission, the counselor arranged to talk with Marion and her parents. Marion's father stated he would not hear of Marion's having an abortion. Marion then stated with conviction that she would kill herself. The counselor believed Marion would act on her threat of suicide.

- If your state had a law requiring parental consent for abortion, how would this influence the interventions you would make in this case?
- Might you encounter a conflict between ethics and the law if you were counseling Marion? How would you deal with her suicidal threat?
- Knowing what Marion told you about her parents' values, would you have involved them in this case? Why or why not?
- If you were the school counselor, what would you do to protect Marion from harming herself?
- Would you use Marion's threat of suicide to influence her parents, or would you ignore this threat? Explain.
- Would you try to involve Marion's family priest/minister/rabbi in this situation? Why or why not?
- What other options would you consider?

Case Studies of Other Possible Value Conflicts

In this section we present some case studies of other possible value conflicts. Try to imagine yourself working with each of these clients. How do you think your values would affect your work with them?

✓ **The Case of Paul.** Paul comes to an agency with many difficulties and anxieties, one of which is his antipathy toward interracial marriage. He expresses disappointment in his daughter and in himself as a father because of her engagement to a man of another race. Paul has gone as far as threatening to disinherit her if she marries this man. What this client does not know is that the social worker herself is in an interracial marriage. The therapist discloses this fact and lets him know of her difficulties with what she perceives as his prejudices.

- How do you react to her self-disclosure?
- Would a referral be in order? Why or why not?
- What are your values in this situation, and what might you do or say if you were the counselor?

- What are your reactions if the therapist were to say to Paul, "I am willing to work with you on this problem. I have some personal insights and experience in this situation because I myself am in an interracial marriage. Knowing this, how would it be for you to work with me?"

Your views on racial issues can have an impact on your manner of counseling in certain situations. Think about what your responses to the following statements tell you about how your values might operate in cases pertaining to racial concerns. In the space, put an "A" if you agree more than you disagree with the statement, and put a "D" if you disagree more than you agree.

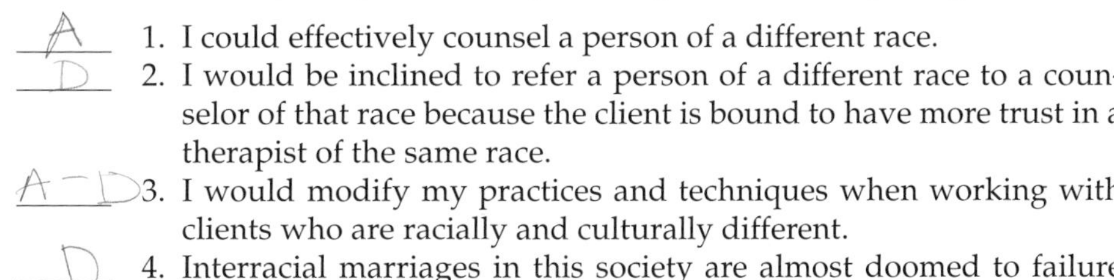

___ 1. I could effectively counsel a person of a different race.
___ 2. I would be inclined to refer a person of a different race to a counselor of that race because the client is bound to have more trust in a therapist of the same race.
___ 3. I would modify my practices and techniques when working with clients who are racially and culturally different.
___ 4. Interracial marriages in this society are almost doomed to failure because of the extra pressures on them.
___ 5. Interracial marriages pose no greater strain on a relationship than do interfaith marriages.
___ 6. I have certain racial (cultural) prejudices that would affect my objectivity in working with clients of a different race (culture) from mine.

The Case of Lupe. Lupe is a social worker in a community mental health agency that is sponsoring workshops aimed at preventing the spread of AIDS. The agency has attempted to involve the local churches in these workshops. One church withdrew its support because the workshops encouraged "safer" sexual practices, including the use of condoms, as a way of preventing AIDS. A church official contended that the use of condoms is contrary to church teachings. Being a member of this church, Lupe finds herself struggling with value conflicts. She believes the teachings of her church and thinks the official had a right to withdraw his support of these workshops. But she is also aware that many people in the community she serves are at high risk for contracting AIDS because of both drug usage and sexual practices. In an attempt to resolve this value conflict, Lupe seeks out several of her colleagues, each of whom responds differently:

Colleague A: I would encourage you to tell your clients and others in the community that you have value conflicts between agency practice and your religious beliefs and, for that reason, you are voluntarily resigning from the agency.

Colleague B: I hope you will be up front with the people you come in contact with by telling them of your values and providing them with adequate referrals so they can get information about prevention of this disease. But you do owe it to them not to steer them in the direction you think they should move.

Colleague C: I think it is best that you not disclose your values or let them know that you agree with the church's views. Instead, work toward changing their behavior and modifying their values directly. After all, in this case the end justifies the means.

Colleague D: More harm can come by your failure to provide necessary information. Even though your values are in sympathy with the church's position, ethically you owe it to the community to teach them methods of safe sex.

If Lupe were to seek you out and ask for your advice, consider what you might say to her. In formulating your position, answer these questions:

- Which of her colleagues comes closest to your thinking, and why?
- With which colleague do you find yourself disagreeing the most, and why?
- Would it be ethical for Lupe not to disclose her values to her clients? Why or why not?
- Given the gravity of this situation and the possibility of the spread of disease, is Lupe ethically bound to provide people who are at high risk with facts and information about prevention?
- What advice would you be inclined to give Lupe, and what does this response tell you about your values?

Shared Life Experiences and Values

To what degree do you share the view that you must have had life experiences similar to those of your clients? You can help people whose experiences, values, and problems are different from yours by tuning in to their feelings and relating them to your own. Counselors need not have experienced each of the struggles of their clients to be effective in working with them. When the counselor and the client connect at a certain level, cultural and age differences can be transcended. Consider for a moment whether you can communicate effectively with these clients:

- An elderly person
- A person of a different racial, ethnic, or cultural group
- A person with a disability
- A delinquent or a criminal
- A person who is abusing alcohol or drugs

It is possible for a relatively young clinician to work effectively with an elderly client. For example, the client may be experiencing feelings of loss, guilt, sadness, and hopelessness. The young counselor can empathize with these feelings even though the counselor's experiences that resulted in some of these same feelings were quite different. It is essential, however, that the counselor be sensitive to the differences in their backgrounds, a subject we examine in Chapter 4.

To facilitate your reflection on whether you need to have life experiences or a value system similar to that of your client, assess what factors in your life would either help or hinder you in establishing a good working relationship with the clients described in the following cases.

 **The Case of Alberto.** Alberto, a Latino client, comes to a community college counseling center on the recommendation of one of his friends. His presenting problem

is depression, chronic sleep disturbance, and the imminent threat of failing his classes. During the initial session you are aware that he is extremely guarded. As a counselor, you may assume that self-disclosure and openness to feelings enhance life. Alberto discloses little about himself or how he is feeling. Although he will answer your questions briefly, you sense that he is withholding much information from you.

- How sensitive are you to your client's sense of privacy? Have you considered that keeping one's thoughts and feelings to oneself might be valued in certain cultures?
- Assume that over time Alberto becomes more self-disclosing and expressive, not only with you but also within his environment. What are the pros and cons of that?
- Is it ethical to encourage Alberto to be more self-disclosing without first understanding the cultural context? Explain.
- How might your intervention reflect your lack of understanding of the importance of the extended family in certain cultures?
- Can you think of some reasons Alberto's cautiousness may be more adaptive than maladaptive?

The Case of Sylvia. At a community clinic, Sylvia, who is 38, tells you that she is an alcoholic. During the intake interview she says, "I feel so much remorse because I've tried to stop my drinking and haven't succeeded. I am fine for a while, and then I begin to think that I have to be a 'perfect' wife and mother. I see all the ways in which I do not measure up—how I let my kids down, the many mistakes I've made with them, the embarrassment I've caused my husband—and then I get so down I feel compelled to drink. I know that what I am doing is self-destructive, but I haven't been able to stop."

- What experiences have you had with alcoholism or its treatment, and how important is that?
- Do you see Sylvia as having a disease? as suffering from a lack of willpower? as an irresponsible, indulgent person? How would your views influence your interventions?
- Does the fact that Sylvia is a woman affect your view of her problem?
- Would you encourage Sylvia to attend Alcoholics Anonymous?
- Is it ethical to treat Sylvia's psychological problems without first attending to her addiction problem?

When you experience discomfort due to a client's very different values or life experiences, you are challenged to extend yourself to develop ways of working with this client. Let us again emphasize that we question the ethics of resorting to a referral in all cases where the therapist experiences discomfort. If you have difficulty relating to people who think differently from the way you do, you need to work on being more open to diverse viewpoints. This openness does not entail accepting other people's values as your own. Instead, it implies being secure enough in your own values that you are not threatened by really listening to, and deeply understanding, people who think differently. Listen to your clients with the intent of understanding what their values are, how they arrived at them, and the meaning these values have for them, and then communicate this acceptance. This acceptance of your clients can significantly broaden you as a person, and it enhances your ability to work with clients. It does not require that you change your values.

The Role of Spiritual and Religious Values in Counseling

Spiritual and religious values and end-of-life decisions are particularly sensitive, controversial, and complex issues as they pertain to counseling. As you read this section and the following one, try to clarify your values in these areas and think about how your views might either enhance or interfere with your ability to establish contact with certain clients.

The field of counseling and psychotherapy is coming to realize the importance of addressing spiritual and religious concerns. There is a growing awareness and willingness to explore spiritual and religious matters within the context of counseling and counselor education programs (Burke et al., 1999; Hagedorn, 2005; Polanski, 2003; Yarhouse & Burkett, 2002). Powers (2005) surveyed the literature on spirituality and counseling and found that very little was being written on this topic prior to the 1950s. However, since the 1970s spirituality and counseling have received increasing attention in the literature, and the professional organizations are recognizing the importance of spiritual issues in counseling practice. In recent years, spirituality and religion have become more prominent in the counseling literature (Hall, Dixon, & Mauzey, 2004; Sperry & Shafranske, 2005). Survey data of both practicing counselors and counselor educators indicate that spiritual and religious matters are therapeutically relevant, ethically appropriate, and potentially significant topics for the practice of counseling in secular settings (Burke et al., 1999; Walker, Gorsuch, & Tan, 2004). Spiritual issues that clients bring to psychotherapy can be basic therapeutic considerations for therapists (Sperry & Shafranske, 2005). As Webb (2005) makes clear in his book, *The Soul of Counseling*, counselors must be prepared to deal with their clients' issues of the human spirit.

Counselors ask just about every imaginable question about a client's life, yet many never think of inquiring about the influence and meaning of spirituality and religion in an individual's life. By not raising the issue, clients may assume that such matters are not relevant for counseling, and counselors may be guilty of excluding an important issue of diversity (Yarhouse, 2003). Religion and spirituality are oftentimes part of the client's problem, and they can also be part of the client's solution. Because spiritual and religious values can play a major part in human life, spiritual values should be viewed as a potential resource in therapy.

Spirituality and religion are critical sources of strength for many clients and provide the bedrock for finding meaning in life. There is growing empirical evidence that our spiritual values and behaviors can promote physical and

Some Thoughts on Spirituality

Some individuals claim to be deeply spiritual, yet they are not affiliated with any formal religion. Here are some viewpoints on the nature of spirituality and how it relates to religion.

- "*Spirituality* refers to a personal inclination or desire for a relationship with the transcendent or God; *religion* refers to the social or organized means by which persons express spirituality." (Grimm, 1994, p. 154)
- "Spirituality refers to a general sensitivity to moral, ethical, humanitarian, and existential issues without reference to any particular religious doctrine. Spiritually oriented individuals are not necessarily affiliated with organized religion." (Genia, 1994, p. 395)
- "We believe spirituality is an innate human quality. Not only is it our vital life force, but at the same time it is also our experience of that vital life force. Although this life force is deeply part of us, it also transcends us. It is what connects us to other people, nature, and the source of life. The experience of spirituality is greater than ourselves and helps us transcend and embrace life situations." (Faiver et al., 2001, p. 2)
- "Spirituality may be defined as: the animating force in life, represented by such images as breath, wind, vigor, and courage. Spirituality is the infusion and drawing out of spirit in one's life. It is experienced as an active and passive process." (*Summit on Spirituality, 1995,* p. 30)
- "Spirituality is also described as a capacity and tendency that is innate and unique to all persons. This spiritual tendency moves the individual toward knowledge, love, meaning, hope, transcendence, connectedness, and compassion. Spirituality includes one's capacity for creativity, growth, and the development of a values system. Spirituality encompasses the religious, spiritual, and transpersonal." (*Summit on Spirituality, 1995,* p. 30)

psychological well-being (Benson & Stark, 1996; Hall, Dixon, & Mauzey, 2004; Richards & Bergin, 1997; Richards, Rector, & Tjeltveit, 1999; Shafranske & Sperry, 2005a). Exploring these values with clients can be integrated with other therapeutic tools to enhance the therapy process.

For some clients, **spirituality** entails embracing a religion. Other clients value spirituality yet do not have ties to a formal religion (see the box titled Some Thoughts on Spirituality). There are many paths toward fulfilling spiritual needs, and it is not your role as a helper to prescribe any particular pathway. Shafranske and Sperry (2005b) make it clear that a spiritual approach to therapy does not impose a particular spiritual worldview on the client; rather, this approach is responsive to clients as whole persons. Shafranske and Sperry (2005a) address how spirituality can affect the course of treatment and alleviate suffering. They write: "The task of the therapist is to identify and to integrate the beliefs, values, and practices involved in the patient's spirituality to enhance coping" (p. 20). Shafranske and Sperry (2005b) caution that spiritually oriented therapy "is not a panacea, nor is it appropriate for every clinical situation; rather, it is intended to complement other forms of psychological and psychiatric treatment for situations in which spirituality or religiosity plays a significant role in a patient's orienting system" (p. 352).

Monitor yourself for subtle ways that you might be inclined to push certain values in your counseling practice. For instance, you could influence clients to embrace a spiritual perspective, or you could influence them to give up certain beliefs that you think are no longer functional for them. It is critical to keep in mind that it is the client's place to determine what specific values to retain or modify.

Contrary to spirituality, **religion** entails a set of codified beliefs that connect us to a God or gods and that influence our daily life. According to Faiver, Ingersoll, O'Brien, and McNally (2001), across the world's diverse cultures are many who find solace through religion, which is the means by which they express their spirituality. Religion is as much an expression of diversity as is race, ethnicity, socioeconomic status, age, gender, or sexual orientation (Yarhouse & Burkett, 2002). Principle E in the *Ethical Principles of Psychologists and Code of Conduct* (APA, 2002) clearly includes religion among many areas of diversity that psychologists are to respect.

Religious Teachings and Counseling

Religious beliefs and practices affect many dimensions of human experience, including how to handle guilt feelings, authority, and moral questions, to name a few. Both religion and counseling help people ponder questions of "Who am I?" and "What is the meaning of my life?" At their best, both counseling and religion are able to foster healing through an exploration of self by learning to accept oneself; by giving to others; by forgiving others and oneself; by admitting one's shortcomings; by accepting personal responsibility; by letting go of hurts and resentments; by dealing with guilt; and by learning to let go of self-destructive patterns of thinking, feeling, and acting.

Although religion and counseling are comparable in a number of respects, some key differences exist. For example, counseling does not involve the imposition of counselors' values on clients, whereas religion often involves teaching doctrines and beliefs to which individuals are expected to conform. Some therapists, from Sigmund Freud to Albert Ellis, have been antagonistic toward religion, and some religious leaders have been equally antagonistic toward psychotherapy. There are religious leaders who have reacted negatively to counseling as a secular force, and psychotherapists who have reacted negatively to religion, describing it as a defense mechanism or as a form of denial.

Although religion, and spirituality in general, is consistently reported as being integral to American's lives, counselors often leave an exploration of religious or spiritual concerns out of the assessment and treatment process (Faiver, O'Brien, & Ingersoll, 2000). In a national survey involving more than 1,000 clinical psychologists, Hathaway, Scott, and Garver (2004) found that the majority believe client religiousness and spirituality is an important aspect of functioning. The majority in this survey also believed they could distinguish between healthy and unhealthy religious functioning, and they reported being familiar with the spiritual beliefs of their client populations. The survey revealed, however, that most clinicians do not routinely incorporate spirituality into the assessment and treatment process. This omission might well limit the effectiveness of therapy for some clients, which would seem to make it a clear ethical issue. Hathaway and colleagues conclude: "Assessment of client religiousness/spirituality should become a more familiar part of the clinical landscape" (p. 103).

Hall, Dixon, and Mauzey (2004) maintain that mental health professionals are increasingly recognizing the importance of incorporating a client's spiritual and religious beliefs into both the assessment and treatment process. Attention to spirituality can be considered in the context of an integrated and holistic effort in helping clients resolve conflicts and improve health, as well as find meaning in dealing with the challenges of living (Shafranske & Sperry, 2005b). If, during the assessment process or later in counseling, clients indicate that they are concerned about any of their religious beliefs or practices, this is a useful focal point for exploration.

Personal Beliefs and Values of Counselors

If mental health practitioners are to effectively serve diverse clients, it is essential that they be capable and prepared to look at spirituality and religion if these are important to their clients. Counselors must understand their own spiritual and religious beliefs if they hope to gain an in-depth appreciation of the beliefs of their clients (Faiver et al., 2001; Hagedorn, 2005).

Your value system influences every facet of your counseling practice, including your assessment strategies, your views of goals of treatment, the interventions used, the topics explored during the sessions, and evaluations of therapy outcomes. No therapy is value free. You have an ethical responsibility to be aware of how your beliefs, or lack thereof, affect your work and to make sure you do not unduly influence your clients.

Your Personal Stance. As you formulate your own position on the place of spiritual and religious values in the practice of counseling, reflect on these questions:

- What connection, if any, do you see between spirituality, religion, and the problems of the client?
- Is there such a thing as professional religious counseling? What are the ethics of guiding a client only within the bounds of your religion? Might this limit a client's choice?
- Do you think it is ever justified for clinicians to introduce or teach their religious or spiritual values to clients and to base their clinical practice on these values?
- What criteria would you use to distinguish between healthy and unhealthy religious functioning of your clients?
- How would you describe the influence of religion or spirituality in your life?
- Are therapists forcing their values on their clients when they decide what topics can be discussed?
- If you have no religious or spiritual commitment, how might this hinder or help you in working with clients who hold strong religious convictions?
- Are you willing to collaborate with clergy or indigenous healers if it appears that clients have questions you are not qualified to answer?

- How does a counselor in a public school deal with spiritual or religious issues that students may bring up? Do parents need to be informed that spiritual issues may be discussed in counseling?

You may believe a client has accepted an unnecessarily strict and authoritarian moral code, but from an ethical perspective, you need to understand what these beliefs mean to your client, whatever your own evaluation of them for yourself might be. Consider the following case as you think about your personal stance on the role of spiritual and religious values in counseling.

✓ **The Case of Kieran.** Kieran is a counselor in private practice who has strong religious beliefs. He is open about this in his professional disclosure statement, explaining that his religious beliefs play a major part in his personal and professional life. Carmel comes to Kieran for counseling regarding what she considers to be a disintegrating marriage. Kieran has strong convictions that favor preserving the family unit. After going through an explanation of the informed consent document, Kieran asks Carmel if she is willing to join him in a prayer for the successful outcome of the therapy and for the preservation of the family. Kieran then takes a history and assures Carmel that everything can be worked out. He adds that he would like to include Carmel's husband in the sessions. Carmel leaves and does not return.

- Do you see any potential ethical violations on Kieran's part?
- If Kieran came to you for consultation, what might you say to him?

Commentary. Although we appreciate Kieran's frankness in presenting his values, we question his approach to Carmel. He does not assess the client's state of mind, her religious convictions, if any, the strength of her convictions, or her degree of comfort with his approach. Carmel may have felt pressured to agree with him in this first session, or she may not have had the strength to disagree openly. The ethical issue is captured in this question: "Did Kieran take care of the client's needs, or did he take care of his own needs at Carmel's expense?"

Including Spiritual and Religious Values in Counseling

Counseling can help clients gain insight into the ways their core beliefs and values are reflected in their behavior. Clients may sometimes discover that they need to reexamine these values. Miranti and Burke (1995) maintain that helpers must be prepared to deal with spiritual issues that lie at the very core of the client's being. The spiritual domain may offer clients in crisis solace and comfort. For many people, it is a major sustaining power that keeps them going when all else fails. The guilt, anger, and sadness that clients experience often results from a misinterpretation of the spiritual and religious realm, which can lead to depression and a sense of worthlessness. Clinicians must remain open and nonjudgmental, for the spiritual beliefs clients hold can be a major source of strength as they make crucial life decisions. Counselors can make use of the spiritual and religious beliefs of their clients to help them explore and resolve their problems (Basham & O'Connor, 2005).

Ethical practice sometimes demands that mental health professionals be willing and able to refer a client to a member of the clergy or an indigenous healer. It is well for practitioners to become knowledgeable about members of the religious community that they can collaborate with and refer clients to when it is appropriate. McMinn and colleagues (1998) outline the therapists' role in collaborating with clergy, but little by way of continuing education is available on the topic of collaboration between counselors and clergy. If a client adheres to religious values and practices, should the therapist get input from the clergy? When is there an ethical responsibility to refer clients for clarification of an issue pertaining to their problem and their faith? McMinn and colleagues write: "Because of the prominence of religious communities in American life, some have referred to organized religion as the 'sleeping giant' when it comes to delivering mental health services" (pp. 564–565). In a later study, McMinn, Aikins, and Lish (2003) concluded that basic competence in collaborating with clergy is sufficient for most practitioners, and that this competence is much like collaboration with physicians and other professionals. They add that "it is important for faculty and supervisors to communicate and model respectful attitudes toward clergy in working with students and supervisees" (p. 202).

Spirituality and religion receive modest attention in mental health training programs and almost none in school counseling programs. In an article dealing with training and education in religion and spirituality within clinical psychology programs, Brawer and colleagues (2002) conclude that most graduate programs address these issues to some degree. Much remains to be done in providing education and training dealing with religious and spiritual issues in counseling. If counselors are to meet the challenge of addressing the role of spirituality in the lives of their clients, they need training in both course work and field work as well as inspiration and leadership from their teachers. Walker, Gorsuch, and Tan (2004) conducted a 26-study meta-analysis of 5,759 therapists and their integration of religion and spirituality in counseling. Most of these therapists surveyed (about 87%) reported that they rarely or never discussed spiritual or religious issues as a part of their graduate training. Walker and colleagues state: "Given the lack of training regarding the integration of religion and spirituality into counseling, it seems that most integration of religion and spirituality in counseling occurs through intrapersonal integration as a result of therapists' own religious or spiritual experience" (p. 76).

A set of competencies in spirituality was developed by the Association for Spiritual, Ethical, and Religious Values in Counseling (ASERVIC) and proposed for inclusion in the Standards of the Council for Accreditation of Counseling and Related Educational Programs (CACREP). These competencies outline the knowledge and skills counselors need to master in order to effectively engage clients in the exploration of their spiritual and religious lives (G. Miller, 1999):

1. Explain the relationship between religion and spirituality, including similarities and differences.
2. Describe religious and spiritual beliefs and practices in a cultural context.

3. Engage in self-exploration of religious and spiritual beliefs in order to increase sensitivity, understanding, and acceptance of diverse belief systems.
4. Describe her or his religious or spiritual belief system and explain various models of religious or spiritual development across the life span.
5. Demonstrate sensitivity and acceptance of a variety of religious or spiritual expressions in client communication.
6. Identify limits of her or his understanding of a client's religious or spiritual expression and demonstrate appropriate referral skills and generate possible referral sources.
7. Assess the relevance of the religious or spiritual domains in the client's therapeutic issues.
8. Be sensitive to and receptive of religious or spiritual themes in the counseling process as befits the expressed preference of each client.
9. Use a client's religious or spiritual beliefs in the pursuit of the client's therapeutic goals as befits the client's expressed preference.

How might these spirituality competencies best be attained? Spirituality and religious frameworks could be included in cultural diversity training for counselors. When educators present a balanced approach to including spirituality and religious issues in training programs, Burke and colleagues (1999) maintain that they are modeling openness to these concerns and to their relevance in counseling. When this openness is not modeled, the chance of unconsciously imposing values and beliefs is increased. Programs need to challenge students to look at what they believe and how their beliefs and values might influence their work.

Some Cautions. Spirituality is an existential issue. Although it is important to be open to dealing with spiritual and religious issues in counseling, counselors should be cautious about introducing religious themes and be aware of the potential for countertransference.

Therapists must guard against making decisions for their clients. Some counselors may push their spiritual or religious beliefs, and others may impose their nonreligious or antireligious attitudes. Walker and colleagues (2004) indicate that most therapists lack formal training in incorporating religious and spiritual dimensions into the counseling process. Because of this lack of training, they caution therapists not to use spiritual and religious interventions inappropriately or to impose their own values on clients. Elsewhere Walker and his colleagues (2005) suggest that training programs incorporate workshops and supervision involving religious and spiritual interventions to teach therapists to use these interventions appropriately and effectively in counseling.

✓ **The Case of Sheila.** Sheila is a rational emotive behavior therapist who claims to be an atheist. She has a strong bias against any kind of spiritual or religious influences, considering these beliefs to be irrational. Her client Brendan describes an unhappy marriage as one of the issues he struggles with. When she suggests to him that perhaps he should consider leaving his marriage, he replies that this is out of the question. He informs her that he has a deep spiritual conviction that this is his destiny. If he were to go against his destiny, he would suffer on some other level. Sheila replies: "Have you ever considered that your convictions may be unhealthy, not only for you but also for your children? Are you willing to look at this?" Brendan seems taken aback. He tells the counselor, "I think that what you just said was not respectful of the way I believe. I am not sure that you can help me." Brendan leaves abruptly.

- How would you assess Sheila's approach?
- Do you see any ethical issues raised in the way Sheila dealt with Brendan? If so, what are the issues?
- Could you see yourself responding as Sheila did? Why or why not?
- Did Sheila take care of her needs or of Brendan's needs?
- Would Sheila necessarily have to agree with Brendan's spiritual beliefs to work with him? Explain.
- How would you work with this client?

Commentary. We have concerns about Sheila describing Brendan's spiritual beliefs as "unhealthy." Brendan's reasons for staying in his marriage (his spiritual values) could have been explored rather than being quickly judged. This kind of approach demonstrates the imposition of the therapist's values, not an exploration of the client's concerns.

✓ **The Case of Rory.** Rory, who has been in counseling for some time with Teresa, sees himself as a failure and cannot move past his guilt. He insists that he cannot forgive himself for his past. He is in great turmoil and berates himself for his aberrant ways. Teresa knows that Rory is a profoundly religious man and asks during one of the sessions: "How would you view and react to a person with a similar struggle as yours? What kind of God do you believe in? Is your God a punitive or loving God? What does your religion teach you about the forgiveness of sin?" Teresa is attempting to utilize Rory's convictions to reframe his thinking. Once he begins to look at his behavior through the eyes of his religious beliefs, his attitudes toward his own behavior change dramatically. Because Rory believes in a loving God, he finally learns to be more forgiving of himself.

- How do you react to how Teresa worked with Rory?
- Would you use Rory's religious beliefs as an intervention? Why or why not?
- By doing this, was Teresa imposing her values? Explain.

Commentary. If Teresa had used her own religious beliefs to reframe Rory's thinking, we would have concerns. If she were his minister, rabbi, or priest, it would be acceptable for her to teach these values. But that is not the role of a counselor. However, Teresa noticed a discrepancy between Rory's religious beliefs and his assessment of his behaviors. By using the client's own belief system, she assisted him in reframing his self-assessment and in the process helped him to be true to his own belief system.

Spiritual and Religious Values in Assessment and Treatment

Traditionally, when a client comes to a therapist with a problem, the therapist explores all the factors that could have contributed to the development of the problem. Even though a client may no longer consider him- or herself to be religious or spiritual, a background of involvement in religion needs to be explored as part of the client's history. To understand the client's concerns, it is essential that counselors understand how the client's religious values and beliefs affect his or her daily life and decision making and how these values and beliefs are related to the issues that bring the client to counseling (Belaire, Young, & Elder, 2005).

A number of writers and researchers believe it is essential to understand and respect clients' religious beliefs and to include such beliefs in their assessment and treatment practice (Belaire et al., 2005; Faiver & O'Brien,1993; Faiver & Ingersoll, 2005; Frame, 2003; Harper & Gill, 2005; Hathaway et al., 2004; Kelly, 1995b; Sperry & Shafranske, 2005). Frame (2003) presents many reasons for conducting assessments when working in the area of spirituality in counseling, some of which include understanding clients' worldviews and the contexts in which they live; assisting clients in grappling with questions regarding the purpose of their lives and what they most value; exploring religion and spirituality as client resources; uncovering religious and spiritual problems; and determining appropriate interventions.

The first step is to include spiritual and religious dimensions as a regular part of the intake procedure and the early phase of the counseling process. Faiver and O'Brien (1993) devised a form to assess the religious beliefs of clients, which they use to glean relevant information on the client's belief system for diagnostic, treatment, and referral purposes. Faiver and O'Brien suggest that the assessment process can include questions pertaining to spiritual and religious issues as they are relevant to a client's presenting problems, questions about the roles religion and spirituality have played or currently play in a client's life, and questions about how religious and spiritual beliefs might be related to the client's cognitive, affective, and behavioral processes. Faiver and Ingersoll (2005) encourage counselors to examine the client's spiritual culture, present circumstances, spiritual and religious beliefs (if any), and worldview. They suggest an assessment format that begins with the global and culminates with the specific. Based on a comprehensive assessment, a determination can be made about the appropriateness of devising a treatment plan that incorporates the client's religious and spiritual beliefs. According to forensic psychologist Rahn Minagawa, by ignoring the client's spirituality and religion, the practitioner is being insensitive to an area of the person's life that may be just as important as his or her ethnicity, cultural background, or sexual orientation. Minagawa believes it also may result in missed opportunities to incorporate the person's religious background or spirituality in promoting the development of insight, change, and cultural awareness (personal communication, August 14, 2003). We strongly support Minagawa's position that religion and spirituality are vital aspects in understanding, assessing, and treating a client.

Assessment is a process of looking at all the potential influences on a client's problem. The exploration of spirituality or religious influences is just as significant as exploring family-of-origin influences. Practitioners should remain finely tuned to their clients' stories and to the reasons clients seek professional assistance.

The Case of Anami. Anami is a counselor in a university counseling center. Tai, a first-generation Asian American client, is caught between the religion of his parents, who are Buddhist, and his emerging beliefs. Since entering the university environment, Tai has begun to question his Buddhist upbringing, yet he has not found anything to replace his parents' values. He feels lost and does not know what to believe.

Anami considers herself to be a holistic counselor, and her client assessments include asking questions about family history, personal history, religious and spiritual upbringing, life turning points, physical health, nutrition, and social relationships. In the process of the assessment, she discovers that many of the issues Tai is struggling with pertain to Buddhism. Anami tells Tai: "I think I can assist you in the things you struggle with, but I have limited knowledge of the Buddhist religion. With your permission I would like to consult on specific matters with a colleague who is a Buddhist. I may also recommend a Buddhist teacher to you to help you clarify some specific beliefs you mentioned in the assessment. Is this acceptable to you?" Tai nods in agreement.

- What do you think of the way Anami handled this case?
- Would you have done anything differently, and if so, what?
- Do you think Anami should have referred Tai because of her lack of familiarity with Buddhism?

Commentary. We find little to disagree with in the way Anami handled the case. We like the way she recognized and acknowledged her limitations, for being willing to educate herself on these matters, and also for being willing to consult with someone who has greater expertise than she does.

End-of-Life Decisions

End-of-life decisions have become an increasingly controversial issue since the Death with Dignity Act became law in Oregon in 1997. Do people who are terminally ill, have an incurable disease, or are in extreme pain have a right to choose the time and the means of their own death by seeking aid-in-dying (Herlihy & Watson, 2004)? Werth and Holdwick (2000) provide definitions for some key concepts related to this issue. **Rational suicide** means that a person has decided—after going through a decision-making process and without coercion from others—to end his or her life because of extreme suffering involved with a terminal illness. **Aid-in-dying** consists of providing a person with the means to die; the person self-administers the death-causing agent, which is a lethal dose of a legal medication. **Hastened death** involves speeding up the dying process, which can entail withholding or withdrawing life support.

The three of us attended an all-day workshop on "End-of-Life Decisions" for a variety of helping professionals. The program consisted of a panel of presenters from different disciplines: clinical psychology, philosophy, medicine, psychiatry, social work, and law. What struck us was the complexity of this topic in practice. Although many of us search for the best answers to difficult life-and-death situations, there are few simple answers. We came away from the conference with an increased awareness and appreciation of the challenging nature of working with people who are dying. It reinforced our belief in how critical it is for helping professionals to be clear about their own values on a range of issues pertaining to end-of-life care. It also reinforced our belief in the importance of having *advance directives* and a *living will* in place. **Advance directives** pertain to decisions people make about end-of-life care that are designed to protect their self-determination when they reach a point in their lives when they are no longer able to make decisions of their own about their care. A **living will** is a formal, written statement that specifies a person's preferences for end-of-life care.

Although there are no easy answers to right-to-die questions, Albright and Hazler (1995) remind us that counselors *do* face these situations *with* their clients. Counselors can assist their clients in making decisions within the framework of clients' own beliefs and value systems. Herlihy and Watson (2004) emphasize the willingness of counselors to examine their own values and beliefs to determine whether they are able and willing to consider a request for aid-in-dying. They state: "It is important that you have confronted your own fears about death and dying so that you do not project these onto your clients" (p. 179).

Mental health professionals must be prepared for working with those who are dying, and with their family members. Herlihy and Watson (2004) maintain that counselors will need to struggle with the ethical quandaries of how to balance the need to protect client rights to autonomy and self-determination with meeting responsibilities to the legal system, all the while remaining true to their own moral and ethical values.

At this point in time, you might consider the following questions: "What is your position on an individual's right to decide about matters pertaining to living and dying? What religious, ethical, and moral beliefs do you hold that would allow you to support a client's decision about ending his or her life under certain circumstances? How might your beliefs get in the way of assisting your client in making his or her own decision?" Your role as a counselor is to assist clients in making the best decision in the context of their own values. However, be knowledgeable of the laws of the state where you practice and the ethical guidelines of your professional organization concerning an individual's freedom to make end-of-life decisions.

Studies of attitudes toward suicide reveal sharp divisions of opinion regarding the meaning of the decision to end one's life. Some regard this as a basic personal right, whereas others consider it morally wrong (Neimeyer, 2000). In their article on the need for ethical reasoning regarding physician-assisted suicide, Kiser and Korpi (1996) suggest that mental health professionals may need to reconsider their views of suicide and how to treat suicidal clients. Instead of considering all individuals who are contemplating suicide as being "mentally ill" persons who should be prevented from ending their lives, certain individuals should be viewed as being capable of making autonomous and rational decisions about ending their life. Therapists can explore alternatives to suicide and, at the same time, be attentive to the client's autonomy and freedom of choice.

There are arguments both in favor of and in opposition to rational suicide. Most arguments favoring rational suicide center on the premise that individuals should have the right to make appropriate decisions about their lives when they are terminally ill. A study examined the attitudes of counselors toward rational suicide and found that about 80% of the respondents believed it was possible for a client to make a decision that death was his or her best option (Rogers, Guellette, Abbey-Hines, Carney, & Werth, 2001). The counselors in this study identified the most typical circumstances under which they would consider a decision to commit suicide as being rational as follows: (a) terminal illness, (b) severe physical pain, (c) a nonimpulsive consideration of alternatives, and (d) an unacceptable quality of life.

Some who favor rational suicide also provide guidelines for determining whether a suicide is rational (Abeles & Barlev, 1999; Farberman, 1997). Based on a survey of ethicists, suicidologists, and forensic psychologists, Werth (1996) provides a set of criteria to evaluate whether a person's suicide or hastened death is rational:

- The person considering suicide has an unremitting and hopeless condition.
- The person is acting under his or her own free will—is under no outside pressure to make the choice.
- The person has engaged in a sound decision-making process that includes consultation with a mental health professional who can make an assessment of mental competence; exploration of the person's values regarding suicide; consideration of the impact on significant others; and discussions with objective others (medical and religious professionals) and with significant others.

When these steps are followed, Werth concludes that an informed and rational choice can be made.

Arguments against assisted suicide focus on a client's religious and spiritual beliefs. As Herlihy and Watson (2004) indicate, religious institutions are often part of a person's life from the time he or she is born. Their religious belief systems may exert a major influence on the way individuals live and on their views pertaining to their own death. Many of the religions of the Western world oppose assisted suicide or **euthanasia,** which literally means "good death."

Suicide: A Free and Rational Choice?

In March 1990 Bruno Bettelheim, a well-known psychoanalyst and author, surprised the psychological community when he took his own life. In an interview with Celeste Fremon (1991), Bettelheim had shared some of his views on the right to take one's own life. He told Fremon that although he was not afraid of dying he did fear suffering. As people grow older, he contended, there is a greater likelihood that they will be kept alive without a purpose. At age 86, Bettelheim was no longer able to do most of the things that brought him enjoyment and meaning, such as hiking, reading, and writing, and he made a decision to end his life.

As a counselor, you need to be willing to discuss end-of-life decisions when clients bring such concerns to you. If you are closed to any personal examination of this issue, you may interrupt these dialogues, cut off your clients' exploration of their feelings, or attempt to provide clients with your own solutions based on your values and beliefs.

In the Netherlands physician-assisted suicide is a legal means of ending one's life (Kiser, 1996), but in the United States physician-assisted suicide is a highly controversial issue. The Supreme Court has held that there is not a constitutional right to aid-in-dying but has left the resolution of whether to allow physician-assisted suicide to the individual states. Although Oregon's Death With Dignity Act was first passed in 1994, it did not go into effect until 1997. Subsequently, both Washington and California placed measures legalizing assisted suicide on their state ballots—both initiatives failed.

Role of Professionals in Helping Clients With End-of-Life Decisions

Psychological services are useful for healthy individuals who want to make plans about their own future care. Such services are also beneficial to individuals with life-limiting illnesses, families experiencing the demands of providing end-of-life care, bereaved individuals, and health care providers who are experiencing stress and burnout (Haley et al., 2003). Mental health practitioners need to acquire knowledge about the psychological, ethical, and legal considerations in end-of-life care. They can have a key role in helping people make choices regarding how they will die and about the ethical issues involved in making those choices (Kleespies, 2004). Although physician-assisted suicide is an option in only one state (Oregon), other end-of-life decisions can be made more broadly, such as refusing all treatment. Does a therapist have an ethical responsibility to explore the client's decision to refuse treatment? Even though it is not against the law to refuse treatment, this decision could be made based on misinformation or a misunderstanding. Thus, a counselor would want to assess the nature of the information upon which the client is making the decision. Just as in the Oregon statute a psychological assessment is required to rule out depression, it is equally important to assess for depression when clients decide to forgo treatment.

Albright and Hazler (1995) acknowledge that counselors will be faced with difficult decisions on what actions to take with clients struggling with end-of-life decisions. They suggest the following interventions to provide direction for clients struggling with these kinds of decisions:

- Learn as much as possible about the course of clients' illnesses, prognoses, and available treatments.
- Know the clients' family support systems and what their views are regarding end-of-life decisions.
- Realize that clients who are near death often need help coping with their psychological pain as well as their physical suffering. Explore clients' fears about dying, the impact of their religious beliefs on their decision or how religion provides them with meaning, and assist them in achieving closure on any unfinished business with others.
- Assume the role of a resource person for these clients.
- Help clients understand the importance of various personal and formal documents associated with the end of life.
- Regardless of the decisions clients make, offer compassion, acceptance, and understanding related to the difficulties in dealing with life and death issues.
- Realize the role of offering comfort to loved ones and friends after the death.

Werth and Holdwick (2000) suggest some additional steps therapists can take. These include giving prospective clients information about the limitations of confidentiality as it applies to assisted death, if applicable; making full use of consultation throughout the process; keeping risk management–oriented notes; and assessing the impact of external coercion on clients' decision making.

Policy Statement on End-of-Life Decisions

Both the American Psychiatric Association and the American Medical Association have opposed physician-assisted suicide (Werth & Gordon, 2002), but few other professional organizations have developed specific guidelines for end-of-life decisions (Werth, 1999a). One exception is the National Association of Social Workers (1994a), which developed a policy statement pertaining to client self-determination in end-of-life decisions. This statement is based on the principle of client self-determination, the premise that choice should be intrinsic to all aspects of life and death. According to the NASW document, end-of-life decisions are the choices individuals make about terminal conditions regarding their continuing care or treatment options. These options include aggressive treatment of the medical condition, life-sustaining treatment, medical intervention intended to alleviate suffering (but not to cure), withholding or withdrawing life-sustaining treatment, voluntary active euthanasia, and physician-assisted suicide. A terminal condition is one where there is no reasonable chance of recovery and where the application of life-sustaining procedures would serve only to postpone the end of life. Here are some excerpts from the NASW report:

> Social workers have an important role in helping individuals identify the end-of-life options available to them. This role must be performed with full

> knowledge of and compliance with the law and in accordance with the *NASW Code of Ethics.*
>
> Social workers should be well informed about living wills, durable power of attorney for health care, and legislation related to advance health care directives.
>
> A key value for social workers is client self-determination. Competent individuals should have the opportunity to make their own choices but only after being informed about all options and consequences. Choices should be made without coercion. Therefore, the appropriate role for social workers is to help patients express their thoughts and feelings, to facilitate exploration of alternatives, to provide information to make an informed choice, and to deal with grief and loss issues.
>
> Social workers should be free to participate or not participate in assisted-suicide matters or other discussions concerning end-of-life decisions depending on their own beliefs, attitudes, and value systems. If a social worker is unable to help with decisions about assisted suicide or other end-of-life choices, he or she has a professional obligation to refer patients and their families to competent professionals who are available to address end-of-life issues.
>
> It is inappropriate for social workers to deliver, supply, or personally participate in the commission of an act of assisted suicide when acting in their professional role. Doing so may subject the social worker to criminal charges. If legally permissible, it is not inappropriate for a social worker to be present during an assisted suicide if the client requests the social worker's presence. The involvement of social workers in assisted suicide cases should not depend on race or ethnicity, religion, age, gender, economic factors, sexual orientation, or disability. ("End of Life Decisions.")

In its revised *Code of Ethics,* ACA (2005) addresses end-of-life care for terminally ill clients. Regarding quality of care, ACA offers this guideline:

> Counselors strive to take measures that enable clients (1) to obtain high quality end-of-life care for their physical, emotional, social and spiritual needs; (2) to exercise the highest degree of self-determination possible; (3) to be given every opportunity possible to engage in informed decision making regarding their end-of-life care; and (4) to receive complete and adequate assessment regarding their ability to make competent, rational decisions on their own behalf from a mental health professional who is experienced in end-of-life care practice. (A.9.a.)

There is also a guideline pertaining to competence, choice, and referral:

> Recognizing the personal, moral and competence issues related to end-of-life decisions, counselors may choose to work or not work with terminally ill clients who wish to explore their end-of-life options. Counselors provide appropriate referral information to ensure that clients receive the necessary help. (A.9.b.)

The ACA also addresses confidentiality issues when working with these clients:

> Counselors who provide services to terminally ill individuals who are considering hastening their own deaths have the option of breaking or not breaking

> confidentiality, depending on applicable laws and the specific circumstances of the situation and after seeking consultation or supervision from appropriate professional and legal parties. (A.9.c.)

The policy statement of NASW and the end-of-life care standards of the ACA provide social workers and counselors with some general guidelines by which they can examine the ethical and legal issues pertaining to end-of-life decisions.

A Counselor's Responsibilities

What is the role of mental health professionals in counseling people who are facing the end of life? If a therapist's values do not allow for the possibility of a hastened death as the best option for an individual, Werth and Holdwick (2000) believe this therapist should not be obligated to provide professional services for a client who brings up this issue.

Another question being raised by experts in the field is, "Who should be trained to provide assistance for people contemplating rational suicide and hastened death decisions?" Silverman (2000) is not convinced that all students and professionals should be trained for situations and careers that they probably will not encounter in their practices. Silverman's contention raises some questions. Although some practitioners may not regularly encounter clients who are considering rational suicide, how can they ethically function when a long-term client might bring up an end-of-life decision? If the request for assistance in hastening the end of life came from a new client, perhaps a therapist could refer this client. But a referral can be much more difficult with a long-term client who brings up ending his or her life. First, would the client follow through in making an appointment with a new therapist? Second, if the therapist was able to discuss the situation with the client, there is always the possibility that this person might change his or her mind.

The mental health professions face the challenge of formulating ethical and procedural guidelines on right-to-die issues, especially in light of advances in medical technology, the aging of the population, and the AIDS epidemic. Need we say again that Oregon is the only state that allows physician-assisted suicide. There are legal prohibitions regarding assisted suicide in all other states, and mental health professionals have to deal with this reality. However, in all states patients are free to choose not to seek treatment to prolong life. Even though practitioners may not have to deal with assisted suicide, they still may be involved in end-of-life decisions. We agree with Herlihy and Watson's (2004) position that "there will be a growing need for specially trained, culturally competent, and ethical counselors to assist clients with end-of-life decision making" (p. 181). Now let's examine some specific cases involving end-of-life decisions.

✓ **The Case of Festus.** A counselor has been seeing a client named Festus who has been diagnosed with an aggressive and painful cancer. After a series of chemotherapy treatments and pain medication, Festus tells the counselor that nothing seems to work and that he has decided to end his life. They discuss his decision for several sessions, examining all aspects, and Festus becomes even clearer about his decision to end his life. Here are four counselors' responses to the decision Festus has made.

Counselor A: Both the law and my code of ethics require that I report this matter.

Festus: Do what you have to do. If you report me, I will simply say that I was not seriously considering it, and I won't see you any more.

Counselor B: I have a great deal of difficulty accepting your decision. I am asking you not to take any action for at least 3 weeks to give us time to talk about this further. Are there possibly ways for you to find meaning in your life in spite of your suffering?

Counselor C: Although the law requires that I report you, it does not seem like the right or effective thing to do. Our relationship has come to mean a lot to both of us, especially at a time like this. You could always stop seeing me and kill yourself anyhow. I will continue to see you as long as you choose to come, and I will help you deal with your pain in any way that I can.

Counselor D: Write a letter to me terminating therapy. Once I receive the letter, our relationship is over.

Consider each of these approaches, and then clarify what you would do in this situation by answering these questions.

- What are your thoughts about each counselor's response? Which one comes closest to your thinking?
- What would you want to say to Festus?
- Is it ethical to impose your values on Festus in this case? Why or why not?
- Do you think the state has the right to decide how individuals with terminal illnesses will die?

Commentary. Many therapists are likely to struggle with what they see as a conflict between choosing the ethical as opposed to the legal path. Following a strictly legal course, the therapist would be free from any lawsuit, and the counselor could exercise his or her duty to protect. However, after a mandatory 72-hour hold for psychiatric evaluation, Festus would be released and free to do whatever he had intended to do.

We do not suggest that you ignore the law, but when you encounter this kind of case, the proper course is not always clear. If you do not report, you may be thinking of the client's autonomy, self-determination, and welfare. You could reason that your client is of sound mind and that he has a right to decide not to live in extreme pain. You could also think about providing him with the maximum degree of support as long as he wants this. However, if you do not report him and he does end his life, the family could sue you for breach of your professional duty. If you do report, and he terminates his therapy, you will not be in a position to offer support or to help him in other ways. If you follow the letter of the law, your therapeutic relationship with this client is most probably ended.

✓ **The Case of Bettina.** Bettina lives at boarding school and has made several suicidal overtures. Because these attempts were judged to be primarily attention-getting gestures, her counselor feels manipulated and does not report them to Bettina's parents. During the last of these attempts, however, Bettina seriously hurts herself and ends up in the hospital.

- Do you see any conflict between what is ethically right and what is legally right in this situation?
- Did the counselor take the "cry for help" too lightly?
- What are the ethical and legal implications for the counselor in deciding that Bettina's attempts were more manipulative than serious and therefore should be ignored?
- What can a counselor do in a situation in which he or she determines that the attempts are manipulative rather than serious?
- If the counselor told Bettina that she was going to inform the girl's parents about these suicidal attempts and Bettina had responded by saying that she would quit counseling if the counselor did so, what do you think the counselor should do?

Issues Involved in End-of-Life Decisions. Although the cases of Festus and Bettina are different, they both raise similar issues of balancing what is ethically right with what is legally required. The codes of ethics of all the professional organizations promote client autonomy and self-determination. However, the law prohibiting assisted suicide does not honor a person's right to self-determination. Mental health professionals are confronted with a potential ethical dilemma when there is a legal prohibition to self-determination. The longer the client-therapist relationship has existed, the greater the complexity of the problem. This is an example of a situation where you might be following a legal course, but some might consider you to be unethical for not respecting a client's choice. If you follow what you consider to be an ethical course that is in conflict with the law, then you face serious legal consequences.

- Do counselors have the responsibility and the right to forcefully protect people from the potential harm their own decisions may bring?
- Do helpers have an ethical right to block clients who have clearly chosen death over life? Do counselors have an ethical duty to respect clients' decisions?
- What are a counselor's legal obligations if a client decides to commit suicide?
- What should be done if what seems ethically right is not legal?
- If a course of action is legal but does not seem like the most ethical path to choose, what would you do?
- Once a therapist determines that a significant risk exists, must some action be taken?
- What are the consequences of failing to take steps to prevent clients from ending their lives?
- When do factors such as a client's age, a client's level of competence, and the special circumstances of each case make a difference?

Chapter Summary

This chapter has addressed a variety of value-laden counseling situations and issues. Our intent has been to focus attention on the ways your values and those of your clients, the codes of ethics, and the legal system can affect your counseling relationships.

There is widespread interest in the spiritual and religious beliefs of both counselors and clients and in how these beliefs and values can be an integral part of the therapeutic relationship. Because spiritual and religious values play a vital role in the lives of many who seek counseling, these values can be viewed as a valuable resource in therapy rather than as something to be ignored. In short, spirituality is a major source of strength for many clients and an important factor in promoting healing and well-being. It is important for clinicians to be open to addressing spiritual and religious issues in the assessment and therapeutic process. However, practitioners must guard against making decisions for their clients. A counselor's role is not to prescribe a particular pathway to clients in fulfilling their spiritual needs but to help clients clarify their own pathway.

End-of-life decisions are another area in which counselors need to clarify their values. The subject of end-of-life decisions has become increasingly controversial since the Death With Dignity Act became law in Oregon in 1997. There are arguments both in favor of and in opposition to rational suicide. Generally, the arguments favoring rational suicide center on the premise that terminally ill individuals have a fundamental right to make appropriate decisions about their lives. Mental health professionals have the challenge of clarifying their own beliefs and values pertaining to end-of-life decisions so that they can assist their clients in making decisions within the framework of clients' beliefs and value systems. In this matter, the counselor's role is to assist clients in making the best possible decisions in light of their own value system. However, it is essential to be aware of state laws and codes of ethics concerning an individual's freedom to make end-of-life decisions.

It is unlikely that mental health professionals can be neutral in the area of values. They may choose to acknowledge their values when they are related to issues their clients are struggling with. It takes honesty and courage to recognize how your values affect the way you counsel, and it takes wisdom to determine when you are not able to work effectively with a client due to a clash of values. Ongoing introspection and discussions with supervisors or colleagues are necessary to determine how to make optimal use of your values in the therapeutic relationship.

Suggested Activities

1. Have a panel discussion on the topic "Is it possible for counselors to remain neutral with respect to their clients' values?" The panel can also discuss different ways in which counselors' values may affect the counseling process.

2. Invite several practicing counselors to talk to your class about the role of values in counseling. Invite counselors who have different theoretical orientations. For example, you might ask a behavior therapist and a humanistic therapist to talk to your class at the same time on the role of values.

3. For a week keep a record of situations where your values guide your actions. Prioritize your values as they are reflected in your record. How do you think these values might influence the way you work with others?

4. In pairs discuss counseling situations that might involve a conflict of values. Then choose a specific situation to role play, with one student playing the part of the client and the other playing the part of the counselor.

5. Many case examples given in this chapter address a wide variety of value issues. In small groups, select two or three of these vignettes and discuss how you, as a group, might address the ethical issues raised in each of these cases.

6. In pairs, talk to your partner about the circumstances in which you would consider referring a client to another professional because of a value conflict between you and your client. Can you think of ways to effectively manage this value conflict other than by making a referral?

7. Some counselors believe terminally ill clients have the ultimate right to determine if, how, and when they will end their life. Other counselors believe their obligation is to assist clients in finding meaning in life regardless of a particular set of circumstances. In two groups argue for and against rational suicide addressing both ethical and legal issues.

8. In this exercise one student acts as the counselor and the other as the client. The task of the counselor is to try to persuade the client to do what the counselor thinks would be best for the client. Then switch roles; afterward discuss what this process was like for you.

Ethics in Action CD-ROM Exercises

9. In video role play #4, The Divorce, it is clear that the counselor has an agenda for the client, who has decided to leave her husband and get a divorce. The counselor's focus is on the welfare of her children. The client feels misunderstood and does not think the counselor is helping her. Have one student role play Gary (the counselor in the video) while another student role plays his supervisor. As the supervisor, explore the issues you see being played out.

10. In video role play #5, Doing It My Way, Sally (the counselor) is attempting to influence her client to think about the effect of her behavior on her parents. Charlae is seeking increased independence and wants to break away from her parents. Sally is concerned about what Charlae's parents' reaction might be if she moves out without involving her parents in this decision. Have one student role play the counselor, while another student becomes Sally's supervisor. Through role playing, demonstrate how you might approach the counselor as her supervisor. What would you most want Sally to consider?

11. In video role play #6, The Promiscuous One, the client (Suzanne) is having indiscriminate sexual encounters, and her counselor (Richard) expresses concern for Suzanne when he learns about her sexual promiscuity. Richard

then focuses on how Suzanne's behavior plays out the recurring theme of abandonment by her father, while she thinks there is no connection. If you were Suzanne's counselor, how would you deal with the situation as she presents it? Is it ethically appropriate for you to strongly influence your client to engage in safe sex practices? Demonstrate how you would approach Suzanne through role playing.

12. In video role play #7, The Affair, the client (Natalie) shares with her counselor that she is struggling with her marriage and is having a long-term affair. The counselor (Janice) says, "Having an affair is not a good answer for someone—it just hurts everyone. I do not think it is a good idea." How would your values influence your interventions in this situation? Have one student role play the counselor and show how he or she might work with Natalie. In a second role play, have one student become the counselor's supervisor and demonstrate what issues you might explore with Janice.

InfoTrac® College Edition Resources

For additional readings, explore InfoTrac College Edition, our online library. Key words are listed in a form that enables the search engine to locate a wider range of articles in the online university library. Key words should be entered exactly as shown, including asterisks, "Wl," "W2," "AND," and other search engine tools. Go to http://www.infotrac-college.com and select these key word searches:

(therap* N6 value*) NOT medic* NOT physic*
psych* N6 value*
spiritual N3 value* AND (psych????y OR psychotherapy OR couns*)
relig* N4 value* AND (psych????y OR psychotherapy OR couns*)
end of life decision*
rational N2 suicide
value N3 neutrality AND (psych????y OR psychotherapy OR couns*)
therapeutic N3 neutrality
value* N3 imposition AND (psych????y OR psychotherapy OR couns*)
euthanasia AND (psych????y OR psychotherapy OR couns*) NOT medic* NOT physic*

Chapter 4

Pre-Chapter Self-Inventory

Directions: For each statement, indicate the response that most closely identifies your beliefs and attitudes. Use the following code:

5 = I *strongly agree* with this statement.
4 = I *agree* with this statement.
3 = I am *undecided* about this statement.
2 = I *disagree* with this statement.
1 = I *strongly disagree* with this statement.

____ 1. Well-trained, sensitive, and self-aware therapists who do not impose their own values on clients are better qualified to be multicultural counselors.
____ 2. To counsel effectively, I must be of the same ethnic background as my client.
____ 3. Basically, all counseling interventions are multicultural.
____ 4. I must challenge cultural stereotypes when they become obvious in counseling situations.
____ 5. Contemporary counseling theories can be applied to people from all cultures.
____ 6. With the current emphasis on multiculturalism, counselors are vulnerable to overcorrecting for a perceived imbalance when considering cultural differences.
____ 7. I will be able to examine my behavior and attitudes to determine the degree to which cultural bias might influence the interventions I make with clients.
____ 8. Special guidelines are needed for counseling members of ethnic or racial minority groups.
____ 9. The codes of ethics of most professional organizations contain culturally biased assumptions.
____ 10. The primary function of majority-group counselors is to alert their clients to the choices available to them.
____ 11. An effective mental health practitioner facilitates assimilation of the minority client into society.

Multicultural Perspectives and Diversity Issues

____ 12. Ethical practice demands that counselors become familiar with the value systems of diverse cultural groups.

____ 13. I would have no trouble working with someone from a culture very different from mine because we would be more alike than different.

____ 14. If I just listen to my clients, I will know all I need to know about their cultural background.

____ 15. Client resistance is typically encountered in multicultural counseling and must be overcome before changes can take place.

____ 16. The ability to observe and understand nonverbal communication is an important component of multicultural counseling.

____ 17. Establishing a trusting relationship is more difficult when the counselor and the client come from different cultures.

____ 18. Unless practitioners have been educated about cultural differences, they cannot determine whether they are competent to work with diverse populations.

____ 19. As a condition for licensure, all counselors should have specialized training and supervised experience in multicultural counseling.

____ 20. At this point in my educational career, I feel well prepared to counsel culturally diverse client populations.

____ 21. To be considered competent, I think all counselors need to appreciate the ways that diversity influences the client-counselor relationship and the counseling process itself.

____ 22. A Christian counselor should refer gay, lesbian, and bisexual clients to another professional.

____ 23. Gay and lesbian clients are best served by gay and lesbian counselors.

____ 24. I would have difficulty counseling either a lesbian or gay couple who wanted support in adopting a child.

____ 25. As a counselor, it is my ethical responsibility to learn about referral resources for gay, lesbian, and bisexual clients and to make appropriate referrals if I do not have the knowledge and skills to work effectively with them.

Introduction

In this chapter we narrow our focus to examine the cultural values, beliefs, and assumptions of helping professionals and their clients and discuss how these values may influence therapeutic work. We also discuss sexual orientation and the values surrounding this topic. The emphasis is on the ethical dimensions of understanding the client's worldview and tailoring the therapeutic process to the client's cultural context.

One of the major challenges facing mental health professionals is understanding the complex role cultural diversity plays in their work. In a sense, all counseling interventions are multicultural. Clients and counselors bring a great variety of attitudes, values, culturally learned assumptions, and behaviors to the therapeutic relationship. Some counselors deny the importance of these cultural variables in counseling; others overemphasize the importance of cultural differences, lose their naturalness, and may fail to make contact with their clients.

Cultural sensitivity is not limited to one group but applies to all cultures. There is no sanctuary from cultural bias. For example, White therapists need to be aware of their possible prejudices toward African American clients, just as African American therapists need to be sensitive regarding their attitudes toward White clients. All mental health practitioners must avoid using their own group as the standard by which to assess appropriate behavior in others. In addition, greater differences may exist within the same cultural group than between different cultural groups, and we need to be intraculturally sensitive as well as multiculturally sensitive.

In this chapter we focus on the ethical implications of a multicultural perspective or lack thereof in the helping professions. To ensure that the terms we use in this chapter have a clear meaning, we have provided specific definitions (see the box titled Multicultural Terminology). This field is complex and is developing rapidly, and practitioners need to stay current on these developments.

The Need for a Multicultural Emphasis

Cultural diversity has always been a fact of life in our world. Yet it is only within the past couple of decades that helping professionals have realized that they can no longer ignore the issues involved in serving culturally diverse populations. Multicultural counseling attempts to clarify the role of sociocultural forces in the origin, expression, and resolution of problems (Axelson, 1999). Das (1995) points out that culture influences every aspect of our lives, for it influences our view of social and psychological reality. Multicultural counseling is based on a number of premises identified here by Das (p. 45):

- All cultures represent meaningful ways of coping with the problems a particular group faces.
- All counseling can be regarded as multicultural if culture is defined broadly to include not only race, ethnicity, and nationality but also gender, age, social class, sexual orientation, and disability.

Multicultural Terminology

The word **culture** can be interpreted broadly, for it can be associated with a racial or ethnic group as well as with gender, religion, economic status, nationality, physical capacity or disability, and affectional or sexual orientation. Pedersen (2000) describes culture as including demographic variables such as age, gender, and place of residence; status variables such as social, educational, and economic background; formal and informal affiliations; and the ethnographic variables of nationality, ethnicity, language, and religion. Considering culture from this broad perspective provides a context for understanding that each of us is simultaneously a member of many different cultures. Within group and between group variables define similarities and differences (Pedersen, 2000). Culture can be considered as a lens through which life is perceived. Each culture, through its differences, generates a phenomenologically different experience of reality (Diller, 2004).

Ethnicity is a sense of identity that stems from common ancestry, history, nationality, religion, and race. This unique social and cultural heritage provides cohesion and strength. It is a powerful unifying force that offers a sense of belonging and sharing based on commonality (Axelson, 1999; Lum, 2000).

Ethnic minority group refers to a group of people who have been singled out for differential and unequal treatment and who regard themselves as objects of collective discrimination. These groups have been characterized as subordinate, dominated, and powerless. Thus, minority is often defined by the condition of oppression rather than by numerical criteria. Although the term *minority* has traditionally referred to national, racial, linguistic, and religious groups, it now also applies to women, the elderly, gay men, lesbians, bisexuals, and people with disabilities (Atkinson, 2004).

Multiculturalism is a generic term that indicates any relationship between and within two or more diverse groups. *Cross-cultural, transcultural,* and *intercultural* are terms with similar meanings. We prefer *multicultural* because it more accurately reflects the complexity of culture but avoids any implied comparison. The multicultural perspective in human-service education takes into consideration the specific values, beliefs, and actions conditioned by a client's ethnicity, gender, religion, socioeconomic status, political views, sexual orientation, geographic region, and historical experiences with the dominant culture (Wright, Coley, & Corey, 1989). Multiculturalism provides a conceptual framework that recognizes the complex diversity of a pluralistic society, while at the same time suggesting bridges of shared concern that bind culturally different individuals to one another (Pedersen, 1991, 2000).

Cultural diversity refers to the spectrum of differences that exists among groups of people with definable and unique cultural backgrounds (Diller, 2004).

Multicultural counseling refers to a helping role and process that uses approaches and defines goals consistent with the life experiences and cultural values of clients, balancing the importance of individualism versus collectivism in assessment, diagnosis, and treatment (Sue & Sue, 2003). Arredondo and her colleagues (1996) state that multicultural counselors integrate multicultural and culture-specific awareness, knowledge, and skills in their counseling practices.

Whereas multiculturalism focuses on ethnicity, race, and culture, **diversity** refers to individual differences such as age, gender, sexual orientation, religion, and physical ability or disability. Both multiculturalism and diversity have been politicized in the United States in ways that have often been divisive, but these terms can equally represent positive assets in a pluralistic society.

Diversity-sensitive counseling is a concept that includes age, culture, disability, education level, ethnicity, gender, language, physique, race, religion, residential location, sexual orientation, socioeconomic situation, and trauma (Weinrach & Thomas, 1998).

Cultural empathy pertains to therapists' awareness of clients' worldviews, which are acknowledged in relation to therapists' awareness of their own personal biases (Roysircar, 2004).

continued on next page

Culture-centered counseling is a three-stage developmental sequence, from multicultural awareness to knowledge and comprehension to skills and applications (Pedersen, 2000).

Stereotypes are oversimplified and uncritical generalizations about individuals who are identified as belonging to a specific group.

Racism is any pattern of behavior that, solely because of race or culture, denies access to opportunities or privileges to members of one racial or cultural group while perpetuating access to opportunities and privileges to members of another racial or cultural group (Ridley, 1989, 2005). Racism can operate on both individual and institutional levels, and it can occur intentionally or unintentionally.

Although counselors exhibiting blatantly biased attitudes may be easily identified, many other well-intentioned helpers practice **unintentional racism** (Ridley, 2005). Unintentional racism is often subtle, indirect, and outside our conscious awareness; this can be the most damaging and insidious form of racism (Sue, 2005). Practitioners who presume that they are free of any traces of racism seriously underestimate the impact of their own socialization. Whether these biased attitudes are intentional or unintentional, the result is harmful for both individuals and society. Pedersen (2000) believes that the key to recognizing unintentional racism lies in the willingness of practitioners to continually examine their underlying assumptions.

Cultural racism is the belief that one group's history, way of life, religion, values, and traditions are superior to others (Sue, 2005).

Note about names: There is some concern about how to refer appropriately to certain racial and ethnic groups as preferred names tend to change. For instance, some alternate names for one group are Hispanic, Latino (Latina), Mexican American, or Chicana (Chicano). Realizing that there is no one "right" designation to fit any group, practitioners can show sensitivity to the fact that a name is important; they can ask their clients how they would like to be identified.

- People seek counseling largely because of problems that emerge out of sociocultural conditions.
- Traditional therapy is a particular form of intervention developed in the West to cope with psychological distress.
- All cultures have developed formal or informal ways of dealing with human problems.

The Problem of Cultural Tunnel Vision

A faculty member overheard one of our students inquiring about possibilities for a field work placement in a community agency. The student remarked: "I don't want a placement where I'll have to work with poor people or minority groups." This brief statement revealed much about the student's attitudes and beliefs, and possibly his fears, about working with people who were different from him. If we want students to be more culturally aware, it is essential that we encourage them to explore their attitudes and fears of people who are different from themselves.

Many students come into training knowing only their own culture, which can lead to **cultural tunnel vision**, a perception of reality based on a very limited set of cultural experiences. Due to these limited cultural experiences, they may unwittingly impose their values on unsuspecting clients by assuming that everyone shares these values. At times, student helpers from the majority group have expressed the attitude, explicitly or implicitly, that racial and ethnic minorities are unresponsive to professional psychological intervention because of their lack of motivation to change, which these student helpers label as resistance. They may never stop to think that what they call "resistance" may be a healthy response on the part of the client to the helper's cultural and theoretical bias.

Students are not alone in their susceptibility to cultural tunnel vision. Ridley (2005) develops the thesis that, ironic as it may seem, racism has been present in mental health delivery systems for quite some time. Ridley states that studies from the 1950s to the present have documented enduring patterns of racism in mental health care delivery systems. The impact of racism on various racial groups and the existence of racism in a variety of treatment settings is well documented.

The **culturally encapsulated** counselor exhibits tunnel vision, which is characterized by these traits described by Wrenn (1962, 1985):

- Defines reality according to one set of cultural assumptions
- Shows insensitivity to cultural variations among individuals
- Accepts unreasoned assumptions without proof or ignores proof because that might disconfirm one's assumptions
- Fails to evaluate other viewpoints and makes little attempt to accommodate the behavior of others
- Is trapped in one way of thinking that resists adaptation and rejects alternatives

Years after his formulation of the culturally encapsulated counselor, Wrenn (1985) maintained that cultural encapsulation continued to be a problem for counseling professionals. Pedersen (2003) cautions mental health professionals not to underestimate the power of cultural bias and cultural encapsulation as generic issues in the profession of counseling psychology.

A good place for you to begin to develop a multicultural perspective is by becoming more aware of your own culturally learned assumptions, some of which may be culturally biased (Pedersen, 2003). This will provide a context for understanding how diverse cultures share common ground and also how to recognize areas of uniqueness (Pedersen, 2000). Whether you are aware of it or not, cultural factors are an integral part of the helping process, and culture influences your interventions with those you serve. Pedersen (1994) puts this challenge well when he writes:

> It is no longer possible for good counselors to ignore their own cultures or the cultures of their clients through encapsulation. However, until the multicultural perspective is understood as making the counselor's job easier instead of harder, and increasing rather than decreasing the quality of a counselor's life, little real change is likely to happen. (p. 22)

Learning to Address Cultural Pluralism

Cultural pluralism is a perspective that recognizes the complexity of cultures and values the diversity of beliefs and values. To operate monoculturally and monolingually, as if all our clients were the same, is not in accord with reality, and it can result in unethical and ineffective practice. Pedersen (2000) reminds us that culture is complex, yet this complexity can be viewed as friend rather than foe because it helps us avoid searching for easy answers to hard questions.

Roysircar (2004) emphasizes the importance of cultural self-awareness, which is captured in the motto, "Therapist, know thy cultural self." Roysircar asserts that therapists' cultural self-awareness is essential for effective and culturally relevant therapy. Richardson and Molinaro (1996) maintain that when practitioners learn about their own culture they are moving in the direction of acquiring multicultural competence. They add, "If a counselor accepts this challenge and engages in self-exploration, then learning about the race, cultures, and experiences of clients becomes a manageable process instead of an overwhelming and threatening one" (p. 241).

The Challenges of Reaching Diverse Client Populations

The Association for Multicultural Counseling and Development has developed a set of multicultural counseling competencies (Roysircar et al., 2003), which provides a framework for the effective delivery of services to diverse client populations. In addition, the APA (1993) provides "Guidelines for Providers of Psychological Services to Ethnic, Linguistic, and Culturally Diverse Populations." Mental health professionals are reminded to be aware of how their own culture, life experiences, attitudes, values, and biases influence them. Additionally, practitioners are challenged to go beyond their cultural encapsulation and ask themselves: "Is it appropriate for me to view these clients any differently than I would if they were from my own ethnic or cultural group?" The APA's guidelines challenge practitioners to respect the roles of family members and the community structures, hierarchies, values, and beliefs that are an integral part of the client's culture. Providers should identify resources in the client's family and the larger community and use them in delivering culturally sensitive services. For example, an entire Native American family may come to a clinic to provide support for an individual in distress because many of the healing practices found in Native American communities are centered on the family and the community.

The American Psychological Association has developed *Guidelines on Multicultural Education, Training, Research, Practice, and Organizational Change for Psychologists* (APA, 2003a), which address the knowledge and skills needed for the profession as a result of the sociopolitical changes within the United States. These guidelines provide psychologists with a framework for delivering services to an increasingly diverse population, and they can be useful for helpers in various mental health professions. Summary statements for the six guidelines contained in the document follow:

1. Psychologists are encouraged to recognize that, as cultural beings, they may hold attitudes and beliefs that can detrimentally influence their perceptions of and interactions with individuals who are ethnically and racially different from themselves. (p. 382)

2. Psychologists are encouraged to recognize the importance of multicultural sensitivity/responsiveness to, knowledge of, and understanding about ethnically and racially different individuals. (p. 385)
3. As educators, psychologists are encouraged to employ the constructs of multiculturalism and diversity in psychological education. (p. 386)
4. Culturally sensitive psychological researchers are encouraged to recognize the importance of conducting culture-centered and ethical psychological research among persons from ethnic, linguistic, and racial minority backgrounds. (p. 388)
5. Psychologists are encouraged to apply culturally appropriate skills in clinical and other applied psychological practices. (p. 390)
6. Psychologists are encouraged to use organizational change processes to support culturally informed organizational (policy) development and practices. (p. 392)

These APA's guidelines need to be considered as a working document rather than a dogmatic set of prescriptions. Those who created this evolving document realize that the integration of racial and ethnic factors into psychological theory, practice, and research has only recently begun.

Psychology has traditionally been based on Western assumptions, which have not always considered the influence and impact of racial and cultural socialization (APA, 2003a). Many clients have come to distrust helpers associated with the establishment or with social service agencies because of a history of unequal treatment. These clients may be slow to form trusting relationships with counselors, and mental health professionals may have difficulty identifying with these clients if they ignore the history behind this distrust. Helpers from all cultural groups need to honestly examine their own assumptions, expectations, and attitudes about the helping process. We are all culture-bound to some extent, and it takes a concerted effort to monitor our positive and negative biases so that they do not impede the formation of helping relationships.

Minority clients are underrepresented in mental health services, and many stop coming for help after a session or two. Sue and Sue (2003) suggest that a basic reason for this underutilization of services and early termination is the biased nature of the services themselves. From an ethical perspective, Sue and Sue maintain that mental health professionals have a moral and professional responsibility (1) to become aware of and deal with the biases, stereotypes, and assumptions that undergird their practice; (2) to become aware of the culturally different client's values and worldview; and (3) to develop appropriate intervention strategies that take into account the social, cultural, historical, and environmental influences of culturally different clients.

The medical model of clinical counseling is seldom a good fit for people in the lower socioeconomic class. The child care and transportation challenges alone make it not worth the effort for most people. Clinics in schools on Saturday and in the evening with child care available are part of the answer, and home visits would also benefit this population. The economically disadvantaged cannot take time off from work for medical appointments without loss of pay, yet we continue to provide a middle-class model that many clients cannot use (John Tweton, personal communication, April 2, 2001).

Sometimes cultural traditions contribute to the underutilization of traditional psychotherapeutic services by minority clients. It may not be the style of an Asian American person to seek professional help quickly when faced with a problem. For example, consider Binh's experience of being torn between marrying a person selected by his parents and marrying a woman of his choice. He might first look for a solution within himself through contemplation. If he were unable to resolve his dilemma, he might seek assistance from a family member or a clergy person. Then he might look to some of his friends for advice and support in making the best decision. If none of these approaches resulted in a satisfactory resolution of his problem, Binh might then turn to a mental health professional. The fact that he did not seek counseling services sooner has little to do with resistance or with insensitivity on the part of counselors; Binh was following a route that was congruent with his cultural background.

Some argue that ethnic minority clients who use counseling resources may lose their cultural values in the process. Some culturally encapsulated helpers mistakenly assume that a lack of assertiveness is a sign of dysfunctional behavior that should be changed. Merely labeling a behavior "dysfunctional" reflects a particular value orientation. Practitioners need to consider whether passivity is a problem from the client's culturally learned perspective and whether assertiveness is a useful behavior that the client hopes to acquire.

Ethics Codes From a Diversity Perspective

Most ethics codes mention the practitioner's responsibility to recognize the special needs of diverse client populations. For example, the Feminist Therapy Institute's (2000) code of ethics has four separate guidelines pertaining to cultural diversities and oppressions:

A. A feminist therapist increases her accessibility to and for a wide range of clients from her own and other identified groups through flexible delivery of services. When appropriate, the feminist therapist assists clients in accessing other services and intervenes when a client's rights are violated.

B. A feminist therapist is aware of the meaning and impact of her own ethnic and cultural background, gender, class, age, and sexual orientation, and actively attempts to become knowledgeable about alternatives from sources other than her clients. She is actively engaged in broadening her knowledge of ethnic and cultural experiences, non-dominant and dominant.

C. Recognizing that the dominant culture determines the norm, the therapist's goal is to uncover and respect cultural and experiential differences, including those based on long term or recent immigration and/or refugee status.

D. A feminist therapist evaluates her ongoing interactions with her clientele for any evidence of her biases or discriminatory attitudes and practices. She also monitors her other interactions, including service delivery, teaching, writing, and all professional activities. The feminist therapist accepts responsibility for taking action to confront and change any interfering, oppressing, or devaluing biases she has.

The Canadian Counselling Association's (1999) code of ethics calls for members to respect diversity. The CCA's nondiscrimination standard states:

> Counsellors actively work to understand the diverse cultural background of the clients with whom they work, and do not condone or engage in discrimination based on age, colour, culture, ethnicity, disability, gender, religion, sexual orientation, marital, or socioeconomic status. (B.9.)

The *Ethical Standards for School Counselors* (ASCA, 2004) addresses the role of diversity in school counseling in Section E.2. School counselors are expected to become aware of their own attitudes, cultural values, and biases that can affect their cultural competence. They are also expected to possess knowledge and understanding about how oppression, racism, discrimination, and stereotyping affect them personally and professionally.

In the NASW *Code of Ethics* (1999), cultural competence and recognition of social diversity are clearly linked to ethical practice. Here are two relevant guidelines:

> Social workers should have a knowledge base of their clients' cultures and be able to demonstrate competence in the provision of services that are sensitive to clients' cultures and to differences among people and cultural groups. (1.05.b.)
>
> Social workers should obtain education about and seek to understand the nature of social diversity and oppression with respect to race, ethnicity, national origin, color, sex, sexual orientation, age, marital status, political belief, religion and mental or physical disability. (1.05.c.)

The *Code of Ethics* of the Canadian Association of Social Workers (1994) has this nondiscrimination standard:

> A social worker in the practice of social work shall not discriminate against any person on the basis of race, ethnic background, language, religion, marital status, sex, sexual orientation, age, abilities, socio-economic status, political affiliation or national ancestry. (1.2.)

The APA ethics code (2002) indicates that part of competence implies understanding diversity:

> Where scientific or professional knowledge in the discipline of psychology establishes that an understanding of factors associated with age, gender, gender identity, race, ethnicity, culture, national origin, religion, sexual orientation, disability, language, or socioeconomic status is essential for effective implementation of their services or research, psychologists have or obtain the training, experience, consultation, or supervision necessary to ensure the competence of their services, or they make appropriate referrals. (2.01.b.)

The revised ACA ethics code (2005) infuses issues of multiculturalism and diversity throughout the document. Examples of a few areas where cultural considerations are specifically addressed include sections of the code dealing with the counseling relationship, informed consent, bartering, accepting gifts, confidentiality and privacy, professional responsibility, assessment and diagnosis, supervision, and education and training programs.

We suggest that you take a few moments to review the ethics codes of one or more professional organizations to determine for yourself the degree to which such codes take cultural, ethnic, and racial dimensions into account. From a multicultural perspective, what are the strengths and shortcomings of these codes? What revisions and additions can you think of as a basis for mental health practitioners to function ethically in today's diverse world?

Cultural Values and Assumptions in Therapy

Many therapeutic practices are biased against racial and ethnic minorities and women (Sue, Ivey, & Pedersen, 1996) and often reflect racism, sexism, and other forms of prejudice. Sue and Sue (2003) contend that this ethnocentric bias has been destructive to the natural help-giving networks of minority communities. They suggest that helpers need to expand their perception of mental health practices to include support systems such as family, friends, community, self-help programs, and occupational networks.

Clinicians may misunderstand clients of a different sex, race, age, social class, or sexual orientation. If practitioners fail to integrate these diversity factors into their practice, they are infringing on the client's cultural autonomy and basic human rights, which will reduce the chance of establishing an effective therapeutic relationship. In our opinion, ethical practice requires that practitioners address these diversity factors as they become relevant in the therapy process.

The diversity-sensitive counseling movement focuses attention on the problems of discrimination, oppression, and racism. The ideas put forward by these practitioners have, in recent years, profoundly changed how counselors conceptualize the helping relationship. But this movement is not without its critics. Weinrach and Thomas (1998) believe the diversity-sensitive counseling movement lacks moderation and attempts to superimpose its agenda on counseling practice. In their view, experts in diversity-sensitive counseling (see for example, Atkinson, 2004; Sue & Sue, 2003) have tended to emphasize problems rather than demonstrate how diversity-sensitive practitioners might actually conduct therapy sessions with various client populations. Live demonstrations at conventions or videotaped counseling interviews with a variety of diverse populations across the life span with a range of presenting concerns are two suggestions they put forward: "Without videotaped demonstrations, provided by diversity-sensitive counseling experts, it is unreasonable to expect professional counselors to provide effective diversity-sensitive counseling" (p. 119). Although Weinrach and Thomas (1998) are critical of what they consider to be the rhetoric of the diversity-sensitive counseling movement, which at times tends to be extreme and doctrinaire, they do admit that this movement deserves praise because "it has contributed to the profession's awareness of the broad variety of factors that may influence a client's thoughts, feelings, behaviors, and spirituality" (p. 121). Educational videotapes are now available by some key multicultural experts who have been challenged to demonstrate what they teach. For example, Allen Ivey and Mary Bradford Ivey's Microtraining Associates produces such videotapes.

✓ **The Case of Le.** Stacy is a counselor at a high school. A Vietnamese student, Le, is assigned to her because of academic difficulties. Stacy observes that Le is slow and deliberate in his conversational style, and she immediately assigns him to a remedial speech class. In the course of their conversations, Le discloses that his father is directing him toward applying to college and majoring in a pre-med program. Le is not at all sure that he even wants to attend college. Stacy gives Le a homework assignment, asking him to tell his father that he no longer wants to pursue college plans and is going to follow a direction that appeals to him.

- Was the fact that Le spoke slowly and deliberately an indication that he needed a remedial class in speech?
- Did the therapist's actions reveal respect for the roles of family members, hierarchies, values, and beliefs in the client's culture?
- Was the therapist culturally sensitive when asking Le to directly confront his father? What alternatives might exist?
- Was Stacy too quick in making her assessments, considering that Le was sent to the school counselor by a teacher? Would it have made a difference if he had come voluntarily for guidance?
- How would you have handled this situation?

✓ **The Case of Cynthia.** Ling has recently set up a private practice in a culturally mixed, upscale neighborhood. Cynthia comes to Ling for counseling. She is depressed, feels that life has little meaning, and feels enslaved by the needs of her husband and small children. When Ling asks about any recent events that could be contributing to her depression, she tells him that she has discussed with her husband her desire to return to school and pursue a career of her choosing. She told her husband that she felt stifled and needed to pursue her own interests. Her husband's response was to threaten a divorce if she followed through with her plans. Cynthia then consulted with her pastor, who pointed out her obligations to her family. Ling is aware of his own cultural biases, which include a strong commitment to family and to the role of the man as the head of the household. Although he shows empathy for Cynthia's struggle, he directs her toward considering postponing her own aspirations until her children have grown up. She surrenders to his direction because she feels guilty about asserting her own needs, and she is also fearful of being left alone. Ling then works with her to find other ways to add meaning to her life that would not have such a radical impact on the family.

- Do you see any evidence of bias or unethical behavior in Ling's approach with his client?
- List some of the potential gender and cultural issues in this case. How might you have addressed each of them?

- Ling did not seem to explore the lack of meaning in Cynthia's life. Does that raise an ethical issue? If so, why?
- Could Ling have acted any differently and still have been true to himself and his own cultural values?
- If Ling's client had shared his family values, would his approach have been appropriate for Cynthia?
- Because Ling had different family values from Cynthia's, should he have referred her to another professional?
- Given what you know about your values, how might you have worked with Cynthia if she had been your client?

Western Versus Eastern Values

Eastern and Western are not just geographic terms but also represent philosophical, social, political, and cultural orientations. Within these broad divisions even greater differences can be found, but it seems clear that many Eastern values differ from those common to Western thinkers. Writers in the field of multicultural counseling allege that most contemporary theories of therapy and therapeutic practices are grounded in Western assumptions, yet most of the world differs from mainstream U.S. culture (Ivey, D'Andrea, Ivey, & Simik-Morgan, 2002; Pedersen, 2003; Sue et al., 1996). These writers are critical of the strong individualistic bias of contemporary theories and the lack of emphasis on broader social contexts, such as families, groups, and communities. Professional psychological help is not a typical option for many minority groups. In fact, in most non-Western cultures informal groups of friends and relatives provide the supportive network.

Practitioners who draw from any of the contemporary therapeutic models would do well to reflect on the underlying values of their theoretical orientation. Many of the therapy systems reflect core value orientations of mainstream U.S. culture, which has its roots in the Anglo-Saxon culture of the English who colonized America. Hogan-Garcia (2003) summarizes the underlying values of this culture as being characterized by an emphasis on the patriarchal nuclear family; "getting things done" and keeping busy; measurable and visible accomplishments; individual choice, responsibility, and achievement; self-reliance and self-motivation; the pragmatic notion of "If an idea works, use it"; change and novel ideas; and equality, informality, and fair play. The degree to which these value orientations fit clients from Eastern cultures needs to be carefully considered by practitioners.

In addition to the areas typically covered in the multicultural literature, there is a growing conviction that religion and spirituality needs to be included in counseling practice. Evans (2003) makes such a case: "Nowhere is it more important than in multicultural counseling to be able to include spirituality in counseling, and nowhere is it more important to be open and accepting of diversity" (p. 161). She adds: "It is difficult for counselors to be multiculturally competent if they resist addressing the client's spiritual issues" (p. 170).

Challenging Mental Health Professionals' Stereotypical Beliefs

Helpers may think they are not biased, yet it is possible that many hold stereotypical beliefs that could well affect their practice. Some examples include these statements: "Failure to change stems from a lack of motivation." "People have choices, and it is up to them to change their lives." Many people do not have a wide range of choices due to environmental factors beyond their control. To assume that all these people lack is motivation is simplistic and judgmental and does not encourage exploration of their struggles. Another often held assumption is that "talk therapy" works best. This ignores the fact that many cultures have alternative practices that people rely on for regaining psychological health. Therapists can discover their biases and stereotypes by reflecting on their cultural and race-based thoughts and feelings, both positive and negative (Roysircar, 2004).

Practitioners who counsel ethnic and racial minority clients without an awareness of their own stereotypical beliefs can easily cause harm to their clients. Ethical practice in a multicultural context requires that mental health practitioners be aware of and sensitive to the unique cultural realities of their clients. Furthermore, ethical practice implies that counselors actively deal with attitudinal barriers. The *Code of Professional Ethics for Rehabilitation Counselors* (CRCC, 2001) identifies advocacy as a part of ethical practice:

> Rehabilitation counselors will strive to eliminate attitudinal barriers, including stereotyping and discrimination toward individuals with disabilities and to increase their own awareness and sensitivity to such individuals. (C.1.a.)

Reflect on these issues as you consider the following case example.

✓ **The Case of Claudine.** Claudine takes over as director of a clinic that has a large percentage of Asian immigrants as clients. At a staff meeting she sums up her philosophy of counseling in this fashion: "People come to counseling to begin change or because they are already in the process of change. Our purpose is to challenge them to continue their change. This holds true whether the client is Euro-American, Asian, or some other minority. If clients are slow to speak, our job is to challenge them to speak, because the expectation in American culture is that people deal with problems through talking. Silence may be appropriate in Asian culture, but it does not work in this non-Asian culture. The sooner clients learn this, the better off they are."

- To what extent do you agree or disagree with Claudine's assumptions, and why?
- Do you see any value in the point she is trying to make?

Commentary. Pedersen (2000) would say that Claudine is a culturally encapsulated counselor because she is defining everyone's reality according to her own cultural assumptions and values. She is minimizing cultural differences by imposing her own standards as criteria for judging the behavior of others. In defense of Claudine, there is some truth in her premise regarding a counselor's role in challenging a client to change. However, the key point is that therapists need to first understand the worldview of their clients and then invite them to decide on change that is congruent with their own values and aspirations.

Examining Some Common Assumptions

Unexamined assumptions can be harmful to clients, especially assumptions based on cultural biases. What is good for one is not good for all. Let's look at a few of these commonly held beliefs about the therapeutic environment.

Assumptions About Self-Disclosure. Therapists often assume that clients will be ready to talk about their intimate personal issues, or that self-disclosure is essential for the therapeutic process to work. Patterson (1985b, 1996) contends that there is no basis for empathic understanding by the therapist unless clients are willing to verbalize and communicate their thoughts, feelings, attitudes, and perceptions. He asserts that the inability to self-disclose is something to be overcome, not accepted.

Sue and Sue (2003) point out that most forms of contemporary therapy value one's ability to self-disclose by sharing intimate personal material. The assumption is that self-disclosure is a characteristic of a healthy personality. The converse is that individuals who are reluctant to self-disclose in therapy possess negative traits such as being guarded and mistrustful. However, it is unacceptable in some cultures to reveal personal problems because it not only reflects on the person individually but also on the whole family. There are strong pressures on Asian American clients not to reveal personal concerns to strangers or outsiders. Similar pressures have been reported for Hispanic, American Indian, African American, and many European clients. Therapists need to realize that cultural forces may be operating when clients are slow to disclose personal details. How much value does "talk" therapy hold for certain clients? What are the challenges a counselor faces in working with culturally different groups who emphasize friendship as a precondition to self-disclosure? Indeed, for many clients it seems strange, and even absurd, for them to talk about themselves personally to a professional therapist whom they do not know.

Americans generally value getting to the "bottom line." In many cultures a dance, circumlocutions, and certain rituals may precede intimate disclosures. The tendency of an insensitive professional might be to view these behaviors as either resistance or a waste of time. Helpers need to understand that there are many different ways for clients to make themselves known besides immediately talking about private aspects of their lives. It is easy to blame the client when therapy does not go well, but the challenge is for therapists to adapt. If they cannot connect to clients using the techniques in which they were trained, the challenge for therapists is to learn other ways of connecting with clients or to admit to their inability to function as helpers.

✓ **The Case of Lily.** Lily, a licensed counselor, has come to work in a family-life center that deals with many immigrant families. She often becomes impatient with the pace of her clients' disclosures. Lily decides to teach her clients by modeling for them. With one of her reticent couples she says: "My husband and I have many fights and disagreements. We express our feelings openly and clear the air. In fact, several years ago my husband had an affair, which put our relationship into turmoil. I believe it was my ability to vent my anger and express my hurt that allowed me to work through this terrible event."

- How do you evaluate Lily's self-disclosure? Would such a disclosure be helpful to you if you were her client?
- Might you be inclined to make a similar type of disclosure to your clients? Why or why not?
- In your opinion, is such a disclosure ever appropriate? Why or why not?

Assumptions About Assertiveness. Many clinicians assume that being assertive is better than being nonassertive. They assume that clients are better off if they can behave in assertive ways, such as telling people directly what they think and what they want. In fact, much of therapy consists of teaching clients the skills to take an active stance toward life. Sue and Sue (1985) report a widespread view that Asian Americans are nonassertive and passive. They contend, however, that this assumption has not been supported by research. These authors emphasize that certain traditional counseling practices may act as barriers to effective multicultural helping, and they call for the use of intervention strategies that are congruent with the value orientation of Asian American clients.

Assumptions About Self-Actualization and Trusting Relationships. Another assumption made by mental health professionals is that it is important for the individual to become a fully functioning person. A counselor may focus on what is good for the individual without regard for the impact of the individual's change on the significant people in that person's life or the impact of those significant people on the client. A creative synthesis between self-actualization and responsibility to the group may be a more realistic goal for some clients.

Another assumption pertains to the development of a personal relationship. Mainstream Americans tend to form quick, though not necessarily deep, relationships and perhaps more readily talk about their personal lives than do those in other cultures. This characteristic is reflected in most therapeutic approaches. Although clinicians expect some resistance, they assume that clients will eventually be willing to explore personal issues. In many cultures this kind of a relationship takes a long time to develop. Many Asian Americans, Hispanics, and Native Americans have been brought up not to speak until spoken to, especially when they are with the elderly or with authority figures. A counselor may interpret the client's hesitancy to speak as resistance when it is only a sign of respect.

Assumptions About Nonverbal Behavior. Many cultural expressions are subject to misinterpretation, including appropriate personal space, eye contact, handshaking, dress, formality of greeting, perspective on time, and so forth. Mainstream Americans frequently feel uncomfortable with periods of silence and tend to talk to ease their tension. In some cultures silence may be a sign of respect and politeness rather than a lack of a desire to continue to speak. Silence may be a reflection of fear or confusion, or it may be a cautious expression and reluctance to do what the counselor is expecting of the client. Itai and McRae (1994) suggest that counselors do well to pay attention to the subtle changes in nonverbal communication by the client so that they are able to understand the true meaning of silence and adopt appropriate counseling interventions to deal with the silence. Counselors might also pay attention to their own inner state to understand the source of their discomfort and to avoid making their problem the client's problem.

Students in the helping professions are often systematically trained in a range of microskills that include attending, open communication, observation, hearing clients accurately, noting and reflecting feelings, and selecting and structuring, to mention a few (Ivey & Ivey, 2007). Although these behaviors are aimed at creating a positive therapeutic relationship, individuals from certain ethnic groups may have difficulty responding positively or understanding the intent of the counselor's attitudes and behavior. The counselor whose confrontational style involves direct eye contact, physical gestures, and probing personal questions may be seen as offensively intrusive by clients from another culture.

In Euro-American middle-class culture, direct eye contact is usually considered a sign of interest and presence, and a lack thereof can be viewed as being evasive. However, even in this culture an individual often maintains more eye contact while listening and less while talking. Research indicates that some African Americans may reverse this pattern by looking more when talking and looking slightly less when listening. Among some Native American and Hispanic groups, eye contact by the young is a sign of disrespect. Some cultural groups generally avoid eye contact when talking about serious subjects (Ivey & Ivey, 1999, 2007). Certainly, counselors who interpret a client's lack of eye contact as "resistive" or "avoidant" are not understanding or respecting important cultural differences. Clinicians need to acquire sensitivity to cultural differences to reduce the probability of miscommunication, misdiagnosis, and misinterpretation of behavior.

Assumptions About Directness and Respect. Western therapeutic approaches tend to stress directness, yet in some cultures directness is perceived as a sign of rudeness and something to be avoided. The counselor could assume that a lack of directness is evidence of pathology, or at least a lack of assertiveness, rather than a sign of respect. Although getting to the point immediately is a prized value in Western culture, clients from other cultures may prefer to delay dealing with their problems, or deal with them more indirectly. In some cultures being addressed by one's first name (other than by friends and family) may be considered as disrespectful and being too direct. Deference is oftentimes a sign of respect, which can be misinterpreted as a lack of directness or a manifestation of self-deprecation.

A Personal Case History. Some time ago Marianne Corey and Jerry Corey conducted a training workshop with counselors from Mexico. Marianne was accused by a male participant of being too direct and assertive. He had difficulty with Marianne's active leadership style and indicated that it was her place to defer to Jerry by letting him take the lead. Recognizing and respecting our cultural differences, we were able to arrive at a mutual understanding of different values.

Jerry had difficulty with the participants showing up after the scheduled time and had to accept the fact that we could not follow a rigid time schedule. (For a rigid personality, dealing with this is quite a challenge!) Typically we have thought that if people were late or missed a session, group cohesion would be difficult to maintain. Because the issue was openly discussed in this situation, however, the problem did not arise. We quickly learned that we had to adapt ourselves to the participants' view of time and they to us as well. To insist on interpreting such behavior as resistance would have been to ignore the cultural context.

Addressing Sexual Orientation

Most of the previous discussion on multiculturalism has focused on issues of race and ethnicity. However, the concept of human diversity encompasses much more than racial and ethnic factors; it encompasses all forms of oppression, discrimination, and prejudice, including those directed toward age, gender, religious affiliation, and sexual orientation. In 1973 the American Psychiatric Association stopped labeling **homosexuality,** a sexual orientation in which people seek emotional and sexual relationships with same-gendered individuals, as a form of mental illness. In 1975 the American Psychological Association endorsed this move by recommending that psychologists actively work to remove the stigma that had been attached to homosexuality. Along with these changes came the assumption that therapeutic practices would be modified to reflect this viewpoint: The mental health system had finally begun to treat the *problems* of gay and lesbian people rather than treating *them* as the problem.

The ethics codes of the ACA (2005), the APA (2002), the AAMFT (2001), the CCA (1999), and the NASW (1999) clearly state that **discrimination,** or behaving differently and usually unfairly toward a specific group of people, is unethical and unacceptable. As an example of unfair discrimination, consider APA's (2002) standard:

> In their work-related activities, psychologists do not engage in unfair discrimination based on age, gender, gender identity, race, ethnicity, culture, national origin, religion, sexual orientation, disability, socioeconomic status, or any basis proscribed by law. (3.01)

Lasser and Gottlieb (2004) identify sexual orientation as one of the most chronic and vexing moral debates plaguing our culture. According to Lasser and Gottlieb, many in our society believe that homosexual or bisexual behavior is morally wrong. Many **lesbian, gay,** and **bisexual** (LGB) individuals have internalized such views, and some are significantly troubled regarding their sexual orientation. They add that therapists are faced with various clinical and ethical issues in working with LGB clients. One of these ethical issues involves therapists confronting their own values regarding homosexual or bisexual desire and behavior.

Working with lesbian, gay, and bisexual individuals presents a challenge to counselors who hold strong personal values. Mental health professionals who have negative reactions to homosexuality are likely to impose their own values and attitudes, or at least to convey strong disapproval. Schreier, Davis, and Rodolfa (2005) remind us that no one is exempt from the influence of societal negative stereotyping, prejudice, and even hatefulness toward LGB people. Furthermore, many gay and lesbian people internalize these negative societal messages and experience psychological pain and conflict because of this. We highlight this topic because it illustrates not only the ethical problems involved in imposing values but also the problems involved in effectively addressing the mental health concerns of gay, lesbian, and bisexual clients.

Negative personal reactions, limited empathy, and lack of understanding are common characteristics in therapists who work with LGB clients (Schreier et al., 2005). Before clinical practitioners can change their therapeutic strategies, they must change their assumptions and attitudes toward the sexual orientation of others. Unless helpers become conscious of their own assumptions and possible countertransference, they may project their misconceptions and their fears onto their clients. Therapists are challenged to confront their personal prejudices, myths, fears, and stereotypes regarding sexual orientation. This is particularly important when a client discloses his or her sexual orientation well into an established therapeutic relationship. In such situations prejudicial, judgmental attitudes and behaviors on the part of the therapist will do serious damage to the client.

The American Psychological Association's Division 44 (APA, 2000) has developed a set of guidelines for psychotherapy with lesbian, gay, and bisexual clients that go further than the APA (2002) ethics code prohibiting unfair discrimination based on sexual orientation. The Division 44 guidelines affirm that a psychologist's role is to acknowledge how societal stigma affects clients. The guidelines emphasize assisting clients in overcoming the psychological distress associated with the oppression LGB individuals often experience in this society (Schreier et al., 2005). Any therapist who may work with lesbian, gay, or bisexual people has a responsibility to understand the special concerns of these individuals and is ethically obligated to develop the knowledge and skills to competently deliver services to them.

We summarize the 16 guidelines of APA's Division 44 (Committee on Lesbian, Gay, and Bisexual Concerns Joint Task Force on Guidelines for Psychotherapy with Lesbian, Gay, and Bisexual Clients), which address four main areas of understanding: (1) attitudes toward LGB people and sexual orientation issues, (2) relationships and family concerns, (3) the complex diversity within the LGB community, and (4) the training and education needed to work effectively with this population. As you read these guidelines, think of ways you might implement them in your therapeutic practice.

1. Psychologists understand that homosexuality and bisexuality are not indicative of mental illness.
2. Psychologists are encouraged to recognize how their attitudes and knowledge about lesbian, gay, and bisexual issues may be relevant to assessment and treatment and seek consultation or make appropriate referrals when indicated.
3. Psychologists strive to understand the ways in which social stigmatization poses risks to the mental health and well-being of lesbian, gay, and bisexual clients.
4. Psychologists strive to understand how inaccurate or prejudicial views of homosexuality or bisexuality may affect the client's presentation in treatment and the therapeutic process.
5. Psychologists strive to be knowledgeable about and respect the importance of lesbian, gay, and bisexual relationships.
6. Psychologists strive to understand the particular circumstances and challenges faced by lesbian, gay, and bisexual parents.
7. Psychologists recognize that the families of lesbian, gay, and bisexual people may include people who are not legally or biologically related.
8. Psychologists strive to understand how a person's homosexual or bisexual orientation may have an impact on his or her family of origin and the relationship to that family of origin.
9. Psychologists are encouraged to recognize the particular life issues or challenges that are related to multiple and often conflicting cultural norms, values, and beliefs that lesbian, gay, and bisexual members of racial and ethnic minorities face.
10. Psychologists are encouraged to recognize the particular challenges that bisexual individuals experience.
11. Psychologists strive to understand the special problems and risks that exist for lesbian, gay, and bisexual youth.
12. Psychologists consider generational differences within lesbian, gay, and bisexual populations and the particular challenges that lesbian, gay, and bisexual older adults may experience.
13. Psychologists are encouraged to recognize the particular challenges that lesbian, gay, and bisexual individuals experience with physical, sensory, and cognitive-emotional disabilities.
14. Psychologists support the provision of professional education and training on lesbian, gay, and bisexual issues.
15. Psychologists are encouraged to increase their knowledge and understanding of homosexuality and bisexuality through continuing education, training, supervision, and consultation.
16. Psychologists make reasonable efforts to familiarize themselves with relevant mental health, educational, and community resources for lesbian, gay, and bisexual people.

The LGB guidelines allow practitioners to personally and professionally define the notion of "gay affirmative therapy" by examining their assumptions and attitudes pertaining to sexual orientation (Schreier et al., 2005). These guidelines have relevance to all mental health professionals, not just to psychologists. Which guidelines might most help you in challenging your beliefs and attitudes regarding sexual orientation? Are there any specific attitudes, beliefs, assumptions, and values you hold that might interfere with your ability to effectively counsel lesbian, gay, and bisexual clients? If you personally believe that homosexual relationships are morally wrong, would you be able to work effectively in this area? What would you do if you discovered that your client was in a gay or lesbian relationship after seeing him or her for some length of time? For an excellent treatment on counseling gay, lesbian, bisexual, and transgendered clients or couples, we recommend *Counseling Gay Men and Lesbians: A Practice Primer* (Barret & Logan, 2002).

Value Issues of Gay and Lesbian Clients

Like any other minority group, lesbians, gay men, and bisexuals are subjected to discrimination, prejudice, and oppression when they seek employment or a place of residence. But lesbian, gay, and bisexual clients also have special counseling needs. For instance, the U.S. Department of Defense does not permit openly homosexual individuals to serve in the military, however they may serve so long as they do not disclose their sexual orientation. Counseling an individual in this workplace environment may raise many ethical issues.

Lesbians and gay men often bring to counseling the struggle between concealing their identity and "coming out." Dealing with family members is of special importance to gay couples. They may want to be honest with their parents, yet they may fear hurting them or receiving negative reactions from them. With the reality of the AIDS crisis, gay men often face the loss of friends. Not only do gay men need to deal with death and loss but they may also want to explore their fears of becoming infected. Clinicians who work with gay men need to be able to talk with their clients about safe-sex practices. In short, therapists need to listen carefully to their clients and be willing to explore whatever concerns they bring to the counseling relationship.

✓ **The Case of Myrna and Rose.** Myrna and Rose are seeking relationship counseling, saying that they are having communication problems. They have a number of conflicts that they want to work out. They clearly state that they are comfortable with their sexual orientation, but they need help in learning how to communicate more effectively.

Counselor A. This counselor agrees to see the two women and work with them much as she would with a heterosexual couple. The counselor adds that if at any time the uniqueness of their relationship causes difficulties, it would be up to them to bring this up as an issue. She lets them know that if they are comfortable with their sexual orientation she has no need to explore it.

- What are your reactions to this counselor's approach?

Counselor B. This counselor agrees to see the couple. During the initial session he realizes that he has strong negative reactions toward them. These reactions are so much in the foreground that they interfere with his ability to effectively work with the couple's presenting problem. He tells the two women about his difficulties and suggests a referral. He lets them know that he had hoped he could be objective enough to work with them but that this is not the case.

- Was this counselor's behavior ethical? Is he violating any of the ethics codes in refusing to work with this couple because of their sexual orientation?
- Given his negative reactions, should he have continued seeing the couple, or would this in itself have been unethical?
- Would it be more damaging to the clients to refer them or to continue to see them?
- Is it ethical for the counselor to charge the couple for this session? Explain your point of view.

Counselor C. This counselor agrees to see Myrna and Rose, and during the first session he suggests that they ought to examine their homosexuality. He has concerns about excluding any issues from exploration in determining what the problem really is between them.

- How do you react to the stance of this counselor? Explain.
- Would it have made a difference if, instead of insisting on exploring their sexual orientation, the counselor had said that he had concerns about excluding any issue from possible exploration in therapy?
- Would it make a difference if he routinely made the same stipulation with hetereosexual couples?

In reviewing the approaches of these three counselors, which approach would be closest to yours? To clarify your thinking on the issue of counseling gay and lesbian clients, reflect on these questions:

- Therapists often find that the presenting problem clients bring to a session is not their major problem. Is the counselor justified in bringing up homosexuality as a therapeutic issue?
- Do you see any ethical issue in a heterosexually oriented therapist working with homosexual couples?
- What attitudes are necessary for therapists to be instrumental in helping clients with their sexual orientation?
- Can a counselor who is not comfortable with his or her own sexual identity possibly be effective in assisting clients who are struggling with their sexual identity?

✓ **The Case of Tanya and Liz.** Maxine, a lesbian therapist, is seeing a lesbian couple, Liz and Tanya. It is customary for Maxine to see the partners individually on occasion. During Tanya's first individual session, she confesses to having affairs with several men. Tanya tells Maxine that she sees herself as bisexual, a fact she has not disclosed to Liz. One of the issues introduced by Liz and Tanya was a problem with intimacy. During the individual session, Maxine suggests that this is one more way that Tanya avoids intimacy and begins to explore this issue with her. At the end of the session, Tanya agrees with the therapist's interpretation and agrees to come back for further couples work with Liz.

- If you were the therapist, how would you have handled Tanya's disclosure?
- Do you see anything inappropriate or unethical in Maxine's approach? Why or why not?
- Is this an example of the imposition of the therapist's values? Why or why not?
- How will Maxine deal with the couple now that she shares a secret with Tanya?
- Was Maxine remiss in not exploring these questions: Does Tanya have an intimacy issue with her partner? Is Tanya bisexual? Is Tanya ambivalent about her sexual orientation?

Educating Counselors About Concerns of Gay, Lesbian, and Bisexual Clients

Crawford and his colleagues (1999) remind practitioners that they should not provide care outside of their areas of expertise. Practitioners need to have knowledge of the core issues pertaining to same-gender couples, including relationship and parenting concerns. These researchers conclude that before therapists provide mental health services to gay and lesbian people and their children they should complete formal, systematic training on sexual diversity.

Crawford and colleagues (1999) conducted a study to assess psychologists' attitudes toward gay and lesbian parenting. The results of their study suggest that psychologists who participated in the study held affirming attitudes toward gay and lesbian parenting. In addition, these psychologists appeared to be sensitive to the stigmatization and bias gay and lesbian families encounter. The participants indicated their concern about the level of social support these families would receive in managing the stressors associated with parenthood. The findings of this study seem to suggest that most of the participants do not endorse negative stereotypes of gay and lesbian people and do not perceive them to be a threat to the welfare of children reared in the homes of same-gender couples.

Biaggio and colleagues (2003) have developed guidelines for LGB educational practices in graduate psychology programs. In their review of the literature, they cite several studies that demonstrate a lack of emphasis on LGB issues in professional psychology programs. Biaggio and colleagues provide these useful recommendations for graduate education about LGB issues:

- Integrate and infuse information about sexual orientation and the needs of LGB persons into the professional program.
- Ensure that both faculty and clinical supervisors are informed about the unique needs of LGB clients.

- Encourage research on LGB topics.
- Recruit faculty with LGB expertise and increase faculty knowledge about LGB concerns.
- Strive to make both student and faculty self-awareness a priority.
- Promote contact with the LGB community.

On this last point, we suggest that faculty invite people from the LGB community to talk in their classrooms. If students are able to participate in a dialogue with LGB individuals, the discussion is likely to move from abstract ideas to dealing with real people and real issues. Kessler and Waehler (2005) address issues pertaining to multiple relationships for therapists who work with LGB clients. They recommend that training programs incorporate multicultural and LGB issues into class discussions on multiple relationships and real situations that often arise in practicum sites.

In a survey of clinical psychologists on treating LGB clients, Murphy, Rawlings, and Howe (2002) found that practitioners frequently seek training after they complete their graduate education. Respondents in this survey rated the most important therapeutic issues with LGB clients and identified training that would improve their work with this population. The topics identified in which continuing education would be helpful included coming out, estrangement from family, support system development, and internalized homophobia. Some ways that respondents reported acquiring information on treating LGB clients included reading articles, seeking supervision, and participating in continuing education workshops.

One way to increase your awareness of ethical and therapeutic considerations in working with LGB clients is to take advantage of continuing education workshops sponsored by national, regional, state, and local professional organizations. By participating in such workshops, you can learn about referral resources as well as about specific interventions and strategies that are appropriate for LGB clients. You may not know the sexual orientation of a client until the therapeutic relationship develops, so even if you do not plan to work with a gay or lesbian population, you need to have a clear idea of your own assumptions, attitudes, and values relative to this issue.

A Court Case Involving a Therapist's Refusal to Counsel Homosexual Clients

In their article, "Legal and Ethical Issues in Counseling Homosexual Clients," Hermann and Herlihy (in press) describe the case of *Bruff v. North Mississippi Health Services, Inc.* (2001). This interesting case illustrates the complexity counselors confront when their value system and religious beliefs conflict with the client's presenting problem. This section is based largely on Hermann and Herlihy's provocative article.

In 1996 Jane Doe initiated a counseling relationship with Bruff, a counselor employed at the North Mississippi Medical Center, an employee assistance program provider. After several sessions, Jane Doe informed Bruff that she was a lesbian and wanted to explore her relationship with her partner. Bruff refused on the basis of her religious beliefs, but offered to counsel her in other areas. The client (Jane Doe) discontinued counseling, and her employer filed a complaint with Bruff's agency. Bruff again repeated her reason for refusing to work with Jane Doe and added that she would be willing to work with clients on any areas that did not conflict with her religious beliefs.

Eventually, Bruff was dismissed by her employer. Bruff appealed to an administrator of the medical center who asked her to clarify the situations in which she could not work with a client. She reiterated that she would "not be willing to counsel anyone on any subject that went against her religion" (cited in Hermann & Herlihy, in press). She was offered a transfer to a Christian counseling center, which she refused on the basis that the director of the center was too liberal. She was given another opportunity for a position in the agency, but lost to a more qualified candidate. Another position in the agency became available, but she did not apply, and eventually she was terminated. Bruff filed suit, and a jury trial in a federal court ruled in her favor. However, on appeal the court reversed the jury's findings and found that there was no violation of Bruff's rights. The court noted that the employer had made several attempts to accommodate Bruff but that Bruff remained inflexible.

Hermann and Herlihy (in press) summarize some of the legal aspects of this case:

- The court held that the employer did make reasonable attempts to accommodate Bruff's religious beliefs.
- Bruff's inflexibility and unwillingness to work with anyone who has conflicting beliefs is not protected by the law.
- A counselor who refuses to work with homosexual clients can cause harm to them. The refusal to work on a homosexual client's relationship issues constitutes illegal discrimination.
- Counselors cannot use their religious beliefs to justify discrimination based on sexual orientation, and employers can terminate counselors who engage in this discrimination.

Hermann and Herlihy believe the *Bruff* case sets an important legal precedent. They assert that the appeal's court decision is consistent with the Supreme Court's precedent interpreting employers' obligations to make reasonable accommodations for employees' religious beliefs. Hermann and Herlihy also note that the *Bruff* case raises an ethical issue that counselors often struggle with: When is it appropriate, and on what grounds, to refer a client? Hermann and Herlihy contend that numerous references in the ACA *Code of Ethics* to working effectively with a diverse population could be used as evidence that the counselor is violating the standard of care in the community. Thus a client would likely prevail in a malpractice suit against the counselor.

We raise the following questions in examining the issues involved in this case:

- How do you deal with (or plan to deal with) issues that conflict with your religious beliefs?

- The court held that Bruff was guilty of illegal discrimination. Should she be charged in court with illegal activity?
- Is it possible to provide clients with services consistent with an ethical standard of care if counselors conceal their religious beliefs that homosexuality is wrong?
- What distinction, if any, do you see between prejudice based on one's own private belief system as opposed to a conviction based on the teaching of one's church?
- If you have sharply different moral beliefs from those of your client, is this equivalent to your not being competent to work effectively with this client? Are referrals justified because of major value conflicts?
- How do you determine that your referral will benefit or harm your client?
- Do counselors have an ethical obligation to reveal their religious beliefs prior to the onset of a professional relationship?
- If you are fully disclosing of your limitations and owning them as your problem, are you behaving ethically and legally?
- Should a client ever be surprised with the fact that you cannot continue working on problems that are problematic for you?
- To what degree does your informed consent document protect you from an ethical or legal violation?
- Does your document in which you disclose your limitations protect clients from harm?
- How would you apply the basic moral principles (addressed in Chapter 1) to making ethical decisions in this case?

We find this case very challenging as it exposes ethical issues that have no easy answers and that require a great deal of discussion. A rigid stance on either side of this issue can create a major problem, precluding the kind of discussion this topic requires. In the words of Rumi, the mystic, "Out beyond ideas of wrong-doing and right-doing, there is a field. I'll meet you there."

The *Bruff* case illustrates both ethical and legal issues related to value imposition and conflict of values between counselor and client (see Chapter 3). In a counseling relationship, it is not the client's place to adjust to the therapist's values, yet this counselor maintained that she could not work with clients whose beliefs went against her religious views. Bruff demonstrates a lack of understanding that counseling is not about her but about the client's needs and values. She would clearly benefit from a continuing education program that focused on how to work within the client's experience rather than from what she considered to be moral behavior.

Although we do not challenge Bruff's right to possess her own personal values, we do challenge the manner in which she dealt with the client involved in this case. At a minimum, Bruff should have informed her potential clients in writing (as part of the informed consent document) about her religious convictions and moral opposition pertaining to homosexuality, thereby providing potential clients with an opportunity to consider whether they wanted to work with a counselor holding these views.

We do not believe that all counselors can work effectively with all clients, but we would expect them to avoid using their personal value system as the criteria for how all clients should think and act. We also question whether it was appropriate for this counselor to have a position in a public counseling agency given her inexperience and ineffectiveness working with diverse client populations. Bruff showed inflexibility both in dealing with her clients and in her response to the agency's attempts to accommodate her values by transferring her to another position.

Matching Client and Counselor

Diversity includes factors such as culture, religion, race, ability, age, gender, sexual orientation, education, and socioeconomic level. Is matching client and counselor on the various aspects of diversity desirable or possible? Does the clinician have to share the experiential world of the client to be effective? These are difficult questions to answer, and the research in this area is inconclusive. Some argue that successful multicultural counseling is highly improbable due to the barriers between groups. Others argue that well-trained practitioners, even though they differ from their clients, are capable of providing effective counseling. Pedersen (1991) recognizes the complex diversity of a pluralistic society but also suggests bridges of shared concern that unite culturally different individuals. The therapist and client are both unique and similar. Patterson (1996) asserts that all counseling is multicultural. From his perspective, all clients belong to multiple groups that influence their perceptions, beliefs, attitudes, and behavior. To be effective, practitioners must understand these multiple influences on behavior. This perspective allows room for clinicians to effectively work with clients who differ from themselves in a number of significant respects.

Lee and Ramsey (2006) observe that one pitfall associated with multiculturalism is that some helping professionals may give up in exasperation, asking: "How can I really be effective with a client whose cultural background is different from mine?" When counselors are overly self-conscious about their ability to work with diverse client populations, they may become too analytical about what they say and do. Counselors who are afraid to face the differences between themselves and their clients, who refuse to accept the reality of these differences, who perceive such differences as problematic, or who are uncomfortable working out these differences are likely to fail.

Foster (1998) points out that the more disparate the respective worlds of the client and the therapist, the more the therapeutic work will need to involve a collaborative effort to find meaning and understanding. When therapists markedly differ from a client's culture, race, or class, it is imperative that they understand how their own subjectivity, or their cultural countertransference, enters into this relationship. Foster describes a clinician's cultural countertransferences as a complex and interacting set of "culturally derived personal life values; academically based theoretical/practical beliefs; emotionally driven biases about ethnic groups; and feelings about their own ethnic self-identity" (p. 256). According to Foster, a cross-cultural therapeutic relationship often involves multiple points of potential dissonance for both client and counselor. Both individuals in the therapeutic dyad have diverse assumptions about the world and whether each will be understood by the other. Therapists need to exercise particular caution in applying their assumptions about the world to a client who is culturally different. If therapists lack understanding and insight into the source of their cultural countertransference, the likely result will be impasses, or perhaps even harm, in the therapeutic work. At times, therapists will not be aware of these countertransference attitudes, nor will they recognize the powerful influence their attitudes have on the course of treatment. Although certain subjective attitudes and biases of therapists may not be overt, they are frequently perceived by the client. Cross-cultural dyads are not necessarily problematic, but they pose challenges that need to be addressed if mutual understanding is to be achieved.

Some therapists wonder whether differences should be addressed, and if they are, should the clinician or the client initiate this? La Roche and Maxie (2003) observe that not all differences between client and therapist have the same impact on the therapeutic relationship. A dissimilarity in race may not hold the same weight as differences in religious beliefs, for example. What is crucial is the client's perception of difference in the therapeutic process. Some writers maintain that most clients will not initiate discussions of cultural differences due to the power differential that exists, which means that the therapist should directly address differences. Other writers take the position that it is more appropriate to wait for the client to bring up cultural differences.

Cultural clashes and misunderstandings had painful consequences for a Hmong family, which are detailed in Anne Fadiman's (1997) book, *The Spirit Catches You and You Fall Down*. Even though the cultural clashes were between the helping professions and the family, the same dynamics can be applied to clinicians who work with people who are culturally different from themselves. This book illustrates how well-intentioned people can cause much harm when they do not know and respect cultural differences.

LaRoche and Maxie (2003) make a point that cultural differences are subjective, complex, and dynamic. Clinicians can make a mistake by assuming there is a standard way to work with clients of a certain cultural background. Instead, practitioners need to explore the meanings that clients ascribe to these cultural differences. LaRoche and Maxie describe working with a third-generation Korean American gay client. Do you work with the sexual orientation issue or how his extended family deals with his gayness? We agree that the process is dynamic and that clinicians must stay with the client and be led by the client into the areas that are most important to him or her.

Pedersen (1999) sheds light on the topic of matching client and therapist. He proposes that counselors be trained to hear the self-talk of culturally different clients. Pedersen writes about the various alternative identities that constitute our self-talk. Each person has a thousand or more alternative roles or identities that are collected over a lifetime from various sources. What are the implications of this notion of multiple cultures within each of us? When you meet a client for the first time, realize that there are more than two people in your office. There are thousands of people in that room, and learning to hear and understand their "voices" will make you a more responsive and effective therapist. The greater the cultural dissimilarity between you and your client, the more both of you will be challenged to accurately hear the other's inner voices. According to Pedersen, this notion of a thousand "people" surrounding each of us is what makes multicultural counseling an exciting and essential perspective. He believes counselors can be trained to hear the inner voices of their culturally different clients. What is important is for counselors to learn how to pay attention to a client's salient cultural identity as it changes within the context of a single interview.

Many of you may see it as a daunting task to pay attention to the single voice of a client, let alone a thousand voices within a client! Pedersen's (1999) point, however, is basic to the therapeutic task: "Competence is measured by your ability to know what your client is thinking but not saying. To the extent that a client and yourself are culturally different, the task of hearing the client's voices will be more difficult but just as important" (p. 100). Pedersen's views on learning to understand the client's and the therapist's internal dialogue as a crucial part of the therapeutic dyad casts a new light on the possibility of matching client and counselor. More important than striving to discover the ideal match is the task of learning to monitor this internal dialogue and use it as a basic component of the therapy process. Pedersen emphasizes that becoming a multiculturally competent counselor entails more than following a list of rules. Gaining competence in this area involves more than a shift in thinking, it demands a shift in attitude. The most important aspects of culture-centered counseling can be learned, but not necessarily taught. We can become our own best teachers if we pay attention to the voices within us and within our clients. "If and when we are competent, it is because those inside voices are guiding us toward competence" (p. 100). In our opinion, the voices on both sides of the counseling dyad come from multiple sources, including parents, grandparents, teachers, subcultures, and significant others. If our approach is rigid and concrete, we hear only the spoken content, which diminishes our effectiveness.

It is our position that clinicians can learn to work with clients who differ from them in gender, race, culture, religion, socioeconomic background, physical ability, age, or sexual orientation. But our stance is tempered by certain reservations and conditions. First, clinicians need to have training in multicultural perspectives, both academic and experiential. Second, as in any other counseling situation, it is important that the client and the practitioner agree to develop a working therapeutic relationship. Third, helpers are advised to be flexible in applying theories and techniques to specific situations. The counselor who has an open stance has a greater likelihood of success than someone who rigidly adheres to a single theoretical system.

Fourth, the mental health professional should be open to being challenged and tested. In multicultural counseling clients are more likely to exhibit caution. Some African Americans may perceive White Americans as potential enemies until proven otherwise. They may use many defenses as survival strategies to protect their true feelings. A Euro-American counselor may be perceived to be a symbol of the establishment. Practitioners who think of themselves as culturally competent and sensitive may find it difficult to withstand this kind of testing. If practitioners become excessively defensive in such situations, they will probably be ineffective with the client. If helpers act defensively, they are creating a potential ethical situation that may hurt the client. Clients may feel that the clinician's values or solutions are being imposed on them. It may seem to minority clients that a professional who is not part of the solution to their problem is really part of the problem.

Fifth, it becomes especially important in multicultural counseling situations for counselors to be aware of their own value systems, of potential stereotyping and any traces of prejudice, and of their cultural countertransference. We agree with Foster's (1998) notion of the **cultural countertransference** of therapists; that is, therapists need to develop self-understanding of how their values, feelings, attitudes, and biases influence their work with culturally different clients. Earlier we described those culture-bound counselors who are unintentional racists. In some ways, such counselors can be more dangerous than those who are more open with their prejudices. These counselors may unintentionally enable and empower racism by making it invisible (Sue, 2005). According to Pedersen (2000), unintentional racists must be challenged either to become intentional racists or to modify their racist attitudes and behaviors. The more "overt racism" characteristic of the South is often more accessible than the evasive avoidance of the "liberal North."

The key to changing unintentional racism lies in examining basic assumptions. Two forms of covert racism that Ridley (2005) identifies are color blindness and color consciousness. The counselor who says, "When I look at you, I see a person, not a Black person" may encounter mistrust from clients who have difficulty believing that. Likewise, a therapist is not likely to earn credibility by saying, "If you were not Black, you wouldn't have the problem you're facing." These examples of color blindness and color consciousness are rather extreme, but there are many more subtle variations on these themes. For a thought-provoking analysis of the role of racism in counseling practice, we refer you to Ridley (2005).

Try to identify your own assumptions as you think about these questions:

- Does a counselor need to share the cultural background of the client to be effective?
- If you were to encounter considerable "testing" from a client who is culturally different from you, how might you react? What are some ways in which you could work therapeutically?
- What experiences have you had with discrimination? How would your own experiences either help or hinder you in working with clients who have been discriminated against?
- What stereotypes are you aware of having?

When counselors identify "unusual behavior" in a client, it is important to determine whether such behavior is unusual within the client's cultural context. Clients may become suspicious if they sense the therapist has already come to a conclusion. Rather than suffering from clinical paranoia, these clients may be reacting to the realities of an environment in which they have suffered oppression and prejudice. In such cases, clients' responses may make complete sense. Practitioners who appreciate the context of such perceptions are less likely to pathologize clients and are able to begin working with clients from their experiential framework.

As you read the following case, consider how you could increase your own sensitivity to individuals from cultural groups different from your own.

✓ **The Case of John.** John comes from a lower-middle-class neighborhood in an eastern city, has struggled to get a college degree, and has finally attained a master's degree in counseling. He is proud of his accomplishments and considers himself to be sensitive to his own background and to those who struggle with similar problems. He has moved to the West Coast and has been hired to work in a high school in a neighborhood with a large minority population.

As a high school counselor, John starts a group for at-risk adolescents. His goals for this group are as follows: (1) to instill pride so that group members will see their present environment as an obstacle to be overcome, not suffered with; (2) to increase self-esteem and to challenge group members to fight the negativism they may encounter in their home and school environments; (3) to teach group members to minimize their differences in terms of the larger community (for example, he points out how some of their idioms and ways of speaking separate them from the majority and reinforce differences and stereotypes); and (4) to teach group members how to overcome obstacles in a nonsupportive environment.

John does not work very closely with teachers, administrators, or other school counselors in the district. He views them as being more interested in politics and red tape and as actually giving very little energy to personal counseling in the school. He has little to do with the families of the adolescents, because he sees them as being too willing to accept handouts and welfare and as not being very interested in becoming self-sufficient and independent. He tells his group members: "What you have at home with your families has obviously not worked for you. What you have in this group is the opportunity to change and to have that change appreciated."

- Does John's background and experiences qualify him as a multicultural counselor? Why or why not?
- What are John's assumptions?
- What was John's internal dialogue?
- If John had become familiar with the environment of this particular group, would he have expressed the same goals?
- If you were John's supervisor, how would you work with him?

Commentary. John is a well-intentioned school counselor who overlooks the particular needs of this minority community. We disagree with his axiom that simply because he could obtain a graduate degree (against difficult odds) anybody could have the same success. John made no attempt to become aware of the unique struggles or values of the high school students he serves. He stereotyped the parents of his group members in a very indirect, but powerful fashion. He imposed newly found personal values in terms of language and upward mobility on the group. He set up potential conflicts between group members and their families by the way he downplayed and labeled their families' value systems. John acted insensitively to the families of his group members. His basic mistake was his assumption that what worked for him would work for them.

Multicultural Training for Mental Health Workers

Although referral is sometimes an appropriate course of action, it should not be viewed as a solution to the problem of inadequately trained helpers. Many agencies have practitioners whose cultural backgrounds are less diverse than the populations they serve. With the increasing number of culturally diverse clients seeking counseling, and with the decreasing number of resources to meet these needs, clinicians may not have the luxury of referral. Therefore, we recommend that all counseling students, regardless of their racial or ethnic background, receive training in multicultural counseling and therapy (MCT).

The standards established by the Council for Accreditation of Counseling and Related Educational Programs (CACREP) require that programs provide curricular and experiential offerings in multicultural and pluralistic trends. CACREP standards call for supervised practicum experiences that include people from the environments in which the trainee is preparing to work. It is expected that trainees will study about ethnic groups, subcultures, the changing roles of women, sexism, urban and rural societies, cultural mores, spiritual issues, and differing life patterns.

Characteristics of the Culturally Skilled Counselor

According to Sue and his colleagues (1998; Sue & Sue, 2003), becoming a **culturally skilled counselor** involves three dimensions. The first dimension deals with the practitioner's attitudes and beliefs about race, culture, ethnicity, gender, and sexual orientation; the need to recognize his or her assumptions; the need to monitor personal biases; development of a positive view toward multiculturalism; and understanding how one's values and biases may get in the way of effective helping. It is essential for all counselors to understand the impact of their cultural experiences on their development of self, their perceptions of others who are different, and their preferred theoretical orientation for interventions (Roysircar, 2004). The second dimension recognizes that a culturally competent practitioner is knowledgeable and understanding of his or her own worldview, possesses specific knowledge of the diverse groups with whom he or she works, understands the worldview of culturally diverse clients, and has a basic understanding of sociopolitical influences. The third dimension deals with skills, intervention techniques, and strategies necessary in serving diverse client groups.

Part of multicultural competence entails recognizing our limitations and is manifested in our willingness to (a) seek consultation, (b) participate in continuing education, and (c) when appropriate, make referrals to a professional who is competent to work with a particular client population. La Roche and Maxie (2003) state that acquiring cultural competence is an active and lifelong learning process, rather than a fixed state that is arrived at. They add that this process may include formal training, critical self-evaluation, and questioning of what is occurring in cross-cultural therapeutic partnerships. Roysircar (2004) concludes that counselors can engage in ongoing cultural self-awareness assessment through introspection, reading, and interpersonal learning. Stuart (2004) believes that "culturally competent psychological services require self-reflection, a critically evaluative use of the literature, thoughtful accumulation of personal practice wisdom, and above all, a great sensitivity to the uniqueness of each client" (p. 8).

A major contribution to the counseling profession has been the development of **multicultural competencies,** a set of knowledge and skills that are essential to the culturally skilled practitioner. Initially formulated by Sue and colleagues (1982), they were later revised and expanded by Sue, Arredondo, and McDavis (1992). Arredondo and her colleagues (1996) updated and operationalized these competencies, and Sue and his colleagues (1998) extended multicultural counseling competencies to individual and organizational development. The multicultural competencies have been endorsed by the Association for Multicultural Counseling and Development (AMCD), by the Association for Counselor Education and Supervision (ACES), and recently by the American Psychological Association (APA, 2003a). For an updated and expanded version of these competencies, see *Multicultural Counseling Competencies 2003: Association for Multicultural Counseling and Development* (Roysircar et al., 2003). Refer also to the APA's (2003a) "Guidelines on Multicultural Education, Training, Research, Practice, and Organizational Change for Psychologists." The essential attributes of culturally competent counselors, compiled from the sources just cited, are listed in the box titled Multicultural Counseling Competencies.

✓ **The Case of Talib.** Talib, an immigrant from the Middle East, is a graduate student in a counseling program. During many class discussions, his views on gender roles become clear, yet he expresses his beliefs in a respectful and nondogmatic fashion. Talib's attitudes and beliefs about gender roles are that the man should be the provider and head of the home and that the woman is in charge of nurturance, which is a full-time job. Although not directly critical of his female classmates, Talib voices a concern that these students may be neglecting their family obligations by pursuing a graduate education. Talib bases his views not only on his cultural background but also by citing experts in this country who support his position that the absence of women in the home has been a major contributor to the breakdown of the family. There are many lively discussions between

Multicultural Counseling Competencies

I. Counselor Awareness of Own Cultural Values and Biases

A. With respect to *attitudes and beliefs,* culturally competent counselors:
- believe that cultural self-awareness and sensitivity to one's own cultural heritage is essential.
- are aware of how their own cultural background and experiences have influenced attitudes, values, and biases about psychological processes.
- are able to recognize the limits of their multicultural competencies and expertise.
- recognize their sources of discomfort with differences that exist between themselves and clients in terms of race, ethnicity, and culture.

B. With respect to *knowledge,* culturally competent counselors:
- have specific knowledge about their own racial and cultural heritage and how it personally and professionally affects their definitions of and biases about normality/abnormality and the process of counseling.
- possess knowledge and understanding about how oppression, racism, discrimination, and stereotyping affect them personally and in their work. This allows individuals to acknowledge their own racist attitudes, beliefs, and feelings.
- possess knowledge about their social impact on others. They are knowledgeable about communication style differences, how their style may clash or foster the counseling process with persons of color or others different from themselves, and how to anticipate the impact it may have on others.

C. With respect to *skills,* culturally competent counselors:
- seek out educational, consultative, and training experiences to improve their understanding and effectiveness in working with culturally different populations.
- are constantly seeking to understand themselves as racial and cultural beings and are actively seeking a nonracist identity.

II. Understanding the Client's Worldview

A. With respect to *attitudes and beliefs,* culturally competent counselors:
- are aware of their negative and positive emotional reactions toward other racial and ethnic groups that may prove detrimental to the counseling relationship. They are willing to contrast their own beliefs and attitudes with those of their culturally different clients in a nonjudgmental fashion.
- are aware of stereotypes and preconceived notions that they may hold toward other racial and ethnic minority groups.

B. With respect to *knowledge,* culturally competent counselors:
- possess specific knowledge and information about the particular client group with whom they are working.
- understand how race, culture, ethnicity, and so forth may affect personality formation, vocational choices, manifestation of psychological disorders, help-seeking behavior, and the appropriateness or inappropriateness of counseling approaches.
- understand and have knowledge about sociopolitical influences that impinge on the lives of racial and ethnic minorities.

C. With respect to *skills,* culturally competent counselors:
- familiarize themselves with relevant research and the latest findings regarding mental health and mental disorders that affect various ethnic and racial groups. They should actively seek out educational experiences that enrich their knowledge, understanding, and cross-cultural skills for more effective counseling behavior.

continued on next page

- become actively involved with minority individuals outside the counseling setting so that their perspective of minorities is more than an academic or helping exercise.

III. Developing Culturally Appropriate Intervention Strategies and Techniques

A. With respect to *attitudes and beliefs,* culturally competent counselors:

- respect clients' religious and spiritual beliefs and values, including attributions and taboos, because these affect worldview, psychosocial functioning, and expressions of distress.
- respect indigenous helping practices and respect help-giving networks among communities of color.
- value bilingualism and do not view another language as an impediment to counseling.

B. With respect to *knowledge,* culturally competent counselors:

- have a clear and explicit knowledge and understanding of the generic characteristics of counseling and therapy and how they may clash with the cultural values of various cultural groups.
- are aware of institutional barriers that prevent minorities from using mental health services.
- have knowledge of the potential bias in assessment instruments and use procedures and interpret findings in a way that recognizes the cultural and linguistic characteristics of clients.
- have knowledge of family structures, hierarchies, values, and beliefs from various cultural perspectives. They are knowledgeable about the community where a particular cultural group may reside and the resources in the community.
- are aware of relevant discriminatory practices at the social and the community level that may affect the psychological welfare of the population being served.

C. With respect to *skills,* culturally competent counselors:

- are able to engage in a variety of verbal and nonverbal helping responses. They are able to send and receive both verbal and nonverbal messages accurately and appropriately. They are not tied to only one method or approach to helping but recognize that helping styles and approaches may be culture bound.
- are able to exercise institutional intervention skills on behalf of their clients. They can help clients determine whether a problem stems from racism or bias in others so that clients do not inappropriately personalize problems.
- are not adverse to seeking consultation with traditional healers or religious and spiritual leaders and practitioners in the treatment of culturally different clients when appropriate.
- take responsibility for interacting in the language requested by the client and, if not feasible, make appropriate referrals.
- have training and expertise in the use of traditional assessment and testing instruments.
- attend to and work to eliminate biases, prejudices, and discriminatory contexts in conducting evaluations and providing interventions and develop sensitivity to issues of oppression, sexism, heterosexism, elitism, and racism.
- take responsibility for educating their clients to the processes of psychological intervention, such as goals, expectations, legal rights, and the counselor's orientation.

For the complete description of these competencies, along with explanatory statements, refer to "Operationalization of the Multicultural Counseling Competencies" (Arredondo et al., 1996). Also see Sue and colleagues (1998, chap. 4) and Sue and Sue (2003, chap. 1) for detailed listings of multicultural counseling competencies.

Talib and his classmates, many of whom hold very different attitudes regarding gender roles.

Halfway through the semester, his instructor, Dr. Felice Good, asks Talib to come to her office after class. Dr. Good lets Talib know that she has grave concerns about him pursuing a career in counseling in this country with his present beliefs. She encourages him to consider another career if he is unable to change his "biased convictions" about the role of women. She tells him that unless he can open his thinking to more contemporary viewpoints he will surely encounter serious problems with clients and fellow professionals.

- If you were one of Talib's classmates, what would you want to say to him?
- What assumptions underlie Dr. Good's advice to Talib?
- If you were a faculty member, what criteria would you use to determine that students are not suited for a program because of their values?
- How would you approach a person whose views seem very different from your own? How would you respond to Talib?

Commentary. Dr. Good seemed to assume that because Talib expressed strong convictions he was rigid and would impose his values on his clients. She did not communicate a respect for his value system along with her concern that Talib might impose his values on clients. She did not use this situation as a teaching tool in the classroom to explore the issue of value imposition.

Students who express strong values are often told that they should not work with certain clients. As a result, students may hesitate to expose their viewpoints if they differ from the "acceptable norm." In our view, a critical feature of MCT is the personal development of trainees, which includes helping them clarify a set of values and beliefs concerning culture that increases their chances of functioning effectively in multicultural situations. We try to teach students that having strong convictions is not the same as imposing them on others. Students are challenged to become aware of their value systems and be open to exploring them. However, their role is not to go into this profession to impose these values on others. If trainees maintain a rigid position regarding the way people ought to live, regardless of their cultural background, they may need to be screened out of a program. Ridley, Mendoza, and Kanitz (1994) contend that the scope of training needs to include both the personal and professional development of trainees. In defining a philosophy of MCT, they ask the following questions:

- How far do we go in shifting students' values and beliefs?
- How far do we go in preserving students' values and beliefs?
- How are we to assess the effects of such shifting or preserving of values and beliefs?
- Do we have an ethical responsibility to influence trainees' values and beliefs, or is it an ethical violation of students' rights to their own personal beliefs?
- What are the implications for students who fail to conform to the accepted value system regarding human diversity?

Our Views on Multicultural Training

The first step in the process of acquiring multicultural counseling skills is for students to become involved in a self-exploratory class to help identify any potential blind spots. Ideally, this course would be required of all trainees in the mental health professions and would be taught by someone with experience in multicultural issues. In addition to this introductory course, students could take at least one other course dealing exclusively with multicultural issues and minority groups.

It is also extremely important that a multicultural perspective be integrated throughout the curriculum. When teaching theories and techniques of counseling, for example, instructors can emphasize how such concepts and strategies can be adapted to the special needs of diverse client populations and how some theories may have limited value in working with certain culturally different clients. Wherever possible, representatives of diverse cultures can speak directly to the students about social, economic, and culture-specific factors that may affect mental health treatment.

Trainees would participate in at least one required internship in which they have multicultural experiences or reframe their experiences from a multicultural viewpoint. Ideally, the agency supervisor will be well-versed in the cultural variables of that particular setting and also be skilled in cross-cultural understanding. Students would also have access to both individual and group supervision on campus from a qualified faculty member. Trainees will be encouraged to select supervised field placements and internships that will challenge them to work on gender and cultural concerns, developmental issues, and lifestyle differences. It is important for students to work with people from all walks of life, not just experts in the field. It is our belief that students will learn to become effective multicultural counselors by working with clients with whom they are not necessarily comfortable and who are not "like them." Through well-selected internship experiences, trainees will not only expand their own consciousness but will also increase their knowledge of diverse groups and will have a basis for acquiring intervention skills.

In addition to didactic approaches to acquiring knowledge and skills in multicultural competence, we strongly favor experiential approaches as a way to increase self-awareness and to identify and examine attitudes associated with diversity competence. In their discussion of developing multicultural counseling competencies, Arthur and Achenbach (2002) state that "experiential learning encourages students to consider cultural contexts that influence their own behavior, attitudes, and beliefs and to be reflective about the impact on their professional role" (p. 5). They conclude that experiential learning can help students increase self-awareness and develop a sense of empathy toward clients from culturally diverse backgrounds. Experiential approaches encourage trainees to pay attention to their thoughts, feelings, and actions in exploring their worldviews. We agree with Arthur and Achenbach's contention that experiential learning, in conjunction with other instructional approaches, can assist students in developing self-awareness, knowledge, and skills required for working with culturally diverse client populations. It is also essential for counselors who work extensively with a specific cultural group to immerse themselves in knowledge and approaches specific to that group through reading, cultural events, workshops, and supervised practice.

Finally, we highly recommend that trainees open themselves to people in other cultures through reading and travel. Students can also make use of films and videotapes and can attend seminars and workshops that focus on multicultural issues in the helping professions. Any experiences that will sensitize students to a broad range of life experiences and cultural values will contribute to their effectiveness as counselors. The film *The Color of Fear,* by Lee Mun Wah, is a dramatic challenge to all of us to examine our presumed freedom from prejudice and bias. The same is true for Anne Fadiman's (1997) book, *The Spirit Catches You and You Fall Down*. Additional videotapes on working with diversity can be obtained from Microtraining Associates, by Allen Ivey and Mary Bradford Ivey.

To get the most from your training, we encourage you to accept your limitations and to be patient with yourself as you expand your vision of how your culture continues to influence the person you are today. It is not helpful to overwhelm yourself with all that you do not know. You will not become more effective in multicultural counseling by expecting that you must be completely knowledgeable about the cultural backgrounds of all your clients, by thinking that you should have a complete repertoire of skills, or by demanding perfection. Recognize and appreciate your efforts toward becoming a more effective person and counselor, and remember that becoming a multiculturally competent counselor is an ongoing process. In this process there are no small steps; every step you take is creating a new direction for you in your work with diverse client populations.

Chapter Summary

Over the last decade mental health professionals have been urged to learn about their own culture and to become aware of how their experiences affect the way they work with those who are culturally different. By being ignorant of the values and attitudes of a diverse range of clients, therapists open themselves to criticism and ineffectiveness. Imposing one's own vision of the world on clients not only leads to negative therapeutic outcomes but also constitutes unethical practice.

Culture can be interpreted broadly to include racial or ethnic groups, as well as gender, age, religion, economic status, nationality, physical capacity or handicap, or sexual orientation. We are all limited by our experiences in these various groups, but we can increase our awareness by direct contact with a variety of groups, by reading, by special course work, and by in-service professional workshops. It is essential that our practices be accurate, appropriate, and meaningful for the clients with whom we work. This entails rethinking our theories and modifying our techniques to meet clients' unique needs and not rigidly applying interventions in the same manner to all clients. We encourage you to continue to examine your assumptions, attitudes, and values so that you can determine how they might influence your practice.

Suggested Activities

1. Select two or three cultures or ethnic groups different from your own. What attitudes and beliefs about these cultures did you hold while growing up? In what ways, if any, have your attitudes changed and what contributed to the changes?

2. Which of your values do you ascribe primarily to your culture? Have any of your values changed over time, and if so, how? How might these values influence the way you work with clients who are culturally different from you?

3. What multicultural life experiences have you had? Did you recognize any prejudices? Have you been the object of prejudice? Are you willing to discuss your experiences in class. Interview other students or faculty members who identify themselves as ethnically or culturally different from you. What might they teach you about differences that you as a counselor might benefit from to work more effectively with them?

4. To what degree have your courses and field experience contributed to your ability to work effectively with people from other cultures? What training experiences would you like to have to better prepare you for multicultural counseling?

5. Divide into groups of four in your class for this exercise designed by our colleague, Paul Pedersen. One person role plays a minority client. A second person assumes the counselor role. The third person acts as an alter ego for the client, as the anticounselor. The fourth person acts as an alter ego for the therapist, or the procounselor. You might have the minority client be somewhat reluctant to speak. The counselor can deal with this silence by treating it as a form of resistance, using typical therapeutic strategies. During this time the anticounselor expresses the cultural meaning of the silence. The procounselor shares out loud what he or she imagines the counselor might be thinking. Now, devise a way to deal with silence from this frame of reference without using traditional therapeutic techniques.

6. Minorities are often pressured to give up their beliefs and ways in favor of adopting the ideals and customs of the dominant culture. What do you think your approach would be in working with clients who feel such pressure? How might you work with clients who see their own ethnicity or cultural heritage as a handicap to be overcome?

7. What was your own "internal dialogue" as you read and reflected on this chapter? Share some of this internal dialogue in small group discussions.

8. In small groups, discuss a few of your assumptions that are likely to influence the manner in which you counsel others. Select one of the assumptions discussed in this chapter from the following list that most applies to you. Explore and share your attitudes.

- What assumptions do you make about the value of self-disclosure on the part of clients?
- What are your assumptions pertaining to autonomy, independence, and self-determination?
- To what degree do you assume that it is better to be assertive than to be nonassertive?
- How would you describe a fully functioning person?
- Do you perceive indirectness as being an impediment?
- What other assumptions can you think of that might either help or hinder you in counseling diverse client populations?

9. In small groups, explore what you consider to be the main ethical issues in counseling lesbian, gay, and bisexual clients. Review the set of guidelines for psychotherapy with lesbian, gay, and bisexual clients given on pages 128 and 129. Which of the 16 guidelines would be most helpful for you in challenging your beliefs and attitudes regarding sexual orientation? Are there any attitudes, beliefs, or assumptions you hold that might get in the way of your effectively counseling lesbian, gay, and bisexual clients?

10. Select any one of the many cases described in this chapter, and reflect on how you would deal with this case from an ethical perspective. After you select the case that most interests you, review the steps in the ethical decision-making process described in Chapter 1, and then go through these steps in addressing the issues involved in the case.

11. In small groups, discuss ways for a culturally encapsulated counselor to become more aware of his or her own culturally learned assumptions. Review the list of traits of the culturally encapsulated counselor who exhibits monocultural tunnel vision. What are some of the ways that you might be culturally encapsulated? If you recognize any of these traits in yourself, what do you think you might do about them?

12. *The Color of Fear*, produced and directed by Lee Mun Wah, is an emotional and insightful portrayal of racism in America.* Its aim is to illustrate the type of dialogue and relationships needed if we are to have a truly multicultural society based on equality and trust. After viewing the film in class, share what it brought out in you.

Ethics in Action CD-ROM Exercises

13. In video role play #3, Culture Clash, the client (Sally) directly questions the counselor's background. Role play a situation where a clash between you and a client might develop (such as difference in age, race, sexual orientation, or culture).

14. Refer to the section titled "Becoming an Effective Multicultural Practitioner" in the *Ethics in Action* CD-ROM. Complete the self-examination of

**The Color of Fear* is available from Stir Fry Productions in Oakland, California. The Stir Fry Productions Company provides trained facilitators (in some areas) to assist with discussion after the film is shown.

multicultural counseling competencies. Bring your answers to class and explore in small discussion groups what you need to do to become competent as a counselor of clients whose cultural background differs from your own.

InfoTrac® College Edition Resources

For additional readings, explore InfoTrac College Edition, our online library. Key words are listed in a form that enables the search engine to locate a wider range of articles in the online university library. Key words should be entered exactly as shown, including asterisks, "Wl," "W2," "AND," and other search engine tools. Go to http://www.infotrac-college.com and select these key word searches:

ethic* multicult* couns*
couns* N4 value
(therap* N6 value*) NOT medic* NOT physic*
psych* N6 value*
multicult* N3 train* AND couns*
multicult* N3 couns* N3 competenc*
ethnicity AND (psychology OR psychotherapy)
ethnic W1 minority W1 group AND (psych????y OR psychotherapy OR couns*)
cultural W1 diversity AND (psych????y OR psychotherapy OR couns*)
cultural W1 empathy
culture W1 centered W1 counseling
unintentional W1 racism
cultural W1 racism
cultural W1 encapsulation
cultural W1 pluralism AND (psych????y OR psychotherapy OR couns*)
homosexuality AND (psych????y OR psychotherapy OR couns*) NOT law NOT lawy*
culturally W1 skilled W1 counselor

Pre-Chapter Self-Inventory

Directions: For each statement, indicate the response that most closely identifies your beliefs and attitudes. Use the following code:

5 = I *strongly agree* with this statement.
4 = I *agree* with this statement.
3 = I am *undecided* about this statement.
2 = I *disagree* with this statement.
1 = I *strongly disagree* with this statement.

_____1. If there is a conflict between a legal and an ethical standard, a therapist must always adhere to the ethical standard.

_____2. Practitioners who do not use written consent forms are unprofessional and unethical.

_____3. To practice ethically, therapists must become familiar with the laws related to their profession.

_____4. Clients in therapy should not have access to their clinical files.

_____5. Clients should be made aware of their rights at the outset of a diagnostic or therapeutic relationship.

_____6. It is unethical for a counselor to alter the fee structure once it has been established.

_____7. Ethical practice demands that therapists develop procedures to ensure that clients are in a position to make informed choices.

_____8. Therapists have the responsibility to become knowledgeable about community resources and alternatives to therapy and to present these alternatives to their clients.

Client Rights and Counselor Responsibilities

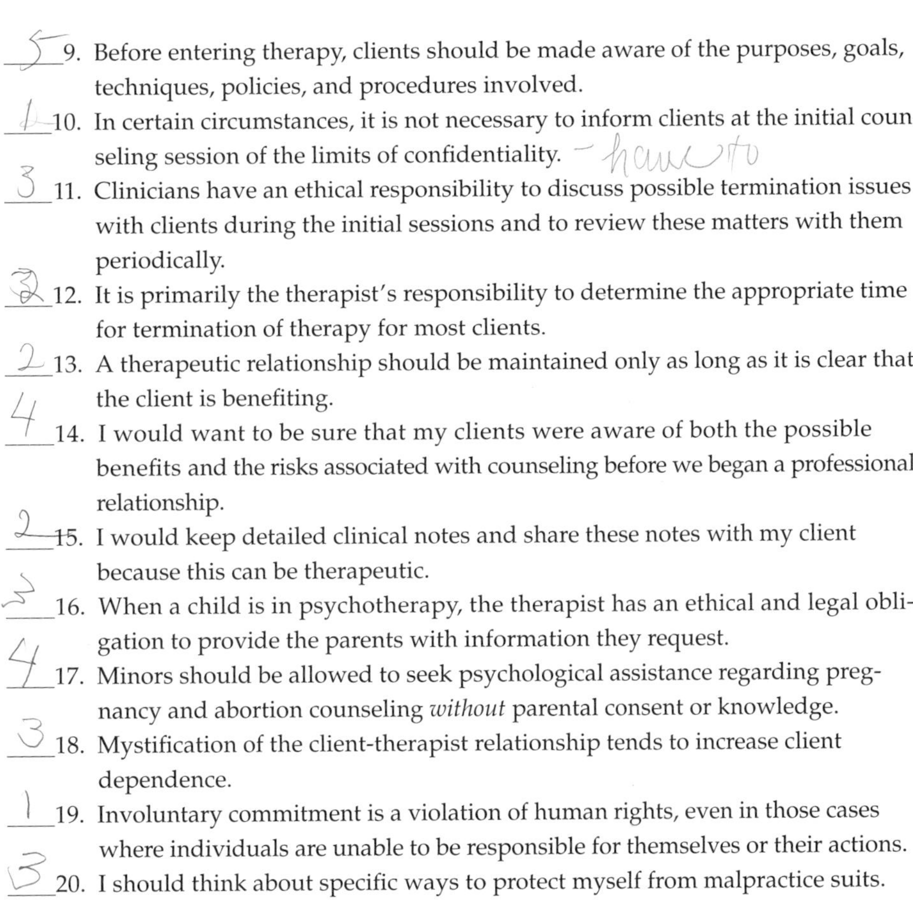

____9. Before entering therapy, clients should be made aware of the purposes, goals, techniques, policies, and procedures involved.

____10. In certain circumstances, it is not necessary to inform clients at the initial counseling session of the limits of confidentiality.

____11. Clinicians have an ethical responsibility to discuss possible termination issues with clients during the initial sessions and to review these matters with them periodically.

____12. It is primarily the therapist's responsibility to determine the appropriate time for termination of therapy for most clients.

____13. A therapeutic relationship should be maintained only as long as it is clear that the client is benefiting.

____14. I would want to be sure that my clients were aware of both the possible benefits and the risks associated with counseling before we began a professional relationship.

____15. I would keep detailed clinical notes and share these notes with my client because this can be therapeutic.

____16. When a child is in psychotherapy, the therapist has an ethical and legal obligation to provide the parents with information they request.

____17. Minors should be allowed to seek psychological assistance regarding pregnancy and abortion counseling *without* parental consent or knowledge.

____18. Mystification of the client-therapist relationship tends to increase client dependence.

____19. Involuntary commitment is a violation of human rights, even in those cases where individuals are unable to be responsible for themselves or their actions.

____20. I should think about specific ways to protect myself from malpractice suits.

Introduction

If we hope to practice in an ethical and legal manner, the rights of clients cannot be taken for granted. In this chapter we deal with ways of educating clients about their rights and responsibilities as partners in the therapeutic process. Special attention is given to the role of informed consent as well as ethical and legal issues that arise when therapists fail to provide for consent. We also deal with some of the ethical and legal issues involved in counseling children and adolescents.

Part of ethical practice is talking with clients about their rights. Depending on the setting and the situation, this discussion can involve the circumstances that led to the client's decision to enter the therapeutic relationship, the responsibilities of the therapist toward the client, the possibility of involuntary hospitalization, the possibility of being forced to submit to certain types of medical and psychological treatment, matters of privacy and confidentiality, the possible ramifications of a *Diagnostic and Statistical Manual of Mental Disorders* (DSM-IV-TR) label, and the possible outcomes and limitations of therapy.

Frequently, clients don't realize that they have rights. Vulnerable and sometimes desperate for help, clients may unquestioningly accept whatever their therapist says or does. There may be an aura about the therapeutic process, and clients may have exaggerated confidence in their therapists, much like the trust patients often have in their physicians. For most people the therapeutic situation is a new one, and they may be unclear about what is expected of them and what they should expect from the therapist. For these reasons we think the therapist is responsible for protecting clients' rights and teaching clients about these rights. The ethics codes of most professional organizations require that clients be given adequate information to make informed choices about entering and continuing the client-therapist relationship (see the box titled The Rights of Clients and Informed Consent for examples from several ethics codes). By alerting clients to their rights and responsibilities, the practitioner is encouraging them to develop a healthy sense of autonomy and personal power.

In addition to the ethical aspects of safeguarding clients' rights, legal parameters also govern professional practice. When we attend workshops dealing with ethical and legal issues in clinical practice, we often hear practitioners expressing their fears of lawsuits. At times it appears that some counselors are more focused on protecting themselves than on helping their clients. You will surely want to protect yourself legally, but we hope you will not allow this reality to immobilize you and inhibit your professional effectiveness. Counseling can be a risky venture, and you must become familiar with the laws that govern professional practice. However, we urge you to avoid becoming so involved in legalities that you cease being primarily interested in the ethical and clinical implications of what you do in your practice.

Ethics Codes

The Rights of Clients and Informed Consent

American Psychological Association (2002)

(a) When obtaining informed consent to therapy as required in Standard 3.10, Informed Consent, psychologists inform clients/patients as early as is feasible in the therapeutic relationship about the nature and anticipated course of therapy, fees, involvement of third parties, and limits of confidentiality and provide sufficient opportunity for the client/patient to ask questions and receive answers.

(b) When obtaining informed consent for treatment for which generally recognized techniques and procedures have not been established, psychologists inform their clients/patients of the developing nature of the treatment, the potential risks involved, alternative treatments that may be available, and the voluntary nature of their participation. (10.01.)

National Association of Social Workers (1999)

Social workers should provide services to clients only in the context of a professional relationship based, when appropriate, on valid informed consent. Social workers should use clear and understandable language to inform clients of the purpose of the service, risks related to the service, limits to service because of the requirements of a third-party payer, relevant costs, reasonable alternatives, clients' right to refuse or withdraw consent, and the time frame covered by the consent. Social workers should provide clients with an opportunity to ask questions. (1.03.)

American Counseling Association (2005)

Counselors explicitly explain to clients the nature of all services provided. They inform clients about issues such as, but not limited to, the purposes, goals, techniques, procedures, limitations, potential risks, and benefits of services; the counselor's qualifications, credentials, and relevant experience; continuation of services upon the incapacitation or death of a counselor; and other pertinent information.

Counselors take steps to insure that clients understand the implications of diagnosis, the intended use of tests and reports, fees, and billing arrangements. Clients have the right to confidentiality and to be provided with an explanation of its limitations (including how supervisors and/or treatment team professionals are involved); to obtain clear information about their records; to participate in the ongoing counseling plans; and to refuse any services or modality change and to be advised of the consequences of such refusal. (A.2.b.)

Feminist Therapy Institute (2000)

A feminist therapist educates her clients regarding power relationships. She informs clients of their rights as consumers of therapy, including procedures for resolving differences and filing grievances. She clarifies power in its various forms as it exists within other areas of her life, including professional roles, social/governmental structures, and interpersonal relationships. She assists her clients in finding ways to protect themselves and, if requested, to seek redress. (II.D.)

The American Mental Health Counselors Association (2000)

Mental health counselors are responsible for making their services readily accessible to clients in a manner that facilitates the clients' abilities to make an informed choice when selecting a provider. This therapeutic responsibility includes a clear description of what the client can expect in the way of tests, reports, billing, therapeutic regime and schedules, and the use of the mental health

continued on next page

counselor's statement of professional disclosure. In the event that the client is a minor or possesses disabilities that would prohibit informed consent, the mental health counselor acts in the client's best interest. (Principle I.J.)

International Association of Marriage and Family Counselors (2002)

Members inform clients (in writing if feasible) about the goals and purposes of counseling, qualifications of the counselor(s), scope and limits of confidentiality, potential risks and benefits of the counseling process and specific techniques and interventions, reasonable expectations for outcomes, duration of services, costs of services, and alternative approaches. (I.O.)

The Client's Right to Give Informed Consent

One of the best ways to protect the rights of clients is to develop procedures to help them make informed choices. **Informed consent** involves the right of clients to be informed about their therapy and to make autonomous decisions pertaining to it. The main purpose of informed consent is to increase the chances that the client will become involved, educated, and a willing participant in his or her therapy. Mental health professionals are required by their ethics codes to disclose to clients the risks, benefits, and alternatives to proposed treatment. The intent of an **informed consent document** is to define boundaries and clarify the nature of the therapeutic relationship. The goal of the informed consent process is to give clients adequate and continuous information so that they may anticipate what they will be asked to consent to in treatment (Wineburgh, 1998).

Informed consent entails a balance between telling clients too much and telling them too little. Although most professionals agree on the ethical principle that it is crucial to provide clients with information about the therapeutic relationship, the manner in which this is done in practice varies considerably among therapists. It is a mistake to overwhelm clients with too much detailed information at once, but it is also a mistake to withhold important information that clients need if they are to make wise choices about their therapy program.

Professionals have a responsibility to their clients to make reasonable disclosure of all significant facts, the nature of the procedure, and some of the more probable consequences and difficulties. All clients have the right to have treatment explained to them. The process of therapy is not so mysterious that it cannot be explained in a way that clients can comprehend how it works. It is essential that clients give their consent *with* understanding. It is the responsibility of professionals to assess the client's level of understanding and to promote the client's free choice. Professionals need to avoid subtly coercing clients to cooperate with a therapy program to which they are not freely consenting. Generally, informed consent requires that the client be competent, have knowledge of what will occur, especially the risks, and give consent to treatment (Anderson, 1996; Bennett et al., 1990; Crawford, 1994; Grosso, 2002).

Legal Aspects of Informed Consent

Three elements are basic to the **legal aspects of informed consent:** capacity, comprehension of information, and voluntariness (Anderson, 1996; Crawford, 1994; Stromberg & Dellinger, 1993). **Capacity** means that the client has the ability to make rational decisions. When this capacity is lacking, a parent or guardian is typically responsible for giving consent. **Comprehension of information** means that therapists must give clients information in a clear way and check to see that they understand it. To give valid consent, it is necessary for clients to have adequate information about both the procedure and the possible consequences. The information must include the benefits and risks of procedures, possible adverse effects from treatment, the risk of forgoing treatment, and available alternative procedures. **Voluntariness** means that the person giving consent is acting freely in the decision-making process and is legally and psychologically able (competent) to give consent. It implies that the professional and the client have discussed the nature of the problem and possible treatments for it. The therapist should explain to competent clients, except those ordered by the court to undergo evaluation or treatment, that they are free to withdraw their consent at any time for any reason.

Educating Clients About Informed Consent

It is a good practice for therapists to employ an educative approach by encouraging clients' questions about assessment or treatment and by offering useful feedback as the treatment process progresses. Here are some questions therapists should answer at the outset of the counseling relationship:

- What are the goals of the therapeutic endeavor?
- What services will the counselor provide?
- What is expected of the client?
- What are the risks and benefits of therapy?
- What are the qualifications of the provider of the services?
- What are the financial considerations?
- To what extent can the duration of therapy be predicted?
- What are the limitations of confidentiality?
- What information about the counselor's values should be provided in the informed consent document so that clients can choose whether they want to enter a professional relationship with this counselor?
- In what situations does the practitioner have mandatory reporting requirements?
- If the person is referred for an assessment or for therapy from the court or from an employer, who is the client?

Informed consent involves disclosure by the practitioner of the necessary information clients will need to make an educated and a free decision of whether or not to become part of a therapeutic relationship. It is essential to give clients an opportunity to raise questions and to explore their expectations of counseling. We view clients as partners with their therapists in the sense that they are involved as fully as possible in each aspect of their therapy. Thus, education about the therapeutic process begins at the intake session and continues to the termination phase. Practitioners cannot assume that clients clearly understand what they are told initially about the therapeutic process. Furthermore, informed consent is not easily completed within the initial session by asking clients to sign forms. On this point, the *Canadian Code of Ethics for Psychologists* (CPA, 2000) indicates that informed consent involves a process of reaching an agreement to work collaboratively rather than simply having a consent form signed (Section 1.17). Educating clients about the therapeutic process is an ongoing endeavor. Properly executed, the informed consent process is a way of engaging the participation of the client. In essence, it can serve as an outline of the rights and responsibilities of the client in the therapeutic process. The more clients know about how therapy works, including the roles of both client and therapist, the more clients will benefit from the therapeutic experience.

Informed consent is also a means of empowering the client, which has clinical as well as ethical significance. Especially in the case of clients who have been victimized, issues of power and control can be central in the therapy process. The process of informing clients about therapy increases the chances that the client-therapist relationship will become a collaborative partnership.

Practitioners are ethically bound to offer the best quality of service available, and clients have a right to know that managed care programs, with their focus on cost containment, may have adverse effects on the quality of care available. Clinicians are expected to provide prospective clients with clear information about the benefits to which they are entitled and the limits of treatment.

Miller (1996b) asserts that quality of care is likely to decline under restrictive managed care programs. In her discussion of the ethics of therapy in a managed care environment, Wineburgh (1998) states that informed consent issues are particularly complicated. Clearly, clients have the right to specific information regarding their treatment under managed care and the limitations of their treatment packages. However, professionals are often restricted by managed care organizational contracts from educating clients about treatment allocation decisions. Managed care contracts often have "gag clauses" that prohibit practitioners from sharing any negative information about managed care policies, including options not covered by the plan. In the managed care environment, consumers in need of therapy may be denied service, clients who are treated may be systematically undertreated, and those with moderate to severe problems requiring longer-term treatment may not receive it. Therapists have an obligation to educate consumers, and managed care programs that promote financial interests to the detriment of quality treatment should be held legally responsible for any adverse impact on clients (Newman & Bricklin, 1991). This discussion of managed care and informed consent presents the therapist with a conundrum. On one hand, you are ethically obligated to give accurate information to the client, and on the other hand, you may be restricted from giving full information to the client by the managed care company. (Chapter 10 includes a detailed discussion of the ethical issues associated with managed care.)

Informed Consent in Practice

How do practitioners assist clients in becoming informed partners? Somberg, Stone, and Claiborn (1993) conducted a survey to assess therapists' practices pertaining to informed consent and found that informed consent procedures need to be considered within the context of the therapist's values, orientation, and work setting. Some practitioners use informed consent forms. Others talk with clients and report these discussions in their files. In either case, it is important to note that both the client and the therapist have the option to revise the therapeutic contract at any time. Due to considerations of documentation, ease of administering, and standardization, Somberg and colleagues recommend using a written approach to informed consent.

Pomerantz and Handelsman (2004) have developed an updated informed consent form that they suggest be executed both verbally and in writing. They state that clients have a right to know what the therapy process entails because they are buying a service from a professional. Some of the topics they have developed include a series of questions pertaining to what therapy is and how it works, the clinician's approach, alternatives, appointments, confidentiality, fees, procedures for filing for insurance reimbursement, and policies pertaining to managed care. Pomerantz and Handelsman believe that an open discussion of a wide range of questions on these topics is "one important facet of a process that will enable clients to make genuinely informed decisions regarding contemporary psychotherapy" (p. 203). Grosso (2002) recommends that the written consent form be designed in the form of a therapeutic contract. In general, client misunderstanding is reduced through the effective use of informed consent procedures, which also tends to reduce the chances a client will file a liability claim. Both the practitioner and the client benefit from this practice.

We have emphasized the importance of the therapist's role in teaching clients about informed consent and encouraging clients' questions about the therapeutic process. With this general concept in mind, put yourself in the counselor's place in the following case. Identify the main ethical issues in this case, and think about what you would do in this situation.

✓ **The Case of Dottie.** At the initial interview the therapist, Dottie, does not provide an informed consent form and touches only briefly on the process of therapy. In discussing confidentiality, she states that whatever is said in the office will stay in the office, with no mention of the limitations of confidentiality. Three months into the therapy, the client exhibits some suicidal ideation. Dottie has recently attended a conference at which malpractice was one of the topics of discussion, and she worries that she may have been remiss in not providing her client with adequate information about her services, including confidentiality and its limitations. She hastily reproduces an informed consent document that she received at the conference and asks her client to sign the form at the next session. This procedure seems to evoke confusion in the client, and he makes no further mention of suicide. After five more sessions, he calls in to cancel an appointment and does not schedule another appointment. Dottie does not pursue the case further.

- What are the ethical and legal implications of the therapist's practice? Explain your position.
- If you had been in Dottie's shoes, what might you have done?
- Would you have contacted this client after he canceled? What are your thoughts about Dottie not doing that?

The Content of Informed Consent

One of the main aims of the first meeting is to establish rapport and create a climate of safety in the therapeutic situation. As mentioned earlier, the challenge is to provide clients with just the right amount of information for them to make informed choices. Providing too much information at the initial meeting can impede clients from becoming active participants in the therapy process. The types and amounts of information, the specific content of informed consent, the style of presenting information, and the timing of introducing this information must be considered within the context of state licensure requirements, work setting, agency policies, and the nature of the client's concerns. The content of informed consent is also determined by the specific client population being served. It should be added that there is no assurance that practitioners can avoid legal action, even if they do obtain written informed consent. Rather than focusing on legalistic documents, we suggest that you develop informed consent procedures that increase client understanding and foster client-counselor dialogue about the therapeutic partnership.

Topics selected for discussion during early counseling sessions are best guided by the concerns, interests, and questions of the client. Let's look in more detail at some of the topics about which clients should be informed.

The Therapeutic Process

Although it may be difficult to give clients a detailed description of what occurs in therapy, some general ideas can be explored. We support the practice of letting clients know that counseling might open up levels of awareness that could cause pain and anxiety. Clients who require long-term therapy need to know that they may experience changes that could produce disruptions and turmoil in their lives. Some clients may choose to settle for a limited knowledge of themselves rather than risking this kind of disruption, and this should be respected. We believe it is appropriate to use the initial sessions for a frank discussion of how change happens. Clients should understand the procedures and goals of therapy, especially if any unusual or experimental approaches or techniques are to be employed. It is their right to refuse to participate in certain therapeutic techniques. It is important that clients know that they can terminate therapy when they decide to, yet it is advisable to discuss the matter of termination with the therapist.

Background of the Therapist

Therapists might provide clients with a description of their training and education, their credentials, licenses, any specialized skills, their theoretical orientation, the types of clients and types of problems in which they have competence, and the types of problems that they cannot work with effectively. State licensure boards often make giving this information a legal requirement. If the counseling will be done by an intern or a paraprofessional, clients should be aware of this. Likewise, if the provider will be working with a supervisor, this fact should be made known to the client. This description of the practitioner's qualifications, coupled with a willingness to answer any questions clients have about the process, reduces the unrealistic expectations clients may have about therapy. It also reduces the chances of malpractice actions. It is essential that you disclose to potential clients in advance certain values you hold, especially those values that might make it difficult for you to maintain objectivity. Examples of such conflicts would be issues pertaining to religion, abortion, divorce, sexual orientation, and end-of-life decisions. If clients are made aware of these values, this may help them decide whether to work with you.

Costs Involved in Therapy

It is essential to provide information about all costs involved in psychological services at the beginning of these services, including methods of payment. Clients need to be informed about how insurance reimbursement will be taken care of and any limitations of their health plan with respect to fees. If fees are subject to change, this should be made clear in the beginning.

Most ethics codes have a standard pertaining to establishing fees (see the ethics codes box titled Establishing Professional Fees). Matters of finance are delicate and, if handled poorly, can easily result in problems between client and therapist. Thus the manner in which fees are handled has much to do with the tone of the therapeutic partnership.

Some professional codes of ethics recommend a sliding fee standard because the financial resources of clients are variable. In addition to adjusting fees to what clients can afford, many professionals provide services to some clients for little or no financial compensation, making their services available to some who could not otherwise afford help.

Ethics Codes

Establishing Professional Fees

American Counseling Association (2005)

In establishing fees for professional counseling services, counselors consider the financial status of clients and locality. In the event that the established fee structure is inappropriate for a client, counselors assist clients in attempting to find comparable services of acceptable cost. (A.10.b.)

American Association for Marriage and Family Therapy (2001)

Marriage and family therapists make financial arrangements with clients, third party payors, and supervisees that are reasonably understandable and conform to accepted professional practices.

Commission on Rehabilitation Counselor Certification (2001)

Rehabilitation counselors will clearly explain to clients, prior to entering the counseling relationship, all financial arrangements related to professional services including the use of collection agencies or legal measures for nonpayment. (J.4.a.)

National Association of Social Workers (1999)

When setting fees, social workers should ensure that the fees are fair, reasonable, and commensurate with the service performed. Consideration should be given to the client's ability to pay. (1.13.a.)

American Psychological Association (2002)

(a) As early as is feasible in a professional or scientific relationship, psychologists and recipients of psychological services reach an agreement specifying compensation and billing arrangements.
(b) Psychologists' fee practices are consistent with law.
(c) Psychologists do not misrepresent their fees.
(d) If limitations to services can be anticipated because of limitations in financing, this is discussed with the recipient of services as early as is feasible.
(e) If the recipient of services does not pay for services as agreed, and if psychologists intend to use collection agencies or legal measures to collect the fees, psychologists first inform the person that such measures will be taken and provide that person an opportunity to make prompt payment. (6.04.)

The Length of Therapy and Termination

Part of the informed consent process involves providing clients with information about the length of treatment and the termination of treatment. Regardless of the length of treatment, it is important for clients to be prepared for a termination phase.

Many agencies have a policy limiting the number of sessions provided to clients. These clients should be informed at the outset that they cannot receive long-term therapy. Under a managed care system, clients are often limited to 6 sessions, or a specified amount for a given year, such as 20 sessions. The limited number of sessions needs to be brought to their attention more than once. Furthermore, clients have the right to expect a referral so that they can continue exploring whatever concerns initially brought them to therapy. If referrals are not possible but the client still needs further treatment, the therapist should explain other alternatives available to the client.

Because practitioners differ with respect to an orientation of long-term versus short-term therapy, it is important to inform clients of the basic assumptions underlying your orientation. In a managed care setting, practitioners will need to have expertise in assessing a client's main psychological issues quickly, and matching each client with the most appropriate intervention. They will also need to acquire competency in delivering brief interventions.

Health maintenance organizations (HMOs) exert considerable influence over basic decisions that affect the therapy process, including length of treatment, number of sessions, the amount of money that will be reimbursed, and even the content of therapy (Smith & Fitzpatrick, 1995). If a health maintenance organization and the therapist disagree about the number of sessions required for effective therapy, the therapist might do well to request in writing from the HMO representative the reasons for not allowing further treatment. Part of informing clients about the therapeutic process entails giving them relevant facts about brief interventions that may not always meet their needs. Clients have a right to know how their health care program is likely to influence the course of their therapy as well as the limitations imposed by the program.

A central concern associated with termination is avoiding abandonment of a client. Clinical records should give evidence that they were not terminated inappropriately. It is useful to document the nature of a client's termination, including who initiated the termination, how this was handled, the degree to which initial goals were met, and referrals provided when appropriate.

Clients have a right to expect that their therapy will end when they have realized the maximum benefits from it or have obtained what they were seeking when they entered it. The issue of termination needs to be openly explored by the therapist and the client, and the decision to terminate ultimately should rest with the client.

Consultation With Colleagues

Student counselors generally meet regularly with their supervisors and fellow students to discuss their progress and any problems they encounter in their work. It is good policy for counselors to inform their clients that they may be receiving supervision on their cases. Experienced clinicians often have scheduled consultation meetings with their peers to focus on how they are serving clients. Even though it is ethical for clinicians to discuss their cases with other professionals, it is wise to routinely let clients know about this. Clients will then have less reason to feel that the trust they are putting in their counselors is being violated.

Interruptions in Therapy

Most ethics codes specify that therapists should consider the welfare of their clients when it is necessary to interrupt or terminate the therapy process. For example, this is the NASW (1999) guideline:

> Social workers who anticipate the termination or interruption of service to clients should notify clients promptly and seek the transfer, referral, or continuation of services in relation to the clients' needs and preferences. (1.16.e.)

It is a good practice to explain at the first contact with clients the possibilities for both expected and unexpected interruptions in therapy and how they might best be handled. A therapist's absence might appear as abandonment to some clients, especially if the absence is poorly handled. As much as possible, therapists should make plans for any interruptions in therapy, such as vacations or long-term absences. When practitioners plan vacations, ethical practice entails providing clients with another therapist in case of need. Clients need information about the therapist's method of handling emergencies as part of their orientation to treatment. Practitioners will need to obtain a client's written consent to provide information to their substitutes. McGee (2003) recommends that therapists include in their informed consent document the name of at least one professional colleague who is willing to assume their professional responsibilities in the event of an emergency, such as the therapist becoming incapacitated through injury or death. Who will maintain their files should also be addressed at this time.

Benefits and Risks of Treatment

Clients should have some information about both the possible benefits and the risks associated with a treatment program. Due to the fact that clients are largely responsible for the outcomes of therapy, it is a good policy to emphasize the role of the client's responsibility. Clients need to know that no promises can be made about specific outcomes, which means that ethical practitioners avoid giving guarantees of cures to clients.

Alternatives to Traditional Therapy

According to the ethics codes of some professional organizations, clients need to know about alternative helping systems. Therefore, it is a good practice for therapists to learn about community resources so they can present these alternatives to a client. Some alternatives to psychotherapy include self-help programs, stress management, programs for personal-effectiveness training, peer self-help groups, indigenous healing practices, bibliotherapy, 12-step programs, support groups, and crisis-intervention centers.

This information about therapy and its alternatives can be presented in writing, through an audiotape or videotape, or during an intake session. An open discussion of therapy and its alternatives may, of course, lead some clients to choose sources of help other than therapy. For practitioners who make a living providing therapy services, asking their clients to consider alternative treatments can produce financial anxiety. However, openly discussing therapy and its alternatives is likely to reinforce many clients' decisions to continue therapy. Clients have a right to know about alternative therapeutic modalities (such as different theoretical orientations and medication) that are known to be effective with particular clients and conditions.

Tape-Recording or Videotaping Sessions

Many agencies require that interviews be recorded for training or supervision purposes. Clients have a right to be informed about this procedure at the initial session, and it is important that they understand why the recordings are made, how they will be used, who will have access to them, and how they will be stored. Therapists sometimes make recordings because they can benefit from listening to them or by having colleagues listen to their interactions with clients and give them feedback. It is essential for trainees or counselors to secure the permission of clients before making any kind of electronic recording.

Clients' Right of Access to Their Files

Clinical records are kept for the benefit of clients. Remley and Herlihy (2005) maintain that clients have a legal right to inspect and obtain copies of records kept on their behalf by professionals. Clients have the ultimate responsibility for decisions about their own health care and also have the right of access to complete information with respect to their condition and the care provided. A professional writes about a client in descriptive and nonjudgmental ways. A clinician who operates in a professional manner should not have to worry if his or her notes were to become public information or be read by a client.

Some clinicians question the wisdom of sharing counseling records with a client. They may operate on the assumption that their clients are not sophisticated enough to understand their diagnosis and the clinical notes, or they may think that more harm than benefit could result from disclosing such information to clients. Rather than automatically providing clients access to what is written in their files, some therapists give clients an explanation of their diagnosis and the general trend of what kind of information they are recording.

Other clinicians are willing to grant their clients access to information in the counseling records they keep, especially if clients request specific information. ACA's (2005) guideline on this matter is this:

> When clients request access to their records, counselors provide assistance and consultation in interpreting counseling records. (B.6.e.)

The Canadian Counselling Association (1999) provides this guidance pertaining to access to records:

> Counsellors understand that clients have a right of access to their counselling records, and that disclosure to others of information from these records only occurs with the written consent of the client and/or when required by law. (B.7.)

Giving clients access to their files seems to be consistent with the consumer-rights movement, which is having an impact on the fields of mental health, counseling, rehabilitation, and education. One way to reduce the growing trend toward malpractice suits and other legal problems is to allow clients to see their medical records, even while hospitalized. Later in this chapter we discuss procedures for keeping records.

Rights Pertaining to Diagnostic Classifying

One of the major obstacles for some therapists to the open sharing of files with clients is the need to give clients a diagnostic classification as a requirement for receiving third-party reimbursement for psychological services. Some clients are not informed that they will be so classified, what those classifications are, or that the classifications and other confidential material will be given to insurance companies. Clients also do not have control over who can receive this information. For example, in a managed care system office workers will have access to specific information about a client, such as a diagnosis. Ethical practice involves informing clients that a diagnosis can become a permanent part of their file. Indeed, a diagnosis can have ramifications in terms of costs of insurance, long-term insurability, and employment. With this information, clients are at least in the position to decline treatment with these restrictions. Some clients have the means to pay for the kind of therapy they want and may choose not to use a third-party payer.

Greenhut (1991) contends that therapists often make clients worse by attaching labels to them. She believes therapy sometimes becomes the exploitation of the exploited. For example, in treating incest survivors, rape victims, and those who have been physically abused, therapists can further oppress these victims by assigning them labels such as co-dependent, narcissistic, borderline, eating disordered, or chronically depressed. There is a danger in viewing a client entirely in terms of a diagnostic classification, or in viewing a disorder as being static, with the end result that the client is left with the notion of being labeled forever. Greenhut urges therapists to encourage their clients to act on the basis of what they believe is best for themselves and, thus, to move beyond their labels. However, it is essential for therapists to have assessment skills and to know that clients' behaviors can fit patterns or categories that may assist in the development of a treatment plan.

The Nature and Purpose of Confidentiality

Clients should be educated regarding matters pertaining to confidentiality, privileged communication, and privacy (which we discuss in Chapter 6). Therapists are expected to inform clients of the limitations of confidentiality from the outset of the professional relationship. The *Code of Ethics of the American Mental Health Counselors Association* (2000) has the following principle pertaining to confidentiality:

> At the outset of any counseling relationship, mental health counselors make their clients aware of their rights in regard to the confidential nature of the counseling relationship. They fully disclose the limits of, or exceptions to, confidentiality, and/or the existence of privileged communication, if any. (3.a.)

Putting this principle into action not only educates clients but also promotes trust on the client's part. The effectiveness of the client-therapist relationship is built on a foundation of trust. If trust is lacking, it is unlikely that clients will engage in significant self-disclosure and self-exploration.

Part of establishing trust involves making clients aware of how certain information will be used and whether it will be given to third-party payers. Pomerantz and Handelsman (2004) indicate that clients have a right to expect answers from the therapist on questions such as these: "How do governmental regulations, such as federal Health Information Portability and Accountability Act (HIPAA) regulations, influence the confidentiality of records? How much and what kind of information will you be required to give the insurance company about therapy sessions?"

Clients in a managed care program need to be told that the confidentiality of their communications will be compromised to some extent. It is especially critical that clients be informed that the managed care organization has the power to limit reimbursement for services. Thus therapists are often required to release confidential information to determine how much treatment is deemed necessary (Wineburgh, 1998). Some therapists are concerned that clients will not engage in self-disclosure if they know that confidential information is given to a managed care organization. It is unethical for therapists to withhold the limits of confidentiality from clients in this context (Kremer & Gesten, 1998). Clearly, when a practitioner contracts with a third-party payer, a client's records come under the scrutiny and review of the system doing the reimbursing. Therapists are required to secure written consent from their clients for any disclosure made to an insurance company. Some clients may want to safeguard their privacy and confidentiality by seeking treatment that does not involve third-party reimbursement.

All the professional codes have a clause stating that clients have a right to know about any limitations of confidentiality from the outset. For example, this is NASW's (1999) guideline:

> Social workers should discuss with clients and other interested parties the nature of confidentiality and limitations of clients' right to confidentiality. Social workers should review with clients circumstances where confidential information may be requested and where disclosure of confidential information may be legally required. This discussion should occur as soon as possible in the social worker-client relationship and as needed throughout the course of the relationship. (1.07.e.)

If you have clients who will be participating in online counseling, they have a right to know about the limits of confidentiality pertaining to this service. An ACA (2005) guideline (A.12.g.) addresses issues related to the difficulty of maintaining the confidentiality of electronically transmitted communications.

As you will see in Chapter 6, confidentiality is not an absolute. Certain circumstances demand that a therapist disclose what was said by a client in a private therapy session or disclose counseling records.

The Professional's Responsibilities in Record Keeping

From an ethical, legal, and clinical perspective, an important responsibility of mental health practitioners is to keep adequate records on their clients. The standard of care for all mental health professionals requires keeping current records for all professional contacts. Record keeping serves multiple purposes.

From a clinical perspective, record keeping provides a history that a therapist can use in reviewing the course of treatment. From a legal perspective, state or federal law may require keeping a record, and many practitioners believe that accurate and detailed clinical records can provide an excellent defense against malpractice claims. From a risk management perspective, record keeping may be the standard of care (Behnke, 2005). Rivas-Vazquez and colleagues (2001) contend that the documentation of clinical services has taken on unprecedented importance for mental health professionals. From their perspective, the main objectives of documentation practices are: (a) to structure quality care, (b) to decrease liability exposure, and (c) to fulfill requirements for reimbursement.

Moline, Williams, and Austin (1998) list a number of arguments for keeping records, including these points:

- Record keeping has become a "standard of care" practice set by most professional organizations.
- Adequate clinical records often serve as a counselor's defense against malpractice claims or in the event of being charged with an ethical violation.
- A clinical record can serve clients by reflecting their condition at a particular time.
- Records document that treatment occurred.
- Records can be useful for clients in the event of transferring to a new counselor or school.
- Records can help counselors improve their skills and provide more effective treatment for clients.
- Federal and/or state law may require the practice of record keeping.

Record Keeping From a Clinical Perspective

Maintaining clinical notes has a dual purpose: (a) to provide the best service possible for clients, and (b) to provide evidence of a level of care commensurate with the standards of the profession. Although keeping records is a basic part of a counselor's practice, Remley and Herlihy (2005) suggest that it is critical to balance the need to maintain adequate records with the obligation to provide quality counseling services: "Counselors who find themselves devoting inordinate or excessive amounts of time creating and maintaining records probably need to reevaluate how they are spending their professional time and energy" (p. 119).

At times, therapists may operate on the assumption that keeping clinical records is not an effective use of the limited time they have, which means they would likely adopt a minimalist approach to record keeping. Clinicians may not keep notes because they can remember what clients tell them, because they are concerned about violating a client's confidentiality and privacy, because they do not want to assume a legalistic stance in their counseling practice, or because they do not have time to keep notes on their clients. Regardless of the reason for not keeping records, Schaffer (1997) claims that it is a serious mistake. Lack of adequate records may deprive clients of data needed for treatment. For example, clients may need to transfer to another therapist, or the therapist may die or retire. If notes were not kept, both the client and the therapist can be hurt.

Some therapists choose to devote their time to delivering service to clients rather than recording process and progress notes. However, these notes are an important part of practice. **Progress notes** are a basic part of the clinical records and are required. These notes are behavioral in nature and address what people say and do. Progress notes contain information on diagnosis, functional status, symptoms, treatment plan, consequences, alternative treatments, and client progress. **Process notes,** or psychotherapy notes, deal with client reactions such as transference and the therapist's subjective impressions of a client. Other areas that might be included in the process notes are intimate details about the client; details of dreams or fantasies; sensitive information about a client's personal life; and a therapist's own thoughts, feelings, and reactions to clients. Process notes are not meant to be readily or easily shared with others. They are intended for the use of the practitioners who created them. Information essential for treatment should not be included in process notes. For example, excluded from process notes are diagnosis, treatment plan, symptoms, prognosis, and progress.

It is important to note that the law requires clinicians to keep a separate clinical record (progress notes) on all clients, but the law *does not* require keeping psychotherapy (process) notes. The privacy rule allows clinicians to keep two sets of records, but it does not mandate it. The idea of two sets of records is that one set (progress notes) is more general, less private, and more readily accessible to insurers and clients. The other set (process notes) is more private and for the use of the therapist. If a therapist does keep process notes, they must be kept separately from the individual's clinical record.

A client's clinical record is not the place for a therapist's personal opinions or personal reactions to the client, and record keeping should reflect professionalism. If a client misses a session, it is a good practice to document the reasons. In writing progress notes, use clear behavioral language. Focus on describing specific and concrete behavior and avoid jargon. It may help to assume that the contents of this record might someday be read in a courtroom with the client present. Although professional documentation is expected to be thorough, it is best to keep notes as concise as possible. Be mindful of the dictum, "If you did not document it, then it did not happen." Record client and therapist behavior that is clinically relevant. Include in clinical records interventions used, client responses to treatment strategies, the evolving treatment plan, and any follow-up measures taken.

Remley and Herlihy (2005) assert that it is possible to keep adequate records *and* provide quality treatment. They point out that adequate records can benefit the client. Some of these benefits include continuity of care when a client is transferred from one professional to another, helping clients assess their progress, and the creation of an accurate history of a client's diagnosis and treatment.

✓ **The Case of Noah.** Noah is a therapist in private practice who primarily sees relatively well-functioning clients. He considers keeping records to be basically irrelevant to the therapeutic process for his clients. As he puts it: "In all that a client says to me in one hour, what do I write down? And for what purpose? If I were seeing high-risk clients, then I certainly would keep notes. Or if I were a psychoanalyst, where everything a client said matters, then I would keep notes." One of his clients, Sue, who had watched a television talk show in which clients rights were discussed, asked to see her file. Noah had to explain his lack of record keeping to Sue.

- What do you think of Noah's philosophy on record keeping? Do you consider it unethical? Why or why not?
- Taking into consideration the kind of clientele Noah sees, is his behavior justified? If you disagree, what criteria would you use in determining what material should be recorded?
- What if a legal issue arises during or after Sue's treatment? How would documenting each session help or not help both the client and the counselor?
- Assuming that some of Noah's clients will move to other locales and see new therapists, does the absence of notes to be transferred to the new therapist have ethical implications? Is it a burden and expense on the clients to have to cover old ground?
- How do you react to Noah's opinion that keeping notes is irrelevant in his practice? Explain.
- If it had no relevance in a court of law, would you still keep notes? Why or why not?

Record Keeping From a Legal Perspective

According to Rivas-Vazquez and his colleagues (2001), the adage "if it is not documented, it did not happen" has never been more relevant than in today's climate of heightened awareness of potential liability exposure. These authors outline the specific domains required for comprehensive documentation practices. Professional ethics codes also outline the requirements of good record keeping (see the ethics codes box titled Record Keeping). It is a wise policy for counselors to document their actions in crisis situations such as cases involving potential danger of harm to oneself, others, or physical property. However, it is not in the best interests of clients for counselors to be more concerned about record keeping as a self-protective strategy than they are to providing quality services to clients.

According to Grosso (2002), in some states it is unethical and illegal for mental health professionals to fail to keep clinical records. Appropriate mental health records are the best form of defense. Grosso adds that such records can quash an investigation by lending weight to the therapist's appropriate application of the standards of practice, selection of client, assessment, diagnosis, treatment plan, consultation(s), and treatment notes. Adequate records can support the best interests of the client and also demonstrate that a practitioner delivered services according to the standard of care expected of a professional.

Two useful books on documentation are *Documentation in Counseling Records* (Mitchell, 2001) and *Documenting Psychotherapy: Essentials for Mental*

Ethics Codes

Record Keeping

National Association of Social Workers (1999)

(a) Social workers should take reasonable steps to ensure that documentation in records is accurate and reflective of the services provided.
(b) Social workers should include sufficient and timely documentation in records to facilitate the delivery of services and to ensure continuity of services provided to clients in the future.
(c) Social workers' documentation should protect clients' privacy to the extent that it is possible and appropriate, and should include only that information that is directly relevant to the delivery of services.
(d) Social workers should store records following the termination of service to ensure reasonable future access. Records should be maintained for the number of years required by state statutes or relevant contracts. (3.04.)

American Psychological Association (2002)

Psychologists create, and to the extent the records are under their control, maintain, disseminate, store, retain, and dispose of records and data relating to their professional and scientific work in order to (1) facilitate provision of services later by them or by other professionals, (2) allow for replication of research design and analyses, (3) meet institutional requirements, (4) ensure accuracy of billing and payments, and (5) ensure compliance with law. (6.01)

Canadian Counselling Association (1999)

Counsellors maintain records in sufficient detail to track the sequence and nature of professional services rendered and consistent with any legal, regulatory, agency, or institutional requirement. They secure the safety of such records and, create, maintain, transfer, and dispose of them in a manner compliant with the requirements of confidentiality and the other articles of this Code of Ethics. (B.6.)

Health Practitioners (Moline, Williams, & Austin, 1998). Moline and colleagues suggest that the practice of keeping adequate records is more than a way to lessen the chance of malpractice action: "We firmly believe that good record keeping supports the therapist in conducting professional duties and thus assists in providing appropriate care for clients. This consideration, we believe, outweighs any legal deliberation" (p. ix).

Schaffer (1997) suggests that practitioners who fail to maintain adequate clinical records are putting themselves in great ethical and legal peril. Keeping records is not only required in all settings but is perhaps the least expensive and most effective form of liability insurance as well. Failing to keep records deprives practitioners of evidence they will need to defend themselves should they become involved in a malpractice or disciplinary action. Even if a mental health provider acts reasonably and keeps good records, there is no complete guarantee that he or she will not be sued. Occasionally a competent practitioner will even be found liable for damages. As unfair as it seems, the law sometimes imposes a legal responsibility on professionals that they did not know they had (Mary Hermann, personal communication, March 10, 2005).

The Committee on Professional Practice and Standards of APA adopted a set of guidelines for record keeping in February 1993 (see Canter et al., 1994, Appendix B). These guidelines include a caution against tampering with case notes and some advice on content and style.

Case notes should *never* be altered or tampered with after they have been entered into the client's record. Tampering with a clinical record after the fact can cast a shadow on the therapist's integrity in court. Enter notes into a client's record as soon as possible after a therapy session, and sign and date the entry. If you are keeping client notes in a computer, it is essential that your program has a time and date stamp so that if your records are subpoenaed there will be no question of adding or deleting material at a later date.

The content and style of a client's records are often determined by agency or institutional policy, state counselor licensing laws, or directives from other regulatory bodies. The particular setting and the therapist's preference may determine how detailed the records will be. Riemersma (2000) states that there are no hard and fast rules as to the contents of records. She does add that therapists are advised to keep records in such a manner that the records could hold up to scrutiny if challenged.

Record Keeping for Managed Care Programs

Most states and agencies require clinicians to keep records. In addition, this is a requirement of managed care programs, and practitioners have to learn how to write and maintain notes about their client's progress. A managed care program may audit a practitioner's reports at any time. By law, managed care practitioners are required to keep accurate charts and notes and must provide this information to authorized chart reviewers. Ideally, good record-keeping practices will help practitioners provide quality service to their clients.

Although there is no specific legal statute that establishes the content of mental health records, the law describes the minimum information that these records must contain, which includes the following: client-identifying information; client's chief complaints, including pertinent history; objective findings from the most recent physical examination; intake sheet; documentation of referrals to other providers, when appropriate; findings from consultations and referrals to other health care workers; pertinent reports of diagnostic procedures and tests; signed informed consent for treatment form; diagnosis, when determined; prognosis, including significant continuing problems or conditions; the existence of treatment plans, containing specific target problems and goals; signed and dated progress notes; types of services provided; precise times and dates of appointments made and kept; termination summary; the use and completion of a discharge summary; and release of information obtained (Canter et al., 1994; Grosso, 2002). A managed care company may demand a refund for services rendered when the records do not contain a complete description of all the services rendered.

Special Issues for School Counselors

In some counseling settings, it may be difficult to keep up with record keeping. For example, in school counseling a student-to-counselor ratio of 400-to-1 (or more) is not uncommon. How realistic is it to expect a school counselor to be able to keep detailed notes on every contact with a student? Birdsall and Hubert (2000) indicate that a well-kept record may be useful to demonstrate that the quality of counseling provided was in line with an acceptable standard of care. Keeping records is particularly important in cases involving moderate to severe social or emotional problems. Maintaining records on parent contacts is also essential. School counselors are also cautioned on the importance of safeguarding the confidentiality of any records they keep.

The *Ethical Standards for School Counselors* (ASCA, 2004) addresses the issue of recording keeping on students:

> The professional school counselor:
>
> (a) Maintains and secures records necessary for rendering professional services to the student as required by laws, regulations, institutional procedures and confidentiality guidelines.
>
> (b) Keeps sole-possession of records separate from students' educational records in keeping with state laws. (A.8.)

School counselors need to be concerned about both administrative and clinical records. Administrative records are the cumulative files on students that are available to other school personnel. Clinical records are the case notes documenting important events regarding a counseling relationship with a student (Remley & Hermann, 2000). At times, school counselors may need to educate teachers about what to enter into a student's cumulative folder. One of our colleagues reports that he had to ask teachers to rewrite their observational reports to remove judgmental terms such as "lazy" or "bully." School records are open for parents to review, and it is essential to refrain from making negative comments concerning parents in administrative records. These records also follow the students to other schools and can provide slanted opinions. All school staff and counselors need to stick to the facts and limit their personal judgments (John Tweton, personal communication, April 2, 2001).

School counselors need to understand the provisions of the Family Educational Rights and Privacy Act of 1974. This federal law requires that schools receiving federal funds provide access to all school records to parents of students under the age of 18 and to students themselves once they reach 18. This law outlines a method for releasing records to clients. Student records are not to be released to third parties without the written consent of parents of minors, or the written consent of adult students (Remley & Hermann, 2000).

Securing Records Now and in the Future

Clients' records must be handled confidentially. ACA's (2005) *Code of Ethics* provides guidelines for storing, transferring, sharing, and disposing of clinical records (see Section B.6.). Counselors have the responsibility for storing client records in a secure place and exercising care when sending records to others by mail or through electronic means.

Remember that the information in the client's record belongs to the client, and a copy may be requested at any time. It is mandatory to treat a client in an honest and non-demeaning fashion, and it is also expected that records will be kept in an accurate and respectful manner. Mental health practitioners bear the ultimate responsibility for what they write, how they store and access records, what they do with these records, and when and how they destroy them (Nagy, 2005). Clinicians are ethically and legally required to keep records in a secure manner and to protect client confidentiality. They are also responsible for taking reasonable steps to establish and maintain the confidentiality of information based on their own delivery of services, or the services provided by others working under their supervision.

Depending on one's place of practice and the types of records kept, clients' records must be maintained for the period of time required by relevant federal, state, and local laws. Organization policy often prescribes guidelines for maintaining records, including a time frame. Practitioners need to consider relevant laws and the policies of the work setting in determining how long to retain a client's records. Behnke, Preis, and Bates (1998) recommend the practice of keeping records as long it is reasonably possible. They suggest retaining records for a period of 10 years following termination of treatment, and 10 years after a minor client has turned 21. They also recommend keeping a brief summary of a client's treatment once the client's complete records are destroyed. Moline, Williams, and Austin (1998) state that how long records need to be retained is a matter of state law. Because regulations vary from state to state, Moline and her colleagues advise practitioners to find out the specific time period for retention of records that is required by the jurisdiction in which they practice.

Whether records are active or inactive, counselors are expected to maintain and store them safely and in a way in which timely retrieval is possible. Extra care should be taken if information is stored on computer disks. Failure to maintain adequate client records could be the basis of a malpractice claim because it breaches the standard of care expected of a mental health professional (Anderson, 1996).

It is wise to think about what will happen to your clinical records after your death or if you are otherwise incapacitated. The law does not specify how records are to be handled upon a therapist's death, but Riemersma (2000) suggests that you give thought to how you expect your records to be handled before it is too late for you to be involved in the decision making. Here are some questions to consider:

- Who will have access to your records in the event of your death?
- Should your clients be given an opportunity to obtain their records, or should they be given the opportunity to have their records transferred to another therapist?
- Should the records be placed in the custody of another health care professional with the clients so notified?

- Should the records be destroyed immediately, with or without giving your clients the opportunity to retrieve the records?
- Do you have a therapist in the community who is willing to take over your practice in the case of your death?

It is important to find answers to these questions if you want to safeguard your estate, for a client can bring suit against your estate after your death. Even death does not shield us from a malpractice suit!

Ethical Issues in Online Counseling

In this section we consider a few of the key ethical issues in the use of online counseling and the many forms of service delivery via the Internet. **Behavioral telehealth,** electronic consultation between consumers and mental health providers, is now part of the counseling literature. This rapidly developing field involves both potential benefits and risks, and just as with any new practice area, practitioners have a primary duty to consider the best interests of the client, to strive to do no harm, and to adhere to legal requirements (Koocher & Morray, 2000). Ultimately, it is the responsibility of mental health professionals to examine the ethical, legal, and clinical issues related to the use of technology (Maheu & Gordon, 2000).

VandenBos and Williams (2000) agree that mental health professionals must make decisions about how they wish to incorporate delivery of services via the Internet into their practices, but they also maintain that professional associations should develop standards for these services. Likewise, Sampson, Kolodinksy, and Greeno (1997) take the position that it is the responsibility of the professional associations to evaluate and revise their ethical standards to maximize the benefits and minimize the limitations of using online counseling: "The counseling profession cannot afford to wait until the information highway is fully operational to decide how to best use this technology" (p. 211). We agree with these writers who call upon the professional organizations to exert their influence in designing effective guidelines for online counseling and other forms of behavioral telehealth.

The *Code of Ethics of the American Mental Health Counselors Association* (AMHCA, 2000) includes guidelines for Internet online counseling that address issues pertaining to confidentiality, client and counselor identification, client waiver, establishing the online counseling relationship, competence, and legal considerations. The APA (2002) ethics code states that psychologists who offer services via electronic transmission inform clients/patients of the risks to privacy and limits of confidentiality (4.02). The Canadian Counselling Association (CCA, 1999) offers this guideline pertaining to the use of technology:

> Counsellors recognize that their ethical responsibilities are not altered, or in any way diminished, by the use of technology for the administration of evaluation and assessment instruments. Counsellors retain their responsibility for the maintenance of the ethical principles of privacy, confidentiality, and responsibility for decisions regardless of the technology used. (D.5.)

The ACA (2005) ethics code states that counselors are expected to inform clients of the benefits and limitations of using technology in the counseling process (A.12.a).

Ritterband and colleagues (2003) indicate that ethical and legal issues must be addressed when using Internet interventions, including privacy, confidentiality, data validity, credentials of professionals using these interventions, potential misuse of Internet interventions, and equality of Internet access.

Advantages and Disadvantages of Counseling via the Internet

Most experts agree that what is being currently offered via Internet counseling cannot be considered traditional psychotherapy, yet many think this form of service delivery may have possibilities for consumers who are reluctant to seek more traditional treatment (Rabasca, 2000a). On this point, Chang and Yeh (2003) speak to the issue of traditional psychotherapy and Asian American men, contending that this population tends to underutilize mental health services. Chang and Yeh point out that this fact reflects more the inadequacies of traditional psychotherapy than the absence of need in this population. They suggest that online groups enable men to be less constrained by masculine stereotypes by offering a more anonymous context for expressing their emotions and personal concerns.

Ritterband and colleagues (2003) show that the provision of health care over the Internet is rapidly evolving and that it provides a potentially beneficial means of delivering treatment that may be unobtainable otherwise. They indicate that the benefits of using Internet interventions are vast because of the potential for greater numbers of people to receive services. Ritterband and colleagues write that Web-based treatment interventions offer an opportunity for practitioners to provide specific behavioral treatments that are tailored to individuals who may need to seek professional assistance from their own homes. However, they also indicate that Internet interventions must first demonstrate feasibility and efficacy through rigorous scientific testing.

There are advantages and disadvantages in using Internet technology to deliver counseling services. Riemersma and Leslie (1999) suggest these advantages for consumers of Internet counseling:

- Some consumers want brief, convenient, and anonymous therapy service.
- Some clients may be reached by online counseling who would not be willing to participate in traditional therapy.
- For persons with physical disabilities, online services are more accessible.
- This form of counseling is suited to a problem-solving approach, which appeals to many consumers.
- Clients who experience anxiety when talking face-to-face with a therapist, or clients who are extremely shy, may feel more comfortable dealing with their problems by means of a computer.

In addition, Sampson, Kolodinsky, and Greeno (1997) identify some benefits to therapists who deliver counseling services online:

- Access to clients in rural areas
- Facilitates assigning, completing, and assessing client homework
- Enhances record keeping
- Expands the pool of referral services
- Increases flexibility in scheduling
- Increases options for supervision and case conferencing
- Enhances collection of research data

Freeny (2001) has learned from his practice that online therapy presents a number of therapeutic and ethical concerns, especially with clients in crisis. He underscores the dilemmas clinicians face between honoring the client's desire for anonymity and a therapist's clinical need to be able to respond in an appropriate and timely manner in crisis situations. There are ethical problems involved in using online counseling to deal with a serious crisis, a psychotic individual, or even someone who needs more than a behavioral intervention. According to Freeny, another disadvantage is that insurance companies have not recognized online counseling for reimbursement. Freeny admits that there will be errors as electronic therapy develops, yet he maintains that the risks are worth taking.

Simply having a technology available does not mean that it is appropriate for every client, or perhaps for any client. The potential benefits need to be greater than the potential risks for clients to ethically justify any form of technology that is used for counseling purposes. Here are some of the disadvantages we see:

- Inaccurate diagnosis or ineffective treatment may be provided due to lack of behavioral clues.
- Confidentiality and privacy cannot be guaranteed.
- Therapists' duty to warn or protect others is restricted.
- Clients who are suicidal, suffering extreme anxiety or depression, or who are in crisis do not receive adequate immediate attention.
- Anonymity enables minors to masquerade as adults seeking treatment.
- Transference and countertransference issues are difficult to address.
- Complex long-term psychological problems are not likely to be successfully treated.

Legal Issues and Regulation of Online Counseling

Because providing counseling services over the Internet is relatively new and controversial, a host of legal questions will not be addressed until lawsuits are filed pertaining to its use, or misuse, in counseling practice. Foxhall (2000) states that the most pressing issue regarding behavioral telehealth or Internet counseling is whether it is legal for a mental health practitioner who is licensed in one state to treat a client in another state by telephone or over the Internet. In addition, if therapists do not know where the client is, how can they call for help in the case of an emergency? If a malpractice suit should take place, which state would have jurisdiction? These are some of the thorny problems raised by online counseling.

No state legislature has yet addressed Internet counseling, although some states have begun restricting physician practice across state lines (Foxhall, 2000). Riemersma and Leslie (1999) point out that, under California law, licensed mental health professionals are not prohibited from providing professional services over the Internet or by other technological means, and they are not aware of any malpractice lawsuits involving Internet counseling. However, it is a mistake to conclude that the use of services over the Internet is risk free. Riemersma and Leslie write that therapists who choose to offer professional services over the Internet will have to give careful thought to ways of limiting their legal liability and to reducing potential harm to their clients.

Competent Counseling Online

Practitioners need to consider their level of competence in delivering services over the Internet, determine what kinds of services they can and cannot appropriately offer, and assess the benefits and risks of this form of service delivery. Therapists who choose to counsel clients online should acquire special training regarding counseling via the Internet.

Riemersma and Leslie (1999) recommend that therapists address these issues specific to the online counseling environment:

- Evaluate and diagnose a client at the beginning of treatment, ideally through an initial face-to-face session, to determine whether the client is a good candidate for online counseling.
- Require the client to be evaluated by a physician to rule out a physical cause for the client's psychological problem prior to initiating Internet counseling.
- Fully inform the client of the limits and expectations of the online relationship.
- Develop a plan for how emergencies will be dealt with.
- Address with the client, in advance, the limitations involved in confidentiality over the Internet and discuss what actions might be taken in the event that confidentiality is compromised.
- Discuss with the client, in advance, how situations involving technological failure will be handled.

Behavioral health care professionals are using a wide variety of Internet technologies to deliver counseling and therapy, including e-mail. However, neither the appropriateness nor the efficacy of using e-mail for clinical interventions has been proven by empirical research (Rabasca, 2000a). This absence of research data makes it impossible to objectively evaluate the benefits and the efficacy of using e-mail as a clinical intervention (Maheu & Gordon, 2000). Freeny (2001) contends that practitioners who offer online services should be technically competent enough to coach clients on ways to make sure communications are secure and private.

The matter of competence and appropriateness of services is more complex than meets the eye. Ritterband and colleagues (2003) state that "developing Internet interventions is an arduous, sometimes tedious, and always time-intensive process" (p. 530). They describe the following steps involved in developing Internet interventions:

- Identify problem areas
- Ascertain effectiveness of established treatment
- Consider legal and ethical issues
- Transform treatment elements using engaging Internet components
- Personalize intervention by identifying elements that can be tailored
- Incorporate feedback as a measure of treatment success
- Construct Internet program
- Test Internet program

According to Ritterband and colleagues, the use of the Internet is likely to grow in importance as a powerful dimension of successful psychobehavioral treatment. In forecasting future directions, they write:

> It is unlikely that Internet interventions will replace face-to-face psychotherapy: however, this technology may be helpful in the treatment of some psychological problems that might otherwise go untreated. It is also possible that such interventions may enhance traditional therapy as an adjunctive component. (p. 533)

Our Perspective on Online Counseling

Therapists do not have to choose between Internet counseling and traditional face-to-face counseling. Technology can be used in the service of clients and can address some unique needs, especially if therapists combine online and personal sessions. For example, therapists might require three to six face-to-face sessions to determine the client's suitability for online counseling and to establish a working therapeutic relationship. This will increase the likelihood that online services will be effective. During these face-to-face sessions, time could be allocated for orienting the client to the counseling process and securing informed consent, taking the client's history, conducting an assessment and formulating a diagnostic impression, collaboratively identifying counseling goals, developing a general treatment plan, and formulating a specific plan of action. As the action plan is carried out following these initial sessions, Internet sessions could be used to monitor specific homework assignments. Depending on the client's needs and situation, there might be face-to-face sessions scheduled at regular intervals along with online counseling. Integrating traditional counseling with online counseling in this way can accommodate consumers who would not take advantage of counseling delivered exclusively by face-to-face sessions due to financial considerations or restrictions imposed by traveling long distances.

From our perspective, counseling services restricted to e-mail or online technology have limitations. We have reservations about the effectiveness of online counseling for clients with deeply personal concerns or interpersonal issues. Most clinical problems involve a complexity of variables that require human-to-human interaction. At the present time, we do not think online counseling should be used as an exclusive or primary means of delivering services, but it can have value if it is used as a supplement to face-to-face counseling.

Some fields of counseling seem better suited for online work than others. For example, career counseling and educational counseling involve gathering information and processing this information. In this endeavor, technology may have some useful applications. Graduate training and continuing education in appropriate technological applications for professional practice are needed (McMinn et al., 1999).

Freeny (2001) contends that online counseling "will soon explode into modern clinical treatment, and therapists must have the courage to face up to its implications" (p. 70). As with any kind of counseling, online counseling needs to be done ethically, legally, and competently. If you were to make online counseling part of your practice, what ethical considerations might you be faced with? What are the challenges that you think most need to be addressed in this area? Regardless of the kind of technology employed, it is our hope that therapists will always use it as a means to the end of enhancing clients' goals rather than as an end in itself.

Working With Children and Adolescents

Consistent with the increasing concern over the rights of children in general, more attention is being paid to issues such as the minor's right of informed consent. Here are some of the legal and ethical questions faced by human service providers who work with children and adolescents:

- Can minors consent to treatment without parental knowledge and parental consent?
- To what degree should minors be allowed to participate in setting the goals of therapy and in providing consent to undergo it?
- What are the limits of confidentiality in counseling with minors?
- What does informed consent consist of in working with minors?

We will consider some of these questions in this section and focus on the rights of children when they are clients.

The Right to Treatment

The parent's right to information about his or her child is different from a right to have access to a child's records. The general rule is that a parent is entitled to general information from the counselor about the child's progress in counseling. In most states, for a minor to enter into a counseling relationship, it is necessary to have informed parental or guardian consent or for counseling to be court ordered (Lawrence & Kurpius, 2000). However, there are exceptions to this general rule. Informed consent of parents or guardians may not be legally required when a minor is seeking counseling for dangerous drugs or narcotics, for sexually transmitted diseases, for pregnancy and birth control, or for an examination following alleged sexual assault of a minor over 12 years of age (Lawrence & Kurpius, 2000). The justification for allowing children and adolescents access to treatment without parental consent is that some minors might not otherwise seek needed treatment. Some children and adolescents who seek help when given independent access might not do so without the guarantee of privacy.

In the case of school counselors, it is not necessary to obtain parental consent unless a state statute requires this. Many schools have a student handbook, a part of which typically describes information about counseling services available to students. This handbook is often sent to parents at the beginning of a school year as a way to provide them with school rules and policies, as well as general information about various services offered by the school. In the section on counseling, some handbooks give examples of individual and group counseling activities. For example, counseling sessions may focus on themes such as improving study habits, time management, making good choices, substance abuse prevention, anger management, career development, and other personal or social concerns. At the end of a handbook, there is typically a page that asks for parents' signatures indicating their consent for their children to use services provided by the school. Such a procedure is a means of securing blanket consent. At times, specific approval may be required if children want to participate in special counseling (such as a children of divorce group). If parents have questions about any counseling activities, they could be given the name of a person to contact at the school. If they do not want their children to receive any kind of counseling, this could be indicated at the end of the handbook on the signature page. Remley and Herlihy (2005) suggest that parents who object to their child's participation in counseling probably have a legal right to do so.

Counselors faced with the issue of when to accept minors as clients without parental consent must consider various factors. Is the parent or the child the primary client? What is the competence level of the minor? What are the potential risks and consequences if treatment is denied? What are the chances that the minor will not seek help or will not be able to secure parental permission for needed help? How serious is the problem? What are the laws pertaining to providing therapy for minors without parental consent? If practitioners need to make decisions about accepting minors without parental consent, they should know the relevant statutes in their state. They would also be wise to consult with other professionals in assessing the ethical issues involved in each case.

A detailed account of factors to consider in the informed consent process in working with children and adolescents is included in the box titled Sample Informed Consent Document. Although this sample form is quite lengthy, you may find it useful to refer to as a template when developing your own informed consent document.

Informed Consent of Minors

Minors are not always able to give informed consent. On this matter the guideline provided by the APA (2002) is as follows:

> For persons who are legally incapable of giving informed consent, psychologists nevertheless (1) provide an appropriate explanation, (2) seek the individual's assent, (3) consider such persons' preferences and best interests, and (4) obtain appropriate permission from a legally authorized person, if such substitute consent is permitted or required by law. When consent by a legally authorized person is not permitted or required by law, psychologists take reasonable steps to protect the individual's rights and welfare. (3.10.b.)

Sample Informed Consent Document

Informed Consent Regarding Out-Patient Child or Adolescent Psychotherapy

Kim Vander Dussen, Psy. D., Clinical Psychologist

California law requires that parents or legal guardians of clients be provided with information to allow them to make informed decisions regarding their child's participation in psychotherapy. This document provides information on risks and benefits of psychotherapy, medical concerns, assessment, the need for children and adolescents to have confidential psychotherapy, collateral contacts, treating children of separated or divorced families, professional records, confidentiality from third parties, evaluating the accuracy of children's disclosures and memory, implications of knowledge of children's disclosures and memory for psychotherapy and related legal issues, alternative treatments, diagnoses, treatment plan, length of treatment, psychotherapy fees, cancellations, and emergencies. Please read this information carefully. Ask your therapist any questions you may have. As these issues are understood, please initial in the places provided.

Initial here if this section has been read and understood_____

Background of Clinician

I am a licensed psychologist, licensed by the California Board of Psychology. I have a Doctorate in Clinical Psychology, a Master's of Arts in Clinical Psychology, a Bachelor of Science in Human Services, and a Bachelor of Arts in Psychology. I have had a great deal of training and supervision in play therapy as well as training in art therapy and sandtray/sandplay therapy. I am a Registered Play Therapist Supervisor and am also enrolled in a certificate program for Infant and Toddler Mental Health. I have experience working with individual adults, groups, families, and children. I am not certified or qualified to practice biofeedback, neurofeedback, or EMDR.

Risks and Benefits of Psychotherapy

Most children receiving psychotherapy are experiencing psychological problems that cause internal distress and/or problems in relationships. The goal of psychotherapy is reduction of such problems. However, some individuals experience an exacerbation of problems or different problems in the course of psychotherapy.

These problems can include increases in anxiety, depression, sadness, sleep disturbances, eliminatory disorders, intrusive thoughts, flashbacks, self-destructive or angry impulses, behavior problems, social problems, academic problems, suicidality, and problems in family relationships. Hospital care or residential treatment may be necessary.

Children in psychotherapy benefit from having a support system, including family, friends, a supportive school environment, and in some cases, religious affiliations. Expressive activities, such as play, art, writing, music, exercise, are also important for the mental health of children. Other treatment modalities such as family therapy, group therapy, 12-step groups, support groups, and medication may be helpful. Referrals can be provided to help develop a support system at your request.

In most cases, therapy eventually improves a child's sense of well-being and one's relationships. In some cases, children obtain little or no benefit from therapy, or become worse. It is not always possible to predict the outcome for an individual. Given this knowledge, the decisions to begin, continue, or terminate therapy for your child generally belong to a child's parents. In some cases, the decision is that of the child at a certain age, such as in cases involving issues of child abuse, sexual assault, substance abuse, birth control, pregnancy, sexually transmitted diseases, and severe psychological need. These decisions may be evaluated with one's therapist. Clients may also obtain independent consultation for a second opinion at any time.

continued on next page

It is also important to consider that if a genuine mental health issue is present, and psychotherapy is recommended, but not pursued, that a child may experience a worsening of symptoms and decrease in overall functioning.

Initial here if this section has been read and understood ______

Medical Concerns

Your child's psychotherapist is not a medical doctor and can therefore not recognize or diagnose medical conditions. It is essential that you obtain a medical examination for your child to determine any medical origins of your psychological problems, e.g., neurological disorders, endocrinological abnormalities, glucose and insulin imbalances, effects of toxins, infectious disease, gastrointestinal disorders, side effects of medication, etc.

Not being a medical doctor, your child's psychotherapist cannot prescribe psychiatric medication but will refer you for psychiatric consultation if this appears to be indicated.

Initial here if this section has been read and understood _______

Assessment

Psychotherapists must conduct both an initial and ongoing assessment of children to understand their psychological needs. It is essential that you cooperate with this assessment process by completing all forms, questionnaires, and psychological tests provided to you and by meeting with your child's therapist, with or without your child present, as your child's therapist indicates. Please be completely open and honest with your child's therapist about all influences that may be affecting your child, even if doing so is painful or embarrassing. Therapists usually cannot tell when parents or children deliberately conceal things. Therapists can only help children with problems to the extent that they are provided with the whole truth.

Initial here if this section has been read and understood _______

The Need for Children and Adolescents to Have Confidential Psychotherapy

As a parent or guardian of a child receiving psychotherapy, your child's psychotherapist will involve you in helping your child to the fullest extent possible. However, the content of your child's sessions must be confidential in order to enable your child to confide in his or her therapist and for therapy to be effective.

In treatment of adolescents, there are many issues that therapists have no opportunity to address unless adolescents trust that communication in therapy will not be shared with parents or guardians. These issues include use of cigarettes, alcohol, and drugs, sexual concerns or behavior, involvement in gangs, cutting classes or truancy, school failure, unauthorized time with peers, and criminal activity. Your adolescent's therapist will work to help him or her behave in ways that are not self-destructive, that do not limit his or her options for the future, and that are considerate of others. If any of these issues rise to the level of serious, imminent danger to self or to others, parents and/or appropriate authorities will be notified.

Initial here if this section has been read and understood _______

Collateral Contact With Parents and Others

Your contract with your child's psychotherapist is collateral, that is, auxiliary to your child's treatment for the purpose of assisting in your child's treatment. Your child's therapist is not treating you and has no therapeutic obligation to you. Therefore, your communication with your child's psychotherapist is not privileged or confidential. Your child's therapist will provide you with psychotherapy referrals if you request such referrals or if he or she believes that therapy would better help you help your child.

Initial here if this section has been read and understood _______

continued on next page

Treating Children of Separated or Divorced Parents

In families of separation and divorce, children's psychotherapists work to help them cope adaptively with the forces acting upon their lives. Treating children in these contexts is difficult because:

1. Both parents usually have different views of the forces acting upon the child and the child's needs.
2. Parents' views may be affected by their own psychological experiences, issues, and needs.
3. Both parents usually fear that the child's psychotherapist will side with the other parent.
4. Both parents usually fear that the child's psychotherapist will make custody or visitation recommendations that are not in the best interest of the child or parent.

For these reasons, your child's psychotherapist has instituted the following policies in treating children of separated or divorced parents who share legal custody.

1. Both parents must consent to treatment, ideally before the first session with the child, or shortly thereafter.
2. Both parents will be offered "equal time" in face-to-face or phone contacts as much as realistically possible, unless this is contraindicated, such as cases in which the therapist judges that contact with one or both parents might negatively affect the child (e.g., if there is a concern related to parental abuse or threats to the child).
3. Your child's therapist will not communicate with attorneys for either parent or guardian.
4. Any information provided by one parent may be shared with the other parent by the child's therapist.
5. Your child's psychotherapist will not provide custody or visitation recommendations to the court, mediator, and/or psychologist conducting a family psychological evaluation. If the child has a court representative (attorney, guardian ad litem, or other advocate) or if requested by both parents or ordered by the court, your child's therapist may discuss observations about the child with these parties.

These policies may not apply when a parent resides out of the area or is incarcerated, when parent-child contact is limited by a court (Juvenile, Family, or Guardianship) or court representative (i.e., County Services Agency social worker), when there is substantial evidence that a parent might be physically or psychologically harming or damage the therapeutic relationship, or when a parent fails to respond to the therapist's attempts to establish contact with that parent.

Initial here if this section has been read and understood ________

Confidentiality From Third Parties (Other Than Parents)

Psychotherapy is confidential from parties other than parents with important exceptions:

1. Information may be released to designated parties by written authorization of clients, parents, or legal guardians.
2. When parents seek reimbursement for psychotherapy from insurance companies or other third parties, information, including psychological diagnoses, and in many cases, explanations of symptoms and treatment plans, and in rare cases, entire client records, must be provided to the third party. If health coverage is provided by the parent's employer, the employer may have access to such information. Insurance companies usually claim to keep psychological diagnoses confidential, but may enter this information into national medical information databanks, where it may be accessed by employers, other insurance companies, etc., and may limit future access to disability insurance, life insurance, jobs, etc. Your child's therapist will provide you with copies of reports submitted to insurance companies at your request.

continued on next page

3. Psychotherapists are required to release information obtained from children or from collateral sources (other individuals involved in a client's psychotherapy, such as parents, guardians, spouses) to appropriate authorities to the extent to which such disclosure may help to avert danger to a psychotherapy client or to others, e.g., imminent risk of suicide, homicide, or destruction of property that could endanger others.
4. Psychotherapists are required to report suspected past or present abuse or neglect of children, adults, and elders, including children being exposed to domestic violence, to the authorities, including Child Protection and law enforcement, based on information provided by the client or collateral sources.
5. If children participate in psychotherapy in compliance with a court order, psychotherapists are required to release information to the relevant court, social service, or probation departments.
6. Your child's psychotherapist must release information, which may include all notes on your child's psychotherapy and contact with collateral sources, in response to a court order, and may also be required to do so in response to a legitimate subpoena.
7. Psychotherapists often consult with other professionals on cases, and teach or write about the psychotherapy process, but disguise identifying information when doing so. Please indicate to your therapist if you wish to place restrictions on consultation, teaching, or writing related to your case.
8. Psychotherapists reserve the right to release financial information to a collection agency, attorney, or small claims court, if you are delinquent in paying your bill.
9. Cell phone and e-mail communication can be intercepted by third parties. These forms of communication are reserved for urgent or time-sensitive matters. Psychotherapists are required to make a record of each client contact. E-mail communications are printed in full and become part of a client's file.

Initial here if this section has been read and understood _______

Professional Records

Psychotherapy laws and ethics require that California licensed psychotherapists keep treatment records. Professional records can be misinterpreted and/or upsetting to untrained readers. Your child and you are entitled to receive a copy of these records unless your therapist believes that seeing them would be emotionally damaging to you or your child, in which case your therapist will review them together with your child or with you or will send them to a mental health professional of your choice, to allow you or your child to discuss the contents. Clients will be charged copying costs plus $2.00 a minute for professional time spent responding to information requests.

Your child's record includes a copy of the signed informed consent form, acknowledgement of receipt of privacy policy and practices, progress notes, any release of protected health information, and copies of your superbill. Records are kept in a locked file cabinet.

Initial here if this section has been read and understood _______

Alternative Treatments

Other treatment approaches are available as an alternative, or as an adjunct, to individual child psychotherapy. These include family therapy, group therapy, 12-step groups and support groups, medication, expressive therapies (e.g., art, writing, psychodrama), cognitive therapy, behavior modification, guided imagery, Eye Movement Desensitization and Reprocessing (EMDR), Accelerated Information Processing (AIP), Traumatic Incident Reduction (TIR), Electroencephalograph (EEG) Spectrum Therapy, careful use of hypnosis and guided imagery, and nutritional consultation.

Initial here if this section has been read and understood _______

continued on next page

Fee for Psychotherapy

Psychotherapy sessions and collateral contacts: $______ per 45–50 minutes, including any time missed by being late. Payment is due at each session.
Phone calls exceeding 10 minutes once a week: $4.00 per minute.
Letters and reports: $____ per hour.
Attendance and Participation in school IEP meeting. ____ per hour. Travel time is charged at hourly rate as well, but adjusted if travel is less than one hour.

I understand that payment is due at the end of each session. I agree to cooperate with procedures required to collect third-party payments. If I receive a third-party payment, I agree to turn it over to my therapist as soon as possible.

Initial here if this section has been read and understood _______

Cancellations

I understand that my child's psychotherapist reserves an appointment time for my child. I agree to call 24 hours in advance if I must cancel a session in order to allow my child's therapist to reschedule his or her time. If I provide less than 24 hours notice of a cancellation, unless a sudden medical emergency has occurred, I will pay the regular session fee of $_____.

Initial here if this section has been read and understood _______

Emergencies

I may telephone my child's therapist in an emergency. My child's therapist is not always immediately available by phone and may not be available in the late evening. If unavailable, my therapist will return my call as soon as possible. If I cannot reach my therapist, I can call the 24-hour Crisis Team at __________. When my child's therapist is out of town, and if I am not also seeing another mental health professional, such as a psychiatrist, my child's therapist will provide me with phone numbers of alternate sources of help.

Initial here if this section has been read and understood _______

Psychotherapy Contract for Parents or Guardians of Child Clients

I have read the above information, have asked questions as needed, and understand the issues related to risks and benefits of psychotherapy, medical concerns, assessment, the need for children and adolescents to have confidential psychotherapy, collateral contacts with parents and others, treating children of separated or divorced families, professional records, confidentiality from third parties, evaluating the accuracy of children's disclosures and memory, implications of knowledge of children's disclosures and memory for psychotherapy and related legal issues, alternative treatments, my child's diagnoses and treatment plan, length of psychotherapy, fee for psychotherapy, emergencies, and cancellations.

If you have any questions and complaints regarding the practice of your therapy, you may contact the appropriate governing board. Contact the Board of Psychology at 800-633-2322 or (916) 263-2699, 1422 Howe Avenue, Suite 22, Sacramento CA 95825-3236.

Initial here if this section has been read and understood _______

Length of Psychotherapy

Some psychological problems in children can be alleviated in a few sessions. Other problems require years of treatment. It is often difficult to predict the length of therapy needed. Some disorders cannot be properly treated within the limitations of some health insurance policies. Generally, hospitalization should be as brief as possible to limit disruptions to a child's life.

continued on next page

The decision to terminate therapy belongs to the parent or legal guardian, except in cases in which the decision is that of the child at a certain age, e.g., cases involving issues of child abuse, substance abuse, birth control, pregnancy, and severe need.

Terminating therapy with a child should be done over a number of sessions, particularly in cases of a long-term therapeutic relationship. Should you or your child decide to terminate therapy prior to the child's therapist's recommendation, it is important that your child have a final meeting with his or her therapist.

If your child's therapist believes you are terminating your child's therapy before adequate treatment has been received for your child's psychological problems, your child's therapist will provide you with referrals for other therapists or you may choose to continue therapy with your current therapist.

Some managed health care plans provide benefits for only a time-limited course of psychotherapy. Some companies have contracts with therapists that prohibit clients to remain in therapy with a therapist beyond the designated time-frame. If your therapist believes your child needs further psychotherapy after this period, your therapist will provide referrals to other therapists with whom your child can continue treatment.

Initial here if this section has been read and understood _______

I agree to treatment for my child based on my informed wish to proceed.

Print Name	Signature	Relationship to the Child	Date
Client Name	Signature		Date
Kim Vander Dussen, Psy. D.			Date

The ACA (2005) also addresses this topic:

> When counseling minors or persons unable to give voluntary consent, counselors seek the assent of clients to services, and include them in decision-making as appropriate. Counselors recognize the need to balance the rights of clients to make choices, their capacity to give consent or assent to receive services, and parental or familial legal rights and responsibilities to protect these clients and make decisions on their behalf. (A.2.d.)

Lawrence and Kurpius (2000) recommend that, whenever possible, counselors involve the parents in the initial meeting with their child to arrive at a clear, mutual agreement regarding the nature and extent of information that will be provided to them. This policy makes it possible to create clear boundaries for sharing information and establishes a three-way bond of trust. Lawrence and Kurpius state: "Involving the parents in the creation of mutually agreed upon guidelines for disclosure and motivating the minor client to disclose on his or her own are two positive strategies that benefit the parents and the client and protect the counselor" (p. 134). To work effectively with a minor it is often necessary to involve the parents in the treatment process. The *Ethical*

Standards for School Counselors (ASCA, 2004) addresses the matter of responsibilities to parents:

> The professional school counselor respects the rights and responsibilities of parents/guardians for their children and endeavors to establish, as appropriate, a collaborative relationship with parents/guardians to facilitate the student's maximum development. (B.1.a.)

According to Benitez (2004), counselors who work with minors are frequently challenged in balancing the minor's need for confidentiality and parents' desires for information about the minor's counseling. Benitez claims that it is a wise policy for practitioners to make it clear to parents of minors that effective counseling requires a sense of trust in the therapist. A therapist who works with minors can inform parents that information will be shared, as he or she deems it appropriate.

Although minor clients have an *ethical* right to privacy and confidentiality in the counseling relationship, the law still favors the rights of parents over their children. Parents and guardians usually have a *legal* right to information pertaining to counseling sessions with their children, although a court may hold otherwise due to specific state statutes (Remley & Herlihy, 2005). In cases when parents or legal guardians become involved in the counseling process, counselors must acknowledge that these adults have authority over minors (Remley & Hermann, 2000). However, from an *ethical* perspective, therapists who work with children and adolescents have the responsibility to provide information that will help minor clients become active participants in their treatment. It is a good policy to provide minors with treatment alternatives and to enlist their participation in defining goals for their therapy. There are both ethical and therapeutic reasons for involving minors in their treatment. By giving them the maximum degree of autonomy within the therapeutic relationship, the therapist demonstrates respect for them. Also, it is likely that therapeutic change is promoted by informing children about the process and enlisting their involvement in it.

If children lack the background to weigh risks and benefits and if they cannot give complete informed consent, therapists should still attempt to provide some understanding of the therapy process. If formal consent cannot be obtained, then even partial understanding is better than proceeding with therapy without any attempt to explain the goals and procedures of the process (Margolin, 1982).

At this point we suggest that you think about some of the legal and ethical considerations in providing counseling for minors.

- Many parents argue that they have a right to know about matters that pertain to their adolescent daughters and sons. They assert, for example, that parents have a right to be involved in decisions about abortion. What is your position?
- If the state in which you practice has a law requiring parental consent for abortion, how would this influence your interventions with minors who were considering an abortion?

- Some people argue for the right of minors to seek therapy without parental knowledge or consent because needed treatment might not be given to them otherwise. When, if at all, would you counsel a minor without parental knowledge and consent?
- What kinds of information should be provided to children and adolescents before they enter a therapeutic relationship?
- If therapists do not provide minors with the information necessary to make informed choices, are they acting unethically? Why or why not?

Counseling Reluctant Children and Adolescents

Some young people simply resent not having a choice about entering a therapeutic relationship. Adolescents often resist therapy because they become the "identified patient" and the focus is on changing them. These adolescents are frequently aware that they are only *part* of the problem in the family unit. Although many minors indicate a desire to participate in treatment decisions, few are given the opportunity to become involved in a systematic way. The message here is that resistance to therapy can at least be minimized if therapists are willing to openly and nondefensively explore the reasons behind this resistance.

The Case of Frank. Frank was expelled from high school for getting explosively angry at a teacher who, according to Frank, had humiliated him in front of his class. Frank was told that he would not be readmitted to school unless he sought professional help. His mother called a therapist and explained the situation to her, and the therapist agreed to see him. Although Frank was uncomfortable and embarrassed over having to see a therapist, he was nevertheless willing to talk. He told the therapist that he knew he had done wrong by lashing out angrily at the teacher but that the teacher had provoked him. He said that although he was usually good about keeping his feelings inside, this time he had "just lost it."

After a few sessions, the therapist determined that there were many problems in Frank's family. He lived with an extreme amount of stress, and to work effectively with Frank it would be essential to see the entire family. Indeed, he did have a problem, but he was only part of the problem. He was covering up many family secrets, including a verbally abusive stepfather and an alcoholic mother. Hesitantly, he agreed that it would be a good idea to have the entire family come in for therapy. When the therapist contacted the parents, they totally rejected the idea of family therapy. The mother asserted that the problem was with Frank and that the therapist should concentrate her efforts on him. A few days before his next scheduled appointment his mother called to cancel, saying that they had placed Frank in homebound study and that he therefore no longer required counseling.

- What are the ethical responsibilities of the therapist in this situation?
- Should Frank be seen as a condition of returning to school?
- What other strategies could the therapist have used?
- What would you have done differently, and why?
- Should the therapist have seen Frank and the teacher?

- Should the therapist have encouraged Frank to continue his therapy even if his family refused to undergo treatment?

Commentary. One ethical problem in this case was the treatment of the individual as opposed to the treatment of the family. There was an alcoholism problem within the family. Frank's expulsion from school could have been more a symptom of the family dysfunction than of his own disturbance. Indeed, he did need to learn anger management, as both the school and the mother contended, yet more was going on within this family that needed attention. In this case it might have been best for the therapist to stick to her initial convictions of family therapy as the treatment of choice. If the parents would not agree to this, she could have made a referral to another therapist who would be willing to see Frank in individual counseling. In many states the therapist would be required to make a child abuse report to the Child Protective Services because of the alleged verbal and emotional abuse.

Specialized Training for Counseling Children and Adolescents

Because minors are a special client population, distinct education, training, and supervised practice are required for counselors who expect to work with minor clients (Lawrence & Kurpius, 2000). The ethics codes of the major professional organizations specify that it is unethical to practice in areas for which one has not been trained. Many human-service professionals have been trained and supervised in "verbal therapies," but there are distinct limitations in applying these therapeutic interventions to children. Practitioners who want to counsel children may have to acquire supervised clinical experience in play therapy, art and music therapy, and recreational therapy. These practitioners also must have a knowledge of developmental issues pertaining to the population with which they intend to work. They need to become familiar with laws relating to minors, to be aware of the limits of their competence, and to know when and how to make appropriate referrals. It is essential to know about community referral resources, such as Child Protective Services. Therefore, it is important not to begin counseling with minors without requisite course work and supervision by a specialist in this area.

Counselors working with children and adolescents must also have special training to deal with issues such as confidentiality. Therapists cannot guarantee to minors blanket confidentiality. If the parents or guardians of minors request information about the progress of the counseling, the therapist may be expected to provide some feedback. Remley and Herlihy (2005) state that in some circumstances counselors will determine that parents or guardians must be given information that a minor client has disclosed in a counseling session. For example, if counselors make the judgment that a minor client is at risk of harm (to self or others), they are required to inform the minor's parents. Counselors are called upon to strike an appropriate balance between revealing too much and too little information to parents. However, it is important that counselors be aware that there is the distinct possibility that counselors could be held legally accountable if a minor client engaged in self-inflicted injury or if he or she harms another person. Counselors also have a duty to protect property when a minor makes a serious threat to destroy it. Because state laws pertaining to confidentiality with minor clients are not uniform, it is essential for counselors to be familiar with the statutes and laws of the jurisdiction in which they practice (Lawrence & Kurpius, 2000).

Information that will or will not be disclosed to parents or guardians must be discussed at the outset of therapy with both the child or adolescent and the parent or guardian. If the matter of confidentiality is not clearly explored with all parties involved, it is almost certain that problems will emerge in the course of therapy.

Involuntary Commitment and Human Rights

The practice of involuntary commitment of people to mental institutions raises difficult professional, ethical, and legal issues. Practitioners must know their own state laws and must be familiar with community resources before taking measures leading to involuntary hospitalization. Good practice involves consulting with professional colleagues to determine the appropriate length and type of treatment (Austin, Moline, & Williams, 1990). The focus of our discussion here is not on specific legal provisions but on the ethical aspects of involuntary commitment.

Under the social policy of "deinstitutionalization," which has gained popularity over the past 25 years, involuntary commitment is sought only after less restrictive alternatives have failed. The main purpose of involuntary hospitalization is to secure treatment for clients rather than to punish them. As it applies to mental health practices, the legal doctrine of using the "least restrictive alternative" requires that treatment be no more harsh, hazardous, or intrusive than necessary to achieve therapeutic aims and to protect clients and others from physical harm (Bednar et al., 1991). Professionals are sometimes confronted with the responsibility of assessing the need to commit clients who pose a serious danger either to themselves or to others. The growing trend is for courts to recognize the therapist's duty to commit such clients. Under most state laws, involuntary civil commitment is based on the following criteria: mental illness, dangerousness to self or others, disability, refusal to consent, treatability, incapacity to decide on treatment, and compliance with the "least restrictive" criterion (Bednar et al., 1991).

Bennett and his colleagues (1990) offer these specific recommendations pertaining to the commitment process:

- Be familiar with your state laws and regulations pertaining to both voluntary and involuntary commitment.
- If you notice that a client's condition is deteriorating, consider consulting with colleagues.
- Carefully consider what you hope to obtain in recommending commitment. Assess the degree to which your client is a danger to self or others.

- Before deciding on a course leading to commitment, consider other options. Also, consider the advisability of referring your client to another professional for evaluation or treatment.
- Ask yourself how commitment might affect the client's attitude toward you as a therapist and toward therapy in general.
- If hospitalization is involuntary, know the procedural steps that must be followed under your state laws.
- Make certain that you can offer reasons for commitment.

Making a decision to commit a client is a serious matter that has implications for you, your client, and members of the client's family. It is essential that you obtain consultation if there is any doubt about the proper course to follow. You need to raise many questions about the appropriateness of choosing commitment over other alternatives. Some writers emphasize practices such as conducting ongoing psychiatric and psychosocial assessments and documenting all examinations and consultations in the client's record. Practitioners are advised to protect themselves from liability associated with involuntary hospitalization by documenting all the steps they take in making this decision (Austin et al., 1990; Bednar et al., 1991).

Malpractice Liability in the Helping Professions

How vulnerable are mental health professionals to malpractice actions? What are some practical safeguards against being involved in a lawsuit? In this section we examine these questions and encourage you to develop a prudent approach to risk management in your practice. It is easy to be anxious over the possibility of being sued, but this is not likely to bring out the best in us as practitioners. We want our discussion of malpractice to lead you to an increased awareness of the range of professional responsibilities and suggest ways to meet these responsibilities in an ethical fashion.

What Is Malpractice?

The word **malpractice** means "bad practice." Malpractice is the failure to render professional services or to exercise the degree of skill that is ordinarily expected of other professionals in a similar situation. Malpractice is a legal concept involving negligence that results in injury or loss to the client. **Professional negligence** can result from unjustified departure from usual practice or from failing to exercise due care in fulfilling one's responsibilities.

Practitioners are expected to abide by legal standards and adhere to the ethics codes of their profession in providing care to their clients. Unless practitioners take due care and act in good faith, they are liable to a civil lawsuit for failing to do their duty as provided by law. The primary problem in a negligence suit is determining which **standards of care** to apply to determine whether a clinician has breached a duty to a client. Clinicians are judged according to the standards that are commonly accepted by the profession. Practitioners need not be infallible, but they are expected to possess and exercise the knowledge, skill, and judgment common to other members of their profession. It is a good policy for practitioners to maintain a reasonable view of the realities involved in dealing with high-risk clients. No matter how ethical and careful you try to be, you can still be accused of malpractice. However, the more careful and ethical you try to be, the less likely you are to be successfully sued. The best defense against becoming embroiled in a malpractice suit is to practice quality client care.

To succeed in a malpractice claim, these four elements of malpractice must be present: (1) a professional relationship between the therapist and the client must have existed; (2) the therapist must have acted in a negligent or improper manner, or have deviated from the "standard of care" by not providing services that are considered "standard practice in the community"; (3) the client must have suffered harm or injury, which must be demonstrated; and (4) there must be a legally demonstrated causal relationship between the practitioner's negligence or breach of duty and the damage or injury claimed by the client. It should be noted that anyone, at any time, can file a suit against you. Even if the suit does not succeed, it can take a toll on you in terms of time and money. You may have to spend many hours preparing and supplying documents and responding to requests for information. However, the burden of proof that harm actually took place is the client's, and the plaintiff must demonstrate that all four elements applied in his or her situation. Let us take a closer look at each of these elements. This discussion is based on an adaptation of the work of several writers (Anderson, 1996; Austin et al., 1990; Bednar et al., 1991; Bennett et al., 1990; Calfee, 1997; Crawford, 1994).

1. **Duty.** There are two aspects of establishing a legal duty: one is the existence of a special relationship, and the other is the nature of that special relationship. A duty exists when a therapist implicitly or explicitly agrees to provide mental health services.
2. **Breach of duty.** After the plaintiff proves that a professional relationship did exist, he or she must show that the duty was breached. Practitioners have specific responsibilities that involve using ordinary and reasonable care and diligence, applying knowledge and skill to a case, and exercising good judgment. If the practitioner failed to provide the appropriate standard of care, the duty was breached. This breach of duty may involve either actions taken by the therapist or a failure to take certain precautions.
3. **Injury.** Plaintiffs must prove that they were harmed in some way—physically, relationally, psychologically—and that actual injuries were sustained. Examples of such injuries include wrongful death (suicide), loss (divorce), and pain and suffering. Plaintiffs must show proof of actual injury.
4. **Causation.** Plaintiffs must demonstrate that the professional's breach of duty was the proximate cause of the injury they suffered. The test in this case lies in proving that the harm would not have occurred if it were not for the practitioner's actions or omissions.

In the case of suicide, for example, two factors determine a practitioner's liability: foreseeability and reasonable care. Most important is *foreseeability,* which involves assessing the level of risk. Failing to conduct a comprehensive risk assessment and to document this assessment would be a major error on the therapist's part. If you are not competent to make such an assessment, then a referral is mandatory so that an assessment can be made. Practitioners need to demonstrate that their judgments were based on data observed and that these judgments were reasonable. The second factor in liability is whether *reasonable care* was provided. Once an assessment of risk is made, it is important to document that appropriate precautions were taken to prevent a client's suicide.

Reasons for Malpractice Suits

The most frequent reasons for disciplinary actions for psychologists from 1983 to 2001 were related to sexual misconduct and unprofessional conduct/negligent practice. Other specific areas that constituted grounds for disciplinary actions included conviction of crimes, fraudulent acts, inadequate record keeping, breach of confidentiality, improper or inadequate supervision, impairment, failure to comply with continuing education requirements, and fraud in applying for license (Kirkland, Kirkland, & Reaves, 2004.)

In their review of the literature on grounds for disciplinary actions against psychologists, Knapp and VandeCreek (2003a) identify the following issues: violations of sexual boundaries, nonsexual multiple relationships, incompetence, breaches of confidentiality, abandonment, inadequate supervision, inadequate record keeping, and child custody disputes.

Malpractice is generally limited to six kinds of situations: (1) the procedure used by the practitioner was not within the realm of accepted professional practice; (2) the practitioner employed a technique that he or she was not trained to use; (3) the professional did not use a procedure that would have been more helpful; (4) the therapist failed to warn others about and protect them from a violent client; (5) informed consent to treatment was not obtained or not documented; or (6) the professional did not explain the possible consequences of the treatment (Anderson, 1996). Mitchell (2001) states that malpractice suits against clinicians continue to increase. According to Mitchell, lawsuits that raise questions about treatment or diagnosis are becoming increasingly common.

Many areas of a therapist's practice could lead to a legal claim, but we will focus on the types of professional negligence that most often put therapists at legal risk. The following discussion of these risk categories is an adaptation of malpractice liability and lawsuit prevention strategies suggested by various writers (Anderson, 1996; Calfee, 1997; Crawford, 1994; Kennedy et al., 2003; Kirkland et al., 2004; Knapp & VandeCreek, 2003a; Mitchell, 2001; Stromberg & Dellinger, 1993; Swenson, 1997; VandeCreek & Knapp, 2001).

Failure to Obtain or Document Informed Consent. Therapists need to recognize that they can be liable for failure to obtain appropriate informed consent even if their subsequent treatment of the client is excellent from a clinical perspective. Although written informed consent may not be needed legally, it is wise to have clients sign a form to acknowledge their agreement with the terms of the proposed therapy. Without a written document, it may be very difficult to ascertain whether counselors communicated clearly and effectively to clients about the therapeutic process and whether clients understood the information.

Client Abandonment. Courts have determined that the following acts may constitute abandonment: failure to follow up on the outcomes with a client who has been hospitalized; consistently not being able to be reached between appointments; failure to respond to a request for emergency treatment; or failure to provide for a substitute therapist during vacation times. Clients have a case for abandonment when the facts indicate that a therapist unilaterally terminated a professional relationship and that this termination resulted in some form of harm. Under managed care plans, therapists may be accused of abandonment when they terminate a client based on the allocated number of sessions rather than on the therapeutic needs of the client. The codes of ethics apply to practitioners, not to managed care systems.

Marked Departures from Established Therapeutic Practices. If counselors employ unusual therapy procedures, they put themselves at risk. They bear the burden of demonstrating a rationale for their techniques. If it can be shown that their procedures are beyond the usual methods employed by most professionals, they are vulnerable to a malpractice action. If it is unlikely that an expert can be found to testify to the acceptability of a certain treatment approach, it would be prudent not to employ this approach (Calfee, 1997).

Practicing Beyond the Scope of Competency. Mental health practitioners have been held liable for damages for providing treatment below a standard of care. If the client follows the treatment suggested by a professional and suffers damages as a result, the client can initiate a civil action. Professional health care providers should work only with those clients and deliver only those services that are within the realm of their competence. Accepting a case beyond the scope of a counselor's education and training is not only a breach of ethics but also can result in a malpractice suit. If counselors have any doubts about their level of competency to work with certain cases, they should receive peer input or consultation. If a counselor is accused of unethical practice, the counselor must prove that he or she was properly prepared in that area of practice (Chauvin & Remley, 1996). Counselors who want to augment their skills can participate in continuing education, take additional graduate course work, and work under the direct supervision of a colleague who has clinical experience with such cases (Calfee, 1997).

Misdiagnosis. Giving a diagnosis that the therapist is not qualified or licensed to render could leave the practitioner vulnerable to an allegation of malpractice (Anderson, 1996). It is generally not the court's role to question the therapist's diagnosis. However, in cases where it can be shown through the therapist's records that a diagnosis was clearly unfounded and below the standard of care, a case of malpractice might be successful. In court an expert witness is often questioned to determine whether the therapist used appropriate assessment procedures and arrived at an appropriate diagnosis. It is wise for mental health practitioners to require a prospective client to undergo a complete physical examination, as the results of this examination might have a bearing on the client's diagnosis and affect his or her treatment (Calfee, 1997).

Repressed or False Memory. A memory is considered false if it is arrived at through the bias and intervention techniques of the therapist, rather than it being the client's actual memory. Therapists have been sued and found guilty of such induced memories. Anderson (1996) cites the example of a jury in Ramsey County, Minnesota, that awarded more than $2.6 million to a woman who claimed she was injured by false memories of abuse induced after her psychiatrist suggested that she suffered from a multiple personality disorder, which most likely was the result of repeated sexual abuse by relatives. Certainly, the style in which a therapist questions a client can influence memories, particularly for young children. Repeated questioning can lead a person to believe in a "memory" that did not occur. A trusted therapist who suggests past abuse as a possible cause of problems or symptoms can greatly influence the client.

What is the best course for you to follow when you suspect that past sexual abuse is related to a client's present problem? How can you best protect the client, the alleged abuser, and other family members, without becoming needlessly vulnerable to a malpractice suit? Anderson recommends following these basic clinical and ethical principles (pp. 54–55):

- Be attentive to the kinds of questions you ask clients.
- Remain nonjudgmental and demonstrate empathy as you talk to a client about possible memories of abuse.
- Avoid prejudging the truth of the client's reports.
- Make use of standard assessment and treatment techniques.
- Avoid pressuring the client to believe events that may not have actually occurred.
- Do not suggest to clients that they terminate the relationship precipitously.

If you are not specifically trained in child abuse assessment and treatment, consult with a supervisor or a professional with expertise in this area, or refer the client for a clinical assessment.

Unhealthy Transference Relationships. The importance of understanding how transference and countertransference play out in the therapy relationship was considered in Chapter 2. The mere existence of countertransference feelings is not an ethical and legal issue. However, if a therapist's personal reactions to a client cannot be managed effectively, an abuse of power is likely, and this can have both ethical and legal ramifications. In cases involving mishandling of a client's transference or a counselor's countertransference, allegations have included sexual involvement with clients, inappropriate socialization with clients, getting involved with clients in a business situation, and burdening clients with a counselor's personal problems. When a therapist gets involved in multiple relationships with a client, it is always the client who is more vulnerable to the abuse of power. When a client cannot be served in a professional manner due to a practitioner's personal feelings about him or her, it is the therapist's responsibility to seek consultation, to undergo personal therapy, and if necessary, to refer the client to another counselor (Calfee, 1997).

Sexual Misconduct with a Client. Related to the topic of unhealthy transference relationships is the area of sexual misconduct, one of the most common grounds for malpractice suits. It is *never* appropriate for therapists to become sexually and intimately involved with clients. This topic is explored in detail in Chapter 7. Court cases suggest that no act is more likely to create legal problems for therapists than engaging in a sexual relationship with a client. Furthermore, initial consent of the client will not be a defense against malpractice actions. Even in the case of sex between a therapist and a former client, courts do not easily accept the view that therapy has ended. More often than not, the court considers that a therapist has taken advantage of the client by changing a professional relationship into a sexual one (Stromberg & Dellinger, 1993).

Failure to Control a Dangerous Client. Therapists may have a duty to intervene in cases where clients pose a grave danger to themselves or to others. However, it is difficult to determine when a given client actually poses a danger to self or others. As Perlin (1997) reminds us, negligence lies in the therapist's failure to warn a third party who is threatened by imminent danger, not in the failure to predict violence. We discuss this topic in greater detail in Chapter 6.

Most states require mental health professionals to warn intended victims of potential harm. State statutes were promulgated to protect mental health professionals who breach confidentiality to report danger to others as well as to protect the public. Even in states where such a warning is not legally mandated, ethical practice demands a proper course of action on the therapist's part.

Just as professionals often have a duty to warn and protect in cases of clients who pose a danger to others, therapists also may have to warn when a client poses a danger to self. A therapist can be liable in a wrongful death claim if the therapist failed to diagnose a client's suicidal condition and if the therapist failed to act in a way to prevent the suicide. However, the courts recognize that suicide and assaultive acts are difficult to predict, which means that liability for failing to anticipate such acts is relatively uncommon. Liability may be imposed, however, if the professional's decision can be shown to have departed from accepted professional practice or standards, or when the therapist did not base his or her assessment and treatment on sound clinical principles (Stromberg & Dellinger, 1993).

VandeCreek and Knapp (2001) observe that some scholars have expressed concern that the duty to warn and protect obligations would greatly limit therapeutic options in treating dangerous clients. To this concern, VandeCreek and Knapp reply: "We have seen no evidence to support this worry. Rather, good clinical practice continues to be the best risk management strategy for the management of dangerous patients" (p. 54).

Risk Management

Risk management is the practice of focusing on the identification, evaluation, and treatment of problems that may injure clients, lead to filing of an ethics complaint, or lead to a malpractice action. One of the best precautions against malpractice is personal and professional honesty and openness with clients. Providing quality professional services to clients is the best preventive step you can take. Although you may not make the "right choice" in every situation, it is crucial that you know your limitations and remain open to seeking consultation in difficult cases.

Calfee (1997) stresses the importance of understanding risk management techniques that can reduce the practice of unethical behavior and minimize the chance of litigation. She describes risk management as a four-step process whereby practitioners (1) identify potential risk areas, (2) evaluate whether the risk area is serious enough to merit further attention, (3) employ preventive and risk control strategies in their work, and (4) review treatments periodically to ascertain their effectiveness. Here are some additional recommendations for improving risk management:

- Become aware of local and state laws that pertain to your practice, as well as the policies of any agency for whom you work. Keep up to date with legal and ethical changes by becoming actively involved in professional organizations and attending risk management workshops (Kennedy et al., 2003).
- Make use of treatment contracts that present clients with written information on confidentiality issues, reasons for contacting clients at home, fees and payment plans, a policy on termination, and suicide provisions (Kennedy et al., 2003). Review this information with the client and document informed consent with a signature.
- Present information to your clients in clear language and be sure they understand the information. Realize that there is a wide variation in age of consent, depending on what the client is consenting to.
- Provide clients with a professional disclosure statement that addresses basic policies and boundary issues in the counseling relationship. Recognize that the disclosure statement forms a contract between you and your client (Chauvin & Remley, 1996).
- Explain your diagnosis, the treatment plan, and its risks and benefits in sufficient detail to be sure the client understands it, and document this as well.
- Clearly define issues pertaining to fees at the outset of therapy. If it is your practice to increase your fees periodically, tell clients that fees are subject to change with notice.
- Collect fees for your professional services on a regular basis. Fee disputes are a frequent basis of complaints lodged against counselors (Chauvin & Remley, 1996).

- Clients should be informed that they have the right to terminate treatment any time they choose.
- Restrict your practice to clients for whom you are qualified by virtue of your education, training, and experience.
- Refer clients whose conditions are obviously not within the scope of your competence. If you are in doubt, seek peer input to determine whether you are practicing outside the scope of your competency (Austin et al., 1990; Calfee, 1997; Pope & Vasquez, 1998).
- Carefully document your clients' treatment process. Document reasons for a client's termination and any referrals or recommendations given (Kennedy et al., 2003).
- Maintain adequate business and clinical records.
- Develop clear and consistent policies and procedures for creating, maintaining, transferring, and destroying client records (Remley & Herlihy, 2005).
- Recognize your ethical, professional, and legal responsibility to preserve the confidentiality of client records.
- Keep clients' complete records for the time period required in your state.
- Report any case of suspected child abuse, elder, or dependent abuse as required by law.
- Before engaging in any dual or multiple relationships, seek consultation and talk with your client about the possible repercussions of such a relationship. Carefully assess and consider any potential dangers to both your client and yourself, especially unfulfilled expectations and lack of objectivity (Herlihy & Corey, 2006b).
- Exercise caution in situations where you are considering engaging in bartering with clients. Realize that such exchanges can lead to problems on both your clients' and your part.
- In deciding whether or not to accept a gift, consider the relevant cultural and clinical issues.
- Although you can be friendly and personal with clients, keep your relationships professional.
- Do not engage in sexual relationships with current or former clients or with current supervisees or students.
- Not keeping your appointments may feel like abandonment to a client. If you have to miss a session, be sure to call the client.
- Be sure to provide coverage for emergencies when you are going away. Have some way to be reached in times of crisis.
- When in doubt, consult with colleagues and document the discussions. Because the legal standard is based on the practices of fellow professionals, the more consensus you have, the better chance you have of prevailing in a suit. Before consulting with others about a specific client, obtain consent from the client for the release of information.
- In cases where you have limited experience or encounter cultural barriers, consult with a colleague experienced in treating this population and, if necessary, refer the client (Bennett et al., 1990).
- In accepting or making referrals, carry out your responsibility to obtain or transfer information pertaining to a client (Austin et al., 1990).

- Get training in the assessment of clients who pose a danger to themselves or others, or have an experienced and competent therapist to whom you can refer. Knowing the danger signs of potentially suicidal and violent clients is the first step toward prevention.
- Consult when you are working with a suicidal client. Clearly document the nature of the consultation, including the topics discussed (Kennedy et al., 2003).
- If you make a professional determination that a client is dangerous, take the necessary steps to protect the client or others from harm (Austin et al., 1990; Bednar et al., 1991; Perlin, 1997).
- Obtain written parental or guardian consent when working with minors. This is good practice even if this consent is not required by state law. Have referral sources for minors when you determine situations that are beyond your scope of practice.
- Recognize that a mental health professional is a potential target for a client's anger or transference feelings. Keep the lines of communication open with clients, allowing them to express whatever they feel to you (Chauvin & Remley, 1996).
- Be especially attentive to how you react to your clients and monitor your countertransference.
- Treat your clients with respect by attending carefully to your language and your behavior.
- Avoid undue influence over clients. Recognize that it is possible for you to unintentionally influence a client in an inappropriate way (Bennett et al., 1990).
- Have a theoretical orientation that justifies the techniques you employ.
- Be clear about what psychotherapy can and cannot do. When initiating a new form of therapy or different method of treatment, be sure you can support the choice of treatment (Calfee, 1997).
- Realize that prevention is a less expensive option than a successful defense against a malpractice suit (Swenson, 1997).
- Carry adequate professional-liability insurance.

This list of risk management strategies may appear overwhelming. Our intention is to remind you of appropriate actions and also to provide a checklist to expand your awareness of ethical and professional behavior. Most ethical practitioners will already be taking these steps. The best way to reduce the chance of being sued is to know the ethical and legal standards and to follow them. If you develop too many forms of self-protection, however, the therapeutic relationship may be negatively affected. Because of your exaggerated cautiousness, your client may be reluctant to engage in the self-disclosure that is a critical aspect of the therapy process. Increased use of the legal system may lead to excessive caution on the part of therapists because of their concern about being sued. With the encroachment of malpractice issues into ethical thinking, there is increasing emphasis on doing what is safest for the therapist rather than what is best for the client.

It is worth noting that malpractice claims are not reserved exclusively for the irresponsible practitioner. Clients may make allegations of unethical conduct or file a legal claim due to negligence, even though the counselor may have acted ethically and appropriately. As Williams (2000) has noted, there are false complaints against psychotherapists who become victimized by the "victims." Williams reminds us that risk management is based on the assumption that practitioners can control their exposure to lawsuits and licensing complaints by monitoring their behaviors. However, reasonable risk management strategies may not prevent false accusations. Williams states: "Psychotherapists must be prepared to face allegations motivated by factors other than a legitimate quest for justice. Greed, vengeance, escape from unwanted treatment, mental illness, false memories, and misunderstandings about the procedures of psychotherapy are all factors that can bring about lawsuits, criminal charges, or licensing board complaints" (p. 81).

Course of Action in a Malpractice Suit

Even though you practice prudently and follow the guidelines previously outlined, you may still be sued. In the event that you are sued, consider these recommendations by Bennett and his associates (1990):

- Treat the lawsuit seriously, even if it represents a client's attempt to punish or control you.
- Do not attempt to resolve the matter with the client directly, because anything you do might be used against you in the litigation.
- Consult with your professional organization's legal counsel. If you consult with an attorney, prepare summaries of any pertinent events about the case that you can use.
- Become familiar with your liability policy, including the limits of coverage, and contact your insurance company immediately.
- Never destroy or alter files or reports pertinent to the client's case.
- Do not discuss the case with anyone other than your attorney. Avoid making self-incriminating statements to the client, or to his or her attorney, or the press.
- Determine the nature of support available to you from professional associations to which you belong.
- Do not continue a professional relationship with a client who is bringing a suit against you.

It is of the utmost importance to obtain legal assistance if the licensing board has opened an investigation. This usually occurs before the filing of a malpractice claim and can be just as devastating as a lawsuit. You should be aware that the licensing board is an advocate for the consumer, not for the provider (Rahn Minagawa, personal communication, August 14, 2003). If you face going to court, you would do well to have some basic knowledge and take steps to prepare yourself for your appearance. Helpful resources for understanding legal matters pertaining to mental health practices, for avoiding counselor malpractice, and for preparing for court are Remley (1991) and Crawford (1994).

Legal Liability in an Ethical Perspective

Legal liability and ethical practice are not identical, but they do overlap in many cases. Legal issues give substance and direction to the evolution of ethical issues. Because ethics complaints may lead to civil or criminal lawsuits, Chauvin and Remley (1996) believe the legal aspects of an ethical complaint dictate how counselors must conduct themselves. Thus, clinicians need to know the relationship between ethics complaints and lawsuits, how boards process complaints, and the importance of seeking legal consultation.

If you are involved in a malpractice action, an expert case reviewer will probably evaluate your clinical records to determine if your practice reflected the appropriate standard of care. Records are vital to review the course of treatment. The manner in which you document treatment is likely to determine the outcome of a case (Mitchell, 2001). The case reviewer will probably look for deviations from your process of reasoning and application of knowledge in trying to determine whether there has been a gross deviation from the standards. As a practitioner, you cannot guarantee the outcome, but you are expected to demonstrate that you applied a reasonable and scientifically based approach to the present problem of your client (Rahn Minagawa, personal communication, August 14, 2003). Although you are not expected to be perfect, it is beneficial to evaluate what you are doing and why you are practicing as you are.

Chapter Summary

The ethics codes of all mental health organizations specify the centrality of informed consent. Clients' rights can best be protected if therapists develop procedures that aid their clients in making informed choices. Legally, informed consent entails the client's ability to act freely in making rational decisions. The process of informed consent includes providing information about the nature of therapy as well as the rights and responsibilities of both therapist and client. A basic challenge therapists face is to provide accurate and sufficient information to clients yet at the same time not to overwhelm them with too much information too soon. Informed consent can best be viewed as an ongoing process aimed at increasing the range of choices and the responsibility of the client as an active therapeutic partner.

In addition to a discussion of the rights of clients, this chapter has considered the scope of professional responsibility. Therapists have responsibilities to their clients, their agency, their profession, the community, the members of their clients' families, and themselves. Ethical dilemmas arise when there are conflicts among these responsibilities, for instance, when the agency's expectations conflict with the concerns or wishes of clients. Members of the helping professions need to know and to observe the ethics codes of their professional organizations, and they must make sound judgments within the parameters of acceptable practice. We have encouraged you to think about specific ethical issues and to develop a sense of professional ethics and knowledge of state laws so that your judgment will be based on more than what "feels right."

Associated with professional responsibilities are professional liabilities. If practitioners ignore legal and ethical standards or if their conduct is below the expected standard of care, they may be sued. Practitioners who fail to keep adequate records of their procedures are opening themselves to liability. Certainly, it is realistic to be concerned about malpractice actions, and professional practices that can reduce such risks have been described. However, it is our hope that practitioners do not become so preoccupied with making mistakes and self-protective strategies that they render themselves ineffective as clinicians.

Suggested Activities

1. In small groups, create an informed consent document. What does your group think clients must be told either before therapy begins or during the first few sessions?

2. In small groups, explore the rights clients have in counseling. One person in each group can serve as a recorder. When the groups reconvene for a general class meeting, the recorders for the various groups share their lists of clients' rights on a 3-point scale: 3 = Extremely important; 2 = Important; 1 = Somewhat important. What rights can your class agree on as the most important?

3. Select some of the open-ended cases presented in this chapter to role play with a fellow student. One of you chooses a client you feel you can identify with, and the other becomes the counselor. Conduct a counseling interview. Afterward, talk about how each of you felt during the interview and discuss alternative courses of action that could have been taken.

4. Providing clients with access to their files and records seems to be in line with the consumer-rights movement, which is having an impact on the human-service professions. What are your own thoughts on providing your clients with this information? What information would you want to share with your clients? In what ways might you go about providing them with this information? What might you do if there were a conflict between your views and the policies of the agency that employed you?

5. Consider inviting an attorney who is familiar with the legal aspects of counseling practice to address your class. Here are some possible questions for consideration: What are the legal rights of clients in therapy? Legally, what are the main responsibilities of therapists? What are some of the best ways to become familiar with laws pertaining to counselors? What are the grounds for lawsuits, and how can counselors best protect themselves from being sued?

6. Interview practicing counselors about some of their most pressing ethical concerns in carrying out their responsibilities. How have they dealt with these ethical issues? What are some of their legal considerations? What are their concerns, if any, about malpractice suits?

7. Discuss your concerns about professional liability. What can you do to lessen the chances of being accused of not having practiced according to acceptable standards?

Ethics in Action CD-ROM Exercises

8. In video role play #7, The Affair, a counselor states, "Having an affair is not a good answer for someone—it just hurts everyone. I just don't think it is a good idea." If you held such a view, should this be a part of your informed consent document? In what value areas might you have difficulty maintaining objectivity? Are there situations in which you would want to get your client to adopt your position?

9. In video role play #4, on divorce, some interesting points are raised about the rights of clients to know about your values as a counselor if these values influence your approach to counseling them. The client has decided to leave her husband and get a divorce. She tells her counselor that she doesn't want to work on her marriage anymore. The counselor responds: "I hate to hear that. What about your kids? Who will be the advocate for them?" She says, "If I am happy, they will be happy. I will take care of my kids." The counselor concludes by asking, "Is divorce the best way to take care of your children?" If you were counseling couples or families, what would you want to tell clients about your values pertaining to matters such as faithfulness in relationships and divorce? In class, role play a situation in which you are meeting a client (or a couple) for the first session. What would you want to tell them about your role as a counselor? Would you reveal the core values you hold that could either enhance or interfere with their therapeutic progress?

10. In video role play #1, Teen Pregnancy, the client is a 13-year-old who just found out she is pregnant. She begs the counselor not to tell her parents. In this situation, what are the rights of the minor client? What rights do the parents have for access to certain information? What ethical and legal issues are involved in this case? What role would parental consent laws play in this case? What kind of informed consent process would you implement if you were counseling minors?

 InfoTrac® College Edition Resources

For additional readings, explore InfoTrac College Edition, our online library. Key words are listed in a form that enables the search engine to locate a wider range of articles in the online university library. Key words should be entered exactly as shown, including asterisks, "Wl," "W2," "AND," and other search engine tools. Go to http://www.infotrac-college.com and select these key word searches:

informed w1 consent AND (psych????y OR psychotherapy OR couns*) NOT medic* NOT phys*

record* N3 couns* OR record* N3 therap* NOT medic* NOT phys*
mental health managed care
malpractice N3 liability AND (psych????y OR psychotherapy OR couns*) NOT law
involuntary commitment AND (psych????y OR psychotherapy OR couns*) NOT law NOT lawy*
repressed W1 memory W1 syndrome
false W1 memory AND (psych????y OR psychotherapy OR couns*)
online N3 couns* OR online N3 psych????y
behavioral N3 telehealth
standard W2 care AND (psych????y OR psychotherapy OR couns*) NOT law NOT lawy*
risk W1 management AND (psych????y OR psychotherapy OR couns*) NOT law NOT lawy* NOT medic*

Chapter 6

Pre-Chapter Self-Inventory

Directions: For each statement, indicate the response that most closely identifies your beliefs and attitudes. Use the following code:

5 = I *strongly agree* with this statement.
4 = I *agree* with this statement.
3 = I am *undecided* in my opinion about this statement.
2 = I *disagree* with this statement.
1 = I *strongly disagree* with this statement.

_____ 1. I am uncertain about how much to tell my clients about confidentiality.
_____ 2. There are no situations in which I would disclose what a client had told me without the client's permission.
_____ 3. Absolute confidentiality is necessary if effective psychotherapy is to occur.
_____ 4. If I were working with a client whom I had assessed as potentially dangerous to another person, it would be my duty to warn the possible victim.
_____ 5. Once I make an assessment that a client is suicidal or at a high risk of carrying out self-destructive acts, it is my ethical and legal obligation to take appropriate action.
_____ 6. Counselors could evoke guilt to discourage clients from suicidal action.
_____ 7. If a suicidal client does not want my help or actively rejects it, I would be inclined to leave the person alone.

Confidentiality: Ethical and Legal Issues

____ 8. As a helping professional, it is my responsibility to report suspected child abuse, regardless of when it occurred.

____ 9. The reporting laws pertaining to child abuse sometimes prevent therapy from taking place with the abuser.

____ 10. I think reporting child abuse should be left to the judgment of the therapist.

____ 11. To protect children from abuse, strict laws are necessary, and professionals should be penalized for failing to report abuses.

____ 12. If my client is HIV-positive, I have a legal duty to warn all of the person's identifiable sexual partners if my client refuses to disclose his or her HIV status to them.

____ 13. In counseling HIV-positive clients, I would be inclined to maintain confidentiality because failing to do so could erode the trust of my clients.

____ 14. If an HIV-positive client refused to disclose his or her HIV status to a partner, I would explore with my client the reasons for not doing so.

____ 15. Using cell phones jeopardizes confidentiality.

____ 16. Communication via electronic mail is fraught with privacy problems.

____ 17. If it became necessary to break a client's confidentiality, I would inform my client of my intended action.

____ 18. I would find the evaluation and management of suicidal risk stressful.

____ 19. I view it as unethical for therapists to employ coercive measures aimed at preventing suicide.

____ 20. I believe that it is easy to invade a client's privacy unintentionally.

Introduction

Perhaps the central right of a client is the guarantee that disclosures in therapy sessions will be protected. As you will see, however, you cannot make a blanket promise to your clients that *everything* they talk about will *always* remain confidential. Consider the ethical and legal ramifications of confidentiality, and inform your clients from the outset of therapy of those circumstances that limit confidentiality.

Landmark court cases have shed new light on the therapist's duty to warn and to protect both clients and others who may be directly affected by a client's behavior. You have both ethical and legal responsibilities to protect innocent people who might be injured by a dangerous client. You also have responsibilities to assess and intervene effectively with clients who are likely to try to take their own lives. To help you think about your position when dealing with potentially dangerous or suicidal clients, we offer some guidelines and case illustrations.

The more you consider the legal ramifications of confidentiality, the clearer it becomes that most matters are not neatly defined. Even if therapists have become familiar with local and state laws that govern their profession, this legal knowledge alone is not enough to enable them to make sound decisions. Each case is unique, for there are many subtle points in the law and at various times conflicting ways to interpret the law. Professional judgment always plays a significant role in resolving cases, from both an ethical and a legal perspective.

Confidentiality, Privileged Communication, and Privacy

An important obligation of practitioners in the various mental health professions is to maintain the confidentiality of their relationships with their clients (see the ethics codes box titled Confidentiality in Clinical Practice for some specific guidelines). Confidentiality is a complex obligation, with several exceptions and nuances, and both legal and ethical implications must be considered (Benitez, 2004). Become familiar with the legal protection afforded to the privileged communications of your clients as well as the limits of this protection.

Confidentiality

Confidentiality, privileged communication, and privacy are related concepts, but there are important distinctions among them. **Confidentiality** is the foundation of safe therapy (Grosso, 2002). As a general rule, psychotherapists are prohibited from disclosing confidential communications to any third party unless mandated or permitted by law to do so. Therapists are advised to err on the side of being overly cautious in protecting the confidentiality of their clients, unless faced with a mandatory exception to confidentiality such as reporting child abuse or elder abuse (Benitez, 2004). Confidentiality is rooted in a client's right to privacy, and in most states therapists have a legal duty not to disclose information about a client.

Ethics Codes

Confidentiality in Clinical Practice

American Counseling Association (2005)

At initiation and throughout the counseling process, counselors inform clients of the limitations of confidentiality and seek to identify foreseeable situations in which confidentiality must be breached. (B.1.d.)

American Psychological Association (2002)

Psychologists have a primary obligation and take reasonable precautions to protect confidential information obtained through or stored in any medium, recognizing that the extent and limits of confidentiality may be regulated by law or established by institutional rules or professional or scientific relationship. (4.01.)

American School Counselor Association (2004)

The professional school counselor informs students of the purposes, goals, techniques and rules of procedure under which they may receive counseling at or before the time when the counseling relationship is entered. Disclosure notice includes the limits of confidentiality such as the possible necessity for consulting with other professionals, privileged communication, and legal or authoritative restraints. The meaning and limits of confidentiality are clearly defined in developmentally appropriate terms to students. (A.2.a.)

Canadian Counselling Association (1999)

Counselling relationships and information resulting therefrom are kept confidential. However, there are the following exceptions to confidentiality:

- when disclosure is required to prevent clear and imminent danger to the client or others;
- when legal requirements demand that confidential material be revealed;
- when a child is in need of protection. (B.2.)

National Association of Social Workers (1999)

Social workers should protect the confidentiality of all information obtained in the course of professional service, except for compelling professional reasons. The general expectation that social workers will keep information confidential does not apply when disclosure is necessary to prevent serious, foreseeable, and imminent harm to a client or other identifiable person. In all instances, social workers should disclose the least amount of confidential information necessary to achieve the desired purpose; only information that is directly relevant to the purpose for which the disclosure is made should be revealed. (1.07.c.)

American Mental Health Counselors Association (2000)

Mental health counselors have a primary obligation to safeguard information about individuals obtained in the course of practice, teaching, or research. Personal information is communicated to others only with the person's written consent or in those circumstances where there is a clear and imminent danger to the client, to others or to society. Disclosure of counseling information is restricted to what is necessary, relevant and verifiable. (Principle 3.)

American Association for Marriage and Family Therapy (2001)

Marriage and family therapists have unique confidentiality concerns because the client in a therapeutic relationship may be more than one person. Therapists respect and guard confidences of each individual client.

continued on next page

International Association of Marriage and Family Counselors (2002)

Members recognize that the proper functioning of the counseling relationship requires that clients must be free to discuss any information, including secrets with the counselor, and counselors must be free to obtain pertinent information beyond that which is volunteered by the client. Members make it understood to all parties in marriage and family counseling that information shared in individual sessions need not be shared with other parties. Absent exceptions, this protection of confidentiality applies to all situations, including initial contacts by a potential client, the fact that a counseling relationship exists, and to all communications made as part of the relationship between a counselor and clients. (II.A.)

Clients have the right to expect that communications will be kept within the bounds of the professional relationship (Behnke et al., 1998). Mental health professionals have an ethical responsibility, as well as a legal and professional duty, to safeguard clients from unauthorized disclosures of information given in the therapeutic relationship. Professionals must not disclose this information except when authorized by law or by the client to do so. Hence, there are limitations to the promise of confidentiality. Court decisions, for example, have underscored the therapist's duty to warn and to protect the client or others, even if it means breaking confidentiality. Also, because confidentiality is a client's right, psychotherapists may legally and ethically reveal a client's confidences in those cases where a client waives this right. It needs to be emphasized that confidentiality belongs to the client, and counselors generally do not find it problematic to release information when the client requests that they do so. Challenges arise, however, when third parties demand that counselors release confidential information that clients do not want released (Glosoff et al., 2000).

The APA (2002) ethics code provides the following guidelines for disclosure of confidential information:

> (a) Psychologists may disclose confidential information with the appropriate consent of the organizational client, the individual client/patient, or another legally authorized person on behalf of the client/patient unless prohibited by law. (4.05.a.)

The ACA (2005) has a new ethical standard for counselor advocacy that has implications for confidentiality. Although counselors are ethically expected to advocate for their clients by working to remove potential barriers and obstacles that might inhibit client access to services or inhibit client growth (A.6.a.), counselors must obtain client consent before engaging in advocacy on behalf of an identifiable client (Herlihy & Corey, 2006c).

Privileged Communication

Privileged communication is a legal concept that generally bars the disclosure of confidential communications in a legal proceeding (Committee on Professional Practice and Standards, 2003). In other words, therapists can refuse to answer questions in court or refuse to produce a client's records in court. All states have enacted into law some form of psychotherapist-client privilege, but the specifics of this privilege vary from state to state. Only privileged communication that is established by statute can protect clients from disclosure in a legal proceeding (Glosoff et al., 2000). These laws ensure that clients' disclosures of personal and sensitive information will be protected from exposure by therapists in legal proceedings.

Again, this privilege belongs to the client and is designed for the client's protection rather than for the protection of the mental health professional, regardless of his or her license (DeBell & Jones, 1997). If a client knowingly and rationally waives this privilege, the professional has no legal grounds for withholding the information. Professionals are obligated to disclose information that is necessary and sufficient when the client requests it, but only the information that is specifically requested and only to the individuals or agencies that are specified by the client.

The basic principles of privileged communication have been reaffirmed by case law. On June 13, 1996, the United States Supreme Court ruled that communications between licensed psychotherapists and their clients in the course of diagnosis or treatment are privileged and therefore protected from forced disclosure in cases arising under federal law. The Supreme Court ruling in *Jaffee v. Redmond* (1996), written by Justice John Paul Stevens, states that "effective psychotherapy depends upon an atmosphere of confidence and trust in which the patient is willing to make frank and complete disclosure of facts, emotions, memories, and fears." According to Newman (1996), the high court's ruling recognizes the societal value of psychotherapy and the importance of confidentiality to successful treatment. This decision may signal the broadening of a trend toward stronger privileged communication statutes.

Generally speaking, the legal concept of privileged communication does *not* apply to group counseling, couples counseling, marital and family therapy, or child and adolescent therapy. Members of a counseling group can assume that they could be asked to testify in court concerning certain information revealed in the course of a group session, unless there is a statutory exception. In states where no law exists to cover confidentiality in group therapy, courts are most likely to use the ethics codes of the professions regarding confidentiality. If a situation arises, therapists may need to demonstrate the means they used to create safety for the group members. One way of doing this is by using a written group contract, which can clearly state that members have the responsibility for maintaining confidentiality of others in the group (Grosso, 2002).

Similarly, couples therapy and family therapy are not subject to privileged communication statutes in many states. In the case of child and adolescent clients, there are restrictions on the confidential character of disclosures in the counseling relationship. No clear judicial trend has emerged for communications that are made in the presence of third persons. It is best for therapists to assume that such communications are not privileged by law. Therapists should inform their clients of the ethical need for confidentiality and the lack of legal privilege concerning disclosures made in the presence of third persons (Anderson, 1996). Although confidentiality is not *legally* protected in the presence of a third person, from an *ethical* perspective, confidentiality is still applicable when three or more clients are involved.

It is a good policy to inform clients about confidentiality and its exceptions from the beginning of the professional contact and to remain open to discussing this matter as the situation may warrant later in the professional relationship. Clients have a right to be informed about any limitations on confidentiality in group work, child and adolescent therapy, couples and family therapy, and organizational consulting (Nagy, 2005).

Glosoff and colleagues (2000) stress that counselors need to stay abreast of both statutes and case law. They give the following suggestions for counselors who are asked to divulge confidential client information in a legal proceeding:

- Make use of informed consent statements regarding the parameters of confidentiality.
- Inform clients of the situation and involve them in the process.
- Take reasonable steps to protect client confidentiality.
- If information is required to be disclosed, provide only minimal disclosure.
- With permission, contact the client's attorney.
- Document all action taken and what information was disclosed.
- Make it a practice to consult with colleagues regarding clinical judgments and with attorneys regarding legal obligations.

Privacy

Privacy, as a matter of law, refers to the constitutional right of an individual to decide the time, place, manner, and extent of sharing oneself with others (Stromberg et al., 1993). Practitioners should exercise caution with regard to the privacy of their clients. It is easy to invade a client's privacy unintentionally. Examples of some of the most pressing situations in which privacy is an issue include an employer's access to an applicant's or an employee's psychological tests, parents' access to their child's school and health records, and a third-party payer's access to information about a client's diagnosis and prognosis.

It is of paramount importance to respect the privacy of your clients and to always exercise caution in discussing your work publicly. Nagy (2005) states that you must not reveal identifying information about clients, orally or in writing, or even the fact that they consult you, without their formal consent. He adds that you need to understand state and federal laws pertaining to privacy and the rules of your employment setting as well, and how they might affect your work in therapy, research, consulting, and supervision.

If counselors have occasion to meet clients outside of the professional setting, it is essential that they do not violate their privacy. This is especially true in small towns, where such meetings can be expected. In such cases, it is a good practice to talk with your client and discuss how you might interact in these possible meetings. Consider what you might do in the following case.

The Case of Erica. Helena is a counselor in the student services department at a community college. She has been counseling Erica for several months for a variety of problems around her body image and eating behaviors. One evening Helena and a friend go out to a local cafe for a light meal and a coffee. Helena is surprised when the waitress comes up to her cheerily and says hello. She looks up and realizes it is Erica. She chats briefly with Erica who then takes her order and goes off to serve other customers. Erica has made no mention of counseling or any aspect of their relationship in another context. Helena's friend then asks who Erica is and how she knows her?

- If you were the counselor, would you introduce Erica to your friend? If so how?
- If you were the counselor, how would you answer your friend's question?
- If Erica began to discuss her sessions with you, what would you do?

Most professional codes of ethics contain guidelines to safeguard a client's right to privacy, such as this ACA (2005) standard: "Counselors respect client rights to privacy. Counselors solicit private information from clients only when it is beneficial to the counseling process" (B.1.b.).

Another example of the privacy standard, designed to minimize intrusions on privacy, is found in the APA (2002) ethics code:

> Psychologists disclose confidential information without the consent of the individual only as mandated by law, or where permitted by law for a valid purpose such as to (1) provide needed professional services; (2) obtain appropriate professional consultations; (3) protect the client/patient, psychologist, or others from harm; or (4) obtain payment for services from a client/patient, in which instance disclosure is limited to the minimum that is necessary to achieve the purpose. (4.05.b.)

One other area where privacy is an issue involves practitioners who also teach courses, offer workshops, write books and journal articles, and give lectures. If these practitioners use examples from their clinical practice, it is of the utmost importance that they take measures to adequately disguise their clients' identities. Additionally, those who teach counseling courses need to explain to their students that they should adequately disguise identities of their clients in any reports they give in class. Of course, students' personal comments in class are also to be kept confidential.

We think it is a good practice to inform clients if you are likely to use your clinical experience in writing or in lectures. One relevant guideline on this issue of privacy is given by NASW (1999):

> Social workers should respect clients' right to privacy. Social workers should not solicit private information from clients unless it is essential to providing service or conducting social work evaluation or research. Once private information is shared, standards of confidentiality apply. (1.07.a.)

Confidentiality and Privacy in a School Setting

Managing confidentiality is one of the most challenging issues facing school counselors (Isaacs & Stone, 1999). School counselors need to balance their ethical and legal responsibilities with three groups: the students they serve, the parents or guardians of those students, and the school system. When minors are unable to give informed consent, parents or guardians provide this informed consent, and they may need to be included in the counseling process.

Because school counselors are part of an educational community, they often consult with parents, teachers, and administrators. In these consultations, school counselors need to make clear that their primary client is the student (Glosoff & Pate, 2002). Birdsall and Hubert (2000) warn school counselors of their responsibility to safeguard a student's right to privacy when teachers or principals ask counselors to divulge student confidences.

School counselors are ethically obliged to respect the privacy of minor clients and maintain confidentiality, yet this obligation may be in conflict with laws regarding parental rights to be informed about the progress of treatment and to decide what is in the best interests of their children (Glosoff & Pate, 2002). An ASCA (2004) guideline indicates that the school counselor "recognizes his/her primary obligation for confidentiality is to the student but balances that obligation with an understanding of the legal and inherent rights of parents/guardians to be the guiding voice in their children's lives" (A.2.g.). School counselors need to approach parents as allies or partners in the counseling process (Glosoff & Pate, 2002).

School counselors have an ethical responsibility to ask for client permission to release information, and they should clearly inform students of the limitations of confidentiality and how and when confidential information may be shared. The ASCA (2004) guideline regarding parents is that the school counselor "informs parents/guardians of the counselor's role with emphasis on the confidential nature of the counseling relationship between the counselor and student" (Section B.2.a.). Although school counselors may be required to provide certain information to parents and school personnel, they need to do so in a manner that will minimize intrusion of the child's or adolescent's privacy and in a way that demonstrates respect for the counselee. To the degree possible, school counselors aim to establish collaborative relationships with parents and school personnel.

Laws regarding confidentiality in school counseling differ. In some states, therapists in private practice are required to demonstrate that attempts have been made to contact the parents of children who are younger than 16, whereas school counselors are not required to do so. Schools that receive federal funding are generally bound by the provisions of the Family Educational Rights and Privacy Act of 1994 (FERPA). It is essential that school counselors exercise discretion in the kind and extent of information they reveal to parents or guardians about their children. Counselors working in schools are not required by FERPA to make their personal records available or to disclose the substance of confidential counseling sessions to parents (Anderson, 1996).

School personnel may operate under different guidelines regarding confidentiality, and they may not understand the mental health professions' requirements. A trainee or intern in a school who is being supervised for licensure is bound by both the profession's ethics codes and state regulations; therefore, supervisors at this level have a particular obligation to assist trainees and interns in negotiating difficulties regarding confidentiality, informed consent, and treatment expectations in schools (Terrence Patterson, personal communication, October 26, 2004).

✓ **The Case of Donna.** Donna, a school counselor, shifted her career from private practice to counseling in an elementary school. She was particularly surprised by the differences between private practice and school counseling with respect to confidentiality issues. She remarked that she was constantly fielding questions from teachers such as: "Whom do you have in that counseling group?" "How is Johnny doing?" "It's no wonder this girl has problems. Have you met her parents?"

Although Donna talked to the teachers about the importance of maintaining a safe, confidential environment for students in counseling situations, she would still receive questions from them about students, some of whom were not in their classes. In addition to the questions from teachers, Donna found that she had to deal with inquiries from school secretaries and other staff members, some of whom seemed to know everything that was going on in the school. They would ask her probing questions about students, which she, of course, was not willing to answer. For example, although she would not tell a secretary whom she was counseling, a teacher might have told the secretary that she was seeing one of his students. One secretary asked her: "Why are you working with Jimmy Smith? He doesn't have as many problems as some of the other students!"

Donna observed that principals and parents also asked for specific information about the students she was seeing. She learned the importance of talking to everyone about the need to respect privacy. If she had not exercised care, it would have been easy for her to say more than would have been ethical to teachers, staff members, and parents. She also learned how critical it was to talk about matters of confidentiality and privacy in simple language with the schoolchildren she counseled.

If you were an elementary school counselor, how might you address these questions?

- If you were asked some of the questions that were posed to Donna, how would you respond?
- How might you protect the privacy of the students and at the same time avoid alienating the teachers and staff members?
- How might you explain the meaning of confidentiality and privacy to teachers? staff members? parents? administrators? the children?

✓ **The Case of Jeremy.** Jeremy, a third grade boy in an elementary school, reports to his school counselor that he was with his mother when she stole a dress from a store. Jeremy also reports that after he and his mother left the store, she told him that she at times stole food because she couldn't afford it. Jeremy requests that the counselor not say anything to his mother because she has been very depressed about not having a job. After the session, the counselor initiates a conversation with Jeremy's fourth grade sister, who is a student in the same school, to further explore the allegation of the mother's stealing.

- Was this school counselor behaving inappropriately by initiating a conversation with a client's sibling to further explore an alleged crime?
- As a counselor, do you have a legal obligation in this case?
- What would you have done if you were counseling Jeremy?

A Case of Academic Dishonesty. Mr. Simon, a high school counselor, is told by Ginger, a student, that she and some friends have stolen a chemistry final exam. Ginger requests that Mr. Simon not say a word about it to anyone because she is presently failing chemistry and needs to do well on the final exam to pass the course and graduate from high school. Mr. Simon decides not to divulge any information, respecting the student client's request to maintain confidentiality.

- What are your thoughts about Mr. Simon's decision not to divulge any information?
- How might this dilemma for Mr. Simon raise questions concerning the limits to confidentiality?
- What might you have done if you were the counselor in this situation?
- Can school policies be included as you explain the limits to confidentiality to students in your role as a school counselor? Why or why not?

Ethical and Legal Ramifications of Confidentiality and Privileged Communication

The ethics of confidentiality rest on the premise that clients in counseling are involved in a deeply personal relationship and have a right to expect that what they discuss will be kept private. The compelling justification for confidentiality is that it is necessary to encourage clients to develop the trust needed for full disclosure and for the other work involved in therapy. Surely no genuine therapy can occur unless clients trust that what they say is confidential.

When it does become necessary to break confidentiality, it is a good practice to inform the client of the intention to take this action and also to invite the client to participate in the process. This step may preserve the therapeutic relationship and create the opportunity to resolve the issue between the individuals concerned (Mappes et al., 1985). For example, most states now have statutes that require professionals who suspect any form of child, elder, or dependent-adult abuse to report it to the appropriate agencies, even when the knowledge was gained through confidential communication with clients. The failure to report often includes substantial fines, and even imprisonment (Ahia & Martin, 1993). Professionals who report suspected child, elder, or dependent-adult abuse are immune from prosecution for breaching confidentiality. **Mandatory reporting** is designed to encourage reporting of any suspected cases of child, elder, or dependent-adult abuse; thus, therapists are advised to err on the side of reporting in uncertain circumstances (Benitez, 2004).

Exceptions to Confidentiality and Privileged Communication. The circumstances under which confidentiality cannot be maintained are not clearly defined by accepted ethical standards, and therapists must exercise their own professional judgment. When assuring their clients that what they reveal will ordinarily be kept confidential, therapists should point out that they have obligations to others besides their clients. All of the major professional organizations have taken the position that practitioners must reveal certain information when there is clear and imminent danger to an individual or to society; therapists are bound to act in such a way as to protect others from harm. The ASCA's (2004) ethical standard states this clearly:

> The professional school counselor keeps information confidential unless disclosure is required to prevent clear and imminent danger to the student or others or when legal requirements demand that confidential information be revealed. Counselors will consult with appropriate professionals when in doubt as to the validity of an exception. (A.2.b.)

It is the responsibility of therapists to clarify the ethical and legal restrictions on confidentiality. Consider these exceptional circumstances in which it is permissible to share information with others in the interest of providing competent services to clients:

- When the client consents to disclosure
- When reimbursement or other legal rules require disclosure
- When clerical assistants handle confidential information, as in managed care
- When the counselor consults with experts or peers
- When the counselor is working under supervision
- When other mental health professionals request information and the client has given consent to share
- When other professionals are involved in a treatment team and coordinate care of a client

Remley and Herlihy (2005) provide a detailed discussion of exceptions to confidentiality and privileged communication. Among the conditions that warrant disclosure of information shared in the counseling relationship are these legally mandated exceptions to confidentiality and privileged communication:

- Disclosure is ordered by a court
- Clients file complaints against their counselors
- Clients claim psychological damage in a lawsuit
- Civil commitment proceedings are initiated

Remley and Herlihy underscore the importance of consultation (and documentation) whenever practitioners are in doubt about their obligations regarding confidentiality or privileged communication.

The limitations of confidentiality may be greater in some settings and agencies than in others. If clients are informed about the conditions under which confidentiality may be compromised, they are in a better position to decide whether to enter counseling. If clients are involved in involuntary counseling, they can decide what they will disclose in their sessions. It is generally accepted that clients have a right to understand in advance the circumstances under which therapists are required or allowed to communicate information about the client to third parties. Unless clients understand the exceptions to confidentiality, their consent to treatment is not genuinely informed.

If you breach confidentiality in an unprofessional manner (in the absence of a recognized exception), you open yourself to both ethical and legal sanctions, including expulsion from a professional association, loss of certification, license revocation, and a malpractice suit. To protect yourself against such liability, Ahia and Martin (1993) recommend taking the following actions. As part of the written informed consent process, let your clients know about all counseling procedures and policies, including confidentiality and its exceptions. Become familiar with all applicable ethical and legal guidelines pertaining to confidentiality, including state privilege laws and their exceptions, child, elder, and disabled abuse reporting requirements, and the parameters of the duty-to-warn exceptions in your state.

The Case of Larry. Larry, 14 years old, is sent to a family guidance clinic by his parents. During the first session the counselor sees Larry and his parents together. She tells the parents in his presence that what she and Larry discuss will be confidential and that she will not feel free to disclose information acquired through the sessions without his permission. The parents seem to understand that confidentiality is necessary for trust to develop between their son and his counselor.

At first Larry is reluctant to come in for counseling. Eventually, as the sessions go on, he discloses that he has a serious drug problem. Larry's parents know that he was using drugs at one time, but he has told them that he is no longer using them. The counselor listens to anecdote after anecdote about Larry's use of illegal drugs, about how "I get loaded at school every day," and about a few brushes with death when he was under the influence of drugs. Finally, she tells Larry that she does not want the responsibility of knowing he is experimenting with illegal drugs and that she will not agree to continue the counseling relationship unless he stops using them. At this stage she agrees not to inform his parents, on the condition that he quits using drugs, but she does tell him that she will be talking with one of her colleagues about the situation.

Larry apparently stops using drugs for several weeks. However, one night while he is under the influence of methamphetamine he has a serious automobile accident. As a result of the accident, Larry is paralyzed for life. Larry's parents angrily assert that they had a legal right to be informed that he was seriously involved in drug use, and they file suit against both the counselor and the agency.

- What is your general impression of the way Larry's counselor handled the case?
- Do you think the counselor acted in a responsible way toward herself? the client? the parents? the agency?
- If you were convinced that Larry was likely to hurt himself or others because of his drug use and his emotional instability, would you have informed his parents, even at the risk of losing Larry as a client? Why or why not?

- Which of the following courses of action might you have taken if you had been Larry's counselor? Check as many as you think are appropriate:

_____ State the legal limits on you as a therapist during the initial session.
_____ Consult with the supervisor of the agency.
_____ Refer Larry for psychological testing to determine the degree of his emotional disturbance.
_____ Refer Larry to a psychiatrist for treatment.
_____ Continue to see Larry without any stipulations.
_____ Insist on a session with Larry's parents as a condition of continuing counseling.
_____ Inform the police or other authorities.
_____ Document your decision-making process with a survey of pertinent research.

- What potential ethical violations do you see in this case?

Three Short Cases. The following cases deal with ethical and legal aspects of confidentiality. What do you think you would do in each of these situations?

1. You are a student counselor. For your internship you are working with college students on campus. Your intern group meets with a supervisor each week to discuss your cases. One day, while you are having lunch in the campus cafeteria with three other interns, they begin to discuss their cases in detail, even mentioning names of clients. They joke about some of the clients they are seeing, while nearby are other students who may be able to overhear this conversation. What would you do in this situation?

_____ I would tell the other interns to stop talking about their clients where other students could overhear them and to continue their conversation in a private place.
_____ I would bring the matter up in our next practicum meeting with the supervisor.
_____ I would not do anything because the students who could overhear the conversation would most likely not be that interested in what was being said.

2. You are leading a counseling group on a high school campus. The members have voluntarily joined the group. In one of the sessions several of the students discuss the drug use on their campus, and two of them reveal that they sell illegal substances to their friends. You discuss this matter with them, and they claim that there is nothing wrong with using these drugs. They argue that most of the students on campus use drugs, that no one has been harmed, and that there isn't any difference between using drugs (which they know is illegal) and using alcohol. What would you do in this situation?

_____ Because their actions are illegal, I would report them to the police.
_____ I would do nothing because their drug use doesn't seem to be a problem for them, and I would not want to jeopardize their trust in me.

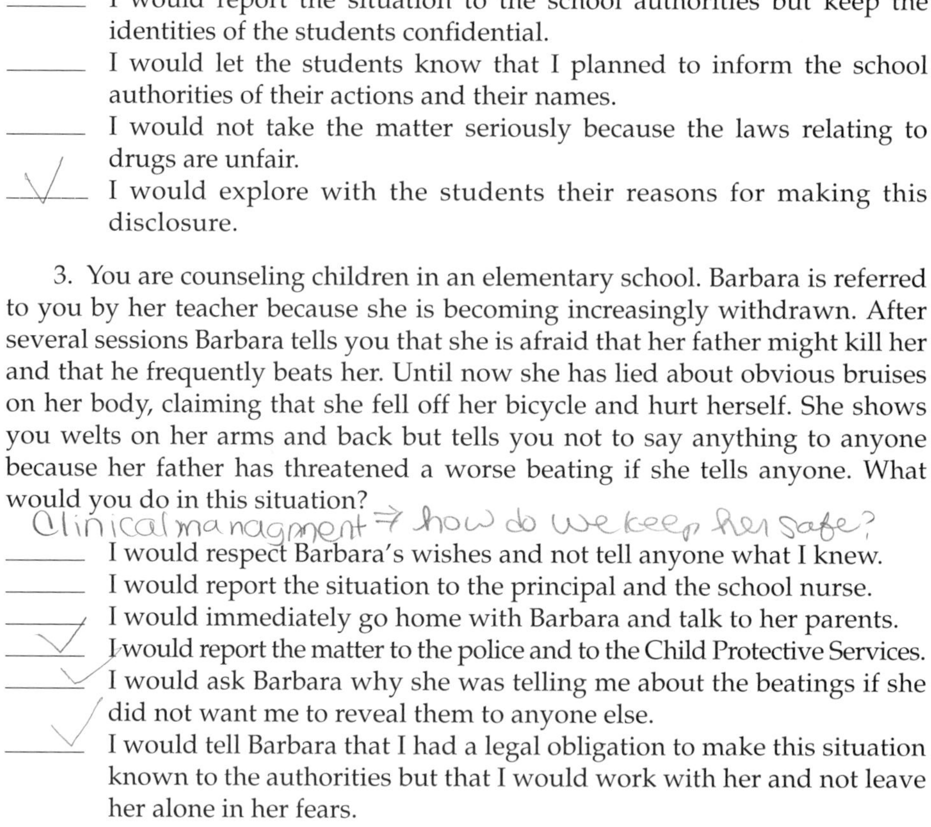

______ I would report the situation to the school authorities but keep the identities of the students confidential.

______ I would let the students know that I planned to inform the school authorities of their actions and their names.

______ I would not take the matter seriously because the laws relating to drugs are unfair.

______ I would explore with the students their reasons for making this disclosure.

3. You are counseling children in an elementary school. Barbara is referred to you by her teacher because she is becoming increasingly withdrawn. After several sessions Barbara tells you that she is afraid that her father might kill her and that he frequently beats her. Until now she has lied about obvious bruises on her body, claiming that she fell off her bicycle and hurt herself. She shows you welts on her arms and back but tells you not to say anything to anyone because her father has threatened a worse beating if she tells anyone. What would you do in this situation?

______ I would respect Barbara's wishes and not tell anyone what I knew.

______ I would report the situation to the principal and the school nurse.

______ I would immediately go home with Barbara and talk to her parents.

______ I would report the matter to the police and to the Child Protective Services.

______ I would ask Barbara why she was telling me about the beatings if she did not want me to reveal them to anyone else.

______ I would tell Barbara that I had a legal obligation to make this situation known to the authorities but that I would work with her and not leave her alone in her fears.

Privacy Issues With Telecommunication Devices

The use of the telephone, answering machines, voice mail, pagers, faxes, cellular phones, and e-mail can pose a number of potential ethical problems regarding the protection of privacy of clients. Mental health practitioners need to exercise caution in discussing confidential or privileged information with anyone over the telephone. Remley and Herlihy (2005, pp. 273–274) offer these guidelines for counselors using the telephone:

- Do not acknowledge that clients are receiving services or give out information regarding clients to unknown callers.
- Strive to verify that you are actually talking to the intended person when you make or receive calls in which confidential information will be discussed.
- Be aware that there is no way to prevent your conversation from being recorded or monitored by an unintended person.
- Be professional, brief, and very careful in talking about confidential information over the telephone.

- Avoid making any comments that you would not want your client to hear or that you would not want to repeat in a legal proceeding.

There are also privacy issues involved in using answering machines, voice mail, pagers, and cellular telephones. Remley and Herlihy offer a number of suggestions to protect the privacy of clients:

- Do not allow unauthorized persons to hear answering machine messages in your office as they are being left or retrieved.
- If you use voice mail or an answering service, ensure that your access codes are not disclosed to unauthorized persons.
- When you leave a message on an answering machine, be aware that the intended person may not be the one who retrieves your message. A family member may retrieve a personal message you left for a client.
- If you are talking to a client by cellular phone, assume that he or she is not in a private place. Also, realize that your conversation may be intercepted by an unauthorized person.
- If you use a pager or a cell phone to send text messages, exercise caution. In sending a text message to a client, be mindful of ensuring your client's privacy by exercising the same caution you would if you were sending a voice mail message.

Using fax machines and e-mail to send confidential material is another source of potential invasion of a client's privacy. It is the counselor's responsibility to make sure fax and e-mail transmissions arrive in a secured environment in such a way as to protect confidential information. Before sending a confidential fax or e-mail, it is a good idea to make a telephone call to ensure that the appropriate person will be able to retrieve this information in a safe and sensitive manner (Cottone & Tarvydas, 2003).

Frankel (2000) states that he will not use e-mail to provide services unless all of the following conditions are met: having an existing professional relationship with a client; providing the client with informed consent about the use of e-mail and its attendant confidentiality; and limiting the e-mail exchange to giving a client basic information such as an appointment. Because e-mail is notoriously unsafe in the way that most people use it, Freeny (2001) contends that security and privacy issues in the use of e-mail must be disclosed in detail to clients.

It should not be assumed that e-mail is private, because e-mail messages can easily be accessed by people other than their intended recipients (Shapiro & Schulman, 1996). Good practice dictates that you do not send clients e-mail messages at their workplace because they have no right to privacy in that situation. Furthermore, the courts have ruled that e-mail sent or received on computers used by employees is considered to be the property of the company, and therefore, privacy and confidentiality do not exist. Employees may have the illusion that they own the contents of their home computers, but it is just an illusion (Rahn Minagawa, personal communication, August 14, 2003). Since there is no reasonable expectation of confidentiality for e-mail, clients need to have input regarding how they want communication to be handled so that their privacy is protected.

This discussion of privacy may appear to be mere common sense, but we have become so accustomed to relying on technology that careful thought is not always given to subtle ways that privacy can be violated. Exercise caution and pay attention to ways that you could unintentionally breach the privacy of your clients when using these forms of communication. Apprise your clients of potential problems of privacy regarding a wide range of technology and discuss how they might best contact you between office visits and how you might leave messages for them. Take preventive measures so that both you and your clients have an understanding and agreement about these important concerns.

Implications of HIPAA for Mental Health Providers

The **Health Insurance Portability and Accountability Act of 1996 (HIPAA)** was passed by Congress to promote standardization and efficiency in the health care industry and to give patients more rights and control over their health information. HIPAA includes provisions designed to encourage electronic transactions and requires certain new safeguards to protect the security and confidentiality of health information. The new privacy regulations protect patients by limiting the ways that covered entities can use patients' medical information and other individually identifiable health information. The privacy rule requires health plans and other covered entities to establish policies and procedures to protect the confidentiality of protected health information about their patients.

What is a **covered entity**? Jensen (2003b) explains that there are three types of covered entities: health plans, health care clearinghouses, and health care providers who transmit health information by electronic means. To determine that you are a "covered entity," you need to answer affirmatively to all three of these questions:

1. Are you a health care provider?
2. Do you transmit information electronically?
3. Do you conduct covered transactions?

According to Jensen, if you do not answer "yes" to all of these questions, or if you do not employ someone to conduct the covered transactions for you, then you are not a covered entity and HIPAA does not apply to you.

If you want to avoid becoming a covered entity, Jensen (2003e) offers these suggestions:

- Do not use your computer to conduct one of the standard/covered transactions.
- Use only your telephone, the mail, or your fax machine.

- Avoid hiring a person to do your billing services to clients if he or she conducts one of the standard/covered transactions electronically.
- Do not allow health plans to communicate with you electronically.
- Make certain that health plans communicate with you about clients only by phone, mail, or fax machine.

In his article, "HIPAA Overview," Jensen (2003b) describes the four components of HIPAA: (1) privacy requirements, (2) electronic transactions, (3) security requirements, and (4) national identifier requirements. Let's examine each in more detail.

Privacy requirements. The Privacy Rule of HIPAA provides patients with rights concerning how their health information is used and disclosed by health care providers who fall within the domain of HIPAA. The Privacy Rule requires practitioners to take reasonable precautions in safeguarding patient information. Providers are expected to have a working knowledge of and guard patients' rights to privacy in disclosure of information, health care operations, limiting the disclosure of protected information, payment matters, protected health information, psychotherapy notes and a patient's medical record, and treatment activities.

Electronic transactions. HIPAA aims at creating one national form of communication, or "language," so that health care providers can communicate with one another electronically in this common language.

Security requirements. Minimum requirements are outlined in HIPAA that are designed to safeguard confidential information and prevent unauthorized access to health information of patients.

National identifier requirements. It is essential that covered entities be able to communicate with one another efficiently. Health care providers and health plans are required to have national identification numbers that identify them when they are conducting standard transactions.

Only mental health providers who fall within the definition of *covered entity* are subject to HIPPA requirements. Those providers who do not fall within this scope of practice are not required to comply with HIPAA requirements, unless they choose to do so (Jensen, 2003e).

Handerscheid, Henderson, and Chalk (2002) state that HIPAA privacy requirements are meant to protect confidential patient information irrespective of the form in which the information is stored. To comply, covered entities first need to review their routine business practices to assess how well patient information is protected against inappropriate disclosures. The second step involves modifying business policies or practices once any problems are detected. The third step involves working with consumers to inform them of their rights, advise them about providing written authorization for release of information, and describe grievance procedures clients can use if they believe their privacy has been violated. (For more background on HIPAA, see United States Department of Health and Human Services, 2003.)

The Duty to Warn and to Protect

Mental health professionals, spurred by the courts, have come to realize that they have a double professional responsibility: to protect other people from potentially dangerous clients and to protect clients from themselves. When considering these duties, Mitchell (2001) states that those in the counseling profession often have to weigh these conflicting principles:

- The client's right to privacy versus the therapist's responsibility to protect society
- The client's right of confidentiality versus the therapist's obligation to protect the community from violent behavior
- The client's right to die versus the therapist's obligation to save lives

Mitchell makes it clear that there is a delicate balance between a client's right and the public good. In this section we look first at therapists' responsibilities to warn and to protect potential victims and then at the problems posed by suicidal clients.

The Duty to Protect Potential Victims

Practitioners need to integrate legal and professional issues into their clinical practices in such a manner that care of clients is not compromised. Bednar and his colleagues (1991) maintain that counselors must exercise the ordinary skill and care of a reasonable professional in (1) identifying those clients who are likely to do physical harm to third parties, (2) protecting third parties from those clients judged potentially dangerous, and (3) treating those clients who are dangerous.

One of the most difficult tasks therapists grapple with is deciding whether a particular client is dangerous. Although practitioners are not generally legally liable for their failure to render perfect predictions of violent behavior of a client, a professionally inadequate assessment of client dangerousness can result in liability for the therapist, harm to third parties, and inappropriate breaches of client confidentiality. Therapists faced with potentially dangerous clients should take specific steps to protect the public and to minimize their own liability. They should take careful histories, advise clients of the limits of confidentiality, keep accurate notes of threats and other client statements, seek consultation, and record steps they have taken to protect others. Indeed, it is extremely difficult to decide when breaching confidentiality to protect potential victims is justified.

Most states permit (if not require) therapists to breach confidentiality to warn or protect victims. In addition, many states grant therapists protection from being sued for breaching confidentiality if the therapist can demonstrate that he or she acted in good faith to protect third parties (Stromberg, Schneider, & Joondeph, 1993). Ahia and Martin (1993) state that there is clearly no exact way to determine who is a reasonably identifiable victim who must be warned of the dangerous behavior of a client. Clinicians are advised to consult with a supervisor or an attorney because they may be subject to liability for either failing to warn those entitled to warnings or warning those who are not entitled.

The responsibility to protect the public from dangerous acts of violent clients entails liability for civil damages when practitioners neglect this duty by (1) failing to diagnose or predict dangerousness, (2) failing to warn potential victims of violent behavior, (3) failing to commit dangerous individuals, or (4) prematurely discharging dangerous clients from a hospital (APA, 1985). The first two of these legally prescribed duties are illustrated in the case of *Tarasoff v. Board of Regents of the University of California* (1976), which has been the subject of extensive analysis in the psychological literature. The other two duties are set forth in additional landmark court cases.

The *Tarasoff* Case. In August 1969 Prosenjit Poddar was a voluntary outpatient at the student health service at the University of California, Berkeley and was in counseling with a psychologist named Moore. Poddar had confided to Moore his intention to kill an unnamed woman (who was readily identifiable as Tatiana Tarasoff) when she returned from an extended trip in Brazil. In consultation with other university counselors, Moore made the assessment that Poddar was dangerous and should be committed to a mental hospital for observation. Moore later called the campus police and told them of the death threat and of his conclusion that Poddar was dangerous. The campus officers did take Poddar into custody for questioning, but they later released him when he gave evidence of being "rational" and promised to stay away from Tarasoff. He was never confined to a treatment facility. Moore followed up his call with a formal letter requesting the assistance of the chief of the campus police. Later, Moore's supervisor asked that the letter be returned, ordered that the letter and Moore's case notes be destroyed, and asked that no further action be taken in the case. Tarasoff and her family were never made aware of this potential threat.

Shortly after Tarasoff's return from Brazil, Poddar killed her. Her parents filed suit against the Board of Regents and employees of the university for having failed to notify the intended victim of the threat. A lower court dismissed the suit in 1974, the parents appealed, and the California Supreme Court ruled in favor of the parents in 1976, holding that a failure to warn an intended victim was professionally irresponsible. The court's ruling requires that therapists breach confidentiality in cases where the general welfare and safety of others is involved. This was a California case, and courts in other states are not bound to decide a similar case in the same way.

Under the *Tarasoff* decision, the therapist must first accurately diagnose the client's tendency to behave in dangerous ways toward others. This first duty is judged by the standards of professional negligence. In this case the therapist did not fail in this duty. He even took the additional step of requesting that the dangerous person be detained by the campus police. But the court held that simply notifying the police was insufficient to protect the identifiable victim (Laughran & Bakken, 1984).

In the first ruling, in 1974, the lower court cited a **duty to warn,** but this duty was expanded by the 1976 California Supreme Court ruling, which said:

"When a therapist determines, or pursuant to the standards of his profession should determine, that his patient presents a serious danger of violence to another, he incurs an obligation to use reasonable care to protect the intended victim against such danger." Attorney Bonnie Benitez (2004) sets out the following key points of *Tarasoff* and the duty to warn:

- Therapists have a duty to warn when a client communicates to them a serious threat of physical violence against an identified victim or victims.
- The duty is discharged by the therapist making reasonable efforts to communicate the threat to the victim or victims and to a law enforcement agency.
- Therapists who make such a warning are granted immunity from any liability that may arise should the client carry out his or her threat.
- Therapists are not expected to predict violence of their clients.
- If therapists fail to warn when a threat has been made, they may be liable not only for the harm to the intended victim, but also to other victims who may be injured if the threat is carried out.

Therapists can protect others through traditional clinical interventions such as reassessment, medication changes, referral, or hospitalization. Other steps therapists may take include warning potential victims, calling the police, or informing the state child protection agency. Negligence lies in the practitioner's failure to warn a third party of imminent danger, not in failing to predict any violence that may be committed. Stromberg, Schneider, and Joondeph (1993) indicate that courts and legislatures tend to be sympathetic toward interns in the mental health professions in terms of predicting violence, identifying potential victims, and requiring therapists to protect third parties. In fact, few reported decisions have found mental health professionals actually liable for failing to protect a threatened third party. Because psychology is not an exact science, predicting the likelihood of future dangerousness cannot be done in a highly reliable manner.

The *Tarasoff* decision made it clear that client confidentiality can be readily compromised; indeed, "the protective privilege ends where the public peril begins" (cited in Perlin, 1997). As Bednar and his colleagues (1991) indicate, the mental health professional is a double agent. Therapists have ethical and legal responsibilities to their clients, and they also have legal obligations to society. These dual responsibilities sometimes conflict, and they can create ambiguity in the therapeutic relationship. State courts and legislatures vary in their interpretations of *Tarasoff*, and practitioners remain uncertain about the nature of their duty to protect or to warn. However, the codes of ethics of most mental health professions incorporate this concept, and it is generally assumed that the duty to warn and to protect is a national legal requirement.

In their assessment of *Tarasoff*, Knapp and VandeCreek (1982) make the point that variations in state laws make the procedures involved in the "duty to warn" a difficult matter. In the *Tarasoff* case, the identity of the victim was known. However, therapists are often concerned about legal responsibility when the identity of the intended victim is unknown. What are the therapist's obligations in cases of generalized statements of hostility? What is the responsibility of the therapist to predict future violence? Knapp and VandeCreek recommend that "psychotherapists need only follow reasonable standards in predicting violence. Psychotherapists are not liable for the failure to warn when the propensity toward violence is unknown or would be unknown by other psychotherapists using ordinary skill" (pp. 514–515). Their point is that therapists should not become intimidated by every idle fantasy, for every impulsive threat is not evidence of imminent danger. In their opinion recent behavioral acts can best predict future violence.

Knapp and VandeCreek suggest that practitioners consider other alternatives to diffuse the danger and, at the same time, satisfy their legal duty. They recommend seeking consultation with other professionals who have expertise in dealing with potentially violent people and documenting the steps taken. VandeCreek and Knapp (2001) recommend that therapists do well to adhere to risk management strategies in dealing with dangerous patients. In particular, therapists need to be especially careful about grounds for liability including abandonment; failure to consult, refer, or coordinate treatment with a physician; maintaining adequate records; and responding appropriately if a suit is filed.

At the time the *Tarasoff* decision was issued it was binding only in California, and therapists in other states did not know whether courts in their states would comply with this decision (VandeCreek & Knapp, 2001). Not all states have embraced the *Tarasoff* doctrine. In 1999 the members of the Texas Supreme Court unanimously rejected the *Tarasoff* duty (*Thapar v. Zezulka*, 1999). Basing its decision on the Texas statute governing the legal duty of mental health professionals to protect clients' confidentiality, the court found that it was unwise to impose a duty to warn on mental health practitioners.

Zur (2005) points out that in July 2004 a California appeals court decision extended the interpretation of the *Tarasoff* warning law. In *Ewing v. Goldstein* (2004) the court expanded the warning to include a family member who believes a patient to pose a risk of grave bodily injury to another person. This court decision means that licensed therapists in California could be held liable for failure to issue a *Tarasoff* warning when the information regarding the dangerousness of a client comes from a client's family member rather than from the client. Zur recommends that California therapists add this recent court decision to their informed consent document. In his discussion of the *Ewing* and *Tarasoff* cases, Jensen (2005) synopsizes the court ruling as follows:

> Communication from a patient's "family member" to the patient's therapist, made for the purpose of advancing the patient's therapy, may create a duty upon the therapist to warn an intended victim of the patient's threatened violent behavior. (p. 33)

The *Bradley* Case. A second case illustrates the duty not to negligently release a dangerous client. In *Bradley Center v. Wessner* (1982) the patient, Wessner, had been voluntarily admitted to a facility for psychiatric care. Wessner was upset over his wife's extramarital affair. He had repeatedly threatened to kill her and her lover and had even admitted to a therapist that he was carrying a weapon in his car for that purpose. He was given an unrestricted weekend pass to visit his children, who were living with his wife. He met his wife and her lover in the home and shot and killed them. The children filed a wrongful death suit, alleging that the psychiatric center had breached a duty to exercise control over Wessner. The Georgia Supreme Court ruled that a physician has a duty to take reasonable care to prevent a potentially dangerous patient from inflicting harm (Laughran & Bakken, 1984).

The *Jablonski* Case. A third legal ruling underscores the duty to commit a dangerous individual. The intended victim's knowledge of a threat does not relieve therapists of the duty to protect, as can be seen by the decision in *Jablonski v. United States* (1983). Meghan Jablonski filed suit for the wrongful death of her mother, Melinda Kimball, who was murdered by Philip Jablonski, the man with whom she had been living. Earlier, Philip Jablonski had agreed to a psychiatric examination at a hospital. The physicians determined that there was no emergency and thus no basis for involuntary commitment. Kimball later again accompanied Jablonski to the hospital and expressed fears for her own safety. She was told by a doctor that "you should consider staying away from him." Again, the doctors concluded that there was no basis for involuntary hospitalization and released him. Shortly thereafter Jablonski killed Kimball. The Ninth U.S. Circuit Court of Appeals found that failure to obtain Jablonski's prior medical history constituted malpractice. The essence of *Jablonski* is a negligent failure to commit (Laughran & Bakken, 1984).

The *Hedlund* Case. The decision in *Hedlund v. Superior Court* (1983) extends the duty to warn to anyone who might be near the intended victim and who might also be in danger. LaNita Wilson and Stephen Wilson had received psychotherapy from a psychological assistant, Bonnie Hedlund. During treatment Stephen Wilson told the therapist that he intended to harm LaNita Wilson. Later he did assault her, in the presence of her child. The allegation was that the child had sustained "serious emotional injury and psychological trauma."

In keeping with the *Tarasoff* decision, the California Supreme Court held (1) that a therapist has a duty first to exercise a "reasonable degree of skill, knowledge, and care ordinarily possessed and exercised by members [of that professional specialty] under similar circumstances" in making a prediction about the chances of a client's acting dangerously to others and (2) that therapists must "exercise reasonable care to protect the foreseeable victim of that danger." One way to protect the victim is by giving a warning of peril. The court held that breach of such a duty with respect to third persons constitutes "professional negligence" (Laughran & Bakken, 1984).

In the Hedlund case the duty to warn of potentially dangerous conduct applied to the mother, not to her child, against whom no threats had been made. However, the duty to exercise reasonable care could have been fulfilled by warning the mother that she and her child might be in danger.

The *Jaffee* Case. In *Jaffee v. Redmond* (1996) the U.S. Supreme Court ruled that communications between licensed psychotherapists and their clients are privileged and therefore protected from forced disclosure in cases arising under federal law. The 7–2 decision in this case represented a victory for mental health organizations because it extended the confidentiality privilege.

An on-duty police officer, Mary Lu Redmond, shot and killed a suspect while attempting an arrest. The victim's family sued in federal court, alleging that the victim's constitutional rights had been violated. The court ordered Karen Beyer, a licensed clinical social worker, to turn over notes she made during counseling sessions with Redmond after the shooting. The social worker refused, asserting that the contents of her conversations with the police officer were protected against involuntary disclosure by psychotherapist-client privilege. The court rejected her claim of psychotherapist-client privilege, and the jury awarded the family $545,000.

The Court of Appeals for the Seventh Circuit then reversed this decision and concluded that the trial court had erred by refusing to afford protection to the confidential communications between Redmond and Beyer. Jaffee, an administrator of the victim's estate, appealed this decision to the Supreme Court.

The Supreme Court upheld the appellate court's decision, clarifying for all federal court cases, both civil and criminal, the existence of the privilege. The Court recognized a broadly defined psychotherapist-client privilege and further clarified that this privilege is not subject to the decision of a judge on a case-by-case basis. The Court's decision to extend federal privilege (which already applied to psychologists and psychiatrists) to licensed social workers leaves the door open for inclusion of other licensed psychotherapists, such as licensed professional counselors, mental health counselors, and licensed marriage and family therapists. The issues in this case are critical for psychotherapists, and it is expected that this decision will have far-reaching consequences for licensed psychotherapists and their clients (Hinnefeld & Towers, 1996; Morrissey, 1996; Newman, 1996; Seppa, 1996).

In discussing the impact on the law of the *Jaffee v. Redmond* case, Shuman and Foote (1999) indicate that the case is not constitutionally based. Instead, *Jaffee* is an interpretation of the Federal Rules of Evidence that apply in actions tried in federal courts. Thus, *Jaffee* applies only in federal cases, both civil and criminal, governed by the Federal Rules of Evidence. Knapp and VandeCreek (1997) conclude that more work needs to be done in extending equal protection to clients across all states. In that way therapists will better be able to inform their clients about the limits to confidentiality. Glosoff and colleagues (1997) support this point of view, saying there needs to be a consistent definition of privilege because therapists may be liable in a legal claim for breach of duty if they neglect to *accurately* describe the limits of confidentiality to their clients.

DeBell and Jones (1997) state that *Jaffee* does not appear to cover couples, family, and group therapy. It might be reasonable to argue that couple and family therapy are no different than individual therapy in this regard, but a problem arises when one party is willing to divulge or requests the therapist to divulge the information. Likewise with group therapy, it is essential that group therapists be familiar with the laws of their own states in regard to privilege in group therapy (DeBell & Jones, 1997).

Implications of Duty to Warn and to Protect for School Counselors

In her doctoral dissertation on legal issues in counseling, Hermann (2001) describes the multiple interpretations of the *Tarasoff* duty and the lack of case law as it pertains to the duty to warn and protect in situations of potential violence in school settings. The basic standard of care for school counselors is clear; courts have uniformly held that school personnel have a duty to protect students from foreseeable harm (Hermann & Remley, 2000). School personnel may need to act on student reports of their peers' plans related to intended violence. Furthermore, school officials may be held accountable if a student's writing assignments contain evidence of premeditated violence.

Hermann and Finn (2002) contend that school counselors are legally and ethically obligated to work toward preventing school violence. They state that school counselors may find themselves legally vulnerable because of their role in determining whether students pose a risk of harm to others and deciding on appropriate interventions with these students. Current case law reveals that all indicators of potential violence should be taken seriously.

Hermann (2002) found that 63% of the school counselors in her study believed they were well prepared to determine whether a student posed a danger to others. Preventing students from harming other students seems to be implicit in the duty of school personnel. Courts have consistently found that school counselors have a duty to exercise reasonable care to protect students from foreseeable harm, but they are only exposed to legal liability if they fail to exercise reasonable care (Hermann & Remley, 2000).

In the short space of one month in 2001, two major shooting incidents took place within the same school district in San Diego, California. Both of these events resulted in intense national media coverage and raised the question of how these tragedies might have been prevented. In the first event the boy doing the shooting had told a couple of his friends of his intentions, and they searched his knapsack for a gun, which they could not find. The shooter insisted he was joking, and his friends failed to report the matter because they did not want to get him in trouble. He later killed 2 and injured 13 others on the campus. In the second incident, no one was killed, but several were injured. In this case, the student had made prior threats of violence.

School counselors are increasingly being forced to deal with incidents and threats of violence by students (Isaacs, 1997). Costa and Altekruse (1994) recommend that school counselors make an assessment of dangerousness by evaluating the student's plans for implementing the violent act and the student's ability to carry out the act. Waldo and Malley (1992) advise gathering the necessary information to make a determination about the student's potential dangerousness, and when faced with potential dangerousness, counselors should consult with other mental health professionals and with legal counsel about the state's most recent position on *Tarasoff*-type cases. Given the context of emerging case law and the violent climate of today's schools, Hermann and Remley (2000) assert that school counselors would do well to take every threat of violence seriously.

Many schools are now searching students for weapons, which has resulted in protests from some that schools are infringing on students' constitutional rights. On this point, Hermann and Remley report that in the wake of public outrage at school violence constitutional rights are being restricted at the schoolhouse gates:

> As school violence and school security increase, students are likely to continue to engage in court battles against educators seeking lost constitutional protections. And educators face even more litigation as those injured seek to find someone to blame for the unfortunate societal phenomenon of guns and violence in schools. (p. 439)

The central ethical concern surrounding this issue involves the commitment of mental health professionals to develop organized prevention efforts in response to school violence. Although many psychologists are involved in assessing and treating at-risk youth for violent behavior, Evans and Rey (2001) report that efforts are not often directed toward organized prevention of violence and delinquency. Not only are psychologists being asked to shed light on the community's understanding of the causes of high-profile incidences of violence, but they are increasingly being asked what they might do to help prevent youth violence, both in and out of the school. Evans and Rey believe practicing psychologists represent a critical resource to school districts in designing and implementing a comprehensive violence prevention program. They outline a collaborative program between a model school and a mental health clinic that can be replicated in a variety of settings.

Guidelines for Dealing With Dangerous Clients

Most counseling centers and community mental health agencies now have guidelines regarding the duty to warn and protect when the welfare of others is at stake. These guidelines generally specify how to deal with emotionally disturbed individuals, violent behavior, threats, suicidal possibilities, and other circumstances in which counselors may be legally and ethically required to breach confidentiality.

The question raised by these documents is, "What are the responsibilities of counselors to their clients or to others when, in the professional judgment of the counselor, there is a high degree of probability that a client will seriously harm another person or destroy property?" Understandably, many counselors find it difficult to predict when clients pose a serious threat to others. Clients are encouraged to engage in open dialogue in therapeutic relationships, and many clients express feelings or thoughts about doing physical harm to others. But few of these threats are actually carried out, and counselors should not be expected to routinely reveal all threats. Breaking confidentiality can seriously harm the client-therapist relationship as well as the relationship between the client and the person "threatened." Such disclosures should be carefully evaluated; counselors should exercise reasonable professional judgment and apply practices that are commonly accepted by professionals in the specialty.

In most cases therapists will not have advanced warning that a client is dangerous. Therefore, it is essential for therapists to be prepared to take action when they are presented with dangerous situations. We offer the following suggestions:

- Examine your informed consent document. Is it clear in terms of the forfeiture of privilege because of a threat of violence to self or others?
- Know how to contact the legal counsel of your professional organization.
- Familiarize yourself with professionals who are experienced in dealing with violence and know how to reach them.
- In the initial interview, if there is any hint of violence in the client's history, request clinical records from previous therapists, if they exist.
- Take at least one workshop in the assessment and management of dangerous clients.
- Determine that the limits of your professional liability insurance are adequate.

If you have prepared yourself for the eventuality of a dangerous client, you will have a better sense of what to do in these circumstances.

Truscott, Evans, and Mansell (1995) present a model for clinical decision making to determine the best interventions for dealing with dangerous outpatient clients that takes into account the degree of risk of violence and the strength of the therapeutic alliance. They suggest a periodic informal assessment of the therapeutic alliance and maintenance of detailed case notes pertaining to the alliance. Some specific aspects of the therapeutic relationship to be assessed include the level of trust between client and clinician, the client's perception of feeling understood and accepted, indication of working toward shared goals, and notes on the helpfulness of therapy and the value of the therapeutic process.

From the vantage point of limiting therapist exposure to duty to protect liability, Monahan (1993) emphasizes the role of documentation as a risk management strategy. As was mentioned in Chapter 5, under no circumstances should clinicians alter client records. If asked under oath whether any part of the records have been altered and such entries later come to light, the clinician is guilty of perjury, a criminal offense. Monahan writes:

> It is, in short, much better to admit that you did not keep good records and hope that the jury believes you when you tell them what happened than to manufacture good records after the fact at the cost of your own integrity and credibility. (p. 248)

Now let's explore two case examples. As you think about these cases, ask yourself how you would assess the degree to which Marvin and Matt are potentially dangerous. What would you do if you were the therapist in each case?

✓ **The Case of Marvin.** Marvin has been seeing Robin, his counselor, for several months. One day he comes to the therapy session inebriated and very angry. He has just found out that a close friend is having an affair with his wife. He is deeply wounded over this incident. He is also highly agitated and even talks about killing the friend who betrayed him. As he puts it, "I am so damn mad I feel like getting my gun and shooting him." Marvin experiences intense emotions in this session. Robin does everything she can to defuse his rage and to stabilize him before the session ends. The session continues for about 2 hours (instead of the usual hour), and she asks him to call her a couple of times each day to check in. Before he leaves, she contracts with him that he will not go over to this man's house and that he will not act out his urges. Because of the strength of the therapeutic relationship, she assessed Marvin as not being a violent person and decided not to follow through with the duty to warn. He follows through and calls her every day. When he comes to the session the following week, he admits to still being in a great deal of pain over his discovery, but he no longer feels so angry. As he puts it, "I am not going to land in jail because of this jerk!" He tells Robin how helpful the last session was in allowing him to get a lot off his chest.

- Do you think Robin followed the proper ethical and legal course of action in this case?
- Did she fulfill her responsibilities by making sure that Marvin called her twice a day?
- Some would say that she should have broken confidentiality and warned the intended victim. What do you think? Explain your reasoning.
- What criteria could you use to determine whether the situation is dangerous enough to warn a potential victim? What is the fine line between overreacting and failing to respond appropriately in this kind of case?
- If Robin had sought you out for consultation in this case immediately after the session at which Marvin talked about wanting to kill his friend, how would you have advised her?

The Case of Matt. Matt is a high school student who seems to have the potential for violence. During his sessions with you, he talks about his impulses to hurt others and himself, and he describes times when he has seriously beaten his girlfriend. He tells you that she is afraid to leave him because she thinks he will beat her even more savagely. He later tells you that sometimes he gets so angry that he feels like killing her. You believe Matt could seriously harm and possibly even kill this young woman. Which of the following would you do? Check all that apply.

______ 1. I would notify Matt's girlfriend that she might be in grave danger.
______ 2. I would notify the police or other authorities.
______ 3. I would keep Matt's threats to myself, because I could not be sure that he would act on them.
______ 4. I would seek a second opinion from a colleague.
______ 5. I would inform my director or supervisor.
______ 6. I would refer Matt to another therapist.
______ 7. I would arrange to have Matt hospitalized.

Would you answer differently if Matt showed real promise in therapy and seemed to really want to change his behavior?

The Duty to Protect Suicidal Clients

In the preceding discussion we emphasized the therapist's obligation to protect others from dangerous individuals. The guidelines and principles outlined in that discussion often apply to the client who poses a danger to self, but some courts have found there is not the same duty in cases of suicide as in cases of violence (Mary Hermann, personal communication, March 10, 2005). As part of the informed consent process, therapists must inform clients that they have an ethical and legal obligation to break confidentiality when they have good reason to suspect suicidal behavior. Even if clients argue that they can do what they want with their own lives, including taking them, therapists have a legal **duty to protect** suicidal clients. The crux of the issue is knowing when to take a client's hints seriously enough to report the condition. Certainly not every mention of suicidal thoughts or feelings justifies extraordinary measures.

The evaluation and management of suicidal risk can be a source of great stress for therapists. Clinical practitioners must face many troublesome issues, including their degree of influence, competence, level of involvement with a client, responsibility, legal obligations, and ability to make life-or-death decisions. Remley and Herlihy (2005) state that counselors can be accused of malpractice for neglecting to take action to prevent harm when a client is likely to commit suicide, yet they are also liable if they overreact by taking actions that violate a client's privacy when there is not a justifiable basis for doing so. The law does not require practitioners to always make correct assessments of suicide risk, but therapists do have a legal duty to make assessments from an informed position and to carry out their professional obligations in a manner comparable to what other reasonable professionals would do in similar situations. If a counselor makes a determination that a client is at risk for suicide, the counselor should take the least intrusive steps necessary to prevent the harm. In such cases, consultation with colleagues and documentation are of critical importance (Remley & Herlihy, 2005).

School Counselor Liability for Student Suicide

Suicide by a student is perhaps the greatest tragedy on a campus, and one that shocks the entire school community. Recognizing signs of potential suicide and preventing suicide certainly have to be among the major challenges school counselors face. School counselors are expected to be aware of the warning signs of suicidal behavior and need to have the skills necessary to assess a student's risk for suicide (Capuzzi & Gross, 2000).

In her study of legal issues encountered by school counselors, Hermann (2002) reports the most prevalent legal issue involves school counselors making a determination whether students are suicidal. Hermann found that almost three fourths (72%) of the school counselors surveyed believed they were well prepared to determine whether a client was suicidal. In a study of school counselors' concerns about student suicide, King and colleagues (1999) found that only 38% of the high school counselors surveyed believed they could determine if a student was at risk for committing suicide. King and colleagues (2000) also studied (1) whether high school counselors knew the risk factors associated with suicidal behavior, and (2) whether these counselors knew the appropriate steps to take in intervening with a student who expressed suicidal ideation, had a specific plan, and had the lethal means to carry out the plan. King and colleagues found that the majority of the high school counselors surveyed were knowledgeable about risk factors of adolescent suicide and knew the appropriate steps to take when a student gave indications of suicidal ideation. Many of the respondents also reported that they did not believe they could identify a student at risk for suicide. This discrepancy may result from the reality of the very large numbers of students that school counselors are assigned, which makes it difficult for counselors to have personal knowledge about the majority of the students for whom they are responsible. King and colleagues made a number of suggestions based on their findings:

- Counselors need to educate school employees, especially teachers, about the risk factors associated with adolescent suicide.
- Counselors might institute peer assistance programs to help identify students at risk for suicide.
- It would be useful for school counselors to have increased access to training programs geared to acquiring information about student suicide.
- Given the legal duty to protect students who may pose a danger to themselves, school counselors would do well to take the initiative in obtaining continuing education on recent developments in the field of student suicide to help limit their legal liability.
- Professional journals and professional conferences need to continue highlighting the issue of student suicide.
- Counselor education programs need to better prepare future school counselors to recognize students at risk for suicide.

Court Cases. In school settings, courts have found a special relationship between school personnel and students. Hermann (2001) has documented this, and our discussion is based on her work. One of the first cases that addressed school counselor liability for student suicide was *Eisel v. Board of Education* (1991). In this case, 13-year-old Nicole was involved in Satanism. Nicole made a suicide pact with another student, who subsequently shot Nicole and then shot herself. Fellow students had told their school counselor that Nicole wanted to take her own life. When the school counselor confronted Nicole about her suicidal intentions, she denied making any such statements. The counselor did not attempt to contact Nicole's parents. In *Eisel* the court found that school counselors have a duty to use reasonable means to attempt to prevent a suicide when they know about a student's suicidal intentions. The reasoning of the court was that an adolescent is more likely to share thoughts of suicide with friends than with a school counselor, teacher, or parent. The court found that reasonable care would have included notifying Nicole's parents that their daughter was at risk for suicide. Although the suicide occurred off the school premises, the court held that legally the school could be held liable for failure to exercise reasonable care to prevent a foreseeable injury.

Even if the risk of the student actually committing suicide is remote, the possibility may be enough to establish a duty to contact the parents and to inform them of the potential for suicidal behavior. Courts have found that the burden involved in making a telephone call is minor considering the risk of harm to a student who is suicidal. In short, school personnel are advised to take every suicide threat seriously and to take every precaution to protect the student.

The courts have addressed the need for training school employees in suicide prevention. The *Wyke v. Polk County School Board* (1997) case involved a 13-year-old named Shawn, who attempted suicide two times at school before finally killing himself at home. School officials were aware of the suicide attempts, yet they failed to notify Shawn's mother. During the trial, several experts in the field of suicide prevention testified about the need for suicide prevention training in schools, including mandatory written policies requiring parental notification, holding students in protective custody, and arranging for counseling services. The experts who testified at the trial believed the school board failed to provide adequate training for school personnel. Without training, school personnel will most likely underestimate the lethality of suicidal thoughts, statements, and attempts. The conclusion of this expert testimony was that Shawn would not have committed suicide if the employees had been adequately trained. Persuaded by this input, the court held that the school could be found negligent for failing to notify the decedent's mother.

If you are aiming for a career as a school counselor, you will need more than this basic knowledge regarding your ethical and legal obligations to respond in a professional manner in situations where students may pose a danger to themselves or others. Continuing education is of the utmost importance, as is your willingness to seek appropriate consultation when you become aware of students who are at risk.

✓ **The Case of Rupe.** Rupe, a 16-year-old high school student, is being seen by the school psychologist, Vernon, at the request of his parents. Rupe's school work has dropped off, he has become withdrawn socially, and he has expressed to his parents that he has thought of suicide, even though he has not made a specific plan. After the psychologist has seen Rupe for several weeks of individual counseling, his concerned parents call and ask how he is doing. They wonder whether they should be alert to possible suicide attempts. Rupe's parents tell Vernon that they want to respect confidentiality and are not interested in detailed disclosures but that they want to find out if they have cause for worry. Without going into detail, Vernon reassures them that they really do not need to worry.

- Is Vernon's behavior ethical? Would it make a difference if Rupe were 25 years old?
- Does Vernon have an ethical obligation to inform Rupe of the conversation with his parents?
- If the parents were to insist on having more information, does Vernon have an obligation to say more?

- If Vernon provides details to the parents, does he have an obligation to inform Rupe before talking with his parents?
- Other than doing what this school psychologist did, do you see other courses of action?
- If Rupe were indeed suicidal, what ethical and legal obligations would Vernon have toward the parents? Would he have to inform the school principal?

Guidelines for Assessing Suicidal Behavior

Although it is not possible to prevent every suicide, it is possible to recognize the existence of common crises that may precipitate a suicide attempt and reach out to people who are experiencing these crises. Counselors must take the "cry for help" seriously. Therapists need to have the necessary knowledge and skills to intervene once they make an assessment that a client is suicidal (Fujimura, Weis, & Cochran, 1985). Several researchers have suggested factors to consider when making an assessment (Capuzzi, 2002; Capuzzi & Gross, 2000; Fujimura et al., 1985; Peruzzi & Bongar, 1999; Pope, 1985b; Remley, 2004; Sommers-Flanagan & Sommers-Flanagan, 1995; Wubbolding, 2006). In an assessment interview, especially focus on evaluating depression, suicide ideation, suicide intention, and suicide plans. In crisis counseling, assess your clients for suicidal risk during the early phase of therapy, and keep alert to this issue during the course of therapy. Danger signs, such as those listed here, should be evaluated:

- Take direct verbal warnings seriously, as they are one of the most useful single predictors of a suicide. Be sure to document your actions.
- Pay attention to previous suicide attempts, as these are the best single predictor of lethality.
- Identify clients suffering from depression, a characteristic common to all suicide victims. Sleep disruption, which can intensify depression, is a key sign. For people with clinical depression the suicide rate is about 20 times greater than that of the general population.
- Be alert for feelings of hopelessness and helplessness, which seem to be closely associated with suicidal intentions. Explore the client's ideational and mood states. Individuals may feel desperate, guilt-ridden, and worthless.
- Explore carefully the interpersonal stressor of loss and separation, such as a relationship breakup or the death of a loved one.
- Monitor severe anxiety and panic attacks.
- Determine whether the individual has a plan. The more definite the plan, the more serious is the situation. Suicidal individuals should be asked to talk about their plans and be encouraged to explore their suicidal fantasies.
- Identify clients who have a history of severe alcohol or drug abuse, as they are at greater risk than the general population. Alcohol is a contributing factor in one fourth to one third of all suicides.
- Be alert to client behaviors such as giving away prized possessions, finalizing business affairs, or revising wills.

- Determine whether clients have a history of previous psychiatric treatment or hospitalization. Clients who have been hospitalized for emotional disorders are more likely to be inclined to suicide.
- Assess the client's support system. If there is no support system, the client is at greater risk.

In addition to these factors, be aware of the categories of people who have an increased risk of suicide. Suicide is the 8th leading cause of death in the United States. For the elderly, it is the 13th, and for young people between the ages of 15 and 24, it is the 3rd leading cause of death (Rosenberg, 1999). Men are 3 times more likely than women to commit suicide (the rate rises rapidly until age 35 and is also high for men over 65). Single people are twice as likely as married people to commit suicide. And finally, factors such as unemployment increase the risk of suicide.

Wubbolding (2006) suggests raising the following questions as an approach to assessment of lethality and to open a frank discussion of whether further intervention is necessary:

- Is there a plan?
- Has the person seriously thought about death?
- Does the person have the means available to kill him- or herself?
- Who could stop him or her?
- What kind of emotional support is available in the family, at home, or elsewhere?

Therapists have the responsibility to prevent suicide if they can reasonably anticipate it. Once it is determined that a client is at risk, the professional is legally required to break confidentiality and take appropriate action. Liability generally arises when a counselor fails to act in such a way as to prevent the suicide or when a counselor does something that might contribute to it.

According to Sommers-Flanagan and Sommers-Flanagan (1995), two processes offer safeguards against malpractice liability in suicidal cases: consultation and documentation. Consultation gives professionals working with suicidal clients the support they need in dealing with the most stressful of all clinical activities. Consultation also provides feedback about the degree to which standards of practice are being met. Documentation is especially important when working with suicidal individuals, and practitioners who conduct suicide assessments should document these steps in the process:

- Conduct a thorough assessment
- Obtain a relevant history
- Obtain previous treatment records
- Directly evaluate suicidal thoughts
- Consult with one or more professionals
- Discuss the limits of confidentiality with the client
- Implement appropriate suicide interventions
- Provide resources to the client
- Contact authorities and family members if a client is at high risk for suicide

The final decision about the degree of suicidal risk is a subjective one that demands professional judgment. According to VandeCreek and Knapp (2001), in evaluating liability courts assess the reasonableness of professional judgment in treating a suicidal person. If a client demonstrates suicidal intent, and the therapist does not exercise reasonable precautions, there are grounds for liability. VandeCreek and Knapp provide this advice regarding therapist liability:

> The courts will not hold the psychotherapist liable only because a patient committed suicide. Instead, the plaintiffs must prove that the psychotherapists were negligent in their assessment or treatment. Psychotherapists can demonstrate the adequacy of their treatment through consulting with other psychotherapists and documenting treatment decisions carefully. (p. 34)

In his discussion of legal issues associated with suicide, Remley (2004) states that although therapists are not required to predict all suicide gestures or attempts, they are expected to exercise sound judgment in making clinical decisions, and their reasoning needs to be recorded in their notes.

The Case for Suicide Prevention. Suicidal individuals often hope that somebody will listen to their cry for help. Many are struggling with short-term crises, and if they can be given help in learning to cope with the immediate problem, their potential for suicide can be greatly reduced.

Expectations for action by mental health professionals dealing with suicidal clients differ depending on the setting. In school settings, the law imposes a duty to take precautions to protect students who may be suicidal. A similar standard exists in hospital settings. However, legal opinions are not consistent when addressing suicidal clients in outpatient settings. It should be noted that successful lawsuits have been brought against therapists who did not follow standard procedures to protect a client's life (Austin et al., 1990). The following are recommendations for managing suicidal behavior (see Austin et al., 1990; Bednar et al., 1991; Bennett et al., 1990; Bonger, 2002; Fujimura et al., 1985; Peruzzi & Bongar, 1999; Pope, 1985b; Pope & Vasquez, 1998; Remley, 2004; Rosenberg, 1999; Sommers-Flanagan & Sommers-Flanagan, 1995):

- Know how to determine whether a client may be at risk for attempting suicide.
- Know your personal limits; recognize the stresses involved in working with suicidal clients and the toll that they take on you personally.
- Work with the suicidal client to create a supportive environment.
- Attempt to secure a contract from the client that he or she will not try to commit suicide, either intentionally or unintentionally.
- Periodically collaborate with colleagues and ask for their views regarding the client's condition. Consult with as many colleagues as possible when making difficult decisions and document these discussions.
- Specify your availability to your clients; let them know how they can contact you during your absences.
- Obtain training for suicide prevention and for crisis-intervention methods.
- Keep up to date with current research, theory, and practice.

- Realize that you may have the responsibility to prevent suicide if the act can be reasonably foreseen.
- Recognize the limits of your competence and know when and how to refer.
- Consider hospitalization, weighing the benefits, the drawbacks, and the possible effects. If the client does enter a hospital, pay particular attention to the increased risk of suicide immediately after discharge.
- Be clear and firm with the client, and do not allow yourself to be manipulated by threats. Give clear messages to the client.
- For services that take place within a clinic or agency setting, ensure that clear and appropriate lines of responsibility are explicit and are fully understood by everyone.
- Work with clients so that dangerous instruments are not within easy access. If the client possesses any weapons, make sure that they are in the hands of a third party.
- Consider increasing the frequency of the counseling sessions.
- Work with clients' strengths and desires to remain alive.
- Attempt to communicate realistic hopes.
- Be willing to communicate your caring. Suicidal people sometimes interpret the unwillingness of others to listen as a sign that they do not care. People may be driven to suicide by an avoidance of the topic on the part of the listener. Remember that caring entails some specific actions and setting of limits on your part.
- As much as possible, involve the client in the decisions and actions being taken. It is important for clients to share in the responsibility for their ultimate decisions.
- Attempt to develop a supportive network of family and friends to help clients face their struggles. Discuss this with clients and enlist their help in building this resource of caring people.

Remember that clients are ultimately responsible for their own actions and that there is only so much that you can reasonably do to prevent self-destructive actions. Even though you take specific steps to lessen the chances of a client committing suicide, the client may still take this ultimate step.

The Case Against Suicide Prevention. Now that we have looked at the case for suicide prevention, we explore another point of view. Szasz (1986) challenges the statement that mental health professionals have an absolute professional duty to try to prevent suicide. He presents the thesis that suicide is an act of a moral agent who is ultimately responsible, and he opposes coercive methods of preventing suicide, such as forced hospitalization. Szasz argues that by attempting to prevent suicide mental health practitioners often ally themselves with the police power of the state and resort to coercion, therein identifying themselves as foes of individual liberty and responsibility. When professionals assume the burden of responsibility of keeping clients alive, they deprive their clients of their rightful share of accountability for their own actions. Szasz believes that it is the client's responsibility to choose to live or to die. He opposes policies of suicide prevention that minimize the responsibility of individuals for killing themselves and supports policies that maximize their responsibility for doing so. Szasz contends, "we should make it more difficult for suicidal persons to reject responsibility for deliberately taking their own lives and for mental health professionals to assume responsibility for keeping such persons alive" (p. 810).

Szasz is not claiming that suicide is always good or that it is a morally legitimate option; rather, his key point is that the power of the state should not be used to prohibit an individual from taking his or her own life. The right to suicide implies that we must abstain from empowering agents of the state to coercively prevent it.

A new dimension has been added to the suicide prevention debate with the passage of Oregon's Right to Die legislation, which enables a person following standard guidelines with physician assistance to hasten the advent of death. Basic to this proposition is the assumption that not every person contemplating suicide is mentally incompetent. In other words, an argument has been made for rational suicide. (See Chapter 3 for more on this topic.)

Your Stance on Suicide Prevention. Considering the arguments for and against suicide prevention, what is your stance on this complex issue? You may want to review the discussion on personal values in Chapter 3 when considering this issue. Where do you stand with respect to your ethical obligations to recognize, evaluate, and intervene with potentially suicidal clients? To what degree do you agree with the guidelines discussed in this chapter? Which guidelines make the most sense to you? Do you take a contrary position on at least some cases of suicide? How do you justify your position? To what extent do you agree or disagree with the contention of Szasz that current policies of suicide prevention displace responsibility from the client to the therapist and that this needlessly undermines the ethic of self-responsibility? What are your thoughts on Oregon's Right to Die law? After clarifying your own values underlying the professional's role in assessing and preventing suicide, reflect on the following case of a client who is contemplating suicide. If Emmanuel were your client, what actions would you take?

✓ **The Case of Emmanuel.** Emmanuel is a middle-aged widower who complains of emptiness in life, loneliness, depression, and a loss of the will to live any longer. He has been in individual therapy for 7 months with a clinical psychologist in private practice. Using psychodiagnostic procedures (both objective tests and projective techniques), she has determined that Emmanuel has serious depressive tendencies and is potentially self-destructive. In their sessions he explores the history of his failures, the isolation he feels, the meaninglessness of his life, and his feelings of worthlessness and depression. With her encouragement he experiments with new ways of behaving in the hope that he will find reasons to go on living. Finally, after 7 months of searching, he decides that he wants to take his own life. He tells his therapist that he is convinced he has been deluding himself in thinking that anything in his life will change for the better and that he feels good about deciding to end his life. He informs her that he will not be seeing her again.

The therapist expresses her concern that Emmanuel is very capable of taking his life at this time because so far he has not been able to see any light at the end of the tunnel. She acknowledges that the decision to commit suicide is not a sudden one, for they have discussed this wish for several sessions, but she lets him know that she wants him to give therapy more of a chance. He replies that he is truly grateful to her for helping him to find his answer within himself and that at least he can end his life with dignity in his own eyes. He says firmly that he does not want her to attempt to obstruct his plans in any way. She asks that he postpone his decision for a week and return to discuss the matter more fully. He tells her he isn't certain whether he will keep this appointment, but he agrees to consider it.

The therapist does nothing further. During the following week she hears from a friend that Emmanuel has committed suicide.

- What do you think of the way the therapist dealt with her client?
- What might you have done differently if you had been Emmanuel's therapist?
- How do you think your viewpoint regarding suicide would influence your approach with Emmanuel?
- Which of the following actions might you have pursued if you had been Emmanuel's counselor?

______ Committed him to a state hospital for observation, even against his will, for 72 hours

______ Consulted with another professional as soon as he began to discuss suicide as an option

______ Respected his choice of suicide, even if you did not agree with it

______ Informed the police and reported the seriousness of his threat

______ Informed members of his family of his intentions, even though he did not want you to

______ Bargained with him in every way possible in an effort to persuade him to keep on trying to find some meaning in life

Discuss in class any other steps you might have taken in this case.

Concluding Thoughts. In his discussion of malpractice liability for the suicidal client, Swenson (1997) writes that suicidal clients, like dangerous clients, pose a high risk for therapists. Although prediction of both danger to others and to self is difficult, courts impose liability on therapists who predict incorrectly. According to Benitez (2004), there is no *Tarasoff* duty to report when a client is threatening suicide. However, therapists are *permitted* to breach confidentiality if they believe it is necessary to prevent the threatened danger. Swenson (1997) asserts that therapists must warn if it is the best way to prevent a suicide. Given this caution, are you inclined to modify your stance on the issue of suicide prevention? If so, how?

Protecting Children, the Elderly, and Dependent Adults From Harm

Whether you work with children or adults in your practice, you are expected to know how to assess potential abuse and to report it in a timely fashion. Privileged communication does not apply in cases of child abuse and neglect, nor does it apply in cases of elder and dependent adult abuse. If children, the elderly, or other dependent adults disclose that they are being abused or neglected, the professional is required to report the situation under penalty of fines and imprisonment. If adults reveal in a therapy session that they are abusing or have abused their children, the matter must be reported. Such matters constitute a situation of **reportable abuse.**

In 1974 Congress enacted the National Child Abuse Prevention and Treatment Act (PL 93-247), which defines child abuse and neglect as follows:

> Physical or mental injury, sexual abuse or exploitation, negligent treatment, or maltreatment of a child under the age of eighteen or the age specified by the child protection law of the state in question, by a person who is responsible for the child's welfare, under circumstances which indicate that the child's health or welfare is harmed or threatened thereby.

In most states a human resources department has responsibilities in cases of abuse, neglect, or exploitation of both children and adults. Increasingly, states are enacting laws that impose liability on professionals who fail to report abuse or neglect of children, the elderly, and other dependent adults. States also provide immunity by law from civil suits that may arise from reporting suspected child abuse and neglect, or of abuse of the elderly or other dependent adults, if the reports are made in good faith. Some states require that professionals complete continuing education workshops on assessment of abuse and proper reporting as a condition of license renewal.

In 2003 more than 550,000 elderly people were reported abused or neglected in the United States, but the actual number may be four or five times higher than this (Egan, James, & Wagner, 2004). The National Center on Elder Abuse (NCEA, 2003) states that about 90% of elderly people live either alone or with loved ones or caretakers. Abusers of elderly people can be anyone they depend on or come into contact with. The major types of elder abuse are physical abuse, sexual abuse, psychological abuse, neglect, abandonment, and financial or material exploitation. **Physical abuse** involves the use of physical force that often results in bodily injury, physical pain, or impairment. **Sexual abuse** consists of nonconsensual sexual contact of any kind with an elderly person. **Psychological or emotional abuse** involves inflicting anguish, pain, or distress through verbal or nonverbal acts. This kind of abuse might include verbal assaults, insults, threats, intimidation, humiliation, and harassment. **Neglect** is the failure of caregivers to fulfill their responsibilities to the elderly. This may consist of the refusal or failure to provide an elderly person with basic necessities such as food, water, clothing, shelter, medicine, personal safety, and comfort. Neglect can be either intentional or unintentional, and can be either self-inflicted or inflicted by others. Older people, especially those who live alone, may suffer from self-neglect. This can be the result of chronic illness, depression, financial problems, or an elderly individual's unwillingness to ask for help (Egan et al., 2004). **Abandonment** involves the desertion of an elderly person by a person who has assumed responsibility for being a caregiver. **Financial or material exploitation** is defined as the illegal or improper use of an elder's funds, property, or assets. The National Center on Elder Abuse is dedicated to educating the public about elder abuse, neglect, and exploitation and its tragic consequences. NCEA is an internationally recognized resource for policy leaders, practitioners, prevention specialists, researchers, advocates, families, and concerned citizens.

One of the reviewers of this book made the observation that not enough people talk about elder abuse and the legal obligation to report abuse and neglect. We agree that abuse of the elderly and other vulnerable adults deserves the same kind of attention that is paid to abuse of children. Mental health providers have an ethical and legal obligation to protect children, the elderly, and dependent adults from abuse and neglect.

Mandatory reporting laws differ from state to state. In Pennsylvania, for example, therapists are required to file a report if the client is a child who appears to be the victim of abuse. If the client is the abuser, however, the mandatory reporting law does not apply. In New York therapists must report abuse whether they learn about the situation from the child in therapy, the abuser who is in therapy, or a relative. In 1989 Maryland changed its law, and it now requires therapists to report both present and past cases of child abuse that are revealed by adult clients in therapy.

How effective are state laws in inducing professionals to report suspected child abuse? Many professionals do not adhere to mandatory reporting laws. In a study to assess psychologists' decisions to report suspected child abuse, Kalichman and Craig (1991) found that the age of the child, the child's behavior during a clinical interview, and the type of abuse influenced their decisions. They found that clinicians may decide not to report due to concerns about the potential negative effect reporting may have on therapy and that clinicians are hesitant to report unless they are fairly certain abuse is occurring. Hermann (2002) found that 91% of school counselors believed they were well prepared to determine whether to report suspected child abuse.

A study on confidentiality and its relation to child abuse reporting indicated that respondents were inconsistent in their procedures for informing clients of the limits of confidentiality (Nicolai & Scott, 1994). The findings of this study suggest the need to reassert the importance of providing clients with detailed information about the limits of confidentiality from the onset of therapy. Nicolai and Scott maintain that continuing education and peer review processes should emphasize the ethical and legal obligations pertaining to child abuse reporting. The focus on training and supervision needs to be on both the associated risks as well as the benefits involved in reporting child abuse.

Although therapists are likely to accept their professional responsibility to protect innocent children, elderly persons, and dependent persons from physical and emotional mistreatment, they may have difficulty determining how far to go in making a report. It is often difficult to reconcile ethical responsibilities with legal obligations. Therapists may think they have been placed in the predicament of behaving either unethically (by reporting and thus damaging the therapy relationship) or illegally (by ignoring the mandate to report all cases of suspected child or elder abuse). Sometimes therapists are uncertain about when they need to report an incident. Is it necessary to report adult clients who admit having abused a child years ago or who were abused as minors themselves? The laws of some states now require therapists to report disclosures by adult clients about child sexual abuse that occurred years before treatment.

Clinicians must develop a clear position regarding the assessment and reporting of child, elder, and dependent adult abuse. To clarify your ethical stance in dealing with the duty to protect children, the elderly, and other dependent adults from abuse or neglect, consider these questions:

- How well prepared do you think you are in determining whether to report suspected abuse of a child, an elderly person, or a dependent adult?
- Would you consider cultural factors in determining whether a situation indicates actual abuse? How would you account for cultural differences in assessing abuse?
- Some state laws require reporting all child abuse, regardless of when it occurred. What are your thoughts about such laws? Do they always serve to protect children from abuse?
- Can you think of ways in which you could file a report on an adult abuser and continue working with the client therapeutically?
- What struggles, if any, have you encountered with respect to following the laws regarding reporting child, dependent adult, or elder abuse?
- If you follow the law in all cases, are you also following an ethical course? What potential conflicts are there between doing what is legal and what is ethical?
- If an adult admits having abused a child, what are your thoughts about a therapist who argues that keeping the client in therapy is the best way to help him or her work through this problem, even if it means failing to report the abuse to authorities?
- Do you think therapists should have some flexibility in deciding when it would be best to make a report? Why or why not?

To help you clarify your position with respect to situations involving child abuse, consider the following two case examples. In the first case, ask yourself how far you should go in reporting suspected abuse. Does the fact that you have reported a matter to the officials end your ethical and legal responsibilities? In the second case, look for ways to differentiate between what is ethical and what is legal practice. Ask yourself what you would be inclined to do if you saw a conflict between ethics and the law.

✓ **The Case of Martina.** Martina, a high school counselor, has reason to believe that one of her students is being physically abused. As part of the abuse, critical medication is being withheld from the student. Martina reports the incident to Child Protective Services and gives all the information she has to the caseworker. She follows up the phone conversation with the caseworker with a written report. A week later, the student tells her that nothing has been done.

- Has Martina adequately fulfilled her responsibility by making the report? Does she have a responsibility to report the agency for not having taken action?
- If the agency does not take appropriate action, does Martina have a responsibility to take other measures?
- Would it be ethical for Martina to take matters into her own hands and to call for a family session or make a house call, especially if the student requests it?
- Does Martina have an obligation to inform the administration? Does the school have a responsibility to see that action is taken?

✓ **The Case of Sally.** One night, in a moment of rare intoxication, a father stumbles into his 12-year-old daughter's bedroom and briefly fondles her. Sally's cries bring her mother into the room, and the incident does not go further. Later, the father does not recall the incident. There has been no previous history of molestation. During therapy the family is able to talk openly about the incident and is working through the resulting pain. Because of this incident, the father has enrolled in a substance abuse program. The family is adamant that this situation should not be reported to social services. The therapist knows that the statute in her state clearly specifies that she is required to report this incident, even if it had happened in the past and no further incidents had occurred. Listen to the inner dialogue of the therapist as she debates the pros and cons of reporting the incident, and think about your reactions to each course of action she considers:

There are many hazards involved if I don't report this incident. If this family ever broke up, the mother or daughter could sue me for having failed to report what happened. I would be obeying the law and protecting myself by reporting it, and I could justify my actions by citing the requirement of the law.

But this occurred on one occasion, and the father was intoxicated. The daughter was frightened by the incident, but she seems to be able to talk about it in the family now. If I obey the law, my actions may be more detrimental to the family than beneficial.

But the law is there for a reason. It appears that a child has been abused—that is no minor incident—and there was trauma for some time afterward.

What is the most ethical thing to do? I would be following the law by reporting it, but is that the most ethical course in this case? Is it the best thing for this family now, especially as none of the members want it reported? My ethical sense tells me that my interventions should always be in the best interests of all three members of this family.

I am required to report only if I suspect or believe that abuse has occurred. Some could argue that no abuse has taken place, which is what the parents seem to indicate by their behavior.

The family is now in therapy with me. If I do make a report, the family might terminate therapy. Is reporting this situation worth risking that chance?

Child protective agencies are often overburdened, and only the most serious cases may be given attention. Because no abuse is presently going on, I wonder if this case will be followed up. Will it be worth risking the progress that has been made with this family?

As an alternative to reporting this matter to the authorities, I could document a clinical plan of action that addresses therapeutic interventions with the father and also the well-being of the others. This course of action might be the best way to meet my legal and ethical obligations in this particular case.

Before I act, perhaps I should consult an attorney for advice on how to proceed. Or I could call Child Protective Services to find out what I must do. Maybe I should call the Board of Ethics of my professional organization and get some advice on how to proceed.

I don't know what action to take. Maybe I should consult with a colleague before I take any definite action.

Commentary. This case illustrates some of the difficulties counselors can find themselves in when their inner ethical sense conflicts with the law or an ethics code. This counselor must struggle with herself to determine whether she will follow her clinical intuitions by doing what she thinks is in the best interests of this family or whether she will do what is required by the law. If she simply reported this case, she would be taking the most conservative route. Her actions would be characterized by compliance with the law and adherence to the ethics code of her profession. However, she may not be putting ethical considerations in the forefront.

If the therapist called the ethics committee of her professional organization or a colleague, she would be acting on a slightly higher level of ethical functioning because of her willingness to consult. Consulting colleagues is always recommended in cases such as this one. The consultation process would help from a legal perspective as well. If other professionals agreed with her course of action, she would have a good chance of demonstrating that she had acted in good faith and that she had met the professional standards of her peers. In addition, consulting colleagues would provide her with one or more different perspectives on a difficult case.

The therapist is acting on the highest level of ethical functioning in examining all the factors and special circumstances of this family before acting. She is struggling to act appropriately, not just to protect herself, and is truly concerned with the best interests of everyone in the family. The welfare of the family members does not require her to violate the law, yet it does require her to think beyond merely obeying the law. It would be good for her to keep in mind that she has the legal obligation to report the situation.

It may still be possible for her to continue her therapeutic relationship with the family even if she decides to make a report. If this therapist approached you for consultation, what suggestions would you give her? What are your views about this case? What might you do if you were the therapist in this situation?

✓ **A Case of Protecting an Elderly Client.** Emily, an elderly client, takes great pride in her independence, her ability to take care of herself, and in not being a burden to her family. Her therapist, Tom, is impressed with her independent spirit. Emily eventually divulges to Tom several episodes of missing that the gas flame was left on in the kitchen. She laughs it off by saying, "I guess I'm not perfect." Every so often, Emily discloses similar episodes of forgetfulness that have potential lethal consequences. Tom becomes increasingly concerned and suggests that she include her family in her problem. Emily lets Tom know that this is not an option because her family has wanted her to move to a nursing home. Emily is adamant in her refusal to go along with their plan. She tells Tom, "If you make me leave my home, there is no point in living."

- If you were Emily's counselor, what course of action would you take?
- What ethical, legal, and medical issues can you identify in this case?
- Is there any duty to warn in this situation?

A Case of Protecting a Dependent Adult. You are working with individuals with mental disabilities, many of whom are institutionalized. One of your clients, Mike, who has a severe mental disability and lives in a residential home, leads you to believe that he is being sexually abused by at least one member of the staff. You are not really sure about this because it is difficult to separate fact from fantasy when talking with him about other things.

- What steps would you take to separate fact from fantasy?
- Are you required to make a report to protective services so that they can determine the validity of the allegation?
- Could you be legally liable for not making a report to protective services?

Confidentiality and HIV/AIDS-Related Issues

AIDS affects a large population with diverse demographics and continues to gain prominence as a public health and social issue. All mental health practitioners will inevitably come in contact with people who have AIDS, with people who have tested positive as carriers of the virus, or with people who are close to these people.

People who have tested HIV-positive (and those who have contracted AIDS) are usually in need of short-term help. They need to find a system to support them through the troubled times they will endure. Those who are HIV-positive live with the anxiety of wondering whether they will come down with this incurable disease. Many of these individuals also struggle with the stigma attached to AIDS. They live in fear not only of developing a life-threatening disease but also of being discovered and rejected by society and by friends and loved ones. In addition to feeling different and stigmatized, they typically have a great deal of anger, which is likely to be directed toward others, especially those who have given them the virus. Those at risk are often angry at health professionals as well. Because such clients are particularly vulnerable to being ostracized and suffering discrimination, it is critical that professionals obtain their informed consent and educate them about their rights and responsibilities.

Therapists need to be very clear in their own minds about the limits of confidentiality, matters of reporting, and their duty to warn and to protect third parties, and they need to communicate their professional responsibilities to their clients from the outset. If therapists decide that they cannot provide competent services to HIV-infected people, it is ethically appropriate that they refer these clients to professionals who can provide assistance. We recommend that you review the earlier discussion in this chapter regarding the therapist's duty to warn and to protect as it applies to people who have AIDS or are HIV-positive.

As a counselor you may indeed work with clients who are HIV-positive. You might accept a client and establish a therapeutic relationship only to find out months later that this person had recently tested positive. If this were the case, would it be ethical to terminate the professional relationship and make a referral? Would the ethical course be to become informed so that you could provide competent help? What would be in the best interests of your client? If you are counseling HIV-positive individuals, do you have a duty both to your clients and to their sexual partners? Do you have an ethical responsibility to warn and protect third parties in cases of those who are HIV-positive and who are putting others at risk by engaging in unprotected sex or needle sharing? If you do your best to convince your client to disclose his or her HIV status to a partner, and if your client refuses to share this information, what course of action might you take? As you think about these questions, consider your ethical responsibilities to respond to this population *before* you encounter possible difficult situations. The three cases described here are designed to help you clarify your position on the ethical dimensions of counseling clients who have AIDS or are HIV-positive. For a comprehensive discussion of many of the topics explored in this section, we recommend *Ethics in HIV-Related Psychotherapy: Clinical Decision Making in Complex Cases* (Anderson & Barret, 2001).

The Case of Al and Wilma. Al and Wilma are seeing Sarina for couples counseling. After a number of sessions Wilma requests an individual session, in which she discloses that she has tested HIV-positive as a result of an affair. Sarina finds herself in a real dilemma: She has concerns for the welfare of the couple, but she is also concerned about Wilma's painful predicament, especially because Wilma has a sincere desire to make her relationship work. Part of Sarina's quandary is that she did not tell the couple her policy about handling confidentiality for private sessions.

- Does Sarina have a duty to warn Al? Why or why not?
- Would such a duty supersede any implied confidentiality of the private session?
- What are some of the potential ethical violations in the manner in which Sarina handled this case?
- Would it be more therapeutic for Sarina to persuade Wilma to disclose her condition to Al rather than taking the responsibility for this disclosure herself?
- If Wilma refused to inform her husband, should Sarina discontinue therapy with the couple? If she were to discontinue working with them, how might she ethically explain her decision?

- If she felt obligated to continue therapy with the couple, how would she handle the secret, and what would be the ethical implications of her practices?
- Are there factors in this situation that would compel Sarina to treat Wilma's secret differently from other major secrets in couples therapy?

The Case of Paddy. Paddy has been seeing a counselor for several months to deal with his depression. He comes to one session in a state of extreme anxiety. He has been in a gay relationship with Christopher for 15 years. On a recent business trip Paddy had a sexual encounter with another man. Paddy is now worried that he may have contracted HIV, but he refuses to be tested. He is terrified of confirming his fear that he is HIV-positive. The counselor encourages Paddy to challenge his fears and be tested. He also encourages him to discuss this matter with Christopher. Paddy steadfastly refuses to consider either of the counselor's suggestions. When the counselor asks Paddy what he wants from him, he replies that he wants to be reassured that he is merely overreacting. He also would like to get over feeling depressed most of the time.

- What are the ethical dilemmas in this case?
- Are there any legal ramifications?
- How would you work with Paddy? Would you try to convince him to be tested, and would this be ethical? Would you try to persuade him to tell Christopher, and would your persuasion be ethical?
- What kind of referral might you make? What if Paddy refused a referral you suggested but insisted on continuing to see you?
- How would you help him achieve his stated goal for seeing you? Do you have enough information to accomplish that goal?
- What values of yours might come into play in dealing with this situation?
- If Paddy consented to being tested and was found to be HIV-positive but still refused to disclose this fact to his partner, what ethical and legal concerns would now come into play? How would you proceed with this new information?
- If Paddy did not have a life-threatening disease but instead contracted a sexually transmitted disease (genital herpes), would your course of action be any different? If so, what would you do?

The Case of Hershel. Hershel is a vice-president in a large company. He is married and has young children. Hershel's job necessitates transcontinental travel several times a year. During these trips he spends time with a lover. On his last trip he confided that one of the men that he had recently been sexually involved with had received an HIV-positive diagnosis. Hershel is panic stricken and seeks the help of a counselor, Blanche, who immediately recommends that he be tested. He follows her recommendation, and his test results are negative. He is elated and now sees no reason to continue therapy. Blanche makes no attempt to persuade him to explore other issues. She has no expertise in the treatment of AIDS clients and lacks essential knowledge pertaining to the latest AIDS research.

- Blanche appeared to take the ethical course in suggesting that Hershel be tested for AIDS, but was one test sufficient? What else needed to be done?
- Given this therapist's level of knowledge about AIDS, should she have referred Hershel? Explain.
- Did the therapist have a duty to warn his wife of the potential life-threatening situation to which she was now exposed?
- If Hershel had disclosed to Blanche that he and his wife were planning on having more children, how might that have affected the complexity of this case?
- Did Blanche have an ethical obligation to get him to discuss the matter with his wife because of the risk to her health? Explain.
- What course of action would you have taken in this case?

Ethical and Legal Considerations in AIDS-Related Cases

In the past few years much has been written about the conditions under which confidentiality might be breached in AIDS-related therapy situations. Courts have not applied the duty to warn to cases involving HIV infection, and therapists' legal responsibility in protecting sexual partners of HIV-positive clients remains unclear. Practitioners have few legal guidelines to help them determine when or how to inform a potential victim of the threat of HIV transmission (Erickson, 1993). Despite the lack of legal guidance on this issue, Erickson contends that there is some basis to consider this an exception to confidentiality issue. Calculated risks can be taken to ensure that unsuspecting individuals are protected from the definite possibility of infection by a contagious, life-threatening disease.

The following guideline from the ACA (2005) ethics code outlines the ethical responsibility of practitioners who might deal with HIV-positive clients who are unwilling to inform their sexual or needle-sharing partners of their HIV status:

> When clients disclose that they have a disease commonly known to be both communicable and life-threatening, counselors may be justified in disclosing information to identifiable third parties, if they are known be at demonstrable and high risk of contracting the disease. Prior to making a disclosure, counselors confirm that there is such a diagnosis and assess the intent of clients to inform the third parties about their disease or to engage in any behaviors that may be harmful to an identifiable third party. (B.2.b.)

This guideline places the responsibility on the counselor for examining a number of issues and eventually arriving at the best decision in a given case. It states that counselors *may be justified* in disclosing information to a third party who is at risk, yet counselors are not necessarily *obligated* to take this course of action. In fact, this is an example of where what is ethically appropriate may conflict with what is legally acceptable. Rahn Minagawa, a forensic psychologist, (personal communication, November 14, 2004) reports that this guideline is in direct conflict with state law in California, which places the practitioner who divulges this confidential information at risk for fines, civil penalties, incarceration, and loss of license.

A different standard pertaining to contagious, fatal diseases is given in the *Code of Professional Ethics for Rehabilitation Counselors* (CCRC, 2001). Note that this guideline does include references to legal requirements:

> Rehabilitation counselors will become aware of the legal requirements for disclosure of contagious and fatal diseases in their jurisdiction. In jurisdictions where allowable, a rehabilitation counselor who receives information will confirm that a client has a disease known to be communicable and/or fatal. If allowable by law, the rehabilitation counselor will ascertain that the client has not already informed the third party about his or her disease and that the client is not intending to inform the third party in the immediate future. (B.1.d.)

Until a landmark court case determines a precedent, mental health professionals will have to continue to struggle with doing what they think is morally and ethically right without any guarantee of legal protection.

Duty to Protect versus Confidentiality. Earlier in this chapter we discussed the principles involved in situations where therapists may have a duty to warn and to protect innocent victims. There have been some attempts to apply the *Tarasoff* decision to AIDS-related cases (Ahia & Martin, 1993; Cohen, 1997; Erickson, 1993; Gray & Harding, 1988; Hoffman, 1991a; Knapp & VandeCreek, 1990; Lamb et al., 1989; McGuire et al., 1995; Melton, 1988; Morrison, 1989; Totten, Lamb, & Reeder, 1990). The duty to warn and to protect *may* arise when a counselor has reason to believe that an HIV-positive client intends to continue to have unprotected sex, or to share needles, with unsuspecting but reasonably identifiable third parties (Ahia & Martin, 1993).

The HIV-positive duty to warn decision is one of the more controversial and emotion-laden issues practitioners might encounter. For practitioners who work with HIV-positive clients, the choice is often between protecting the client-therapist relationship and breaching confidentiality to protect at-risk populations. This situation can put practitioners in a moral, ethical, legal, and professional dilemma. The duty to warn and to protect third parties is especially difficult because counselors face not only ethical and legal issues surrounding confidentiality of client communications but also specific statutory prohibitions against disclosure of HIV information (Ahia & Martin, 1993; VandeCreek & Knapp, 1994).

State laws differ regarding HIV and the limits of confidentiality, and the law is often different for medical professionals than for licensed psychotherapists. According to Pennsylvania law, therapists may not break confidentiality to warn that a client poses a threat to others through HIV/AIDS. Instead, therapists are expected to persuade clients to change their behavior voluntarily (VandeCreek & Knapp, 1994). Some state laws forbid any disclosure of HIV status to third parties, and others allow some disclosure to at-risk third parties by physicians and psychiatrists but not by other mental health professionals. However, under many state laws, therapists who disclose a person's HIV-status to an unauthorized third party are subject to criminal charges and to malpractice action as well. Other states have yet to address this issue by statute. Thus, it is crucial to know the laws in your state in this matter.

Two thirds of the states have enacted legislation specifying limits to confidentiality regarding an individual's HIV status (Melchert & Patterson, 1999). Montana is the only state that protects mental health practitioners from liability in making good faith disclosures to third parties at risk for HIV infection. In Texas, all therapists are given protection against liability for disclosing this information to a spouse. Although therapists may be morally obligated to warn third parties who are at risk for HIV infection, Melchert and Patterson report that no state requires health care professionals to make such warnings. Furthermore, very few states (Montana and Texas) offer legal protection against liability for practitioners who break client confidentiality to warn third parties at risk. Therapists need to carefully consider any applicable state laws that might restrict or guide reporting options.

Cohen (1997) contends that the HIV dilemma can be resolved by referring to legal precedent, state statutes, and professional codes of ethics. Counselors who disclose information about their client's HIV status to endangered third parties will break client-counselor confidentiality. However, counselors who keep this confidentiality may fail to prevent serious and preventable harm to the third party. Cohen proposes these ethical guidelines for deciding when to disclose confidential information about a client's HIV status:

- When there are sufficient factual grounds for considering risk of harm to the third party to be high
- When the third party is at risk of death or substantial bodily harm
- When the harm to the third party is not likely to be prevented unless the counselor makes the disclosure
- When the third party cannot reasonably be expected to foresee or comprehend the high risk of harm to self

Preserving client confidentiality is a serious moral, ethical, and legal obligation. Cohen states that the case for breaching confidentiality must be strong before disclosure is justifiable.

Do *Tarasoff* Principles Apply in AIDS-Related Psychotherapy? McGuire and colleagues (1995) assert that *Tarasoff* guidelines may be helpful in identifying critical factors in the ethical dilemma of having a client who is HIV-positive and who refuses to disclose his or her HIV status or otherwise warn sexual partners. They suggest that therapists should be extremely cautious regarding breaching confidentiality and should first consider less intrusive means of dealing with HIV-positive clients who indicate that they are not using safe sex practices and are not warning their partners of their HIV status. Several researchers have addressed breaching confidentiality related to the danger to others posed by HIV-positive clients (Ahia & Martin, 1993; Erickson, 1993; Lamb et al., 1989; McGuire et al., 1995). They provide these recommendations for therapists:

- All limits to confidentiality should be discussed with the client at the onset of treatment. When this is done early in the therapeutic relationship, it is less likely that therapists will lose clients because of breaching confidentiality.

The implications of disclosing confidentiality, as well as other alternatives, can be explored with HIV-positive clients within the counseling context at this time.

- Therapists must be aware of the state laws regarding their professional interactions with HIV-positive clients and know the HIV confidentiality law of their state. Therapists should be aware that some state laws prohibit warning identifiable third parties of partners who are HIV-positive.
- Therapists need to keep current with regard to relevant medical information related to the transmission of HIV, know which sexual practices are safe and which are not, and encourage their clients to practice safe sex. Because sharing a contaminated needle is another major means of HIV transmission, therapists should be up to date on approaches to drug education.
- Practitioners can seek training for intervening in the crises facing HIV-positive clients and those with AIDS.
- Therapists need to be aware of their own attitudes, biases, and prejudices as they relate to individuals who are at a higher risk of becoming infected.
- Therapists should speak directly and openly with their clients about their concerns regarding the danger of certain behaviors and the risk to third parties. They can use the therapeutic process to educate their clients as to the effects their behavior can have on others, teach safe sex practices, obtain commitments from the client to notify partners, and offer help in communicating information to partners.
- If the client continues to resist using safe sex practices or refuses to inform partners, then the therapist needs to determine what course of action to follow.
- Practitioners should consult with knowledgeable peers or attorneys, or both, to determine that their intended course of action is ethically and legally sound.
- If all other options have been exhausted and the therapist has decided to breach confidentiality by warning an identified partner, the client should generally be informed of this intention, and the therapist should attempt to obtain the client's permission.
- In disclosing HIV information, therapists need to follow the statutory guidelines and safeguard the client's privacy as much as possible.

Several writers have applied *Tarasoff* as a framework for examining decisions about breaking confidentiality and protecting third parties (Grosso, 2002; Lamb et al., 1989; McGuire et al., 1995; Totten et al., 1990). Therapists have a duty to protect when the following three conditions are met:

- There must be a *special client-therapist relationship* that entails the practitioner's responsibility for the safety of the client and also of other parties whom the therapist knows to be threatened by the client.
- *Clear and imminent danger* must exist. It is important to be certain that the client is HIV-positive. The degree of dangerousness of a client who has tested HIV-positive depends on several factors: the client's medical diagnosis, the extent to which the person engages in high-risk behaviors, and the use of safe sex techniques aimed at reducing the chances of transmission of the virus.

Assessing dangerousness calls for an in-depth discussion of the client's drug use and sexual practices.

- There must be an *identifiable victim.* The duty to protect would probably extend to partners of an exclusive relationship but would not include anonymous partners unknown to the therapist. HIV-positive clients may have been sexually involved with many people in the past and may now have multiple sexual partners. This matter is complicated by the fact that the virus can remain dormant for years. Who are the potential victims? How should the therapist decide whom to inform?

If an HIV-infected individual is engaging in high-risk behavior with an identifiable, unsuspecting partner, then it appears that the three criteria under the *Tarasoff* decision may be met. However, many states have not adopted *Tarasoff*, which places the professional responsibility on each practitioner to examine his or her personal and professional values in weighing the ethical, legal, and moral implications of any proposed course of action.

Special Training on HIV-Related Issues

Mental health professionals have an ethical obligation to be knowledgeable about HIV and AIDS so they can ask the right questions. You can start by reading about AIDS-related issues and by attending a workshop on the subject. You can also contact one of the many clinics throughout the country, which are useful resources for treatment and referrals. In many communities, groups of volunteers have been organized to work with AIDS clients.

Werth and Carney (1994) emphasize the importance of incorporating HIV-related issues into graduate student training. They cite several surveys that show that most students are not receiving HIV-related training in their graduate programs and are unprepared to handle ethical, legal, and professional issues pertaining to HIV situations. Specifically, on the topic of the duty to protect versus confidentiality, they find the reaction of their students is to breach confidentiality too soon, without giving adequate consideration to other alternatives or to the potential consequences. In training students in this area, Werth and Carney review case scenarios, discuss the implications of the *Tarasoff* case, and review ethical and legal cases. They pose the following questions for discussion:

- What is the therapist's role (watchdog, change agent, client advocate)?
- To whom does the therapist have a primary responsibility?
- How is this situation similar or different from the *Tarasoff* case?
- What options and courses of action are available?
- Where can the therapist go for consultation?

In summary, dealing responsibly with the dilemmas posed in this section demands an awareness of the ethical, legal, and clinical issues involved in working with clients with HIV/AIDS. There are no simple solutions to the many complex issues practitioners may face, and this topic is surely one of the more challenging ones. Consulting with both colleagues and attorneys is an excellent practice that can help you make appropriate decisions.

Chapter Summary

Along with their duties to clients, therapists also have responsibilities to their agency, to their profession, to the community, to the members of their clients' families, and to themselves. Ethical dilemmas involving confidentiality arise when there are conflicts between responsibilities. Members of the helping professions should know and observe the ethics codes of their professional organizations and make sound judgments that are within the parameters of acceptable practice. We have encouraged you to think about specific ethical issues and to develop a sense of professional ethics and knowledge of state laws so that your judgment will be well-founded.

Court decisions have provided an expanded perspective on the therapist's duty to protect the public. As a result of the *Tarasoff* case, therapists are now becoming aware of their responsibility to the potential victims of a client's violent behavior. This duty spans interventions from warnings to threatened individuals to involuntary commitment of clients. Therapists are vulnerable to malpractice action when they demonstrate negligent failure to diagnose dangerousness, negligent failure to warn a known victim once such a diagnosis has been made, negligent failure to commit a dangerous person, or negligent failure to keep a dangerous client committed.

Therapists also have a duty to protect clients who are likely to injure or kill themselves. Practitioners must develop skills in making accurate assessments of potentially suicidal persons. Once a client is diagnosed as a danger to him- or herself, the therapist is responsible for preventing suicide by acting in professionally acceptable ways. A dissenting opinion on this issue is that of Szasz, who challenges the assumption that therapists should be held accountable for a client's decision to die. He believes suicide is an ultimate right and responsibility of the client and that it is unethical for therapists to employ coercive measures aimed at preventing it.

All states have laws that require professionals to report child, elder, and dependent adult abuse whenever they suspect or discover it in the course of their professional activities. Clients have a right to know that therapists are legally and ethically bound to breach confidentiality in situations involving child, elder, or dependent adult abuse. Therefore, this must be included in your informed consent document.

The duty to protect has also been applied to HIV/AIDS cases. Because state laws vary on breaching confidentiality to warn victims of a client's HIV status, practitioners are advised to know their state laws and to consult professional colleagues, and perhaps an attorney, before they take the action of informing an identified partner of an HIV-infected client. This should be the last option, implemented only after less obtrusive measures have failed, and only if the disclosure does not conflict with state law.

Suggested Activities

1. In small groups discuss the cases and guidelines presented in this chapter on the duty to protect victims from violent clients. If you found yourself faced with a potentially dangerous client, what specific steps might you take to carry out this duty?

2. Structure a class debate around the arguments for and against suicide prevention. Consider debating a specific case of a client who is terminally ill with AIDS and decides that he wants to end his life because of his suffering and because there is no hope of getting better.

3. Ask several students to investigate the laws of your state pertaining to confidentiality and privileged communication and present their findings to the class. What kinds of mental health providers in your state can offer their clients privileged communication? What are the exceptions to this privilege? Under what circumstances are you legally required to breach confidentiality? Regarding confidentiality in counseling minors, what state laws should you know?

4. In small groups discuss specific circumstances in which you would break confidentiality, and see whether you can agree on some general guidelines.

5. Discuss some ways in which you can prepare clients for issues pertaining to confidentiality. How can you teach clients about the purposes of confidentiality and the legal restrictions on it? Examine how you would do this in various situations, such as school, group work, couples and family counseling, and counseling with minors.

6. In a class debate, have one side take the position that absolute confidentiality is necessary to promote full client disclosure. The other side can argue for a limited confidentiality that still promotes effective therapy.

Ethics in Action CD-ROM Exercises

7. Refer to role play #6, The Promiscuous One, and think of ways to reenact a role play with different students demonstrating a variety of ways to deal with this woman who is having unprotected casual sexual encounters. If she told you that she just found out that she is HIV-positive—and that she absolutely does not intend to reveal this news to her husband—what would your stance be? Would you protect the client's confidentiality? Or would you see this as a duty to warn and protect case? Devise alternative role plays showing a variety of approaches for dealing with the ethical and legal dimensions in this case.

 InfoTrac® College Edition Resources

For additional readings, explore InfoTrac College Edition, our online library. Key words are listed in a form that enables the search engine to locate a wider range of articles in the online university library. Key words should be entered exactly as shown, including asterisks, "Wl," "W2," "AND," and other search engine tools. Go to http://www.infotrac-college.com and select these key word searches:

confidentiality N3 couns* OR confidentiality N3 psych????y
privileged W1 communication AND (psych????y OR psychotherapy OR couns*)
privacy AND (psych????y OR psychotherapy OR couns*) NOT medic* NOT law
limits W2 confidentiality
duty W2 warn AND (psych????y OR psychotherapy OR couns*)
duty W2 protect AND (psych????y OR psychotherapy OR couns*)
suicid* client*
suicid* therap*
suicide W1 prevention AND (psych????y OR psychotherapy OR couns*)
confid* AND HIV
confid* AND AIDS
mandat* W1 report* AND (psych????y OR psychotherapy OR couns*)
HIPPA AND (psych????y OR psychotherapy OR couns*)
tarasoff AND (psych????y OR psychotherapy OR couns*)
child W1 abuse AND physical AND (psych????y OR psychotherapy OR couns*) NOT pediatric* NOT medic*
child W1 abuse AND sexual AND (psych????y OR psychotherapy OR couns*) NOT pediatric* NOT medic*
child W1 abuse AND psychologic* AND (psych????y OR psychotherapy OR couns*) NOT pediatric* NOT medic*
child W1 abuse AND neglect AND (psych????y OR psychotherapy OR couns*)

Pre-Chapter Self-Inventory

Directions: For each statement, indicate the response that most closely identifies your beliefs and attitudes. Use the following code:

5 = I *strongly agree* with this statement.
4 = I *agree* with this statement.
3 = I am *undecided* about this statement.
2 = I *disagree* with this statement.
1 = I *strongly disagree* with this statement.

_____ 1. A good therapist gets involved in the client's case without getting involved with the client emotionally.

_____ 2. Nonerotic touching is best avoided in counseling because it can easily be misunderstood by the client.

_____ 3. Therapists who hug clients of only one sex are guilty of sexist practice.

_____ 4. Although it may be unwise to form social relationships with clients while they are in counseling, there should be no ethical or professional prohibition against social relationships after counseling ends.

_____ 5. If I were a truly ethical professional, I would never be sexually attracted to a client.

_____ 6. If I were counseling a client who was sexually attracted to me, I would refer this client to another counselor.

_____ 7. I might be inclined to barter my therapeutic services for goods if a client could not afford my fees.

_____ 8. If a client initiated the possibility of exchanging services in lieu of payment, I would consider bartering as an option.

_____ 9. Sexual involvement with a client is never ethical, even after therapy has ended.

Managing Boundaries and Multiple Relationships

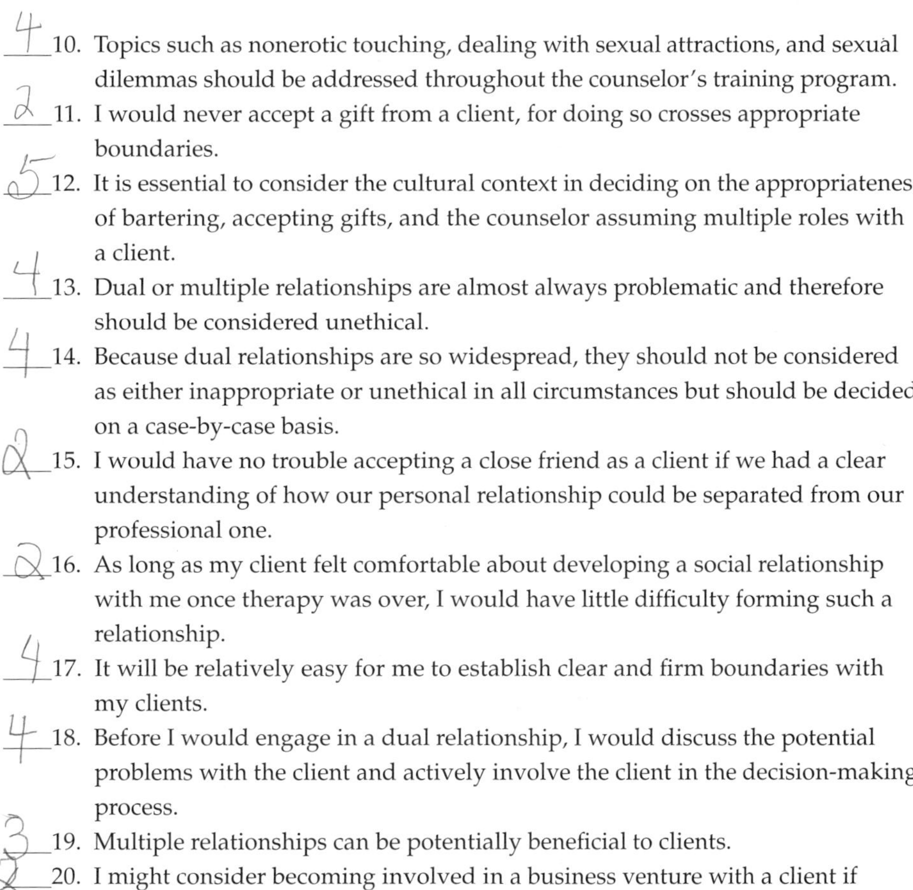

____10. Topics such as nonerotic touching, dealing with sexual attractions, and sexual dilemmas should be addressed throughout the counselor's training program.

____11. I would never accept a gift from a client, for doing so crosses appropriate boundaries.

____12. It is essential to consider the cultural context in deciding on the appropriateness of bartering, accepting gifts, and the counselor assuming multiple roles with a client.

____13. Dual or multiple relationships are almost always problematic and therefore should be considered unethical.

____14. Because dual relationships are so widespread, they should not be considered as either inappropriate or unethical in all circumstances but should be decided on a case-by-case basis.

____15. I would have no trouble accepting a close friend as a client if we had a clear understanding of how our personal relationship could be separated from our professional one.

____16. As long as my client felt comfortable about developing a social relationship with me once therapy was over, I would have little difficulty forming such a relationship.

____17. It will be relatively easy for me to establish clear and firm boundaries with my clients.

____18. Before I would engage in a dual relationship, I would discuss the potential problems with the client and actively involve the client in the decision-making process.

____19. Multiple relationships can be potentially beneficial to clients.

____20. I might consider becoming involved in a business venture with a client if I were convinced that doing so would not harm my client.

Introduction

Ethical concerns are often raised when clinicians blend their professional relationship with another kind of relationship with a client. These *multiple* or *dual relationships* are addressed by the ethics codes of most professional organizations, which stress thinking of the best interests of clients when considering boundary issues. At times, this determination is not easy to make.

The APA (2002) ethics code defines a **multiple relationship** as existing when a practitioner is in a professional role with a person in addition to another role with that same individual, or with another person who is close to that individual. Dual or multiple relationships can also occur when professionals assume two or more roles at the same time or sequentially with a client. This may involve assuming more than one professional role (such as instructor and therapist) or blending a professional and nonprofessional relationship (such as counselor and friend or counselor and business partner). **Dual relationships** also include providing therapy to a relative or a friend's relative, socializing with clients, becoming emotionally or sexually involved with a client or former client, combining the roles of supervisor and therapist, having a business relationship with a client, borrowing money from a client, or loaning money to a client. Mental health professionals must learn how to effectively and ethically manage multiple relationships, including dealing with the power differential that is a basic part of most professional relationships, managing boundary issues, and striving to avoid the misuse of power (Herlihy & Corey, 2006b).

Sometimes it is difficult to understand the rationale behind prohibitions, and some boundary limitations may seem arbitrary. Many of the ethics codes are based on reactions to violations rather than being well-thought-out codes based on the diagnosis of the client and the nature of the so-called dual relationship. Codes can provide some guidelines, but good judgment, the willingness to reflect on one's practices, and being aware of one's motivations are critical dimensions of an ethical practitioner.

Mental health professionals often fail to heed warning signs in their relationships with clients. They may not have paid sufficient attention to the potential problems involved in boundary crossings, or they may have innocently crossed boundaries that led to problems for both the client and themselves.

The underlying theme of this chapter is the need for therapists to be honest and self-searching in determining the impact of their behavior on clients. Some of the issues and cases we present may seem clear-cut to you, but others are not. In ambiguous cases it becomes a personal challenge to make an honest appraisal of your behavior and its effect on clients. Consider this key question: Whose needs are being met, the therapist's or the client's? To us, behavior is unethical when it reflects a lack of awareness or concern about the impact of the behavior on clients. Some counselors may place their personal needs above the needs of their clients, engaging in more than one role with clients to meet their own financial, social, or emotional needs.

This chapter focuses on boundary issues in counseling practice, dual and multiple relationships, role blending, a variety of nonsexual dual relationships, and sexual issues in therapy. We also examine the more subtle aspects of sexuality in therapy, including sexual attractions and the misuse of power. Multiple relationship issues cannot be resolved with rules alone; therapists must think through the ethical and clinical dimensions involved in a wide range of boundary concerns.

Dual and Multiple Relationships

The codes of ethics of most professional organizations warn of the potential problems of dual and multiple relationships (see the ethics codes box titled Dual and Multiple Relationships). These codes caution professionals against any involvement with clients that might impair their judgment and objectivity, affect their ability to render effective services, or result in harm or exploitation to clients. Although most of the ethics codes mention both sexual and nonsexual dual relationships, the law does not specifically address dual relationships, except for sex with clients (Grosso, 2002).

Writing from a legal perspective, Hermann (2006) indicates that dual relationships exist on a continuum ranging from boundary crossings for a client's benefit to sexual dual relationships that cause major harm to a client. The legal implications pertaining to dual relationships depend on the nature of the relationship and whether the client suffers harm. The mere existence of a dual relationship does not, in itself, constitute malpractice; rather, it is harming or exploiting a client that is unethical. In cases where a client suffers harm or is exploited due to a dual relationship, the client could file a malpractice lawsuit against the mental health provider. Hermann concludes that it is a wise practice for counselors to avoid dual relationships to the extent possible and to document precautions taken to protect clients when such relationships are unavoidable.

Differing Perspectives

There is a wide range of viewpoints on dual relationships. If you are intent on clarifying your position on this issue, you will encounter conflicting advice. Some writers focus on the problems inherent in dual relationships. St. Germaine (1993) maintains that although dual relationships are not always harmful to clients it is essential for professionals to recognize the potential for harm associated with any kind of blending of roles. She mentions that errors in judgment may occur when a professional's self-interest becomes involved. Pope and Vasquez (1998) contend that dual relationships tend to impair the therapist's judgment, increasing the potential for conflicts of interest, exploitation of the client, and blurred boundaries that distort the professional nature of the therapeutic relationship. Pope and Vasquez note that therapists often try to justify, trivialize, or discount their practices of engaging in more than one role with clients. Therapists may block out awareness of the potential for serious harm; may focus on the beneficial aspects of such relationships; may assert that these practices are widely prevalent, inevitable and unavoidable, and reflect

Ethics Codes

Dual and Multiple Relationships

American Association for Marriage and Family Therapy (2001)

Marriage and family therapists are aware of their influential position with respect to clients, and they avoid exploiting the trust and dependency of such persons. Therapists, therefore, make every effort to avoid conditions and multiple relationships with clients that could impair professional judgment or increase the risk of exploitation. When the risk of impairment or exploitation exists due to conditions or multiple roles, therapists take appropriate precautions. (4.1.)

National Association of Social Workers (1999)

Social workers should not engage in dual or multiple relationships with clients or former clients in which there is a risk of exploitation or potential harm to the client. In instances when dual or multiple relationships are unavoidable, social workers should take steps to protect clients and are responsible for setting clear, appropriate, and culturally sensitive boundaries. (1.06.c.)

Feminist Therapy Institute (2000)

A feminist therapist recognizes the complexity and conflicting priorities inherent in multiple or overlapping relationships. The therapist accepts responsibility for monitoring such relationships to prevent potential abuse of or harm to the client. (III.A.)

National Organization for Human Services (2000)

Human service professionals are aware that in their relationships with clients, power and status are unequal. Therefore, they recognize that dual or multiple relationships may increase the risk of harm to, or exploitation of, clients, and may impair their professional judgment. However, in some communities and situations it may not be feasible to avoid social or other nonprofessional contact with clients. Human service professionals support the trust implicit in the helping relationship by avoiding dual relationships that may impair professional judgment, increase the risk of harm to clients, or lead to exploitation.

Canadian Psychological Association (2000)

Avoid dual or multiple relationships and other situations that might present a conflict of interest or that might reduce their ability to be objective and unbiased in their determinations of what might be in the best interests of others. (III.33.)

Manage dual or multiple relationships that are unavoidable due to cultural norms or other circumstances in such a manner that bias, lack of objectivity, and risk of exploitation are minimized. This might include obtaining ongoing supervision or consultation for the duration of the dual or multiple relationship, or involving a third party in obtaining consent. (III.34.)

Canadian Association of Social Workers (1994)

Social workers shall not have a business relationship with a client, borrow money from a client, or loan money to a client.

American School Counselor Association (2004)

[The school counselor] avoids dual relationships that might impair his/her objectivity and increase the risk of harm to the student (e.g., counseling one's family members, close friends or associates). If a dual relationship is unavoidable, the counselor is responsible for taking action to eliminate or reduce the potential for harm. Such safeguards might include informed consent, consultation, supervision and documentation. (A.4.a.)

continued on next page

American Counseling Association (2005)

Counselor-client non-professional relationships with clients, former clients, their romantic partners, or their family members should be avoided, except when the interaction is potentially beneficial to the client. (A.5.c.)

When a counselor–client nonprofessional interaction with a client or former client may be potentially beneficial to the client or former client, the counselor must document in case records, prior to the interaction (when feasible), the rationale for such an interaction, the potential benefit, and anticipated consequences for the client or former client and other individuals significantly involved with the client or former client. Such interactions should be initiated with appropriate client consent. Where unintentional harm occurs to the client or former client, or to an individual significantly involved with the client or former client, due to the nonprofessional interaction, the counselor must show evidence of an attempt to remedy such harm. Examples of potentially beneficial interactions include, but are not limited to, attending a formal ceremony (e.g., a wedding or graduation); purchasing a service or product provided by a client or former client (excepting unrestricted bartering); hospital visits to an ill family member, mutual membership in a professional association, organization, or community. (A.5.d.)

American Psychological Association (2002)

(a) A multiple relationship occurs when a psychologist is in a professional role with a person and (1) at the same time is in another role with the same person, (2) at the same time is in a relationship with a person closely associated with or related to the person with whom the psychologist has the professional relationship, or (3) promises to enter into another relationship in the future with the person or a person closely associated with or related to the person.

A psychologist refrains from entering into a multiple relationship if the multiple relationship could reasonably be expected to impair the psychologist's objectivity, competence, or effectiveness in performing his or her functions as a psychologist, or otherwise risks exploitation or harm to the person with whom the professional relationship exists.

Multiple relationships that would not reasonably be expected to cause impairment or risk exploitation or harm are not unethical.

(b) If a psychologist finds that, due to unforeseen factors, a potentially harmful multiple relationship has arisen, the psychologist takes reasonable steps to resolve it with due regard for the best interests of the affected person and maximal compliance with the Ethics Code.

(c) When psychologists are required by law, institutional policy, or extraordinary circumstances to serve in more than one role in judicial or administrative proceedings, at the outset they clarify role expectations and the extent of confidentiality and thereafter as changes occur. (3.05.)

tradition; and may emphasize the right of clients to enter into relationships of their choice. Such rationalizations enable the professional to avoid responsibility for designing acceptable alternative approaches.

Those who take a more moderate view see the entire discussion of dual relationships as subtle and complex, defying simplistic solutions or absolute answers. Tomm (1993) believes standards in the ethics codes that address dual relationships tend to be narrow and deceptive. He points out that simply avoiding dual relationships does not prevent exploitation. Counselors can misuse their power and influence in a variety of ways that can harm clients. Tomm contends that maintaining interpersonal distance focuses on the power differential, promotes an objectification of the therapeutic relationship, and tends to promote a vertical hierarchy in the relationship.

Moleski and Kiselica (2005) point out that many counselors are rethinking their traditional approach to the therapeutic process, and hence are entering into more secondary relationships, which have an impact on the counseling relationship. Despite certain clinical, ethical, and legal risks, some blending of roles is unavoidable, and it is not necessarily unethical or unprofessional. None of the codes of ethics of any of the professional organizations state that nonsexual dual relationships are unethical, and most of them acknowledge that some are unavoidable (Lazarus & Zur, 2002).

Although the codes of ethics of most professions warn against engaging in nonsexual dual relationships, not all such relationships can be avoided, nor are they necessarily harmful (Herlihy & Corey, 2006b). For example, "mentoring" involves blending roles, yet both mentors and learners can certainly benefit from this relationship. Castro, Caldwell, and Salazar (2005) point out that mentors often balance a multiplicity of roles, some of which include teacher, counselor, role model, guide, and friend. They add that the mentoring relationship is a personal one, in which both mentor and mentee may benefit from knowing the other personally and professionally. Castro and colleagues emphasize the importance of maintaining boundaries between mentorship and friendship, which requires vigilance of the power differential and how it affects the mentee. They contend that the focus of mentoring is always on the mentee's personal and professional development.

There are many clear benefits of mentoring relationships, but a spectrum of ethical concerns also are associated with these relationships. Ethical problems are likely to arise if the mentor's role becomes blurred, so that he or she is more of a friend than a mentor (Warren, 2005). After reviewing the literature on the topic of dual and multiple relationships, Herlihy and Corey (2006b) conclude that there is no clear consensus regarding nonsexual dual relationships in counseling. It is the responsibility of practitioners to monitor themselves and to examine their motivations for engaging in such relationships.

Factors to Consider Before Entering Into a Multiple Relationship

Younggren and Gottlieb (2004) suggest applying an ethically based, risk-managed, decision-making model when practitioners are analyzing a situation involving the pros and cons of a multiple relationship. They "acknowledge that these types of relationships are not necessarily violations of the standards of professional conduct, and/or the law, but we know enough to recommend that they have to be actively and thoroughly analyzed and addressed, although not necessarily avoided" (p. 260). Younggren and Gottlieb recommend that practitioners address these questions to make sound decisions about multiple relationships (pp. 256–257):

- Is entering into a relationship in addition to the professional one necessary, or should I avoid it?
- Can the dual relationship cause harm to the client?
- If harm seems unlikely, would the additional relationship prove beneficial?
- Is there a risk that the dual relationship could disrupt the therapeutic relationship?
- Can I evaluate this matter objectively?

In answering these questions, practitioners need to carefully assess the risk for conflicts of interest, loss of objectivity, and implications for the therapeutic relationship. Counselors must discuss with the client the potential problems involved in a multiple relationship, and it is good practice to actively involve the client in the decision-making process. If the dual relationship is judged to be appropriate and acceptable, the therapist should document the entire process, including having the client sign an informed consent form. In addition, therapists would do well to adopt a risk-management approach to the problem. This involves a careful review of various issues such as diagnosis, level of functioning, therapeutic orientation, community standards and practices, and consultations with professionals who could support the decision. Younggren and Gottlieb conclude with this advice: "Only after having taken all these steps can the professional consider entering into the relationship, and he or she should then do so with the greatest of caution" (p. 260).

Moleski and Kiselica (2005) believe dual relationships range from the destructive to the therapeutic. Although some dual relationships are harmful, other secondary relationships complement, enable, and enhance the counseling relationship. Moleski and Kiselica encourage counselors to examine the potential positive and negative consequences that a secondary relationship might have on the primarily counseling relationship. They suggest that counselors should consider forming dual relationships only when it is clear that such relationships are in the best interests of the client.

Boundary Issues

Certain behaviors of professionals have the potential for creating a dual relationship, but they are not inherently considered to be dual relationships. Examples of these behaviors include accepting a client's invitation to a special event such as a graduation; bartering goods or services for professional services; accepting a small gift from a client; attending the same social, cultural, or religious activities as a client; or giving a supportive hug after a difficult session. Some writers (Gabbard, 1994, 1995, 1996; Gutheil & Gabbard, 1993; Smith & Fitzpatrick, 1995) caution that engaging in boundary crossings paves the way to boundary violations and to becoming entangled in complex multiple relationships. Gutheil and Gabbard (1993) distinguish between boundary crossings (changes in role) and boundary violations (exploitation of the client at some level). A **boundary crossing** is a departure from commonly accepted practices that could potentially benefit clients, whereas a **boundary violation** is a serious breach that results in harm to clients. They note that not all boundary crossings should be considered boundary violations. Interpersonal boundaries are fluid; they may change over time and may be redefined as therapists and clients continue to work together. Yet behaviors that stretch boundaries can become problematic, and boundary crossings can lead to a pattern of blurring of professional roles. The key is to take measures to prevent boundary crossings from becoming boundary violations.

Establishing and Maintaining Appropriate Boundaries. Consistent yet flexible boundaries are often therapeutic and can help clients develop trust in the therapy relationship. Borys (1994) suggests that many clients require the structure provided by clear and consistent boundaries. Such a structure is like "a buoy in stormy, chaotic seas" (p. 270).

Strasburger, Jorgenson, and Sutherland (1992) contend that therapists who push nonsexual boundaries are more likely to become sexually involved with clients. They recommend avoiding this slippery slope to prevent sexual misconduct. Inherent in the concept of the "slippery slope" is the notion that clinicians need to exercise caution before entering into all types of multiple relationships, even if they are not harmful in themselves.

Lamb and Catanzaro (1998) summarize areas where nonsexual relationships can prove to be ethically questionable. Particularly problematic boundary behaviors include social, financial, or workplace relationships with current or former clients; business relationships with current or former clients; multiple relationships with clients, students, or supervisees; and physical touching of current or former clients, students, or supervisees.

Fay (2002) presents a different view on boundaries in psychotherapy, contending that more emphasis needs to be placed on closeness rather than distance, and on intimacy rather than boundaries or barriers to intimacy. He states that the purpose of ethical standards is to discourage behavior that does not promote client welfare, yet restrictions on behavior that is not exploitive curtail therapeutic possibilities. Fay writes: "Ethics is not in the boundaries; it is more comprehensively in the way you treat a suffering or struggling human being—your ability and willingness to act in a caring, empathic, competent and nonexploitive manner" (p. 131).

Conventional wisdom emphasizes the need for stability in the client-therapist relationship. Ira Orchin (2004), a psychologist in private practice, stretches boundaries by taking therapy outdoors. Orchin maintains that going outside the office challenges therapists to manage more fluid boundaries and novel situations, but that doing so often has definite therapeutic benefits. He believes that an outdoor session can be an appropriate way to create ceremonies and rituals to mark transitions, celebrate achievements, and encourage transformation. Orchin claims that this effective intervention has assisted many of his clients in getting through an impasse in their therapy and moving therapy forward. This approach is an example of a boundary crossing that could have therapeutic benefits if it is carefully applied to certain clients and specific situations.

Role Blending. A concept related to that of maintaining appropriate boundaries is **role blending,** or combining roles and responsibilities. Certainly, blending some roles is indefensible, such as blending the roles of therapist and lover or therapist and business partner. But other roles that professionals play involve an inherent duality. For example, counselor educators serve as instructors, but they sometimes act as therapeutic agents for their students' personal development. At different times, counselor educators may function in the role of teacher, therapeutic agent, mentor, evaluator, or supervisor. The roles supervisors play are another example. Although supervision and psychotherapy are two different processes, they share some common aspects. The supervisor may need to assist supervisees in identifying ways that their personal dynamics are blocking their ability to work effectively with clients. Herlihy and Corey (2006b) assert that role blending is inevitable in the process of educating and supervising counselor trainees and that this role blending can present ethical dilemmas that involve a loss of objectivity or conflicts of interest. They state that role blending is not necessarily unethical, but it does call for vigilance on the part of the professional to ensure that exploitation does not occur.

Functioning in more than one role involves thinking through potential problems before they occur and building safeguards into practice. Whenever a potential for negative outcomes exists, professionals have a responsibility to design safeguards to reduce the potential for harm. Herlihy and Corey (2006b) and St. Germaine (1993) identify the following measures aimed at minimizing the risks inherent in dual or multiple relationships:

- Maintain healthy boundaries from the outset.
- Secure the informed consent of clients and discuss with them both the potential risks and benefits of dual relationships or any kind of blending of roles.
- Remain willing to talk with clients about any potential problems and conflicts that may arise.
- Seek supervision or consult with other professionals when dual relationships become particularly problematic or when the risk for harm is high.
- Document any dual relationships in clinical case notes.
- When necessary, refer clients to another professional.

In *Boundary Issues in Counseling: Multiple Roles and Responsibilities,* Herlihy and Corey (2006b) identify ten key themes surrounding multiple roles in counseling. These themes summarize the critical issues practitioners face in thinking about dual and multiple relationships.

1. Multiple relationship issues affect virtually all mental health practitioners, regardless of their work setting or clientele.
2. All professional codes of ethics caution practitioners about the potential exploitation in dual relationships, and more recent codes acknowledge the complex nature of these relationships.
3. Not all multiple relationships can be avoided, nor are they necessarily always harmful.

4. Multiple role relationships challenge us to monitor ourselves and to examine our motivations for our practices.
5. Whenever you consider becoming involved in a dual or multiple relationship, seek consultation from trusted colleagues or a supervisor.
6. Few absolute answers exist to neatly resolve dual or multiple relationship dilemmas.
7. The cautions for entering into dual or multiple relationships should be for the benefit of our clients or others served rather than to protect ourselves from censure.
8. In determining whether to proceed with a dual or multiple relationship, consider whether the potential benefit outweighs the potential for harm. To the extent possible, include the client in making this consideration.
9. It is the responsibility of counselor preparation programs to introduce boundary issues and explore multiple relationship questions. It is important to teach students ways of thinking about alternative courses of action.
10. Counselor education programs have a responsibility to develop their own guidelines, policies, and procedures for dealing with multiple roles and role conflicts within the program.

The maintenance of appropriate and useful boundaries with clients is of the utmost importance in the work of psychotherapists. Professionals often get into trouble when their boundaries are poorly defined and when they attempt to blend roles that do not mix well. A gradual erosion of boundaries can lead to very problematic multiple relationships that bring harm to clients. Gabbard (1994) cites the **slippery slope phenomenon** as one of the strongest arguments for carefully monitoring boundaries in psychotherapy. This argument is based on the premise that certain actions will inevitably lead to a progressive deterioration of ethical behavior. Furthermore, if professionals do not adhere to rigid standards, their behavior may foster relationships that are sexual or in some way harmful to clients. To avoid going down a slippery slope, therapists are advised to have a therapeutic rationale for every boundary crossing and to question behaviors that are inconsistent with their theoretical approach (Pope, Sonne, & Holroyd, 1993; Smith & Fitzpatrick, 1995). But Twemlow (1997) argues that the concept of exploitation is often used far too broadly so that it now prohibits all nontraditional methods of treatment: "It has become clear to me that an individual assessment is the cornerstone of a logical and sensitive answer to the question of whether a particularly slippery slope has truly been slippery for the particular patient" (p. 360).

The Ban on Nonsexual Dual Relationships

Within the last 10 years the trend in state licensure boards has been to prohibit dual relationships, including nonsexual dual relationships (O'Laughlin, 2001). Some state licensure rules prohibit therapists from engaging in any kind of dual relationship that *may* impair the professional judgment of the therapist or that *may* be potentially exploitive of clients. According to O'Laughlin, prohibiting relationships that are *potentially* exploitive or that *might* impair objectivity or competency gives licensing boards a great deal of power and raises serious concerns about violating constitutional freedoms. O'Laughlin contends that "not every dual relationship creates a conflict of interest and not all conflicts of interest will inevitably result in a breach of the client's trust" (p. 729). He concludes that rather than prohibiting dual relationships what should be prohibited is exploitation of clients.

The California Board of Behavioral Sciences (BBS) engaged in a discussion about whether dual relationships should be specifically named as unprofessional conduct in the licensing laws for marriage and family therapists and for clinical social workers. The rationale given by the BBS was that in a large number of dual relationship cases action is taken against licensed practitioners. The California Association of Marriage and Family Therapists (CAMFT) stated its opposition to any amendment to the licensing laws that would concretize dual relationships as unprofessional conduct. CAMFT claimed that dual relationships are not always unethical or unprofessional, and that dual relationships are often unavoidable, especially in smaller or rural communities (CAMFT, 2004a, pp. 5–6).

Although some state licensure boards do not specifically label any dual relationship as unprofessional conduct, some therapists demonstrate unprofessional conduct by failing to establish and maintain clear boundaries. Here are two examples of dual relationships that were subject to disciplinary actions against licensed practitioners:

- A licensed marriage and family therapist was charged with failing to maintain clear boundaries and engaging in a dual relationship with a client. The therapist simultaneously maintained a professional relationship and a close personal relationship with the client, which included social, religious, and familial behavior. It was found that this impaired the therapist's judgment and resulted in the exploitation of the client, to her extreme detriment (CAMFT, 2001, p. 40).
- A licensed clinical social worker was required to surrender her license after being charged with participating in dual relationships with a client. The therapist had related to the client as a personal and social friend, invited the client to a dinner party, exchanged gifts with the client, and confided personal information to the client (CAMFT, 2001, p. 40).

Zur (1999) points out that some therapists will exploit dual relationships with clients regardless of prohibitions by licensure boards. Further, he contends that avoiding all dual relationships puts therapists in unrealistic and inappropriate power positions vis-à-vis their clients and leads to increased isolation of therapists. Appropriate dual relationships, in contrast, are essential to some therapeutic approaches, and these relationships can alter the power differential between therapist and client in ways that enhance the healing process.

Commentary. Prohibiting all forms of multiple relationships does not seem to be the best answer to the problem of exploitation of clients. Zur (1999) writes that during his graduate school training he was warned over and over never to engage in any kind of dual relationship. Here are some of the "nevers" he heard: never indulge in boundary crossing, never touch a client, never go to coffee or have lunch with a client, never treat a spouse or a friend of a client, never meet clients in social situations, and never join the same synagogue or church as a client. We agree with Zur's (2000a) contention that the professions have possibly gone too far in their attempts to regulate dual relationships.

Think about the circumstances in which you may decide upon flexible boundaries. How might certain dual or multiple relationships be unavoidable at times, and what can you do in these situations? What kinds of relationships might place you in professional jeopardy? Consider how refusing to attend a social event of a client could complicate the therapeutic relationship. In your struggle to determine what constitutes appropriate boundaries, you are likely to find that occasionally role blending is inevitable. Therefore, it is crucial to learn how to manage boundaries, how to prevent boundary crossings from turning into boundary violations, and how to develop safeguards that will prevent harm or exploitation of clients.

Controversies on Boundary Issues

Lazarus (1998, 2001) states that a general proscription against dual relationships has led to unfair and inconsistent decisions by state licensing boards, brought sanctions against practitioners who have done no harm, and sometimes impeded a therapist's ability to perform optimum work with a client. He argues for a case-by-case, nondogmatic evaluation of boundary questions when deciding whether to enter into a secondary relationship:

> The therapist is to be fully accountable and must ponder issues such as potential risks of harming the patient, possible conflicts of interest, whether or not a dual relationship will impair the therapist's judgment, if the patient's rights or autonomy will be infringed upon, and whether the therapist will gain a personal advantage over the client. (1998, p. 24)

Lazarus (1994a, 2001) contends that some well-intentioned ethical standards can be transformed into artificial boundaries that result in destructive prohibitions and undermine clinical effectiveness. Moreover, he believes some dual relationships can enhance treatment outcomes. In this section we present Lazarus's key arguments along with some responses to those ideas.

When taken too far, Lazarus argues that some well-intentioned guidelines can backfire. He admits that he has socialized with some clients, played tennis with others, taken walks with some, respectfully accepted small gifts, and given gifts (usually books) to clients. Lazarus emphasizes that he is clearly opposed to any form of disparagement, exploitation, abuse, harassment, or sexual contact with clients. Indeed, certain boundaries are essential. Rather than being driven by rules, however, Lazarus calls for a process of negotiation in many areas of nonsexual multiple relationships that some would contend are in the forbidden zone.

Lazarus's (1994a) keynote article caused a good deal of controversy, as can be seen by the number of authors who were invited to respond. These authors included Bennett, Bricklin, and VandeCreek (1994), Brown (1994), Gabbard (1994), and Gutheil (1994).

Bennett, Bricklin, and VandeCreek (1994) remind us of the unfortunate reality that too many practitioners have difficulty distinguishing where appropriate boundary lines should be drawn. Bennett and his colleagues agree with Lazarus that competent therapists will use clinical judgment rather than a cookbook approach when working with clients, but they fear that less experienced therapists will misinterpret his position as granting them license to minimize the importance of respecting boundary issues in therapy.

In her response to Lazarus's article, Brown (1994) maintains that the goal of ethical decision making is to take a position where potential for abuse and exploitation are minimized. She recognizes how easy it is for therapists to misuse the power they have and suggests that therapists consider the impact of their behavior on clients. Brown questions the clinical purpose of Lazarus's extra-office encounters with his clients—playing tennis, eating meals, and going for walks—and wonders if he has taken into account the entire therapeutic relationship before deciding to engage in any of these extra-office contacts. She states that violations of boundaries tend to profoundly imbalance the power of an already power-imbalanced relationship by placing the needs of the more powerful person, the therapist, in a paramount position.

Gabbard (1994) fears that Lazarus is "teetering on the precipice." Failing to establish clear boundaries can be very dangerous to both the client and the therapist. Gabbard sees boundaries as providing safety for clients: "Professional boundaries provide an envelope within which a warm, empathic holding environment can be created" (p. 285).

Gutheil (1994) criticizes Lazarus for not considering the potential impact of his interventions on the client. He also stresses his belief that sound risk management is not antithetical to spontaneity, warmth, humanitarian concerns, or flexibility of approach, as Lazarus contends. One of Gutheil's main points is that sound and valid risk management principles need to rest on a solid clinical foundation.

In Lazarus's rejoinder (1994b) he comments that the major difference between his views and those of the respondents is that they dwell mainly on the potential *costs and risks,* whereas he focuses mainly on the potential *advantages* that may occur when certain boundaries are transcended. Elsewhere Lazarus (2001) asserts that there is a widespread sense of mass hysteria where clinicians and licensing boards incorrectly assume that consumers are protected by declaring all forms of dual relationships as harmful, exploitive, and inevitably resulting in sexual misconduct. Lazarus writes: "Too many therapists see only a negative and hazardous side to all dual relationships. They claim that harm is inevitable, faulty clinical judgments will ensue, and in terms of risk management, great dangers lurk behind every corner" (p. 16). Lazarus thinks that professionals who hide behind rigid boundaries often fail to be of genuine help to their clients.

Advantages of Boundary Crossings

Boundary crossings can often be extremely helpful, whereas boundary violations are usually harmful. Many therapists confuse the two. Therapy is often shortchanged by the tendency to practice defensively, to allow the fear of attorneys and licensing boards to dictate how we treat our clients. It is imperative not to exploit, disparage, abuse, or harass a client, and to steer clear of any sexual contact. We must also appreciate the significance of confidentiality, integrity, respect, and informed consent. All the rest of the ethical rules, codes, and regulations are negotiable. Thus, contrary to the opinions of most therapists, nonsexual dual relationships can often enhance the process and outcome of psychotherapy.

Arnold Lazarus (personal communication, April 25, 2005) provided us with the following cases in which he contends that boundary crossings had positive outcomes rather than harming or exploiting the client. As you read Lazarus's thoughts on the advantages of selected boundary crossings, ask yourself where you stand on this issue.

✓ **The Case of Pete.** A few minutes before noon, my client Pete, whom I was scheduled to see from 11 a.m. to 12 p.m. was focusing on some highly significant issues. I said to him: "What's your program like for the rest of the afternoon?" He said that he had to attend a 4 p.m. meeting, whereupon I said: "I have nothing scheduled until 1:30. Should we pick up some sandwiches from the local deli, come back here, and continue for another hour at no extra cost to you?" He enthusiastically agreed.

As I had anticipated, Pete seemed to be more relaxed and open while munching sandwiches and sipping iced tea, so that pertinent information emerged much sooner than might have been the case had we adhered to the traditionally accepted therapist-client relationship. Subsequently, Pete emphasized how much my largesse had meant to him. That "sandwich session" seemed to be a turning point in the course of his therapy and appeared to have consolidated our working alliance.

I should underscore that the invitation to extend the session and "break bread" was not issued capriciously. Boundary crossings should occur only when they are likely to be helpful to the client. The therapist needs to consider potential benefits, drawbacks, and probable risks beforehand (see Lazarus & Zur, 2002).

✓ **The Case of Rita.** Rita, a young woman who had graduated from a prestigious law school felt inferior, considered herself "a loser," and generally belittled herself. She had received years of traditional insight therapy, and whatever gains may have accrued, self-confidence was not one of them. I was using a cognitive-behavior therapy approach, and we were making headway. Possibly because she was now exuding a sense of confidence and competence, a few fortunate events came together. She obtained a position with a law firm in which the senior partner was very supportive. She developed an intimate relationship with a man, which further helped to bolster her ego. She prepared a legal brief that enabled her firm to win an important case. Nevertheless, to use a football analogy, she was still not in the end zone. She felt that I and I alone really understood her "decrepitude." If her boss, her boyfriend, or anyone else were privy to the information she had shared with me, they would demean and reject her. So when she volunteered to critique a rather lengthy book chapter I was working on at the time, I decided to cross a boundary and accepted her offer. (I had mentioned this project *en passant* when she was discussing the rigors of preparing legal briefs.) My sense was that had I played by the rules and declined her offer—no matter how politely and graciously—this would only have reinforced her self-denigration. When the page proofs subsequently arrived, I made a point of showing her how many of her excellent literary suggestions had been incorporated. A few months later, I crossed another boundary. When one of my associates needed an attorney with expertise in Rita's domain, I referred him to her. This proved to her that despite knowing about her previous shortcomings, I nevertheless had respect for her and held her in high regard. This was a turning point. "If you believe in me, there's every reason for me to believe in myself," she declared.

Commentary. In much of the literature on boundaries, the focus is on negative outcomes. Phrases such as "protecting the client," "minimizing the potential for abuse and exploitation," "teetering on the precipice," and the "slippery slope phenomenon" abound. The assumption seems to be that without ethical rules and regulations all practitioners would be violating the rights of clients. We are in agreement with Lazarus that this focus on the negative, emphasizing what the practitioner cannot do, can also be detrimental to the client. Greenspan (2002) expresses similar sentiments, and she is doubtful that the admonition to eschew all dual relationships achieves the objective of protecting clients and promoting healing. Elsewhere Greenspan (1994) states:

> The standard of care itself conspires against the genuine meeting of persons that is the real *sine qua non* of healing. It keeps patient and professional separate even when they do not wish to be. It makes authenticity feel like a bad and dangerous thing. (pp. 199–200)

Zur's (2000a) statement that the real focus ought to be on preventing exploitation to the client is especially relevant here. For instance, consider some of the advantages of out-of-office encounters between school counselors and students. By attending a student's school play, musical recital, or sports event, the counselor can do a lot to build a relationship with a student. We recommend that counselors ask this question: "In what way is what I am contemplating in the best interests of the client?"

Imagine that you were required to videotape all your sessions with clients and maintain them as your records. Would your behavior with your clients be different in any way? What do you do now that you might hesitate to do if your colleagues were to view your videotaped sessions? Would you be pleased to have your work with the client published? Would you welcome oversight from your peers? If you would not be comfortable with such oversight, take time to examine what makes you uncomfortable.

Consider the client population with whom you are dealing as this will certainly influence the kinds of boundaries of which you need to be sensitive. Not all clients are alike. Age, diagnosis, and culture are key elements that need to be considered in establishing boundaries. A second element is the character of the therapist. In our opinion, the therapist's character and values have more influence than training and orientation. Consider how boundaries were respected in your family of origin and how you manage boundaries in your own personal life. How sensitive are you to the boundaries of others in your personal life? If we establish and maintain appropriate boundaries in our personal lives, it is unlikely that we will be indifferent to boundaries in our professional lives, or unwittingly ignore them.

Before you read about the various forms of multiple relationships therapists may encounter, clarify your thinking on these issues:

- What do you think of Lazarus's contention that certain boundaries can diminish therapeutic effectiveness?
- What are your reactions to Lazarus's claim that some dual relationships and boundary crossings tend to enhance treatment outcomes?
- Do you think nonsexual dual relationships necessarily lead to exploitation, sex, or harm? What are your thoughts about the "slippery slope" phenomenon?
- Do you think the ethics codes of the various professional organizations are reasonable as they pertain to boundary issues, nonprofessional relationships, and multiple relationships?
- What kinds of boundaries do you maintain in your personal life?
- Might certain dual relationships alter the power differential between you and your client in such a manner as to facilitate better health and healing?
- How can you assess the impact your interventions and behavior have on your client?
- Would you allow your fear of a malpractice suit to alter the way you deal with boundaries with clients? If so, what are you doing that could be viewed as being unethical?
- What topics pertaining to managing boundaries, multiple roles, and multiple relationships would you want to address with your clients from the initial session?

As you read the rest of this chapter, ask yourself what challenges you might encounter in managing multiple relationships.

Managing Multiple Relationships in Small Communities

In small communities, including rural communities, mental health practitioners and school counselors have far greater challenges dealing with multiple relationships than those who work in urban areas. Practitioners who work in small communities often have to blend several professional roles and functions.

They may attend the same church or community activities as the clients they serve. In an isolated area a priest or a minister may seek counseling for a personal crisis from the only counselor in the town—someone who also happens to be a parishioner. Consider the roles of these two psychologists who practice in rural settings.

- Dr. Gib Condie lives in Powell, Wyoming, a community of about 5,000 where he holds the multiple roles of psychologist, neighbor, friend, and spiritual leader. As a school psychologist, he is faced with the challenge of balancing multiple roles and relationships in his community. He is also a Mormon bishop to 400 people in Powell. Condie believes that the many benefits associated with a rural practice far outweigh the challenges (cited in Kennedy, 2003, p. 67).
- Dr. Dan Goodkind offers psychological services to an underserved rural community 170 miles outside of Salt Lake City. This Utah psychologist finds that practicing in a rural area poses unique ethical dilemmas. Because the area has limited psychological services, neighbors or friends can become his next clients. Even though he tries to avoid seeing personal acquaintances professionally, this cannot always be avoided (cited in Dittmann, 2003).

Schank and Skovholt (1997) conducted interviews with psychologists who live and practice in rural areas and small communities and found that they all acknowledged concerns involving professional boundaries. Some of the major themes were the reality of overlapping social or business relationships, the effects of overlapping social relationships on members of the psychologist's own family, and the dilemma of working with more than one family member as clients or with clients who have friendships with other clients. For them to be accepted, many of these psychologists found they had to work within the existing community system. Although the psychologists knew the content of the ethics codes, they admitted that they often struggle in choosing how to apply those codes to the ethical dilemmas they face in rural practice.

Sleek (1994) also describes ethical dilemmas that are unique to rural practice. For example, if a therapist shops for a new tractor, he risks violating the letter of the ethics code if the only person in town who sells tractors happens to be a client. However, if the therapist were to buy a tractor elsewhere, this could strain relationships with the community because of the value rural communities place on loyalty to local merchants. Or consider clients who wish to barter goods or services for counseling services. Some communities operate substantially on swaps rather than on a cash economy. This does not necessarily have to become problematic, yet the potential for conflict exists in the therapeutic relationship if the bartering agreements do not work well.

Campbell and Gordon (2003) address some of the unique aspects of rural practice and offer strategies for evaluating, preventing, and managing multiple relationships in rural practice. They point out that the APA ethics code offers three helpful criteria in making decisions about multiple relationships: risk of exploitation, loss of therapist objectivity, and harm to the professional relationship. They also mention that in the everyday professional practice in rural areas, prospective multiple relationships do not often fit precisely into a single ethical category. Campbell and Gordon conclude:

> Multiple relationships in rural practice are inevitable because of the limited number of rural practitioners, access difficulties, characteristics of rural communities, and characteristics of psychologists who practice in these communities. Although the best practice is to abstain from multiple roles and boundary compromises, there are situations in which avoidance of involvement may result in no psychological care for a large portion of the rural community. (p. 434)

A Case of a Multiple Relationship in a Small Community. Millie is a therapist in a small community, and one day she experienced heart pain. The fire department was called, and the medic on the team turned out to be her client, Fred. To administer proper medical care, Fred had to remove Millie's upper clothing. During subsequent sessions, neither Fred nor Millie discussed the incident, but both exhibited a degree of discomfort with each other. After a few more sessions, Fred discontinued his therapy with Millie.

- Can this case be considered an unavoidable dual relationship? Why or why not?
- What might Millie have done to prevent this outcome?
- If Millie had decided to acknowledge the discomfort they both felt in the session, should she have addressed her discomfort first or should she have started with Fred's?

The Challenge of Practicing in a Small Community*

I (Marianne Schneider Corey) would like to share my experience in conducting a private practice in a small community. I practiced for many years as a marriage and family therapist in a small town. This situation presented a number of ethical considerations involving safeguarding the privacy of clients.

I discussed with my clients the unique variables pertaining to confidentiality in a small community. I informed them that I would not discuss professional concerns with them should we meet at the grocery store or the post office, and I respected their preferences regarding interactions away from the office. Knowing that they were aware that I saw many people from the town, I reassured them that I would not talk with anyone about who my clients were, even when I might be directly asked. Another example of protecting my clients' privacy pertained to the manner of depositing checks at the local bank. Because the bank employees knew my profession, it would have been easy for them to identify my clients. Again, I talked with my clients about their preferences. If they had any discomfort about my depositing their checks in the local bank, I arranged to have them deposited elsewhere.

Practicing in a small town inevitably meant that I would meet clients in many places. For example, the checker at the grocery store might be my client; the person standing in line before me at the store could be a client who wants to talk about his or her week; at church there may be clients or former clients in

*This section is presented from the private practice of Marianne Corey.

the same Bible study group; in restaurants a client's family may be seated next to the table where my family is dining, or the food server could be a client; and on a hiking event I may discover that in the group is a client and his or her partner. Even in urban areas, therapists will occasionally encounter their clients in any of these situations. However, in a rural area such meetings are more likely to occur. All of these examples present possible problems unless these situations are managed effectively. Neither my clients nor I experienced problems in such situations because we had talked about the possibility of such meetings in advance. Being a practitioner in a small community demands flexibility, honesty, and sensitivity. In managing multiple roles and relationships, it is not very useful to rely on rigid rules and policies; you must be ready to creatively adapt to situations as they unfold.

The examples I have given demonstrate that what might clearly not be advisable in an urban area might just as clearly be unavoidable in a rural area. This does not mean that rural mental health professionals are free do whatever they please. The task of managing boundaries is more challenging in rural areas, and to a greater extent practitioners are called upon to examine what is in the best interests of their client.

Now consider the following questions:

- What ethical dilemmas do you think you would encounter if you were to practice in a rural area?
- Are you comfortable discussing possible outside contacts with clients up front and are you able to set guidelines with your clients?
- What are some of the advantages and disadvantages of practicing in a small community?
- Is there more room for flexibility in setting guidelines regarding social relationships and outside business contacts with clients in a small community?

Bartering for Professional Services

When a client is unable to afford therapy, he or she may offer a **bartering** arrangement, exchanging services in lieu of paying a fee. For example, a mechanic might exchange work on a therapist's car for counseling sessions. However, if the client was expected to provide several hours of work on the therapist' car in exchange for one therapy session, this client might become resentful over the perceived imbalance of the exchange. If the therapist's car was not repaired properly, the therapist might resent that client. This would damage the therapeutic relationship. In addition, problems of another sort can occur with dual relationships should clients clean house, perform secretarial services, or do other personal work for the therapist. Clients can easily be put in a bind when they are in a position to learn personal material about their therapists. The client might feel taken advantage of by the therapist, which could damage his or her therapy. Certainly, many problems can arise from these kinds of exchanges for both therapists and clients.

Ethics Codes

Bartering

American Counseling Association (2005)

Counselors may barter only if the relationship is not exploitive or harmful and does not place the counselor in an unfair advantage, if the client requests it, and if such arrangements are an accepted practice among professionals in the community. Counselors consider the cultural implications of bartering and discuss relevant concerns with clients and document such agreements in a clear written contract. (A.10.d.)

American Psychological Association (2002)

Barter is the acceptance of goods, services, or other nonmonetary remuneration from clients/patients in return for psychological services. Psychologists may barter only if (1) it is not clinically contraindicated, and (2) the resulting arrangement is not exploitative. (6.05.)

American Association for Marriage and Family Therapy (2001)

Marriage and family therapists ordinarily refrain from accepting goods and services from clients in return for services rendered. Bartering for professional services may be conducted only if: (a) the supervisee or client requests it, (b) the relationship is not exploitative, (c) the professional relationship is not distorted, and (d) a clear written contract is established. (7.5.)

National Association of Social Workers (1999)

Social workers should avoid accepting goods or services from clients as payment for professional services. Bartering arrangements, particularly involving services, create the potential for conflicts of interest, exploitation, and inappropriate boundaries in social workers' relationships with clients. Social workers should explore and may participate in bartering only in very limited circumstances where it can be demonstrated that such arrangements are an accepted practice among professionals in the local community, considered to be essential for the provision of service, negotiated without coercion and entered into at the client's initiative and with the client's informed consent. Social workers who accept goods or services from clients as payment for professional services assume the full burden of demonstrating that this arrangement will not be detrimental to the client or the professional relationship. (1.13.b.)

Ethical Standards on Bartering

Most ethics codes now address the complexities of bartering (see the ethics codes box titled Bartering). We agree with the general tone of these standards, although we would add that bartering should be evaluated within a cultural context. In some cultures and in certain communities, bartering is an accepted practice.

Before bartering is entered into, both parties should talk about the arrangement, gain a clear understanding of the exchange, and come to an agreement. It is also important that problems that might develop be discussed and that alternatives be examined. Using a sliding scale to determine fees or making a referral are two possible alternatives that might have merit. Bartering is an example of a dual relationship that we think allows some room for practitioners, in collaboration with their clients, to use good judgment and consider the cultural context in the situation. Both Holly Forester-Miller and Lawrence Thomas write about their views on the benefits of bartering when clients cannot afford to pay for psychological services.

Forester-Miller (2006) writes about the difficulties involved in avoiding dual relationships in rural communities. She reminds counselors that values and beliefs may vary significantly between urban dwellers and their rural counterparts and suggests that counselors need to work to ensure that they are not imposing values that come from a cultural perspective different from that of their clients. She uses bartering as an example of one way of providing counseling services in some regions to individuals who could not otherwise afford counseling. Forester-Miller gives an example of adapting her practices in the Appalachian culture, where individuals pride themselves on being able to provide for themselves and their loved ones. Forester-Miller once counseled an adolescent girl whose single-parent mother could not afford her usual fee, nor could she afford to pay a reduced fee, and even a small amount would be a drain on this family's resources. When Forester-Miller informed the mother that she would be willing to see her daughter for free, the mother stated that this would not be acceptable to her. However, she asked the counselor if she would accept a quilt she had made as payment for counseling the daughter. The mother and the counselor discussed the monetary value of the quilt and decided to use this as payment for a specified number of counseling sessions. Forester-Miller reports that this was a good solution because it enabled the adolescent girl to receive needed counseling services and gave the mother an opportunity to maintain her dignity in that she could pay her own way.

Thomas (2002) is a psychologist who believes bartering is a legitimate means of helping out a person with financial difficulties. He maintains that bartering should not be ruled out simply because of the slight chance that a client might initiate a lawsuit against the therapist. His view is that if we are not willing to take some risks as psychotherapy professionals, then we are not worthy of our position. Along with taking risks, Thomas believes that venturing into any dual relationship requires careful thought and judgment. He contends that the vast majority of professional work should be paid by the usual monetary means, yet he adds that when this is not possible due to a client's economic situation, allowances should be made so that psychological services might be available. In making decisions about bartering, the most salient issue is the "higher standard" of considering the welfare of the client. Bartering can be one way of providing help to those in financial straits who do not qualify for insurance reimbursement. Thomas recommends a written contract that spells out the nature of the agreement between the therapist and client, which should be reviewed regularly. Documenting the arrangement can clarify agreements and can also help professionals defend themselves if this becomes necessary. Thomas admits that bartering is a troublesome topic, yet he emphasizes that the role of our professional character is to focus on the higher standard—the best interests of the client.

Making a Decision About Bartering

Bartering is not prohibited by ethics or law, but most legal experts frown on the practice. Woody (1998), who is both a psychologist and an attorney, argues against the use of bartering for psychological services. He suggests that it could be argued that bartering is below the minimum standard of practice. Woody suggests that if you enter into a bartering agreement with your client, you will have the burden of proof to demonstrate that (a) the bartering arrangement is in the best interests of your client; (b) is reasonable, equitable, and undertaken without undue influence; and (c) does not get in the way of providing quality psychological services to your client. Because bartering is so fraught with risks for both client and therapist, Woody believes prudence dictates that it should be the option of last resort. He concludes that bartering is a bad idea and should be avoided: "No matter how carefully a bartering agreement is structured, the psychologist remains vulnerable" (p. 177). Even if the client needs special financial arrangements or suggests bartering as a solution to his or her financial problem, the therapist is always left with the liability. Woody also takes a dim view of providing *pro bono* services in cases of financial hardship.

If you decide to participate in a bartering arrangement with a client, you would need to report the bartered services or goods as income to the Internal Revenue Service. Therefore, it is important to use the fair market value of the goods or services, because the IRS will in all likelihood apply this standard (Rahn Minagawa, personal communication, August 14, 2003).

Therapists who are considering entering into a bartering arrangement would do well to consider Hall's (1996) recommendations prior to establishing such an arrangement:

- Evaluate whether the bartering arrangement will put you at risk of poor professional judgment or have a negative impact on your performance as a therapist.
- Determine the value of the goods or services in a collaborative fashion with the client at the outset of the bartering arrangement.
- Determine the appropriate length of time for the barter arrangement.
- Document the bartering arrangement, including the value of the goods or services and a date on which the arrangement will end or be renegotiated.

Woody (1998) presents some additional guidelines to clarify the bartering arrangements:

- Minimize any unique financial arrangements.
- If bartering is used for psychological services, it is better to exchange goods rather than services.
- Both you and your client should reach a written agreement for the compensation by bartering.
- If a misunderstanding begins to develop, the matter should be dealt with by a mediator, not by you and your client.

To these recommendations we add the importance of consulting with experienced colleagues, a supervisor, or your professional organization if you are considering some form of bartering in lieu of payment for therapy services. It may be worthwhile to contact the American Barter Exchange for their guidelines for bartering arrangements. We highly recommend a straightforward discussion with your client about the pros and cons of bartering in your particular situation, especially as it may apply to the standards of your community. We agree with Thomas (2002), who recommends creating a written contract that specifies hours spent by each party and all particulars of the agreement. If you still have doubts about the agreement, consult with a contract lawyer. Once potential problems have been identified, consult with colleagues about alternatives you and your client may not have considered. Ongoing consultation and discussion of cases, especially in matters pertaining to boundaries and dual roles, provide a context for understanding the implications of certain practices. Needless to say, these consultations should be documented.

Your Stance on Bartering. Consider a situation in which you have a client who cannot afford to pay even a reduced fee. Would you be inclined to engage in bartering goods for your services? What kind of understanding would you need to work out with your client before you agreed to a bartering arrangement? Would your decision be dependent on whether you were practicing in a large urban area or a rural area? How might you take the cultural context into consideration when making your decision?

Consider these cases and apply the ethical standards we have summarized to your analysis. What ethical issues are involved in each case? What potential problems do you see emerging from these cases? What alternatives to bartering can you think of?

The Case of Barbara. Barbara is 20 years old and has been in therapy with Sidney for over a year. She has developed respect and fondness for her therapist, whom she sees as a father figure. She tells him that she is thinking of discontinuing therapy because she has lost her job and simply has no way of paying for the sessions. She is obviously upset over the prospect of ending the relationship, but she sees no alternative. Sidney informs her that he is willing to continue her therapy even if she is unable to pay. He suggests that as an exchange of services she can become the baby-sitter for his three children. She gratefully accepts this offer. After a few months, however, Barbara finds that the situation is becoming difficult for her. Eventually, she writes a note to Sidney telling him that she cannot handle her reactions to his wife and their children. It makes her think of all the things she missed in her own family. She writes that she has found this subject difficult to bring up in her sessions, so she is planning to quit both her services and her therapy.

- What questions does this case raise for you?
- How would you have dealt with this situation?
- Was it unethical for the therapist to suggest that Barbara baby-sit for him?
- Did Sidney adequately consider the nature of the transference relationship with this client?
- Do you see any solutions for this dilemma?

The Case of Olive Isle. Olive Isle is a massage therapist in her community. Her services are sought by many professionals, including Giovani, a local psychologist. In the course of a massage session, she confides in him that she is experiencing difficulties in her marriage. She would like to discuss with him the possibility of exchanging professional services. She proposes that in return for marital therapy she will give both him and his wife massage treatments. An equitable arrangement based on their fee structures can be worked out. Giovani might make any one of the following responses:

Response A: That's fine with me, Olive. It sounds like a good proposal. Neither one of us will suffer financially because of it, and we can each benefit from our expertise.

Response B: Well, Olive, I feel okay about the exchange, except I have concerns about the dual relationship.

Response C: Even though our relationship is nonsexual, Olive, I do feel uncomfortable about seeing you as a client in marital therapy. I certainly could refer you to a competent marital therapist.

- What are your thoughts on these responses?
- What are your thoughts about Olive's proposal? What are the ethical implications in this case?
- If you were in this situation, how would you deal with Olive?

The Case of Exchanging Services for Therapy. Bryce is a counselor in private practice and has been seeing a client for a few months. Jana is hard working, dedicated to personal growth, and is making progress in treatment. At her last session she expressed concern regarding the $100 per hour fee and her ability to continue funding her sessions. Jana suggested that Bryce consider allowing her husband's pool company to provide summer pool cleaning service for the months of May through August for Bryce's home pool in return for her continued sessions. The fees would be basically equitable, and Bryce is seriously considering this agreement to assist Jana in her ability to continue counseling.

- Does this arrangement seem like a reasonable request to you?
- What ethical issues related to this situation might cause you concern?
- Which ethical standards apply to this situation?

Commentary. Accepting goods and services from clients in return for counseling services is discouraged in counseling relationships, and the case of Barbara demonstrates one of the pitfalls of this practice. In the case of Olive Isle and Giovani, one wonders why bartering for services was even suggested. If their fee structures are so similar, a fee-for-service arrangement will avoid needless entanglements. The case of Bryce and Jana is less clear-cut. While bartering with a client is not expressly prohibited in the code of ethics, it certainly leaves room for the relationship between client and counselor to be reframed. It is important that the arrangement was suggested by Jana and not by Bryce. It would be beneficial for Bryce to consider some consultation in reviewing the pros and cons of this proposal prior to making a decision. If he decides to participate in this bartering arrangement, he will need to have an explicit written contract of the agreed upon terms of exchange.

Giving or Receiving Gifts

Few professional codes of ethics specifically address the topic of giving or receiving gifts in the therapeutic relationship. The AAMFT (2001) does have such a guideline:

> Marriage and family therapists do not give to or receive from clients (a) gifts of substantial value or (b) gifts that impair the integrity or efficacy of the therapeutic relationship. (3.10.)

The latest version of the ACA ethics code (2005) added a new standard on receiving gifts.

> *Receiving Gifts.* Counselors understand the challenges of accepting gifts from clients and recognize that in some cultures, small gifts are a token of respect and showing gratitude. When determining whether or not to accept a gift from clients, counselors take into account the therapeutic relationship, the monetary value of the gift, a client's motivation for giving the gift, and the counselor's motivation for wanting or declining the gift. (A.10.e.)

Lavish gifts certainly present an ethical problem, yet we can go too far in the direction of trying to be ethical and, in so doing, actually damage the therapeutic relationship. Some therapists include a policy statement on matters such as not accepting gifts from clients in their informed consent document, so that there will not be a question on this matter. Rather than establishing a hard and fast rule, our preference is to evaluate each situation on a case-by-case basis. A number of factors need to be considered in making a decision of whether to accept gifts from clients. Let's examine a few of these areas in more detail.

- *What is the monetary value of the gift?* Most mental health professionals would agree that accepting a very expensive gift is inappropriate and unethical. It would also be problematic if a client offered tickets to the theater or a sporting event and wanted you to accompany him or her to this event.
- *What are the clinical implications of accepting or rejecting the gift?* It is important to recognize when accepting a gift from a client is clinically contraindicated and that you be willing to explore this with your client. Certainly, knowing the motivation for a client's overture is critical to making a decision. For example, a client may be seeking your approval, in which case the main motivation for giving you a gift is to please you. Accepting the gift without adequate discussion would not be helping your client in the long run.
- *When in the therapy process is the offering of a gift occurring?* Is it at the beginning of the therapy process? Is it at the termination of the professional relationship? It is more problematic to accept a gift at an early stage of a counseling relationship because doing so may be a forerunner to creating lax boundaries.

- *What are your own motivations for accepting or rejecting a client's gift?* Some counselors will accept a gift simply because they do not want to hurt a client's feelings, even though they are not personally comfortable doing so. Counselors may accept a gift because they are unable to establish firm and clear boundaries. Other counselors may accept a gift because they actually want what a client is offering.
- *What are the cultural implications of offering a gift?* In working with culturally diverse client populations, clinicians often discover that they need to engage in boundary crossing to enhance the counseling relationship (Moleski & Kiselica, 2005). The cultural context does play a role in evaluating the appropriateness of accepting a gift from a client. Sue (2006) points out that in the Asian cultures gift giving is a common practice to show respect, gratitude, and to seal a relationship. Although such actions are culturally appropriate, Western-trained professionals may believe that accepting a gift would distort boundaries, change the relationship, and create a conflict of interest. However, if a practitioner were to refuse a client's gift, it is likely that this person would feel insulted or humiliated and the refusal could damage both the therapeutic relationship and the client. If you are opposed to receiving gifts and view this as a boundary crossing, address this issue in your informed consent document.

One of the reviewers of this book stated that students sometimes give school counselors gifts. Such gifts are usually inexpensive, if purchased, or are something made in an art or shop class. He indicates that he could accept the gift and display the gift in his office. If you were a school counselor, would you be inclined to accept inexpensive gifts? Would you display a gift in your office? How would you respond if other students (your clients) or teachers asked you who made the gift that is on display? Under what circumstances, if any, might you be inclined to give a student a gift?

✓ **The Case of Tomoko.** Tomoko, a Japanese client, presents a piece of jewelry to her counselor, Joaquin. Tomoko says she is grateful for all that her counselor has done for her and that she really wants him to accept her gift, which has been in her family for many years. In a discussion with the counselor, Tomoko claims that giving gifts is a part of the Japanese culture. Joaquin discusses his dilemma, telling Tomoko that he would like to accept the gift but that he has a policy of not accepting gifts from clients. He reminds her of this policy, which was part of the informed consent document she signed at the beginning of the therapeutic relationship. Tomoko is persistent and lets Joaquin know that if he does not accept her gift she will feel rejected. She is extremely grateful for all Joaquin has done for her, and this is her way of expressing her appreciation.

Put yourself in this situation with Tomoko. What aspects would you want to explore with your client before accepting or not accepting her gift?

- Do you see a difference between accepting a gift during therapy or at the end of therapy?

- Would it be important to consider your client's cultural background in accepting or not accepting the gift?
- What might you say to Tomoko if she told you that in her culture it is expected that you will reciprocate in some way if you accept her gift?
- How would you deal with Tomoko if she were insistent that you recognize her token of appreciation?
- If you find that clients frequently want to give you gifts, would you need to reflect on what you might be doing to promote this pattern?

✓ **The Case of Accepting a Gift.** A counselor, Aiden, has just completed a six-unit workshop to increase his multicultural competence. In the course of the workshop, emphasis is placed on sensitivity to giving and receiving gifts in various cultures. Several months later, one of Aiden's counselees, Sunmie, is terminating a 2-year therapeutic relationship with him. At the last session she surprises him with a very beautiful and obviously expensive piece of art. Aiden is rendered speechless for a moment, and then he recalls the workshop that spoke about the etiquette of receiving gifts in certain cultures. He then decides to accept the gift. As Sunmie is leaving, she lets him know that she would be very honored if he would attend the birthday party for her daughter so that he could meet the entire family.

- How would you apply the ethics code to Aiden's situation?
- How would you respond to Sunmie in this situation?
- What steps would you take in making an ethical decision in this case?
- Might there be an ethical issue in refusing the gift? Explain.

✓ **A Case of Disciplinary Action Against a Therapist.** In 2005 a licensed marriage and family therapist (whom we will call Judy) was charged with gross negligence in her treatment of a client in that she blurred therapeutic boundaries by creating a dual relationship (CAMFT, 2005, p. 50). In fact, there were multiple charges against Judy. The therapist repeatedly gave gifts to her client and received gifts from the client. Shortly after therapy began with a married woman, Judy began disclosing an increasing amount of personal information about herself to her client, including details of her sex life. Judy encouraged the client to increase her sessions to twice a week. These sessions often lasted 2 to 3 hours, and sometimes beyond midnight. Judy invited her client to spend a weekend with her at her home. During this weekend, the therapist smoked marijuana in the client's presence and invited her to smoke it also. During this same weekend, the therapist had a massage in her living room at home and started to undress in front of her client.

This case illustrates how lax boundaries can contribute to a number of ethical violations.

- Would you ever consider giving a gift to a client?
- How much personal information do you think you would share with a client? In what circumstances might you do so?

Social Relationships With Clients

Do social relationships with clients necessarily interfere with therapeutic relationships? Some would say no, contending that counselors and clients are able to handle such relationships as long as the priorities are clear. They see social contacts as particularly appropriate with clients who are not deeply disturbed and who are seeking personal growth. Some peer counselors, for example, maintain that friendships before or during counseling are actually positive factors in establishing trust.

Other practitioners take the position that counseling and friendship should not be mixed. They argue that attempting to manage a social and professional relationship simultaneously can have a negative effect on the therapeutic process, the friendship, or both. Here are some reasons for discouraging the practice of accepting friends as clients or of becoming socially involved with clients: (1) therapists may not be as challenging as they need to be with clients they know socially; (2) counselors' own needs to be liked and accepted may lead them to be less challenging, lest the friendship or social relationship be jeopardized; (3) counselors' own needs may be enmeshed with those of their clients to the point that objectivity is lost; and (4) counselors are at greater risk of exploiting clients because of the power differential in the therapeutic relationship.

Few professional ethics codes specifically mention social relationships with clients. One exception is that of the Canadian Counselling Association (1999), which has the following standard pertaining to relationships with former clients:

> Counsellors remain accountable for any relationships established with former clients. Those relationships could include, but are not limited to those of a friendship, social, financial, and business nature. Counsellors exercise caution about entering any such relationships and take into account whether or not the issues and relational dynamics present during the counselling have been fully resolved and properly terminated. In any case, counselors seek consultation on such decisions. (B.11.)

Cultural Considerations

The cultural context can play a role in evaluating the appropriateness of dual relationships that involve friendships in the therapy context. In writing about dual relationships from an African perspective, Parham and Caldwell (2006) question Western ethical standards that discourage dual and multiple relationships and claim that such standards can prove to be an obstacle or hindrance in counseling African American clients. In an African context, therapy is not confined to a practitioner's office for 50-minute sessions. Instead, therapy involves multiple activities that might include conversation, playful activities, laughter, shared meals and cooking experiences, travel, rituals and ceremony, singing or drumming, storytelling, writing, and touching. Parham and Caldwell view each of these activities as having the potential to bring a "healing focus" to the therapeutic experience.

In a similar spirit, Sue (2006) makes it clear that some cultural groups may value multiple relationships with helping professionals. Some of Sue's points are worth considering in determining when multiple relationships might be acceptable:

- In some Asian cultures it is believed that personal matters are best discussed with a relative or a friend. Self-disclosing to a stranger (the counselor) is considered taboo and a violation of familial and cultural values. Thus some Asian clients may prefer to have the traditional counseling role evolve into a more personal one.
- Clients from many cultural groups prefer to receive advice and suggestions from an expert. They perceive the counselor to be an expert, having higher status and possessing superior knowledge. To work effectively with these clients, the counselor may have to play a number of different roles, such as advocate, adviser, change agent, and facilitator of indigenous support systems. Yet counselors may view playing more than one of these roles as engaging in dual or multiple relationships. (See Chapter 13 for a more extensive discussion of alternatives to traditional roles for professionals who work in the community.)

Forming Relationships With Former Clients

On the topic of establishing friendships with former clients, Grosso (2002) states that mental health professionals are not legally or ethically prohibited from entering into a nonsexual relationship with a client after the termination of therapy. However, Grosso adds that the ethics codes address friendships with former clients, stating that difficulties might arise for both the client and the therapist. For example, a former client might feel taken advantage of, which could result in a complaint against the therapist. Grosso points out that therapists need to know that it is their responsibility to evaluate the impact of entering into such relationships.

Although forming friendships with former clients may not be unethical or illegal, the practice could be unwise. The safest policy is probably to avoid developing social relationships with former clients. O'Laughlin (2001) reports that some state licensing boards view social relationships with former clients much the same as sexual relationships with former clients. Some state regulations have posttherapy bans on both of these relationships for at least 2 years or more after termination of therapy. This social relationship restriction bars a therapist and a client from dating, becoming friends, or getting married.

In the long run, former clients may need you more as a therapist at some future time than as a friend. If you develop a friendship with a former client, then he or she is not eligible to use your professional services in the future. Additionally, in many situations the imbalance of power never changes. Even in the social relationship, you are either seen as a therapist, or you behave as a therapist. Mental health practitioners should be aware of their own motivations, as well as the motivations of their clients, when allowing a professional relationship to evolve into a personal one. We question helpers who rely on their professional position as a way to meet their social needs. Furthermore, therapists who are in the habit of developing relationships with former clients may find themselves overextended and come to resent the relationships they sought out or consented to. Perhaps the crux of the situation involves the therapist being able to establish clear boundaries regarding what he or she is willing to do. Consider this case example.

The Case of a Former Client. Imagine a former client of yours, who while in therapy with you, requested to meet you in the park because the client found the office environment cold and unfriendly. A year after the termination of therapy, the client calls you and invites you to a party saying, "It would mean a lot to me for you to come."

- What are your immediate reactions?
- What would you say to your former client?
- Would the fact that the client had invited you to meet in the park during your therapy sessions cause you to hesitate about going to the party?

Your Position on Socializing with Current or Former Clients. There are many types of socializing, ranging from going to a social event with a client to having a cup of tea or coffee with a client. There are differences between a social involvement initiated by a client and one instigated by a therapist. Another factor to consider is whether the social contact is ongoing or occasional. The degree of intimacy is also a factor. For instance, there is a difference between meeting a client for coffee as opposed to a candlelight dinner. In thinking through your own position on establishing a dual relationship with a current client, consider the nature of the social function, the nature of your client's problem, the client population, the setting where you work, the kind of therapy being employed, and your theoretical approach. If you are psychoanalytically oriented, you are likely to adopt stricter boundaries and will be concerned about infecting the transference relationship should you blend any form of socializing with therapy. If you are a behavior therapist helping a client to stop smoking, it may be possible to have social contact at some point. Weigh the various factors and consider this matter from both the client's and the therapist's perspective.

Certainly, there are problems when professional and social relationships are blended. Such arrangements demand a great deal of honesty and self-awareness on the part of the therapist. No matter how clear the therapist is on boundaries, if the client cannot understand or cannot handle the social relationship, such a relationship should not be formed—with either current or former clients. When clear boundaries are not maintained, both the professional and the social relationship can sour. Clients may well become inhibited during therapy out of fear of alienating their therapist. They may fear losing the respect of a therapist with whom they have a friendship. They may censor their disclosures so that they do not threaten this social relationship.

Ethics codes generally do not address the issue of friendships with former clients. What are your thoughts on this topic? What are the therapist's obligations to former clients? Should the focus be on all relationships with former clients or only those that are exploitative? Should ethics codes address nonromantic and nonsexual posttherapy relationships specifically? Under what circumstances might such relationships be unethical? When do you think these relationships might be considered ethical?

Sexual Attractions in the Client-Therapist Relationship

Are sexual attractions to be expected in therapy? In a pioneering study, "Sexual Attraction to Clients: The Human Therapist and the (Sometimes) Inhuman Training System," Pope, Keith-Spiegel, and Tabachnick (1986) developed the theme that there has been a lack of systematic research into the sexual attraction of therapists to their clients. They provide clear evidence that attraction to clients is a prevalent experience among both male and female therapists and investigated the following questions:

- What is the frequency of sexual attraction to clients by therapists?
- Do therapists feel guilty or uncomfortable when they have such attractions?
- Do they tend to tell their clients about their attractions?
- Do they consult with colleagues?
- Do therapists believe their graduate training provided adequate education on attraction to clients?

Pope and his colleagues studied 585 respondents, and only 77 reported never having been attracted to any client. The vast majority (82%) reported that they had never seriously considered actual sexual involvement with a client. An even larger majority (93.5%) reported never having had sexual relations with their clients. Therapists gave a number of reasons for having refrained from acting out their attractions to clients, including a need to uphold professional values, a concern about the welfare of the client, and a desire to follow personal values. Fears of negative consequences were mentioned, but they were less frequently cited than values pertaining to client welfare. Those who had some graduate training in this area were more likely to have sought consultation (66%) than were those with no such training.

Since this pioneering study there has been more research on this topic (see Downs, 2003; Lamb, Catanzaro, & Moorman, 2003; Pope 1994; Pope et al., 1993). According to Pope, Sonne, and Holroyd (1993), the tendency to treat sexual feelings as if they are taboo has made it difficult for therapists to acknowledge and accept attractions to clients. They found that the most common reactions of therapists to sexual feelings in therapy were these:

- Surprise, startle, and shock
- Guilt
- Anxiety about unresolved personal problems
- Fear of losing control
- Fear of being criticized

- Frustration at not being able to speak openly—or at not being able to make sexual contact
- Confusion about tasks
- Confusion about boundaries and roles
- Confusion about actions
- Fear or discomfort at frustrating the client's demands

Given these reactions, it is not surprising that many therapists want to hide rather than to acknowledge and deal with sexual feelings by consulting a colleague or by bringing this to their own therapy.

There is a distinction between finding a client sexually attractive and being preoccupied with this attraction. Surely it can happen that we find ourselves being physically attracted to some clients more than others. However, as therapy proceeds, this generally becomes less and less of an issue, and the attraction is less likely to determine how we treat our clients. If you find yourself sexually attracted to your clients, it is important that you examine these feelings. If you are frequently attracted, you need to deal with this issue in your own therapy and supervision. If this happens, consider these questions: "What is going on in my own life that may be creating this intense sexual attraction? What am I not taking care of in my personal life?" We recommend Irvin Yalom's (1998) book, *Lying on the Couch: A Novel*, for an interesting discourse on the slippery slope of sexual attraction between therapists and clients.

Educating Counselor Trainees

Many training programs spend too little time addressing how to deal with sexual attraction to clients (Hamilton & Spruill, 1999; Housman & Stake, 1999; Pope, 1987; Pope et al., 1986; Pope et al., 1993; Rodolfa et al., 1990; Samuel & Gorton, 1998; Vasquez, 1988; Wiederman & Sansone, 1999). Moreover, little attention has been given to the ethical aspects of nonerotic physical contact (see Holub & Lee, 1990, in a later section in this chapter).

Although transient sexual feelings are normal, intense preoccupation with clients is problematic. Pope and colleagues (1986) found that 57% of the psychologists in their study sought consultation or supervision when attracted to a client. Housman and Stake (1999) found that 50% of the doctoral students in their study reported having experienced a sexual attraction to a client; only half of these students had chosen to discuss the attraction with a supervisor. Seeking help from a colleague or supervision or personal therapy can give therapists access to guidance, education, and support in handling their feelings. Pope, Sonne, and Holroyd (1993) believe that exploration of sexual feelings about clients is best done with the help, support, and encouragement of others. They maintain that practice, internships, and peer supervision groups are ideal places to talk about this issue but that this topic is rarely raised.

Counselors need to ask themselves how they set boundaries when sexual attraction occurs. Practitioners who have difficulty setting and keeping appropriate boundaries in their personal life are more likely to encounter problems in establishing appropriate boundaries with their clients. Heiden (1993) writes that counselors must ask themselves about how they treat clients in different ways, especially with reference to time spent, intimacy, and touch. It is well for counselors to think about how their own needs for intimacy are being met by clients.

Housman and Stake (1999) surveyed sexual ethics training and student understanding of sexual ethics in clinical psychology doctoral programs and found that 94% of the students had received sexual ethics training. Programs provided an average of 6 hours of training. Their findings also call attention to the importance of addressing sexual issues in therapy early in students' training. Sexual feelings for clients are common among students as well as professional practitioners. It was concluded that most students in training do not understand that sexual attractions for clients are normal. Housman and Stake's findings suggest that only half the students who are attracted will seek supervision. They note that even if students refrain from acting on their sexual feelings for clients, they may withdraw emotionally from their clients to avoid feelings they believe are unacceptable. It is crucial that students acknowledge these feelings to themselves and their supervisors and take steps to deal effectively with them. Housman and Stake emphasize the importance of broadening sexual ethics training to address both the emotional and cognitive aspects of attractions in the therapeutic relationship.

Wiederman and Sansone (1999) concur that deliberate attention to sexuality issues during training is required for the development of competent mental health professionals. Ideally, this training would involve accurate information and firsthand experience. Hamilton and Spruill (1999) believe it is crucial to increase students' awareness of sexual attraction before they begin seeing clients. They recommend including this topic as a basic component in a preparatory clinical skills course. This training needs to create the expectation that sexual attractions will arise in therapy and to create an atmosphere of trust in which students feel as free as possible to disclose these feelings and experiences in their supervision. If students are not presented with normalizing information, they are likely to continue to regard sexual feelings as proof of a troubled therapy relationship. Hamilton and Spruill conclude: "Feelings of sexual attraction must be openly discussed as a normal reaction to the type of closeness that characterizes psychotherapy, and appropriate therapeutic boundaries must be clearly explained and strictly enforced" (p. 325).

We think training programs have a responsibility to help students identify and openly discuss their concerns pertaining to sexual dilemmas in counseling practice. Prevention of sexual misconduct is a better path than remediation. Ignoring this subject in training sends a message to students that the subject should not be talked about, which will inhibit their willingness to seek consultation when they encounter sexual dilemmas in their practice.

Suggestions for Dealing With Sexual Attractions

Jackson and Nuttall (2001) provide the following recommendations regarding sexual attractions to minimize the likelihood of sexual transgressions by clinicians:

- Learn to recognize sexual attractions and how to deal with these feelings constructively and therapeutically.

- Seek professional support during times of personal loss or crisis.
- Make it a practice to examine and monitor feelings and behaviors toward clients.
- Know the difference between sexual attraction to clients and acting out.
- Learn about the possible adverse consequences for clients and therapists who engage in sexual activity.
- Establish and maintain clear boundaries with clients by dealing with a client's sexual advances firmly and consistently.
- Terminate the therapeutic relationship when sexual feelings obscure objectivity.

Put Yourself in This Situation. Imagine that you are sexually attracted to one of your clients. You are aware that your client has feelings toward you and might be willing to become involved with you. You often have difficulty paying attention during sessions because of your attraction. Which of the following options most closely aligns with what you would do?

- I can ignore my feelings for the client and my client's feelings toward me and focus on other aspects of the relationship.
- I will tell my client of my feelings of attraction, discontinue the professional relationship, and then begin a personal relationship.
- I will openly express my feelings toward my client by saying: "I'm glad you find me an attractive person, and I'm attracted to you as well. But this relationship is not about our attraction for each other, and I'm sure that's not why you came here."
- If there was no change in the intensity of my feelings toward my client, I would arrange for a referral to another therapist.
- I would consult with a colleague or seek professional supervision.

Can you think of another direction in which you might proceed? Why would you choose this direction?

✓ **The Case of Adriana.** Adriana's husband, a police officer, was killed in the line of duty, leaving her with three school-age boys. She seeks professional help from Clint, the school social worker, and explores her grief and other issues pertaining to one son who is acting out at school. She seems to rely on the social worker as her partner in supporting her son. After 2 years the son is ready to move on to high school. She confesses to Clint that she is finding it increasingly difficult to think of not seeing him anymore. She has grown to love him. She finds herself constantly thinking about him, and she wonders if they could continue to see each other socially, maybe even romantically.

At first Clint is taken aback. But he also realizes that throughout the relationship he has come to admire and respect Adriana, and he discloses his fondness for her. He explains to her that because of their professional relationship he is bound by ethical guidelines not to become involved with parents socially or romantically. He proposes to her that they not see each other for a year. If their feelings persist, he will then consider initiating a personal relationship. Adriana expresses her disappointment at the year's delay but agrees to the stipulation.

- What are your thoughts about Clint's way of handling the situation?
- If Clint was attracted to Adriana but had withheld this information for therapeutic reasons, how would you react?
- If Clint has no feelings of attraction or desire to continue any sort of relationship but said what he did to avoid a difficult ending, would his actions be ethical?
- If you were in a similar situation and did not want to pursue the relationship, how might you deal with your client's disclosure?

Sexual Relationships in Therapy: Ethical and Legal Issues

The issue of erotic contact in therapy is not simply a matter of whether or not to have sexual intercourse with a client. Even if you decide intellectually that you would not engage is such intimacies, it is important to realize that the relationship between therapist and client can involve varying degrees of sexuality. Therapists may have sexual fantasies, they may behave seductively with their clients, they may influence clients to focus on sexual feelings toward them, or they may engage in physical contact that is primarily intended to satisfy their sexual desires. Sexual overtones can distort the therapeutic relationship and become the real focus of the sessions. It is crucial that practitioners learn to differentiate between having sexual feelings and acting on them. We need to be aware of the effects of our sex-related socialization patterns and how they may influence possible countertransference reactions.

During the past decade a number of studies have documented the harm that sexual relationships with clients can cause. As you will see in Chapter 9, there has also been considerable writing on the damage done to students and supervisees when educators and supervisors enter into sexual relationships with them. Later in this section we discuss these negative effects on clients that typically occur when the client-therapist relationship becomes sexualized.

Ethical Standards on Sexual Contact With Clients

Sexual relationships between therapists and clients continue to receive considerable attention in the professional literature. Sexual relationships with clients are clearly unethical, and all of the major professional ethics codes have specific prohibitions against them (see the ethics codes box titled Sexual Contact and the Therapeutic Relationship). Additionally, most states have declared such relationships to be a violation of the law. If therapists have had a prior sexual relationship with a person, many of the ethics codes also specify that they should not accept this person as a client. It is clear from the statements of the major mental health organizations that these principles go beyond merely condemning sexual relationships with clients. The existing codes are explicit with respect to sexual harassment and sexual relationships with clients, students, and supervisees. However, they do not, and maybe they cannot, define some of the more subtle ways that sexuality may be a part of professional relationships.

Ethics Codes

Sexual Contact and the Therapeutic Relationship

- "Sexual intimacy with clients is prohibited" (AAMFT, 2001, 1.4.).
- "Sexual activity with a current or former patient is unethical" (American Psychiatric Association, 2001, 2.1.).
- "Sexual or romantic counselor–client interactions or relationships with current clients, their romantic partners, or their family members are prohibited" (ACA, 2005, A.5.a.).
- "The social worker shall not have a sexual relationship with a client" (CASW, 1994, 4.3.).
- "Psychologists do not engage in sexual intimacies with current clients/patients" (APA, 2002, 10.05.).
- "Psychologists do not engage in sexual intimacies with individuals they know to be close relatives, guardians, or significant others of current clients/patients. Psychologists do not terminate therapy to circumvent this standard" (APA, 2002, 10.06.).
- "Psychologists do not accept as therapy clients/patients persons with whom they have engaged in sexual intimacies" (APA, 2002, 10.07.).
- "Social workers should under no circumstances engage in sexual activities or sexual contact with current clients, whether such contact is consensual or forced" (NASW, 1999, 1.09.a.).
- "Social workers should not provide clinical services to individuals with whom they have had a prior sexual relationship. Providing clinical services to a former sexual partner has the potential to be harmful to the individual and is likely to make it difficult for the social worker and individual to maintain appropriate professional boundaries" (NASW, 1999, 1.09.d.).

Sexual misconduct is considered to be one of the more serious of all ethical violations for a therapist, and it is also one of the most common allegations in malpractice suits (see APA, 2003b). Therapist-client sexual contact is arguably the most disruptive and potentially damaging boundary violation (Smith & Fitzpatrick, 1995).

The Scope of the Problem

The report of the APA (2003b) Ethics Committee reveals that the major area of sexual dual relationship allegations continues to be male psychologists with adult female clients. Sexual misconduct played a role in 53% of the complaints opened by the APA in 2002, and all of these sexual dual relationships involved male psychologist–female client complaints. In a study that focused on psychologists who had sexual relationships with clients, supervisees, and students, Lamb, Catanzaro, and Moorman (2003) found that 3.5% reported at least one sexual boundary violation. Of the total sample in the study, 2% reported a sexual boundary violation with a client, 1% with a supervisee, and 3% with a student. The majority of these violations occurred after the professional relationship had ended (50% after therapy, 100% after supervision, and 54% after teaching). Of the sample, 84% were older male psychologists who engaged in sexual relationships with female clients, supervisees, and students.

In her review of research on the sexually abusive therapist, Olarte (1997) likewise notes that a majority of sexual boundary violations (approximately 88%) occur between male therapists and female clients. According to Olarte, the typical composite of a therapist who becomes involved in sexual boundary violations is a middle-aged man who is experiencing personal distress, is isolated professionally, and overvalues his healing abilities. His methods are unorthodox, and he inappropriately discloses personal information that is irrelevant to therapy.

Many professional journals review disciplinary actions taken against therapists who violate ethical and legal standards, and most of these cases involve sexual misconduct. Brief summaries of a few of these cases provide a picture of how therapists can manipulate clients to meet their own sexual or emotional needs.

- A clinical social worker engaged in unprofessional conduct when he exchanged a romantic kiss with a client. The clinician used his relationship with another client to further his own personal, religious, political, or business interests. He engaged in a sexual relationship with a former client, less than 3 years after termination of the professional relationship (CAMFT, 2004b, p. 49).
- A licensed marriage and family therapist engaged in inappropriate sexually based discussions and sexual relationships with a client. The therapist discussed intimate aspects of his personal life with his client, engaged in multiple relationships with the client, watched a sexually explicit movie with her, and accepted a nude photograph of the client. He failed to schedule appointments with the client at appropriate times, scheduling them instead for the evening hours. He failed to refer her to another therapist (CAMFT, 2004c, p. 50).
- A licensed psychologist was charged with gross negligence in using vulgar language with clients and suggesting that they hug and/or kiss him on the cheek, even though doing so made his clients uncomfortable (California Department of Consumer Affairs, Board of Psychology, 1999, pp. 12–13).
- A licensed psychologist, who was a professor, was charged with gross negligence and unprofessional conduct in using his position as a professor to take advantage of a student that involved both giving the student a back massage and inappropriate sexually touching (California Department of Consumer Affairs, Board of Psychology, 1999, pp. 12–13).
- A licensed counselor treated a female client for about 10 years. The counselor asked his client how she felt about taking her clothes off during therapy sessions. She indicated that she would feel very embarrassed. About 3 months later, he urged her to remove her clothing, proposing to use "Reichian" therapy. The client removed her clothes, except her underwear, but told her counselor about her discomfort in doing this. He assured her that this technique would help her in dealing with her sexual problems. Later, she agreed to take off all her clothes and was nude during her sessions. This occurred between 6 and 12 times and constituted gross negligence on the counselor's part (CAMFT, 1996b, p. 25).
- A licensed counselor told a female client that she needed to have and to express her oedipal sexual feelings toward her father as a child in a safe place,

that he would be that safe place, that she should have sexual feelings for someone other than her father, and that she needed to be sexually attracted to him. During a session in the early phase of her therapy, the counselor instructed the client to sit on his lap and tell him what she wanted to do with him sexually. Later the counselor kissed the client on the mouth. Although she did not experience this kiss as sexual, she did not feel it was right. The therapist later tried to convince her that the kiss was on the cheek and not on the lips. She eventually terminated therapy because she felt that the situation surrounding the kiss operated against any therapeutic gain in continuing therapy with this counselor (CAMFT, 1996c, p. 34).

As serious as sexual misconduct is, it is a mistake to overemphasize this form of boundary violation. Sexual violations are currently given priority consideration, and rightly so, yet many other violations are just as egregious, including client abandonment, mismanaging suicidal clients, misuse of the power differential with the student in academic settings, and financial ruin resulting from a business relationship with a treating therapist (Orr, 1997).

The Case of Wayne. A recently divorced 29-year-old high school counselor, Wayne, is assigned the senior class. An attractive 17-year-old senior girl, Kelly, works in the counseling office as a student assistant. She eventually comes to see Wayne as a father figure and becomes infatuated with him. Later during her senior year of high school, Kelly and Wayne share their sexual attraction and fondness for each other. Wayne goes out of his way to get her accepted at the state university, where he has performed consulting activities. After Kelly graduates from the university they get married.

- What potential ethical and legal issues are involved in this case?
- Is the fact that Wayne used his influence to get Kelly accepted in a university itself an ethical concern?
- Assuming Kelly and Wayne wait until she is no longer a student at the high school, and assuming she has now turned 18, are any ethical or legal issues involved?
- If Wayne were to seek you out for consultation regarding this case, what input might you give him?

At-Risk Therapists

In the Lamb, Catanzaro, and Moorman (2003) study of professionals who engaged in sexual boundary violations, respondents cited concurrent dissatisfaction in their own lives as a risk factor leading to sexual misconduct. In their study on sexual boundary violations, Jackson and Nuttall (2001) note that it is critical for clinicians to become aware of their own history and the impact it may have on their relationships with clients. They contend that, although sexual exploitation of clients by therapists is the result of a complex set of factors, one of these factors is a childhood history of severe sexual abuse in the background of offending male therapists.

Jackson and Nuttall conclude that therapists can minimize their potential for sexual boundary violations through a process of self-examination and being willing to seek ongoing support. They urge high-risk clinicians to avoid the isolation of private practice, closely monitor their boundaries with clients, obtain ongoing professional supervision, and seek their own therapy to address any remaining abuse-related issues. In our opinion, these suggestions will only work with those therapists who recognize they have a problem and want to change.

Harmful Effects of Sexual Contact With Clients

Studies continue to demonstrate that clients who are the victims of sexual misconduct suffer dire consequences. Erotic contact is totally inappropriate and is an exploitation of the relationship by the therapist. Most practitioners view sexual contact with clients as being illegal, unprofessional, unethical, and clinically harmful.

Bouhoutsos and colleagues (1983) assert that when sexual intercourse begins, therapy as a helping process ends. When sex is involved in a therapeutic relationship, the therapist loses control of the course of therapy. Sexual contact is especially disruptive if it begins early in the relationship and if it is initiated by the therapist. Of the 559 clients in their study who became sexually involved with their therapists, 90% were adversely affected. This harm ranged from mistrust of opposite-gender relationships to hospitalization and, in some cases, suicide. Other effects of sexual intimacies on clients' emotional, social, and sexual adjustment included negative feelings about the experience, a negative impact on their personality, and a deterioration of their sexual relationship with their primary partner. Bouhoutsos and her colleagues conclude that the harmfulness of sexual contact in therapy validates the ethics codes barring such conduct and provides a rationale for enacting legislation prohibiting it.

Olarte (1997) identifies the harmful effects of sexual boundary violations: distrust of the opposite sex, distrust for therapists and the therapeutic process, guilt, depression, anger, feeling of rejection, suicidal ideation, and low self-esteem. It is generally agreed that sexual boundary violations remain harmful to clients no matter how much time elapses after termination of therapy.

Legal Sanctions Against Sexual Violators

Not only does sexualizing a therapy relationship result in harm to clients, but therapists who engage in sexual activity with clients (or former clients) risk negative consequences for themselves, both personally and professionally. Among these consequences are being the target of a lawsuit, being convicted of a felony, having their license revoked or suspended by the state, being expelled from professional organizations, losing their insurance coverage, and losing their jobs. Therapists may also be placed on probation, be required to undergo their own psychotherapy, be closely monitored if they are allowed to resume their practice, and be required to obtain supervised practice.

A number of states have enacted legal sanctions in cases of sexual misconduct in the therapeutic relationship, making it a criminal offense. These states include California, Colorado, Florida, Georgia, Idaho, Maine, Michigan, Minnesota, Missouri, New Hampshire, New Mexico, North Dakota, Rhode Island, Texas, Washington, and Wisconsin. Other jurisdictions are working toward passage of similar laws, and most will eventually pass some type of legislation to curb therapists' sexual misconduct (Reaves, 2003).

Professionals cannot argue that their clients seduced them. Even if clients behave in seductive ways, it is clearly the professional's responsibility to keep appropriate boundaries. Regardless of the client's pathology, the responsibility to hold to ethical standards in a therapy relationship rests solely with the therapist (Olarte, 1997).

Criminal liability is rarely associated with the practices of mental health professionals. However, some activities can result in arrest and incarceration, and the number of criminal prosecutions of mental health professionals is increasing. The two major causes of criminal liability are sex with clients (and former clients) and fraudulent billing practices (Reaves, 2003). In California, the law prohibiting sexual activity in therapy applies to two situations: (1) the therapist has sexual contact with a client during therapy, and (2) the therapist ends the professional relationship primarily to begin a sexual relationship with a client. Therapists who have sex with clients are subject to both a prison sentence and fines (California Department of Consumer Affairs, 2004). For a first offense with one victim, an offending therapist would probably be charged with a misdemeanor, with a penalty of a sentence up to one year in county jail and a fine up to $1,000. For second and following offenses, therapists may be charged with misdemeanors or felonies. For a felony charge, offenders face up to 3 years in prison, or up to $10,000 in fines, or both. In addition to criminal action, civil action can be taken against therapists who are guilty of sexual misconduct. Clients may file a civil lawsuit to seek money for damages or injuries suffered and for the cost of future therapy sessions (California Department of Consumer Affairs, 2004).

Assisting Victims in the Complaint Process

Each of the mental health professional associations has specific policies and procedures for reporting and processing ethical and professional misconduct. (Chapter 1 lists these organizations and provides contact information.) Mental health professionals have an obligation to help increase public awareness about the nature and extent of sexual misconduct and to educate the public about possible courses of action. The California Department of Consumer Affairs (2004) booklet, *Professional Therapy Never Includes Sex*, describes ethical, legal, and administrative options for individuals who have been victims of professional misconduct.

Although the number of complaints of sexual misconduct against therapists has increased, individuals are still reluctant to file complaints for disciplinary action against their therapists, educators, or supervisors. Many clients do not know that sexual contact between counselor and client is unethical and illegal. They are often unaware that they can file a complaint, and they frequently do not know the avenues available to them to address sexual misconduct. Each of the following options has both advantages and disadvantages, and it is ultimately up to the client to decide the best course of action.

Clients can file an ethical complaint with a professional association or with the therapist's licensing board. If a complaint is filed with a professional association and the allegation is proven, the association will likely recommend disciplinary action that may result in revoking the therapist's membership. When this action is taken, other members in the association will be informed of this member's unethical behavior. However, this action does not prevent the therapist from practicing.

Administrative action begins with the client filing a complaint with the therapist's licensing board, which has the power to discipline a therapist using the administrative law process. Depending on the violation, the board may revoke or suspend a license. When a license is revoked, the therapist cannot legally practice. In those cases where sexual misconduct is admitted or proven, most licensing boards will revoke a therapist's license.

Legal alternatives include civil suits or criminal actions. A malpractice suit on civil grounds seeks compensatory damages for the client for the cost of treatment and for the suffering involved. Criminal complaints are processed based on state and federal statutes.

Sexual Relationships With Former Clients

What are the ethics of having a sexual relationship once therapy has ended? What do the ethics codes have to say with respect to sexual relationships with former clients? Most professional organizations prohibit their members from engaging in sexual relationships with former clients because of the potential for harm. Some organizations specify a time period, and others do not. Most state that in the exceptional circumstance of sexual relationships with former clients—even after a 2- to 5-year interval—the burden of demonstrating that there has been no exploitation clearly rests with the therapist. (For guidelines for particular professional associations, refer to the ethics codes box titled Sexual Relationships With Former Clients.)

When considering initiating such a relationship, many factors must be evaluated. These include the amount of time that has passed since termination of therapy, the nature and duration of therapy, the circumstances surrounding termination of the professional-client relationship, the client's personal history, the client's competence and mental status, the foreseeable likelihood of harm to the client or others, and any statements or actions by the therapist suggesting a plan to initiate a sexual relationship with the client after termination.

With regard to timing issues, one question that is always unclear is when the professional relationship actually ended (Foster, 1996). Foster summarizes some points made by Gary Schoener, who raises some very useful questions to help practitioners evaluate posttermination relationships:

Ethics Codes

Sexual Relationships With Former Clients

Canadian Counselling Association (1999)

Counsellors avoid any type of sexual intimacies with clients and they do not counsel persons with whom they have had a sexual relationship. Counsellors do not engage in sexual intimacies with former clients within a minimum of three years after terminating the counselling relationship. This prohibition is not limited to the three year period but extends indefinitely if the client is clearly vulnerable, by reason of emotional or cognitive disorder, to exploitative influence by the counselor. Counsellors, in all such circumstances, clearly bear the burden to ensure that no such exploitative influence has occurred, and to seek consultative assistance. (B.12.)

American Psychological Association (2002)

(a) Psychologists do not engage in sexual intimacies with former clients/patients for at least two years after cessation or termination of therapy.

(b) Psychologists do not engage in sexual intimacies with former clients/patients even after a two-year interval except in the most unusual circumstances. Psychologists who engage in such activity after the two years following cessation or termination of therapy and of having no sexual contact with the former client/patient bear the burden of demonstrating that there has been no exploitation, in light of all relevant factors, including (1) the amount of time that has passed since therapy terminated; (2) the nature, duration, and intensity of the therapy; (3) the circumstances of termination; (4) the client's/patient's personal history; (5) the client's/patient's current mental status; (6) the likelihood of adverse impact on the client/patient; and (7) any statements or actions made by the therapist during the course of therapy suggesting or inviting the possibility of a posttermination sexual or romantic relationship with the client/patient. (10.08.)

American Counseling Association (2005)

Sexual or romantic counselor–client interactions or relationships with former clients, their romantic partners, or their family members are prohibited for a period of five years following the last professional contact. Counselors, before engaging in sexual or romantic interactions or relationships with clients, their romantic partners, or client family members after five years following the last professional contact, demonstrate forethought and document (in written form) whether the interactions or relationship can be viewed as exploitive in some way, and/or whether there is still potential to harm the former client; in cases of potential exploitation and/or harm, the counselor avoids entering such an interaction or relationship. (A.5.b.)

Commission on Rehabilitation Counselor Certification (2001)

Rehabilitation counselors will not engage in sexual intimacies with former clients within a minimum of 5 years after terminating the counseling relationship. Rehabilitation counselors who engage in such relationships after 5 years following termination will have the responsibility to examine and document thoroughly that such relations do not have an exploitative nature, based on factors such as duration of counseling, amount of time since counseling, termination circumstances, client's personal history and mental status, adverse impact on the client, and actions by the counselor suggesting a plan to initiate a sexual relationships after termination. Rehabilitation counselors will seek peer consultation prior to engaging in a sexual relationship with a former client. (A.5.b.)

National Association of Social Workers (1999)

Social workers should not engage in sexual activities or sexual contact with former clients because of the potential for harm to the client. If social workers engage in conduct contrary to this prohibition

continued on next page

or claim that an exception to this prohibition is warranted due to extraordinary circumstances, it is social workers—not their clients—who assume the full burden of demonstrating that the former client has not been exploited, coerced, or manipulated, intentionally or unintentionally. (1.09.c.)

American Association for Marriage and Family Therapy (2001)

Sexual intimacy with former clients is likely to be harmful and is therefore prohibited for two years following the termination of therapy or last professional contact. In an effort to avoid exploiting the trust and dependency of clients, marriage and family therapists should not engage in sexual intimacy with former clients after the two years following termination or last professional contact. Should therapists engage in sexual intimacy with former clients following two years after termination or last professional contact, the burden shifts to the therapist to demonstrate that there has been no exploitation or injury to the former client or to the client's immediate family. (1.5.)

- What was the length and level of therapeutic involvement?
- How much transference, dependency, or power inequity remains after termination?
- Was there any deception or coercion, intentional or unintentional, by the therapist indicating that sex is generally acceptable after termination of therapy?
- Was there an actual termination? Was the decision to terminate a mutual one? Did the therapist end the professional relationship to make it possible to enter into a romantic or sexual relationship with a client?
- Who initiated posttermination contact?
- What was the extent of the discussion of the pros and cons of engaging in a romantic or sexual relationship?
- What kind of consultation, if any, took place?

Some counselors maintain, "Once a client, always a client." Although a blanket prohibition on sexual intimacies, regardless of the time that has elapsed since termination, might clarify the issue, some would contend that this measure is too extreme. Others point out that there is a major difference between an intense, long-term therapy relationship and a less intimate, brief-term one. A blanket prohibition ignores these distinctions.

It is essential that the therapist be willing to seek consultation or personal therapy to explore his or her motivations and the possible ramifications of transforming a professional relationship into a personal one. Bennett and his colleagues (1990) offer several suggestions to those considering initiating a relationship with a former client:

- Be aware that developing a personal relationship with a former client is illegal in some jurisdictions and that therapists have been sued for malpractice for engaging in this practice.
- Reflect on the reasons for termination. If you, the client, or both of you experienced an attraction before ending therapy, was the professional relationship terminated for an appropriate reason or so that a sexual relationship could develop?

- Ask yourself about the potential benefits and risks of developing a personal relationship with a former client.
- Before initiating such a relationship, consider discussing the matter with a colleague. If you are unwilling, then you are a danger to yourself and your clients.

What is Your Position? At this point, reflect on your own stance on the controversial issue of forming sexual relationships once therapy has ended. Consider these questions in clarifying your position:

- Should counselors be free to formulate their own practices about developing sexual relationships with former clients? Give your reasons.
- Does the length and quality of the therapy relationship have a bearing on the ethics involved in such a personal relationship? Would you apply the same standard to a long-term client with an intense transference relationship and a brief therapy client who worked on personal growth issues for six weeks?
- Would you favor changing the ethics codes to include an absolute ban on posttermination sexual relationships regardless of the length of time elapsed? Why or why not?
- Are sexual relationships with former clients unethical regardless of the elapsed time or the type of therapy? Are there any exceptions that might justify developing an intimate relationship with a former client?
- What ethical guidelines would you suggest regarding intimate relationships with former clients?
- Although it might not be illegal in your state, what are the potential consequences of engaging in sex with former clients? Explain.
- React to the statement, "Once a client, always a client."

Commentary. We believe the statement "Once a client, always a client" is a dogmatic pronouncement that should be subject to discussion. An absolute ban on all sexual relationships with former clients implies that diagnosis and treatment are irrelevant. Is a client who is seen for two sessions to be considered on equal footing with a client who may have been in therapy for 5 years? Clearly there is concern when a therapist marries a former client and, indeed, doing so might be unwise. Yet making all actions that may be unwise into "clearly unethical actions" seems excessive.

A Special Case: Nonerotic Physical Contact With Clients

Although acting on sexual feelings and engaging in erotic contact with clients is unethical, nonerotic contact is often appropriate and can have significant therapeutic value. It is important to stress this point because some counselors perceive a taboo against touching clients. Therapists may hold back when they feel like touching their clients compassionately. They may feel that touching can be misinterpreted as sexual or exploitative; they may be afraid of their impulses or feelings toward clients; they may be afraid of intimacy; or they may believe that to express closeness physically is unprofessional. With the current attention being given to sexual harassment and lawsuits over sexual misconduct in professional relationships, some counselors are likely to decide that it is not worth the risk of touching clients at all, lest their intentions be misinterpreted. Although touching does not necessarily constitute a dual relationship, we include this discussion here because certain kinds of touching can lead to dual relationships. A therapist's touch can be a genuine expression of caring, or it can be done primarily to gratify the therapist's own needs.

There are two sides to the issue of touching. Some clinicians oppose any form of physical contact between counselors and clients on the grounds that it can promote dependency, can interfere with the transference relationship, can be misread by clients, and can become sexualized. On the other side, Rabinowitz (1991), in writing about a men's therapy group, cites research findings indicating that appropriate touching can foster self-exploration, increase verbal interaction, increase the client's perception of the expertness of the counselor, and produce more positive attitudes toward the counseling process.

Holub and Lee (1990) assert that the decision to touch or not to touch clients involves more than considering its effectiveness in helping clients or engaging them in therapy. They maintain that this decision should also include deliberating over the correctness, motivations, and interpretations of the touching. The power differential between therapist and client should be considered, and touching often elicits different feelings in men than it does in women. The practice of male therapists' touching only female clients might be interpreted as sexist or at least as poor judgment, and perhaps a sign of future boundary violations.

Rabinowitz (1991) states that it may be safer for a hug to occur in group therapy rather than in individual counseling because there are witnesses to the context of the touching, leaving less room for misinterpretation. However, counselors are still responsible for being sensitive to each member of the group and for avoiding meeting their own needs at the expense of the members. Rabinowitz adds: "Despite the cultural taboo for men to engage in physical touching, the act of embracing another man, in the context of the therapy group, does seem to encourage the expression of deeper feelings and lessen the isolation men often feel in our competitive society" (p. 576).

If touching is consistently and actively used in therapy, Bennett and his colleagues (1990) suggest that it is wise to explain this practice to clients and their families, if appropriate, before therapy begins. They recommend that practitioners consider how clients are likely to react to touching and that they ask themselves these questions:

- How well do I know the client?
- What makes me think that touch is indicated?
- Could the touch be misinterpreted by the client (or the client's family) as a sexual overture?
- Is touching appropriate in this circumstance?

In our view, it is critical to determine whose needs are being met when it comes to touching. If it comes from the therapist alone, and not from the context of the therapeutic relationship, it needs to be carefully examined. If touching occurs, it should be a spontaneous and honest expression of the therapist's feelings. It should not be done as a technique. It is unwise for therapists to touch clients if this behavior is not congruent with what they feel. A nongenuine touch will be detected by clients and could erode their trust in the relationship.

Counselors need to be sensitive to those circumstances when touching could be counterproductive. There are times when touching clients can distract them from what they are feeling, or when clients do not want to be touched. This is often the case with clients who come from a background of physical or sexual abuse. There are also times when a touch given at the right moment can convey far more empathy than words can. Therapists need to be aware of their own motives and to be honest with themselves about the meaning of physical contact. They also need to be sensitive to factors such as the client's readiness for physical closeness, the client's cultural understanding of touching, the client's reaction, the impact such contact is likely to have on the client, and the level of trust that they have built with the client.

Practitioners need to formulate clear guidelines and consider appropriate boundaries, but touch can be a therapeutic means to healing. It is sad that the legal climate discourages the appropriate use of this medium of reaching clients. Think about your position on the ethical implications of the practice of touching as part of the client-therapist relationship by answering these questions:

- What criteria could you use to determine whether touching your clients was therapeutic or countertherapeutic?
- Do you think some clients may never be open to touching in therapy?
- How could you honestly answer the question, "Are my own needs being met at the expense of my client's needs?" What might you do if you hugged a client whom you felt needed this kind of physical support and the client suggested that you were meeting your own needs?
- To what degree do you think your professional training has prepared you to determine when touching is appropriate and therapeutic?
- What factors should you consider in determining the appropriateness of touching clients? (Examples are age, gender, the type of client, the nature of the client's problem, and the setting in which the therapy occurs.)
- Imagine your first session with a same-gender client who is crying and in a state of crisis. Might you be inclined to touch this person? Would it make a difference if the client asked you to hold him or her? Would it make a difference if this client were of the opposite gender? of the same gender?
- If you are favorably inclined toward the practice of touching clients, are you likely to restrict this practice to opposite-gender clients? to same-gender clients? to clients of either gender to whom you are attracted? Explain.
- What would you do if your client wanted a hug, but you were resistant to doing it? How would you explain yourself to the client?

✓ **The Case of Ida.** Tu Chee is a warm and kindly counselor who routinely embraces his clients, both male and female. One of his clients, Ida, has had a hard life, has had no success in maintaining relationships with men, is now approaching her

40th birthday, and has come to him because she is afraid that she will be alone forever. She misreads his friendly manner of greeting and assumes that he is giving her a personal message. At the end of one session when he gives his usual embrace, she clings to him and does not let go right away. Looking at him, she says: "This is special, and I look forward to this time all week long. I so much need to be touched." He is surprised and embarrassed. He explains to her that she has misunderstood his gesture, that this is the way he is with all of his clients, and that he is truly sorry if he has misled her. She is crestfallen and abruptly leaves the office. She cancels her next appointment.

- What are your thoughts on this counselor's manner of touching his clients?
- If Tu Chee explained at the outset of therapy that his touching was part of his style, would that have been more acceptable?
- Was the manner in which he dealt with Ida's embrace ethically sound?
- Would you follow up with Ida about canceling her appointment?

Commentary. In our opinion, this case is a good example of a situation in which the counselor was more concerned with the bind he was in than the bind his client was in. The nature of a therapist's work is to take care of the client's difficulty first. How would you have responded?

Chapter Summary

This chapter has put ethical issues pertaining to multiple relationships into perspective. We have emphasized that dual and multiple relationships are neither inherently unethical nor always problematic. Such relationships are always unethical, however, when they result in exploitation or harm to clients. We have attempted to avoid being prescriptive and have summarized a range of recommendations offered by others to reduce the risk of boundary crossings and boundary violations—recommendations we expect will increase the chances of protecting both the client and the therapist.

Although ethics codes provide general guidance, you will need to weigh many specific variables in making decisions about what boundaries you need to establish in your professional relationships. The emphasis in this chapter has been on guidelines for making ethical decisions about nonsexual dual and multiple relationships. Nonsexual dual relationships are often complex and defy simplistic solutions. To promote the well-being of their clients, clinicians are challenged with balancing their own values and life experiences with ethics codes as they make choices regarding how to best help their clients (Moleski & Kiselica, 2005).

Sexual relationships with clients are obviously unethical and detrimental to clients' welfare. It is unwise, unprofessional, unethical, and in many states illegal to become sexually involved with clients. However, it is important that you not overlook some of the more subtle and perhaps insidious behaviors of the therapist that may in the long run cause serious damage to clients. This is not to say that as a counselor you are not also human or that you will never be attracted to certain clients. You are imposing an unnecessary burden on yourself if you believe that you should not have such feelings for clients or if you try to convince yourself that you should not have more feeling toward one client than toward another. What is important is how you decide to manage these feelings as they affect the therapeutic relationship. Referral to another therapist is not necessarily the best solution, unless it becomes clear that you can no longer be effective with a certain client. Instead, you may recognize a need for consultation or, at the very least, for an honest dialogue with your colleagues. If for some reason your feelings of attraction become known to the client, it is essential that the client be assured that they will not be acted upon. If this creates a problem for the client, a referral should be discussed.

Becoming a therapist does not make you perfect or superhuman. We want to stress the importance of reflecting on what you are doing and on whose needs are primary. A willingness to be honest in your self-examination is your greatest asset in becoming an ethical practitioner. As was mentioned earlier, it is always good to keep in mind whether you would act differently if your colleagues were observing you.

Suggested Activities

1. Investigate the ethical and legal aspects of dual relationships as they apply to the area of your special professional interests. Look for any trends, special problems, or alternatives. Once you have gathered some materials and ideas, present your findings in class.
2. Some say that dual relationships are inevitable, pervasive, and unavoidable and have the potential to be either beneficial or harmful. Form two teams and debate the core issues. Have one team focus on the potential benefits of dual relationships and argue that they cannot be dealt with by simple legislative or ethical mandates. Have the other team argue the case that dual relationships are unethical because they have the potential for bringing harm to clients and that there are other and better alternatives.
3. Write a brief journal article on your position on dual relationships in counseling. Take some small aspect of the problem, develop a definite position on the issue, and present your own views.
4. What are your views about forming social relationships with clients during the time they are in counseling with you? after they complete counseling?
5. What guidelines would you employ to determine whether nonerotic touching was therapeutic or countertherapeutic? Would the population you work with make a difference? Would the work setting make a difference? How comfortable are you in both receiving and giving touching? What are your ethical concerns about touching?
6. Take some time to review the ethics codes of the various professional associations as they apply to two areas: (a) dual relationships in general and (b) sexual intimacies with present or former clients. Have several students team up to analyze different ethics codes, make a brief presentation to the class, and then lead a discussion on the code's value.

7. Review the discussion on sexual relationships with former clients. Form two teams and debate the issue of whether sexual and romantic relationships with former clients should be allowed after some period of time has elapsed.

8. Form small groups to explore the core issues involved in some of the cases in this chapter. Role play the cases, and then discuss the implications. Acting out the part of the therapist and the client is bound to enliven the discussion and give you a different perspective on the case. Feel free to embellish on the details given in the cases.

9. Divide the class into a number of small groups, and develop your own case illustrating some ethical dilemma in the general area of dual relationships. Come up with a title for your case, creative names for the therapist and the client, and interesting points that will make the case a good discussion tool. Each group can act out its case in class and lead a general discussion.

Ethics in Action CD-ROM Exercises

10. Using segment 3 of the CD-ROM (boundary issues), bring your completed responses to the self-inventory to class for discussion.

11. In video role play #8, The Picnic, the client (Lucia) would like to meet with the counselor (John) at the park down the street for their counseling sessions so she can get to know him better and feel closer to him. She could bring a lunch for a picnic. John is concerned about creating an environment that would help Lucia the most, and she says, "That (meeting in the park) would really help me." Through role playing, demonstrate how you would establish and maintain boundaries with Lucia if she were your client.

12. In video role play #9, The Friendship, at the last therapy session the client (Charlae) says she would like to continue their relationship because they have so much in common and she has shared things with the counselor (Natalie) that she has not discussed with anyone else. Natalie informs Charlae that this puts her in a difficult situation and she feels awkward. Charlae says, "What if we just go jogging together a couple of mornings a week?" Assume your client would like to meet with you socially and this is the final therapy session. Via role playing, demonstrate how you would handle such a request from a former client who is interested in developing a social relationship with you.

13. In video role play #10, The Disclosure, the counselor (Conrad) shares with the client (Suzanne) that he has been thinking about her a lot and that he is attracted to her. Suzanne responds with, "You are kidding, right?" She says she came to him because she was having problems with men taking advantage of her and not respecting her. She has bared her soul to him, and now she feels devalued. Suzanne suggests possibly seeing another counselor, but Conrad thinks they can work it out. What are your thoughts about the way the counselor (Conrad) shared his feelings with the client? If you were sexually attracted to a client, what course of action would you follow? Role play the way you would deal with a client who disclosed to you that he or she found you "quite attractive." Assume that you also found this client "quite attractive."

14. In video role play #11, The Architect, the client (Janice) lost her job and can no longer pay for counseling sessions. She suggests providing architecture services for work on his house. The counselor (Jerry) suggests they discuss the pros and cons and that he wants to be sure that this is in her best interests. He mentions the code of ethics that discourages bartering. Jerry talks about issues of value and timeliness of services. Put yourself into this scene. Assume your client lost her job and could no longer pay for therapy. She suggests a bartering arrangement for some goods or services you value. Role play how you would deal with her. What issues would you want to explore with your client?

15. In video role play #12, Tickets for Therapy, the client (John) shows his appreciation for his counselor (Marianne) by giving her tickets to the theater. John says, "I got tickets for you so you can go and enjoy it and have a good time." Marianne talks about why she cannot accept the tickets, in spite of the fact that she is very appreciative of his gesture. Put yourself in the counselor's place. What issues would you explore with John? Might you accept the tickets, under any circumstances? Why or why not? Demonstrate, through role playing, what you would say to the client.

InfoTrac® College Edition Resources

For additional readings, explore InfoTrac College Edition, our online library. Key words are listed in a form that enables the search engine to locate a wider range of articles in the online university library. Key words should be entered exactly as shown, including asterisks, "Wl," "W2," "AND," and other search engine tools. Go to http://www.infotrac-college.com and select these key word searches:

dual relationship* couns*
dual relationship* psych????y
multiple relationships AND (psych????y OR psychotherapy OR couns*)
bartering AND (psych????y OR psychotherapy OR couns*)
gift W1 giving AND (psych????y OR psychotherapy OR couns*)
social W1 relationship* client*
social W1 relationship* therap*
sexual W1 attraction client*
sexual W1 relation* client*
physical W1 touching AND (psych????y OR psychotherapy OR couns*)
boundar* N2 crossing AND (psych????y OR psychotherapy OR couns*)
boundar* N2 violation AND (psych????y OR psychotherapy OR couns*)

Pre-Chapter Self-Inventory

Directions: For each statement, indicate the response that most closely identifies your beliefs and attitudes. Use the following code:

5 = I *strongly agree* with this statement.
4 = I *agree* with this statement.
3 = I am *undecided* about this statement.
2 = I *disagree* with this statement.
1 = I *strongly disagree* with this statement.

____ 1. Counselors are ethically bound to refer clients to other therapists when working with them is beyond their professional training.
____ 2. Ultimately, practitioners create their own ethical standards.
____ 3. Possession of a license or certificate from a state board of examiners shows that a person has therapeutic skills and is competent to practice psychotherapy.
____ 4. Professional licensing protects the public by setting minimum standards of preparation for those who are licensed.
____ 5. The present processes of licensing and certification encourage the self-serving interests of the groups in control instead of protecting the public from incompetent practice.
____ 6. Continuing education course work should be a requirement for renewal of a license to practice psychotherapy.

Professional Competence and Training

____7. It is unethical for counselors to practice without continuing their education.

____8. Institutions that train counselors should select trainees on the basis of both their academic record and the degree to which they possess the personal characteristics of effective therapists (as determined by current research findings).

____9. The arguments for licensing psychotherapists outweigh the arguments against licensing.

____10. Candidates applying for a training program have a right to know the criteria for selecting trainees.

____11. Once students are admitted to a graduate training program, that program should assess them at different times to determine their suitability for completing the degree.

____12. Trainees who display rigid and dogmatic views about human behavior, and who are not responsive to remediation, should be dismissed from a training program.

____13. It is unethical for a program to train practitioners in only one therapeutic orientation without providing an unbiased overview of other theoretical systems.

____14. The process of licensing tends to pit professional specializations against one another.

____15. I might not seek out workshops, seminars, courses, and other postgraduate learning activities if continuing education were not required to maintain my license to practice.

Introduction

In this chapter we focus on the ethical and legal aspects of professional competence and the education and training available for mental health professionals. We discuss issues related to professional licensing and certification as well as approaches to continuing education.

Ability is not an easy matter to assess. Competence is a process rather than something that is achieved once and for all. To maintain their competence in a meaningful way, practitioners need to be interested in keeping up to date in their field and enhancing their skills. Continuing education is particularly important in emerging areas of practice.

Practitioners can develop competence both as a generalist and as a specialist. A generalist is a practitioner who is able to work with a broad range of problems and client populations. A specialist is a worker who has developed competence in a particular area of practice such as drug and alcohol counseling, eating disorders, or career development.

The education and training of mental health professionals is given special attention because of the unique ethical issues involved. Indeed, ethical issues must be considered from the very beginning, starting with admission and screening procedures for graduate programs. One key issue is the role of training programs in safeguarding the public when it becomes clear that a trainee has problems that are likely to interfere with professional functioning.

Therapist Competence: Ethical and Legal Aspects

In this section we examine **therapist competence,** or the skills and training required to effectively treat clients in a specific area of practice. We discuss what it is, how we can assess it, and what some of its ethical and legal dimensions are. We explore these questions: What ethical standards exist that offer guidance in determining competence? What ethical issues are involved in training therapists? To what degree is professional licensing an accurate and valid measure of competence? What are the ethical responsibilities of mental health professionals to continue to upgrade their knowledge and skills?

Competence is both an ethical and a legal concept. From an ethical perspective, competence is required of practitioners if they are to avoid doing harm to their clients. Even though mental health professionals may not intend harm to clients, lack of competence is often a major contributing factor in harm done to clients. From a legal standpoint, incompetent practitioners are vulnerable to malpractice suits and can be held legally responsible in a court of law (Corey & Herlihy, 2006c).

Perspectives on Competence

We begin this discussion of competence with an overview of specific guidelines from various professional associations. They are summarized in the ethics codes box titled Professional Competence. These guidelines leave several questions unanswered. What are the boundaries of one's competence, and how do professionals know when they have exceeded them? How can practitioners determine whether they should accept a client when their experience and training might be questionable? What should be the minimal degree required for entry level professional counseling? To be competent to practice with a variety of client populations, does a counselor have to be both a generalist and a specialist?

These questions become more complex when we consider the criteria used in evaluating competence. In our opinion, assessing competence is an extremely difficult task. What are the criteria for the assessment? How do you measure the competence and objectivity of the assessors? Many people who complete a doctoral program lack the skills or knowledge needed to carry out certain therapeutic tasks. Obviously, a degree or a license alone does not guarantee competence for any and all psychological services.

When is a therapist ready to practice independently? Is the number of supervised hours a sufficient criterion to evaluate a practitioner's readiness to practice independently? The results of one study indicate that psychology training directors are divided in their opinions of when trainees are competent to practice independently and what constitutes minimal competence (Rodelfa, Ko, & Petersen, 2004).

As a beginning counselor, if you were to refer all the clients with whom you encounter difficulties, you would probably have few clients. You must assess how far you can safely go with clients and recognize when to refer clients to other specialists or when to seek consultations with other professionals. You are not alone when you have doubts about your general level of competence. In fact, it is not at all unusual for even highly experienced therapists to wonder seriously at times whether they have the personal and professional abilities needed to work with some of their clients. It is more troubling to think of therapists who rarely question their competence. Thus, difficulty working with some clients does not by itself imply incompetence, nor does lack of difficulty imply competence.

One way to develop or upgrade your skills is to work with colleagues or professionals who have more experience. You can also learn new skills by going to conferences and conventions, by taking additional courses in areas you do not know well and in theories that you are not necessarily drawn to, and by participating in workshops that combine didactic work with supervised practice. The feedback you receive can give you an additional resource for evaluating your readiness to undertake certain therapeutic tasks. In addition to having a basic preparation as a generalist, you might also want to acquire advanced training in a specialty area, a topic we deal with later in this chapter.

Making Referrals

It is essential for professionals to know from the outset the boundaries of their own competence and to refer clients to other professionals when working with them is beyond their professional training or when personal factors would

Ethics Codes

Professional Competence

American Association for Marriage and Family Therapy (2001)

Marriage and family therapists do not diagnose, treat, or advise on problems outside the recognized boundaries of their competencies. (3.11.)

International Association of Marriage and Family Counselors (2002)

Members do not attempt to diagnose or treat problems beyond the scope of their abilities and training. While developing new skills in specialty areas, marriage and family counselors take steps to ensure the quality of their work through training, supervision, and peer review. (III.D.)

American Psychological Association (2002)

Psychologists provide services, teach, and conduct research with populations and in areas only within the boundaries of their competence, based on their education, training, supervised experience, consultation, study, or professional experience. (2.01.a.)

American Psychiatric Association (2001)

A psychiatrist who regularly practices outside his or her area of professional competence should be considered unethical. Determination of professional competence should be made by peer review boards or other appropriate bodies. (2.3.)

American School Counselor Association (2004)

The professional school counselor monitors personal well-being and effectiveness and does not participate in any activity that may lead to inadequate professional services or harm to a student. (E.1.b.)

Feminist Therapy Institute (2000)

A feminist therapist will contract to work with clients and issues within the realm of her competencies. If problems beyond her competencies surface, the feminist therapist utilizes consultation and available resources. She respects the integrity of the relationship by stating the limits of her training and providing the client with the possibilities of continuing with her or changing therapists. (IV.B.)

A feminist therapist recognizes her personal and professional needs and utilizes ongoing self-evaluation, peer support, consultation, supervision, continuing education, and/or personal therapy. She evaluates, maintains, and seeks to improve her competencies, as well as her emotional, physical, mental, and spiritual well-being. When the feminist therapist has experienced a similar stressful or damaging event as her client, she seeks consultation. (IV.C.)

National Association of Social Workers (1999)

Social workers should accept responsibility or employment only on the basis of existing competence or the intention to acquire the necessary competence. (4.01.a.)

Social workers should strive to become and remain proficient in professional practice and the performance of professional functions. Social workers should critically examine, and keep current with, emerging knowledge relevant to social work. Social workers should routinely review professional literature and participate in continuing education relevant to social work practice and social work ethics. (4.01.b.)

continued on next page

Canadian Association of Social Workers (1994)

A social worker shall have and maintain competence in the provision of a social work service to a client. (3.)

The social worker shall not undertake a social work service unless the social worker has the competence to provide the service or the social worker can reasonably acquire the necessary competence without undue delay, risk, or expense to the client. (3.1)

Canadian Counselling Association (1999)

Counsellors limit their counselling services and practices to those which are within their professional competence by virtue of their education and professional experience, and consistent with any requirements for provincial and national credentials. They refer to other professionals, when the counselling needs of clients exceed their level of competence. (A.3.)

American Counseling Association (2005)

Counselors practice only within the boundaries of their competence, based on their education, training, supervised experience, state and national professional credentials, and appropriate professional experience. Counselors gain knowledge, personal awareness, sensitivity, and skills pertinent to working with a diverse client population. (C.2.a.)

American Mental Health Counselors Association (2000)

The maintenance of high standards of professional competence is a responsibility shared by all mental health counselors in the best interests of the public and the profession. Mental health counselors recognize the boundaries of their particular competencies and the limitations of their expertise. Mental health counselors only provide those services and use only those techniques for which they are qualified by education, techniques or experience. Mental health counselors maintain knowledge of relevant scientific and professional information related to the services they render, and they recognize the need for on-going education. (Principle 7.)

interfere with a productive working relationship. With rare exceptions, you should be able to determine whether you are competent to treat a given client by the end of the initial interview. Both you and your client need to know if therapy is limited to a specified number of sessions. The client should be made aware of this at the intake session.

Because the counseling process can be unpredictable at times, counselors will sometimes encounter situations in which the ethical path to follow is to refer a client due to a lack of competence in a particular area. For example, consider the case of Quan, whose presenting problem was anxiety pertaining to academic success in college. This was within the scope of her school counselor's training. However, later in the course of therapy Quan became very depressed and engaged in self-mutilation and other forms of self-destructive behavior. Quan's counselor recognized that these symptoms and behaviors reflected a problem area that was outside the scope of his expertise. Ethical practice required that he make a referral to another professional who was competent to treat Quan's problems. Of course, before taking this action he would seek consultation and perhaps obtain supervision from an expert. He could not continue to counsel Quan if the source of her symptoms was beyond his training to assess or if her behavior posed a threat to her life.

Possessing the expertise to effectively work with a client's problem is one benchmark, but other circumstances might also make you wonder if a referral is in order. You and a client may decide that because of value conflicts or for some other reason your relationship is not productive. The client may want to continue working with another person rather than discontinue counseling. For these and other reasons, you will need to develop a framework for evaluating when to refer a client, and you will need to learn how to make this referral in such a manner that your client will be open to accepting your suggestion rather than being harmed by it. We hope you would not see referring a client with whom you have difficulty as a cure-all. Clients can be negatively affected when you refer them too quickly. If you make frequent referrals, then you may need to examine your perception of your level of competence. In this case, you may need to refer yourself for further help. Consider a referral as a final intervention after you have exhausted other interventions including consulting. Most codes of ethics have a guideline pertaining to conditions for making a referral, for example:

> Social workers should refer clients to other professionals when other professionals' specialized knowledge or expertise is needed to serve clients fully or when social workers believe they are not being effective or making reasonable progress with clients and additional service is required. (NASW, 1999, 2.06.a.)

✓ **The Case of Helen.** To make the art of referral more concrete, consider the following exchange between a client and her counselor. Helen is 45 years old and has seen a counselor at a community mental health center for six sessions. She suffers from periods of depression and frequently talks about how hard it is to wake up to a new day. In other respects it is very difficult for Helen to express what she feels. Most of the time she sits silently during the session. The counselor decides that Helen's problems warrant long-term therapy that he doesn't feel competent to provide. In addition, the center has a policy of referring clients who need long-term treatment to therapists in private practice. The counselor therefore approaches Helen with the suggestion of a referral:

Counselor: Helen, during your intake session I let you know that we are generally expected to limit the number of our sessions to six visits. Since today is our sixth session, I'd like to discuss the matter of referring you to another therapist.

Helen: Well, you said the agency generally limits the number of visits to six, but what about exceptions? I mean, after all, I feel as if I've just started with you, and I really don't want to begin all over again with someone I don't know or trust.

Counselor: I can understand that, but you may not have to begin all over again. I could meet with the therapist you'd be continuing with to talk about what we've done these past weeks.

Helen: I still don't like the idea at all. I don't know whether I'll see another person if you won't continue with me. Why can't I stay with you?

Counselor: I think you need more intensive therapy than I'm trained to offer you, and, as I've explained, I'm expected to do only short-term counseling.

Helen: Intensive therapy! Do you think that my problems are that serious?

Counselor: It's not just a question of you having serious problems. I am concerned about your prolonged depressions, and we've talked about my concerns over your suicidal fantasies. I'd just feel much better if you were to see someone who is trained to work with depression.

Helen: I think you've worked with me just fine. If you won't let me come back, then I'll just forget counseling.

This exchange reflects a common problem.

- What do you think of the way Helen's counselor approached her? Would you have done anything differently?
- Is it possible that the counselor was not clear enough regarding the limitation of six visits?
- Would you have waited until the sixth session to remind her of termination?
- If you were Helen's counselor, would you agree to continue seeing her if she refused to be referred to someone else? Why or why not?

Ethical Issues in Training Therapists

Training is a basic component of practitioner competence. Our discussion of the central ethical and professional issues in training is organized around questions pertaining to selection of trainees, content of training programs, and best approaches to training.

Selection of Trainees

A core ethical and professional issue involves formulating policies and procedures for selecting appropriate candidates for a training program. Here are some issues to consider:

- What criteria should be used for admission to training programs?
- Should the selection of trainees be based solely on traditional academic standards, or should it take into account factors such as personal characteristics, character, and psychological fitness?
- To what degree is a candidate for training open to learning and to considering new perspectives?
- Does the candidate have problems that are likely to interfere with training and with the practice of psychotherapy?
- What are some ways to increase applications to programs by diverse groups of candidates?
- How open are training programs to diversity? How open are they to including people who will challenge them as trainers?
- How thorough should an orientation to a program be? What should it include?

- How does a program determine the psychological fitness of a candidate?
- When the selection committee has determined that the applicant is not suitable due to serious psychological impairment, how willing is the administration to support the committee's decision?
- If there is a lack of administrative support, when is it the responsibility of the relevant professional organization to intervene?

Training programs have an ethical responsibility to establish clear selection criteria, and candidates have a right to know the nature of these criteria when they apply. Although grade-point averages, scores on the Graduate Record Examination (GRE), and letters of recommendation are often considered in the selection process, relying on these measures alone does not provide a comprehensive picture of a candidate. In her study of program directors' perceptions of admission screening measures and indicators of student success, Leverett-Main (2004) found that program directors rated standard screening measures such as GRE scores and letters of recommendation as ineffective. The personal interview was identified as the most effective screening measure currently used. Practicum and internship performances were considered to be the most effective measures of graduate student success.

Factors such as personality characteristics, character, and psychological fitness are important variables that need to be considered in selecting applicants. On this matter, Johnson and Campbell (2002) write: "There is currently no consistent approach to screening for character and fitness during graduate school admission; similarly, there is no consistent approach to effectively addressing problems with character and fitness once they are revealed" (p. 50). In a later study, Johnson and Campbell (2004) point to the problem of predicting who will become effective practitioners. They state that "currently, no research in psychology demonstrates the efficacy of a screening approach to character and fitness" (p. 406). This being said, Johnson and Campbell still maintain that being competent requires both moral character and personal psychological fitness. Although character and fitness alone are not enough to ensure competence, Johnson and Campbell point out that their absence greatly increases the risk of both impairment and incompetence. They argue that a lack of psychological fitness threatens to undermine a practitioner's ability to reliably and effectively serve clients.

In addition to the factors just discussed, we think it is important to meet with applicants in some kind of personal or group interview process. We have participated in group screening interviews with candidates applying for a counseling program and found that the group format has some advantages over individual interviews. One of these advantages is being able to observe applicants interacting with others in the group and see how they present their ideas on a range of specific topics. Although some faculty will protest the time it takes to conduct individual and group interviews as part of the admissions process, it is considerably less time and effort than is expended in dealing with even one problematic student who is admitted and who later faces dismissal from a program for some nonacademic reason.

Many programs ask candidates to write a detailed essay that includes their reasons for wanting to be in the program, their professional goals, an assessment of their personal assets and liabilities, and life experiences that might be useful in their work as counselors. A number of programs have both faculty members and graduate students on the reviewing committee. If many sources are considered and if more than one person makes the decision about whom to select for training, there is less likelihood that people will be screened out on the basis of the personal bias of one individual. Leverett-Main (2004) concluded the following in her study of screening procedures:

> The creation of a structured interview format for counselor education screening committees, including defined questions and rating scales that are consistently administered to all applicants, may improve the screening process and assist screening committees to select graduate students who will succeed both in the classroom and as future counselors. (p. 218)

As part of the screening process, ethical practice implies that candidates are given information about what will be expected of them if they enroll in the program. Just as potential therapy clients have a right to informed consent, students applying for a program have a right to know the material they will be expected to learn and the manner in which education and training will take place. The language in the informed consent document must be unambiguous, and the criteria for successful completion of the program needs to be easily understood by all concerned. The Canadian Counselling Association (1999) calls for those in charge of training programs to take responsibility for orientation to all core aspects of the program, "including a clear policy with respect to all supervised practice components, both those simulated and real" (F.c.). With this kind of orientation to a program, students are better equipped to decide whether they want to be a part of it.

Screening can be viewed as a two-way process. As faculty screen candidates and make decisions on whom to admit, candidates may also be screening the program to decide if this is right for them.

✓ **The Case of Leo.** Julius is on a review committee in a graduate counseling program. Leo has taken several introductory courses in the program, and he has just completed an ethics course with Julius. It is clear to this professor that Leo has a rigid approach to human problems, particularly in areas such as interracial marriage, same-gender relationships, and abortion. Over the course of the semester, Leo appeared to be either unwilling or unable to modify his thinking. When challenged by other students in the class about his views, Leo argued that certain behaviors were simply "wrong" and that it was the task of the counselor to help the client see this. In meeting with the committee charged with determining whether candidates should be advanced in the program, Julius expresses his strong concern about retaining Leo in the program. His colleagues share this concern, and Leo is denied advancement.

- What concerns, if any, do you have about the manner in which this case was handled? Were any of Leo's rights violated?

- Was it made clear to Leo that when he expressed his ideas in his classes they could be held against him? If not, is there an ethical issue in that situation?
- Did the committee decide too early in the program that Leo would not change his ideas and attitudes in the course of his education?
- Were any other avenues open in dealing with Leo short of disqualifying him from the program?
- If Leo's values reflected his minority cultural background, would that make a difference? Would the committee be culturally insensitive for rejecting him from the program?
- What if Leo said that when he eventually obtained his license he intended to work exclusively with people from his cultural and religious background? Should he be denied the opportunity to pursue a degree in counseling if his career goal is to work with a specific population that shares his views and values?
- Using the criteria seemingly espoused by this selection committee, would a minister from a conservative background who was attempting to get a master's degree in counseling be rejected?
- If you were on the committee, how would you handle candidates who seemed to exhibit racism, homophobia, and rigid thinking?

Content of a Program

What is the content of a training program, and how is it decided? Is the curriculum determined by the preferences of the faculty, or is it based on the needs of future clients, or both? Some programs are structured around a specific theoretical orientation in two ways: first, by the school itself having a specific orientation, and second, by insisting that students subscribe to one theory at some point in their training. Other programs have a broader content base and are aimed at training generalists who will be able to step into future positions that present evolving challenges. Some think that all specialty training should be abolished. They are concerned about training practitioners in only one therapeutic orientation (without also providing unbiased introductions to other models). There is merit in an analytically trained therapist's learning about alternative approaches such as behavior therapy or a systemic model. By the same token, a behavior therapist and a systemic therapist need to be able to recognize the role of transference and countertransference in the therapeutic process. It is important that therapists know when a particular approach is contraindicated, especially if it is their own specialty. From an ethical perspective, counselor educators and trainers are expected to present varied theoretical positions. Training programs would do well to offer students a variety of therapeutic techniques and strategies that can be applied to a wide range of problems with a diverse clientele.

We recommend that students be exposed to the major contemporary counseling theories and that they be taught to formulate a rationale for the therapeutic techniques they employ. It is a good idea to teach students the strengths and limitations of these contemporary counseling theories. Some writers point out the limitations of basing training mainly on these standard counseling models and call for training in alternative theoretical positions that apply to diverse client populations (Sue et al., 1996). For an overview of the contemporary counseling theories see Corey, 2005b; Corsini and Wedding, 2005; Ivey et al., 2002; Seligman, 2001; and Sharf, 2004.

In deciding what to teach, certain questions are worth considering:

- Is the curriculum inclusive of many cultures, or is it culturally biased?
- Is there a universal definition of mental health, or is mental health determined by cultural influences?
- Should therapy help clients adjust to their culture? Or might it encourage them to find ways of making the changes they want within their culture?
- Does the curriculum give central attention to the ethics of professional practice?
- Is it ethical to leave out training in ethics? Is it enough to hope that ethical issues will be addressed through the supervision process alone?
- What is the proper balance between academic course work and supervised clinical experience?
- What core knowledge should be taught in counselor education programs?
- What is the appropriate balance between basic preparation and advanced specialization?

In training programs for various mental health professions, general content areas are part of the core curriculum, which are generally outlined by CACREP (2001) standards. For example, in counseling programs the following areas are typically required for all students: professional orientation, human growth and development, social and cultural foundations, counseling theory and practice, group counseling, lifestyle and career development, appraisal of individuals, and research and evaluation.

It is our opinion that training programs need to be designed so that students can acquire a more thorough understanding of themselves as well as acquire theoretical knowledge. Ideally, students will be introduced to various content areas, will acquire a range of skills they can utilize in working with diverse clients, will learn how to apply theory to practice through supervised fieldwork experiences, and will learn a great deal about themselves personally. A good program does more than impart knowledge and skills essential to the helping process. In a supportive and challenging environment, the program encourages students to build on their life experiences and personal strengths and provides opportunities for expanding their awareness of self and others.

Ethics education deserves prominent attention in any program geared to educating and training mental health practitioners. Down's (2003) study suggests that counselor trainees receive inconsistent ethics education. Approximately 30% of the respondents in Down's study report having a separate ethics course. Most of the study's participants received their ethics education through supervision. In their survey investigating ethics education practices in CACREP-approved counselor education programs, Urofsky and Sowa (2004) found that ethics education is combined with legal issues in 39% of the programs; 31% of the programs have a stand alone ethics course; and 11% of the programs report that ethics is infused in various courses in the curriculum. Urofsky and Sowa state that "ethics education is a fairly well-established aspect of the general counselor education curriculum" (p. 44). It is interesting to note that 92% of the responding counselor educators believe that they are adequately prepared to teach an ethics course in the counseling program. Seventy-nine percent of the counselor educators either agree or strongly agree with the statement: "Students feel better able to conduct ethical clinical practice after completing a counseling ethics course" (p. 42).

Although ethics is supposedly incorporated in a number of required courses, seminars, supervision, and practicum and internship experiences, we believe the lack of systematic coverage of ethical issues will hinder students, both as trainees and later as professionals. The topics we address in this book deserve a separate course as well as infusion throughout all courses and supervised fieldwork experiences. Elsewhere we address the teaching of ethics courses in human services and counseling in detail (Corey, Corey, & Callanan, 2005).

How Can We Best Train?

Programs for educating and training counselors should be built on the foundation of the natural talents and abilities of the students. Ideally, as we have said, counselor educators and supervisors teach students the knowledge and skills they need to work effectively with diverse populations. In addition, students need a core set of attitudes and values that are congruent with carrying out their role as helping professionals. In his provocative article "Can Psychotherapists Transcend the Shackles of Their Training and Superstitions?" Lazarus (1990) contends that formal education and training in psychological diagnosis and treatment often undermine the natural talents and skills of trainees. Of course, Lazarus does not believe that training necessarily erodes natural talent, but he does warn that "one of the main shackles under which many therapists labor comes from the almost endless list of proscriptions that they are handed" (p. 353).

We think Lazarus (2001) makes an excellent point in calling for training programs "to avoid instilling a fear of lawsuits in students and terrorizing them about the dangers of running afoul of licensing agencies" (p. 16). Lazarus writes:

> Some therapists create such highly sanitized treatment environments that they lose sight of human and humane concerns. Instead of producing frightened conformists, our training programs should focus on turning out caring and enterprising helpers who have the confidence to think for themselves. (p. 16)

In our view, one of the best ways to teach students how to effectively relate to a wide range of clients, many of whom will differ from themselves, is for faculty to model healthy interpersonal behavior. It is imperative that counselor educators and supervisors display cohesive relationships among themselves and treat students in a respectful, collegial manner. This is not always the case, however. In some programs the faculty performs somewhat like a dysfunctional family with unaddressed interpersonal conflict, and even hostile behavior.

Students are sometimes drawn into these dynamics, being expected to take sides. In an effective program, differences are discussed openly, and there is an atmosphere of genuine respect and acceptance of diversity of perspectives. If a faculty practices the principles they teach, they are demonstrating powerful lessons about interpersonal relating that students can apply to their personal and professional lives.

- What would you do if you found yourself in a program characterized by dysfunctional behavior?
- How would you react to a student who said, "I don't care what they do; I just want to get my degree and get out of here"?
- If you were concerned about the ethics of this program as a student, what actions would be open to you besides quitting?

Effective programs combine academic and personal learning, weave together didactic and experiential approaches, and integrate study and practice. A program structured exclusively around teaching academics does not provide important feedback to students on how they function with clients. In experiential learning and in fieldwork, problem behaviors of trainees will eventually surface and can be ameliorated. Evaluation is an important component of this process, and we turn to this topic next.

Evaluating Knowledge, Skills, and Personal Functioning

Evaluation Criteria and Procedures

Every training institution has an ethical responsibility to screen candidates so the public will be protected from incompetent practitioners. Programs clearly have a dual responsibility: to honor their commitment to the students they admit and to protect future consumers who will be served by those who graduate. Just as the criteria for selecting applicants to a program should be clear, the criteria for successful completion and the nature of the evaluation process need to be spelled out as clearly and objectively as possible.

Students need to know that their knowledge and skills, clinical performance, and interpersonal behaviors will be evaluated at different times during the program. Informing students on these matters implies that academic programs have written policies that are available to students before they are admitted to a program. However, despite accreditation policies, 54% of the professional psychology programs do not have written guidelines for intervening with problematic students (Vacha-Haase et al., 2004).

Lamb, Cochran, and Jackson (1991) recommend that trainees be informed about evaluation criteria and procedures as part of the orientation to the program. It should be made known to students "When, how, by whom, and by what form" their evaluations will occur (p. 291). Lamb and colleagues also recommend that the evaluation criteria include the following broad aspects of professional functioning: (a) knowledge and application of professional standards;

(b) competency; and (c) personal functioning (such as self-awareness, use of supervision, and coping with stress).

We strongly support the standards for performance evaluation of the ACA, NASW, and APA (see the ethics codes box titled Evaluating Student Performance). In addition to evaluating candidates when they apply to a program, we favor periodic reviews to determine whether trainees should be retained. Regarding evaluations of students in a program, the CACREP standard (2001) states:

> The program faculty conduct a developmental, systematic assessment of each student's progress throughout the program, including consideration of the student's academic performance, professional development, and personal development.

Students need feedback on their progress so they can build on their strengths or remediate problem areas. Ideally, trainees will also engage in self-evaluation to determine whether they are "right" for the program and whether the program is suitable for them. The first goal of an evaluation of candidates is to assess progress and correct problems. If shortcomings are sensitively pointed out to trainees in a timely way, they can often correct them.

Assessing graduate students to determine whether they have the knowledge and skills required to function effectively as practitioners is essential. Forrest and colleagues (1999) identify these categories of professional competence that might be considered as part of the evaluation process: academic skills, assessment skills, clinical judgment, clinical skills, ethics, interpersonal skills, intrapersonal skills, response to supervision, and theoretical skills. One approach

Ethics Codes

Evaluating Student Performance

American Counseling Association (2005)

Counselors clearly state to students, prior to and throughout the training program, the levels of competency expected, appraisal methods, and timing of evaluations for both didactic and clinical competencies. Counselor educators provide students with ongoing performance appraisal and evaluation feedback throughout the training program. (F.9.a.)

National Association of Social Workers (1999)

Social workers who have the responsibility for evaluating the performance of others should fulfill such a responsibility in a fair and considerate manner and on the basis of clearly stated criteria. (3.03.)

American Psychological Association (2002)

In academic and supervisory relationships, psychologists establish a timely and specific process for providing feedback to students and supervisees. Information regarding the process is provided to the student at the beginning of supervision. (7.06.a.)

Psychologists evaluate students and supervisees on the basis of their actual performance on relevant and established program requirements. (7.06.b.)

to evaluating trainees' professional competence is to require an oral examination judged by experienced professionals in the community who have no other connection to the university. Many states require a similar oral examination to obtain a license as a mental health professional. This type of comprehensive exam would help protect clients by ensuring that beginning counselors are adequately trained and prepared to enter private or agency practice.

Responsibility of Professional Organizations

The standards for evaluating student performance provided by the various professional organizations are quite general and do not specify what constitutes "incompetent professional performance." It would be helpful if CACREP identified the specifics of what constitutes "satisfactory personal and professional development." We believe professional organizations have a key role to play in specifying minimum standards of competence by providing a clear definition of what it means for a candidate to be found unsuitable. This protects both future clients and students who may be facing dismissal from a program. Furthermore, it protects the counseling faculty and administration by having the backing of a professional organization. The absence of such specific guidelines from the professions puts the responsibility solely on faculty to develop these standards. Oftentimes training programs have little power or support when designing criteria and procedures for dismissing students who fail to meet minimal performance standards.

Ideally, we would like to see each professional organization develop specific guidelines pertaining to students' successful completion of a program: NASW for social worker students, AAMFT for students in marital and family therapy programs, APA for students in clinical and counseling psychology, and ACA for students in counselor education programs. Faculty in these respective professional training programs would then have the backing of their professional associations in determining their own specific set of evaluation procedures to be used in making decisions regarding retaining or dismissing students.

Evaluation of Interpersonal Behaviors, Personal Characteristics, and Psychological Fitness

It is essential to evaluate trainees' professional behavior, clinical performance, and psychological fitness to identify those interpersonal behaviors and personality characteristics that are likely to influence trainees' ability to effectively deliver mental health services. The CACREP standards (2001) specify psychological fitness as a key characteristic of a professional counselor:

> Fitness implies psychological health, including the following variables: self-awareness, self-acceptance, self-knowledge, self-confidence, courage, resilience, purpose in life, balance, moderation, and emotional stability.

Johnson and Campbell (2002) consider the issue of character and fitness criteria for professional psychologists, stating that psychology training programs devote only cursory attention to these facets. Johnson and Campbell (2004) define **character** as the honesty and integrity with which a person deals with others. Character includes virtues such as integrity (honesty and consistency in behavior), prudence (evidence of good judgment), and caring (respect and sensitivity to the welfare of others). **Psychological fitness** pertains to emotional stability and can be evidenced by the presence of personality adjustment, absence of psychological disorder, and appropriate use of substances.

Johnson and Campbell found that training directors are very concerned about both character and fitness. However, a major problem faced by training programs in evaluating the character and fitness of applicants and current students is the lack of consensus regarding the presence of character and fitness. As they point out, it is easier to identify the absence of character and fitness than it is to confirm their existence. They note that there is no existing research bearing on the practices that programs employ in evaluating character and fitness, either during the application process or during the training itself.

When it comes to the matter of evaluative processes to identify trainees with problems, the research literature remains minimal. There is a lack of clear, shared, and consistent language to represent the different types of problematic behaviors (Forrest et al., 1999). Addressing this matter, Vacha-Haase and colleagues (2004) contend: "Confusion regarding the definitions of *distressed, impaired,* or *problematic* student behaviors has been rampant. Not only have these terms been used interchangeably for the past several decades, but a review of the literature provides no singular definition" (p. 115). It is clear that the faculty of each training program needs to develop clear definitions and evaluation criteria in assessing the psychological fitness of trainees.

Oliver and colleagues (2004) contend that research aimed at developing and refining an empirically supported model for systematically evaluating impairment would be helpful. They suggest the term **professional impairment** as a useful concept that emphasizes the specific difficulties that may impede or interfere with carrying out professional responsibilities. Some of these difficulties might include deficient knowledge, limited clinical skills, inadequate technical skills, poor judgment, and disturbing interpersonal attributes.

Sometimes students have personal characteristics or problems that interfere with their ability to function effectively, yet when this is pointed out to them, they may deny the feedback they receive. A program has an ethical responsibility to take action rather than simply pass on a student with serious academic or personal problems. Elman and Forrest (2004) take the position that training programs need to establish written policies regarding the way that personal psychotherapy might be recommended and required with respect to the remediation of a student's problems. They further state:

> Training programs need to reduce their ambivalence about involvement in personal psychotherapy when it is used for remediation. The challenge is to provide developmentally appropriate educational experiences for trainees in a safe learning environment while protecting the public by graduating competent professionals. (p. 129)

The CACREP standards (2001) stress the importance of establishing an institutional due process policy that addresses actions to be taken when evaluations indicate that a student is not appropriate for the program. In such instances, faculty should assist in facilitating the student's transition out of the program and, if possible, into a more appropriate area of study (II. F.).

Gatekeeper Role of Faculty in Promoting Competence

A key role of clinical training faculty is to promote and facilitate competence and professional behavior of their students. A major problem faced by educators in these training programs is identifying, dealing with, and possibly dismissing students who are not making satisfactory progress toward professional competence (Oliver et al., 2004). The academic faculty in a professional program generally has a **gatekeeper's role,** protecting consumers by identifying and intervening with graduate students who exhibit problematic behaviors (Vacha-Haase et al., 2004). These authors state that until recently there has been very little examination of problematic student behavior or the evaluation and dismissal of students in professional programs. Given the increased awareness of possible damage caused by counselors who do not possess the personal qualities of effective counselors, it is reasonable to assume that faculty will have to serve as gatekeepers for the profession (Lumadue & Duffey, 1999).

Forrest and her colleagues (1999) summarize the ethical obligation of faculty members and clinical supervisors in overseeing trainees' work:

> Ethical standards mandate that educators and trainers: (a) attend to the possibility that their trainees' personal problems might lead to harm of others; (b) make sure that trainees are not harming clients or others under their care; (c) attend to the possibility that trainees may misuse their influence; (d) evaluate whether trainees are performing services responsibly, competently, and ethically; (e) articulate a clear set of professional standards; and (f) evaluate trainees based on these relevant and established requirements. (p. 636)

Bemak, Epp, and Keys (1999) address the harmful consequences and suggest a model for intervention and possible dismissal of impaired students in graduate training programs. In their review of the literature, Forrest and colleagues (1999) found these common categories for dismissal: poor academic performance, poor clinical performance, poor interpersonal skills, and unethical behavior. Psychological reasons for dismissal included factors such as emotional instability, personality disorder, psychopathology, and unprofessional demeanor.

It is not always possible to rely on screening procedures during the admission process to identify students who do not have the necessary personality characteristics to become competent clinicians (Kerl et al., 2002). It is essential to operationally define the personality characteristics that are likely to impede a student's ability to practice effectively. In fairness to students, counseling faculty need to develop objective evaluation procedures and processes to communicate to students both their strengths and areas needing improvement with respect to interpersonal behavior and clinical performance. If a student initiates a legal challenge regarding his or her professional performance, it is essential for faculty and program administrators to show documentation of the student's lack of competency (Kerl et al., 2002).

Gaubatz and Vera (2002) investigated whether formalized gatekeeping procedures and program-level training standards influence the rates at which deficient trainees are graduated from counseling programs. Their findings indicated that programs with formalized standards and procedures reduce the number of deficient students it graduates. Gaubatz and Vera conclude:

> Formalized gatekeeping procedures may be an essential component of ethically sound professional training. If we, as counselor educators, are committed to training qualified counselors, we should hold ourselves accountable for implementing measures that have been shown empirically to improve the quality of our graduates. Formalized gatekeeping procedures appear to do exactly that. (p. 304)

✓ **The Case of a Discouraged Professor.** Prudence was a student at a university with a 48-unit master's degree program in counseling. This core degree and a few additional classes qualified a graduate to apply for the licensed professional counselor examination once the required supervised internship hours were completed. Prudence was identified by the faculty as having a level of affect that could be termed a complete lack of empathy. In counseling dyads, group process experiences, and classroom exercises it became clear that Prudence was unable to make empathic connection. Academically, Prudence received good grades; she completed the reading, wrote satisfactory papers, and took examinations as well as most. It was in the behavioral dimension—such as reflective listening, being able to establish client rapport, and demonstrating empathic understanding—that her lack of skill was noted.

Prudence progressed through most of the graduate program and entered an intensive group process course, which was a requirement of the program. The professor in this didactic training environment noted Prudence's barriers to building effective counseling relationships and made two or three interventions. These interventions included direct discussion with Prudence as well as referral and recommendation for personal counseling. At the end of the semester, Prudence's behaviors and skills had not improved, and by some measures they had actually deteriorated. The grade for the group process class was the only grade Prudence needed to complete her degree program. After many hours of soul searching, the professor decided that this student should not be allowed to advance because her lack of empathic understanding and her typically bizarre responses in counseling dyads made her, as a potential counseling professional, a risk to others. He gave Prudence a failing grade, which meant that Prudence would not receive her degree without successfully repeating the group process class.

Prudence responded by suing both the professor and the university. An investigation was completed at the university by the academic senate. In addition to the professor and the student, several members of the faculty and many individuals from the group process class were called as witnesses. The senate overruled the professor's grade and awarded a master's degree in counseling to Prudence. Today she is a licensed professional counselor.

Discouraged by the lack of support from the university, the professor reduced his teaching to part time and retired at the first available opportunity. In reflecting on this case, what implications can you draw?

- If this student was able to pass all of her other courses, was it justified to block her from a master's degree based on her performance in this one group process course?
- What are your thoughts about the actions taken by the administration?
- Is it the responsibility of professional accrediting agencies to intervene in a situation such as this?
- Did other professors who had noticed Prudence's lack of empathy have an ethical responsibility to address this issue with her earlier in her graduate course work?

Dismissing Students for Nonacademic Reasons

From our perspective, faculty who are in the business of training counselors should be credited with the ability to have accurate perceptions and observations pertaining to personality characteristics that are counterproductive for becoming effective counselors. When a student has good grades but demonstrates dysfunctional interpersonal behavior, indicating serious unresolved conflicts, action needs to be taken. Dismissal from a program is a measure of last resort. We would hope this option would not be employed unless all other attempts at remediation had failed.

Legal Deterrents to Dismissing Students

Some of the barriers to taking the action of dismissing students from a program include difficulties in giving clear evidence to support the decision to dismiss a student; the lack of adequate procedures in place to support a dismissal decision; concern about the psychological distress for faculty and students; concern about the heightened resistance and defensiveness in the trainee; the potential for receiving criticism from other faculty or supervisors who were not involved in the trainee's remediation; and lack of administrative support (Forrest et al., 1999).

Perhaps the major deterrent to dismissing a student is the fear of legal reprisal by that student. Bernard and Goodyear (2004) have noted that faculty in training programs have traditionally been concerned about their legal standing if they decide to dismiss a student from a program on what they consider "nonacademic" reasons. After their review of the literature on evaluating the competence of trainees, Forrest and her colleagues (1999) came to the conclusion that "we are struggling to understand and implement our responsibilities as gatekeepers for professional quality control" (p. 679). At times, there is a reluctance on the part of counselor educators and administrators to pursue dismissal of students who have interpersonal or clinical skills deficits. This is especially true if the concerns are about personal characteristics or problematic behavior, even in cases where the faculty are in agreement regarding the lack of suitability of a given student. However, in cases of those students who are unable to adhere to professional standards or who lack clinical competence, it is critical that they not be allowed to complete a graduate program. If it can be demonstrated that a program failed to adequately train an individual, the university may be held responsible for the harm the graduate inflicts on clients (Custer, 1994; Kerl et al., 2002).

Custer (1994) describes a lawsuit involving a master's level counselor who graduated from Louisiana Tech's College of Education. A female therapy client filed suit against Louisiana Tech, claiming that the program allowed an incompetent practitioner to graduate from the program. The client claimed that her life had been destroyed by incompetent therapy. The claim was that the program itself was inadequate in that it simply did not adequately prepare her counselor. The counselor was named in the malpractice action along with her supervisor and the university. The initial lawsuit was settled in 1994 for $1.7 million. A case such as this makes it clear that specific competency standards for retaining and graduating counseling students are not only useful but necessary.

Court Cases on Dismissing Students From a Program

Mary Hermann summarized a court case pertaining to dismissing a student for nonacademic reasons (cited in Remley et al., 2002). In *Board of Curators of the University of Missouri v. Horowitz* (1978), the United States Supreme Court considered a case brought by a student who had been dismissed from medical school, in spite of the fact that she had excellent grades. The decision to dismiss the student was based on the faculty's determination that she was deficient in clinical performance and interpersonal relationship skills. Prior to the dismissal, on several occasions, the faculty expressed dissatisfaction with the student's clinical work and informed her that she faced dismissal if she did not exhibit clear improvement. The student continued to receive unsatisfactory evaluations on her clinical work. Prior to the student's dismissal from medical school, she was evaluated by seven independent physicians in the community, all of whom agreed with the medical school professors that her clinical skills were unsatisfactory.

After being dropped from the program, the student filed a lawsuit claiming that her dismissal from medical school violated her constitutional rights. In reviewing the case, the Supreme Court considered that the student had been informed of the faculty's dissatisfaction with her clinical performance, and the student knew that unless she made significant improvement in this area, she would be dismissed from the program. The Court held that the decision to dismiss the student from medical school was based on a careful and deliberate evaluation by the faculty, and thus the student's dismissal was not a violation of her constitutional rights.

The model described for medical students would be an excellent model for counselor education programs to adopt in dealing with a student identified as lacking the necessary qualifications to be an effective helper. Using this model, the problematic student would be evaluated both at the university and in the community, where a number of experienced practitioners would review the findings of the faculty and administration.

In *Shuffer v. Trustees of California State University and Colleges* (1977), a California court addressed a complaint similar to that of the medical student described previously. The student plaintiff was enrolled in a master's degree program in counseling. The faculty determined that Shuffer's work in a practicum was unsatisfactory, and she was required to take a second practicum. The court held that a faculty may require students to complete special requirements as long as the requirements are not arbitrary.

A case presented at an ACES conference by Remley and colleagues (2002) illustrates the difficulty of implementing procedures for dismissing students for nonacademic reasons. The university went to great lengths to identify the problem areas and to develop a remediation plan for the student. The faculty offered the student an opportunity to challenge the grade in one class. The decision was made not to advance the student candidacy. The letter was returned as undeliverable, and a lawsuit was filed against the faculty and the university. The lawsuit was dismissed with prejudice (cannot be refiled) based on an executed confidential settlement agreement.

Systematic Procedures in Evaluation Student Performance

Kerl and colleagues (2002) describe the importance of designing systematic procedures for training programs to evaluate students' professional performance. When dismissal from a program is based on interpersonal or clinical incompetence, Kerl and colleagues underscore the importance of sound systematic academic evaluation and adherence to procedural and substantive due process. These authors argue that in counselor education programs the evaluation of students' interpersonal and clinical skills is part of the overall assessment of their academic performance. They conclude that courts have consistently viewed personal characteristics or behaviors as basic to academic performance, which makes this an academic issue. Kerl and colleagues describe an evaluation instrument, Professional Counseling Performance Evaluation (PCPE), designed by the counseling faculty at Southwest Texas State University to provide feedback to students on their progress in meeting professional standards and to document deficiencies that are serious enough to result in dismissal from the program.

The PCPE is provided to all students as a part of admissions and discussed during program orientation. The PCPE is completed for each student in every experiential course. Students receive a copy of the evaluation and have an opportunity to discuss their ratings with the faculty member at the end of each course. Kerl and colleagues state that using the PCPE throughout the program has resulted in significantly fewer students finding out about their problematic behavior as they reach the end of their program and significantly fewer dismissals from the program.

Kerl and colleagues describe a legal challenge by a student who was dismissed from the counseling program at Southwest Texas State University. The student exhibited poor impulse and anger control, unethical behavior, and inadequate counseling skills. This student had received three completed PCPE's that identified significant reservations by faculty members regarding the student's professional performance competency. Suggestions for improvement were given to the student at the time each PCPE was shared and discussed with the student. The student failed to follow through with remediation plans and filed suit against the university and the counseling program. Kerl and colleagues describe the outcome of this case:

> The court ruled that the student was provided adequate due process, that the university had the obligation to uphold professional standards, that the university's policies and procedures were enunciated in the graduate catalog and other departmental documents, and that the faculty had followed these procedures. (pp. 330–331)

This court decision identified professional performance competence as an academic concern. The use of the PCPE (along with the clear standards, policies, and procedures developed by the faculty) played a key role in the court's judgment that ruled in favor of the university on all counts (Kerl et al., 2002).

Seattle University's Department of Counseling and School Psychology has developed what we consider to be an excellent form designed to assess students' personal and professional competencies at several junctures in their program. With the permission of the faculty and dean of this program, we are reproducing their assessment form, which is a good model for informing students about expectations of the program and for providing students with regular feedback on both their personal and professional development (see the box titled Personal and Professional Competencies).

Professional Licensing and Credentialing

Most states have established specific requirements of supervised practice beyond the receipt of a master's or doctoral degree for licensing and certification in areas such as clinical social work, clinical or counseling psychology, rehabilitation counseling, mental health counseling, and couples and family therapy. Most licenses are generic in nature, meaning the holder of the license is assumed to have minimal competence in the general practice of counseling or clinical work. In this section we focus on issues pertaining to competence both as a generalist and in an advanced specialization, including basic assumptions of the practice of licensing, arguments for and against licensing and certification for mental health professionals, and the debate over specialty certification.

Purposes of Legislative Regulation of Practice

Sweeney (1995) describes credentialing as an approach to identifying individuals by occupational group, involving at least three methods: registry, certification, and licensure. In its simplest form, **registry** is generally a voluntary listing

Personal and Professional Competencies

The counseling faculty, Department of Counseling and School Psychology, College of Education, Seattle University, believes that counseling students must be able to demonstrate basic counseling skills and be knowledgeable of a variety of counseling theories. Additionally, they must be able to integrate the learned skills with their own developed philosophical and theoretical constructs. The faculty knows the role of the school counselor, mental health counselor, and post-secondary counselor to be, and, therefore, expects students to meet 18 *Personal and Professional Competencies*. Each student is assessed at candidacy, prior to internship, and at the end of each quarter of the three-quarter internship. Students are aware of the *Personal and Professional Competencies* when they enter the program and know that they will be evaluated as to whether or not they meet these competencies. At the end of internship, the student must have met each competency.

Student ________________________________ Date______________

__School __Mental Health __Post-Secondary __Certification-only
__On-going/optional __Candidacy/required __Pre-Internship/required

MC = Meets competency **NM** = Does not meet competency **NO** = Not observed or documented
Shaded column = on-going or at candidacy; non-shaded = pre-internship

A. Counseling Skills and Abilities	MC		NM		NO	
1. The student counselor creates a safe clinical setting with appropriate boundaries regarding such issues as the professional relationship, meeting times and location.						
2. The student counselor listens to the client and conveys the primary elements of the client's story.						
3. The student counselor responds to client feelings, thoughts and behaviors in a therapeutic manner using appropriate counseling responses.						
4. The student counselor communicates empathy by expressing the perspective of the client, when appropriate.						
5. The student counselor stays in the here and now, when appropriate.						
6. The student counselor is intentional by responding with a clear understanding of the therapeutic purpose.						
B. Professional Responsibility	**MC**		**NM**		**NO**	
7. The student counselor follows professional codes of ethics, the Seattle University Student Honesty Code, civil laws; demonstrates analysis and resolution of ethical						

continued on next page

issues; and relates to peers, professors, and clients in a manner consistent with professional standards.						
8. The student counselor demonstrates sensitivity to real and ascribed differences of client and counselor roles and manages role differences therapeutically.						
9. The student counselor demonstrates the ability to match appropriate interventions to the presenting clinical profile in a theoretically consistent manner and provides only those services and applies only those techniques for which the student is qualified, or is in the process of being qualified, through education, training and experience.						
10. The student counselor has a commitment to social justice and demonstrates a respect for individual differences, including those related to age, gender, race, ethnicity, culture, national origin, religion, sexual orientation, disability, language, and socioeconomic status.						
11. The student counselor articulates an understanding of how and when a counselor may take a leadership role.						
12. The student counselor articulates how regional, national and international issues affect the role of the counselor.						
C. Personal Responsibility	**MC**		**NM**		**NO**	
13. The student counselor demonstrates an awareness of the student's own belief systems, values, needs and limitations and the effect of these on personal and professional behavior.						
14. The student counselor demonstrates the ability to receive, integrate and utilize feedback from peers, faculty, teaching assistants, and supervisors.						
15. The student counselor demonstrates appropriate behavior in and out of the classroom and is dependable regarding assignments, attendance, and deadlines.						
16. The student counselor takes responsibility for personal and professional behavior.						
17. The student has an accurate assessment of personal and professional competencies.						
18. The student exhibits appropriate levels of self-assurance and confidence.						

continued on next page

19. The student counselor expresses thoughts and feelings effectively both orally and in writing.						
20. The student counselor demonstrates the ability to manage the stresses of a demanding profession by developing effective coping skills, that include professional and personal support systems.						

Comments (refer to specific competency):

Orientation (*to be signed at the new student orientation*)
By signing below, the student is certifying that the student understands: 1) the personal and professional competencies listed above; 2) that the student is expected to meet these competencies; and 3) that the student *may* be evaluated at any time; and *will* be evaluated at candidacy and prior to internship using this document.

Student Date

Faculty Date

(copy to student file)

Candidacy (*to be signed at the meeting with the student advisor at candidacy*)
By signing below, the student is certifying that the student has met with the student's advisor and 1) has discussed the student's candidacy status; 2) understands competencies that have not been meet; 2) has a strategy for meeting unmet criteria; 3) and understands that unmet competencies are expected to be met before the student finished the program.

Student Date

Faculty Date

Disposition or recommendation:

Pre-Internship (*to be signed at a meeting with the student advisor at the discretion of the student or the advisor prior to internship*)
By signing below, the student is certifying that the student has met with the student's advisor and 1) has discussed the student's pre-internship status; 2) understands competencies that have not been meet; 2) has a strategy for meeting unmet criteria; 3) and understands that unmet competencies are expected to be met before the student finished the program.

Student Date

Faculty Date

Disposition or recommendations:

We thank the counseling faculty, Department of Counseling and School Psychology, College of Education, Seattle University, for granting us permission to reproduce the form they use in their program.

of individuals who use a title or provide a service. Registration represents the least degree of regulation of practice. Both certification and licensure involve increased measures designed to regulate professional practices.

Although licensing and certification differ in their purposes, they have some features in common. Both require applicants to meet specific requirements in terms of education and training and acceptance from practicing professionals. Both also generally rely on tests to determine which applicants have met the standards and deserve to be granted a credential.

Certification is a voluntary attempt by a group to promote a professional identity. Certification confirms that the practitioner has met a set of minimum standards established by the certification agency. Some types of certification are required for practicing in a certain setting. For example, in most states school counselors must obtain a certificate in order to practice. Although certification gives practitioners the right to use a specific title, it does not ensure quality practice, nor does it govern practice (Hosie, 1995).

Unlike certification, **licensure statutes** determine and govern professional practice. Licensure acts, sometimes called practice acts, specify what the holder of the license can do and what others cannot do (Remley, 1995). Licensure is generally viewed as the most desirable form of legislative regulation of professional practice because it tends to highlight the uniqueness of an occupation and restricts both the use of the title and the practice of an occupation (Sweeney, 1995).

Licensure and certification assure the public that practitioners have completed minimum educational programs, have had a certain number of hours of supervised training, and have gone through some type of evaluation and screening. Licenses and certifications do not, and probably cannot, ensure that practitioners will competently do what their credentials permit them to do. The main advantages of licensure and certification are the protection of the public from grossly unqualified and untrained practitioners and the formal representation to the public that practitioners are part of an established profession.

Most licenses and credentials are generic; that is, they usually do not specify the clients or problems practitioners are competent to work with, nor do they specify the techniques that they are competent to use. A licensed psychologist may possess the expertise needed to work with adults yet lack the training necessary to work with children. The same person may be qualified to do individual psychotherapy yet have neither the experience nor the skills required for family counseling or group therapy. Most licensing regulations do specify that licensees are to engage only in those therapeutic tasks for which they have adequate training, but it is up to the licensee to put this rule into practice. Such a broad definition of practice also applies to many other professions.

Arguments For and Against Professional Licensing and Credentialing

Four main arguments have been put forth in favor of legislation to regulate the delivery of mental health services. The first is that the public is protected by setting minimum standards of service and holding professionals accountable if they do not measure up. This argument contends that the consumer would be harmed by the absence of such standards because incompetent practitioners can cause long-term negative consequences. Second, the regulation of practitioners is designed to protect the public from its ignorance about mental health services. This argument rests on the assumption that the consumer who needs psychological services typically does not know how to choose an appropriate practitioner or how to judge the quality of services received. Most people do not know the basic differences between a licensed professional counselor, a licensed psychologist, a psychiatrist, a licensed clinical social worker, and a licensed marital and family therapist. Third, because insurance companies frequently reimburse clients for the services of licensed practitioners, licensing means that more people can afford mental health care. Fourth, there is the view that licensing allows the profession to define for itself what it will and will not do. In fact, licensure itself is perceived to enhance the profession and is a sign of maturity.

The arguments for licensure revolve around the contention that the consumer's welfare is better safeguarded with legal regulation than without it. Those who challenge this assumption often maintain that licensing is designed more as a self-serving measure that creates monopolistic helping professions than as a protection for the public from misrepresentation and incompetence (Davis, 1981). Others are skeptical when it comes to setting up criteria for regulating mental health practitioners. Carl Rogers (1980) maintained that as soon as criteria are set up for certification the profession inevitably becomes frozen in a past image. He noted that there are as many certified charlatans as there are uncertified competent practitioners. Another drawback to licensing, from his viewpoint, is that professionalism builds up a rigid bureaucracy. Merrill (2003) uses the term "licensure anachronisms" to identify these rigid rules and asserts that there is a need for a change in licensure practices. Each state regulates its own standards and practices regarding granting of licenses to psychologists. Interstate reciprocity that would allow a licensed psychologist to practice in a state other than the one that granted the license is rare. Licensing boards claim that their function is to protect the consumer, but Merrill contends that licensing bodies sometimes carry out self-serving and arbitrary actions rather than performing this function.

We have observed that the process of licensing often contributes to professional specializations' pitting themselves against one another. Instead of fostering a collaborative spirit between licensed clinical social workers and licensed marriage and family therapists or between licensed psychologists and licensed professional counselors, the licensing process of each group too often promotes working in the opposite direction. We wonder if the protection of consumers is the main motivation of some licensing boards or whether their motivation may be to limit the number of practitioners. Furthermore, the examinations used to determine competence may have questionable validity. Although we are not opposed to the concept of professional licensing, we do have serious concerns about the criteria and the processes that are often used to determine who is competent to practice and the manner in which candidates are assessed.

Specialties Within the Mental Health Professions

Some training programs offer specialty training and encourage students to enroll in a specific track at all levels of education, from associate of arts to doctoral programs. For example, students can be trained and certified as substance abuse counselors in associate of arts programs. At the master's level counseling program, students can specialize in a given area such as school counseling, rehabilitation counseling, or marriage and family counseling. Doctoral programs offer specializations in community and multicultural counseling, organizational development, and human development, to mention a few. At the doctoral level specializations also exist within each of the major mental health professions of social work, marriage and family therapy, clinical psychology, counseling psychology, and counselor education.

Should states adopt legislation to regulate the practice of counseling specializations? Some argue in favor of specialty licensing, and others argue against it. Although Remley (1995) sees a need to recognize counselors who possess specialized knowledge and training, he opposes state regulation of the practice of counseling specializations as being not in the best interests of either the public or the profession. Remley contends that only the general practice of counseling should be regulated by the state; specialty practice should be addressed through credentialing. Hosie (1995) challenges the assumption that specialties are necessary to provide competent practice to specific client types. He makes a case for basic preparation required to be a competent generalist rather than viewing advanced specialization as necessary for employment as a counselor and for competent practice with clients.

Professionals who argue for the need for specializations within the counseling field point to the current realities and complexities of counseling practice in diverse settings, with various client problems, and with a range of client populations. Practitioners who have expressed concern over certification of specialties are asking for a basis to bring unity to the counseling field. It is our hope that consumers are not forgotten in the heated debates surrounding certification and licensure issues and professional specialties. Also, we hope these issues will not separate professionals.

Continuing Education and Demonstration of Competence

Most professional organizations support efforts to make continuing education a mandatory condition of relicensing (see the ethics codes box titled Continuing Education Requirements). Professionals are encouraged to engage in ongoing education and training in their specializations. According to Nagy (2005), this means that professionals should stay on top of new developments in their area and keep their skills sharp.

Most mental health professionals are required to demonstrate, as a basis for relicensure or recertification, that they have completed a minimal number of continuing education activities. As a condition for relicensure as a social worker, psychologist, or a marriage and family therapist, most states now

Ethics Codes

Continuing Education Requirements

American Mental Health Counselors Association (2000)

Mental health counselors recognize the need for continued education and training in the area of cultural diversity and competency. Mental health counselors are open to new procedures and sensitive to the diversity of varying populations and changes in expectations and values over time. (7.c.)

American Counseling Association (2005)

Counselors recognize the need for continuing education to acquire and maintain a reasonable level of awareness of current scientific and professional information in their fields of activity. They take steps to maintain competence in the skills they use, are open to new procedures, and keep current with the diverse populations and specific populations with whom they work. (C.2.f.)

American Psychological Association (2002)

Psychologists planning to provide services, teach, or conduct research involving populations, areas, techniques, or technologies new to them undertake relevant education, training, supervised experience, consultation, or study. (2.01.c.)

National Association of Social Workers (1999)

Social work administrators and supervisors should take reasonable steps to provide or arrange for continuing education and staff development for all staff for whom they are responsible. Continuing education and staff development should address current knowledge and emerging developments related to social work practice and ethics. (3.08.)

American Association for Marriage and Family Therapy (2001)

Marriage and family therapists pursue knowledge of new developments and maintain competence in marriage and family therapy through education, training, or supervised experience. (3.1.)

American School Counselors Association (2004)

The professional school counselor strives through personal initiative to maintain professional competence including technological literacy and to keep abreast of professional information. Professional and personal growth are ongoing throughout the counselor's career. (E.1.c.)

American Psychiatric Association (2001)

Psychiatrists are responsible for their own continuing education and should be mindful of the fact that theirs must be a lifetime of learning. (5.1.)

require specific courses and a minimum number of hours of continuing education. For example, licensed psychologists and marriage and family therapists in California are required to complete a 6-hour course in ethics and the law as a part of the 36 hours of continuing education for every renewal period (which occurs every 2 years).

Individual practitioners have an ethical responsibility to seek out ways to keep current with new developments in their field, and administrators of mental health agencies also have responsibilities to provide continuing education activities for the staff. Some of these activities can take the form of in-service workshops and training at the agency site; other activities will require therapists to go outside the agency.

To assume that our skills never deteriorate or that we know everything we need to know upon graduation is naive. If we rarely or never seek continuing education, how do we justify this lack of initiative? Learning never ceases; new clients present new challenges. New areas of knowledge and practice demand ongoing education. Even recent graduates may have significant gaps in their education that will require them to take workshops or courses in the future. You may also need to seek supervision in working with various client populations or to acquire skills in certain therapeutic modalities. For example, your job may require you to conduct groups, yet your program may not have included even one group course in the curriculum. When continuing education is tailored to your personal and professional needs, it can keep you on the cutting edge of your profession.

Consider the following case of a therapist who believes that competence can be attained once and for all.

✓ **The Case of Conrad.** Dr. Conrad Hadenuf has been a licensed psychologist for 20 years and has always maintained a busy practice. He sees a wide variety of clients. As a condition of license renewal, he is required to attend a 15-hour retraining program on substance abuse. He is indignant. "I have a Ph.D., I have 3,000 hours of supervised experience, and I have years of experience with all sorts of problems," he says. "This is just a money-making gimmick for those who want to generate workshops!" Knowing that he has no choice if he wants to retain his license, Conrad grudgingly attends the workshop, sits in the back of the room, takes no notes, takes longer breaks than scheduled, and leaves as soon as the certificates of attendance are available.

- What are your reactions to Conrad's statements? Is his rationale for not wanting to participate in the workshops justified?
- Although Conrad might claim that he has no desire to deal with substance abuse, can he realistically say that he will never be confronted with clients with substance abuse problems?
- How do you view mandated continuing education as a condition for license renewal?
- Are practitioners being ethically responsible to their clients if they never actively participate in the required continuing education courses?

Clarifying your Stance. We hope you will think of ways to maintain and enhance your competence. Use the following questions to clarify your thinking on the issues we have raised. What is your own strategy for remaining professionally competent?

- What effects on individual practitioners do you think the trend toward increased accountability is likely to have? How might this trend affect you?
- Do you think it is ethical to continue practicing if you do not continue your education? Why or why not?

- What are some advantages and disadvantages to using continuing education programs solely as the basis for renewing a license? Is continuing education enough? Explain.
- What are your reactions to competence examinations (oral and written) for entry level applicants and as a basis for license renewal? What kinds of examinations might be useful?
- Should evidence of continuing education be required (or simply strongly recommended) as a basis for recertification or relicensure?
- If you support mandatory continuing education, who should determine the nature of this education? What standards could be used in making this determination?
- What kinds of continuing education would you want for yourself? Through what means do you think you can best acquire new skills and keep abreast of advances in your field?

Review, Consultation, and Supervision by Peers

Peer review is an organized system by which practitioners within a profession assess one another's services. Peer review provides some assurance to consumers that they will receive competent services. In addition to providing peer review, colleagues can challenge each other to adopt a fresh perspective on problems they encounter in their practice. Regarded as a means rather than an end in itself, peer review has as its ultimate goals not only to determine whether a practitioner's professional activity is adequate but also to ensure that future services will be acceptable. Peer review continues a tradition of self-regulation.

Borders (1991) described the value of structured peer groups that foster the development of skills, conceptual growth, participation, instructive feedback, and self-monitoring. Peer-supervision groups are useful for counselors at all levels of experience. For trainees, peer groups offer a supportive atmosphere and help them learn that they are not alone with their concerns. For counselors in practice, they provide an opportunity for continued professional growth.

Peer-consultation groups can also function as an informal and voluntary form of review in which individual cases and ethical and professional issues are examined (Lewis, Greenburg, & Hatch, 1988). These groups provide additional safeguards to consumers and a greater measure of accountability. Furthermore, being part of a peer-consultation group offers reassurance to practitioners who are concerned about malpractice litigation.

Consider your own stance as you answer these questions about peer review and peer consultation:

- Can you think of both advantages and disadvantages to basing license renewal strictly on peer-review procedures?
- Who determines the qualifications of the peer reviewer? What criteria should be used to determine the effectiveness of counseling practice?

- What are your thoughts about a peer-consultation group for yourself? If you would like to be involved in such a group, how might you take the initiative to form one?

Commentary. Before closing this discussion of competence, we want to mention the danger of rarely allowing yourself to experience any self-doubt and being convinced that you can handle any therapeutic situation. Sidney Jourard (1968) made a comment many years ago that still seems timely. Jourard warns about the delusion that one has nothing new to learn. He maintains that exciting workshops or contact with challenging colleagues can keep therapists growing. He urges professionals to find colleagues whom they can trust so that they can avoid becoming "smug, pompous, fatbottomed and convinced that they have the word. [Such colleagues can] prod one out of such smug pomposity, and invite one back to the task" (p. 69).

We support the view that supervision is a useful tool throughout one's career. Along with Jourard, we also see the development of competence as an ongoing process, not a goal that counselors ever finally attain. This process involves a willingness to continually question whether you are doing your work as well as you might and to search for ways of becoming a more effective person and therapist.

Chapter Summary

The welfare of clients is directly affected by ethical issues in the training of therapists and in the debate over whether professional licensure and credentialing are adequate measures of competence. Counselors must acquire new knowledge and skills throughout their professional career. This is particularly true for practitioners wishing to develop a specialty area dealing with certain client populations or problems.

A core ethical and professional issue in training involves the question of how to develop policies and procedures for selecting the candidates who are best suited for the various mental health professions. The challenge is to adopt criteria for choosing people who have the life experiences that will enable them to understand the diverse range of clients with whom they will work. The personal characteristics of trainees, such as attitudes, beliefs, character, and psychological fitness, are critical in deciding whom to admit to training programs.

Another important issue is the effectiveness of professional licensing and credentialing as a sign of an individual's competence. Although most practitioners will need to acquire competence as generalists, the counseling profession has been characterized by the emergence of specialty areas of practice. These areas of specialization need to be clarified without destroying the unity within the profession. The issues are complex, yet the goal is to focus licensure and certification more on protecting consumers than on protecting professional specializations. Increased collaboration among the various mental health professions can enhance this process.

Suggested Activities

1. Invite several practicing counselors to talk to your class about the ethical and legal issues they encounter in their work. You might have a panel of practitioners who work in several different settings and with different kinds of clients.

2. In small groups explore the topic of when and how you might make a referral. Role play a referral, with one student playing the client and another the counselor. After a few minutes the "client" and the other students can give the "counselor" feedback on how he or she handled the situation.

3. In small groups explore what you think the criteria should be for determining whether a therapist is competent. Make up a list of specific criteria, and share it with the rest of the class. Are you able as a class to come up with some common criteria for determining competence?

4. Several students can look up the requirements for licensure or certification of the major mental health specializations in your state. What are some of the common elements? Present your findings to the class.

5. Work out a proposal for a continuing education program as a small group activity. Develop a realistic model to ensure competency for professionals once they have been granted a license. What kind of design most appeals to you? a peer-review model? competency examinations? taking courses? other ideas?

6. Assume that you are applying for a job or writing a résumé to use in private practice. Write your own professional disclosure statement in a page or two. Bring your disclosure statements to class and have fellow students review what you have written. They can then interview you, and you can get some practice in talking with "prospective clients." This exercise can help you clarify your own position and give you valuable practice for job interviews.

7. As a class project several students can form a committee to investigate some of the major local and state laws that apply to the practice of psychotherapy. You might want to ask mental health professionals what major conflicts they have experienced between the law and their professional practice.

8. Form a panel to discuss procedures for selecting appropriate applicants for your training program. Your task as a group is to identify specific criteria for candidates. Consider these questions: In addition to grade-point averages, scores on the Graduate Record Examination, and letters of recommendation, what other procedures and criteria might you establish? Would you recommend individual interviews? interviews conducted in small groups? What life experiences would your group look for? What personal qualities are essential? What attitudes, values, and beliefs would be congruent with becoming a counseling professional? What personal characteristics, if any, would you use as a basis for rejecting an applicant? What process should the program use in making selections?

9. Assume that you are a graduate student who is part of the interviewing team for applicants for your training program. Identify six questions to pose to all applicants. What are you hoping to learn about the applicants from your questions?

10. Interview professors or practitioners in schools, agencies, or work settings that interest you. Ask them what they most remember about their training

programs. What features were most useful for them? What training do they wish they had had more of, and what would they like to have had less of? How adequately do they think their graduate program prepared them for the work they are now doing? What continuing education experiences do they most value?

11. Have several students role play a licensing board to interview candidates for a professional license. Make up a list of questions to pose to the examinees. Several students in the class can volunteer to sit for the interview. This role play can be repeated.

12. Consider the advantages of forming a peer-support group within one of your own classes. Several of you could make a commitment to meet to explore ways to get the most from your training and education. The group could also study together and exchange ideas for future opportunities.

Ethics in Action CD-ROM Exercises

13. Reflect on all of the role-playing situations enacted in the *Ethics in Action* CD-ROM. Putting yourself in the place of the counselor, can you think of any situations in which you would determine that a referral is in the best interests of your client? Consider situations such as sharp value differences between you and your client, a lack of multicultural competence in a particular case, a client to whom you were sexually attracted, or a client who cannot pay you because of losing employment. Select an area where you could envision yourself making a referral and role play this with another student as the client. Assume that your client does not want to accept the referral and insists on remaining with you.

InfoTrac® College Edition Resources

For additional readings, explore InfoTrac College Edition, our online library. Key words are listed in a form that enables the search engine to locate a wider range of articles in the online university library. Key words should be entered exactly as shown, including asterisks, "Wl," "W2," "AND," and other search engine tools. Go to http://www.infotrac-college.com and select these key word searches:

therap* N3 competence
training therap* AND (psych????y OR psychotherapy OR couns*) NOT medic*
continuing education for mental health workers
education psych*
training AND psychotherapy AND research
techniques in couns* NOT medic*
professional AND licensing AND (psych????y OR couns* OR mental W1 health) NOT medic*
credentialing mental health
psychological N3 fitness AND competence
professional W2 impairment
gatekeeper* N2 role* AND (psych????y OR psychotherapy OR couns*)

Chapter 9

Pre-Chapter Self-Inventory

Directions: For each statement, indicate the response that most closely identifies your beliefs and attitudes. Use the following code:

5 = I *strongly agree* with this statement.
4 = I *agree* with this statement.
3 = I am *undecided* about this statement.
2 = I *disagree* with this statement.
1 = I *strongly disagree* with this statement.

____ 1. To protect the client, the supervisor, and the supervisee, ethical guidelines are needed to govern the conduct of counselor supervisors.

____ 2. Supervisors should be held legally accountable for the actions of the trainees they supervise.

____ 3. Supervisors have the responsibility to monitor and assess a trainee's performance in a consistent and careful manner.

____ 4. Working under supervision is one of the most important components of my development as a competent practitioner.

____ 5. Supervisors must be sure that trainees fully inform clients about the limits of confidentiality.

____ 6. Supervision is best focused on my progress as a practitioner rather than on the client's problems.

____ 7. Ideally, supervisory sessions are not aimed at providing therapy for the trainee.

____ 8. It is clearly unethical for counselor educators to date their students or other students who are involved in the training program.

____ 9. It is acceptable for a supervisor or educator to date former students, once they have completed the program.

Issues in Supervision
Consultation

_____10. Supervisees and trainees have a right to know what is expected of them and how they will be evaluated. They also have a right to periodic feedback and evaluation from supervisors so that they have a basis for improving their clinical skills.

_____11. It is unethical for counseling supervisors to operate in multiple roles such as mentor, adviser, teacher, and evaluator.

_____12. Ethically, supervisors need to clarify their roles and to be aware of potential problems that can develop when boundaries become blurred.

_____13. It is unethical for supervisors or counselor educators to provide therapy to a current student or supervisee.

_____14. Personal information that trainees share in supervision should remain confidential and never be shared with other faculty members.

_____15. Supervisors have a role in advocating for their supervisees and clients in the educational and training settings within which they practice.

_____16. Before initiating a contract, consultants may ethically investigate the goals of the agency to determine whether they can support them.

_____17. When consultants become aware of value clashes that cannot be resolved, ethical practice dictates that they decline to negotiate a contract.

_____18. Consultants need to make an ethical determination that they are sufficiently trained to offer the services they contract to perform.

_____19. In consulting it is almost impossible to avoid dual relationships, because the work involves blending teaching skills and counseling skills as needed in the situation.

_____20. Ethical practice requires that consultants inform their consultees about the goals and process of consultation, the limits to confidentiality, the voluntary nature of consultation, the potential benefits, and any potential risks.

Introduction

Supervision is an integral part of training helping professionals and is one of the ways in which trainees can acquire the competence needed to fulfill their professional responsibilities. Supervision is perhaps the most important component in the development of a competent practitioner. It is within the context of supervision that trainees begin to develop a sense of their professional identity and to examine their own beliefs and attitudes regarding clients and therapy.

Supervision is a process that involves a supervisor overseeing the professional work of a trainee with four major goals: (1) to promote supervisee growth and development, (2) to protect the welfare of the client, (3) to monitor supervisee performance and to serve as a gatekeeper for the profession, and (4) to empower the supervisee to self-supervise and carry out these goals as an independent professional (Haynes, Corey, & Moulton, 2003).

As we mentioned in Chapter 8, professional competence is not attained once and for all. Being a competent professional demands not only continuing education but also a willingness to obtain periodic supervision when faced with ethical or clinical dilemmas. By consulting experts, practitioners show responsibility in obtaining the assistance necessary to provide the highest quality of care for clients. As practitioners, we can never know all that we might like to know, nor can we attain all the skills required to effectively intervene with all client populations or all types of problems. This is where the processes of supervision and consultation come into play.

Mental health professionals are often expected to function in the roles of both supervisor and consultant. To carry out these roles ethically and effectively requires proper training. The skills used in counseling are not necessarily the same as those needed to adequately supervise trainees or to advise other helping professionals, which implies a need for specific training in how to supervise. Supervision is a well-defined area that is rapidly becoming a specialized field in the helping professions with a developing body of research and an impressive list of publications, and ethical and professional standards are an integral part of the profession of supervision. This chapter explores dilemmas frequently encountered in the fields of supervision and consultation and provides some guidelines for ethical and legal practice in these areas.

Ethical Issues in Clinical Supervision

The relationship between the clinical supervisor and the trainee (or student) is of critical importance in the development of competent and responsible therapists. If we take into consideration the dependent position of the trainee and the similarities between the supervisory relationship and the therapeutic relationship, the need for guidelines describing the rights of trainees and the responsibilities of supervisors becomes obvious. Although specific guidelines for ethical behavior between a supervisor and trainee have not been delineated in the ethics codes of all professional associations, two organizations have produced guidelines specific to supervision issues. The Association for Counselor Education and Supervision has developed "Ethical Guidelines for Counseling Supervisors" (ACES, 1993, 1995), which address issues such as client welfare and rights, supervisory role, and program administration role. The National Association of Social Workers created "Guidelines for Clinical Social Work Supervision" (NASW, 1994b), which addresses the purpose and intent of supervision, qualifications of supervisors, conduct of supervision, legal issues, and ethical issues.

Some critical ethical issues in supervision include balancing the rights of the clients, the rights and responsibilities of supervisees, and the responsibilities of supervisors to both supervisees and their clients. Many of the ethical standards pertaining to the client-therapist relationship also apply to the supervisor-supervisee relationship. **Informed consent in supervision** is as essential as informed consent in counseling (which was discussed in Chapter 5). It is beneficial to discuss the rights of supervisees from the beginning of the supervisory relationship, in much the same way as the rights of clients are addressed early in the therapy process. If this is done, the supervisee is empowered to express expectations, make decisions, and become an active participant in the supervisory process. Giordano, Altekruse, and Kern (2000) have developed a comprehensive statement titled "Supervisee's Bill of Rights" (see box), which is designed to inform supervisees of their rights and responsibilities in the supervisory process.

The Supervisor's Roles and Responsibilities

Supervisors have a responsibility to provide training and supervised experiences that will enable supervisees to deliver ethical and effective services. Supervisors must be well trained, knowledgeable, and skilled in the practice of clinical supervision (Vasquez, 1992). If they do not have training in clinical supervision, it will be difficult for supervisors to ensure that those they supervise are functioning effectively and ethically.

Supervisors are ultimately responsible, *both ethically and legally,* for the actions of their trainees. Therefore, they are cautioned not to supervise more trainees than they can responsibly manage at one time. They must check on trainees' progress and be familiar with their caseloads. Just as practitioners keep case records on the progress of their clients, supervisors should maintain records pertaining to their work with trainees.

Clinical supervisors have a position of influence with their supervisees; they operate in multiple roles as teacher, mentor, consultant, counselor, sounding board, adviser, administrator, evaluator, recorder, and empowerer (Haynes et al., 2003). It is essential that supervisors monitor their own behavior so as not to misuse the inherent power in the supervisor-supervisee relationship. According to Sherry (1991), supervisors are ethically vulnerable for three main reasons: (1) the power differential between the participants, (2) the "therapy-like" quality of the supervisory relationship, and (3) the conflicting roles of the supervisor and supervisees. He points to the multiple roles supervisors are expected to play. Although the requirements of these roles overlap in some

Supervisee's Bill of Rights*

Nature of the Supervisory Relationship

The supervisory relationship is an experiential learning process that assists the supervisee in developing therapeutic and professional competence. A professional counselor supervisor who has received specific training in supervision facilitates professional growth of the supervisee through:

- monitoring client welfare
- encouraging compliance with legal, ethical, and professional standards
- teaching therapeutic skills
- providing regular feedback and evaluation
- providing professional experiences and opportunities

Expectations of Initial Supervisory Session

The supervisee has the right to be informed of the supervisor's expectations of the supervisory relationship. The supervisor shall clearly state expectations of the supervisory relationship that may include:

- supervisee identification of supervision goals for oneself
- supervisee preparedness for supervisory meetings
- supervisee determination of areas for professional growth and development
- supervisor's expectations regarding formal and informal evaluations
- supervisor's expectations of the supervisee's need to provide formal and informal self-evaluations
- supervisor's expectations regarding the structure and/or the nature of the supervisory sessions
- weekly review of case notes until supervisee demonstrates competency in case conceptualization

The supervisee shall provide input to the supervisor regarding the supervisee's expectations of the relationship.

Expectations of the Supervisory Relationship

1. A supervisor is a professional counselor with appropriate credentials. The supervisee can expect the supervisor to serve as a mentor and a positive role model who assists the supervisee in developing a professional identity.
2. The supervisee has the right to work with a supervisor who is culturally sensitive and is able to openly discuss the influence of race, ethnicity, gender, sexual orientation, religion, and class on the counseling and the supervision process. The supervisor is aware of personal cultural assumptions and constructs and is able to assist the supervisee in developing additional knowledge and skills in working with clients from diverse cultures.
3. Since a positive rapport between the supervisor and supervisee is critical for successful supervision to occur, the relationship is a priority for both the supervisor and supervisee. In the event that relationship concerns exist, the supervisor or supervisee will discuss concerns with one another and work towards resolving differences.
4. Therapeutic interventions initiated by the supervisor or solicited by the supervisee shall be implemented only in the service of helping the supervisee increase effectiveness with clients. A proper referral for counseling shall be made if appropriate.

continued on next page

5. The supervisor shall inform the supervisee of an alternative supervisor who will be available in case of crisis situations or known absences.

Ethics and Issues in the Supervisory Relationship

1. **Code of Ethics & Standards of Practice.** The supervisor will insure the supervisee understands the *American Counseling Association Code of Ethics* and legal responsibilities. The supervisor and supervisee will discuss sections applicable to the beginning counselor.
2. **Dual Relationships.** Since a power differential exists in the supervisory relationship, the supervisor shall not utilize this differential to their gain. Since dual relationships may affect the objectivity of the supervisor, the supervisee shall not be asked to engage in social interaction that would compromise the professional nature of the supervisory relationship.
3. **Due Process.** During the initial meeting, supervisors provide the supervisee information regarding expectations, goals and roles of the supervisory process. The supervisee has the right to regular verbal feedback and periodic formal written feedback signed by both individuals.
4. **Evaluation.** During the initial supervisory session, the supervisor provides the supervisee a copy of the evaluation instrument used to assess the counselor's progress.
5. **Informed Consent.** The supervisee informs the client she is in training, is being supervised, and receives written permission from the client to audio tape or video tape.
6. **Confidentiality.** The counseling relationship, assessments, records, and correspondences remain confidential. Failure to keep information confidential is a violation of the ethical code and the counselor is subject to a malpractice suit. The client must sign a written consent prior to counselor's consultation.
7. **Vicarious Liability.** The supervisor is ultimately liable for the welfare of the supervisee's clients. The supervisee is expected to discuss with the supervisor the counseling process and individual concerns of each client.
8. **Isolation.** The supervisor consults with peers regarding supervisory concerns and issues.
9. **Termination of Supervision.** The supervisor discusses termination of the supervisory relationship and helps the supervisee identify areas for continued growth and explore professional goals.

Expectations of the Supervisory Process

1. The supervisee shall be encouraged to determine a theoretical orientation that can be used for conceptualizing and guiding work with clients.
2. The supervisee has the right to work with a supervisor who is responsive to the supervisee's theoretical orientation, learning style, and developmental needs.
3. Since it is probable that the supervisor's theory of counseling will influence the supervision process, the supervisee needs to be informed of the supervisor's counseling theory and how the supervisor's theoretical orientation may influence the supervision process.

Expectations of Supervisory Sessions

1. The weekly supervisory session shall include a review of all cases, audio tapes, video tapes, and may include live supervision.
2. The supervisee is expected to meet with the supervisor face-to-face in a professional environment that insures confidentiality.

Expectations of the Evaluation Process

1. During the initial meeting, the supervisee shall be provided with a copy of the formal evaluation tool(s) that will be used by the supervisor.

continued on next page

2. The supervisee shall receive verbal feedback and/or informal evaluation during each supervisory session.
3. The supervisee shall receive written feedback or written evaluation on a regular basis during beginning phases of counselor development. Written feedback may be requested by the supervisee during intermediate and advanced phases of counselor development.
4. The supervisee should be recommended for remedial assistance in a timely manner if the supervisor becomes aware of personal or professional limitations that may impede future professional performance.
5. Beginning counselors receive written and verbal summative evaluation during the last supervisory meeting. Intermediate and advanced counselors may receive a recommendation for licensure and/or certification.

***Source:** Maria A. Giordano, Michael K. Altekruse, & Carolyn W. Kern, Supervisee's Bill of Rights (2000).

cases, they may also conflict. Supervisors are faced with the responsibility of protecting the welfare of the clients, the supervisees, the public, and the profession. Sherry maintains that the clients' welfare comes first, followed by that of the supervisees. Because supervision is like therapy in some ways, Sherry reminds us that there is a risk of harm to both the client and the supervisee from a supervisor's blurred objectivity, impaired judgment, or exploitation. Supervisors are responsible for ensuring compliance with relevant legal, ethical, and professional standards for clinical practice (ACES, 1993, 1995). The main purposes of ethical standards for clinical supervision are to provide behavioral guidelines to supervisors, to protect supervisees from undue harm or neglect, and to ensure quality client care (Bernard & Goodyear, 2004). Supervisors can demonstrate these ethical guidelines through the behavior they model in the supervisory relationship.

Supervisor Responsibilities to Supervisees and their Clients. Here are some responsibilities of supervisors to supervisees and some specific ways in which supervisors can promote counselor development:

- State the specific objectives of supervision.
- Formulate a sound supervisory contract that clarifies the expectations and parameters of the supervision agreement.
- Negotiate mutual decisions, rather than make unilateral decisions, about the needs of the trainee.
- Perform the role of teacher or consultant as appropriate.
- Clarify the supervisory role.
- Integrate knowledge of supervision with one's personal talents or areas of expertise.
- Meet with supervisees on a regular basis to give ongoing evaluation and feedback.
- Evaluate the supervisee's role and conceptual understanding of the therapeutic process.

- Promote the supervisee's ethical and legal knowledge and behavior.
- Interact with counselor trainees in a manner that facilitates their self-exploration, problem-solving ability, and confidence.
- Provide supervisees with guidance in the assessment and treatment of their clients.
- Recognize issues of cultural diversity, including ethnicity or race, gender, sexual orientation, age, disabilities, and religion, and integrate that recognition into their work with trainees.
- Assist supervisees in recognizing their personal limitations so as to protect the welfare of their clients.
- Be aware of the clients being treated by supervisees.
- Teach and model ethical and professional behavior.
- Be familiar with the techniques being employed by the trainees.
- Be sensitive to possible cues that might indicate a client is at risk.
- Maintain confidentiality of clients.
- Maintain the confidentiality of supervisees, and explain the parameters of confidentiality in the supervisory relationship.
- Maintain documentation of supervision.

Supervisors have an evaluative role, and at times faculty members need to be apprised of students' progress. However, personal information that supervisees share in supervision should generally remain confidential. At the very least, supervisees have a right to be informed about what will and will not be shared with others on the faculty. Because supervisors best teach by modeling, it is essential that they demonstrate ethical standards for practice. They need to put ethics in the foreground of their supervisory practices, which can best be done by treating supervisees in a respectful, professional, and ethical manner. One of the best ways for supervisors to model professional behavior for supervisees is to deal appropriately with confidentiality issues pertaining to supervisees. The primary responsibility of supervisors "is to model what they aspire to teach" (Bernard & Goodyear, 2004, p. 72).

Methods of Supervision. The standards of the APA (2002), NASW (1994b, 1999), ACA (2005), and ACES (1993, 1995) require that supervisors demonstrate a conceptual knowledge of supervisory methods and techniques and that they be skilled in using this knowledge to promote the development of trainees. It is essential that supervisors have a clearly developed model of supervision and the methods they employ. We believe that the most important element in the supervisory process is the kind of person the supervisor is. The methods and techniques supervisors use are more likely to be helpful if an effective and collaborative working relationship with supervisees has been established. In much the same way that effective therapists create a climate in which clients can explore their conflicts, supervisors need to establish a collaborative relationship that encourages trainees to reflect on what they are doing.

Supervision can be accomplished in a variety of ways. Here Feist (1999) describes some commonly used methods of supervision:

- *Self-report* is one of the most widely used supervisory methods, yet it may be the least useful. This procedure is limited by the supervisee's conceptual and observational ability.
- *Process notes* build on the self-report by adding a written record explaining the content of the session and the interactional processes.
- *Audiotapes* are a widely used procedure that yields direct and useful information about the supervisee.
- *Videotape* recording allows for an assessment of the subtleties of the interaction between the supervisee and the client.
- *Live supervision,* which is conducted by the supervisor during the supervisee's session with a client, provides the most accurate information about the therapy session.

Verbal exchange and direct observation are the most commonly used forms of supervision. In verbal exchange, the supervisor and supervisee discuss cases, ethical and legal issues, and personal development. Direct observation methods involve a supervisor actually observing a supervisee's practice. Direct observation, even though it demands time and effort, provides a more accurate reflection of the skills and abilities of the supervisee (Haynes et al., 2003).

Styles of Supervision. Supervisees at different stages in their professional development may require different styles of supervision. Overholser (1991) points out that an important element in the supervisory process is balancing a directive style and a permissive one. A supervisor's task is to strive for an optimal level of challenge and support. The hope is that the supervisor will promote autonomy without overwhelming the supervisee. Although supervisees may need more direction when they begin their training, it is a good idea to foster a reflective and questioning approach that leads to self-initiated discovery. Overholser applies the Socratic method to supervision, assuming that trainees achieve more insight when they discover a relationship on their own rather than having it explained to them. The Socratic supervisor functions more as a catalyst for exploration than as a lecturer and helps trainees realize that the answers lie within themselves.

When we supervise, we focus on the dynamics between ourselves and our trainees as well as the dynamics between supervisees and their clients. Here we see a parallel process operating between a counseling model and a supervisory model. Supervisees can learn ways to conceptualize what they are doing with their clients by reflecting on what they are learning about interpersonal dynamics in the supervisory relationship. Although the trainee's ability to assess and treat a client's problems is important, in supervision we are more concerned with the interpersonal aspects that are emerging. In our view, supervisors do well to look beyond the cases trainees bring to the supervisory sessions and focus on the interpersonal dimensions.

As supervisors we oversee the work of our supervisees and help them refine their own insights and clinical hunches. Rather than placing the emphasis on teaching supervisees by giving them information, we strive to help them identify their own intuitions and insights. Instead of using our words with supervisees' clients, we hope supervisees will find their own words and develop their voice. Our style of supervision is reflected by the questions we explore: What are you wanting to say to your clients? What direction do you think is most appropriate to take with your clients? What is going on with you as you listen to your clients? How are you reacting to your clients? How is your behavior affecting them? Which clients bring out your own resistances? How are your values manifested by the way you interact with your clients? How might our relationship, in these supervisory sessions, mirror your relationships with your clients? Are you feeling free enough to bring into these supervisory sessions any difficulties you are having with your clients?

Although we see supervision as a separate process from psychotherapy and do not attempt to make training sessions into therapy sessions, the supervisory process can be therapeutic and growth producing. One of the most important goals for clinical supervisors is to promote the supervisee's self-awareness and ability to recognize personal characteristics that could have a negative impact on the therapeutic relationship (Vasquez, 1992). We might add that this goal of promoting self-awareness and independence of supervisees may be inhibited by the emphasis on the supervisor's legal responsibilities and the threat of being involved in a malpractice suit. Because supervisors are responsible for whatever happens to the supervisees' clients, some supervisors may tend to be more directive and controlling. As a way to resolve this dilemma, supervisors might discuss this struggle with their supervisees and with colleagues. Being concerned about liability issues should not prevent supervisors from giving their best efforts to guiding their supervisees.

Ethical Practices of Clinical Supervisors

Ladany and colleagues (1999) reviewed the literature identifying key ethical guidelines for clinical supervision and conducted a study that examined ethical practices of supervisors. The results of the study indicate that 51% of the 151 supervisees sampled reported what they considered to be at least one ethical violation by their supervisors. The ethical guidelines most frequently violated involved adequate performance evaluation, confidentiality issues relevant to supervision, and ability to work with alternative perspectives. Let's examine some specific ethical guidelines included in the study along with the results.

- *Performance evaluation and monitoring supervisee activities.* It is expected that the supervisor will review actual counseling sessions via videotape or audiotapes and will read the supervisee's case notes; the supervisor should provide ongoing feedback to supervisees. In evaluating supervisors, this was the most frequent ethical violation reported by the supervisees. One third of the study participants perceived that their supervisors did not provide adequate evaluations of their counseling performances.
- *Confidentiality in supervision.* Supervisors are to appropriately handle confidentiality issues in the supervisory relationship. Eighteen percent of the supervisees reported that confidentiality issues were not handled appropriately by their supervisors.

- *Ability to work with alternative perspectives.* Eighteen percent of the supervisees reported that their supervisors were not receptive to theoretical approaches other than their own.
- *Session boundaries and respectful treatment.* Supervisors are to demonstrate respect for supervisees by establishing and maintaining appropriate boundaries. Of all of the participants, 13% reported that their supervisors did not ensure adequate session conditions or respect.
- *Orientation to professional roles.* It is expected that the role and responsibilities of the supervisor and supervisee will be clearly defined. Nine percent of respondents reported that their supervisors never explained the roles and responsibilities of the supervisee and the supervisor.
- *Expertise/competency issues.* The supervisor has the responsibility for making appropriate disclosures to the supervisee when the supervisor or supervisee does not possess the competence to deal with a particular case or situation. Nine percent of the supervisees viewed their supervisors as lacking competence regarding the clients the supervisees were treating.
- *Disclosure to clients.* It is the responsibility of supervisors to ensure adequate disclosure of the supervisee's training status to the supervisee's clients. Eight percent of the supervisees reported that their supervisors did not address the issue of how they were to disclose their student status to clients. In some instances, supervisees were instructed to refer to themselves as staff and not as students or trainees.
- *Modeling ethical behavior and responding to ethical concerns.* Eight percent of the supervisees reported that modeling and responding to ethical concerns were not provided by their supervisors.
- *Crisis coverage and intervention.* In the event of a crisis, the supervisor is to provide adequate communication with the supervisee and is to provide appropriate supervisory support and guidance. Although crisis intervention methods are taught in the classroom, it is in the context of supervision where the practical reality of crisis work is best learned. Seven percent of the supervisees contended that crisis procedures and policies were not explained to them by supervisors or by the agency where they were doing their fieldwork.
- *Multicultural sensitivity toward clients and supervisees.* It is the responsibility of supervisors to deal appropriately with racial, ethnic, cultural, sexual orientation, and gender issues concerning both clients and supervisees. Seven percent of the supervisees reported that their supervisors were multiculturally insensitive in reference to clients and also that they were multiculturally insensitive to them as supervisees.
- *Dual roles.* It is the responsibility of the supervisor to handle role-related conflicts in an appropriate and ethical manner. Supervisees may be affected by the multiple roles in which supervisors are engaged, and this blending of roles may influence the supervision process. In this study, 6% of the supervisees reported ethical violations pertaining to dual roles.
- *Termination and follow-up issues.* Supervisors have the responsibility of ensuring the continuity of a client's care and of preventing abandonment of a client. Five percent of supervisees believed their supervisors did not handle termination and follow-up issues appropriately.

- *Differentiating supervision from psychotherapy.* In the supervisory relationship, it is expected that a supervisee's personal issues will be dealt with appropriately and that referrals will be made to a therapist when a supervisee experiences a personal problem that interferes with providing adequate care to the client. According to the participants in this study, only 5% believed that their supervisor failed to adhere to this ethical guideline.
- *Sexual issues.* One percent of the supervisees reported that their supervisors were inappropriate regarding sexual or romantic issues in the supervisory relationship.

Ladany and his colleagues (1999) conclude that clinical supervisors may be in need of education and training regarding ethical guidelines in supervision. Their findings also indicate that supervisors' unethical behaviors often are not noticed or monitored by the agency that employs them.

Competence of Supervisors

Clinical supervisors are more vulnerable and at risk for ethical and legal liability than they were 20 years ago. Yet only recently has the standard for qualifying to be a clinical supervisor included formal course work and supervision of one's work with supervisees. Currently, most psychology and counselor education programs offer a course in supervision at the doctoral level, and some programs provide training for supervisors at the master's level (Polanski, 2000). However, many supervisors do not have formal training in supervision and may rely on their previous supervisory experience as trainees and their clinical knowledge to inform their practice as supervisors (Bernard & Goodyear, 2004; Getz, 1999). Supervisors who are unable to demonstrate that they have achieved competence in clinical supervision are at risk in the litigious environment of today's clinical practice (Miars, 2000).

From both an ethical and legal standpoint, it is essential that supervisors have the education and training to adequately carry out their roles. In their exploratory study of supervision training for professional counselors, McMahon and Simons (2004) found that supervision training significantly aided practicing professional counselors in acquiring confidence and increasing self-awareness, supervisory skills and techniques, and theoretical and conceptual knowledge of supervision. In short, this study showed that supervision training provided to practicing counselors can make a difference. Course work in theories of supervision, working with difficult supervisees, working with culturally diverse supervisees, and methods of supervision provide a good foundation. The counselor licensure laws in a number of states (Arkansas, Louisiana, Ohio, South Carolina, and Texas) now stipulate that licensed professional counselors who practice supervision are required to have relevant training experiences and course work in supervision. Licensed professional counselors in Ohio who are applying for status as counseling supervisors are required to have a minimum of 3 years of practice as a licensed counselor prior to their application (Polanski, 2000). In California the supervised hours of marriage and family therapy interns and psychology interns are not recognized unless the supervisor has been in practice for at least 2 years and has had at least one continuing education course of 6 hours in supervision every 2-year cycle. Social workers and psychologists in California are now required to complete formal course work in supervision to be qualified to function as clinical supervisors. In Florida, those who want to supervise are required to complete a 16-hour course on supervision if they have not had a graduate course in supervision.

For practitioners to qualify as supervisors in Oregon, a three-credit semester course or a 30-hour continuing education course is minimal, and supervision for supervisors is highly desirable (Miars, 2000). In addition to course work, counselors need to have training in supervision. Unfortunately, many do not have the academic training and background to deal with the challenges they will face as supervisors. It is essential that these supervisors acquire the specific knowledge and skills they lack through continuing education. Supervisors must stay current with the changes in policies and regulations pertaining to supervision because regulations change from time to time.

Polanski (2000) makes a case for teaching supervision at the master's level. Course work in supervision for counselors entering the field can teach them how to ask for what they need and influence their own supervision experiences. They are able to learn about the importance of mutuality in the supervision relationship. In short, students receiving this training become educated consumers of supervision, and they have a better understanding of the practice of supervision when they take such a role in the future.

Gizara and Forrest (2004) examined the process by which experienced supervisors identified and intervened with impaired trainees. Their study underscored the point that simply being a competent clinician does not make you a competent supervisor. The supervisory role requires many skills and values that are different from those of the therapeutic relationship. Many of the supervisors in this study stated that their training did not prepare them for the complex task of dealing with problematic trainees. Supervisors described a sense of discomfort with the responsibility involved in making decisions in cases of impaired supervisees. The study reveals a clear need for academic programs and agencies to formally address the evaluative nature of supervision. Gizara and Forrest recommend:

> (a) making supervision courses with supervision practice mandatory; (b) engaging students in prolonged examination of professional standards of practice; (c) developing students' abilities not only to recognize ethical responsibilities but also be able to tolerate the difficulty of these situations and knowing how to engage in an effective process of addressing those responsibilities; and (d) demonstrating for students and actively developing a professional norm of shared responsibility for confronting inadequate competence. (p. 138)

In addition to specialized training in methods of supervision, supervisors also need to have an in-depth knowledge of the specialty area in which they will provide supervision. Storm (1994) contends that this expertise is often lacking in those supervising trainees in marriage and family therapy. Storm concludes that the unique context of this specialty practice creates difficulties for untrained supervisors as they attempt to carry out their roles in an ethical and effective manner. It is unethical for supervisors to offer supervision in areas that are beyond the scope of their practice. On this matter, the NASW (1999) ethical guideline is clear:

> Social workers who provide supervision or consultation should have the necessary knowledge and skill to supervise or consult appropriately and should do so only within their areas of knowledge and competence. (3.01.a.)

When supervisees are working outside the area of competence of the supervisor, it is the responsibility of the supervisor to arrange for competent clinical supervision of the cases in question (Cobia & Boes, 2000).

Some of the personal attributes that have been consistently identified as helpful in supervisors include humor, empathy, respect, genuineness, personal warmth, supportive attitudes, ability to confront, immediacy, concern for supervisee growth and well-being, concern for clients' welfare, availability for self-reflection, flexibility and openness to new ideas and approaches to cases, courage, tolerance, and openness to various styles of learning. In short, good supervisors tend to be available, accessible, affable, and able. The general picture of the good supervisor reveals an individual who is a technically competent professional with good human relations skills and effective organizational-managerial skills (Haynes et al., 2003).

This discussion would not be complete without considering supervisor impairment or incompetence. At times, supervisors may be unable to effectively carry out their supervisory roles due to personal or external factors or because of physical and psychological depletion. Much as the case of impaired therapists discussed in Chapter 2, impaired supervisors may do harm to trainees.

Muratori (2001) considers impairment of a supervisor from a trainee's perspective and describes a continuum of ineffective supervisors from those who may be improved through guided supervision to those who are clearly impaired. Signs of supervisor impairment might include boundary violations, misuse of power, sexual contact with supervisees, substance abuse, extreme burnout, or diminished clinical judgment.

According to Muratori, it is critical to be aware of the reality that supervisors are in an evaluative position vis-à-vis their trainees, which limits trainees' options in deciding what to do in situations of incompetent supervision. Trainees need to consider the power differential inherent in the supervisory relationship, their level of development as counselor trainees, and the personalities of both the supervisor and the supervisee. Muratori asserts that trainees who have an impaired supervisor may have few desirable options. Even assertive supervisees must carefully weigh their options for action with an impaired supervisor because of the possible consequences that could be associated with the supervisor's misuse of power.

Have you considered what you might do if you had to deal with an impaired supervisor? Put yourself in Melinda's shoes as you reflect on the following case provided by Michelle Muratori.

The Case of Melinda. Melinda, a second year master's student, was thrilled when she found out she had been selected to do a 1-year internship at her college's counseling center. She was hopeful that this experience would help launch her career as a college counselor upon completion of her degree. Unfortunately, a few weeks into the first semester Melinda began to suspect that her on-site supervisor, Kathy, was impaired. Although Kathy was personable at times, her mood seemed to fluctuate in an unpredictable manner. On several occasions Kathy berated Melinda during supervision for not taking her direction. Melinda was starting to develop autonomy as a counselor, which was appropriate at this point in her training. Nevertheless, whenever she expressed her own ideas, Kathy appeared to feel threatened and angry. Not surprisingly, Melinda started to question her own abilities and felt reluctant to talk openly about her cases during supervision sessions. Aware that she had an ethical responsibility to provide her clients with an acceptable standard of care, she began to worry that the inadequate supervision she was receiving might compromise her ability to provide proper services to her clients. She asked herself, "Should I confront Kathy and tell her that I need more guidance from her? If I do that, will I compromise my chances of finishing the program since Kathy has the power to fail me? If I tell anyone about what's happening, will they think I am just being a difficult and rebellious supervisee?" Ultimately, Melinda took the risk of consulting with a professor in her program and transferred to a new supervisor. Although she felt angry that she received such poor supervision from Kathy, she reported factual information only to her professor and did not vent her negative feelings. Despite some fallout from this experience, Melinda was able to complete the program and pursue her career as a college counselor.

- What are your impressions of how Melinda handled the situation?
- How would you know if a supervisor is impaired? Would your stage of development as a counselor trainee influence the way you perceived a supervisor's behavior?
- If your supervisor appeared to be impaired or ineffective, how would you handle the situation? Would you confront the person directly, discuss the problem with other supervisors or professors, or try to ignore it and make the most out of a bad situation? Explain.
- If you took action, would you have any fear of retribution from your impaired supervisor? How could you minimize the risks associated with taking action?
- If one of your peers complained to you that his or her supervisor was impaired, how do you think you would react? Would you be inclined to notify the department chair or other supervisors about this or let your peer work out the problem? What are the pros and cons of these two options?

Legal Aspects of Supervision

Three legal considerations in the supervisory relationship are informed consent, confidentiality and its limits, and liability. First, supervisors must see that trainees provide the information to clients that they need to make informed choices. Clients must be fully aware that the counselor they are seeing is a trainee, that he or she is meeting on a regular basis for supervisory sessions, that the client's case may be discussed in group supervision meetings with other trainees, and that sessions may be taped or observed. As Bernard and Goodyear (2004) indicate, by virtue of supervision, supervisors have a relationship with the trainee's clients. Therefore, it is necessary that the client be informed of that relationship in detail.

Cobia and Boes (2000) suggest that supervisors make use of professional disclosure statements for supervision so that supervisees are informed of the potential benefits, risks, and expectations of entering into the supervisory relationship. In much the same way that therapists provide their clients with a professional disclosure statement, it is wise for supervisors to inform supervisees about the relevant aspects of the supervision process.

McCarthy and colleagues (1995), advocating for informed consent as a crucial aspect of clinical supervision, recommend addressing the following areas in a written informed consent document: purpose of supervision, professional disclosure statement, practical issues, supervision process, administrative issues, ethical and legal issues, and statement of agreement. By attending to informed consent in the supervision process, the professional development of supervisees will be enhanced and quality client care will be fostered. Sutter, McPherson, and Geeseman (2002) also recommend a written contract for supervision even though such contracts may not be legally binding. The agreement informs the supervisee of the expectations and responsibilities of both parties in the supervisory relationship and benefits both the supervisor and supervisee. In addition, supervisory contracts can increase the quality of care for clients receiving psychological services.

Second, supervisors have a legal and ethical obligation to respect the confidentiality of client communications. Supervision involves discussion of client issues and review of client materials, and it is essential that supervisees respect their clients' privacy by not talking about their clients outside of the context of supervision. By their own behavior, supervisors have a responsibility to model for supervisees appropriate ways of talking about clients and keeping information protected and used only in the context of supervision (Bernard & Goodyear, 2004). Supervisors must make sure that both supervisees and their clients are fully informed about the limits of confidentiality, including those situations in which supervisors have a duty to warn or to protect.

Third, supervisors ultimately bear legal responsibility for the welfare of those clients who are counseled by their trainees. In addition to being ethically vulnerable, supervisors are legally vulnerable to the work performed by those they are supervising. It is incumbent upon supervisors to understand the legal ramifications of their supervisory work. To carry out their ethical and legal responsibilities, supervisors are required to be familiar with each case of every supervisee. Failure to do this is to invite legal action. This requirement may not be practical in the sense that supervisors cannot be cognizant of all details of every case, but they should at least know the direction in which the cases are being taken. Harrar, VandeCreek, and Knapp (1990) indicate that supervisors bear both direct liability and vicarious liability. **Direct liability** can be incurred if supervisors are derelict in the supervision of their trainees, if they give trainees inappropriate advice about treatment, or if they give tasks to trainees that exceed their competence. **Vicarious liability** pertains to the responsibilities that supervisors have because of the actions of their supervisees. From both a legal and ethical standpoint, trainees are not expected to assume final responsibility for clients; rather, their supervisors are legally expected to carry the decision-making responsibility and liability.

Just as therapists are vulnerable to clients who may decide to press forward with malpractice actions, so are supervisors open to malpractice litigation against them by the supervisees' clients. Guest and Dooley (1999) point out that this has resulted in the reluctance of some professionals to agree to take on supervisory functions. Guest and Dooley suggest that supervisors would do well to practice risk management in supervision much as they do in their therapy practice with clients.

Haynes and colleagues (2003) recommend an organized approach to managing the multiple tasks in the supervisory process. They identify the following risk management practices for supervisors:

- Don't supervise beyond your competence.
- Evaluate and monitor supervisees' competence.
- Be available for supervision consistently.
- Formulate a sound supervision contract.
- Maintain written policies.
- Document all supervisory activities.
- Consult with appropriate professionals.
- Maintain a working knowledge of ethics codes, legal statutes, and licensing regulations.
- Use multiple methods of supervision.
- Have a feedback and evaluation plan.
- Purchase and verify professional liability insurance coverage.
- Evaluate and screen all clients under your supervisee's care.
- Establish a policy for ensuring confidentiality.
- Incorporate informed consent in practice.

For a list of ethical and legal questions supervisors would do well to ask themselves, see *Clinical Supervision: A Handbook for Practitioners* (Fall & Sutton, 2004, pp. 8–11). For a useful treatment of legal aspects of supervision, see *Managing Clinical Supervision: Ethical and Legal Risk Management* (Falvey, 2002).

Special Issues in Supervision for School Counselors

Crespi, Fischetti, and Butler (2001) state that the viability of clinical supervision as a tool to enhance school counseling has received little attention. Page, Pietrzak, and Sutton (2001) found that only 13% of school counselors were receiving individual clinical supervision and only 10% were receiving group clinical supervision. Page and colleagues report that the majority of counselors desired clinical supervision but did not receive it. Although administrative supervision is generally available, clinical supervision is less frequently provided to school counselors (Herlihy, Gray, & McCollum, 2002).

Supervision is an effective way to assist school counselors in maintaining and enhancing their clinical skills development. Supervision can provide ongoing consultation regarding ethical and legal issues and can offer a professional support system that may prevent stress and burnout (Herlihy et al., 2002). With increasing numbers of problems and a greater responsibility for the mental health needs of children and adolescents, it makes sense for schools to carefully examine ways to develop clinical supervision programs dealing with treatment issues. Crespi and colleagues (2001) outline these advantages of clinical supervision as an approach to personal and professional development:

- Clinical supervision provides a means for creating an interdisciplinary discussion of children's and adolescents' mental health and for utilizing an array of interventions for different children with different problems.
- Supervision provides much needed support and guidance when school counselors deal with difficult situations.
- Supervision offers a consistent vehicle to upgrade and refine assessment and counseling skills, and it offers a framework from which to review case interventions.

One excellent way to build supervision opportunities in school settings is to establish community linkages between local schools and university faculty. Faculty in counselor preparation programs are in a good position to advise and educate school counselors on innovations in counseling that can be applied to schools. Herlihy and her colleagues (2002) address several ethical and legal issues that arise in school counselor supervision: competence to supervise, confidentiality, relationship boundaries, accountability and liability, and evaluation and performance.

With respect to competence to supervise, few school counselors have received formal preparation in supervision. Other mental health professionals often provide supervision to school counselors, yet they may not have a complete understanding of the school counselor's setting or the developmental needs of students. Even in cases where the clinical supervisor is appropriately prepared, he or she may not work in the same site as the counselor being supervised. This situation does not allow for direct observation of the counselor's performance. Most schools have only one counselor, or even a half-time counselor, which raises the issue of how realistic it is to hire a counseling supervisor in these cases.

School counselors generally do not choose their clinical supervisors. From a legal vantage point, school counselors would not likely be held accountable if a supervisor were to inappropriately disclose information about school-age children to teachers or administrators. However, in such situations school counselors have an ethical responsibility to address concerns they have about their supervisor's actions. If a supervisor has evaluative authority with counselors, this can place these counselors in a vulnerable position.

Boundary issues in the supervisory relationship need to be considered. An example of a dual relationship might involve the clinical supervisor also serving as the administrative supervisor for the school counselor. Another boundary issue pertains to including a discussion of the supervisee's personal concerns in the supervisory sessions. At times, it may be necessary to address a supervisee's personal issues, especially if these concerns are having an impact on his or her ability to work effectively with clients. However, the challenge is to maintain the appropriate boundaries involved in helping the supervisee identify and understand how personal issues may be interfering with effectively delivering services without changing the supervisory relationship into a therapy relationship.

Regarding accountability and liability, administrative supervisors or employers (such as the school principal) have direct control over the actions of counselors in the school. This means that administrative supervisors are legally liable for the actions of the school counselors they hire, evaluate, and may fire. Clinical supervisors, however, are not directly responsible for the actions of school counselors because they do not have the authority to hire and fire. Still, it is essential that clinical supervisors limit their vicarious liability by clarifying their role to the school counselor, the principal, or the director of guidance. This is best done by both written documents signed by all parties and a discussion of the documents. It is also important that clinical supervisors refrain from interfering with an administrative supervisor's authority over the school counselor.

With respect to evaluation, clinical supervisors need to thoroughly discuss at the outset of supervision the evaluation process and procedures with the school counselors they are supervising to minimize later misunderstandings. According to Herlihy and colleagues (2002), the main goal of supervision for school counselors is to help them develop skills in self-evaluation that they can continue to use throughout their careers.

Herlihy and her colleagues offer the following recommendations to those who provide administrative and clinical supervision to school counselors:

- Clinical supervisors should obtain specific course work in supervision.
- As a way to expand the pool of supervisors for school counselors, a peer-supervision program could be instituted in the school district.
- Clinical supervisors can collaborate with counselor educators at nearby universities.
- Supervisors can work with school administrators in developing school policies that support school counselors in obtaining supervision.
- Clinical supervisors should know and review the codes of ethics of relevant professional organizations and stay informed about laws pertaining to counseling and supervision.
- Supervisors have a role in protecting the confidentiality of student clients of the school counselor.
- Supervisors are expected to maintain appropriate relationship boundaries with their supervisees.
- As a protection from legal liability, it is a good idea for supervisors to obtain their own professional liability insurance.

Multicultural Issues in Supervision

Ethical supervision must include the ways in which diversity factors can influence the process. In addition to course work, supervisors need a framework to approach differences in culture, race, gender, socioeconomic status, religion, and other variables pertaining to clients being seen by trainees (Falender & Shafranske, 2004). The ACA's (2005) code of ethics dealing with supervision states that "Counseling supervisors are aware of and address the role of multiculturalism/diversity in the supervisory relationship" (F.2.b).

Multicultural supervision encompasses a broad definition of culture that includes race, ethnicity, socioeconomic status, sexual orientation, religion, gender, and age (Fukuyama, 1994). Supervisors who are functioning ethically and competently are cognizant of and address the salient issues that apply to multicultural supervision (Bernard, 1994). Supervisors have an ethical responsibility to become aware of the complexities of a multicultural society (see Chapter 4). In this section we take a closer look at some of these issues as they relate to supervision.

Racial and Ethnic Issues

There is a price to be paid for ignoring racial and ethnic factors in supervision. If supervisors do not assist supervisees in addressing racial and ethnic issues, their clients may be denied the opportunity to explore these issues in their therapy. Cook (1994) calls for routinely including discussions of racial identity attitudes as part of both therapy and supervisory relationships. The supervisor's recognition of racial issues can serve as a model for supervisees in their counseling relationships. Reflecting on racial interactions in supervision offers a cognitive framework for supervisees to generalize to their counseling practices.

Priest (1994) focuses on the supervisor's role in enhancing the supervisee's respect for diversity. Because of the power dynamics inherent in the supervisory relationship, Priest believes it is the supervisor's responsibility to serve as the catalyst for facilitating discussions about multicultural issues. He points out that too often supervisors emphasize client similarities and minimize racial and cultural differences. If trainees do not understand the cultural context in which their clients live, Priest believes the chances are increased that trainees' behavior will result in clients prematurely terminating counseling.

Toward Multiculturally Effective Supervision. In her pilot study to define the issues in multicultural supervision with visible ethnic minority trainees, Fukuyama (1994) explored critical incidents in multicultural supervision. Respondents were asked how to make supervision more multiculturally sensitive and effective. Here are some of their suggestions:

- Have supervisors initiate discussion of multicultural issues as a basic part of supervision.
- Provide increased training for supervisors in working with multicultural issues, including opportunities to tape supervision sessions for self-reflection.

- Provide more supervisors with multicultural experience.
- Involve all personnel within an agency in multicultural training.
- Train supervisors to develop a genuine respect for and acceptance of cultural diversity. Caution them about the problems involved in trying to be "politically correct" and overemphasizing diversity issues.
- Provide a training model for "prejudice reduction" that could be used with trainees' clients to help them deal with racism and prejudice.
- Discuss multicultural issues in an intern seminar under the supervisor's guidance.

It is essential that supervisors receive training in multicultural issues, including having course work, practical experiences in supervision, research activities, and multicultural counseling (Fukuyama, 1994; Priest, 1994).

Constantine (1997) proposes a framework to facilitate learning multicultural competencies in supervision relationships. Semistructured questions are used to assist trainees in identifying their own cultural group identities and acknowledging the extent to which these identities influence their interactions in both supervision and counseling relationships. Ideally, this framework is introduced during the early stages of the supervision relationship because it helps to establish rapport between supervisors and supervisees. It also highlights the importance of paying attention to multicultural issues in the supervision process, and it sensitizes students to ethical issues. In using Constantine's framework, supervisors and supervisees discuss their responses to this series of questions:

- What are the main demographic variables that make up my cultural identity?
- What worldviews—assumptions and values—do I bring to the supervision relationship based on my cultural identity?
- What value systems are inherent in my approach to supervision? What strategies and techniques do I use in supervision?
- What knowledge and skills do I possess about the worldviews of supervisors (supervisees) who have different cultural identities from me?
- What are some of the issues and challenges I face in working with supervisors (supervisees) who are culturally different from me? How do I address these issues?
- In what ways would I like to improve my abilities in working with culturally diverse supervisors (supervisees)?

Although this framework was initially developed for use in the early stages of the supervision process, Constantine (1997) states that it can be used to help supervisors and supervisees continue their discussion of multicultural concerns and differences throughout the supervisory relationship.

Implications for Training and Supervision. Bernard (1994) suggests the following parameters of training and supervision to achieve multicultural competence:

- Supervisees must be at least as multiculturally sensitive as their clients, and supervisors must be at least as multiculturally competent as their supervisees.

- Training programs need to determine a trainee's readiness for clinical experience and for entry level practice.
- Supervisors need to understand both developmental supervision models and racial identity models. It is essential that supervisors acquire skills in knowing when and how to challenge supervisees on multicultural issues.
- Supervisors themselves need to seek consultation if they hope to enhance their own multicultural development.

On a more personal note, one of our former students, who is now in a doctoral program in counseling, shared her views with us about the importance of including multicultural considerations in supervision. She reported an experience in a group supervision session with a fellow student (an Asian American whom we will call Hoa). The supervisor, who was generally a sensitive person, perceived Hoa's quiet nature in a negative light and questioned her level of empathy. Hoa attributed her style of relating to colleagues and clients to her cultural background. This is but one example of how supervisors may hold assumptions that are out of their awareness that can be detrimental to both supervisees and to their clients. This also illustrates the need for supervisors to challenge their own blind spots, which can often be achieved by participating in their own supervision.

To develop the knowledge and skills to work effectively in multicultural counseling situations, trainees need to understand their own level of racial and cultural identity. Furthermore, they need to recognize how their attitudes and behaviors affect their clients. Good supervision will enable trainees to explore the impact that diversity issues may have on their counseling style.

Spiritual Issues

Spirituality has come to be considered a multicultural issue and a critical issue for counselor supervision. Bishop, Avila-Juarbe, and Thumme (2003) state that integrating spiritual issues in supervision enhances the supervision process. There is considerable and increasing literature on the role of spirituality in counseling, yet supervisors and counselors continue to struggle with accepting it as significant in the therapeutic process (Zinnbauer & Pargament, 2000). Spirituality in supervision has received little attention in the literature (Polanski, 2003), but Bishop and colleagues (2003) maintain that for the supervision process to be effective supervisors must be open and willing to address spiritual issues when they are of significance to the supervisee or his or her clients. In addressing the role of spirituality in supervision, Polanski (2003) claims that appropriate, holistic client care often includes the religious or spiritual beliefs of a client in the therapeutic process. Thus supervision is a useful forum for teaching and learning how to address spirituality in counseling. Polanski concludes: "It is clear that counselors not only need to become aware of potential spiritual issues in their clients, but they must also be comfortable in managing these issues clinically" (p. 139).

In our view, spirituality is an important factor to be explored and not ignored in supervision. We want to emphasize that exploring spirituality does not mean imposing spirituality on either clients or supervisees.

Gender Issues

Carta-Falsa and Anderson (2001) describe a collaborative model of clinical supervision based on a genuine dialogue between supervisor and supervisee in which the supervisee is seen as resourceful and the supervisor reinforces the strengths of the supervisee. In this paradigm, power is shared between the supervisor and supervisee. Together they participate in acquiring, sharing, and reshaping knowledge. According to Carta-Falsa and Anderson, this collaborative spirit leads to an empowered relationship that is characterized by a sense of safety. This sense of trust and security forms the basis for increased risk taking, higher levels of performance, and greater individual confidence.

Gender issues occupy a central place in the supervision process. Both feminist supervision and multicultural supervision pay attention to the power dynamic in the supervisory relationship as well as to the relationship between client and counselor. For example, instead of the supervisor telling supervisees what to do, the supervisor can help supervisees think about their clients in new ways, formulate their own interpretations, and devise their own interventions. Porter and Vasquez (1997) describe the **feminist supervision** model as a collaborative respectful process characterized by a balance between supervisory responsibility and supervisee autonomy. Porter and Vasquez identify nine principles that guide feminist supervision (pp. 162–167):

1. Feminist supervisors are proactive in analyzing power dynamics and differentials between supervisor and supervisee, model the use of power in the service of the supervisee, and vigilantly avoid abuses of power. This principle is a hallmark of feminist supervision as it addresses the power dynamics of the supervisory relationship. It is the supervisor's responsibility to address the power differential in the supervisory relationship and, to the extent possible, minimize it.
2. Feminist supervision is based on a mutually respectful and collaborative relationship. This does not imply an equal relationship, however, because supervisors do have evaluative responsibilities. Supervisees are provided with informed consent, and diversity perspectives are encouraged. To the extent possible, supervisees develop learning goals and objectives and choose client populations with whom to work.
3. Feminist supervisors facilitate reflexive interactions and supervisee self-examination by modeling openness, authenticity, reflexivity, and the value of lifelong learning and self-examination. Supervisors are willing to explore their own motivations, attitudes, and potential countertransference that could affect the supervisory relationship.
4. Supervision occurs in a social context that attends to and emphasizes the diversity of women's lives and context. Unfortunately, the world does not attend to women's lives equally with men's lives. One of the tasks of feminist supervision is to balance the need for attention to and redefinition of women's gender roles without excluding or demonizing men.
5. Feminist supervisors attend to the social construction of gender and the role of language in maintaining a gendered society. Feminist supervisors are

attuned to external factors as well as internal dynamics that influence the client's concerns. For example, if a client has an eating disorder, supervisors will suggest that it is important to consider societal messages about women's bodies. Feminist supervisors look for the supervisee's social constructions of gender that might influence their work with their clients. An example here would be a supervisee who assumes that a female client is dysfunctional if she does not conform to the traditional view of a woman as mother, caretaker, and homemaker.

6. Another hallmark of feminist supervision is that supervisors advance and model the principle of advocacy and activism. Supervisors guide their supervisees into thinking about their role and power in influencing the systems in which they work. Feminist supervisors are aware of the fine balance between imposing their beliefs and being apolitical in supervision.

7. Feminist supervisors maintain standards that ensure their supervisees' competent and ethical practice. Supervisors help their supervisees to appreciate the complex nature of ethical dilemmas, and they discuss ways to prevent ethical breaches. Furthermore, they assume responsibilities for challenging sexist and racist attitudes and behaviors of their supervisees, including the negative use of stereotypes and the misuse of diagnoses.

8. Feminist supervisors attend to the developmental shifts occurring in the supervisory process and provide input as a function of the skill level, developmental level, and maturational level of the supervisee. Supervisors encourage both accountability and independence on the part of their supervisees as they develop maturity and competencies. Supervisors monitor their own authoritarian supervisory practices.

9. Feminist supervisors advocate for their supervisees and clients in the educational and training settings within which they practice. Supervisors recognize that the feminist tenet of working for social change often originates in their own institution.

Do you see any distinction between these feminist principles and the principles of any effective approach to supervision? Are there any distinct aspects to feminist supervision? In your view, how are the concerns of the feminist supervision model reflecting broader multicultural concerns? To what degree is supervision ethical if it does not take into consideration gender issues and cultural issues?

Multiple Roles and Relationships in the Supervisory Process

The ACES standards (1993, 1995) state that counseling supervisors are expected to possess the personal and professional maturity to play multiple roles. **Multiple-role relationships in supervision** occur when a supervisor has concurrent or consecutive professional or nonprofessional relationships with a supervisee in addition to the supervisor-supervisee relationship. Although multiple roles and relationships are common in the context of training and supervision, it is essential for supervisors to thoroughly discuss and process issues relevant to these multiple roles with their supervisees (Ladany et al., 1999). Ethically, supervisors need to clarify their roles and to be aware of potential problems that can develop when boundaries become blurred. As Herlihy and Corey (2006b) point out, unless the nature of the supervisory relationship is clearly defined, both the supervisor and the supervisee may find themselves in a difficult situation at some point in their relationship. If the supervisor's objectivity becomes impaired, the supervisee will not be able to make maximum use of the process. If the relationship evolves into a romantic one, the entire supervisory process is destroyed, with the supervisee sooner or later likely to allege exploitation.

The crux of the issue of multiple-role relationships in the training and supervisory process is the potential for abuse of power. Like therapy clients, students and supervisees are in a vulnerable position and can be harmed by an educator or supervisor who exploits them, misuses power, or crosses appropriate boundaries. The ACA (2005) has a standard pertaining to relationship boundaries with supervisees:

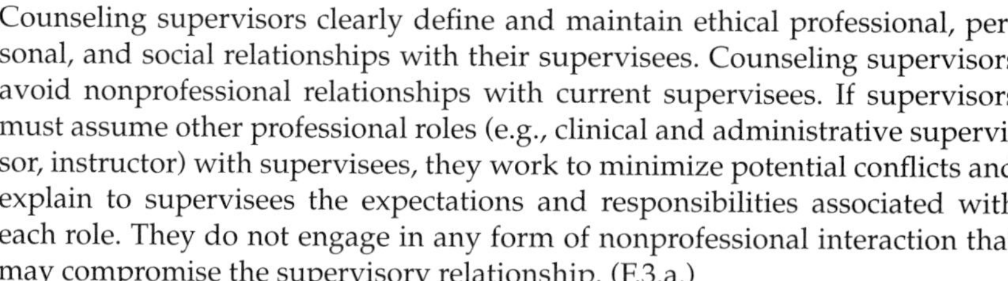

> Counseling supervisors clearly define and maintain ethical professional, personal, and social relationships with their supervisees. Counseling supervisors avoid nonprofessional relationships with current supervisees. If supervisors must assume other professional roles (e.g., clinical and administrative supervisor, instructor) with supervisees, they work to minimize potential conflicts and explain to supervisees the expectations and responsibilities associated with each role. They do not engage in any form of nonprofessional interaction that may compromise the supervisory relationship. (F.3.a.)

In their study of faculty-student relationships, Bowman, Hatley, and Bowman (1995) assessed both faculty and student perceptions regarding dual or multiple relationships in mentoring, friendships, monetary interactions, informal social interactions, and romantic-sexual relationships. They admit that certain multiple relationships are unavoidable in most training programs. Rather than viewing multiple relationships as inherently unethical, Bowman and her colleagues propose that it is best to examine the behavior of the persons who are involved in these relationships. Apart from sexual dual relationships with students and supervisees, which are clearly unethical, a wide range of dual and multiple relationships exist that are part and parcel of supervision and training of therapists. It is misleading to mix these nonsexual dual or multiple relationships with unethical sexual relationships. At its best, professional training is responsible for teaching skills that enable the supervisor to ethically manage situations involving multiple roles and relationships.

Burian and O'Connor Slimp (2000) point out that multiple-role relationships may at first appear benign, and sometimes even beneficial, yet they pose some risks to interns and training staff. For example, the mentoring that occurs between faculty and students (and between supervisors and supervisees) often includes social elements, which can be beneficial to the trainee. Burian and O'Connor Slimp's decision-making model pertaining to social multiple-role relationships between interns and their trainers is designed to raise awareness of the issues involved in these relationships and provide a basis for evaluating their potential for harm. These authors suggest ending or postponing the social relationship if more than a minimal risk of harm exists. The ultimate ethical responsibility rests with the individual with the greatest power.

In their discussion of faculty-student dual relationships, Biaggio, Paget, and Chenoweth (1997) note that overlapping roles are to be expected. They add that faculty-student relationships are not static. Students progress from the beginning stages, to graduation, and to becoming colleagues with faculty members. Biaggio and her colleagues present three general guidelines for faculty to attend to in maintaining ethical relationships with students. First, faculty need to recognize the potential for harm in dual relationships with their students, and they need to be aware that they hold a position of power and authority over students. Because dual and overlapping relationships are unavoidable in educational settings, careful monitoring is essential so that students are not harmed.

Second, a framework is necessary for evaluating appropriate and inappropriate conduct. An ethical relationship with a student is one in which these conditions are met: (a) educational standards are maintained, (b) educational experiences are provided for the student, and (c) care is taken to avoid exploitation of the student. Third, emphasis is placed on establishing and maintaining a climate for ethical relationships between faculty and students. Perhaps most important is that faculty and administrators model appropriate and ethical relationships with other professionals, students, and clients. When faculty model ethical behavior, they bring about increased awareness of ethical concerns in both educational and professional settings.

Both faculty and supervisors play a critical role in helping counselor trainees understand the dynamics of balancing multiple roles and managing dual relationships. Although students may learn about dual relationships during their academic work, it is generally not until they are engaged in fieldwork experiences and internships that they are required to grapple with these boundary issues (Herlihy & Corey, 2006b).

Supervisors must not exploit students and trainees or take unfair advantage of the power differential that exists in the context of training. Managing multiple roles ethically is the responsibility of the supervisor. A point that we made earlier needs to be reiterated. Supervisors have a much better chance of managing boundaries in their professional work if they are able to take care of their boundaries in their personal lives. Supervisors who are able to establish appropriate personal and professional boundaries are in a good position to teach students how to develop appropriate boundaries for themselves. Next we look at sexual dual relationships in training and supervision.

Sexual Intimacies During Professional Training

In their national survey on sexual intimacy in counselor education and supervision, Miller and Larrabee (1995) found that counseling professionals who were sexually involved with a supervisor or an educator during their training later viewed these experiences as being more coercive and more harmful to a working relationship than they did at the time the actual sexual involvement occurred. Perceptual changes took place over time with respect to how students were affected by becoming sexually involved with people who were training them, which raises questions about their willingness to freely consent to such relationships and how prepared they were to deal with the ethics of such intimacies. Moreover, it seems clear that educators and supervisors have professional power and authority long after direct training ends.

In their study of psychologists who reflected on their sexual relationships with clients, supervisees, and students, Lamb, Catanzaro, and Moorman (2003) found that 1% of the total sample reported a sexual boundary violation with a supervisee and 3% of the total sample reported a sexual boundary violation with a student. The majority of these violations occurred after the professional relationship had ended (100% after supervision and 54% after teaching). The respondents in the study were asked to identify the circumstances or reasons that influenced their decisions to pursue these sexual relationships, and three general types emerged:

- "No harm, thus I proceeded" (40% of the responses).
- "Consulted and/or negotiated" (32% of the responses).
- "Continued although I knew the behavior was problematic and/or unethical" (28% of the responses). Approximately half of the respondents indicated that they terminated the professional relationship (therapist, supervisor, teacher) so that they might initiate or continue the sexual relationship.

Similar to Miller and Larrabee's (1995) survey, Hammel, Olkin, and Taube (1996), who studied student-educator sexual involvement in doctoral training programs in psychology, found that respondents were, in retrospect, more likely to view sexual relationships as coercive, ethically problematic, and a hindrance to the working relationship compared to how they viewed them at the time they occurred. Clear power differentials exist between educators and students. The typical relationship is between an older male professor and a younger female graduate student. Both Miller and Larrabee (1995) and Hammel and his colleagues (1996) take the position that engaging in sexual behavior with students and supervisees is highly inappropriate and contrary to the spirit of the ethics codes of most professional organizations and educational institutions (see the ethics codes box titled Sexual Relations Are Prohibited Between Supervisor and Trainee).

Supervisory relationships have qualities in common with instructor-student and therapist-client relationships. In all of these professional relationships, it is the professional who occupies the position of power. Thus, it is the professional's responsibility to establish and maintain appropriate boundaries and to explore with the trainee (student, supervisee, or client) ways to prevent potential problems associated with boundary issues. If problems do arise, the professional has the responsibility to take steps to resolve them in an ethical manner.

The core ethical issue is the difference in power and status between educator and student or supervisor and supervisee and the exploitation of that power. When supervisees first begin counseling, they are typically naive and uninformed with respect to the complexities of therapy. They frequently regard

Ethics Codes

Sexual Relations Are Prohibited Between Supervisor and Trainee

Association for Counselor Education and Supervision (1993)

Supervisors should not participate in any form of sexual contact with supervisees. Supervisors should not engage in any form of social contact or interaction which would compromise the supervisor-supervisee relationship. Dual relationships with supervisees that might impair the supervisor's objectivity and professional judgment should be avoided and/or the supervisory relationship terminated. (2.10.)

American Counseling Association (2005)

Sexual or romantic interactions or relationships with current supervisees are prohibited. (F.3.b.)

Commission on Rehabilitation Counselor Certification (2001)

Rehabilitation counselors will not engage in sexual relationships with students or supervisees and will not subject them to sexual harassment. (G.1.b.)

National Association of Social Workers (1999)

Social workers should not engage in any dual or multiple relationships with supervisees in which there is a risk of exploitation of or potential harm to the supervisee. (3.01.c.)

American Association for Marriage and Family Therapy (2001)

Marriage and family therapists do not engage in sexual intimacy with students or supervisees during the evaluative or training relationship between the therapist and student or supervisee. Should a supervisor engage in sexual activity with a former supervisee, the burden of proof shifts to the supervisor to demonstrate that there has been no exploitation or injury to the supervisee. (4.3.)

International Association of Marriage and Family Counselors (2002)

Members who provide supervision respect the inherent imbalance of power in supervisory relationships. Thus, they actively monitor and appropriately manage multiple relationships. They refrain from engaging in relationships or activities that increase risk of exploitation, or that may impair the professional judgment of supervisees. Sexual intimacy with students or supervisees is prohibited. (VII.B.)

American Psychological Association (2002)

Psychologists do not engage in sexual relationships with students or supervisees who are in their department, agency, or training center or over whom psychologists have or are likely to have evaluative authority. (7.07.)

The American Psychiatric Association (2001)

Sexual involvement between a faculty member or supervisor and a trainee or student, in those situations in which an abuse of power can occur, often takes advantage of inequalities in the working relationship and may be unethical because:

a. Any treatment of a patient being supervised may be deleteriously affected.
b. It may damage the trust relationship between teacher and student.
c. Teachers are important professional role models for their trainees and affect their trainees' future professional behavior. (4.14.)

their supervisors as experts, and their dependence on their supervisors may make it difficult to resist sexual advances. Supervisees may disclose personal concerns and intense emotions during supervision, much as they might in a therapeutic situation. The openness of supervisees and the trust they place in their supervisors can be exploited by supervisors who choose to satisfy their own psychological or sexual needs at the expense of their supervisees.

Assume that you are a trainee. During your individual supervision sessions the supervisor frequently acts flirtatious toward you. You get the distinct impression that your evaluations will be more favorable if you "play the game." What course of action might you take in such a situation? Is there a difference between sexual harassment and consensual sexual relationships, or are all sexual advances in unequal power relationships really a form of sexual harassment? Can there ever be consensual sex in such a situation?

The Case of Augustus. Augustus meets weekly with his professor, Amy, for individual supervision. With only 3 weeks remaining in the semester, Augustus confesses to having a strong attraction to Amy and says he finds it difficult to maintain professional distance with her. Amy discloses that she, too, feels an attraction. But she is sensitive to the professional boundaries governing their relationship, and she tells him it would be inappropriate for them to have any other relationship until the semester ends. She lets him know that she would be open to further discussion about a dating relationship at that point. Even though he will still be in the program, Amy says that she will no longer have a supervisory role with him, nor will she be evaluating his status in the program.

- What are your thoughts on this situation? List them and explain.
- Do you think Amy handled her attraction to Augustus in the best way possible? Explain your response.
- If you were a colleague of Amy's and heard about this situation from another student, what would you do?
- Is the fact that Amy will no longer be supervising Augustus sufficient to eliminate the imbalance of power in the relationship? Do you think it would be appropriate for them to date each other while he is still a student in the program? after he graduates?

Commentary. We wonder how Amy's sexual attraction toward Augustus affected her supervision prior to acknowledging these feelings. We also wonder about her motivation for disclosing her attraction with only three supervisory sessions remaining. The sexual attractions were most likely influencing supervision, even before being acknowledged. Rather than disclosing her feelings of attraction, it would have been more appropriate for Amy to seek consultation once she became aware of her attraction.

Trainees do need to have a safe environment in which they can discuss sexual attractions they may be having for their clients. They need to be reassured that these feelings in themselves are human and harmless but that acting on them is always inappropriate and unethical. For this safe climate to be created, supervisors need to be competent in addressing sexual attraction and boundary issues. Supervisors also need to be assertive in bringing these issues up in supervision, and they need to be aware of how their own feelings toward supervisees might affect the supervisory relationship (Falender & Shafranske, 2004).

Ethical Issues in Combining Supervision and Counseling

Supervisors play multiple roles in the supervision process, and the boundaries between therapy and supervision are not always clear. In the literature on supervision, there seems to be basic agreement that the supervision process should concentrate on the supervisee's professional development rather than on personal concerns and that supervision and counseling have different purposes. However, there is a lack of consensus and clarity about the degree to which supervisors can ethically deal with the personal issues of supervisees. Supervisory relationships are a complex blend of professional, educational, and therapeutic aspects. This complex process can become increasingly complicated when supervisors are involved in certain multiple roles with trainees. It is the supervisor's responsibility to help trainees identify how their personal dynamics are likely to influence their work with clients, yet it is not the proper role of supervisors to serve as personal counselors for supervisees. Combining the roles of supervising and counseling often presents conflicts (Corey & Herlihy, 2006b; Pope & Vasquez, 1998; Whiston & Emerson, 1989), and the ACA (2005) guideline expressly prohibits this dual role:

> If supervisees request counseling, supervisors provide them with acceptable referrals. Counselors do not provide counseling services to supervisees. Supervisors address interpersonal competencies in terms of the impact of these issues on clients, the supervisory relationship, and professional functioning. (F.5.c.)

As personal problems or limitations become evident, training professionals are ethically obliged to encourage and challenge trainees to face and deal with these barriers that could inhibit their potential as helpers (Herlihy & Corey, 2006b). However, this discussion should emanate from the work of the trainee with the client. Sometimes the personal concerns of the supervisee are part of the problem presented in supervision. In such cases, the safety and welfare of the client would require the supervisor to pay some attention to the supervisee's personal issue. Supervision could involve assisting the supervisee in identifying personal concerns so that these concerns do not become the client's problem. Although discussing a trainee's personal issues may appear to be similar to therapy, the purpose is to facilitate the trainee's ability to work successfully with clients. When personal concerns are discussed in supervision, the goal is not to solve the trainee's problem. This generally requires further exploration in personal therapy that is beyond the scope of supervision. If the trainee needs or wants personal therapy, the best course for a supervisor to follow is to make a referral to another professional. We now consider two specific cases.

The Case of Hartley. During a supervision hour, Hartley confides to his supervisor that his 5-year personal relationship has just ended and that he is in a great deal of pain. As he describes in some detail what happened, he becomes very emotional. Hartley expresses his concern about his ability to work with clients, especially those who are struggling with relationships. Here are how five supervisors might have dealt with Hartley's concerns:

Supervisor A: I'm sorry you're hurting, but I feel the need to use this time to help you work with your clients. I can see no way for you to refer your clients at this point without serious repercussions for them.

Supervisor B: [After listening to Hartley for some time and acknowledging his pain] I know it is difficult for you to work with your clients. I know you are in therapy, and I suggest that you increase the frequency of your sessions to give yourself an opportunity to deal with your own pain.

Supervisor C: That must be very painful. Do you want to talk about it? Because what is going on with you interferes with your ability to be present with clients, I think it is essential that we work with your pain. [The more the supervisor works with Hartley's pain, the more they tap into other problems in his life. Three weeks later the supervision time still involves Hartley's hurt and crisis.]

Supervisor D: I see you are very affected by the changes in your life. I am glad that you can see how this may affect your work with clients. Can we spend a little time discussing how your experience may create a problem in your dealings with clients?

Supervisor E: This is obviously very difficult and emotional for you. What specifically are you afraid may happen with you when helping clients with similar problems?

- Which of the five responses comes closest to your own, and why?
- How might you have responded to Hartley?
- Do you think any of these five responses crossed the boundary between supervision and personal therapy? Explain.

The Case of Greta. Ken is a practicing therapist as well as a part-time supervisor in a counseling program. One of his supervisees, Greta, finds herself in a personal crisis after she learns that her mother has been diagnosed with terminal cancer. Much of her internship placement involves working with hospice patients. She approaches Ken and lets him know that she feels unable to continue doing this work. He is impressed with her therapeutic skills and thinks it would be most unfortunate for her to interrupt her education at this point. He also assumes that he can more effectively deal with her personal crisis because of their trusting relationship. For the next four supervision sessions, Ken focuses almost exclusively on Greta's personal problems. As a result of his help, Greta recovers her stability and is able to continue working with the hospice patients, with no apparent adverse effects for either them or her.

- What are your thoughts on the problem and the solution Ken chose? Explain.
- What are your reactions to Ken blending the roles of supervisor and counselor?

- What potential ethical issues, if any, would you see if Ken had recommended that Greta temporarily discontinue her field placement and enter therapy with him in his private practice?
- If Ken recommended that Greta see another therapist for her personal therapy but she refused on the ground that he knew her best, would that make a difference?
- Do you see another way of dealing with this situation?
- Is it ever appropriate for supervisors to blend the roles of supervisor and therapist? Why or why not?

Commentary. It is our position that the emphasis of supervision needs to be on the enhancement of supervisees' work with their clients. Because we believe in the notion of countertransference, we think trainees' own issues can be stimulated by their clients. Falender and Shafranske (2004) suggest that if countertransference is unrecognized and not managed, it has deleterious effects on both therapeutic and supervisory relationships. They contend that addressing countertransference is one of the central tasks of supervision. Falender and Shafranske believe that the exploration of countertransference is best accomplished on the foundation of a well-established supervisory relationship in which consideration of personal factors are encouraged and modeled by the supervisor. We agree with the position that attending to the personal dynamics of trainees is a necessary part of supervision. For instance, with Greta, we would attend to the pain that is triggered by her work, yet we would not explore in an in-depth way the unfinished business she might have with her mother. With Hartley, we would be sensitive to his pain, yet we would not pursue the historical roots of his problem. Supervision typically focuses on the here and now. Past concerns are more appropriately explored in personal therapy.

One of the reviewers of this book raises a significant point regarding time limitations. Weekly supervisory sessions of about one hour never provide enough time to cover administrative, ethical, legal, logistical, and clinical issues of clients. If personal issues raised by a supervisee are salient to the supervisee's work, the supervisor needs to determine how these issues will be handled by the supervisee outside the supervisory session (Terrence Patterson, personal communication, October 26, 2004).

Educators Who Counsel Students

As we mentioned in Chapter 2, many professional programs strongly recommend, if not require, a personal therapeutic experience. Some programs expect students to undergo individual therapy for a time, and other programs provide a growth group experience. At the very least, students have a right to know of these requirements before they make a commitment to begin a program. Further, we believe students should generally be allowed to decide what type of therapeutic experience is most appropriate for them.

Many ethics codes address the advisability of educators and supervisors offering their services as therapists to students and supervisees. For example, the AAMFT (2001) code states that "Marriage and family therapists do not provide therapy to current students or supervisees" (4.2.). The ACA (2005) code states that "Counselor educators do not serve as counselors to current students unless this is a brief role associated with a training experience" (F.10.e.). Although the practice of faculty members' providing counseling for current students for a fee is unethical, some situations are not so clear-cut. Once students complete a program, for example, what are the ethics of a psychology professor taking them on as clients? Can it still be argued that the prior role as educator might negatively affect the current role as therapist? If the former student and the professor/therapist agree that there are no problems, is a therapeutic relationship ethically justified? To clarify your position on this issue, reflect on this case.

The Case of Brent. A psychology professor, Hilda, teaches counseling classes, supervises interns, and also provides individual therapy at the university counseling center. One of her graduate students, Brent, approaches her with a request for personal counseling. Even though she tells him of her concern over combining roles, he is persuasive and adds that he trusts her and sees no problem in being both her student and her counselee.

- What issues, if any, ethical or otherwise, do you see in this case?
- Would it make a difference if Brent had approached her for counseling after he had completed the course with her?
- Would the situation take on a different dimension if the professor had a private practice and charged Brent a fee for her service?
- Assume that Hilda was leading a therapy group during the semester and that Brent wanted to join the group. Is being a client in a group different from being an individual client?
- Do you see any potential for exploitation in this case?
- Would it make a difference if there was a lack of availability of other counseling resources in the area?

The Case of Laura. Laura, a master's level graduate student in a counseling program, has completed a "Social and Cultural Foundations of Counseling" course that was very personal and required a lot of self-reflection and journaling. During this course, she had the opportunity of listening to and talking with two lesbian women who had been living in an open, committed relationship for 15 years. In meeting these people, she decided it was time for her to "come out" too. She started with a close friend who had known her all her life, but it did not go well. Her friend was shocked and very disapproving, and they have not talked to each other since the disclosure. She is also wondering whether she should now tell her parents because she is afraid her former friend will say something to someone in the small town in which they live, and it will get back to her parents anyway. She does not want to lose them too.

Laura is now failing her "Methods of Research" course because she has missed a lot of classes struggling with this issue. She needs more time and help to catch up, but her instructor, a "born-again" Christian, is unsympathetic, and she does not want to tell him what is going on for fear of having to endure a lecture about her "sins" from this man. She has been confiding in one professor, a licensed professional counselor, who is both a supervisor of her practicum and an instructor in her courses. The professor acknowledges what a difficult decision she is facing with regard to telling her parents and others, and she lets the student know that she is available to talk to her any time the student needs a friendly ear. She also tells Laura about a lesbian counselor who has a private practice in the area. Laura is not ready to see someone she does not know, and she is reluctant to be seen going to a counselor who is known to be gay or lesbian.

The professor does nothing to persuade her differently and reminds Laura that she is available at any time. She also inquires whether Laura would like her to talk to the "Methods of Research" instructor—without disclosing more than the fact that the student is having a hard time right now and could use some help and understanding. Laura accepts this offer.

- Do you approve or disapprove of how the professor worked with Laura?
- What are the dual relationship issues involved here, and how would you resolve them?
- Do you think the professor/counselor was engaged in appropriate social activism or in boundary violations?
- What ethical issues are raised in this case?
- If Laura were your student, how might you have dealt with this situation?

Clarifying Your Stance. Identify the potential ethical and legal issues raised in the following brief scenarios, and consider how you would address them.

- Your supervisor does not provide what you consider to be adequate supervision. You are left mainly on your own with a difficult caseload. The staff members where you work also have overwhelming caseloads. When you do get time with a supervisor, he or she also seems overwhelmed with responsibilities. Thus, you do not get enough time to discuss your cases. What would you be inclined to do?
- You have a conflict with your supervisor over the most ethical way to deal with a client. What would you do?
- You do not get adequate feedback on your performance as a trainee. At the end of the semester your supervisor gives you a negative evaluation. What potential ethical and legal issues might be involved? What might you do or say?
- Do you think it is unethical for supervisors to initiate social or sexual relationships with trainees after they have graduated (and when the supervisors have no professional obligations to the trainees)? Explain your position.
- If during the course of your supervision you became aware that personal problems were interfering with your ability to work effectively with clients, what would you be inclined to do?
- What are the main problems with multiple relationships in supervision? What potential problems do you see, and how might you resolve them? Do

you think all such relationships in supervision should be minimized or even avoided entirely?

- What possible benefits, if any, do you see when supervisors combine a multiplicity of roles such as teacher, mentor, counselor, consultant, evaluator, and supervisor?

Special Issues in Consultation

According to A. M. Dougherty (2005), there is no widespread agreement on the definition of consultation. There is general agreement that the goal of all consultation is to solve problems or to attend to a situation that needs attention. Dougherty defines **consultation** as "a process in which a human service professional assists a consultee with a work-related (or caretaking-related) problem with a client system, with the goal of helping both the consultee and the client system in some specified way" (p. 11). Consultation is a specialized professional process, and it is being carried out by many different groups in diverse work settings, which presents some unique ethical challenges.

Consultants often work with individuals and small groups in schools, agencies, and businesses and share expertise with others in the helping professions so that they can better serve their own clients. This process is aimed at helping people work more effectively on the individual, group, organizational, or community level. Consultants assist consultees with immediate problems and also try to improve their ability to solve future problems.

Based on a survey of the literature on the nature of consultation, Dougherty found general agreement on these common characteristics of consultation (pp. 11–12):

- The consultant provides indirect service to the client by providing direct service to consultees to better serve their own clients.
- Participation in the consultation process should be voluntary by all the parties involved.
- Consultees have the freedom to decide what they will do with the suggestions and recommendations of the consultant.
- The relationship between the consultee and the consultant, at its best, is a collaboration of peers who are equal in power.
- Consultation is a temporary process. Depending on the type, consultation may range from a single session to multiple sessions.
- Consultation is primarily aimed at problems with work or caretaking as opposed to personal concerns (such as the consultee's marital discord or depression). For example, consultants might provide training workshops for counselors and social workers in an agency. The focus of consultation could be on learning to recognize and deal effectively with job-related stress that can easily interfere with one's professional functions.
- Consultants can take on a variety of roles depending on the nature of consultation and the desired outcomes of consultation.
- Consultation typically occurs in an organizational context.

The Need for Ethical Standards for Consultants

As consultation has become more widely practiced, ethical and legal issues have arisen that demand awareness and preparedness of the consultant's part (A. M. Dougherty, 2005). The ethics codes of most of the mental health professional associations do not sufficiently address the complexity of ethical issues consultants encounter and offer only limited guidelines for the practice of consultation. Consultants are faced with many ethical and legal dilemmas, and they carry a heavy responsibility for their actions and the decisions they make. To effectively make ethical decisions, consultants need more than knowledge of ethical standards; they also must learn how to identify and work through a variety of problematic situations they will encounter.

Ethical issues in consultation have been given increased attention in recent years, and so too have legal issues. Consultants can be sued for malpractice or breach of contract, and it is essential that consultants become aware of the laws affecting their practices and act in a manner that reflects this knowledge (A. M. Dougherty, 2005).

Ethical and Professional Issues in Consultation

A number of ethical and professional issues pertain to consultation in the human-service professions, including values, multiculturalism, consultant competence and training, the consultation relationship, the rights of consultees, and consultation in groups (A. M. Dougherty, 2005). Let's look more closely at each of these ethical issues in consultation. Our discussion is based on material from a variety of sources (A. M. Dougherty, 2005; Jackson & Hayes, 1993; Newman, Robinson-Kurpius, & Fuqua (2002); Remley, 1993; Wallace & Hall, 1996).

Values Issues in Consultation. Consulting involves multiple parties with diverse and often competing interests and priorities, and it can be expected that value conflicts will occur among various sectors within an organization. Because consultation generally occurs in a systems context, what is good for an agency or an organization may not always be good for the individuals employed in that system (Wallace & Hall, 1996).

Ethical practice demands that consultants investigate the goals of an agency before agreeing to offer consultation services so they can determine whether they can fulfill the terms of the contract (Wallace & Hall, 1996). It is essential that consultants understand how their values influence their practice. When consultants become aware of differences in values that cannot be resolved, or a clear difference in expectations, the ethical course to follow is to decline the contract. This approach prevents arriving at an insoluble value conflict in the middle of the consulting contract. Because of differences between the values of the consultant and the agency hiring the consultant, referral is sometimes in order.

Value conflicts can arise at any stage of the consultation process. The challenge of dealing with the balance between the system as a whole and the individuals within it often demands a stance of openness on the consultant's part in addressing different values and in making key choices. It is critical that difficult choices be made *with* consultees rather than *for* them by the consultant acting alone.

Multicultural Issues in Consultation. Most ethics codes specifically mention the practitioner's responsibility to consider the cultural context when delivering professional services, such as this NASW (1999) guideline: "Social workers who provide supervision or consultation are responsible for setting clear, appropriate, and culturally sensitive boundaries" (3.01.b.). Just as cultural awareness is critical in the practice of counseling and supervision, so is it basic to effective consultation (Ingraham, 2000). The ethical practice of consultation requires consultants to demonstrate sensitivity to and respect for cultural differences when they provide their services in a variety of settings.

When consultants lack multicultural awareness and sensitivity, they risk getting lost in their expert role and frequently experience frustration in their attempts to render effective services. They can also create serious problems for the consultee. Furthermore, if consultants do not take diversity factors into account, they place themselves in ethical jeopardy because this neglect can infringe upon the rights of consultees with different worldviews and values (A. M. Dougherty, 2005).

Ingraham (2000) and Jackson and Hayes (1993) state that a broader multicultural training program is needed for consultants. Consultants need training in diverse worldviews, an awareness of differences in reasoning patterns, an understanding of variations in communication patterns, and an awareness of their capabilities to effect change. If students are not exposed to training in the multicultural dimensions of consultation, they will have only a limited ability to reach the diverse client populations they may serve.

Competence and Training in Consultation. It is imperative that consultants have adequate education and training to perform the services for which they intend to contract. Furthermore, they are ethically bound to assume responsibility for keeping abreast of theoretical and technical developments in their field. The codes of ethics of the ACA (2005) and the APA (2002) recommend that consultants deliver only those services that they are competent to perform. Consultants should present their professional qualifications to avoid misrepresenting themselves. Prior to accepting a consulting role, consultants need to decide whether their competence is adequate for a particular project. If consultants realize that they do not have the competence to undertake an assignment, they should decline and make an appropriate referral. Furthermore, consultants need to be reasonably certain that the organization employing them has the resources to give the kinds of help that its clients need and that referral resources are available.

Closely related to the issue of competence is determining whether consultants have an adequate level of training to perform contracted services. Consultants can maintain a high level of professionalism by continuing their education, by attending professional conferences, by consulting with more experienced colleagues, and by obtaining the relevant credentials or licenses for the profession in which they expect to serve as a consultant.

Relationship Issues in Consultation. The consultant-consultee-client relationship is a complex one that needs to be considered in the context of the organization in which the consulting is occurring. The consultee's interests and needs are paramount. The consulting relationship is based on a clear understanding of what the problem is, the goals for change, and the predicted consequences of the interventions selected (ACA, 2005, D.2.b.). Consultants are expected to establish a clear contract with well-defined limits, to respect their contract, and to communicate the terms of the contract to all those participating in consulting activities. Any changes in the contract should be made only through explicit agreement with staff members and the administration.

Some writers recommend using a written consultation contract to set the stage for a successful consulting relationship (Remley, 1993). An alternative to a formal, written contract is a letter of understanding in which the consultant summarizes and confirms the expectations of the consultation agreement (Wallace & Hall, 1996). Both consultants and consultees gain from written documents that spell out the essentials of the agreement, including the nature of the consultation relationship, goals, practical aspects, fees, confidentiality matters, and informed consent issues. The more specific a written contract is, the more useful the document will be to both parties. According to Remley (1993), contracts are best structured in this way:

- Clearly specify the work to be completed by the consultant.
- Identify any work products expected from the consultant.
- Establish a time frame for completing the work.
- Identify lines of authority and the person to whom the consultant is responsible.
- Establish compensation arrangements, including the method of payment.
- Specify any special arrangements agreed upon by the parties.

A good contract is a form of legal protection for both the consultant and the consultee. It can also assist both parties in developing a clear understanding of the terms of the consultation agreement and can be used as a source of reference if misunderstandings emerge at any stage in the consultation process.

An ethical consultant places top priority on the consultee's freedom of choice, which can be compromised by the creation of dependence, by the misuse of power, or by making decisions for consultees. It is essential that consultees be aware that they have the freedom to do whatever they wish with the recommendations of a consultant (Kratochwill & Pittman, 2002). Consultants have a responsibility to protect the freedom of consultees by declining to become involved in activities that require discussion of highly personal issues.

Rights of Consultees. Two central issues involving the rights of consultees are confidentiality and informed consent. Just as in any other professional relationship, absolute confidentiality cannot be guaranteed. The matter of who will have access to the consultant's findings needs to be established before gathering data. Consultants can remind staff members and administrators of the limits of confidentiality established during contract negotiations. Newman and colleagues (2002) suggest that at a minimum consultants make certain that consultees clearly understand what and how information will be used, by whom, and for what purposes.

Consultants who work in schools may need to break confidentiality when there is abusive behavior on a consultee's part, such as a teacher's consistent violation of a school's policy regarding corporal punishment. Likewise, consultants who work in a residential care facility need to assume responsibility for protecting the residents, yet they may also have to report certain incidents or situations to others in the facility. In all settings, those who are participating in the consultation process have a right to know about the limits of confidentiality. It is the consultant's job to ensure that all participants clearly understand the parameters of confidentiality.

Ethical practice requires that consultants inform their consultees about the goals and purpose of consultation, the limits to confidentiality, the potential benefits, any potential risks, the potential outcomes of intervention, and their freedom to decline to participate in the consultation process. As was mentioned in Chapter 5, informed consent is not exclusively accomplished at the outset of a relationship but is best achieved through a continuing discussion of relevant issues. It is a good policy for consultants to put themselves in the place of their consultees and ask themselves what they would want to know. All who are participating have a right to know about the nature and purpose of the consultation process.

Issues Involving Consultation in Groups. The structure of consultation increasingly involves a consultant and a group of consultees. The ethical guidelines for group work discussed in Chapter 12 apply here to the process of consulting in groups. When consultants use group process approaches, it is essential that they be competent in group consultation. Those who participate in consultation in groups have a right to know what will be expected of them. Matters such as self-disclosure, privacy, the boundary between work-related concerns and personal concerns, and the limits of confidentiality are all particularly important.

Three Case Examples of Consulting

✓ **The Case of Lynn.** The principal of a school hires Lynn, a psychologist in private practice, to conduct a communications workshop focusing on improving interpersonal relationships between the faculty and the administration. The workshop is a 2-day intensive group experience involving all teachers and the three administrators in the school. Participants are encouraged to openly express their concerns and difficulties and to focus on possible strategies for improving working conditions. The workshop seems to go well.

The following week, the principal calls Lynn and asks for a meeting. The principal agrees that the workshop seemed successful and says she would be interested in Lynn's assessment of key faculty members. She would like to know more about the natural leaders and the potential troublemakers. Lynn is asked to go through the list of teachers and make an assessment of each person's potential to be helpful or uncooperative.

- What potential ethical issues, if any, are involved in this case?
- As the principal attended the workshop and basically heard everything, would it be permissible for Lynn to give her professional assessment of each person?
- The consultation contract was between the principal and Lynn. What rights, if any, does that fact give the principal?
- What are your reactions to the after-workshop meeting between Lynn and the principal?
- Does informed consent require that all participants know exactly how the information they share will be used?

✓ **The Case of Delilah.** An airline management group is concerned about the loss of working hours because of on-the-job stress. Delilah is hired to provide stress management skills to solve the problem. The contract calls for her to teach specific strategies, such as relaxation, diet, exercise, aerobics, and visualization, with the stated goal of reducing stress and improving efficiency. In the process of teaching employees how to cope with stress, she discovers that many outside personal problems are contributing to their stress. She decides to alter her strategy to include several hours of group counseling to address the personal problems of the participants. In addition, she gives the participants three sources of referral for further professional help.

- Can a consultant unilaterally change the provisions of a contract?
- Should Delilah ignore the personal problems that are contributing to inefficiency on the job because this information was not available to her when the contract was designed?
- Does management have the right to insist on the contract being strictly adhered to? What if management contends that personal problems are best dealt with separately and financed by the employees or their insurance company?
- Is Delilah now involved in a dual relationship as consultant and counselor? Explain your position.

✓ **A Case of a Hidden Agenda.** A state-funded agency employs a team of consultants to conduct human relations training and staff development. Over time, these consultants earn a reputation for working effectively with the lower-level staff. The director of the agency expresses a desire for the consultants to "work on" key members of the upper-level staff who are identified as being particularly troublesome to the agency. The stipulation is that the focus on these key members is not to be disclosed; rather, the impression to be given is that the team is working to improve the overall efficiency of the staff.

- If the consultants accept this contract as it is written, are they being unethical?
- If this hidden agenda is successfully carried out, overall efficiency will be enhanced and the entire agency benefits. Does the end justify the means?

- Assume that a hidden agenda becomes evident to you during the course of a consulting workshop you are giving. What would be the ethical thing to do? Would you disclose to the members that you suspect a hidden agenda? Would you confront the director who had hired you?

Chapter Summary

Counselors are often asked to assume the roles of supervisor and consultant. It is clear that special training is needed to effectively perform the many functions required in these activities. Some of the key ethical issues associated with supervision and consultation involve carrying out professional roles and responsibilities, maintaining clear boundaries between roles, and avoiding the problems created by dual or multiple relationships.

Supervision is one way in which trainees learn how to apply their knowledge and skills to particular clinical situations. It is essential that supervisees receive regular feedback so that they have a basis for honing their skills. Effective supervision deals with the professional as a person and as a practitioner. It is not enough to focus only on the trainee's skills. The supervisory relationship is a personal process, and the supervisee's dynamics are equally important in this process. Although supervision aims at honing the skills of trainees, the welfare of those served by trainees is the primary consideration. Supervisors have both legal and ethical responsibilities to clients, who have a right to competent service regardless of the supervisee's level of training (Welfel, 2006).

Consultation, much like supervision, is a professional specialization that can be carried out with individuals and in small groups with diverse client populations in various work settings. Consultants help human-service workers deliver services to their clients more effectively, but they are not legally responsible for their consultees' clients. Consultants focus on work-related concerns. Ethical and professional issues pertaining to consultation include values, multiculturalism, competence and training, the consulting relationship, the rights of consultees, and consulting in groups.

Suggested Activities

1. Role play a situation that involves a supervisor asking supervisees to get involved in therapy situations that are beyond the scope of their training and experience. One student in class can play the role of a persuasive supervisor who thinks students will learn best by "jumping into the water and learning how to swim." The supervisor can ask trainees to work with a family, lead a therapy group alone, or work with abused children. After the role play, discuss the ethical and clinical issues involved with a focus on ways to deal with inadequate supervision.

2. Set up another role-playing situation. In this case, the supervisor is difficult to reach and rarely keeps his or her appointments with supervisees. One student can play the inaccessible supervisor, and several others can assume the

roles of students who need to meet with their supervisor to discuss difficult cases. How would they deal with this type of supervisor?

3. Investigate some of the community agencies in your area to learn what supervision they offer to interns and to newly hired practitioners. Several students can form a panel to share the results.

4. Form an ethics committee in class to review these two cases dealing with supervision:

- A supervisor has made sexual overtures to several supervisees.
- A supervisor is accepting supervisees as clients in his or her private practice, and the supervisor makes it a practice to date former students in the program.

The ethics committee can present its case in class with appropriate courses of action for each problem area. The others in the class can interact with the committee by providing alternative viewpoints.

5. In dyads or triads, explore your thoughts on the ethical issues raised in the following situations. How might you react in these situations?

- You are aware that a clinical supervisor has made it a practice to have sexual relationships with several of his supervisees. Some of these students are friends of yours, and they tell you that they felt pressure to comply because they were in a vulnerable position. What would you do?
- Several of your friends tell you that a clinical supervisor at the university makes it a practice to date former supervisees. When colleagues confronted him in the past, he maintained that all of these trainees were adults, that none of them were his supervisees when he dated them, and that what he did in his private life was strictly his own business. What is your view of his behavior?
- Imagine yourself as a supervisee in an internship placement in a community agency. Your supervisor at this agency makes inappropriate advances to you. How might you react? What would you do?

6. Assume that you are in a field placement as a counselor trainee in a community agency. The administrators tell you that they do not want you to inform your clients that you are a student intern. They explain that your clients might feel that they were getting second-class service if they found out that you were in training. What would you say and do if you found yourself as an intern in this situation? Would it be ethical to follow this directive and not inform your clients that you are a trainee and that you are receiving supervision? Do you agree or disagree with the rationale of the administrators? Might you accept the internship assignment under the terms outlined if you could not find any other field placements?

7. Interview a consultant to discover how this person was trained and what professional activities he or she typically performs. It would be useful for various students to interview consultants in different settings, such as businesses, public schools, agencies, and private practice. Ask the consultants to share some of the ethical dilemmas they have faced in their work. How did they deal with them?

8. Interview several clinical supervisors to determine what they consider to be the most pressing ethical and legal issues in the supervisory relationship. Here

are some questions you might ask supervisors: What are the rights of trainees? What are the main responsibilities of supervisors? To what degree should supervisors be held accountable for the welfare of the clients who are counseled by their trainees? What kind of specialized training have they had in supervision? Who is the focus of supervision—the client? the trainee? What are some common problems faced by supervisors in effectively carrying out their duties?

Ethics in Action CD-ROM Exercises

9. Reflect on all of the role-playing situations enacted in the *Ethics in Action* CD-ROM. Put yourself in the place of the counselor. Would you seek input from a supervisor in any of these situations? Consider situations such as working with a pregnant teenager who urges you not to tell her parents; becoming aware of countertransference with a client; having a sharp value difference between you and your client; finding yourself attracted to a client; having difficulty establishing and maintaining boundaries with a client. Select the one vignette in the video that you think would be most challenging. A small group of students can offer you peer supervision as you play the role of a counselor struggling with a particularly difficult ethical situation. Ask another student to role play the counselor with an ethical issue you would find challenging. Assume the role of the supervisor of this counselor. What questions would you ask of the counselor? What kinds of suggestions might you offer?

InfoTrac® College Edition Resources

For additional readings, explore InfoTrac College Edition, our online library. Key words are listed in a form that enables the search engine to locate a wider range of articles in the online university library. Key words should be entered exactly as shown, including asterisks, "Wl," "W2," "AND," and other search engine tools. Go to http://www.infotrac-college.com and select these key word searches:

clinic* supervision
ethic* clinical superv*
legal clinical superv*
clinical W1 superv* AND role NOT medic*
clinical W1 superv* AND responsib*
clinical W1 superv* AND competence
clinical W1 superv* AND consultation*
multicult* N3 superv*
multiple N2 role* AND superv*
ethic* AND consultation AND (psych????y OR psychotherapy OR couns*) NOT law NOT medic*
informed N2 consent AND supervision AND (psych????y OR psychotherapy OR couns*)
direct W1 liability AND (psych????y OR psychotherapy OR couns*) NOT medic*

Chapter 10

Pre-Chapter Self-Inventory

Directions: For each statement, indicate the response that most closely identifies your beliefs and attitudes. Use the following code:

5 = I *strongly agree* with this statement.
4 = I *agree* with this statement.
3 = I am *undecided* about this statement.
2 = I *disagree* with this statement.
1 = I *strongly disagree* with this statement.

_____ 1. It is best to adhere to a specific theory of counseling.

_____ 2. I would rather combine insights and techniques derived from various theoretical approaches to counseling than base my practice on a single model.

_____ 3. People are basically capable of and responsible for finding their own solutions to their problems.

_____ 4. What happens in counseling sessions is more my responsibility than it is my client's.

_____ 5. I would find it difficult to work for an agency that expected me to perform functions I didn't think were appropriate to counseling.

_____ 6. I should have the power to define my own role and professional identity as a mental health practitioner.

_____ 7. Clients should always select the goals of counseling.

_____ 8. I would be willing to work with clients who did not seem to have any clear goals or reasons for seeking counseling.

Issues in Theory, Practice, and Research

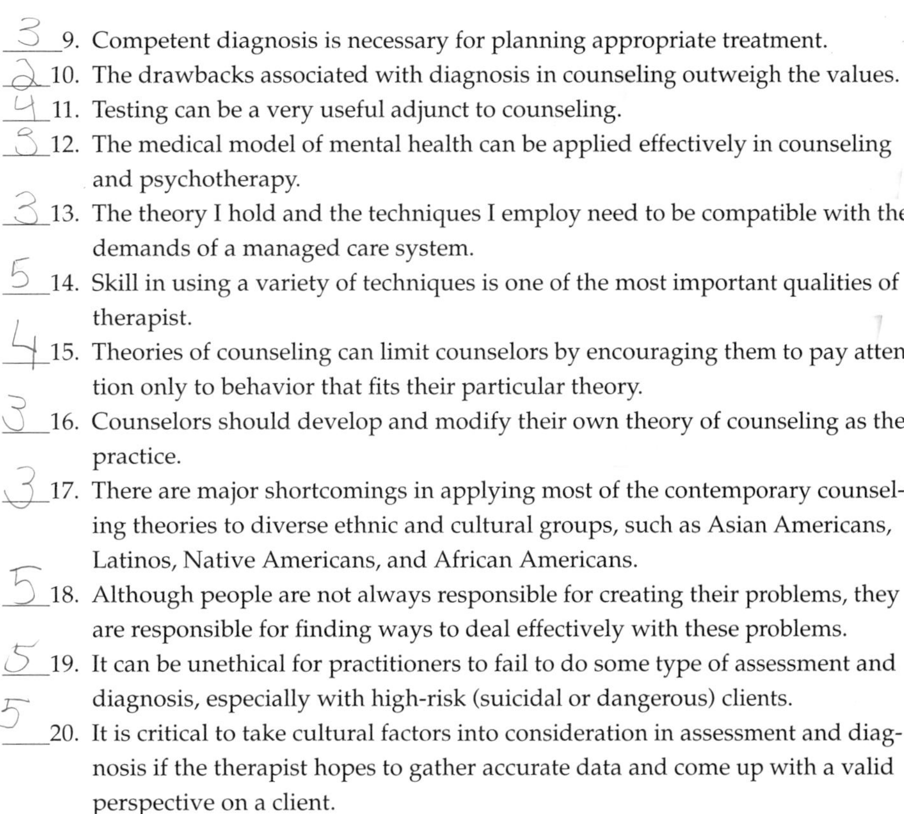

_3_ 9. Competent diagnosis is necessary for planning appropriate treatment.

_2_ 10. The drawbacks associated with diagnosis in counseling outweigh the values.

_4_ 11. Testing can be a very useful adjunct to counseling.

_3_ 12. The medical model of mental health can be applied effectively in counseling and psychotherapy.

_3_ 13. The theory I hold and the techniques I employ need to be compatible with the demands of a managed care system.

_5_ 14. Skill in using a variety of techniques is one of the most important qualities of a therapist.

_4_ 15. Theories of counseling can limit counselors by encouraging them to pay attention only to behavior that fits their particular theory.

_3_ 16. Counselors should develop and modify their own theory of counseling as they practice.

_3_ 17. There are major shortcomings in applying most of the contemporary counseling theories to diverse ethnic and cultural groups, such as Asian Americans, Latinos, Native Americans, and African Americans.

_5_ 18. Although people are not always responsible for creating their problems, they are responsible for finding ways to deal effectively with these problems.

_5_ 19. It can be unethical for practitioners to fail to do some type of assessment and diagnosis, especially with high-risk (suicidal or dangerous) clients.

_5_ 20. It is critical to take cultural factors into consideration in assessment and diagnosis if the therapist hopes to gather accurate data and come up with a valid perspective on a client.

Introduction

Therapists' theoretical positions and conceptual views influence their actual practice. Ideally, theory is meant to help practitioners make sense of what they hear in counseling sessions. Another way of thinking about this issue is to imagine a client asking you to explain your view of counseling in clear and simple terms. Could you tell your client what you most hoped to accomplish and how you would go about it? Ethical practice is grounded in a solid theoretical and research base. Practitioners who operate in a theoretical vacuum, with little or no interest in the practical applications of psychotherapeutic research, may be engaging in behavior that is ethically questionable or at least not very helpful.

This chapter addresses a variety of interrelated ethical issues, such as why a theory has both practical and ethical implications, the goals and techniques that flow from a theoretical orientation, the role of assessment and diagnosis in the therapeutic process, issues in psychological testing, ethical considerations in the practice of managed care, and ethics in research. We examine the impact that managed care is having on counseling practice, and we especially look at the balance between cost containment measures and providing quality care to consumers. We consider the ethical and legal implications of managed care as they apply to informed consent, appropriate levels of care, and outcome expectations for short-term interventions on a range of client problems.

Professional counselors need to be able to conceptualize what they are doing in their counseling sessions and why they are doing it. Sometimes practitioners have difficulty explaining why they use certain counseling procedures. When you first meet a new client, for example, what guidelines would you use in structuring what you will hear? What do you want to accomplish at this initial session? Rank in order of importance the following factors that you would be interested in knowing about your client:

______ The presenting problem (the reason the client is seeking counseling)
______ The client's style of coping with demands, stresses, and conflicts
______ Early experiences as a child, particularly in relation to parents and siblings
______ Ego strength
______ Functional strengths and weaknesses
______ Developmental history
______ The client's struggle with current choices
______ The client's cultural background
______ Goals and agenda for counseling
______ Current support system
______ Motivation to change
______ Level of reality testing

Now examine how you ranked these items. What theoretical approach would your rankings seem to indicate? You might consider how open you are to challenging your theoretical stance and how this openness or lack of it might influence therapeutic outcomes for your clients. Think about how your theoretical viewpoint influences your decisions on questions such as these: What are your goals for counseling? What techniques and interventions would you use to reach your goals? What value do you place on evidence-based treatment techniques? What is the proper place of diagnosis and testing in the counseling process? How do you make provisions for cultural diversity in your assessment and treatment plans? How flexible are you in your approach? Does research have a place in your counseling practice? What connections do you see between theory, practice, and research?

Developing a Counseling Style

Developing a counseling style is more complicated than merely accepting the tenets of a given theory. We believe the theoretical approach you use to guide your practice is an expression of you as a person and springs from your life experience. Further, because a theory of counseling is often an expression of the personality of the theorist and of the therapist, a theoretical approach becomes more useful and meaningful once you have taken a critical look at the theorist who developed it and why it appeals to you. Uncritically following any single theory can lead you to ignore some of the insights that your life and your work open up to you. This is our bias, of course, and many would contend that providing effective therapy depends on following a given theory. Ultimately your counseling orientation and style must be appropriate for the type of counseling you do and the unique needs of your clients.

Theories of counseling are based on worldviews, each with its own values, biases, and assumptions of how best to bring about change in the therapeutic process (Ivey et al., 2002). As we discussed in Chapter 4, contemporary theories of therapeutic practice are grounded in assumptions that are part of Western culture, and they emphasize choice, the uniqueness of the individual, self-assertion, and ego strength. Many of these assumptions are inappropriate for evaluating clients from non-Western cultures that focus on interdependence, downplay individuality, and emphasize being in harmony with the universe. From an Asian perspective, for example, basic life values are associated with a focus on inner experience and an acceptance of one's environment.

Whereas the Western therapeutic approaches are oriented toward individual change, non-Western approaches focus more on the social framework than on development of the individual. The Western model of therapy has limitations when it is applied to many ethnic and cultural groups, such as Asian Americans, Latinos, Native Americans, and African Americans. It is not customary for many client populations to seek professional help, and they will typically turn first to informal systems such as family, friends, and the community.

Sue, Ivey, and Pedersen (1996) believe we need to develop a theory that enables us to work with various cultures. In addition to dealing with the feeling, thinking, and behaving dimensions familiar to Western theorists, a multicultural approach emphasizes the social and cultural context of human existence. This approach takes into account that we are all biological, spiritual, and political beings as well.

When developing or evaluating a theory, a major consideration is the degree to which that perspective helps you understand and organize what you are doing with clients. Does your framework provide a broad base for working with diverse clients in different ways, or does it restrict your vision and cause you to ignore variables that do not fit the theory? Does your theory allow for cultural differences? To what degree are you flexible? If you hold steadfastly to one theory, you might expect your clients to conform to your expectations. It is important, therefore, to evaluate what you are emphasizing in your counseling work. The following questions may help you make this evaluation:

- How did you acquire your theory? Did you incorporate many of the views of your instructors or training supervisors?
- Does your theory evolve and change as you gain clinical experience with a variety of clients?
- What does your approach stress, and why does it appeal to you?
- Does your theory make room for cultural factors? Can you apply your theory to a wide range of clients, many of whom will have different expectations in seeking help?
- Does your theory challenge you to extend your thinking, or does it merely support your assumptions?
- Do you have a responsibility to know many theories and techniques to better serve diverse clients?
- Does your theory have research to support its effectiveness?
- How do you present your theoretical model in your informed consent document?
- In what ways have your life experiences caused you to modify your theoretical viewpoint?

Your assumptions about the nature of counseling and the nature of people have a direct impact on your manner of practice. The goals that you think are important in therapy, the techniques and methods you employ to reach these goals, the way in which you see the division of responsibility in the client-therapist relationship, your view of your role and functions as a counselor, and your view of the place of assessment and diagnosis in the therapeutic process are all largely determined by your theoretical orientation.

Practicing counseling without an explicit theoretical rationale is somewhat like flying a plane without a map and missing crucial instruments. A theoretical orientation is not a rigid structure that prescribes specific steps of what to do in a counseling situation; rather, it is a set of general guidelines that counselors can use to make sense of what they are hearing and what needs to change.

The Division of Responsibility in Therapy

Beginning mental health practitioners may take upon themselves too much responsibility for client outcomes. They may blame themselves for not knowing enough, not having the necessary skill and experience, or not being sensitive enough. They may transmit their performance anxiety to their clients. Overly anxious counselors frequently fail to include clients in the process and outcome of their own therapy.

The question of responsibility is an integral part of the initial sessions and includes involving clients in thinking about their part in their own therapy. One way to clarify the shared responsibility in a therapeutic relationship is by a **contract,** which is based on a negotiation between the client and the therapist to define the therapeutic relationship. A contract (which can be an extension of the informed consent process discussed in Chapter 5) tends to encourage the client and the therapist to specify the goals of the therapy and the methods likely to be employed in obtaining these goals. For certain populations, such as children, legal and ethical considerations need to be taken into account in designing the contract and the treatment plan.

Therapists who work within a managed care context need to discuss with clients how being involved with managed care will influence the division of responsibility among the HMO, the client, and the therapist. The HMO or PPO provider may determine what kinds of problems are acceptable for treatment, how long treatment will last, the number of sessions, and the focus of the work. Under this system, practitioners must be accountable to the managed care company by demonstrating that specific objectives have been met.

From our own perspective, therapy is a collaborative venture of the client and the therapist. Both have serious responsibilities for the direction of therapy, and this needs to be clarified during the initial stages of counseling. Most probably the therapist has the greater responsibility in the initial phase of therapy, especially in exploring the presenting problem and designing the treatment plan. In essence, the therapist has the responsibility to create the environment that allows change to take place. However, as therapy progresses, the responsibility shifts more to the client. Counselors who typically decide what to discuss and are overdirective run the risk of perpetuating their clients' dependence. Clients are to be encouraged to assume as much responsibility as they can. Action-oriented therapies, such as the cognitive-behavioral approaches, emphasize client-initiated contracts and homework assignments as ways in which clients can fulfill their commitment to change. These devices help to keep the focus of responsibility on clients by challenging them to decide what they want from therapy and what they are willing to do to get what they want. It also keeps the therapist more active in the process.

As you consider the range of viewpoints on the division of responsibility in therapy, think about your own position on this issue. Has your position changed over time? If so, in what ways and why?

Deciding on the Goals of Counseling

Therapy without a goal is unlikely to be effective, yet practitioners often fail to devote enough time to thinking about the goals they have for their clients and the goals clients have for themselves. In this section we discuss possible aims of therapy, how goals are determined, and who should determine them. Clinicians' answers to these questions are directly related to their theoretical orientations.

When considering therapeutic goals, it is important to keep in mind the cultural determinants of therapy. The aims of therapy are specific to a particular culture's definition of psychological health. In describing their theory of multicultural counseling and therapy, Sue, Ivey, and Pedersen (1996) develop a number of propositions that underlie their metatheory. Two of these assumptions have particular relevance for the topic of therapeutic goals. Sue and his colleagues claim that multicultural counseling is more effective when counselors use modalities and define goals that are consistent with the life experiences and cultural values of the client. They stress that no single approach is equally effective in working with all client populations. The ultimate goal of training practitioners to be multiculturally competent, regardless of their theoretical orientation, is to expand the range of therapeutic strategies they can apply to culturally diverse client groups. A second proposition of their multicultural theory pertains to its basic goal, which is the liberation of consciousness. This approach goes beyond the limitations of the traditional goals of Western psychotherapy and emphasizes the family, group, and cultural aspects of counseling. Ultimately, this theory considers the person-in-relation and the cultural context as essential aspects in developing appropriate goals for the helping process. This topic was addressed in Chapter 4.

In most therapeutic approaches, effective counseling does not result when the clinician imposes goals; however, some practitioners may believe they know what is best for their clients and persuade their clients to accept their goals. Others are convinced that the specific aims of counseling ought to be determined entirely by their clients. Who sets the goals of counseling is best understood in light of the theory you operate from, the type of counseling you offer, the setting in which you work, and the nature of your clientele. Your theoretical orientation influences general goals, such as insight versus behavior change. If you are not clear about your general goals, your techniques may be random and arbitrary.

Other factors can also affect the determination of goals. For example, if you work with clients in a managed care system, the goals will need to be highly specific, limited to reduction of problematic symptoms, and often aimed at teaching coping skills. When you work in crisis intervention, your goals are likely to be short term and functional, and you may be much more directive. Working with children in a school, you may combine educational and therapeutic goals. As a counselor to the elderly in an institution, you may stress coping skills and ways of relating to others in this environment. What your goals are and how actively you involve your client in determining them will depend to a great extent on the type of counseling you provide and the type of client you see.

✓ **The Case of Leon.** Leon, a 45-year-old aeronautical engineer who is married and has three children, has been laid off after 20 years of employment with the same company. He shows signs of depression, has lost weight, and was referred to you by his primary physician. He has had no previous history of depression, but his father committed suicide at age 50. Leon is not close to his mother or siblings and describes his marriage as lackluster at best. He expresses, without much affect, feelings of abandonment at being terminated after so many years of dedicated service. How would you assess and work with Leon if he were your client? Consider these questions:

- Would Leon's age, ethnicity, and culture be significant factors for you to consider in developing a treatment plan?
- What specific goals would you have in mind as you develop a treatment plan for Leon?
- Would your approach call for a suicide assessment? Why or why not?
- How do you see Leon's support system, and how significant would that be in setting goals?
- To what degree would you involve Leon in creating goals?
- Would you consider Leon's unemployment a significant factor in this case? Would your goals include dealing with that reality?
- How would you assess the outcomes of your work with Leon? What would need to change for you to deem your work with Leon successful? In what ways might you involve Leon in assessing outcomes?

The Use of Techniques in Counseling

Your use of techniques in counseling is closely related to your theoretical model. What techniques, procedures, or intervention methods would you use, and when and why would you use them? Out of anxiety, counselors may try technique after technique in an indiscriminate fashion. Practitioners should have a rationale for using a particular method of intervention and need to have training in the proper use of that technique.

Lambert and Cattani-Thompson (1996) reviewed studies on counseling effectiveness and found little evidence of specific efficacy for particular techniques or counseling theories. However, a number of significant implications for counseling practice did come to light. For example, some specific techniques appear to be more effective with particular symptoms and disorders, especially for certain behavioral disorders. However, Lambert and Cattani-Thompson assert that successful client outcome is largely determined by client characteristics, such as motivation, severity of symptoms, and acceptance of personal responsibility for change. Other predictors of successful outcomes of counseling involve client-therapist relationship factors. Practitioners would do well to pay attention to the way they interact with clients and the manner in which they participate in the therapy, providing high levels of empathy, respect, and collaboration. It appears that the techniques counselors employ, although important, are less crucial to therapy outcomes than are the interpersonal factors operating in the client-counselor relationship.

The purpose of techniques is to facilitate movement in a counseling session, and your techniques really cannot be separated from your personality and your relationship with your client. When practitioners fall into a pattern of mechanically employing techniques, they are not responding to the particular individuals they are counseling. To avoid this pitfall, it is useful to pay attention to the ways you use techniques. You may try a technique you have observed someone else using very skillfully only to find that it does not work well for you. In essence, your techniques need to fit your therapeutic style and your level of training, and they should be tailored to the specific needs of your client. When working with culturally diverse client populations, it is clinically and ethically imperative that you use interventions that are consistent with the values of your client. It is best to adapt your techniques to the needs of your clients rather than to expect your clients to fit your techniques.

Evidence-Based Therapy Practice

Mental health practitioners are frequently challenged with making decisions about what they believe to be the best therapeutic approach or interventions with a particular client. For many therapists this choice is made on the basis of their theoretical orientation. In recent years, however, a shift has occurred toward promoting the use of specific interventions for specific problems or diagnoses based on empirically supported treatments (Cukrowicz et al., 2005; Deegear & Lawson, 2003). Increasingly, clinicians who practice in a behavioral health care system are encountering the concept of **evidence-based practice** (McCabe, 2004). Evidence-based practice (EBP), also called empirically supported treatments (EST), implies that clinicians are accountable to their clients and need to have up-to-date information on what treatments have been demonstrated to work (Edwards, Dattilio, & Bromley, 2004). The managed health care system is a driving force in promoting empirically supported treatments (Deegear & Lawson, 2003). This trend influences psychotherapeutic practice today and may mandate the types of treatments therapists can offer in the future (Wampold & Bhati, 2004). The results of a study conducted by Cukrowicz and her colleagues (2005) lends support to a growing literature indicating that ESTs demonstrate better treatment outcomes than do non-ESTs. In this study, "patients who received ESTs not only got better than those who did not but they also got better with comparatively less therapeutic contact" (p. 335). Results of this study support the idea that "clinicians are well advised to use ESTs as a frontline treatment for their patients in order to remain consistent with ethical practice" (p. 336).

Basing one's psychotherapeutic practices on interventions that have been empirically validated may seem to be the ethical path to take, but business considerations do enter into this picture. Edwards and his colleagues (2004) point out that psychological assessment and treatment is a business involving financial gain and reputation. In seeking to specify the treatment for a specific diagnosis as precisely as possible, health insurance companies are concerned with determining the minimum amount of treatment that can be expected to be effective. There is a pressure for ESTs to be both short and standardized. Treatments are operationalized by reliance on a treatment manual that identifies what is to be done in each therapy session and how many sessions will be required (Edwards et al., 2004).

Some practitioners believe that this approach is mechanistic and does not take into full consideration the relational dimensions of the psychotherapy process. Indeed, relying exclusively on standardized treatments for specific problems may raise another set of ethical issues. One of these issues is the reliability and validity of these empirically based techniques. Human change is complex and difficult to measure unless researchers operationalize the notion of change at such a simplistic level that the change may be meaningless. In addition to the ethical consideration of therapist accountability, we consider other ethical issues involved in mental health managed care later in this chapter.

Assessment and Diagnosis as Professional Issues

Assessment and diagnosis are integrally related to the practice of counseling and psychotherapy. All clinicians, no matter what their theoretical orientation, engage in some form of assessment, which is generally an ongoing part of the therapeutic process. This assessment is subject to revision as the clinician gathers further data during the therapy sessions. Some practitioners consider assessment as a part of the process that leads to a formal diagnosis, both of which they view as essential for treatment planning.

Assessment consists of evaluating the relevant factors in a client's life to identify themes for further exploration in the counseling process. **Diagnosis,** which is sometimes part of the assessment process, consists of identifying a specific mental disorder based on a pattern of symptoms that leads to a specific diagnosis found in the *Diagnostic and Statistical Manual of Mental Disorders* (American Psychiatric Association, 2000), the official guide to a system of classifying psychological disorders and generally referred to as the **DSM-IV-TR.** Both assessment and diagnosis can be understood as providing direction for the treatment process.

Psychodiagnosis (or **psychological diagnosis**) is a general term covering the process of identifying an emotional or behavioral problem and making a statement about the current status of a client. Psychodiagnosis might also include identifying a syndrome that conforms to a diagnostic system such as the DSM-IV-TR. This process involves identifying possible causes of the person's emotional, cognitive, physiological, and behavioral difficulties, leading to some kind of treatment plan designed to ameliorate the identified problem.

Differential diagnosis is the process of distinguishing one form of mental disorder from another by determining which of two (or more) disorders with similar symptoms the person is suffering from. The DSM-IV-TR is the standard reference for distinguishing one form of mental disorder from another; it provides specific criteria for classifying emotional and behavioral disturbances and shows the differences among the various disorders. In addition to describing cognitive, affective, and personality disorders, this revised edition also deals with a variety of other disorders pertaining to developmental stages, substance abuse, moods, sexual and gender identity, eating, sleep, impulse control, and adjustment. The DSM-IV-TR is the most widely used system for identifying, classifying, and describing mental disorders in the world (Wylie, 1995).

Some dispute that diagnosis should be part of the psychotherapeutic process; others see diagnosis as an essential step leading to a treatment plan. Still others view it as an inappropriate application of the medical model of mental health to counseling and therapy (Sleek, 1996). Those who oppose a diagnostic model claim that the DSM labels and stigmatizes people. However, those who designed the DSM assert that it classifies mental disorders, not people (Wylie, 1995).

Theoretical Perspectives on Assessment and Diagnosis

Depending on the theory from which you operate, a diagnostic framework may occupy a key role or a minimal role in your therapeutic practice. Practitioners using a cognitive-behavioral approach and the medical model may place heavy emphasis on the role of assessment as a prelude to the treatment process. The rationale is that specific therapy goals cannot be designed until a clear picture emerges of the client's past and present functioning. Many practitioners whose practices are based on the relationship-oriented approaches tend to view the process of assessment and diagnosis as external to the immediacy of the client-counselor relationship, a process that can remove the therapist from understanding the subjective world of the client. The developmental counseling and therapy model (DCT) is based on the assumption that greater attention needs to be paid to environmental and contextual issues. This approach is grounded on the premise that the individual develops within a family in a community and cultural context (Ivey & Ivey, 1998; Ivey et al., 2005). Regardless of the particular theory espoused by a therapist, both clinical and ethical issues are associated with the use of assessment procedures and diagnosis as part of a treatment plan.

Let's review some of the contemporary theoretical models of counseling and psychotherapy. Our discussion is based on an adaptation of material in *Case Approach to Counseling and Psychotherapy* (Corey, 2005a). We want to emphasize that practitioners within the same theoretical model often differ with respect to the degree to which they employ a diagnostic framework in their clinical practices. Here we give a summary of the way each model addresses assessment and diagnosis.

Psychoanalytic Therapy. Among psychoanalytically oriented therapists, some, though certainly not all, favor psychodiagnosis. This is partly due to the fact that for a long time in the United States, psychoanalytic practice was largely limited to persons trained in medicine. Some of these psychodynamically oriented therapists (Gabbard, 2000) note that in its effort to be theory neutral, the DSM-IV-TR unfortunately eliminated very useful terminology linked to a psychoanalytic perspective.

Adlerian Therapy. Assessment is a basic part of Adlerian therapy. The initial session focuses on developing a relationship based on a deeper understanding of the individual's presenting problem. A comprehensive assessment involves examining the client's lifestyle. The therapist seeks to ascertain the faulty, self-defeating beliefs and assumptions about self, others, and life that maintain the problematic behavioral patterns the client brings to therapy.

Existential Therapy. The main purpose of existential clinical assessment is to understand the personal meanings and assumptions clients use in structuring their existence. This approach is different from the traditional diagnostic framework, for it focuses on understanding the client's inner world, not on understanding the individual from an external perspective.

Person-Centered Therapy. Like existential therapists, person-centered practitioners maintain that the best vantage point for understanding another person is through his or her subjective world. They believe that traditional assessment and diagnosis are detrimental because they are external ways of understanding the client.

Gestalt Therapy. Many Gestalt therapists gather certain types of information about their clients' perceptions to supplement the assessment and diagnostic work done in the present moment. Gestalt therapists attend to interruptions in the client's contacting functions, and the result is a "functional diagnosis" of how individuals experience satisfaction or blocks in their relationship with the environment.

Behavior Therapy. The behavioral approach begins with a comprehensive assessment of the client's present functioning, with questions directed to past learning that is related to current behavior. Practitioners with a behavioristic orientation generally favor a diagnostic stance, valuing observation and other objective means of appraising both a client's specific symptoms and the factors that have led up to the client's malfunctioning. Such an appraisal, they argue, enables them to use the techniques that are appropriate for a particular disorder and to evaluate the effectiveness of the treatment program.

Cognitive-Behavioral Approaches. The assessment used in cognitive-behavioral therapy is based on getting a sense of the client's pattern of thinking. Once self-defeating beliefs have been identified, the treatment process involves challenging specific thought patterns and substituting constructive ones.

Reality Therapy. Reality therapists do not make use of psychological testing and traditional diagnosis. Instead, through the use of skillful questioning, the therapist helps clients make an assessment of their current behavior. This informal assessment encourages clients to focus on what they want from life and to determine whether what they are doing is working for them.

Feminist Therapy. Feminist therapists criticize the current classification system, claiming it emphasizes the individual's symptoms and ignores the social factors that cause dysfunctional behavior. The feminist assessment process emphasizes the cultural context of clients' problems, especially the degree to which clients possess power or are oppressed. They contend that as traditionally practiced, diagnostic systems such as the DSM-IV-TR reflect the dominant culture's definitions of psychology and health. Misdiagnosis and blaming the victim may occur when sociopolitical factors are minimized or ignored. Feminist assessment and diagnosis requires a cooperative and phenomenological approach.

Postmodern Approaches. Solution-focused brief therapy and narrative therapy are two examples of postmodern therapies that do not emphasize formal diagnosis or categorization of individuals. Postmodern approaches do not highlight a client's deficits, problems, failures, and what is wrong with people. Instead, emphasis is placed on an individual's competencies, accomplishments, skills, strengths, and successes. The therapist's assessment and provisional diagnosis are generally arrived at by collaborative conversations with a client.

Systemic Therapies. In most systemic approaches both therapist and client are involved in the assessment process. Some systemic therapists assist clients in tracing the key events of their family history and identifying issues in their family of origin. As a part of the assessment process, individuals may be asked to identify what they learned from interacting with their parents, from observing their parents' interactions with each other, and from observing how each parent interacted with each sibling.

DSM-IV-TR Assessments

Although you may not yet have had to face the practical question of whether to diagnose a client, you will probably need to come to terms with this issue at some point in your work. Regardless of your theoretical orientation, you will most likely be expected to work within the framework of the DSM-IV-TR if you are practicing in a community mental health agency. Because you will need to think within the framework of assessing and diagnosing clients, it is essential that you become familiar with the diagnostic categories and the structure of the DSM-IV-TR.

The DSM-IV-TR is based on a system that involves assessment on several axes, each of which refers to a different domain of information that could be useful for clinicians in planning treatment. The use of the multiaxial system facilitates systematic evaluation with attention to the various forms of mental disorders and general medical conditions, psychosocial and environmental problems, and level of functioning that could possibly be missed if the focus were on assessing a single presenting problem. This comprehensive approach offers a format for organizing and communicating clinical data, for understanding the complexity of clinical situations, and for describing variations among individuals with the same diagnosis (American Psychiatric Association, 2000).

Let us briefly review some of the arguments for and against the use of diagnosis in therapy. Then you can consider how valuable diagnosis is from your point of view.

Arguments for Psychodiagnosis

Practitioners who favor the use of diagnostic procedures argue that such procedures enable the therapist to identify a particular emotional or behavioral disorder, which helps design an appropriate treatment plan. Like putting together a jigsaw puzzle, diagnosis involves piecing together bits of information to build an overall picture of the individual (Sleek, 1996). This approach stems from the medical model of mental health, according to which different underlying causal factors, some of which are biological, produce different types of disorders.

Proponents of traditional diagnosis often make the following points:

- Therapists have a legal, professional, and ethical obligation to assess whether clients may pose a danger to themselves or to others. They also need to screen for disorders that might respond best to a combination of medication and psychotherapy. Diagnosis may alert them to the need for a referral to a physician or a psychiatrist for a medical diagnosis.
- Diagnosis can alert therapists to the existence of a possible neuropsychological problem requiring further neuropsychological assessment.
- To function effectively in most mental health agencies, practitioners must be skilled in understanding and utilizing diagnostic procedures.
- In working with a professional team, diagnosis is essential so that all team members have a common language and a common frame of reference. In other words, diagnosis provides a method of shorthand communication among practitioners.
- Since the DSM-IV was written to be theory neutral, a diagnosis may be helpful to the therapist who wants to consult with other therapists about a given client.
- It may be difficult to formulate a meaningful treatment plan without clearly defining the specific problems that need to be addressed. Diagnosis points the way to possible treatment strategies for specific disorders.
- Diagnosis can provide information about possible causal factors associated with different types of mental disorders.
- There is no insurance reimbursement without an acceptable diagnosis.
- Diagnosis can provide a framework for research into various treatment approaches.

In his article on ethical concerns about diagnosis, Hamann (1994) contends that clinicians in both public and private mental health agencies have the responsibility for diagnosing. Practitioners who work in an agency setting have the initial contact with most clients. They are expected to take a history as part of the intake session to arrive at a diagnosis. Such clinicians often have a caseload of at least 100 clients, and they are expected to define the client's problem and develop a treatment plan to alleviate the problem—typically in one session. From Hamann's perspective, graduate programs involved in training therapists need to teach diagnosis. Because mental health agencies assume that those they employ will be proficient in diagnosis, training programs have a responsibility to see that students acquire competence in understanding a diagnostic framework.

Those who support traditional forms of diagnosis agree that present classification systems have limitations and that some of the problems mentioned by the critics of diagnosis do exist. Rather than abandoning diagnostic classifications altogether, however, they favor updating diagnostic manuals to reflect improvements in diagnosis and treatment procedures.

Although you may not find traditional diagnosis (DSM-IV-TR) necessary or useful in your practice, it is important to know enough about diagnosis to refer a client. For example, once you have made a diagnosis of a client who is chronically depressed with possible suicidal tendencies, you are in a position to make an appropriate referral if you do not have the competence to deal with this problem yourself. Or you can work cooperatively with a physician when your screening indicates an assessment for medication.

Arguments Against Psychodiagnosis

Other professionals see diagnosis as unnecessary or harmful. Carl Rogers (1961) consistently maintained that diagnosis was detrimental to counseling because it tended to pull clients away from an internal and subjective way of experiencing themselves and to foster an objective and external conception of themselves. The result was an increased tendency toward dependence, with clients acting as if the responsibility for changing their behavior rested with the expert and not with themselves.

It is essential to consider cultural factors in both the assessment process and in formulating a diagnosis. If clinicians fail to consider ethnic and cultural factors in certain patterns of behavior, a client may be subjected to an erroneous assessment and diagnosis. Due to the methods used to identify meaning in diagnosis, the cultural and gender aspects of the presenting problem frequently are not considered (Sinacore-Guinn, 1995), and certain behaviors and personality styles may be labeled neurotic or deviant simply because they are not characteristic of the dominant culture. Being adept at psychodiagnosis requires cultural sensitivity; without it the value of your diagnoses will be limited.

Kress, Eriksen, Rayle, and Ford (2005) indicate that some literature and research on cross-cultural assessment and diagnosis reveals the inaccuracy of the DSM system with underrepresented groups. Some literature shows the tendency of some practitioners to overdiagnose, underdiagnose, and misdiagnose clients from marginalized groups. Kress et al. write that "counselors need to carefully consider all aspects of clients' culture in conjunction with clients' past and present life circumstances to avoid misdiagnosis or the use of unnecessary diagnoses" (p. 103).

Ivey and Ivey (1998) propose reframing DSM-IV-TR by paying special attention to the interface of multicultural issues, origin of problems, and treatment. The Iveys suggest that diagnostic systems need more balance and that attention must be focused on the reality of human experience. In their developmental counseling and therapy model, psychological distress is viewed as the result of biological and developmental factors. Although the stressor may be located within the individual, this model calls for inclusion of the broader systemic and cultural contexts as a basis for meaningful assessment. For example, the distress of depression is generally the result of the interaction of the biologically vulnerable person in a social and cultural environment. One such environmental factor is social discrimination. From the developmental perspective, the inclusion of culture-related issues such as race, ethnicity, gender, sexual orientation, and spirituality is essential for accurate assessment and diagnosis. Ivey and Ivey argue that "a diagnosis that is not culture-centered with awareness of multiple contextual issues is incomplete at best and potentially dangerous and misleading" (p. 336).

Therapists who argue against diagnosis make these observations:

- Diagnosis is typically done by an expert observing a person's behavior and experience from an external viewpoint, without reference to what they mean to the client.
- Diagnostic categories can minimize the uniqueness of the client. When clients are categorized, it can lead to imposing labels on them in such a way as to not see their complexity or individuality. Using labels in this way tends to limit vision rather than enhancing understanding of the individual.
- Reducing people to the sum of their symptoms ignores natural capacities for self-healing.
- Because the emphasis of the DSM-IV-TR is on pathology, deficits, limitations, problems, and symptoms, individuals are not encouraged to find and utilize their strengths, competencies, and abilities.
- Diagnosis can lead people to accept self-fulfilling prophecies or to despair over their condition.
- Diagnosis can narrow therapists' vision by encouraging them to look for behavior that fits a certain disease category.
- DSM-IV-TR diagnoses are based on the assumption that distress in a family or social context is the result of individual pathology, whereas a systemic approach views the source of the distress as being within the entire system.
- Although DSM-IV-TR makes some reference to ethnic, cultural, environmental, and class factors in understanding and interpreting dysfunctional behavior, it deals largely with culture-bound syndromes and does not adequately take into account culture, age, gender, and other ways of viewing health and sickness.
- The best vantage point for understanding another person is through his or her subjective world, not through a general system of classification.
- Some disorders, especially those associated with children, depend on adults in homes and schools to give subjective reports that are often self-serving in terms of trying to control the child or to protect themselves.

Some theorists and practitioners favor assessment but argue against the necessity for making DSM-IV-TR diagnoses. Lazarus (2005) is one of these individuals. He takes the position that a comprehensive assessment is essential to treatment, but he finds little value in most DSM-IV-TR psychiatric labels. The core of Lazarus's multimodal therapy approach is conceptualized in terms of the acronym BASIC I. D., which specifies the seven modalities that provide a foundation for designing a treatment plan—behavior, affect, sensation, imagery, cognition, interpersonal relationships, and drugs/biological factors. Lazarus contends that by examining the salient problems across these seven domains of human functioning, the clinician is likely to be far more helpful than those who neglect one or more of these dimensions. Although Lazarus assesses the issues that need to be addressed, he emphasizes specific and interrelated problems. For example, even when one of the problems is bipolar depression, this is noted along with other impediments and treated according to empirically supported data when feasible. What governs Lazarus's therapy is not the label but the specific problems that call for remediation, correction, or elimination (Arnold Lazarus, personal communication, November 16, 2003).

Beutler and Malik (2002) claim that a growing number of mental health professionals question the lack of strong a empirical foundation in the DSM-IV-TR categories. For a more detailed discussion of perspectives that move away from conventional thinking and propose modifications and alternatives, see Beutler and Malik's *Rethinking the DSM*.

Our Position on Assessment and Psychodiagnosis

Both assessment and diagnosis, broadly construed, are legitimate parts of the therapeutic process. The kind of diagnosis we have in mind is the result of a collaborative effort by the client and the therapist, also referred to as co-diagnosis. Both should be involved in discovering the nature of the client's difficulty, a process that commences with the initial sessions and continues until therapy is terminated. Even practitioners who oppose conventional diagnostic procedures and terminology unavoidably make an assessment of clients based on questions such as these:

- What brought the client into therapy?
- What are the client's resources for change?
- What are the client's strengths and vulnerabilities?
- What does the client want from therapy, and how can it best be achieved?
- What should be the focus of the sessions?
- What factors are contributing to the client's problems, and what can be done to alleviate them?
- In what ways can an understanding of the client's cultural background shed light on developing a plan to deal with the problems?
- What role does the client's spirituality play in assessing and treating the problem?
- What specific family dynamics might be relevant to the client's present struggles and interpersonal relationships?
- What kind of support system does the client have?
- What are the prospects for meaningful change?

From our perspective, assessment and diagnosis (either formal or informal) helps the practitioner conceptualize a case and implement treatment. The clinician and the client can discuss key questions as part of the therapeutic process.

Clinicians will develop hypotheses about their clients, and they can talk about these conjectures with them. Diagnosis does not have to be a matter of categorizing clients; rather, practitioners can think more broadly, describe behavior, and think about its meaning. In this way, diagnosis becomes a process of thinking *about* the client *with* the client. Diagnosis can be viewed as a general descriptive statement identifying a client's style of functioning. The therapist can develop hunches about a client's behavioral style and perhaps even share these observations with the client as a part of the therapeutic process.

We favor a collaborative approach to assessment, one that includes the client as a therapeutic partner. After the initial assessment of the client is completed, a decision can be made whether to refer the individual for alternative or additional treatment. If the client is accepted by the therapist, the two can discuss the assessment results. This information can be used in exploring the client's difficulties and in selecting treatment goals. Assessment and diagnosis can be linked directly to the therapeutic process, forming a basis for developing methods of evaluating how well the therapist's procedures are working to achieve the client's goals.

Using DSM-IV-TR nomenclature is a reality that most practitioners must accept, especially if they work within a managed care system. For therapists who are required to work with a diagnostic framework, the challenge is to use diagnosis as a means to the end of providing quality service to clients rather than as an end in itself that leads to a justification for treatment. As one clinician put this struggle: "It's hard *not* to think in terms of DSM when I have to use it every day for managed care. The language seeps into my brain, into the way I look at clients, even when I know better" (Wylie, 1995, p. 68).

Clarifying Your Position. What is your position on diagnosis? The following questions may help you clarify your thinking on this issue:

- After reviewing the arguments for and against psychodiagnosis, what position are you inclined to support? Why?
- Some contend that clients have a right to know their diagnoses as part of informed consent. What do you think of this practice?
- If you do not tell the client the diagnosis, how do you explain that omission from your informed consent?
- Some maintain that clients should not be told their diagnoses because of the possibility of their living up to a self-fulfilling prophecy. What is your thinking on this matter?
- If you were working for an agency that relied on managed care programs, how would you deal with the requirement of quickly formulating a diagnosis and a treatment plan? How would you work with the limitations of being able to see clients for no more than six visits?
- Some writers have taken the position that practitioners should take a stand against classification and coding for the purpose of third-party payments unless clients know of their diagnoses and agree to provide this information to insurance companies. Do you see an ethical issue in this practice?

- Do you agree or disagree that therapists who do not accept the medical model, yet who provide diagnoses for reasons of third-party payments, are compromising their integrity? Are they acting ethically?
- What ethical and professional issues can you raise pertaining to diagnosis? In your view, what is the most critical issue?

Ethical and Legal Issues in Diagnosis

Ethical dilemmas are often created when diagnosis is done strictly for insurance purposes, which often entails arbitrarily assigning a client to a diagnostic classification, sometimes merely to qualify for third-party payment. Many insurance carriers will not pay for treatment that is not defined as an "illness" for which treatment is medically necessary. Wylie (1995) gives the example of the V-codes, a grab bag of diagnostic leftovers at the back of the DSM-IV-TR that rarely qualify for reimbursement. If a therapist treats a couple for marital difficulties and submits a claim with a V-code diagnosis, chances are that the claim will be rejected. Some therapists may agree to see a couple or a family but submit a claim for an individual as the "identified patient," using an acceptable DSM diagnosis. According to Wylie, not only is this practice technically unethical and inaccurate but it may also be illegal.

Hamann (1994) stresses that under no circumstances should clinicians compromise themselves regarding the accuracy of a diagnosis to make it "fit" criteria accepted by an insurance company. This behavior is not only unethical but is also fraudulent. Some practitioners who are opposed to a diagnostic framework take the path of least resistance and give every client the same diagnosis. A related matter is the fact that many insurance companies pay only for psychological services that have been approved under an acceptable diagnosis. Presumably, clients who consult therapists regarding problems that do not fit a standard category will not be reimbursed for their psychotherapy.

With some managed care mental health companies, a therapist may call the company with a diagnosis. A technician then looks up "appropriate" treatment strategies to deal with the identified problem (if, indeed, the diagnosis even meets the criteria for reimbursement). This raises significant ethical issues as important treatment decisions may be made by a nonprofessional who has never seen the client.

Practitioners who submit claims to managed care companies must often wrestle with practical demands versus ethical decision making. If a therapist submits an accurate diagnosis, but one not classified as an illness in the DSM-IV-TR, there will be no reimbursement. However, if the diagnosis is selected mainly on the basis that it is one the company will accept, the therapist might be guilty of deceptive practice. "Therapists are forever trying to fit their diagnosis to the procrustean bed of official DSM terminology and managed care's interpretation of it" (Wylie, 1995, p. 32). It is worth mentioning that professionals who participate in a managed care program are doing so by choice, and thus they also agree to the contracts of the managed care company.

Competence is another central ethical issue in making assessments. Some practitioners do not possess the competence to use DSM diagnosis appropriately.

If therapists do not understand how to work within some kind of diagnostic and assessment framework, and if they do not have a clear picture of the client's problem, it is possible that they will not help the client. We also think it is an ethical (and sometimes legal) obligation of therapists to be mindful that a medical evaluation is many times indicated. This is especially true in dealing with problems such as dementia, schizophrenia, manic-depression, and depression with suicidal ideation. Students need to learn the clinical skills necessary to do this type of screening and referral, which is a form of diagnostic thinking.

Practitioners may cause harm to clients if they treat them in restrictive ways because they have diagnosed them on the basis of a pattern of symptoms. Therapists can actually behave toward clients in ways that make it very difficult for clients to change. Furthermore, it is essential that practitioners who use the DSM-IV-TR be trained in its use. This training requires learning more than diagnostic categories; it involves knowing personality theory, psychopathology, and seeing how they relate to therapeutic practice. Now let us look at two specific cases where diagnosis and treatment options had to be evaluated.

✓ **The Case of Irma.** Irma has just accepted her first position as a counselor in a community agency that is part of a managed care system. An agency policy requires her to conduct an intake interview with each client, determine a diagnosis, and establish a treatment plan—all in the first session. Once a diagnosis is established, clinicians have a maximum of five more sessions with a given client. After 3 weeks, she lets a colleague know that she is troubled by this timetable. Her colleague reassures her that what she is doing is acceptable and that the agency's aim is to satisfy the requirements of the HMO. Irma does not feel reassured and cannot justify making an assessment in so short a time.

- Do you share Irma's concern? Are there ethical difficulties with this agency's policies?
- Is it justified to provide a person with a diagnosis mainly for the purpose of obtaining third-party payment? Explain.
- If Irma retains her convictions, is she ethically obliged to discontinue her employment at this agency? What other alternatives, if any, do you see for her situation?
- In the course of a client's treatment, if the original diagnosis becomes obsolete, would you continue to use that diagnosis simply because your client wishes to see you?

✓ **The Case of Bob.** Bob displays symptoms of insomnia, sadness, lethargy, and hopelessness. After 12 weeks of treatment, Felicita realizes that her client has all the symptoms of a major depression and that he is showing no improvement. She is inclined to double the number of weekly sessions to accelerate her client's progress.

- What do you think of Felicita's plan? Is it justified?
- Should she have done a more thorough assessment earlier in the treatment? Might the results have indicated alternative treatments?

- Is Felicita obligated to refer Bob for a psychiatric evaluation to determine whether antidepressant medication is indicated? Is she obliged to refer him if he so desires?
- What are her ethical obligations if he refuses to see a psychiatrist?
- Do you see any other ethical issues in this case?

Now let's turn to a case that addresses ethical and legal issues pertaining to collecting a fee for conducting an assessment.

✓ **The Case of Jamie.** Jamie's parents ask you to assess their 16-year-old son because they suspect he has a reading disability. You assess Jamie and discover that he does, indeed, have difficulties with reading comprehension when under time pressure. You spend three additional sessions giving enough other assessment instruments to rule out other problems. When you report the findings to Jamie's parents, they say they want you to write a statement about your findings to the SAT board so that Jamie will be given more time to take the test. You write a 10-page report detailing the findings from all the assessment instruments you administered along with detailed background information, yet the SAT board denies the request for more time. Jamie's father is both a physician and a lawyer. He accuses you of not having done a good enough job and refuses to pay your fees.

- How would you respond to Jamie's father's accusations and refusal to pay your fees?
- What legal and ethical actions can you take to collect your fees?
- Can you send the account to a collection agency? Why or why not?
- Are the parents or is Jamie responsible for the fees? Explain.

Commentary. If you send the name and address of the parents to a collection agency, this could be interpreted as a breach of confidentiality. In addition, the lawyer father may initiate a civil suit against you for breach of contract because the SAT board did not find your report persuasive. To avoid such unpleasant situations, we suggest providing clients with a written contract of informed consent that clearly states your fees, the requirement of payment at the time of service, and the product that will be delivered.

Cultural Issues in Diagnosis and Assessment

Cultural sensitivity is essential in making a proper diagnosis, and a range of factors need to be considered in interpreting the assessment process. See the ethics codes box titled Cultural Sensitivity in Assessment for some professional guidelines regarding culturally sensitive diagnosis.

Itai and McRae (1994) recommend caution in diagnosis as it applies to cross-cultural situations, especially when English is not the client's primary language. Some cultural differences are easily misunderstood and misdiagnosed. For example, many Japanese Americans believe that losing emotional control or crying in front of people would mean a loss of face and that one

Ethics Codes

Cultural Sensitivity in Assessment

American Counseling Association (2005)

Counselors recognize that culture affects the manner in which clients' problems are defined. Clients' socioeconomic and cultural experiences are considered when diagnosing mental disorders. (E.5.b.)

American Psychological Association (2002)

When interpreting assessment results, including automated interpretations, psychologists take into account the purpose of the assessment as well as the various test factors, test-taking abilities, and other characteristics of the person being assessed, such as situational, personal, linguistic, and cultural differences, that might affect psychologists' judgments or reduce the accuracy of their interpretations. They indicate any significant limitations of their interpretations. (9.06.)

Commission on Rehabilitation Counselor Certification (2002)

a. Proper Diagnosis. Rehabilitation counselors qualified to provide proper diagnosis of mental disorders will take special care when doing so. Assessment techniques (including personal interview) used to determine client care (e.g., locus of treatment, type of treatment, or recommendation follow-up) will be carefully selected and appropriately used. (F.4.a.)
b. Cultural Sensitivity. Disability, socioeconomic, and cultural experience of clients will be considered when diagnosing mental disorders. (F.4.b.)

should keep unpleasant thoughts private. A therapist could miss the symptom of a major depressive episode if the cultural imperative of not displaying emotion or reporting unpleasant thoughts in public were not considered. Similarly, Japanese Americans tend to consult their parents when making important decisions. Such clients could be misdiagnosed as "Dependent Personality Disorder" if the therapist did not understand the value placed on interdependence, respect, and conformity in Japanese culture.

The APA's (1993) guidelines for serving culturally diverse populations address the importance of modifying assessment and treatment approaches to meet the needs of ethnic minorities, recommending that providers of psychological services "need knowledge and skills for multicultural assessment and intervention" (p. 45), "recognize ethnicity and culture as significant parameters in understanding psychological processes" (p. 46), and "consider not only differential diagnostic issues but also the cultural beliefs and values of the client and his/her community in providing intervention" (p. 46).

DSM-IV-TR incorporates cautions such as these so that misdiagnoses are less likely with culturally diverse populations:

> Diagnostic assessment can be especially challenging when a clinician from one ethnic or cultural group uses the DSM-IV classification to evaluate an individual from a different ethnic or cultural group. A clinician who is unfamiliar with the nuances of an individual's cultural frame of reference may incorrectly judge as psychopathology those normal variations in behavior, belief, or experience

> that are particular to the individual's culture. (American Psychiatric Association, 2000, p. xxxiv)

Whenever clinicians assess clients with different ethnic or cultural backgrounds, it is important to be aware of unintentional bias and to keep an open mind to the possibility of distinctive ethnic and cultural patterns. Kress and colleagues (2005) maintain that clinicians need to strive toward culturally sensitive diagnostic practices because doing so is ethically required and integral to effectively delivering services to diverse client groups. They encourage counselors to conduct a thorough assessment of their clients' cultural realities and to acquire an understanding of the complexity of the nature of the DSM.

In addition to the medical model (DSM) of assessment, there are also comprehensive behavioral, couples, and family assessment models. DSM categories are often irrelevant when assessments done under these models indicate a critical need for treatment. However, insurers will most often deny coverage for non-DSM conditions. Clients need to be informed of the implications of using DSM labels; that is, that this information is being entered into data management systems and has the potential of limiting their future insurability (Terrence Patterson, personal communication, October 26, 2004).

Using Tests in Counseling

As is true of diagnosis and assessment, the proper use of psychological testing in counseling and therapy is the subject of some debate. Generally, those who use therapeutic approaches that emphasize an objective view of counseling are inclined to use testing procedures as tools to acquire information about clients or as resources that clients themselves can use to help them in their decision making. Therapists who employ person-centered and existential approaches tend to view testing in much the same way that they view diagnosis—as an external frame of reference that is of little use to them in counseling situations.

We think the core issue is not whether you will use tests but rather under what circumstances and for what purposes. Tests are available that measure aptitude, ability, achievement, intelligence, values and attitudes, vocational interests, or personality characteristics. Unfortunately, these tests are often misused. They may be given routinely, given without providing feedback to clients, used for the wrong purposes, or given by unqualified testers. Here are some questions that will help you think about the circumstances under which you might want to use tests for counseling purposes.

- What do you know about the tests you may use? It is important for counselors to be familiar with any tests they use and to have taken these tests themselves. They should know the purpose of each test and how it measures what it purports to measure. Sometimes mental health workers find that they are expected to give and interpret tests as a basic function of their job. If they have not had adequate training in this area, they are in an ethical bind. In-service training and continuing education programs are ways of gaining competence in using some psychological assessment devices.

- Do you follow the codes of ethics with respect to competence in working with tests? Are you able to recognize the limits of your competence to use and interpret tests?
- How much involvement should clients have in the selection of tests? Should counselors assume the responsibility, or should clients decide whether they want to take certain tests? Are you ethically required to provide informed consent when administering tests?
- Do you know why you want to use a particular test? Does your agency require that you administer certain tests? Are you giving tests because they will help you understand a client better? Do you administer tests mainly when clients request them? Whatever your reasons, you should be able to state them clearly.
- If clients request testing, do you explore their reasons? Some clients may think that a test will provide them with answers in making important decisions. Clients need to be aware that tests are merely tools that can provide useful information they can then explore in their counseling sessions. They also need to understand what the tests are designed for. These points are particularly relevant in testing culturally diverse populations.
- How do you view test results? Do you believe test scores are true indicators of what is going on with the client? A true test score is only a theoretical possibility, but the standard error of measurement provided with every test score is often overlooked. When test scores are understood as indicating a range of possibilities, they are often helpful in providing a guideline for future work.
- How do you integrate test results into the counseling sessions? In general, it is best to give test *results,* not simply test *scores.* In other words, explore with your clients the meaning the results have for them. Integrate the test results with other information about the client, such as developmental, social, and medical history. Evaluate your clients' readiness to receive and accept certain information and be sensitive to the ways in which clients respond to the information provided. The interpretation and discussion of test data should be understandable and relevant to the needs of ethnically and culturally diverse client populations (APA, 1993).
- Are you concerned about maintaining the confidentiality of test results? Results may be handled in different ways, depending on the purpose and type of each test or on the requirements of the agency where you work. Nevertheless, your clients need to feel that they can trust you and that test results will neither be used against them nor revealed to people who have no right to this information.
- Are you critical in evaluating tests? Too often mistakes are made because counselors have unquestioning faith in tests. Know the limitations of the tests you use, and keep in mind that a test can be useful and valid in one situation but inappropriate in another.

The APA (1993) guidelines for working with diverse populations caution psychologists to consider the validity of a given test and to interpret test data in the context of the cultural and linguistic characteristics of the individual being tested. Be aware of the reference population of the test, and recognize the possible limitations of such an instrument with other populations.

Clients from culturally diverse backgrounds may react to testing with suspicion if tests have been used to discriminate against them in schools and employment. To minimize such negative reactions, it is a good practice to explore a client's views and feelings about testing and to work with him or her in resolving attitudes that are likely to affect the outcome of a test.

The ACA (2005) has developed a number of specific standards governing the ethical use of tests in counseling. Clients being tested should know what the test is intended to discover, how it relates to their situation, and how the results will be used. ACA's (2005) guideline on multicultural issues/diversity in assessment reinforces the need for caution when interpreting tests:

> Counselors use with caution assessment techniques which were normed on populations other than the client. Counselors recognize the effects of age, color, culture, disability, ethnic group, gender, race, language preference, religion, spirituality, sexual orientation, and socioeconomic status on test administration and interpretation, and place test results in proper perspective with other relevant factors. (E.8.)

Many clients seek tests in the hope of finding "answers." It is important to explore why a person wants to take a battery of tests and to teach the person the values and limitations of testing. If that is done, there is less chance the tests will be undertaken in a mechanical fashion or that unwarranted importance will be attributed to the results. Perhaps the most basic ethical guideline for using tests is to keep in mind the primary purpose for which they were designed: to provide objective and descriptive measures that can be used by clients in making better decisions. Additionally, it is wise to remember that tests are tools that should be used in the service of clients, not against clients.

Counseling in a Managed Care Environment

Until the 1980s mental health services were generally purchased under a traditional **fee-for-service approach,** wherein practitioners controlled both the supply and the demand dimensions of service delivery (Cummings, 1995). Practitioners decided what clients needed, how and when to treat them, and how long therapy would last. Individual practitioners billed insurance carriers on a fee-for-service basis, and there was little incentive for practitioners to reduce costs by increasing their efficiency and effectiveness. With large numbers of health care professionals entering the marketplace, the general expectation was that fees would fall. However, the opposite has been the case, and fees have risen.

Rapidly escalating costs, especially in inpatient care, have led third-party payors to demand more effective cost and quality controls (see Acuff et al., 1999; Broskowski, 1991; Cooper & Gottlieb, 2000; Cummings, 1995; Glosoff et al., 1999; Haas & Cummings, 1991; Hering, 2000; Hersch, 1995; Karon, 1995; Miller, 1996c, 1996d; Newman & Bricklin, 1991). The solution was **managed care,** which stressed time-limited interventions, cost-effective methods, and focused on preventive rather than curative strategies. Managed care offered a plan to businesses that would reduce the costs of care (Hersch, 1995), which was easy to sell to businesses. The development of managed care was helped by the failure of mental health professionals to control rising costs of health care services.

Fees for psychological services are often exorbitant, which means that only a small number of people can afford them. On a personal note, consider the case of a student we know who wanted to enter couples therapy. She inquired about the fee schedule and was given this overview by the therapist:

> For a 90-minute session with a couple my fee is $290. I like to see the couple together for the first session to get a sense of how you interact as a couple. Then I see each partner individually for the second and third sessions. In the fourth session, I meet with you as a couple to establish your goals for therapy.

At this point the process has cost the couple $1,160, and if they are lucky, they have identified the goals for their work. This is a good example of an approach to treatment that has contributed to the rise of cost-containment systems for mental health services. As intrusive and arbitrary as managed care can be, it may well be that therapists have otherwise priced themselves out of business.

Fee-for-Service Care Versus Managed Care

Under fee-for-service care, some therapists operate from the assumption, "the longer, the better." The managed care dictum appears to be "the shorter, the better." In both systems, clients are vulnerable to the judgment of others (in the first instance the solo practitioner and in the second the HMO provider) regarding length of treatment, nature of treatment, techniques to be used, and content of treatment sessions. In the fee-for-service approach, individual practitioners determine the costs and the length of treatment without any outside review. To think that this system is not abused would be naive. However, it is equally obvious that managed care does not focus on the best interests of the client. As the managed care model stresses time-limited interventions, cost-effective methods, and a focus on preventive rather than curative strategies, this shift in values has, as Cummings (1995) points out, brought forth a fundamental redefinition of the role of the therapist. Miller (1996b) reports that one major problem with managed care is that clients receiving therapy are undertreated, which leads to underdiagnosing important conditions, dangerously restricting hospital admissions, failing to make referrals, and providing insufficient follow-up. Other writers state that mental health practitioners and managed care companies appear to be worlds apart in their respective set of work values. Mental health professionals are challenged to deal with some unique ethical issues if they work in a managed care environment. MacCluskie and Ingersoll (2001) point out one of these challenges:

> This is not to imply that managed care is unethical care; only that in the context of managed care, the motives for decision making are primarily economic. Economic parsimony does not necessarily constitute unethical behavior unless it sacrifices the sufficiency or quality of care in the process. (pp. 102–103)

Managed care is driven by economics, like any other business. Current managed care practice is characterized more by an interest in reducing costs than by quality of service. Managed care systems are primarily interested in cost containment as a route to profitability and are concerned only secondarily with consumer needs and preferences. Equally untenable are health care professionals' attitudes that the pursuit of profit has no place in the effective delivery of psychological services (Davis & Meier, 2001; Karon, 1995).

Shore (1996) states that managed care makes people powerless, depriving them of basic rights of choice, privacy, and decision making: "Managed care is simply a search on behalf of employers for the cheapest health plan—a search, by the insurer, for the least possible treatment performed by the cheapest, least-trained clinician" (p. 324). It is clear that financial considerations are driving decisions and that the costs of medical care have soared. But does managed care cure the problem or simply create a new problem? What about what is best for the client? Again, Shore is critical of managed care, stating: "Managed care favors clinicians who generate a profit and cause no trouble. Skill, training, and ethics matter less than compliance with managed care procedures" (p. 324).

In her discussion of the ethical issues in managed care, Austad (1996) points out that those who oppose managed care contend that it is inherently unethical because it gives providers a financial incentive to withhold treatment. Furthermore, the financial incentives inherent in managed care tempt both the practitioner and the payor to underserve clients in these ways:

- Deny and limit access to long-term therapy
- Narrow the clients' choice of a therapist
- Disrupt the continuity of care
- Rely on less-qualified providers to provide services
- Use less-qualified providers to review care
- Breach client confidentiality by giving reviewers too much personal information about clients
- Base practices on a business ethic instead of a professional ethic

Despite these problems, Austad is not opposed to managed care, and she makes a convincing case about the myth of long-term psychotherapy as the standard for ideal therapy.

Austad contends that long-term therapy poses real problems for the fair distribution of psychological services to those who need care. Taking the position that what is good for the individual must be tempered by the common good, Austad urges the profession to develop therapy models that provide care to the largest number who need treatment. She believes it is better to give some therapy to those who need it rather than to provide abundant therapy to only a select few. Austad argues that short-term therapy can be highly effective, that it is not inferior to long-term treatment, and that brief therapy enables more people to be served.

Of interest in the discussion of the ethics of managed care is the lack of any strong voice coming from the professional organizations. Although the codes of ethics of these organizations all have guidelines pertaining to the priority of client welfare and competent services, they are essentially silent on the ethics of certain operations of managed care companies. The question we consider to be at the core of this conflict is this: Who is taking care of the client's interests?

Critical Ethical Issues Associated With Managed Care

In a review of the literature, we identified four major areas where ethical dilemmas most commonly surface in a managed care system: (1) informed consent, (2) confidentiality, (3) abandonment, and (4) utilization review. The following discussion is based on key points from a variety of sources (Acuff et al., 1999; Cooper & Gottlieb, 2000; Davis & Meier, 2001; Glosoff et al., 1999; Haas & Cummings, 1991; Hering, 2000; Karon, 1995; MacCluskie & Ingersoll, 2001; Newman & Bricklin, 1991; Younggren, 2000).

Informed Consent. Informed consent is an ongoing process. If you are a practitioner who works within a managed care setting, you need to address these questions:

- What can I do to maintain both ethical standards and high-quality services?
- What concerns are there regarding the ethics of such systems themselves?
- What kind of information does my client have a right to know prior to entering into a professional relationship with me?

Informed consent assumes particular importance under a managed care system, and informed consent forms should state that the managed care company may request a client's diagnosis, results on any tests given, a wide range of clinical information, treatment plans, and perhaps even the entire clinical record of a client. Clinicians who work in a managed care system are ethically bound to ensure that clients understand any policies or arrangements with managed care systems that are pertinent to treatment before entering into a therapeutic relationship (Glosoff et al., 1999).

Acuff and her colleagues (1999) point out that some managed care organizations make it a practice not to provide full, complete, and accurate information to their subscribers. Many clients are not fully aware of how the complexities of managed care arrangements affect their benefits and rights, and it is a mistake to assume that new clients have complete information regarding how the managed care system affects their specific benefit package. For this reason, the informed consent procedure must be very clear (Cooper & Gottlieb, 2000).

Clients have a right to know that there may be other forms of treatment—possibly ones that may be more helpful—that are being denied to them solely for cost-containment reasons. They have a right to know if the therapist is versed in brief therapy, that an outside person is likely to judge what kind of treatment will be given and how many sessions will be allowed, the specific limitations of the plan they are participating in, and who decides the time of termination of therapy. Ethical practice demands that providers inform clients of all of these issues pertaining to their treatment, but managed care practices often fall short of full disclosure.

Confidentiality. Traditionally, confidentiality is considered an ethical and legal duty imposed on therapists to protect client disclosures (see Chapter 5). Within a managed care context, however, confidentiality may no longer be presumed in the therapeutic relationship. Davis and Meier (2001) observe: "While maintaining confidentiality has always been a cornerstone of counseling and psychotherapy, for some managed care companies it is unfamiliar terrain" (p. 42). Managed care shifts the traditional basis for limits on confidentiality to matters pertaining to cost containment (Cooper & Gottlieb, 2000). In exploring confidentiality in managed care, Acuff and her colleagues (1999) contend that without the assurance of confidentiality it is reasonable to assume that many people will not seek treatment, and clients in therapy may withhold crucial information. Although there have always been exceptions to confidentiality, the demand for client information inherent in managed care far exceeds traditional limitations to confidentiality. At the very least, clients should be aware that managed care contracts may require therapists to reveal sensitive client information to a third party who is in a position to authorize initial or additional treatment. Practitioners can no longer assure their clients of confidential therapy at any level. Practitioners have no control over confidential information once it leaves their offices, and many managed care contracts require a practitioner to submit all treatment records before payment is issued. Because of these restrictions on confidentiality, therapists have an obligation to inform clients from the outset of therapy about the relevant limits of confidentiality under their managed care policy (Acuff et al., 1999; Cooper & Gottlieb, 2000).

Hering (2000) has argued that managed care has resulted in the erosion of the traditional sense of confidentiality. HMOs have wide access to client disclosures, and clients cannot be assured that much of what they say will remain confidential. Hering asserts that the managed care company is mainly concerned with cost containment and only gives lip service to a therapist's autonomy and professional judgment. In short, managed care, without any legal intervention, without any research, without any input from professional organizations, has redefined confidentiality.

Abandonment. The codes of ethics of professional organizations state that mental health practitioners do not abandon clients. Traditionally, the matter of termination of therapy is a collaborative effort involving both the client and the therapist. Under managed care programs, termination is generally a matter decided by the managed care provider. Termination does not come out of a collaborative process but out of company policy. Clients may have a sense of abandonment if their therapy ends abruptly. It is the responsibility of therapists to inform clients that the request for additional sessions may or may not be granted by their managed care provider.

In many HMOs, clients are limited to 20 sessions annually, with lifetime cost caps, and they may be denied the care they need if it extends beyond their benefits. Even though a client's policy may allow for up to 20 therapy sessions, the client may be authorized for only 6 sessions. It is essential to apply for additional sessions well in advance of the last authorized visit (Cooper & Gottlieb, 2000). Although these limitations may make financial sense, this situation can become ethically problematic. Haas and Cummings (1991) note that this policy shifts the risk to the therapist. Therapists are ethically and legally obligated to offer a standard of care to clients, and they are not to abandon them. This puts therapists who work with managed care in the position of referring clients if continued therapy is needed.

Although the cost-containment practices of managed care are not necessarily unethical, Acuff and her colleagues (1999) believe that such practices can lead to client abandonment. There are financial incentives to limit treatment even when, in the therapist's view, treatment is clinically indicated and the client wants more treatment.

As an alternative to ending treatment with a client who clearly needs further treatment, therapists could offer pro bono services. However, this might put an unrealistic strain on their ability to survive financially. If referral resources are not readily available, and if therapists are not willing to abandon clients, how can therapists protect their financial interests and still serve the best interests of their clients?

It is anticipated that more consumers of mental health services will file both ethical and legal complaints against therapists because of their willingness to terminate therapy due to decisions made by HMOs (Glosoff et al., 1999). Practitioners are ultimately responsible to their clients in an HMO system, even if the decisions are made by the managed care system.

Utilization Review. Under managed care plans, all treatment is monitored. **Utilization review** refers to the use of predefined criteria to evaluate treatment necessity, appropriateness of therapeutic intervention, and therapy effectiveness. This process may take place before, during, and after treatment (Cooper & Gottlieb, 2000). Acuff and her colleagues (1999) state that utilization management and review involves making decisions regarding types of treatment, setting, and the duration of treatment. They point out that ideally the needs of the client should remain paramount, yet these needs should be met in a cost-effective manner. Utilization review of clients is generally done by way of a written document that is periodically sent to the company. One disadvantage of this form of review is the possibility of the loss of confidentiality, because paper reviews are sent by mail or electronic means. The disadvantage of telephone reviews is finding the time to make the call and then waiting to actually make the connection (Davis & Meier, 2001). One additional potential problem pertaining to utilization review is the competence of the person doing the reviewing. Is the reviewer also a clinician? If not, what makes the individual competent to make a clinical decision?

Other Ethical Issues. Other common problems that must be addressed include matters of financial incentives; diagnosis and assessment; competence; limited client choice of diverse providers; and teaching, training, and supervision of students (Glosoff et al., 1999). Competence is a critical issue. Therapists must be capable of providing time-limited, effective services. Furthermore, therapists will have to assume a pragmatic and theoretically eclectic orientation, as they will need to demonstrate flexibility in the use of effective techniques in dealing with a variety of problems. Therapists who are not competent in short-term interventions should probably avoid involvement in a managed care program. In this system, brief therapy is the norm, regardless of the problem. If counselors are not trained in brief therapy methods, and if clients will not be well served by a limited number of sessions, then counselors need to have skills in making appropriate referrals.

A critical ethical issue involves the divided loyalties therapists experience in attempting to do what is best for the client and the obligation to contain costs and restrict intervention to short-term, highly focused goals. It is important that the welfare of the client does not get put on the back burner in the interests of preserving the financial integrity of the system. Karon (1995) reminds us that competent and ethical therapists are primarily concerned with the well-being of their clients, which is an entirely different criterion from cost effectiveness.

Karon considers psychotherapy under managed health care "a growing crisis and a national nightmare." Although Karon admits that there are legitimate ways to save money without impairing the quality of care, he emphasizes that doing so requires careful thought and research; managed care companies are largely ignoring such reasonable and reasoned approaches. Stating that the aim of managed care is to provide as little psychological care as possible, while giving the appearance of providing adequate mental health care, Karon contends that ethical therapists are bound to encounter dilemmas. In a system where the median number of sessions is five or six, no matter what problem is presented, medication is often relied on to obviate the need for long-term therapy. Davis and Meier (2001) make a further observation of what may ensue from the practices of some managed care companies: "A danger exists that a new hierarchy of psychotherapy will develop with the most skilled therapists unavailable to those with managed care coverage that is not clinician friendly" (p. 52).

Managed Care and Malpractice

Stromberg and Dellinger (1993) assert that two core issues of malpractice apply to managed care: standard of care and therapist liability. Is the standard of care by which a therapist's service is measured different, or lower, in a managed care plan? Some may argue that clients who participate in a less expensive health plan—one that offers only limited coverage for psychological services—should not be in a position to sue therapists who terminate treatment after a predetermined number of sessions. To date, there is no evidence that courts recognize a lower standard of competence for managed care versus fee-for-service care. This means that therapists who work under managed care must still do the best they can to provide the kind of service clients require. Moreover, practitioners have a responsibility to anticipate the limited nature of services, and they should discuss the implications of this with their clients.

Are health care professionals liable for decisions to limit care that are specified by managed care plans? Some court rulings have established an ambiguous but important obligation for therapists: Although therapists need not disregard the utilization review standards of the managed care plan, they are likely to be legally required (1) to provide emergency psychological services regardless of payment, and (2) to energetically seek approval for additional services that the client genuinely needs.

A federal court ruling has implications for therapists who work with managed care companies. Believed to be the first of its kind involving a managed behavioral health care company, the 1996 lawsuit alleged that CIGNA Behavioral Health, Incorporated terminated therapists, purportedly without cause, when therapists requested more sessions for their clients than the managed care company was willing to provide. In their lawsuit, the plaintiffs claimed that in limiting the number of sessions provided the managed care company was substituting its judgment for the therapist's professional judgment, contrary to client welfare and public policy, and that these policies unlawfully prevented psychologists from exercising appropriate standards of care and clinical judgment. Nessman and Herndon (2000) report that this ruling has implications beyond this particular case and CIGNA: "In essence, a federal court determined that if a managed-care company uses 'no cause' terminations to retaliate against providers who advocate for their patients to secure needed care, this would be an illegal act in violation of public policy" (pp. 20–21).

It is clear that managed care has both ethical and legal implications for professional practice. Ethically, therapists must not abandon their clients, and they have a responsibility to render competent services. Legally, it appears that practitioners employed by a managed care unit are not exempt from malpractice suits if clients claim that they did not receive the standard of care they required. Therapists cannot use the limitations of the managed care plan as a shield for failing to render crisis intervention, to make appropriate referrals, or to request additional services from the plan.

The Future of Mental Health Care Delivery

Most who write about managed care seem to agree that the system is here to stay and that therapists will need to become trained or retrained in a body of knowledge and skills applicable to time-efficient and cost-effective therapies. All mental health providers are facing and will continue to face major changes in the manner in which their services are delivered. Clearly, accommodations must be made if professionals expect to survive in the era of managed care.

Rupert and Baird (2004) reported on data from two national surveys pertaining to practitioners in managed care systems and found that managed care was a source of stress, with paperwork and reimbursement issues being the most highly rated stresses. They concluded that "respondents with high managed care caseloads worked longer hours, had more client contact, received less supervision, reported more negative client behaviors, experienced more stress, were less satisfied with their incomes, and scored higher on emotional exhaustion" (p. 185). The potential for burnout for practitioners is obvious and needs to be addressed for the sake of both the practitioners and their clients.

Mental health providers are facing and will continue to face major changes in the manner in which their services are delivered. Clearly, accommodations must be made if professionals expect to survive in the era of managed care.

Various writers have forecast the future of mental health services under managed care. Here is a sampling of their thoughts:

> Overall, experts agree that managed care, in some form, is here to stay, at least in the foreseeable future. . . . It is expected that practitioners will be doing more group therapy, especially psychoeducational groups. Finally, we anticipate that there will be an increase in the effort to use manualized therapy for various diagnostic categories to standardize practice and reduce cost. (Cooper & Gottlieb, 2000, p. 229)

> Managed care works in its present form because we let this dictatorial system keep us feeling helpless and powerless. We have been shamed into abdicating control to a ruthless corporate authoritarian, whose value system is based solely on the profit motive. . . . It is time to stand up and take responsibility for our fear. Let us do what we would advise our own clients to do: empower ourselves before managed care owns any more of us than it already does. (Hering, 2000, p. 38)

We certainly are not wise enough to predict the future of the therapy enterprise under a managed care paradigm. However, under both the old and new systems, clients have had relatively little voice in the decisions made about them. Under the old system, a solo practitioner might tell a client, "Your problem will require at least 2 years of therapy, or longer." With the new system the client is likely to hear, "Your treatment will be limited to six sessions." Regardless of the structure underlying the delivery of services, we believe ethical practice demands that clients be given the maximum voice possible in agreeing to basic aspects of their treatment and in participating in the process of making decisions about the course of their therapy.

Clarifying Your Stance. If you are currently in training to become a mental health services provider, you will surely confront some of these issues. Clarify your position by answering these questions about working in a managed care environment.

- What are the major ethical problems you might face under a managed care program?
- Is your role being determined or restricted by managed care? To what degree are you willing to accept the requirements imposed by a managed care approach?
- How might your ability to establish a working relationship with your clients be affected under managed care?
- How would you educate your clients about the benefits and limitations inherent in a managed care plan? Can you think of ways to increase the chances that your clients will have a voice in the process of their therapy?
- What steps can you take to become competent in rendering cost-effective treatments that do not compromise the welfare of your clients?

Ethical challenges occur routinely in the practice of mental health care. If you are interested in an in-depth treatment of this topic, we recommend *Health*

Care Ethics for Psychologists: A Casebook (Hanson, Kerkhoff, & Bush, 2005), which addresses informed consent, respect for clients' dignity and confidentiality, the balance between client and family rights, and billing for services under managed care.

Ethical Issues in Psychotherapeutic Research

Most of the questions we have raised in this chapter have a direct relationship to a therapist's therapeutic approach. Specialized techniques, the balance of responsibility in the client-therapist relationship, the functions of the therapist, and the goals of treatment are all tied to a therapist's theoretical orientation. But at some point you will probably ask: Does my psychotherapeutic approach or technique work? To answer this question, you need to rely on the findings of psychotherapeutic research.

Boisvert and Faust (2003) examined leading international psychotherapy researchers' views on psychotherapy outcome research. Participants in the study rated level of research evidence for or against various assertions about psychotherapy process and outcomes. Their study revealed some interesting conclusions.

Experts showed strong agreement that research *did support* the following assertions:

- Therapy is helpful to the majority of clients.
- Most people achieve some change relatively quickly in therapy.
- People change more due to "common factors" than to "specific factors" associated with therapies.
- In general, therapies achieve similar outcomes.
- The relationship between the therapist and client is the best predictor of treatment outcome.
- Most therapists learn more about effective therapy techniques from their experience than from the research.
- Approximately 10% of clients get worse as a result of therapy.

Experts showed strong agreement that research *did not support* the following assertions:

- Placebo control groups and waitlist control groups are as effective as psychotherapy.
- Therapist experience is a strong predictor of outcome.
- Long-term therapy is more effective than brief therapy for the majority of clients (p. 511).

Although the ethical implications of conducting research in counseling and psychotherapy are vast, we want to address a few selected issues and encourage you to think about your responsibilities in this area. Consider these questions:

- In conducting research in a counseling setting, is it necessary that participants always give their informed consent? Can you think of situations in which it might be justified not to obtain informed consent for the sake of a better research design?

- Is it ever ethical to use deception in psychological research? Is deception justified if the participants are given accurate details after the research study is completed?
- Can practitioners be considered ethical if they practice without conducting any research on the techniques they use or without having them empirically validated?

Considering Ethics in Research Design

Considering the vast number of studies on psychotherapeutic research, there is little discussion in the literature of the ethical problems encountered in designing and conducting studies. Yet critical ethical issues in this field deserve the careful attention of investigators (Imber et al., 1986). In this section we consider some of these issues, including informed consent, using deception in psychological research, withholding treatment, using placebos, research with training and personal-growth groups, and cultural diversity in research. For further reading in this area we recommend Sales and Folkman (2000).

Informed Consent. We define informed consent as the participant's assent to being involved in a research study after having received full information about the procedures and their associated risks and benefits. In the process of informing research participants about what will be expected of them, it is important to use simple and clear language in addition to any technical language that may be required. Nagy (2005) lists the following elements as being basic to informed consent:

- Description of the research
- Voluntary participation
- Consequences of refusing to participate or dropping out
- Information that would affect one's willingness to participate
- Answering questions raised by participants

The APA (2002) standard on obtaining informed consent of research participants states:

> (a) Psychologists inform participants about (1) the purpose of the research, expected duration, and procedures; (2) their right to decline to participate and to withdraw from the research once participation has begun; (3) the foreseeable consequences of declining or withdrawing; (4) reasonably foreseeable factors that may be expected to influence their willingness to participate such as potential risks, discomfort, or adverse effects; (5) any prospective research benefits; (6) limits of confidentiality; (7) incentives for participation; and (8) whom to contact for questions about the research and research participants' rights. They provide opportunity for the prospective participants to ask questions and receive answers. (8.02.a.)

NASW's (1999) code of ethics focuses on informed consent issues regarding research participants:

> Social workers engaged in evaluation or research should obtain voluntary and written informed consent from participants, when appropriate, without any implied or actual deprivation or penalty for refusal to participate, without undue inducement to participate, and with due regard for participants' well-being, privacy and dignity. Informed consent should include information about the nature, extent, and duration of the participation requested and disclosure of the risks and benefits of participation in the research. (5.02.e.)

Informed consent is important for a variety of reasons: it protects people's autonomy by allowing them to make decisions about matters that directly concern them; it guarantees that the participants will be exposed to certain risks only if they agree to them; it decreases the possibility of an adverse public reaction to experimenting with human subjects; and it helps researchers scrutinize their designs for inherent risks (Lindsey, 1984). The researcher might be guided by asking: "What would clients who are interested in their own welfare need to know before making a decision?" With these points in mind, consider the following situation to determine the ethics of the researcher's behavior.

✓ **The Case of Hannah.** Hannah is committed to designing research procedures to evaluate the process and outcome of her treatment programs. She is convinced that to obtain valid data she must keep the research participants ignorant in many respects. Thus, she thinks it is important that the clients she sees be unaware that they are being studied and be unaware of the hypotheses under investigation. Although she agrees that some ethical issues may be raised by her failure to inform her clients, she believes that good research designs call for such procedures. She does not want to influence her clients and thus bias the results of her study, so she chooses to keep information from them. She contends that her practices are justified because there are no negative consequences or risks involved with her research. She further contends that if she is able to refine her therapeutic techniques through her research efforts with her clients, both they and future clients will be the beneficiaries.

- What are your thoughts about Hannah's ethics and the rationale she gives for not obtaining informed consent?
- Assume that she was interested in studying the effects of therapists' reinforcement of statements by clients during sessions. If the clients knew she was using certain procedures and studying certain behaviors, would it bias the results?
- If the value of the research seems to be greater than the risks involved to participants, do you think researchers are justified in not obtaining the informed consent of participants?

Commentary. Although some of Hannah's contentions have merit, we do not think the ends are justified by the means she employs. She might be justified in withholding some of the details of her research studies (or the hypotheses under investigation), but it seems unethical for her to fail even to mention to her clients that she is actually doing research with them as part of her therapeutic approach. Because Hannah's clients are investing themselves both emotionally and financially in their therapy, they have the right to be informed about procedures that are likely to affect them. Furthermore, they have the right to agree or refuse to be a part of her study. Her approach does not allow them to make that choice.

Using Deception. Individuals who participate in a research project have a right to know what they will be voluntarily agreeing to, as this APA (2002) standard on deception in research makes clear:

> (a) Psychologists do not conduct a study involving deception unless they have determined that the use of deceptive techniques is justified by the study's significant prospective scientific, educational, or applied value and that effective nondeceptive alternative procedures are not feasible.
> (b) Psychologists do not deceive prospective participants about research that is reasonably expected to cause physical pain or severe emotional distress.
> (c) Psychologists explain any deception that is an integral feature of the design and conduct of an experiment to participants as early as is feasible, preferably at the conclusion of their participation, but no later than at the conclusion of the data collection, and permit participants to withdraw their data. (8.07.)

The case against deception in psychological research has been strongly made, and ethics codes prohibit deception that undermines an individual's rights. Deception violates the individual's right to voluntarily choose to participate, abuses the trusting relationship between experimenter and subject, contributes to deception as a societal value, is contrary to the professional roles of educator or scientist, and will eventually erode trust in the profession of psychology (Adair, Dushenko, & Lindsay, 1985). With these points in mind, consider the following situation and determine whether deception is justified.

✓ **The Case of Vincent.** Vincent, a family therapist, routinely videotapes his initial session with families without their knowledge. He does so because he wants to have a basis for comparing the family's behavior at the outset with their behavior at the final session. He assumes that if the family members knew they were being videotaped at the initial session they would behave in self-conscious and fearful ways. At the beginning of therapy he does not think they could handle the fact of being taped. Yet he likes to have families look at themselves on videotape at their final session, at which time he tells them that he taped their initial session and explains why he did not inform them of this procedure.

- Because Vincent eventually does tell families that they were taped at the initial session, do you think he is guilty of deception? Explain.
- To what degree do you think the practice of taping clients without their knowledge affects the trust level in the therapeutic relationship? Are the possible benefits of this practice worth the potential risks to the practitioner's reputation?

Commentary. Vincent's policy of videotaping clients without their knowledge and consent is ethically questionable. Most of the professional codes of the national organizations explicitly state that such a practice is to be avoided. Because the therapeutic relationship is built on goodwill and trust, we oppose any practices that are likely to jeopardize that trust.

Withholding Treatment. Is it ethical to withhold treatment from a particular group so that it can be used as a control group? Consider this situation.

✓ **The Case of Hope.** Hope works with people diagnosed as depressive psychotics in a state mental hospital. In the interest of refining therapeutic interventions that will help depressed clients, she combines therapy and research procedures. Specifically, she employs cognitive-behavioral approaches in a given ward. Her research design specifies treatment techniques for a particular group of patients, and she carefully monitors their rate of improvement as part of the treatment program. Hope says that she believes in the value of cognitive-behavioral approaches for depressive patients, yet she feels a professional and ethical obligation to empirically validate her treatment strategies. For her to know whether the treatment procedures alone are responsible for changes in the patients' behaviors, she deems it essential to have a comparable group of patients who do not receive the treatment. When she is challenged on the ethics of withholding treatment from a particular group of patients on the ward, she justifies her practice on the ground that she is working within the dictates of sound research procedures.

- Some researchers contend that they are necessarily caught in ethical dilemmas if they want to use a control group. Do you see an apparent contradiction between the demands of sound research methodology and sound ethical practice?
- Do you think Hope was acting ethically in withholding treatment so that she could test her therapeutic procedures? Would it be better for her to simply forget any attempts at empirical validation of her procedures and devote her efforts to treating as many patients as she can?
- Would it be ethical for her to use procedures that are untested?

✓ **A Case Using Placebos.** In a second case Hope uses placebo controls. That is, rather than merely denying treatment to a group or keeping members on a waiting list, she meets with a control group whose members think they are receiving therapy but actually are not receiving standard treatment. In short, the group is led to believe that it is benefiting from therapy.

- What are the ethics of using placebos in counseling and clinical research?
- Does the placebo approach by its very nature constitute deception of patients?
- Can you think of any situations that justify the use of this approach?

Research Using Trainee Personal-Growth Groups. In many graduate programs it is common for trainees in counseling internships to participate in personal-growth groups. Sometimes these groups are integrated with training or supervision groups in which the interns are encouraged to explore their own personal issues that arise in conjunction with their placements in the field.

✓ **The Case of Wesley.** Wesley makes it a practice to conduct research on the process and outcomes of the personal-growth groups he leads for counselor trainees. To begin with, all the students in his graduate counseling program are required to attend the sessions of a personal-growth group for a full academic year. In addition to leading these growth groups for trainees, he also teaches theory courses and supervises students writing master's theses and doctoral dissertations. His primary theoretical orientation is Gestalt therapy, with an emphasis on other experiential and role-playing techniques. He expects the students to come to the sessions and be willing to work on personal concerns. These personal concerns often pertain to issues that arise as a result of problems they encounter with difficult client situations in their internship. At the beginning of the group, Wesley asks students to take psychological tests that assess traits such as openness, dogmatism, degree of self-acceptance, level of self-esteem, and other dimensions of personality that he deems to be related to one's ability to counsel others. He again administers these same devices at the end of the year to provide a comparison. During the year he asks a group of experts to observe his trainees in the group sessions at various points. This is done so that outsiders can assess the level of growth of individuals at different points as well as get a sense of the progress of the group as a whole.

As part of informed consent, Wesley tells the trainees what he is attempting to evaluate during the year, and he discusses fully with them the rationale for using outsiders to observe the group. He also promises the students that he will meet with them individually at any time during the semester if they want to discuss any personal issues. He also meets with them individually at the end of the group to discuss changes in scores on the psychological tests. As a way to correct for his bias in the investigation, he submits his research design to a university committee. The function of this committee is to review his design for any ethical considerations and to give him suggestions for improving his study.

- Do you think it is ethical for a program to require student attendance at personal-growth groups? Is it ethical for the leader of such a group to also have these same students in academic classes and to evaluate and supervise them?
- What research practices, if any, would you say are ethically questionable?
- Do you think it is ethically sound to have observers as a part of the design? The students know about these outsiders, but the observers will be part of the process even if some students do not like the idea. Do you see pressure being exerted? If so, is it justified in this case?
- What recommendations can you make for improving Wesley's research design as well as improving the quality of the learning experience for the students?

Cultural Diversity Aspects of Research

Although research is considered basic to the development of theory, cultural factors are often neglected in both research and theory. It is critical that research designs be based on culturally sensitive principles. ACA (2005) has this guideline on diversity in research: "When appropriate to research goals, counselors are sensitive to incorporating research procedures that take into account cultural considerational. They seek consultation when appropriate" (G.1.g.).

The APA's "Guidelines for Providers of Psychological Services to Ethnic, Linguistic, and Culturally Diverse Populations" (1993) calls for a conceptual framework that will enable service providers to organize and accurately assess the value and utility of current and future research involving diverse ethnic and cultural populations. These guidelines include an exploration of several research issues:

- The impact of ethnic and racial similarity in the counseling process
- Minority groups' use of mental health services
- The relative effectiveness of directive and nondirective styles of therapy
- The role of cultural values in treatment
- Appropriate counseling models
- Competence in skills for working with specific ethnic populations

In a discussion of new approaches to cultural diversity, Lee (1997b) contends that research evidence must guide counseling. Based on reviews of what has been accomplished in research on cross-cultural counseling, he proposes the following three areas for future research:

- New process and outcome research in the area of multicultural counseling. Evaluation of culturally responsive methods must be made an integral part of practice in various settings.
- Normal human development research from a cross-cultural perspective. New studies might focus on coping skills among diverse groups of people.
- Research on intragroup differences due to factors such as level of ethnic identity, level of acculturation, and socioeconomic status.

Inventory of Your Position on Research

As a way of concluding this discussion, we suggest that you clarify your own thinking on the matter of balancing scientific rigor with ethical rigor. If you agree more than you disagree with the following statements, place an "A" in the space provided; if you disagree more than you agree, place a "D" in the space. After you have finished the inventory, discuss some of your answers with fellow students.

______ 1. To use therapeutic techniques or interventions that lack a sufficient research base is irresponsible and unethical.

______ 2. Deception is sometimes a necessary aspect of psychological research.

______ 3. Failure to obtain the informed consent of participants in research is always unethical.

______ 4. If a research study contains any risks to the participants, its design should be changed because by its very nature it is unethical.

______ 5. The use of placebo groups can be justified. If these controls are not used, practitioners will have difficulty evaluating the efficacy of the intervention they use.

______ 6. Researchers will ultimately get the best results if they are open and honest about the research design with the participants in the study.

_____ 7. If individuals are "debriefed" afterward, deception during the study can be justified.

_____ 8. Practitioners should use no techniques that have not been empirically shown to be of value.

_____ 9. To produce sound research studies of therapy, we must be willing to tolerate some ethical violations.

_____ 10. It is ethical to justify research in educational settings solely on the basis of the potential benefits of the research itself.

Chapter Summary

Issues in theory, practice, and research are necessarily interrelated. From an ethical perspective, therapists need to anchor their practices to both theory and research. Without a theoretical foundation, practitioners are left with little rationale to formulate therapeutic goals and develop techniques to accomplish these goals. Practitioners are sometimes impatient when it comes to articulating a theory that guides practice. Some rely on a limited number of techniques to deal with every conceivable problem clients may present. However, a good theory helps clinicians understand what they are doing.

We do not advocate that you subscribe to one established theory; therapeutic techniques from many theoretical approaches may be useful in your practice. Ideally, your theoretical orientation will serve as a basis for reflecting on matters such as goals in counseling, the division of responsibility between the client and the counselor in meeting these goals, and techniques that are most appropriate with specific clients in resolving a variety of problems.

Just as clinicians sometimes underuse theory, some do not see the practical value of research. Without understanding how to translate current research findings into their practices, therapists limit themselves in their ability to help clients. Thus, an appreciation of how theory and research can enhance how therapists function can lead to more effective and therefore more ethical practice.

Suggested Activities

1. Do this exercise in dyads. Describe your theoretical stance, and tell your partner how you view human nature. How will this view influence the way you counsel?
2. How do you determine the proper division of responsibility in counseling? In small groups explore diverse viewpoints on this question.
3. If you were applying for a job as a counselor and were asked, "What are the most important goals you have for your clients?" how would you respond?
4. Suppose a client came to you and asked you to administer a battery of interest, ability, and vocational tests. How would you respond? What questions would you ask the client before agreeing to arrange for the testing?

5. Interview at least one practicing therapist and discuss how his or her theoretical orientation influences his or her practice. Ask the practitioner questions raised throughout this chapter. Bring the results of your interview to class.

6. Suppose you were applying for a job in a community mental health center. How would you respond to these questions during the interview:

- Many of our clients represent a range of diverse cultural and ethnic backgrounds. To what degree do you think you will be able to work with them?
- How much do you understand about your own acculturation process? How will this help or hinder you in working with our clientele?
- What will be your biggest challenge in forming trusting relationships with clients who are culturally different from you?

7. In dyads or triads, discuss the position that a thorough assessment and diagnosis is a necessary step in effective counseling practice. Also, discuss the ethics of using a diagnosis exclusively for the purpose of insurance reimbursement.

8. As a small group activity, explore how you would go about getting to know your client during your initial contact. How would you structure future sessions? Explore the following questions:

- Are tests important as a prerequisite to counseling? Would you decide whether to test, or would you allow your client to make this decision?
- How would you incorporate a cultural perspective into your work? How would your client's cultural and ethnic background influence the development of your relationship?
- Would you develop a contract with your client specifying what the client could expect from you and what the client wanted from counseling? Why or why not?
- Would you be inclined to use directive, action-oriented techniques, such as homework assignments? Why or why not?

9. Videotape or tape-record sessions with several clients. Instead of focusing your attention on what your client said or did, examine your own responses and how you relate to clients.

- Do you ask open-ended questions or closed-ended questions, or do you ask questions because you do not know what else to do?
- Do you tend to give advice, and if so, why?
- Do you encourage your clients to fully express what they are feeling before you offer support?
- Do you leave it to your clients to discover what their behaviors mean from their own perspective, or do you tell your clients what certain behaviors mean?
- Do you use techniques primarily to get clients moving, or do you use interventions aimed at enabling clients to explore thoughts or feelings that they bring up?

- Have you yourself experienced the techniques you are using with your clients?
- Do you tend to rely on one theory to guide your choice of techniques, or do you rely on many counseling approaches?

Monitoring your own work in light of these questions can help you discover your counseling style, understand the interventions you make, and evaluate the impact these counseling procedures have on your clients. This willingness to reflect on the effects your interventions have on clients is of the utmost importance.

InfoTrac® College Edition Resources

For additional readings, explore InfoTrac College Edition, our online library. Key words are listed in a form that enables the search engine to locate a wider range of articles in the online university library. Key words should be entered exactly as shown, including asterisks, "Wl," "W2," "AND," and other search engine tools. Go to http://www.infotrac-college.com and select these key word searches:

psychodiagnosis
ethical issue* AND diagnosis AND (psych????y OR psychotherapy OR couns*)
evidence W1 based W1 practice AND (psych????y OR psychotherapy OR couns*)
psychological W1 diagnosis AND (psych????y OR psychotherapy OR couns*)
differential W1 diagnosis AND (psych????y OR psychotherapy OR couns*)
managed W1 care AND (psych????y OR psychotherapy OR couns*) NOT law
utilization W1 review AND (psych????y OR psychotherapy OR couns*)

Chapter 11

Pre-Chapter Self-Inventory

Directions: For each statement, indicate the response that most closely identifies your beliefs and attitudes. Use the following code:

5 = I *strongly agree* with this statement.
4 = I *agree* with this statement.
3 = I am *undecided* about this statement.
2 = I *disagree* with this statement.
1 = I *strongly disagree* with this statement.

____ 1. A person who comes from a troubled family background is generally unlikely to become a good family therapist.

____ 2. I would never divulge in a family session any secrets given to me privately by one of the members.

____ 3. In practicing couples counseling, I would also be willing to see them for individual sessions in addition to conjoint therapy.

____ 4. Counselors have an ethical responsibility to encourage spouses to leave partners who are physically or psychologically abusive.

____ 5. I would not be willing to work with a couple if I knew that one of the individuals was having an affair.

Ethical Issues in Couples and Family Therapy

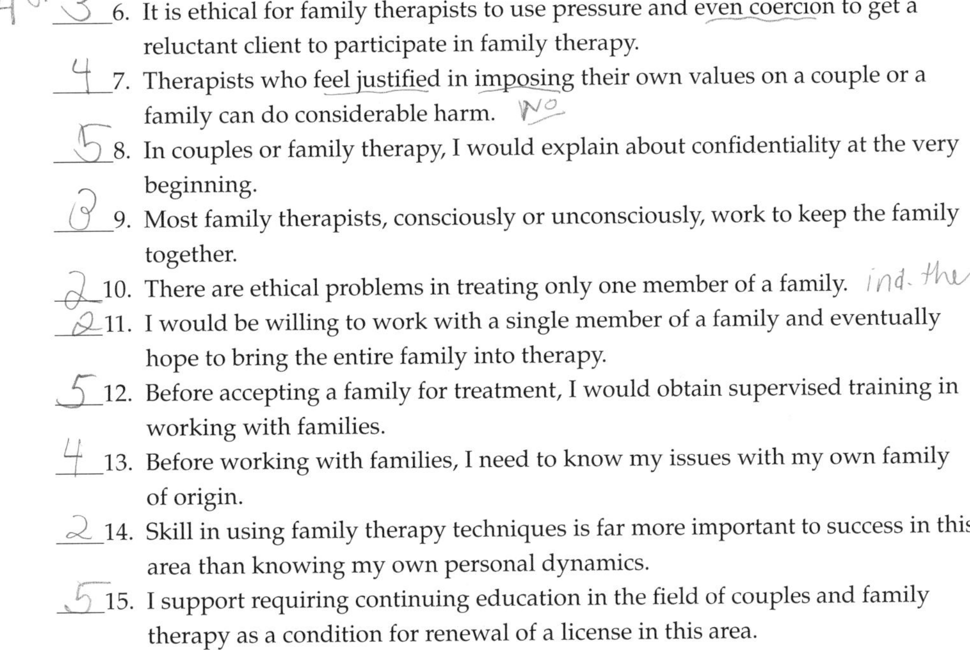

_____ 6. It is ethical for family therapists to use pressure and even coercion to get a reluctant client to participate in family therapy.

_____ 7. Therapists who feel justified in imposing their own values on a couple or a family can do considerable harm.

_____ 8. In couples or family therapy, I would explain about confidentiality at the very beginning.

_____ 9. Most family therapists, consciously or unconsciously, work to keep the family together.

_____ 10. There are ethical problems in treating only one member of a family.

_____ 11. I would be willing to work with a single member of a family and eventually hope to bring the entire family into therapy.

_____ 12. Before accepting a family for treatment, I would obtain supervised training in working with families.

_____ 13. Before working with families, I need to know my issues with my own family of origin.

_____ 14. Skill in using family therapy techniques is far more important to success in this area than knowing my own personal dynamics.

_____ 15. I support requiring continuing education in the field of couples and family therapy as a condition for renewal of a license in this area.

Introduction

Much of the practice of couples and family therapy rests on the foundation of **systems theory,** which views psychological problems as arising from within the individual's present environment and the intergenerational family system. Symptoms are believed to be an expression of dysfunctions within the system, which are passed along through numerous generations. The idea that the identified client's problem might be a symptom of how the system functions, not just a symptom of the individual's maladjustment and psychosocial development, was a revolutionary notion. The family systems perspective is grounded on the assumptions that a client's problematic behavior may (1) serve a function or purpose for the family, (2) be a function of the family's inability to operate productively, or (3) be a symptom of dysfunctional patterns handed down across generations. However, other theoretical frameworks also guide the practice of family therapy, including Bowen's multigenerational family therapy, Satir's human validation process model, Whitaker's experiential approach, structural family therapy, strategic family therapy, and the social construction models of family therapy (Corey, 2005b).

Goldenberg and Goldenberg (2004) urge therapists to view all behavior, including the symptoms expressed by the individual, within the context of the family and society. Although traditional approaches to treating the individual have merit, expanding the perspective to consider clients as members of their family, community, and society may enhance therapists' understanding. The Goldenbergs claim that a systems orientation does not preclude dealing with the individual but does broaden the traditional emphasis to address the roles individuals play in the family.

The systems perspective views the family as a functioning entity that is more than the sum of its members. The family provides the context for understanding how individuals behave. Actions by any individual member influence all the other members, and their reactions have a reciprocal effect on the individual. For instance, an acting-out child may be expressing deep conflicts between the mother and the father and may actually be expressing the pain of an entire family. Family therapists often work with individuals, the couple, and parents and children to get a better understanding of patterns that affect the entire system and to develop strategies for change.

Although contemporary couples and family therapists usually base their clinical practice on a foundation of systems theory, the majority of family therapists integrate concepts and techniques from various theoretical orientations to produce their own blend of methods based on their training, personality, and the population of families they serve (Hanna & Brown, 2004). Nichols and Schwartz (2004) also maintain that family therapy is moving toward integration. They believe that it does not make sense to study only one model and to neglect the insights of others.

Many master's programs in counseling now offer a specialization in relationship counseling or couples and family therapy. Components of the training program in couples and family therapy include the study of systems theory, an examination of family of origin, the use of live supervision, and an emphasis on ethical and professional issues specific to working with couples and families.

Many of the ethical issues we have already discussed take on special significance when therapists work with more than one client. Most graduate programs in couples and family therapy now require a separate course in ethics and the law pertaining to this specialization, with an increased emphasis on ethical, legal, and professional issues unique to a systems perspective. The professional practice of couples and family therapy is regulated by state laws, professional specialty guidelines, ethics codes, peer review, continuing education, managed care, and consultation (Goldenberg & Goldenberg, 2004). Some specific areas of ethical concern for family therapists that we discuss in this chapter include ethical standards of practice, therapist values, therapist responsibility, gender sensitivity, confidentiality, and informed consent and the right to refuse treatment.

Ethical Standards in Couples and Family Therapy

The AAMFT *Code of Ethics* (2001) provides a framework for many of the ethical issues we will consider in this chapter. In addition to the AAMFT code, two useful resources for issues involving couples and family therapy are the *Ethical Casebook for the Practice of Marriage and Family Counseling* (Stevens, 1999) and the American Association for Couples and Family Therapy *Ethics Casebook* (Brock, 1998). In addition, many states have their own professional organizations that outline ethical standards for the practice of couples and family therapy.

We begin our discussion by considering the AAMFT's (2001) code in each of eight core areas, followed by a brief discussion of what this means for therapists.

1. *Responsibility to clients.* "Marriage and family therapists advance the welfare of families and individuals. They respect the rights of those persons seeking their assistance, and make reasonable efforts to ensure that their services are used appropriately" (Principle I).

As the focus of therapy shifts from the individual to the family system, a new set of ethical questions is raised: Whose interests does the family therapist serve? To whom and for whom does the therapist have primary loyalty and responsibility? the client identified as being the problem? the separate family members as individuals? the family as a whole? By agreeing to become involved in family therapy, the members can generally be expected to place a higher priority on the goals of the family as a unit than on their own personal goals.

2. *Confidentiality.* "Marriage and family therapists have unique confidentiality concerns because the client in a therapeutic relationship may be more than one person. Therapists respect and guard confidences of each individual client" (Principle II).

Confidentiality assumes unique significance in the practice of couples and family therapy. This issue arises within the family itself in deciding how to deal with secrets. Incest, extramarital affairs, contagious diseases, or physical or psychological abuse of a partner or children may be involved. Should the therapist attempt to have families explore all their secrets? What are the pros and cons of revealing a family secret when some members are likely to suffer from extreme discomfort if it is disclosed? Family therapists have different perspectives on maintaining confidentiality. Some treat all information they receive from a family member just as if the person were in individual therapy. Others refuse to see any member of the family separately, claiming that doing so fosters unproductive alliances and promotes the keeping of secrets. Still others tell family members that they will exercise their own judgment about what to disclose from an individual session in a couples or family session.

3. *Professional competence and integrity.* "Marriage and family therapists maintain high standards of professional competence and integrity" (Principle III).

This principle implies that clinicians keep abreast of developments in the field through continuing education and clinical experiences. A single course or two in a graduate counseling program is hardly adequate preparation for functioning ethically and effectively as a counselor with couples or families. Here are some questions that can be productively explored: How can therapists know when their own personal problems are likely to hamper their professional work? What are some ways in which therapists can best maintain a level of competence? How can therapists use their values in a constructive fashion?

4. *Responsibility to students and supervisees.* "Marriage and family therapists do not exploit the trust and dependency of students and supervisees" (Principle IV).

The code cautions practitioners to avoid multiple relationships, which are likely to impair clinical judgment. As you saw in Chapters 7 and 9, perspectives differ on how best to handle dual relationships and avoid exploiting the trust and dependency of clients, students, and supervisees. What are your views about dual relationships as they apply to couples and family therapy? students and supervisees? Can you think of a possible dual or multiple relationship that would not interfere with your objectivity or lead to exploitation? What concerns might you have about dual relationships between marriage and family therapists and students or supervisees?

5. *Responsibility to research participants.* "Investigators respect the dignity and protect the welfare of research participants, and are aware of federal and state laws and regulations and professional standards governing the conduct of research" (Principle V).

Researchers must carefully consider the ethical aspects of any research proposal, making use of informed consent procedures and explaining to participants what is involved in any research project. If there is a conflict between research purposes and therapeutic purposes, how would you resolve it? What are some multicultural considerations in doing research in this area? What obstacles do you see to doing research in this area?

6. *Responsibility to the profession.* "Marriage and family therapists respect the rights and responsibilities of professional colleagues and participate in activities that advance the goals of the profession" (Principle VI).

Ethical practice requires measures of accountability that meet professional standards. It is expected that couples and family therapists will contribute time to the betterment of society, including donating services. What would you say about the ethics of those therapists who do not contribute any of their professional time pro bono? What do you see as your ethical obligation to advance the goals of your profession? What activities do you participate in (or expect to participate in) for professional advancement?

7. *Financial arrangements.* "Marriage and family therapists make financial arrangements with clients, third party payers, and supervisees that are reasonably understandable and conform to accepted professional practices" (Principle VII).

Couples and family therapists do not accept payment for making referrals and do not exploit clients financially for services. They are truthful in representing facts to clients and to third parties regarding any services rendered. Ethical practice dictates a disclosure of fee policies at the onset of therapy. What steps would you take to inform your clients about your fee policies? Would you charge for missed appointments? What are some ways in which clients can be exploited financially?

8. *Advertising.* "Marriage and family therapists engage in appropriate informational activities, including those that enable the public, referral sources, or others to choose professional services on an informed basis" (Principle VIII).

Ethical practice dictates that practitioners accurately represent their competence, education, training, and experience in couples and family therapy. Therapists do not advertise themselves as specialists (for example, in sex therapy) without being able to support this claim by virtue of their education, training, and supervised experience. How would you advertise your services? How might you promote yourself as a couples and family practitioner?

Special Ethical Considerations in Working With Couples and Families

Why do couples seek therapy? This question was the basis of a survey of 147 married couples seeking marital therapy, which was conducted by Doss, Simpson, and Christensen (2004). The most commonly reported reasons for seeking couples therapy were problematic communication and lack of emotional affection. Other reasons included the desire to improve the relationship for the sake of the children (19% of couples) and positive feelings for their spouse or relationship (22% of couples).

A number of ethical considerations are unique to couples and family therapy. Because most couples and family therapists focus on the family system as the client rather than on the individual's dynamics, potential ethical dilemmas can arise from the first session, which need to be clarified. Because of the increased complexity of their work, couples and family therapists are faced with more potential ethical conflicts than are practitioners who specialize in individual therapy. Therapists who work with cohabitating couples or multiple family members often encounter dilemmas that involve serving one member's best interest at the expense of another member's interest.

In their interventions, therapists need to consider that the status of one partner or family member does not improve at the expense of the other partner or another family member. Gladding, Remley, and Huber (2001) maintain that therapists can respond to ethical dilemmas over conflicting interests of multiple individuals by identifying the couple or family system as the focus of treatment rather than a single individual as the primary "client." Therapists who function as an advocate of the system avoid becoming an agent of any one partner or family member. Working within a framework that conceptualizes change as affecting and being affected by all family members, practitioners are able to define problems and consider plans for change in the context of the family system.

Gladding and colleagues also address these ethical concerns faced by couples and family counselors (p. 62):

- Can therapists automatically assume the right to define couples' and families' presenting problems in terms of their own therapeutic orientation?
- How much concerted effort can therapists exert in convening all significant family members for therapy sessions?
- Should willing individual relationship partners or several family members seeking assistance go untreated because one individual refuses to participate?
- Under what situations, if any, should therapists impose their control on couples and families? If so, to what extent should they impose it in seeking change in the relationship system?
- How much intrasystem stress should be engendered or allowed to materialize in the pursuit of change?
- What are the ethical implications inherent in employing paradoxical procedures?
- How can the impact of working with couples and families within the larger context of service agency constraints be pursued ethically?

Contemporary Professional Issues

In this section we identify a few of the current professional issues in the practice of couples and family therapy. These include the personal, academic, and experiential qualifications necessary to practice in the field.

Personal Characteristics of the Family Therapist

In Chapter 2 we addressed the significance of the personal characteristics of the therapist as a major factor in creating an effective therapeutic alliance. Self-knowledge is particularly critical for family therapists, especially with regard to family-of-origin issues. When therapists work with a couple or a family, or with an individual who is sorting out a family-of-origin issue, their perceptions and reactions are likely to be influenced by their own family-of-origin issues. Therapists who are unaware of their own vulnerabilities are likely to misinterpret their clients or steer clients in a direction that will not arouse their own anxieties. Therapists who are aware of their own emotional issues are less likely to get entangled in the problems of their clients.

Many trainers of family therapists believe that a practitioner's mental health, as defined by relationships with his or her family of origin, has implications for professional training. It is assumed that trainees can benefit from an exploration of the dynamics of their family of origin because it enables them to relate more effectively to the families they will meet in their clinical practice.

Getz and Protinsky (1994) take the position that personal growth is an essential part of training for couples and family counselors and that knowledge and skills cannot be separated from a helper's internal dynamics and use of self. They write: "Trainees can and should be referred for personal therapy, but their issues, when identified as affecting their work, are addressed preferably in training" (p. 183). Getz and Protinsky point to growing clinical evidence that a family-of-origin approach to supervision is a necessary dimension of training for therapists who want to work with families. They contend that the reactions of therapists to their clients' stories tend to reactivate therapists' old learned patterns of behavior and unresolved problems. Through studying their own family of origin, students are ultimately able to improve their ability to counsel families.

In writing on the personal training of family therapists, Aponte (1994) describes his person/practice model, which is based on the premise that therapy is a personal encounter within a professional framework. Although he acknowledges that theory and technique are essential to the professional practice of family therapy, he stresses that the process is affected wholly through the relationship between therapist and client. For Aponte, training the person of the therapist calls for trainees to examine their personal issues in relation to the therapy they do: "The touching of therapists' and clients' lives in therapy beckons therapists to gain mastery of their personal selves in their clinical relationships" (p. 4).

Educational Requirements for Family Therapy

All couples and family training programs acknowledge that both conceptual knowledge and clinical skills are necessary to become a competent family therapist. As training programs have evolved, major didactic and experiential components have been identified. Family therapy training programs use three primary methods of training: (1) didactic course work; (2) the use of master therapist videotapes plus trainee tapes for postsession viewing by the trainees and supervisors; and (3) regular supervision by an experienced family supervisor who, together with trainees, may watch the session behind a one-way mirror or on videotape (Goldenberg & Goldenberg, 2004). In addition to these methods of training, trainees are now likely to be exposed to a variety of current issues in the field of family therapy. Some of these include gender awareness, cultural sensitivity, and an understanding of the impact of larger systems on family functioning (Goldenberg & Goldenberg, 2004). It is essential for students to gain experience in working with a variety of families from different ethnic and socioeconomic backgrounds who have various presenting problems. A program offering both comprehensive course work and clinical supervision provides the ideal learning situation.

Experiential Qualifications for Family Therapy

In training couples and family therapists, primary emphasis must be given to the quality of supervised practice and clinical experience. Academic knowledge comes alive in supervised practicum and internship experiences, and trainees learn how to use and sharpen their intervention skills. It is through direct clinical contact with families, under close supervision, that trainees develop their own styles of interacting with families. A variety of supervisory methods can be employed to assist trainees in learning by doing, including the use of audiotapes, videotapes, written process notes, co-therapy, corrective feedback by telephone, live supervision, and calling the trainee out of the family session for consultation.

Most graduate programs employ both didactic and experiential methods and supervised practice. Didactic methods include lectures, group discussion, demonstrations, instructional videotapes of family therapy sessions, role playing, and assigned readings. Clinical experience with families is of limited value without regularly scheduled supervisory sessions. Live supervision can be conducted by a supervisor who watches and guides the sessions behind a one-way mirror and offers useful feedback and consultation to the trainee on how he or she is working with a family (Goldenberg & Goldenberg, 2004). Family therapy trainees can also profit from the practice of co-therapy, which provides trainees with opportunities to work closely with a supervisor or a colleague. A great deal of the supervision can take place immediately after and between sessions.

Experiential methods include both personal therapy and working with issues of one's own family of origin. A rationale for personal therapeutic experiences is that such exploration enables trainees to increase their awareness of transference and countertransference, which assists trainees in relating more effectively to the families they will meet in their clinical practice.

If clinicians are seeing families as part of their work, and if their program did not adequately prepare them for competence in intervening with families, they are vulnerable to a malpractice suit for practicing outside the boundaries of their competence. Those practitioners who did not receive specialized training in their program need to involve themselves in postgraduate in-service training or special workshops.

✓ **The Case of Ludwig.** Ludwig is a counselor whose education and training have been exclusively in individual counseling. Ella comes to him for counseling, but, after more than a dozen sessions with Ella, Ludwig realizes that much of her difficulty lies not just with her but with her entire family system. By this time Ludwig has established a strong working relationship with Ella. Because he has no experience in family therapy, he ponders what to do. He thinks of referring Ella to a colleague who is well trained in family therapy, but he realizes that doing so could have a detrimental effect on her. One of Ella's problems has been a sense of abandonment by her parents. He wants to avoid giving her the impression that he, too, is abandoning her. He decides to stay with her and work with her individually. Much of the time is spent trying to understand the dynamics of the family members who are not present.

- Do you agree with Ludwig's clinical decision? Do you agree with his rationale?
- From your perspective, would it have made a difference if he had consulted with Ella? Would it have made a difference if he had consulted with or obtained supervision from a colleague?
- Even though Ludwig was not trained as a family therapist, what if he had decided to see the entire family and attempted to do family therapy for the benefit of his client? Would you be inclined to do that?
- What if Ludwig had been trained in family systems but, when he suggested family sessions to Ella, she refused? What would you do if faced with such a dilemma?
- Assume that Ludwig decided to see each family member individually to learn how each viewed the family system. In this process he discovered a great discrepancy between Ella's description of the family and what the other family members said. Ludwig became convinced that his client was either misreading the family or was not presenting an accurate description of her problem. What is your opinion of his analysis? Does it raise any concerns for you?

Values in Couples and Family Therapy

In Chapter 3 we explored the impact of the therapist's values on the goals and direction of the therapeutic process. We now consider how values take on special significance in counseling couples and families. Values pertaining to marriage, the preservation of the family, divorce, traditional and nontraditional lifestyles, gender roles and the division of responsibility in the family, child rearing, and extramarital affairs can all influence therapists' interventions. Therapists may take sides with one member of the family against another; they may impose their values on family members; or they may be more committed to keeping the family intact than are the family members themselves. Conversely, therapists may have a greater investment in seeing the family dissolve than do members of the family.

The value system of the therapist has a crucial influence on the formulation and definition of the problems the therapist sees in a family, the goals and plans for therapy, and the direction the therapy takes. The International Association of Marriage and Family Counselors (2002) ethics code states: "Members do not impose personal values on families or family members" (I.F.). Counselors who, intentionally or unintentionally, impose their values on a couple or a family can do considerable harm. Ethical issues are raised in establishing criteria of psychosocial dysfunction, assessing the problems of the identified patient in the family context, and devising treatment strategies.

In their discussion of the valuing components of the professional practice of couples and family therapy, Gladding and colleagues (2001) agree with the assumption that the *content* of values is important and cannot be ignored, yet they place emphasis on the *process* of valuing, which includes the values, beliefs, and resultant actions they encompass. They note that too often values are represented as static positions construed as right or wrong rather than as a process that requires continual reconsideration and reclarification. They compare this to the process therapists use to understand cultural diversity. Respect for a client's culture or ethnicity involves initial acceptance of differences, exploration of those differences, and subtle explanations of how a given ethnic group's customs differ from the larger culture. In a like manner, couples and family therapists have the role of assisting couples and families in negotiating the values they want to retain, modify, or discard.

We want to emphasize again that it is not the function of any therapist to make decisions for clients. Family therapists do not decide how members of a family should change. The role of the therapist is to help family members see more clearly what they are doing, to help them make an honest evaluation of how well their present patterns are working for them, and to help and encourage them to make necessary changes.

What values and experiences of yours might influence how you would work with couples and families? To assist you in formulating your personal position, consider two cases that raise value issues that could affect the course of therapy.

The Case of Sharon. Sharon is a 25-year-old client who says, "I'm never going to get married because I think marriage is a drag. I don't want kids, and I don't want to stay with one person forever." Here are the inner dialogues of four therapists regarding her case.

Therapist A: She seems very selfish to me. With her attitude, it's probably a good idea that she doesn't intend to get married. I wonder why she is in therapy?

Therapist B: Well, she doesn't have to be married. Mental health doesn't necessarily require that one be married. I certainly would want to communicate to her that remaining single is acceptable. But I would like to explore with her how she went about making this decision.

Therapist C: Why is she so opposed to marriage? I wonder if she is talking more about her family than marriage?

Therapist D: I feel sorry for her. She must have had some very painful experiences growing up. She must have had a terrible relationship with her father that prevents her from forming healthy relationships now. If I can only get to the underlying problem, I know she will be able to overcome her negative experiences.

- What is your reaction to Sharon's statement?
- What is your reaction to each of the therapist's responses to her?
- What implied value is each therapist expressing?
- Why would you want to challenge (or accept) Sharon's decision?
- In what ways do you think you might work with Sharon differently from the four therapists? If you don't feel comfortable with a commitment to marriage and a family yourself, do you think you could be objective enough to help her explore some of the possibilities she might be overlooking?

The Case of Frank and Judy. During the past few years Frank and Judy have experienced many conflicts in their marriage. Although they have made attempts to resolve their problems by themselves, they have finally decided to seek the help of a professional marriage counselor. Even though they have been thinking about divorce with increasing frequency, they still have some hope that they can achieve a satisfactory marriage.

We will present the approaches of three couples counselors, each holding a different set of values pertaining to marriage and the family. As you read these responses, think about the degree to which each represents what you might say and do if you were counseling this couple.

Counselor A. This counselor believes it is not her place to bring her values pertaining to the family into the sessions. She is fully aware of her biases regarding marriage and divorce, but she does not impose them or expose them in all cases. Her primary interest is to help Frank and Judy discover what is best for them as individuals and as a couple. She sees it as unethical to push her clients toward a definite course of action, and she lets them know that her job is to help them be honest with themselves.

- What are your reactions to this counselor's approach?
- How would you, as a counselor, keep your values from interfering with the therapy process?

Counselor B. This counselor has been married three times herself. Although she believes in marriage, she is quick to maintain that far too many couples stay in their marriages and suffer unnecessarily. She explores with Judy and Frank the conflicts that they bring to the sessions. The counselor's interventions are leading them in the direction of divorce as the desired course of action, especially after they express this as an option. She suggests a trial separation and states her willingness to counsel them individually, with some joint sessions. When Frank brings up his guilt and reluctance to divorce because of the welfare of the children, the counselor confronts him with the harm that is being done to them by a destructive marriage. She tells him that it is too much of a burden to put on the children to keep the family together at any price.

- What, if any, ethical issues do you see in this case? Is this counselor exposing or imposing her values?
- Do you think this person should be a marriage counselor, given her bias?
- What interventions made by the counselor do you agree with? What are your areas of disagreement?

Counselor C. At the first session this counselor states his belief in the preservation of marriage and the family. He feels that many couples take the easy way out by divorcing too quickly in the face of difficulty. He says that most couples have unrealistically high expectations of what constitutes a "happy marriage." The counselor lets it be known that his experience continues to teach him that divorce rarely solves any problems but instead creates new problems that are often worse. The counselor urges Frank and Judy to consider the welfare of their three dependent children. He tells the couple of his bias toward saving the marriage so they can make an informed choice about initiating counseling with him.

- What are your personal reactions toward the orientation of this counselor?
- Do you agree with him stating his bias so obviously?
- What if he were to keep his bias and values hidden from the couple and accept them into therapy? Do you think he could work objectively with this couple? Why or why not?

Commentary. This case shows how the value system of the counselor determined the direction counseling took. The counselor who is dedicated to preserving marriage and family life is bound to function differently from the counselor who puts primary value on the welfare of individual family members. What might be best for one family member is not necessarily in the best interests of the entire family. It is essential, therefore, for counselors who work with couples and families to be aware of how their values influence the goals and procedures of therapy. Ethical practice should challenge clients to look at their own values and to choose a course of action that is best for them.

Gender-Sensitive Couples and Family Therapy

Gender-sensitive couples and family therapy attempts to help both women and men move beyond stereotyped gender roles. Sexist attitudes and patriarchal assumptions are examined for their impact on family relationships. With this approach, family therapy is conducted in an egalitarian fashion, and both therapist and client work collaboratively to empower individuals to choose roles rather than to be passive recipients of gender-role socialization.

All therapists need to be aware of their values and beliefs about gender. In Chapter 4 we discussed the importance of counselors' being aware of how their culture has influenced their personality. The way people perceive gender likewise has a great deal to do with their cultural background. A challenge to all family therapists is to be culturally sensitive, gender sensitive, and to avoid imposing their personal values on individuals, couples, and families. A standard of IAMFC (2002) addresses the issue of cultural factors:

> Members recognize the influence of world view and cultural factors (race, ethnicity, gender, social class, spirituality, sexual orientation, educational status) on the presenting problem, family functioning, and problem-solving skills. Counselors are aware of indigenous healing practices and incorporate them into treatment when necessary or feasible. Members are encouraged to follow the guidelines provided in the Multicultural Competencies. (I.G.)

Counselors who work with couples and families can practice more ethically if they are aware of the history and impact of gender stereotyping as it is reflected in the socialization process in families, including their own. Effective practitioners must continually evaluate their own beliefs about appropriate family roles and responsibilities, child-rearing practices, multiple roles, and nontraditional vocations for women and men. Counselors also must have the knowledge to help their clients explore educational, vocational, and emotional goals that they previously deemed unreachable. The principles of gender-aware therapy have relevance for counselors as they help clients identify and work through gender concepts that have limited them.

Feminist Perspective on Family Therapy

Some feminist therapists have been critical of the clinical practice of family therapy, contending that it has been filled with outdated patriarchal assumptions and grounded on a male-biased perspective of gender roles and gender-defined functions within the family. Feminists assert that our patriarchal society subjugates women, blames them for inadequate mothering, and expects them to accept their contribution to their problem.

A **feminist view of family therapy** focuses on gender and power in relationships and encourages a personal commitment to challenge gender inequity. They espouse a vision of a future society that values equality between women and men. Examining the power differential in their relationships often helps partners demystify differences between them. Feminist family therapists share a number of roles, each of which is based on a specific value orientation: They make their values and beliefs explicit so that the therapy process is clearly understood; they strive to establish egalitarian roles with clients; they work toward client autonomy and client empowerment; and they emphasize commonalities among women. In short, they do have an agenda to challenge traditional gender roles and the impact this socialization has on a relationship and a family.

Feminist therapists do not take a neutral stance with respect to gender roles and power in relationships. They advocate for definite change in the social structure, especially in the area of equality, power in relationships, the right to self-determination, freedom to pursue a career outside the home, and the right to an education.

Therapists can best function in the interests of both female and male clients by challenging them to examine self-contradictions. The therapist's task is to help clients decide who and what they want to be in the context of their lives, not what the therapist thinks they should be. Feminist therapists state that all therapists have values and that they believe it is important to be clear with clients about these values. This is different, however, from imposing values on clients. An imposition of values is inconsistent with viewing clients as their own best experts. Clients should be encouraged to make their own choices, and their choices need to be supported by their therapist.

A Nonsexist Perspective on Family Therapy

Regardless of their particular theoretical orientation, it is incumbent upon family therapists to take whatever steps are necessary to account for gender issues in their practice and to become nonsexist family therapists. Margolin (1982) provides a number of recommendations on how to be a nonsexist family therapist and how to use the therapeutic process to challenge the oppressive consequences of stereotyped roles and expectations in the family. One recommendation is that family therapists examine their own behavior for comments and questions that imply that wives and husbands should perform specific roles and hold a specific status. For example, a therapist can show bias in subtle and nonverbal ways, such as looking at the wife when talking about rearing children or addressing the husband when talking about any important decisions that need to be made. Further, Margolin contends that family therapists are particularly vulnerable to the following biases: (1) assuming that remaining married would be the best choice for a woman, (2) demonstrating less interest in a woman's career than in a man's career, (3) encouraging couples to accept the belief that child rearing is solely the responsibility of the mother, (4) showing a different reaction to a wife's affair than to a husband's, and (5) giving more importance to satisfying the husband's needs than to satisfying the wife's needs. She raises two important questions dealing with the ethics of doing therapy with couples and families:

- How does the therapist respond when members of the family seem to agree that they want to work toward goals that (from the therapist's vantage point) are sexist in nature?
- To what extent is the therapist culturally sensitive, especially when the family's definition of gender-role identities differs from the therapist's view?

As you read the case examples that follow, consider your own values. How do you think about gender, and do your views influence your perception of these cases? How might your values affect your way of counseling in each case?

The Case of Marge and Al. Marge and Al come to marriage counseling to work on the stress they are experiencing in rearing their two adolescent sons. The couple directs the focus toward what their sons are doing and not doing. In the course of therapy, the counselor learns that both Marge and Al have full-time jobs outside the home. In addition, Marge is a full-time mother and homemaker, but her husband refuses to share any domestic responsibilities. Marge doesn't question her dual career. Neither Marge nor Al shows much interest in exploring the division of responsibilities in their relationship. Instead, they focus the sessions on getting advice about how to handle problems with their sons.

- What would you do with their presenting problem, their trouble with their sons? What might the behavior of the sons imply?
- Is it ethical for the therapist to focus only on the expressed concerns of Marge and Al? Does the therapist have a responsibility to challenge this couple to look at how they have defined themselves and their relationship through assumptions about gender roles?

- Can't impose on them if they don't want to fix problem.

- If you were counseling this couple, what might you do? How would your interventions reflect your values in this case?

As you think about this case and the following one, ask yourself how your values regarding traditional wives and mothers might affect your relationship with clients like Marge and Melody.

The Case of Melody. Melody, 38, is married and has returned to college to obtain a teaching credential. During the intake session she tells you that she is experiencing conflicting feelings and is contemplating some major changes in her life. She has met a man who shares her interest and enthusiasm for school as well as many other aspects of her life. She is considering leaving her husband and children to pursue her own interests for a change. Which of the following reactions reflect how you think? Would you verbalize them?

- "Perhaps this is a phase you are going through. It happens to a lot of women who return to college. Maybe you should slow down and think about it."
- "You may have regrets later on if you leave your children in such an impulsive fashion."
- "Many women in your position would be afraid to do what you are thinking about doing."
- "I hate to see you divorce without having some marriage counseling first to determine whether that is what you both want."
- "Maybe you ought to look at the prospects of living alone for a while. The idea of moving out of a relationship with your husband and right into a new relationship with another man concerns me."

If Melody were your client, what values of yours would influence your interventions?

The Case of Naomi. The White family (consisting of wife, husband, four children, and the wife's parents) has been involved in family therapy for several months. During one of the sessions, Naomi (the wife) expresses the desire to return to college to pursue a law degree. This wish causes tremendous resistance on the part of every other member of her family. The husband says that he wants her to continue to be involved in his professional life and that, although he admires her ambitions, he simply feels that it would put too much strain on the entire family. Naomi's parents are shocked by their daughter's desire, viewing it as selfish, and they urge her to put the family's welfare first. The children express their desires for a full-time mother. Naomi feels great pressure from all sides, yet she seems committed to following through with her professional plans. She is aware of the sacrifices that would be associated with her studies, but she is asking for everyone in the family to make adjustments so that she can accomplish some goals that are important to her. She is convinced that her plans would not be detrimental to the family's welfare. The therapist shows an obvious bias by giving no support to Naomi's aspirations and by not asking the family to consider making any basic adjustments. Although the therapist does not openly say that she should give up her plans, his interventions have the result of reinforcing the family's resistance.

- Do you think this therapist is guilty of furthering gender-role stereotypes? Do his interventions show an interest in the well-being of the entire family?
- What are other potential ethical issues in this case?
- Being aware of your own bias regarding gender roles, how would you work with this family?
- Assume that the therapist had an obvious bias in favor of Naomi's plans and even pushed the family to learn to accept her right to an independent life. Do you see any potential ethical issues in this approach? Do you think a therapist can remain neutral in this kind of case? Explain your stance.

Responsibilities of Couples and Family Therapists

Margolin (1982) argues persuasively that difficult ethical questions confronted in individual therapy become even more complicated when a number of family members are seen together. She observes that the dilemma with multiple clients is that in some instances an intervention that serves one person's best interests could burden another family member or even be countertherapeutic. Under the family systems model, for example, therapists do not focus on the individual but on the family as a system. Such therapists avoid becoming agents of any one family member, believing that all family members contribute to the problems of the whole family. Ethical practice demands that therapists be clear about their commitments to each member of the family.

Therapist responsibilities are also a crucial issue in counseling with couples. This is especially true when the partners do not have a common purpose for seeking counseling. How do therapists carry out their ethical responsibilities when one partner comes for divorce counseling and the other wants to work on saving the marriage?

In addition to clinical and ethical considerations, Margolin reminds us that legal obligations may require therapists to put the welfare of an individual over that of a relationship. For example, the law requires family therapists to inform authorities if they suspect child neglect or abuse or become aware of it during the course of therapy. Even though reporting this situation may mean the end of therapy for the family, clearly the therapist's ethical and legal responsibility is to help the threatened or injured person. In the case of domestic violence, clinicians agree that conducting couples therapy while there is ongoing domestic violence presents a potential danger to the abused and is unethical. If the abuser has completed a course of treatment, there may be a possibility of doing therapy with the couple, depending on the assessment provided by the treatment facility. In situations involving domestic violence, there are both ethical and legal issues to consider. In cases where there are conflicts between ethical and legal dimensions of practice, it is especially important for family therapists to seek consultation.

At times couples and family therapists struggle over the issue of when to consult. This is especially true of situations in which a person (or couple or family) is already involved in a professional relationship with a therapist and seeks the counsel of another therapist. What course of action would you take if a husband sought you out for private counseling while he and his wife were also seeing another therapist for marriage counseling? Would it be ethical to enter into a professional relationship with this man without the knowledge and consent of the other professional? What might you do or say if the husband told you that the reason for initiating contact with you was to get another opinion and perspective on his marital situation and that he did not see any point in contacting the other professional?

Confidentiality in Couples and Family Therapy

The principle of confidentiality as it applies to couples and family therapists entails that practitioners not disclose what they have learned through the professional relationship except (1) when mandated by law, such as in cases of physical or psychological child abuse, incest, child neglect, or abuse of the elderly; (2) when it is necessary to protect clients from harming themselves or to prevent a clear and immediate danger to others; (3) when the family therapist is a defendant in a civil, criminal, or disciplinary action arising from the therapy; or (4) when a waiver has previously been obtained in writing. If therapists use any material from their practice in teaching, lecturing, and writing, they take care to preserve the anonymity of their clients. For therapists who are working with families, any release of information must be agreed to by all parties. However, there is an exception to this policy when a therapist is concerned that a family member will harm him- or herself, or will do harm to another person (Green, 2003). Another exception occurs when the law mandates a report.

Therapists have differing views on the role of confidentiality when working with families. One view is that therapists should not divulge in a family session any information given to them by individuals in private sessions. In the case of couples counseling, some practitioners are willing to see each spouse for individual sessions. Information given to them by one spouse is kept confidential. Other therapists, however, reserve the right to bring up certain issues in a joint session, even if one person mentioned the issue in a private session.

Some therapists who work with couples or entire families go further. They have a policy of refusing to keep information secret that was shared individually. Their view is that secrets are counterproductive for effective couples or family therapy. Therefore, "hidden agendas" are seen as material that should be brought out into the open during a couples or family session. Still another view is that therapists should inform their clients that any information given to them during private sessions will be divulged as they see fit in accordance with the greatest benefit for the couple or the family. These therapists reserve the right to use their professional judgment about whether to maintain individual confidences or not, claiming that this gives them more flexibility. Therapists who have not promised confidentiality have more options and thus must carefully consider the therapeutic ramifications of their actions.

Benitez (2004) recommends that therapists who work with couples would do well to develop a policy with regard to information that is shared with the therapist by one member of the couple outside of the presence of the other member of the couple. Benitez advises that this policy should state that such information might be disclosed to the other member of the couple at the therapist's discretion. This frees the therapist from being put in the position of keeping a secret of a client participating in conjoint therapy. However, each person must be informed of this policy in advance and also agree to this policy. According to Benitez, a "no secrets" policy is essential for therapists who offer couples counseling. Couples may need to be frequently reminded of this policy.

As a part of the informed consent process, it is absolutely essential to ethical practice that couples and family therapists clarify their position regarding confidentiality from the outset. The informed consent statement must include clarification as to who is the client and how personal matters that are expressed by a family member to the counselor on an individual basis will be dealt with during the course of family therapy (Smith, 1999). ACA's (2005) standard dealing with couples and family counseling states: "In couples and family counseling, counselors clearly define who is considered 'the client' and discuss expectations and limitations of confidentiality. Counselors seek agreement and document in writing such agreement among all involved parties having capacity to give consent concerning each individual's right to confidentiality and any obligation to preserve the confidentiality of information known" (B.4.b). When informed consent is done properly, family members are in a position to decide whether to participate in therapy and how much to disclose to the therapist. For example, a husband might disclose less in a private session if he knew that the therapist might bring these disclosures out in a conjoint session.

 **A Case of Therapist Quandary.** A husband is involved in individual therapy to resolve a number of personal conflicts, of which the state of his marriage is only one. Later, his wife comes in for some joint sessions. In their joint sessions much time is spent on how betrayed the wife feels over having discovered that her husband had an affair in the past. She is angry and hurt but has agreed to remain in the marriage and to come to these therapy sessions as long as the husband agrees not to resume the past affair or to initiate new ones. The husband agrees to her demands. The therapist does not explicitly state her views about confidentiality, nor does she explain a "no secrets" policy, yet the husband assumes that she will keep to herself what she hears in both the wife's private sessions and his private sessions. During one of the conjoint sessions, the therapist states that maintaining or initiating an affair is counterproductive if they both want to work on improving their marriage. The therapist states a strong preference that they agree not to have affairs during the time they are in therapy.

In a later individual session the husband tells the therapist that he has begun a new affair. He brings this up privately with his therapist because he feels some guilt over not having lived up to the agreement. But he maintains that the affair is not negatively influencing his relationship with his wife and has helped him to tolerate many of the difficulties he has been experiencing in his marriage. He also asks that the therapist not mention this in a conjoint session, for he fears that his wife will leave him if she finds out that he is involved with another woman. Think about these questions in deciding on the ethical course of action:

- The therapist has not explicitly stated her view of confidentiality and has not issued a "no secrets" policy. Is it ethical for her to bring up the husband's new affair in a conjoint session?
- How does the therapist handle her conviction regarding affairs in light of the fact that the husband tells her that it is actually enhancing, not interfering with, the marriage?
- Should the therapist attempt to persuade the husband to give up the affair? Should she persuade the client to bring up this matter himself in a conjoint session? Is the therapist colluding with the husband against the wife by not bringing up this matter?
- Should the therapist discontinue therapy with this couple because of her strong bias? If she does suggest termination and referral to another professional, might not this be tantamount to admitting to the wife that the husband is having an affair? What might the therapist say if the wife is upset over the suggestion of a referral and wants to know the reasons?

Informed Consent in Couples and Family Therapy

In Chapter 5 we examined the issue of informed consent and clients' rights within the framework of individual therapy. Informed consent is a critical ethical issue in the practice of couples and family therapy. Before each individual agrees to participate in family therapy, it is essential that the counselor provide information about the purpose of therapy, typical procedures, the risks of negative outcomes, the possible benefits, the fee structure, the limits of confidentiality, the rights and responsibilities of clients, the option that a family member can withdraw at any time, and what can be expected from the therapist. When therapists take the time to obtain informed consent from everyone, they convey the message that no one member is identified as the source of all the family's problems. Although getting the informed consent of each member of the family is ideal from an ethical point of view, actually carrying out this practice may be difficult. The more thorough and clear the preparation and informed consent process is, the easier it is for families to make decisions regarding their treatment, and as well, the more control the therapist has over future potential problems.

Clients have a right to know that the family system will be the focus of the therapeutic process and to know about the practical implications of this approach. Informed consent can be more complex than it appears. Many times families enter counseling with one person in the family being perceived as the one with the problem or the "identified patient." After therapy commences, however, the entire family becomes the focus of the therapist's intervention. Did these family members truly consent to become clients, or did they perceive their role as consultants? Family members should have opportunities to raise questions and know as clearly as possible what they are getting involved in when they enter family therapy.

Kaplan (2000) uses an informed consent brochure as a basis for establishing a solid therapeutic relationship among participants in family therapy. Here are some of the steps in this informed consent procedure:

- Construct a thorough informed consent brochure.
- Ask the couple or family to arrive early before the first session so they have time to read the brochure.
- Ask the family if they have any questions about the therapeutic process based on their reading of the informed consent brochure.
- Review the policies and rules about confidentiality.
- Request from each family member a written acknowledgment that he or she has reviewed and understood the contents of the brochure.
- Give the family the brochure to take home for further reference.
- Ask about the brochure at the beginning of the second session.

This structured informed consent procedure increases the chances of instilling a sense of trust that is foundational for future therapy sessions.

As a part of any informed consent document, it is essential that the therapist's policy be spelled out regarding the conditions for family therapy to begin. For instance, some family therapists will conduct family sessions even if certain members will not attend. Other family therapists consider it essential that all members of the family participate in the therapy process. This latter bias raises ethical questions about exerting pressure on an individual to participate, even if that person is strongly against being involved. Although coercion of a reluctant person is generally viewed as unethical, many therapists strongly suggest that a reluctant family member participate for a session or two to determine what potential value there might be in family therapy. Some resistance can arise from a family member's feeling that he or she will be the main target of the sessions. This resistance can be lessened and perhaps even eliminated in a short period of time if the therapist refuses to allow the family to use one member as a scapegoat.

There is no professional agreement on whether it is necessary to see all the family for therapy to take place, but we believe it is particularly important when it comes to therapy with children. In so many instances the child is the first family member presented for therapy, which can put an inordinate burden on the child. Including the whole family in therapy provides more protection for the child, and as the whole system corrects itself, the family can become a source of support for the child.

Chapter Summary

The field of couples and family therapy is rapidly expanding and developing. With an expansion in educational programs comes the need for specialized training and experience. A thorough discussion of ethical issues must be part of all such programs. A few of these issues are determining who is the primary client, dealing with confidentiality, policies on handling secrets, providing informed consent, counseling with minors, and exploring the role of values in family therapy.

The task of the therapist is to help a couple or a family explore and clarify their own values, not to influence them to conform to the therapist's value system. Likewise, a key ethical issue is the impact of the therapist's life experiences on his or her ability to practice effectively and objectively. As is true regarding all ethical issues, there is a significant relationship between sound ethical practices and clinical decision making. Family therapists may sometimes experience confusion, for example, regarding the ethical aspects of deciding who will attend family sessions. It is obvious, however, that such decisions cannot be made without a solid foundation in clinical theory and methodology. With increased knowledge and practical experience, therapists can make these ethical decisions with greater certainty. Being open to periodic supervision, seeking consultation when necessary, and being willing to participate in one's own therapy are some ways in which couples and family therapists can refine their clinical skills.

Suggested Activities

1. In the practice of couples and family therapy, informed consent is especially important. As a class discussion topic, explore some of these issues: What are the ethical implications of insisting that all members of a family participate in family therapy? What kind of information should a family therapist present from the outset to all those involved? Are there any ethical conflicts in focusing on the welfare of the entire family rather than on what might be in the best interests of a family member?
2. Investigate the status of regulating professional practice in couples and family therapy in your state. What are the academic and training requirements, if any, for certification or licensure in this field?
3. In a small group, discuss the major ethical problems facing couples and family therapists. Consider issues such as confidentiality, enforced therapy involving all family members, qualifications of effective family therapists, imposing the values of the therapist on a family, and practicing beyond one's competence.
4. Design a project to study your own family of origin. Interview as many relatives as you can. Look for patterns in your own relationships, including problems you currently struggle with, that might stem from your family of origin. What advantages do you see in studying your own family as one way to prepare yourself for counseling families?
5. Imagine that you are participating on a board to establish standards—personal, academic, and experiential—for family therapists. What do you think the minimum requirements should be to prepare a trainee to work with families? What would your ideal training program for couples and family therapists look like?

Ethics in Action CD-ROM Exercises

6. In video role play #4, The Divorce, the client (Janice) has made a decision to leave her husband and get a divorce. She says she does not want to work on her relationship anymore. The counselor (Gary) says he hates to hear that. Janice has not been happy for a long time, and she is tired of her husband's temper and his moods. Gary brings up the kids and asks who will be the advocate for them. Janice thinks that if she is happy they will be happy. She says she will take care of the kids, but that she has to do something with her life. Gary concludes by asking, "Is divorce the best way to take care of them?"

Put yourself in this situation with a client similar to Janice. Assume that your client is experiencing a great deal of ambivalence about getting a divorce, even though she tells you she is convinced that her marital situation is hopeless. She pleads with you to tell her whether she should remain married or get a divorce. What approach might you take? If your client expects you to provide her with an answer, because she is coming to you as the expert, what would you do? Have one student role play the confused client who is searching for an answer and ask several students to give different ways of proceeding with this client.

7. Now let's assume that the client in video role play #4 is struggling with staying versus leaving her husband. Using the responses of Counselors A, B, and C in the text for the case of Frank and Judy (see pages 447–448), have three students role play the counselors and interact with the client in the video.

InfoTrac® College Edition Resources

For additional readings, explore InfoTrac College Edition, our online library. Key words are listed in a form that enables the search engine to locate a wider range of articles in the online university library. Key words should be entered exactly as shown, including asterisks, "Wl," "W2," "AND," and other search engine tools. Go to http://www.infotrac-college.com and select these key word searches:

ethic* AND family w1 therap*
value* AND marri* w1 therapy
gender W1 sensitive AND therapy
confid* AND marital n4 family w1 therapy
systems W1 approach AND family W1 therapy
gender W1 sensitive AND family W1 therapy
femin* AND family W1 therapy

Chapter 12

Pre-Chapter Self-Inventory

Directions: For each statement, indicate the response that most closely identifies your beliefs and attitudes. Use the following code:

5 = I *strongly agree* with this statement.
4 = I *agree* with this statement.
3 = I am *undecided* about this statement.
2 = I *disagree* with this statement.
1 = I *strongly disagree* with this statement.

__2__ 1. Groups are useful mainly as a way to cut costs.
__3__ 2. Ethical practice requires that prospective group members be carefully screened and selected.
__4__ 3. It is important to prepare members so that they can derive the maximum benefit from the group.
__3__ 4. Requiring people to participate in a therapy group raises ethical issues.
__3__ 5. It is unethical to allow a group to exert pressure on one of its members.
__2__ 6. Confidentiality is less important in groups than it is in individual therapy.

Ethical Issues in Group Work

___ 7. Socializing among group members is almost always undesirable.

___ 8. One way of minimizing psychological risks to group participants is to negotiate contracts with the members.

___ 9. A group leader has a responsibility to teach members how to translate what they have learned in the group to their outside lives.

___ 10. It is unethical for counselor educators to lead groups of their students in training.

___ 11. Group psychotherapy cannot be conducted in an ethical manner over the Internet except in very limited circumstances.

___ 12. It is the group leader's responsibility to make prospective members aware of their rights and responsibilities and to demystify the process of a group.

___ 13. Group members should know that they have the right to leave the group at any time.

___ 14. Before people enter a group, it is the leader's responsibility to discuss with them the personal risks involved, especially potential life changes, and help them explore their readiness to face these risks.

___ 15. It is a sound practice to provide written ethical guidelines to group members in advance and discuss them in the first meeting.

Introduction

We are giving group work special attention, as we did with couples and family therapy, because it raises unique ethical concerns. Groups have been increasing in popularity, and in many agencies and institutions they are the primary form of treatment. Along with this increased use of groups has come a rising ethical awareness. Practitioners who work with groups face a variety of situations that differ from those encountered in individual therapy.

In tracing the research trends in group counseling and psychotherapy, Barlow, Fuhriman, and Burlingame (2004) state that empirical research on group counseling has shown that a set of recognizable factors—such as skilled leaders, appropriately referred group members, and defined goals—create positive outcomes in groups. They conclude that group approaches can ameliorate a number of social ills. Research confirms that group treatment is more effective than no treatment, yet group therapy does not appear to be superior to other forms of therapy. A survey of more than 40 years of research shows an abundance of evidence that group approaches are associated with clients' improvement in a variety of settings and situations (Barlow et al., 2004; Burlingame, Fuhriman, & Johnson, 2004).

Although there are some distinct advantages to group therapy, this mode of treatment appears to be underutilized because clients, and some therapists, view group therapy as a second-choice form of treatment. If groups are to flourish, group practitioners face the challenge of educating the public and health care professionals about this therapeutic approach. Clients are less frequently referred for group therapy than they are to individual treatment, and when clients are referred they may not always follow through and join a group (Trull, 2005).

Our illustrations of important ethical considerations in this chapter are drawn from a broad spectrum of groups, including therapy groups, counseling groups, personal-growth groups, psychoeducational groups, and structured groups. Obviously, these groups differ with respect to their member population, purpose, focus, and procedures, as well as in the level of training required for the facilitators of these groups. Although these distinctions are important, all groups face some common concerns: training group leaders, co-leadership issues, the ethical issues surrounding group membership, confidentiality in groups, values, uses and abuses of group techniques, and issues concerning consultation, referral, termination, and follow-up. We address these issues in this chapter.

Training and Supervision of Group Leaders

For competent group leaders to develop, training programs must make group work a priority. Such is not the case in some graduate training programs where not even one group course is required. Although some counselor training programs offer a sequence of two or three courses in group work, most have only one group course (Wilson, Rapin, & Haley-Banez, 2004). Most group courses include both the didactic and experiential aspects of group process.

With proper training in group work, competent practitioners will discover their limitations and recognize the kinds of groups they are competent to lead. Ethical practitioners familiarize themselves with referral resources and refrain from working with client populations that need special assistance beyond their level of competence. For practitioners to become competent group facilitators, specialized training is essential as a way to obtain proficiency and expertise in group process (Markus & King, 2003). When it comes to training doctoral level psychologists, comprehensive training standards have not been universally or rigorously followed. In a survey of group psychotherapy training during predoctoral psychology internships, Markus and King found that, much like graduate school programs, predoctoral clinical psychology internships do not routinely provide adequate group therapy training. The results of this survey suggest that there is a lack of depth and breadth of group therapy didactic offerings to psychology interns.

Professional Training Standards*

The Association for Specialists in Group Work (ASGW) revised the "Professional Standards for the Training of Group Workers" (ASGW, 2000), taking under consideration the "Best Practice Guidelines" (ASGW, 1998) and the "Principles for Diversity-Competent Group Workers" (ASGW, 1999). The ASGW training standards specify two levels of competencies and related training. First is a set of *core knowledge* and *skill competencies* that provide the foundation on which *specialized* training is built. At a minimum, one group course should be included in a training program, and it should be structured to help students acquire the basic knowledge and skills needed to facilitate a group. These group skills are best mastered through supervised practice, which should include a minimum of 10 hours (with 20 hours recommended) of observation and participation in a group experience. Specific course experiences can be developed from the knowledge and skill objectives delineated for these areas: nature and scope of practice; assessment of group members; the planning of group interventions with emphasis on environmental contexts and the implication of diversity; the implementation of specific group interventions; co-leadership practices; evaluation of process and outcomes; and ethical practice, best practice, and diversity-competent practice (Wilson et al., 2004).

Once counselor trainees have mastered these core knowledge and skills domains, they can acquire training in group work specializations in one or more of these four areas: (1) task groups, (2) psychoeducational groups, (3) group counseling, and (4) group psychotherapy. The ASGW standards detail specific knowledge and skill competencies for these specialties and recommend the number of hours of supervised training necessary for each.

*Adapted from "Professional Standards for the Training of Group Workers," adopted January 22, 2000, in *The Group Worker: Association for Specialists in Group Work, 29*(3), (Spring 2000), 1–10. The ASGW is a division of the American Counseling Association, 5999 Stevenson Avenue, Alexandria, VA 22304.

The ASGW's (2000) training standards are the foundation for training group workers in most counselor education programs. The standards of the Council for Accreditation of Counseling and Related Educational Programs (CACREP, 2001) that deal with group work reflect much of this material. Both ASGW and CACREP have articulated minimal guidelines for experiential training. ASGW (2000) recommends 20 hours of observation and participation in a group as a member or a leader, and CACREP (2001) specifies a 10-hour requirement as a participant in a small-group activity. Attempts have been made to integrate the ASGW recommendations with the CACREP standards, outlining supervised clinical experience obtained in both practicum and internship programs. The CACREP standards require experience in individual and group counseling under supervision and, consistent with the ASGW training standards, indicate that at least one fourth of the direct service practicum be devoted to group work.

Whether core training in group work reflects minimal CACREP standards or the more specific ASGW standards, this training alone is not sufficient to prepare counselors for conducting groups on their own. Practitioners must still acquire training in a particular specialization in group work. The current trend in training for group workers focuses on learning group processes by becoming involved in supervised experiences. Both direct participation in planned and supervised small groups and clinical experience in leading various groups under careful supervision are needed to equip leaders with the skills to meet the challenges of group work.

Barlow (2004) describes a conceptual model of how to teach specialized group work competencies using a 3-year plan. Barlow maintains that doctoral training programs could consider layering the teaching of core and specialized skills over a few years. Such skills could be identified as they occur in other courses in the program. Over time, various classes could strategically cover experiential, academic, observational, and supervisory skills. Barlow contends that if this approach were implemented, students would be on their way to developing expertise in group skills.

Our Views on Training Group Workers

Professional codes, legislative mandates, and institutional policies alone will not ensure competent group leadership. Group counselor trainees need to confront the typical dilemmas they will face in practice and learn ways to clarify their views on these issues. This can best be done by including ethics in the trainees' academic program as well as discussing ethical issues that grow out of the students' experiences in practicum, internship, and fieldwork. One effective way to teach ethical decision making is by presenting trainees with case vignettes of typical problems that occur in group situations and encouraging discussion of the ethical issues and pertinent guidelines. We tell both students and professionals who attend our workshops that they will not always have the answers to dilemmas they encounter in their groups. Ethical decision making is an ongoing process that takes on new forms and increased meaning as practitioners gain experience. It is critical that group leaders develop a receptivity to self-examination and to questioning the professionalism of their group practice.

In addition, we highly recommend three other experiences as adjuncts to a training program for group workers: (1) personal experience in a self-exploration group; (2) personal (private) psychotherapy; and (3) supervision.

Self-Exploration Groups. Group leaders need to demonstrate the willingness to do for themselves what they expect members in their groups to do: Expand their awareness of self and the effect of that self on others. As an adjunct to formal course work and internship training, participation in a therapeutic group can be extremely valuable. One of the best ways to learn how to assist group members in their struggles is to be a member of a group yourself. Yalom (2005) strongly recommends a group experience for trainees. Some of the benefits, he suggests, are experiencing the power of a group, learning what self-disclosure is about, coming to appreciate the difficulties involved in self-sharing, learning on an emotional level what one knows intellectually, and becoming aware of one's dependence on the leader's power and knowledge. He cites surveys indicating that 60 to 70% of group therapy training programs offer some type of personal-group experience. About half of these programs offer an optional group, and the other half a mandatory group.

Personal Psychotherapy. Sometimes issues surface in a group experience that may be more appropriately dealt with in personal (individual) therapy. We also encourage individual therapy as a way of enhancing trainees' abilities to understand both themselves and others. Yalom (2005) believes that extensive self-exploration is necessary if trainees are to perceive countertransference feelings, recognize blind spots and biases, and use their personal attributes effectively in groups. Although videotaping, working with a co-leader, and supervision are all excellent sources of feedback, Yalom maintains that personal therapy is usually necessary for fuller understanding and correction.

Supervision. Markus and King (2003) maintain that comprehensive training must include intensive supervision by a competent group therapist. Although Markus and King endorse group supervision of group leader trainees as a powerful cognitive and emotional learning experience, they report that the majority of internships that provide supervision of group trainees tend to use the one-to-one model rather than offer opportunities for group supervision.

Group supervision with group counselors provides trainees with many experiential opportunities to learn about the process and development of a group. In their investigation of group supervision with group counselors, Christensen and Kline (2000) emphasize that supervisees have many opportunities to learn through both participation and observation. Their investigation lent support to the numerous benefits of group supervision, a few of which include enhancement of knowledge and skills; ability to practice techniques in a safe and supportive environment; integration of theory and practice; richer understanding of patterns of group dynamics; opportunities to test one's assumptions;

personal development through connection with others; and opportunities for self-disclosure and for giving and receiving feedback. Results of Christensen and Kline's study supported previous findings of other researchers regarding group supervisory strategies. That is, supervisors need to assume a facilitative role in the supervision group, the stages of group development also apply to a supervision group, and it is important to address both content and process issues throughout group supervision.

Workshops that provide supervision for group trainees help them to develop the skills necessary for effective intervention. Also, this format helps interns learn a great deal about their response to criticism, their competitiveness, their need for approval, their concerns over being competent, and their power struggles. In working with both university students learning about group approaches and professionals who want to upgrade their skills, we often use a 5-day intensive workshop, which we find to be very effective.

As you consider the training of group leaders, ponder these questions for yourself:

- What makes you qualified to lead groups?
- Can you think of safeguards to minimize the potential risks of combining experiential and didactic methods?
- Does ethical practice demand that group leaders receive some form of personal therapy? Should this be group therapy or experience in a personal-growth group?
- What are your reactions to the suggestions we offered for training group workers?

Diversity Issues in Training Group Workers

Given the fact that the U.S. population is characterized by drastically increasing diversity, it is essential that group counselors be culturally competent practitioners (Bemak & Chung, 2004). An integral part of the training of group leaders is promoting sensitivity and competence in addressing diversity in all forms of group work. Being diversity competent is more complex in meaning than "respecting other people." To fully assimilate the meaning into our personal and professional beings, it is important for us to have a common understanding of the principles on which diversity competence is built. The "Principles for Diversity Competent Group Workers" (ASGW, 1999) addresses issues such as racism, classism, sexism, heterosexism, and ableism with sensitivity and skill. These principles emphasize the practitioner's responsibility to have a general understanding of the diverse cultural backgrounds of the group members so interventions are congruent with their worldviews.

Most of the ethics codes of the various professional organizations now give some attention to applying these principles when working with diverse client populations. Guidelines for competence in diversity issues in group practice are discussed in a variety of sources, some of which include Arredondo and colleagues (1996), ASGW (1999), APA (1993), Bemak and Chung (2004), and

DeLucia-Waack and Donigian (2004). Based on these sources, we have adapted the following guidelines for group practice:

- Group counselors emphasize appreciation, respect, and acceptance in cultural and racial identity for all cultures.
- Group counselors strive to understand how their cultural background interrelates with people from other cultural backgrounds.
- Group counselors consider the impact of adverse social, environmental, and political factors in assessing problems and designing interventions.
- Group counselors acquire the knowledge and skills necessary for effectively working with the diverse range of members in their groups. They seek consultation, supervision, and further education to fill any gaps and keep themselves current.
- Group counselors are aware of problems involved in stereotyping and avoid making the erroneous assumption that there are no differences between group members from the same ethnic, racial, or other group.
- Group counselors respect the roles of family and community hierarchies within a client's culture.
- Group counselors assist members in determining those instances when their difficulties stem from others' racism or bias, so they do not inappropriately personalize problems.
- Group counselors inform members about basic values that are implicit in the group process (such as self-disclosure, reflecting on one's life, and taking risks).

An awareness of cultural diversity is particularly important for group work. In Chapter 4 we discussed the characteristics of the culturally competent counselor. If group counselors do not understand how their cultural background influences their own thinking and behavior, there is little chance they can understand how their group members are influenced by their cultural thinking and behavior.

The self-awareness, knowledge, and skill competencies described in Chapter 4 certainly apply to practitioners who work with groups. ASGW (1999) spells out the implications of the principles of diversity training for awareness of self, knowledge, and skills. In working with groups characterized by diversity, practitioners need to be aware of the assumptions they make about ethnic and cultural groups, and they are challenged to adapt their practices to the needs of the members. It is essential that the goals and processes of the group match the cultural values of the members of that group. It is critical that leaders become aware of their potential biases based on age, disability, ethnicity, gender, race, religion, or sexual orientation. Group counselors need to have an understanding of the diversity of cultural worldviews and their potential impact on relationships, behaviors, and clients' willingness to become involved in a group experience. Although it is not realistic to assume that leaders will have knowledge about every culture, it is important that counselors understand that each person participates in a group from his or her own unique perspective (DeLucia-Waack & Donigian, 2004).

Ivey, Pedersen, and Ivey (2001) present the idea of multicultural intentionality, or the ability to work effectively with many varying types of individuals with diverse cultural backgrounds. To the key components of awareness, knowledge, and skills, they add the characteristics of humility, confidence, and recovery skills as critical to effective group leadership. These attributes mean that leaders do not have to possess all the answers, that they can learn from their members and from their own mistakes, and that they can develop confidence in their flexibility in challenging situations. The ability to recover from mistakes gracefully is more important than not making any mistakes.

What awareness, knowledge, and skills do you already possess that you can build on to help you develop the ability to work well with multicultural groups? To what degree are you able to respect the values and worldviews of group participants who may be very different from you? Take an active role in seeking out experiences that will enhance your ability to make connections with diverse group members. For a more detailed treatment of diversity issues in group work, see DeLucia-Waack and Donigian (2004), *The Practice of Multicultural Group Work: Visions and Perspectives From the Field.*

Co-Leadership

If you lead groups, you will probably work with a co-leader at some time. We think there are many advantages to the **co-leader model.** The group can benefit from the insights and feedback of two leaders. The leaders can complement and balance each other. They learn by discussing what goes on in the group and by observing each other's style, and together they can evaluate what has gone on in the group and plan for future sessions. Also, co-leaders can share the responsibilities. While one leader is working with a particular member, the other can be paying attention to others in the group.

The choice of a co-leader is crucial and can have ethical implications. A group can suffer if its leaders are not working effectively together. If the leaders' energies are directed at competing with each other or at some other power struggle or hidden agenda, there is little chance that the group will be effective.

Selection of a co-leader involves more than attraction and liking. Each of the leaders should be secure enough that the group won't have to suffer as one or both of them try to "prove" themselves. We surely don't think it is essential that co-leaders always agree or share the same perceptions or interpretations; in fact, a group can be given vitality if co-leaders feel trusting enough to express their differences of opinion. Mutual respect and the ability to establish a relationship based on trust, cooperation, and support are most important. Also, each person should be autonomous and have his or her own style yet be able to work with the other leader as a team.

In our view it is essential for co-leaders to spend some time together immediately following a group session to assess what has happened. Similarly, we believe that they should meet at least briefly before each session to talk about anything that might affect their functioning in the group.

At this point we ask you to draw up your own guidelines for selecting a co-leader:

- What would you most appreciate in a co-leader?
- If you found that you and your co-leader clashed on many issues and approached groups very differently, what would you do?
- What ethical implications are involved when a great deal of time during the sessions is taken up with power struggles and conflicts between the co-leaders?
- In what ways could you be most helpful to your co-leader?
- How could a co-leader be most helpful to you?

Ethical Issues in Group Membership

How can group leaders make potential members aware of the services they are providing? What information do clients have a right to expect before they decide to attend a group? People have a right to know what they are getting into before they make a commitment to become a part of any group. Informed consent requires that leaders make the members aware of their rights (as well as their responsibilities) as group participants. The section on informed consent in Chapter 5 applies to both individual and group counseling. Refer to that earlier discussion for further details.

Screening and Selection of Group Members

Group leaders are faced with the difficult task of determining who should be included in a group and who should not. Are groups appropriate for all people? To put the question in another way, is it appropriate for *this* person to become a participant in *this* type of group, with *this* leader, at *this* time? To answer this question, some type of **screening,** which involves interviewing and evaluating potential members, is often employed to select suitable members.

Assuming that not everyone will benefit from a group experience—and that some people may be psychologically harmed by certain group experiences—is it unethical to fail to screen prospective group candidates? Many group leaders do not screen participants, for various reasons. Some practitioners are clinically opposed to the notion of using screening as a way of determining who is suitable for a group, and some maintain that they simply do not have the time to carry out effective screening. Others believe that ethical practice demands careful screening and preparation of all candidates.

Unless careful selection criteria are employed, Yalom (2005) argues that group therapy clients may end up discouraged and may not be helped. He maintains that it is easier to identify the people who should be excluded from group therapy than those who should be included. Citing clinical studies, he lists the following as poor candidates for a heterogeneous outpatient intensive therapy group: brain-damaged people, paranoid individuals, hypochondriacs, those who are addicted to drugs or alcohol, acutely psychotic individuals, and antisocial personalities. In terms of criteria for inclusion, he contends that the client's level of motivation to work is the most important variable. From his perspective, groups are useful for people who have problems in the interpersonal domain, such as loneliness, inability to make or maintain intimate contacts, feelings of unlovability, fears of being assertive, and dependency issues.

Clients who lack meaning in life, who suffer from diffuse anxiety, who are searching for an identity, who fear success, and who are compulsive workers might also profit from a group experience. The ACA (2005) identifies the counselor's responsibility for screening prospective group members:

> Counselors screen prospective group counseling/therapy participants. To the extent possible, counselors select members whose needs and goals are compatible with goals of the group, who will not impede the group process, and whose well-being will not be jeopardized by the group experience. (A.8.a)

Screening is most effective when the leader interviews the members and the members also have an opportunity to interview the leader. While prospective group members are being screened, they should be deciding whether they want to work with a particular leader and whether the group in question is suitable for them. Practitioners should welcome the opportunity to respond to any questions or concerns prospective members may have, and they should actively encourage prospective members to raise questions about matters that will affect their participation.

It needs to be mentioned that not all theoretical orientations favor or agree with the notion of screening. For example, practitioners with a transactional analysis orientation often do not conduct screening. Many Adlerians believe screening does not fit with the democratic spirit of their theory. Some maintain that screening is done more for the comfort of the group leader than the good of the client. If a practitioner does not screen because of a theoretical value, we do not think this constitutes unethical practice. Furthermore, in some settings it is impractical to screen members prior to forming a group. In situations where it is not possible to conduct screening interviews, one alternative is to use the initial session to screen participants and to present informed consent guidelines.

Preparing Group Participants

To what extent are group counselors responsible for helping participants to benefit from their group experience? Many practitioners do very little to prepare members for a group. They are opposed to preparation on the grounds that it could inhibit a group's spontaneity and autonomy. Others take the position that members need to be provided with some structure to derive maximum gains.

Yalom (2005) advocates exploring group members' misconceptions and expectations, predicting early problems, and providing a conceptual framework that includes guidelines for effective group behavior. He views this preparatory process as more than the dissemination of information. He contends that it reinforces the therapist's respect for the client, demonstrates that therapy is a collaborative venture, and shows that the therapist is willing to share his or her knowledge with the client. This cognitive approach to preparation has the goals of providing a rational explanation of the group process, clarifying how members are expected to behave, and raising expectations about what the group can accomplish.

In our experience working with groups, we have found that providing members with basic information about group process tends to eliminate some of the difficulties encountered in the early stages of a group. Our preparation procedures apply to most types of groups, with some modifications. At both the screening session and the initial group meeting, we explore the members' expectations, clarify goals and objectives, discuss procedural details, explore the possible risks and values of group participation, and discuss guidelines for getting the most from a group experience (Corey, Corey, Callanan, & Russell, 2004; M. Corey & Corey, 2006). As part of member preparation, we include a discussion of the values and limitations of groups, the psychological risks involved in group participation, and ways of minimizing these risks. We also allow time for dealing with misconceptions that people have about groups and for exploring the fears or resistances the members may have. In most of our groups, members do have certain fears about what they will experience; until we acknowledge these fears and talk about them, very little productive work can occur. Further, we ask members to spend time before they come to the group defining for themselves what they most want to achieve. To make their goals more concrete, we usually ask them to develop a contract that entails areas of concern on which they are willing to work in the group. We also ask them to do some reading and to write about their goals and about the significant turning points in their lives.

At this point, we ask you to write down some things you might do to prepare people for a group. What ethical concerns do you have regarding preparation? What do you think would occur if you did little in the way of preparing group members?

Involuntary Participation

Can involuntary group membership be effective? Are there situations in which it is ethical to require or coerce people to participate in a group? How is informed consent especially critical in groups where attendance is mandatory?

Obviously, voluntary participation is an important beginning point for a successful group experience. Members will make significant changes only to the extent that they actively seek something for themselves. Unfortunately, not all groups are composed of clients who have chosen to be there. In some community agencies and inpatient facilities, the main therapeutic vehicle may be group therapy. People receiving services may be required to attend group sessions, sometimes several times a week. This **involuntary participation** is somewhat akin to compulsory education—people can be forced to attend but not to learn.

When group participation is mandatory, greater effort needs to be directed toward fully informing members of the nature and goals of the group, procedures to be used, the rights of members to decline certain activities, the limits of confidentiality, and what effect their level of participation in the group will have on critical decisions about them outside of the group. When attendance at group sessions is mandatory, group leaders must be certain that group members understand their rights and their responsibilities.

Consider these questions on involuntary membership:

- Do you think members can benefit from a group experience even if they are required to attend? Why or why not?
- What strategy might a leader use to foster more effective group participation while still giving the members true freedom of choice?
- From an ethical perspective, is it required that members of an involuntary group give consent? To what degree should members be informed about the consequences of the quantity or quality of their participation in a group?

Freedom to Leave a Group

Once members make a commitment to be a part of a group, do they have the right to leave at any time they choose? Procedures for leaving a group should be explained to all members during the initial session. Ideally, the leader and the member cooperate to determine whether a group experience is proving to be productive or counterproductive. We take the position that clients have a responsibility to the leader and to other members to explain why they want to leave. There are several reasons for this policy. It can be deleterious to members to leave without having been able to discuss what they considered threatening or negative in the experience. Further, it is unfortunate for members to leave a group because of a misunderstanding about some feedback they have received. Such a termination can be harmful to group cohesion, for the members who remain may think that they caused a particular member's departure. We tell our members that they have an obligation to attend all sessions and to inform us and the group if they decide to withdraw. Although members have a right to leave, we ask them to talk about it out of respect for the needs of the remaining members. If members even consider withdrawing, we encourage them to bring this up for exploration in a session. We do not think it is ethical to use undue pressure to keep these members, and we are alert to other members pressuring a person to stay.

Psychological Risks

The fact that groups can be powerful catalysts for personal change means that they are also risky. Our goal is not to make sure that all members are comfortable as much as to create a safe environment where they can take risks and explore their discomfort. Although we don't think groups can be free of risks, ethical practice demands that group practitioners inform prospective participants of the potential hazards involved in the group experience. However, merely informing participants does not absolve leaders of all responsibility. Group leaders have an ethical responsibility to take precautionary measures to reduce unnecessary psychological risks. ACA's (2005) guideline is this: "In a

group setting, counselors take reasonable precautions to protect clients from physical, emotional, or psychological trauma" (A.8.b). Certain safeguards can be taken during the course of a group to avoid disastrous outcomes. Here are some of the risks that participants should know about (M. Corey & Corey, 2006):

- Members may experience some disruptions in their lives as a result of their work in the group.
- Group participants are often encouraged to be completely open. In this quest for self-revelation, privacy is sometimes surrendered.
- A related risk is group pressure. The participants' right not to explore certain issues or to stop at a certain point should be respected. Also, members should not be coerced into participating in an exercise.
- Scapegoating is another potential hazard in groups. Unchallenged projection and blaming can have dire effects on the target person.
- Confrontation can be used or misused in groups. Harmful attacks on others should not be permitted under the guise of "sharing."
- Even though a counselor may continue to stress the necessity not to discuss with outsiders what goes on in the group, there is no guarantee that all members will respect the confidential nature of their exchanges.

One way to minimize psychological risks in groups is to use a contract, in which leaders specify what their responsibilities are and members specify their commitment to the group by declaring what they are willing to do. If members and leaders operate under a contract that clarifies expectations, there is less chance for members to be exploited or damaged by a group experience.

Of course, a contract approach is not the only way to reduce potential risks, nor is it sufficient in itself to do so. One of the most important safeguards is the leader's training in group process. Group counselors have the major responsibility for preventing needless harm to members. To fulfill this role, group leaders should have a clear grasp of the boundaries of their competence. As a rule, leaders should conduct only those types of groups for which they have been sufficiently prepared. A counselor may be trained to lead a personal-growth or consciousness-raising group but be ill-prepared to embark on a therapy group. Sometimes people who have attended a few intensive groups become excited about doing this type of group as leaders, even though they lack the requisite training. Oftentimes they are overwhelmed and unable to cope with what emerges in the group. Working with an experienced co-leader is one good way to learn and also a way to reduce potential risks.

Confidentiality in Groups

The ethical, legal, and professional aspects of confidentiality (discussed in Chapter 6) have a different application in group situations. Are members of a group under the same ethical and legal obligations as the group leader not to disclose the identities of other members or the content of what was shared in the group? The legal concept of privileged communication generally does not apply in a group setting, unless there has been a statutory exception. Therefore, group counselors have the responsibility of informing members of the limits of confidentiality within the group setting, their responsibilities to other group members, and the absence of legal privilege concerning what is shared in a group (Anderson, 1996). One of the clear ethical responsibilities of members is to respect the communications of others in the group. Benitez (2004) recommends that group practitioners develop a group confidentiality agreement that addresses both the leader's duty of confidentiality and the rules of confidentiality for the group members.

From the beginning of a group we discuss with members the purpose and limits of confidentiality. The APA (2002) standard also recognizes the limits of confidentiality in group therapy: "When psychologists provide services to several persons in a group setting, they describe at the outset the roles and responsibilities of all parties and the limits of confidentiality" (10.03). ACA's (2005) ethics code specifies that "counselors clearly explain the importance and parameters of confidentiality for the specific group being entered" (B.4.a).

How to Encourage Confidentiality. The ASGW (1998) "Best Practice Guidelines" state the following regarding confidentiality:

> Group Workers define confidentiality and its limits (for example, legal and ethical exceptions and expectations; waivers implicit with treatment plans, documentation, and insurance usage). Group Workers have the responsibility to inform all group participants of the need for confidentiality and potential consequences of breaching confidentiality; they must explain that legal privilege does not apply to group discussions (unless provided by state statute). (A.7.d)

Encouraging confidentiality is a special challenge for counselors who offer groups for children and adolescents in school settings. On this matter, ASCA's (2004) *Ethical Standards for School Counselors* provides an important guideline:

> The professional school counselor establishes clear expectations in the group setting and clearly states that confidentiality in group counseling cannot be guaranteed. Given the developmental and chronological ages of minors in schools, the counselor recognizes the tenuous nature of confidentiality for minors renders some topics inappropriate for group work in a school setting. (A.6.c)

Although most writers on ethical issues in group work make the point that confidentiality cannot be guaranteed, they also talk about the importance of teaching group members to avoid breaking confidences. Confidentiality in group situations is not easily enforced. Because members cannot assume that anything they say or hear in the group will remain confidential, they should be able to make an informed choice about how much to reveal.

It is our position that leaders need periodically to reaffirm to group members the importance of not discussing with outsiders what has occurred in the group. We talk with each prospective member about the necessity of maintaining confidentiality to establish the trust and cohesion required if participants are to reveal themselves in significant ways. We discuss this point during the screening interviews, again during the pregroup or initial meetings, at times during the course of a group when it seems appropriate, and again at termination. Most people do not maliciously attempt to hurt others by talking with people outside the group about specific members. However, it is tempting for members to share their experiences with other people, and in so doing they sometimes make inappropriate disclosures. Because of this tendency to want to share with outsiders, we repeatedly caution participants in any type of group about how easily and unintentionally the confidentiality of the group can be compromised.

If you were to lead a group, which of the following measures might you take to ensure confidentiality? Check any of the statements that apply:

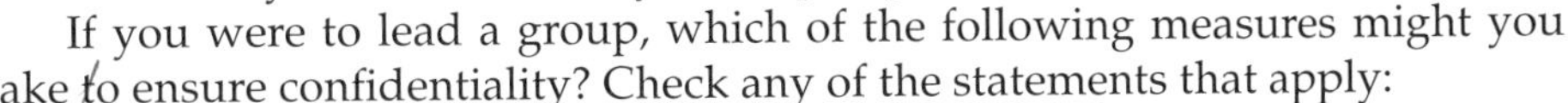

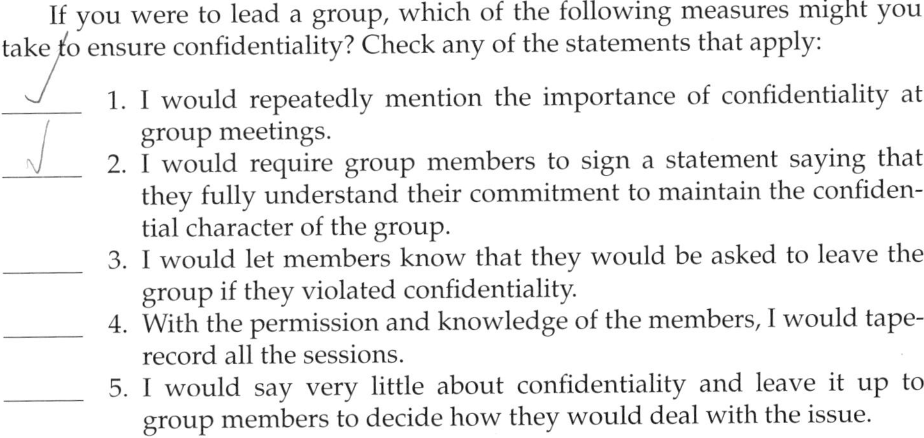

______ 1. I would repeatedly mention the importance of confidentiality at group meetings.

______ 2. I would require group members to sign a statement saying that they fully understand their commitment to maintain the confidential character of the group.

______ 3. I would let members know that they would be asked to leave the group if they violated confidentiality.

______ 4. With the permission and knowledge of the members, I would tape-record all the sessions.

______ 5. I would say very little about confidentiality and leave it up to group members to decide how they would deal with the issue.

Exceptions to Confidentiality. Group counselors have a responsibility to define clearly what confidentiality means, explain its importance, and inform members of the difficulties involved in enforcing it. Although group counselors are expected to stress the importance of confidentiality and set a norm, they are also expected to inform members about its limits. For example, if members pose a danger to themselves or to others, the group leader would be ethically and legally obliged to breach confidentiality. The other limitations for confidentiality, which were discussed in Chapter 6, also apply to group work.

It is a good practice for group workers to give a written statement to each member outlining the nature, purposes, and limitations of confidentiality and acknowledging specific situations that would require the breaching of confidences. It seems that such straightforwardness with members from the outset does a great deal to create trust, for at least members know the consequences of certain revelations to the group.

Of course, it is imperative that those who lead groups become familiar with the state laws that have an impact on their practice. For instance, all states have had mandatory child abuse reporting laws since 1967. Several states also have mandatory elder abuse and dependent adult abuse reporting laws. The great majority of states currently have laws requiring counselors to report clients' threats to harm themselves or others.

If you lead a group at a correctional institution or a psychiatric hospital, you may have to record in a member's chart certain behaviors or verbalizations that he or she exhibits in the group. At the same time, your responsibility to your clients requires you to inform them that you are documenting their verbalizations and behaviors and that this information is accessible to other staff.

Confidentiality with Minors. Do parents have a right to information that is disclosed by their children in a group? The answer to that question depends on whether we are looking at it from a legal, ethical, or professional viewpoint. State laws differ regarding counseling minors. It is important for group leaders to be aware of the laws related to working with minors in the state where they are practicing. Circumstances in which a minor may seek professional help without parental consent, defining an emancipated minor, or the rights of parents (or legal guardians) to have access to the records regarding the professional help received by their minor child vary according to state statutes.

Before any minor enters a group, it is a good practice to obtain written permission from the parents. Such a statement should include a brief description of the purpose of the group, the importance of confidentiality as a prerequisite to accomplishing these purposes, and your intention not to violate any confidences. Although it may be useful to give parents information about their child, this can be done without violating confidences. At the first session it is helpful to inform and discuss with minors their concerns about confidentiality and how it will be maintained. Such practices can strengthen the child's trust in the counselor.

Group leaders have a responsibility in groups that involve children and adolescents to take measures to increase the chances that confidentiality will be kept. It is important to work cooperatively with parents and legal guardians as well as to enlist the trust of the young members. It is also useful to teach minors, using a vocabulary they understand, about the nature, purposes, and limitations of confidentiality. It is a good idea for leaders to encourage members to initiate discussions on confidentiality whenever this becomes an issue for them.

Confidentiality and Online Group Work. Ethical considerations pertaining to confidentiality and the questionable effectiveness of online counseling may be a factor in its limited uses in educational and practice settings (Krieger & Stockton, 2004). Humphreys, Winzelberg, and Klaw (2000) take the position that online group psychotherapy cannot ethically be conducted over the Internet, except in very limited circumstances. Internet group therapy involves typing, recording, copying, and distributing all the "interactions" that take place online. This makes ensuring clients' privacy and confidentiality a very difficult matter. In addition, individuals cannot be reliably identified over the Internet. A person with access to a client's computer could sign into online group counseling by using the password and the name of the actual client. The implications for lack of confidentiality and privacy are obvious here. Because of the difficulty of maintaining the confidential nature of a group, we are opposed to online group counseling on both ethical and clinical grounds.

Humphreys and colleagues (2000) state that some kinds of peer groups and self-help groups do utilize Internet technology, but they add that the astonishing growth in the technology has outpaced the development of formal ethical guidelines for practitioners involved in online groups. Humphreys and colleagues write about a therapist's ethical responsibilities in self-help groups, discussion groups, and support groups that operate on the Internet, and they offer practical strategies for avoiding ethical problems.

Chang and Yeh (2003) provide a theoretical framework and practical guidelines for practitioners to implement online groups to address racial, cultural, and gender issues in working with Asian American men. They emphasize how important it is for group facilitators to set the tone for a group by creating initial ground rules from the outset, especially guidelines for dealing with confidentiality. Chang and Yeh suggest that in closed groups confidentiality can be maximized by instructing participants to avoid disclosing the concerns of other group members to people who are not part of the group. Group members should also be cautioned about not sharing passwords used to access the group with those who are not a part of the group. As the group is beginning, it is essential to address topics such as respectful communication, level of interaction, termination conditions, and opportunities for face-to-face contact.

Values in Group Counseling

Group counselors have the responsibility of being aware of their own values and the potential impact they have on the interventions they are likely to make. However, group counselors are sometimes timid about making their values known lest they influence the direction members are likely to take. Group counselors need to consider when it might be appropriate to expose their beliefs, decisions, life experiences, and values. The leader's central function is to help members find answers that are congruent with their own values, not to short-circuit the members' exploration by providing them with answers. We suggest that you refer to the discussion of value conflicts in Chapter 3 and consider specific areas in which you might be inclined to impose your values in the groups you lead. Reflect on any tendencies you may have to lead your clients in a certain direction, and think about ways to minimize the chances of imposing your values on them.

Certain behaviors of group leaders reveal their values: (a) demonstrating acceptance of the person of the client; (b) avoiding responding to sarcastic remarks with sarcasm; (c) being honest with members rather than harboring hidden agendas; (d) avoiding judgments and labeling of members, and instead describing the behavior of members; (e) stating observations and hunches in a tentative way rather than dogmatically; (f) letting members who are difficult know how they are affecting them in a nonblaming way; (g) detecting their own countertransference reactions; (h) avoiding misuse of their power; (i) providing both support and caring confrontations; and (j) avoiding meeting their own needs at the expense of the members (M. Corey & Corey, 2006).

Uses and Abuses of Group Techniques

Group techniques can be used to facilitate the movement of a group and to deepen and intensify certain feelings. We think leaders should have a clear rationale for using each technique. This is an area in which theory can be a useful guide for practice.

Techniques can also be abused or used in unethical ways. Here are some ways leaders might employ techniques unethically:

- Using techniques with which they are unfamiliar
- Using techniques to enhance their power
- Using techniques whose sole purpose is to create intensity because of the leader's need for intensity
- Using techniques to pressure members, even when they have expressed a desire not to participate in an exercise

We use these guidelines in our practice to avoid abusing techniques in a group:

- Techniques used have a therapeutic purpose and are grounded in some theoretical framework.
- The client's self-exploration and self-understanding is fostered.
- Techniques are devised for each unique client situation, and they assist the client in exploring some form of new behavior.
- Leaders modify their techniques so that they are suitable for the client's cultural and ethnic background.
- Techniques are used to enhance the group process rather than to cover up the leader's incompetence.
- Techniques are introduced in a timely and sensitive manner, and they are abandoned if they are not working.
- The tone of a leader is consistently invitational; members are given the freedom either to participate in or to skip a given experiment.
- Leaders use techniques in which they have received training and supervision.

Although it is unrealistic to expect that leaders will always know exactly what will result from an intervention, they should know how to cope with unexpected outcomes. For example, guided fantasies into times of loneliness as a child or physical exercises designed to release anger can lead to intense emotional experiences. If leaders use such techniques, they must be ready to deal with any emotional release. It is essential that group counselors become aware of the potential for encouraging catharsis to fulfill their own needs. Some leaders push people to express anger because they would like to be able to do so themselves. They develop techniques to focus the group on anger. Although these are legitimate feelings, expressing anger in the group may satisfy the leader's agenda more than it meets the needs of the members. This question ought to be raised frequently: "Whose needs are primary, and whose needs are being met—the members' or the leader's?"

Therapist Competence

How can leaders determine whether they are competent to use a certain technique? Although some leaders who have received training in the use of a technique may hesitate to use it (out of fear of making a mistake), other leaders may not have any reservations about trying out new techniques. It is useful if leaders have experienced these techniques as members of a group and have a clear rationale for using them. Group counselors need to be able to articulate a theoretical orientation that guides the interventions they make in their groups.

Unfinished Business

Another major issue pertaining to the use of group techniques relates to providing immediate help for any group member who shows extreme distress during or at the end of a group session, especially if techniques were used to elicit intense emotions. Although some "unfinished business" promotes growth, there is an ethical issue in the use of a technique that incites strong emotional reactions if the client is abandoned at the end of a session because time has run out. Leaders must take care to allow enough time to deal adequately with the reactions that were stimulated in a session. It is unwise to introduce techniques in a session when there is not enough time to work through the feelings that might result or in a setting where there is no privacy or where the physical setup would make it harmful to employ certain techniques.

Our position on the ethical use of techniques is that group leaders need to learn about potential adverse effects. One way for group leaders to learn is by taking part in groups themselves. By being a group member and first experiencing a range of techniques, a therapist can develop a healthy respect for using techniques appropriately to meet clients' needs. In our training workshops for group leaders, we encourage spontaneity and inventiveness in the use of techniques, but we also stress the importance of striking a balance between creativity and irresponsibility. The reputation of group work has suffered from the actions of irresponsible practitioners, mostly those who use techniques randomly without a clear rationale or without any sense of the potential outcome of techniques. If the group leader has a strong academic background, has had extensive supervised group experience, has participated in his or her own therapy or personal-growth experience, and has a basic respect for clients, he or she is not likely to abuse techniques.

The Consultation and Referral Process

Group counselors need to be aware of their limitations in working with certain types of clients. The willingness to consult with other professionals demonstrates wisdom and good faith on the practitioner's part. For example, diversity-competent group workers are willing to seek consultation with traditional healers and religious or spiritual healers in the treatment of a diverse range of problems of individual members. Group workers actively seek out educational experiences that foster their knowledge and understanding of skills for facilitating groups across differences (ASGW, 1998, 1999).

It is a good practice for leaders to explain to members their policies about consultation. When are they likely to consult? What measures do they take to protect confidentiality? Are they willing to have between-session consultations with group members? When and how might they refer? Here are some guidelines pertaining to the consultation and referral process:

- Group counselors can seek consultation and supervision when they are faced with ethical concerns or difficulties that interfere with carrying out their leadership functions.
- Leaders need to develop sensitivity to situations in which a referral is appropriate.
- Leaders learn about the resources within the community and help members make use of these resources.

As we discussed earlier, one way to protect against a malpractice suit is to demonstrate that consultation procedures were used in dealing with an ethical dilemma. If group leaders consult supervisors or other professionals, they are demonstrating good clinical practice, adhering to ethical guidelines, and minimizing their chances of malpractice.

Issues Concerning Termination

The final phase in the life of a group is critical, for this is when members have the task of consolidating their learning. At this time members need to be able to express what the group experience has meant to them and to state where they intend to go from here. Neglecting the process of termination can easily leave the members stuck and will limit opportunities for members to conceptualize what they learned from a group experience. For many group members endings are difficult because they realize that time is limited in their group. The ending of a group often triggers other losses that members have experienced. Thus, the termination of a group may involve a grieving process. It is important for leaders to focus on the feelings of loss that may permeate the atmosphere. These feelings need to be identified and explored, although they probably cannot be alleviated. Members need to face the reality of termination and learn how to say good-bye. If the group has been truly therapeutic, the members will be able to extend their learning outside the group, even though they may well experience a sense of sadness and loss.

The Termination Phase

The termination phase of a group provides an opportunity for members to clarify the meaning of their experience, to consolidate the gains they have made, and to make decisions about the new behaviors they want to carry away from the group and apply to their everyday lives. The following professional issues are involved in the termination of a group:

- What responsibilities do group leaders have for assisting participants to develop a conceptual framework that will make sense of, integrate, and consolidate what they have learned in their group?
- To what degree is it the leader's responsibility to ensure that members are not left with excessive unfinished business at the end of the group?
- How can group leaders help participants translate what they have learned as a result of the group into their daily lives? Should leaders assume that this translation will occur automatically, or must they prepare members for maximizing their learning?

Typically, the final phase of group work may be the one that leaders handle most ineptly, possibly owing to their lack of training or partly because of their own resistance to termination. Avoiding acknowledgment of a group's termination may reflect discomfort on the leader's part in dealing with endings and separations. When termination is not dealt with, the group misses an opportunity to explore concerns that may affect many members, and the clients' therapy is jeopardized. When learning is not conceptualized, the ability to bring the meaning of the experience to real life is severely diminished.

Follow-Up and Evaluation

Throughout the life of a group, group leaders assist members in assessing their own progress and monitor their style of modeling. In this sense, evaluation is an ongoing process whereby members are taught how to determine if the group is helping them attain their personal goals. But group counselors also must assess both the process and the outcomes of their groups. Once a group has ended, follow-up group sessions provide an opportunity to do this. In our opinion, follow-up activities are useful to the members and to the group counselor as well. Both short-term follow-up (after 1 month) and long-term follow-up (after 3 months to a year) can be invaluable measures of accountability. (For more discussion on termination issues, see M. Corey & Corey, 2006.)

Chapter Summary

Along with the growing popularity of group approaches to counseling and therapy comes a need for ethical and professional guidelines for those who lead groups. There are many types of groups, and there are many possible uses of groups in various settings. In this chapter we have discussed some issues that are related to most groups: How does a leader's theoretical view of groups influence the way a group is structured? What are some key elements in recruiting, screening, selecting, and preparing group members? What ethical, professional, legal, and practical issues concerning confidentiality are involved in any type of group? To what degree should participants be prepared for a group before the group begins? What are some ethical issues in the selection and training of group leaders? In what ways can group techniques be used or abused? What responsibility do group leaders have in terms of follow-up and evaluation? With respect to these and other issues, we have stressed the importance of formulating your own views on ethical practice in leading groups, after carefully considering the best practice guidelines and training standards of ASGW.

Suggested Activities

1. Replicate the initial session of a group. Two students can volunteer to co-lead and approximately eight other students can become group members. Assume that the group is a personal-growth group that will meet for a predetermined number of weeks. The co-leaders' job is to orient and prepare the members by describing the group's purpose, giving an overview of group process concepts, and talking about ground rules for effective group participation. If time allows, members can express any fears and expectations they have about being involved in the group, and they can also raise questions they would like to explore.
2. Practice conducting screening interviews for potential group members. One person volunteers to conduct interviews, and another student can role play a potential group member. Allow about 10 minutes for the interview. Afterward, the prospective client can talk about what it was like to be interviewed, and the group leader can share his or her experience.
3. As part of your job, you are expected to lead a group consisting of involuntary members. How will this fact affect your approach? What might you do differently with this group compared with a group of voluntary members? Have several students play the reluctant members while others practice dealing with them.
4. You are leading a counseling group with high school students. A member comes to the group obviously incoherent and disruptive. How do you deal with him? What might you say or do? Discuss in class how you would deal with this situation, or demonstrate how you might respond by having a fellow student play the part of the adolescent.
5. Again, assume that you are leading a high school counseling group. An angry father who gave written permission for his son's participation comes to your office and demands to know what is going on in your group. He is convinced that his son's participation in the group is an invasion of family privacy. As a group leader, how would you deal with his anger? To make the situation more real and interesting, have someone role play the father.
6. Selecting a good co-leader for a group is important, for not all matches of co-leaders are productive. Form dyads and negotiate with your partner to determine whether the two of you would be effective if you were to lead a group together. You might discuss matters such as potential power struggles, competitiveness, compatibility of views and philosophy, your differing styles

and how they might complement or interfere with each other, and other issues that you think would have a bearing on your ability to work as a team.

InfoTrac® College Edition Resources

For additional readings, explore InfoTrac College Edition, our online library. Key words are listed in a form that enables the search engine to locate a wider range of articles in the online university library. Key words should be entered exactly as shown, including asterisks, "Wl," "W2," "AND," and other search engine tools. Go to http://www.infotrac-college.com and select these key word searches:

training AND group W1 leader*
supervision AND group W1 leader*
co-leadership AND group w1 work AND (psych????y OR psychotherapy OR couns*)
confidentiality AND group* AND (psych????y OR psychotherapy OR couns*)
values AND (group W1 counseling OR group W1 therapy)
screening AND (group W1 counseling OR group W1 therapy)

Chapter 13

Pre-Chapter Self-Inventory

Directions: For each statement, indicate the response that most closely identifies your beliefs and attitudes. Use the following code:

5 = I *strongly agree* with this statement.
4 = I *agree* with this statement.
3 = I am *undecided* about this statement.
2 = I *disagree* with this statement.
1 = I *strongly disagree* with this statement.

_____1. It is important to include people from the client's environment in his or her treatment.

_____2. Community workers need to take an active role in seeking solutions to the social and political conditions related to human suffering.

_____3. Mental health experts need to devote more of their energies to preventing emotional and behavioral disorders rather than just treating them.

_____4. With increasing attention being paid to the community mental health approach and less funding being provided, the role of the professional needs to expand to include a variety of indirect services to clients as well as direct clinical services.

_____5. The use of nonlicensed workers is a valuable, cost-effective, and ethical way to deal with the shortage of professional help and budget constraints.

_____6. Nonlicensed workers who receive adequate training and good supervision are capable of providing many of the direct services that professionals now provide.

_____7. In working with a variety of client groups in the community, it is essential for community workers to be skilled in out-of-office strategies and roles such as change agent, outreach, consulting, and advocacy.

_____8. Human-service workers need to understand the community in which they operate, including its needs, assets, and issues.

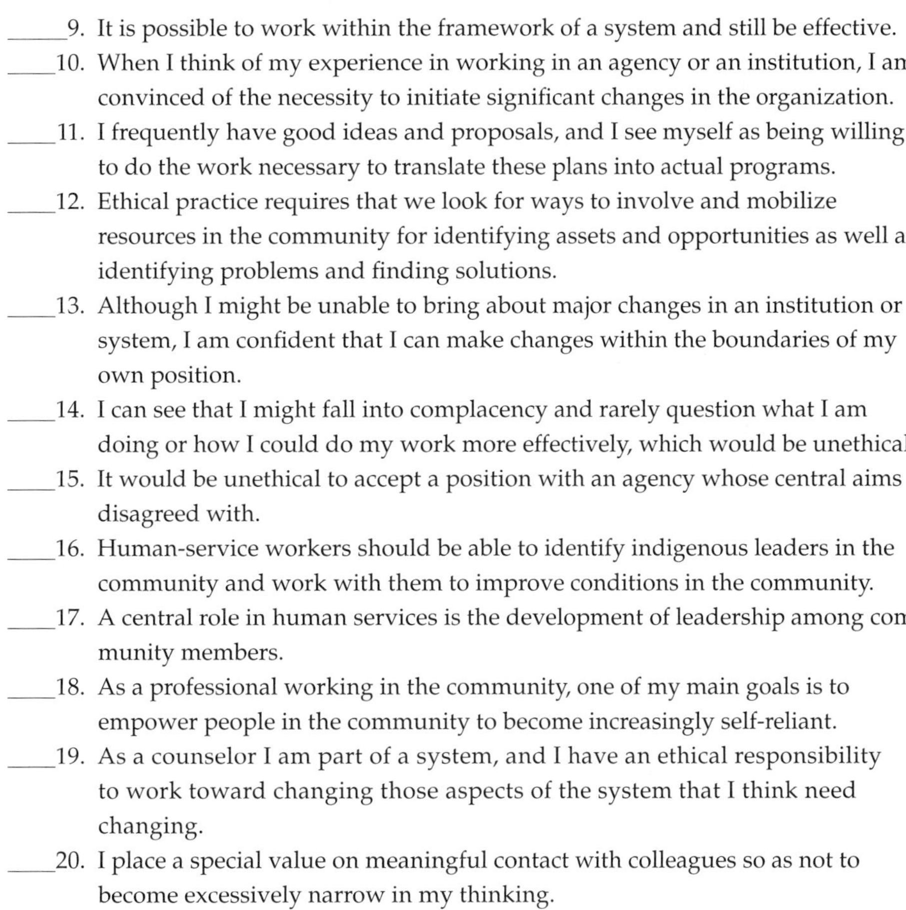

Ethical Issues in Community Work*

_____9. It is possible to work within the framework of a system and still be effective.

____10. When I think of my experience in working in an agency or an institution, I am convinced of the necessity to initiate significant changes in the organization.

____11. I frequently have good ideas and proposals, and I see myself as being willing to do the work necessary to translate these plans into actual programs.

____12. Ethical practice requires that we look for ways to involve and mobilize resources in the community for identifying assets and opportunities as well as identifying problems and finding solutions.

____13. Although I might be unable to bring about major changes in an institution or system, I am confident that I can make changes within the boundaries of my own position.

____14. I can see that I might fall into complacency and rarely question what I am doing or how I could do my work more effectively, which would be unethical.

____15. It would be unethical to accept a position with an agency whose central aims I disagreed with.

____16. Human-service workers should be able to identify indigenous leaders in the community and work with them to improve conditions in the community.

____17. A central role in human services is the development of leadership among community members.

____18. As a professional working in the community, one of my main goals is to empower people in the community to become increasingly self-reliant.

____19. As a counselor I am part of a system, and I have an ethical responsibility to work toward changing those aspects of the system that I think need changing.

____20. I place a special value on meaningful contact with colleagues so as not to become excessively narrow in my thinking.

*We want to acknowledge Mark Homan, instructor of social work at Pima Community College (Tucson, Arizona), for his consultation with us and helpful input in revising this chapter.

Introduction

Working with people who come for "individual" counseling is one way for professionals to promote mental and emotional health. Working in the community involves different skills, some of which include connecting people, developing leadership, inspiring confidence, and promoting a culture of learning (Mark Homan, personal communication, January 20, 2005). Professional helpers can foster real and lasting changes if they have an impact on the total milieu of people's lives in a "systems" approach. The aspirations and difficulties of clients intertwine with those of many other people and, ultimately, with those of the community at large. What occurs in one part of the system affects all parts of the system to some degree. In this chapter we focus on the community itself as the target for change.

Systems theories posit that the identified client's problem might be a symptom of how the family system functions, not just a symptom of the individual's internal dynamics. When the community mental health movement came into existence, it took the family systems perspective a step further and holds that the entire community is the best focus of treatment. By looking at the whole community, it is possible to discover the strengths within the community and to develop ways to bring these strengths to work for the community. Feminist therapy likewise addresses the need to consider the social and cultural context that contributes to a person's problems in order to understand that person. It is our contention that individual, family, community, and feminist perspectives all have a special place as each one addresses a specific and complementary need that is not addressed by the others. These theoretical frameworks need not compete with one another; the field is enriched by all approaches.

The foundation of all ethical practice is promoting the welfare of clients. More often than not, ethical practice requires that we look at the community as a whole to identify assets and opportunities as well as to identify problems and find solutions. If community workers ignore community needs because they seem overwhelming, and overlook the abilities, strengths, and resources within the community, this poses an ethical concern. Practitioners can make ripples within segments of the community even in small ways if they are committed to becoming change agents. It is essential that community workers focus on the capabilities and strengths within a community, for doing so empowers people in the community.

We use the term **community agency** broadly to include any institution—public or private, nonprofit or for-profit—designed to provide a wide range of social and psychological services to the community. Likewise, when we speak of a **community counselor,** we refer to a diverse pool of human-service workers whose primary duties include serving individuals within the community in a variety of community groups. **Community workers** include, but are not limited to, social workers, community organizers and developers, psychologists, psychiatrists, nurses, counselors, couples and family therapists, and human-service workers with varying degrees of education and training.

Whether or not you work in a community agency setting, you need to know how to mobilize community resources. Examine your own commitment to working in the community by thinking about these questions:

- What sense do you have of the social and psychological needs in your community and of the assets and resources within the community to deal with them?
- If clients ask what resources are available to them, would you know where to refer them? Could it be unethical if you did not know?
- What forces within your community exacerbate the problems individuals and groups are experiencing?
- What are the main assets available to empower people in your community?
- What factors contribute to the strength and development of your community?
- How do you see your role in improving your community?

Whereas the traditional approach to understanding and treating human problems focuses on resolution of internal conflicts as a pathway to individual change, the community approach focuses on ways of changing the environmental factors causing individual problems. The community mental health perspective is relevant to all communities, but it is particularly relevant to underserved communities. Although there is some question as to whether there are sufficient mental health professionals to meet the mental health needs of all people in the United States, there is agreement that many geographical regions and client populations are underserved (Robiner & Crew, 2000). DeLeon, Giesting, and Kenkel (2003) state that community health centers, and other community agencies, provide opportunities for graduate psychology students to acquire the culturally sensitive competencies required of them to adequately address the needs and abilities of underserved populations.

A community orientation requires practitioners to design interventions that go beyond the office. Counselors trained in individual therapy who work in the community must develop a more expansive notion of who the client is. "Clients" are primarily constituency group members, residents of target communities, and people who have been marginalized (Hardina, 2004). The community orientation is based on the premise that the community itself is the most appropriate focus of attention, rather than the individual, and also the most potent resource for solutions. As Mark Homan stresses in his teaching, "Healthy communities believe more in their abilities than in their problems" (personal communication, January 20, 2005). The ethical imperative is to do what best serves the "community as the client":

> Just like an individual or a family, a community has resources and limitations. Communities have established coping mechanisms to deal with problems. To promote change in a community, the community must believe in its own ability to change and must take responsibility for its actions or inactions. (Homan, 2004, pp. 24–25)

We also examine an issue of particular importance to the community worker: namely, how the system affects the counselor and how to thrive and survive while working in the system. In examining the counselor's relationship to the community, we address the ethical dimensions of practice. If practitioners are limited in their ability to adapt their roles to the needs of the community, they are not likely to be effective in reaching those who most need assistance.

Ethical Practice in Community Work

The ethics codes of professional practice reinforce the practitioner's responsibility to the community and to society (see the ethics codes box titled Responsibilities to Community and Society). It is left to community workers to identify strategies for becoming more responsive to the community.

Those who engage in community work often encounter ethical dilemmas different from those common to clinical practice. In writing about guidelines for ethical practice in community organization, Hardina (2004) addresses both the contributions and the limitations of the *Code of Ethics* of the National Association of Social Workers (1999). Hardina notes that the ethical principles for social workers outlined in the code of ethics do not begin to cover many of the practical situations community workers encounter.

Community organizers typically work with community residents, constituency groups, local institutions, and government decision makers. Hardina asserts that most community practice activities occur outside traditional agency settings and involve the use of power and influence to bring about social change. One of the primary objectives of community practice is constituency self-determination. Community organizers must first determine the primary recipient of their interventions. Is the client or constituent an individual, a group of people, or society in general? They also need to acquire adequate tools to deal effectively with the ethical dilemmas they encounter in practice.

The Community Mental Health Orientation

The need for diverse and readily accessible treatment programs has been a key factor in the development of the community mental health orientation, which is based on the premise that problem solving does not take place in a vacuum, isolated from the larger social and political influences of society. Environmental factors cause or contribute to the problems of many groups in society, and a process that considers both the individual and the environment is often most beneficial to clients.

The focus of community work is on preventing rather than curing problems. Additionally, members of the community are encouraged to take control of and master their own problems so that traditional intervention will become less necessary (Trull, 2005). Lewis, Lewis, Daniels, and D'Andrea (2003) define **community counseling** as "a comprehensive helping framework of intervention strategies and services that promotes the personal development and well-being of all individuals and communities" (p. 6). They describe the activities

Ethics Codes

Responsibilities to Community and Society

National Organization for Human Services (2000)

Human service professionals keep informed about current social issues as they affect the client and the community. They share that information with clients, groups and community as part of their work. (Statement 11.)

Human service professionals act as advocates in addressing unmet client and community needs. Human service professionals provide a mechanism for identifying unmet client needs, calling attention to these needs, and assisting in planning and mobilizing to advocate for those needs at the local community level. (Statement 13.)

Human service professionals advocate for the rights of all members of society, particularly those who are members of minorities and groups at which discriminatory practices have historically been directed. (Statement 16.)

Canadian Association of Social Workers (1994)

A social worker shall advocate change: (a) in the best interest of the client, and (b) for the overall benefit of society, the environment and the global community. (10)

A social worker shall identify, document and advocate for the elimination of discrimination. (10.1.)

A social worker shall advocate for the equal distribution of resources to all persons. (10.2.)

A social worker shall advocate for the equal access of all persons to resources, services and opportunities. (10.3.)

A social worker shall advocate for a clean and healthy environment and shall advocate the development of environmental strategies consistent with social work principles. (10.4.)

A social worker shall provide reasonable professional services in a state of emergency. (10.5.)

A social worker shall promote social justice. (10.6.)

American School Counselor Association (2004)

The professional school counselor:

(a) Collaborates with agencies, organizations and individuals in the community in the best interest of students and without regard to personal reward or remuneration.

(b) Extends his/her influence and opportunity to deliver a comprehensive school counseling program to all students by collaborating with community resources for student success. (D.2.)

National Association of Social Workers (1999)

(a) Social workers should engage in social and political action that seeks to ensure that all persons have equal access to the resources, employment, services, and opportunities that they require in order to meet their basic human needs and to develop fully. Social workers should be aware of the impact of the political arena on practice, and should advocate for changes in policy and legislation to improve social conditions in order to meet basic human needs and promote social justice.

(b) Social workers should act to expand choice and opportunity for all persons, with special regard for vulnerable, disadvantaged, oppressed, and exploited persons and groups.

(c) Social workers should promote conditions that encourage respect for cultural and social diversity within the United States and globally. Social workers should promote policies and practices that demonstrate respect for difference, support the expansion of cultural knowledge and resources, advocate for programs and institutions that demonstrate cultural competence, and promote policies that safeguard the rights of and confirm equity and social justice for all people.

continued on next page

(d) Social workers should act to prevent and eliminate domination of, exploitation of, and discrimination against any person, group, or class on the basis of race, ethnicity, national origin, color, sex, sexual orientation, age, marital status, political belief, religion, or mental or physical disability. (6.04.)

Feminist Therapy Institute (2000)

A feminist therapist seeks multiple avenues for impacting change, including public education and advocacy within professional organizations, lobbying for legislative actions, and other appropriate activities. (V.A.)

A feminist therapist actively questions practices in her community that appear harmful to clients or therapists. She assists clients in intervening on their own behalf. As appropriate, the feminist therapist herself intervenes, especially when other practitioners appear to be engaging in harmful, unethical, or illegal behaviors. (V.B.)

that make up a comprehensive community counseling model as having the following four components: (1) direct client services, (2) indirect client services, (3) direct community services, and (4) indirect community services. Let's examine each of these components separately.

1. **Direct client services** focus on outreach activities to a population that might be at risk for developing mental health problems. Community counselors provide help to clients either facing crises or dealing with ongoing stressors that impair their coping ability. By reaching out to those schools and communities that would be receptive to help, community workers can offer a variety of personal, career, family, and counseling services to at-risk groups (Lewis et al., 2003). This population would also include referrals from the courts, churches, probation departments, and mandated therapy for drug and alcohol abuse.

2. **Indirect client services** consist of client advocacy and consultation, which involves active intervention for and with an individual or a group. These include, but are not limited to, people without jobs, people without homes, people with disabilities, and persons living with AIDS. Community workers need to become advocates, speaking up on their clients' behalf and actively intervening in their client's situation (Lewis et al., 2003). Advocacy consists of those focused efforts to change existing policy or to influence proposed policy on behalf of specific underrepresented groups (Ezell, 2001). Mark Homan (personal communication, January 20, 2005) has a different point of view on advocacy. He makes a subtle, but important distinction, of working *with* groups, rather than *for* groups. For Homan, advocacy aims at working with groups to build their capacity and power and use it, along with ours, to make change. As much as possible, advocacy involves creating partnerships by working with groups in a collaborative way rather than merely providing services for these groups.

3. **Direct community services** in the form of preventive education are geared to the population at large. Examples of these programs include life planning workshops, value clarification seminars, interpersonal skills training, marriage

education, and teaching parents about their legal rights and responsibilities. Because the emphasis is on prevention, these programs help people develop a wider range of competencies. The focus of preventive programs is on teaching effective living and problem-solving competencies.

4. **Indirect community services** are attempts to change the social environment to meet the needs of the population as a whole and are carried out by influencing public policy. The focus is on promoting systemic change by working closely with those is the community who develop public policy. The overall goal is the reduction of health problems, both mental and physical.

Community counseling calls for practitioners who (a) are familiar with resources within the community that they can refer clients to, when necessary; (b) have a basic knowledge of the cultural background of their clients; (c) possess skills that can be used as needed by clients; (d) have the ability to balance various roles as professionals; (e) are able to identify nonprofessionals in the community who have the ability to be change agents for their community, and (f) have the willingness to be advocates for policy changes in the community.

Roles of Helpers Working in the Community

Ideally, all mental health professionals are committed to promoting change on both individual and community levels; however, they do not all have the same areas of interest and expertise. No matter what setting we choose for our work, we must be aware of the broader context of human problems in order to be effective and therefore ethical. The challenge is to think beyond the needs of the individual to the needs and the strengths of the community at large, in much the same way as practitioners would include the family when addressing the needs of the child.

As we indicated in Chapter 4, to meet the needs of many ethnic and culturally diverse clients, traditional counselors need to have a different vision and master different skills, such as outreach interventions. Delivering services in nontraditional settings may be clinically and ethically indicated and may be beneficial to clients. On this point, Knapp and Slattery (2004) indicate that home-based services are often the only way some people can get services because of transportation problems, mobility issues, or cultural barriers to office-based treatment. Providing home-based services can also lead to ethical challenges in managing professional boundaries. When working in the homes of clients, Knapp and Slattery recommend that therapists emphasize informed consent, especially about therapeutic boundaries.

The outreach approach may include both developmental and educational efforts, such as skills training, stress management, and consultation. Outreach activities also include family preservation services, the goal of which is to develop a treatment plan with a family to maintain children's safety in their own homes. Community counselors also attempt to change the dysfunctional system that is producing problems for individuals, families, and communities.

The focus is on looking at the problem in context rather than dealing only with the problem within the individual.

Alternative Counselor Roles

Rather than operating in a singular role, as is the case with many traditional counselors, the emphasis of the community perspective is on alternative ways of helping clients. Atkinson, Thompson, and Grant (1993) state that the role of psychotherapist is frequently inappropriately applied when working with racial or ethnic minority clients. Atkinson and his colleagues believe the conventional role of psychotherapist is appropriate "only for a client who is highly acculturated and now wants relief from an existing problem that has an internal etiology" (p. 269). Other writers (Sue, Ivey, & Pedersen, 1996; Sue & Sue, 2003) have criticized conventional approaches to therapy because they place undue responsibility on the client for his or her plight. At the extreme, some interventions blame client problems entirely on the individual without regard to contributing environmental factors. Community-oriented counseling emphasizes the necessity for recognizing and dealing with environmental conditions that often create problems for ethnically diverse client groups. This is known as a psychosocial approach or orientation. Atkinson (2004) suggests alternative roles for counselors who work in the community: advocate, change agent, consultant, adviser, facilitator of indigenous support systems, and facilitator of indigenous healing methods.

Advocate. Because ethnic minority clients are often oppressed to some degree by the dominant society, they can be helped by counselors who are willing to speak on their behalf. Mental health practitioners especially need to function as **advocates** for clients who are low in acculturation and who need remediation of a problem that results from discrimination and oppression.

Change Agent. Counselors can confront and bring about change within the system that contributes to, if not creates, many of the problems clients face. In the role of **change agents,** counselors assist clients in recognizing oppressive forces in the community as a source of their problem; they also teach clients strategies for dealing with these environmental problems. A change agent recognizes that healthy communities produce healthy people. The main purpose of community change is fostering healthy communities (Homan, 2004). As a change agent one must sometimes educate organizations to change their culture to meet the needs of the community.

Consultant. Operating as **consultants,** counselors encourage ethnic minority clients to learn skills they can use to interact successfully with various forces within their community. In this role, client and counselor cooperate in addressing unhealthy forces within the system. They work with racial and ethnic minority clients to design preventive programs aimed at eliminating the negative impacts of racism and oppression. The role of consultant can be seen as the role of a teacher. Often the "teacher" is less of a threat and more socially acceptable to members of non-Western cultures than the "counselor," even though the same professional may be performing both functions.

Adviser. The counselor as **adviser** initiates discussions with clients about ways to deal with environmental problems that contribute to their personal problems. For example, recent immigrants may need advice on immigration paperwork, coping with problems they will face in the job market, or problems that their children may encounter at school.

Facilitator of Indigenous Support Systems. All cultural groups have some form of social support aimed at preventing or remediating psychological and social problems. Many ethnically diverse clients, people in rural environments, and older people would not consider seeking professional help in the traditional sense. However, they may be willing to turn to social support systems within their own communities. Community workers need to be aware of cultural factors that may be instrumental in contributing to a client's problem or resources that might help alleviate or solve the client's problem. Counselors can play an important role by encouraging clients to make full use of **indigenous support systems** within their own communities.

Facilitator of Indigenous Healing Systems. Mental health practitioners need to learn what kinds of healing resources exist within a client's culture. In many cultures individuals with problems are more likely to put their trust in traditional healers. For that reason, counselors need to be aware of **indigenous healing systems** and be willing to work collaboratively with them when it is to the benefit of the client. Ignoring these indigenous resources can have a negative effect on the client's welfare, and therefore, has ethical implications. One such example of a conflict between indigenous healing and mainstream medicine is explored in Fadiman's (1997) book, *The Spirit Catches You and You Fall Down*. This conflict resulted in the death of a child.

Constantine and colleagues (2004) present a comprehensive literature review and discuss the cultural relevance of indigenous healing practices in promoting psychological, physical, and spiritual well-being in people of color. They suggest that counselors exercise due care in making referrals to indigenous helping resources that would not jeopardize clients' physical and mental health. Constantine and her colleagues encourage counselors to be open to learning about indigenous healing resources, especially with clients from cultures that may mistrust Western mental health approaches. By assuming an open stance, "counselors may be able to recognize potential similarities and differences between indigenous and Western approaches to helping and may begin to bridge the gaps between traditional helping institutions and the cultures of the individuals they serve" (p. 120).

In summary, it is ethically incumbent on practitioners who work in the community to assume some or all of the alternative roles described here when needed to benefit their clients and provide optimal care.

Some Tasks of Community Counseling

The community counseling approach serves people of all ages and backgrounds and with all types and degrees of problems. To effectively serve this variety of client populations, practitioners need to develop culturally diverse competencies (Hogan-Garcia, 2003). In community counseling, practitioners may find themselves performing some or all of these duties:

- Supporting the needs of minority groups in the community
- Assisting client groups to become true partners with professionals in the development and delivery of services with shared decision-making authority
- Promoting community organization and development activities as fundamental agency responsibilities and seeing that this is reflected in agency budgets
- Actively reaching out to people with special needs and initiating programs aimed at preventing problems rather than merely treating them
- Drawing on and improving the skills of community workers and laypeople to help meet the many different needs and discover and use the many abilities of clients
- Developing strategies to deal effectively with poverty, drug and alcohol abuse, child sexual and physical abuse, and domestic violence
- Developing strategies that will empower the disenfranchised in the community
- Consulting with a variety of social agencies about programs in gerontology, welfare, child care, and rehabilitation, and helping community workers apply psychological knowledge in their work
- Evaluating human-service programs to assess agency intervention efforts
- Advocating and assisting with public and private initiatives that promote the total well-being of clients
- Working with members of a particular community to develop and build on community assets to promote communities and instill self-reliance

Educating the Community

There are many reasons people do not make use of available mental health resources. They may not be aware of their existence; they may not be able to afford these services; they may have misconceptions about the nature and purpose of counseling; they may be reluctant to recognize their problems; they may harbor the attitude that they should be able to take charge of their own lives; they may feel a social stigma attached to seeking professional help; or they may perceive that these resources are not intended for them because the services are administered in a culturally insensitive way. One of the major barriers to clients not making use of social and psychological services is that access to these services is confusing and sometimes humiliating.

One goal of the community approach is to educate the public and attempt to change the attitudes of the community about mental health and the attitudes of those who deliver mental health services. Many people still cling to a very narrow definition of mental illness. Widespread misconceptions include the notion that once people suffer from any kind of emotional disturbance they can never be cured, the idea that people with emotional and behavioral disorders are merely deficient in "willpower," and the belief that the mentally ill are always dangerous and should be separated from the community lest they "contaminate" or harm others. Professionals face real challenges in combating these misconceptions, for unless this is done many people will not seek professional help. Practitioners are ethically bound to actively work at presenting mental health services in a way that is understandable to and respectful of the community at large.

Influencing Policymakers

The challenges facing community workers are often overwhelming, especially with current constraints on funding and the bureaucratic malaise. How can dedicated community workers continue to develop social programs if they are constantly faced with the likelihood that their programs will be cut back or canceled? Sherman and Wenocur (1983) write, "Thus, the workers are put in a double bind, in that they are now held responsible by their clients for help they feel they should, but cannot in fact, provide adequately. Caught in this bind, workers often cannot cope with clients' anger. Worse, they cannot justify their inability to help" (p. 376). There is little room for staff members to come up with innovative social programs when the agencies themselves are concerned with mere survival.

One way community workers can initiate change is by organizing within an agency or even several agencies and developing a collective voice. Practitioners can empower a community to organize political action to influence the state and national government to fulfill their responsibilities. This action may involve providing funds, technical assistance, legal protection, or other support a smaller community requires to flourish (Homan, 2004).

✓ **The Case of a Nonprofit Agency Designed to Educate the Community.** The Coalition for Children, Adolescents and Parents (CCAP) is a community agency aimed at the prevention of adolescent pregnancy. This small grassroots agency in Orange County, California, applies outreach strategies to educate the community as a way to meet a critical need in the community (Hogan-Garcia & Scheinberg, 2000). For the past 20 years, CCAP has served as a model of how to involve the community in a project to enhance the community. From its inception, a high priority has been given to hiring a multiethnic staff that could serve and mirror the community. The staff is committed to understanding each other, rather than allowing their differences to separate them, and staff members meet frequently for cultural sharing as a way to better understand each other and themselves. Those who work at the agency have opportunities to critically examine their ethnocentric assumptions about the world and the community. All the members of the agency staff are committed to clarifying and understanding personal values, beliefs, and behaviors. Because the individuals on the staff believe in the value of understanding cultural diversity, they are able to serve as a bridge between the mainstream and minority communities.

One of the early projects designed by CCAP involved outreach and education in the Latino community to prevent the spread of HIV. A Latina staff member conducted interviews with 30 mothers in the community regarding their understanding of HIV, human sexuality, and teen pregnancy. From this contact with these mothers, a group of leaders (comadres) was formed to educate the community. The women who served as leaders met for monthly meetings, which were held at a neighborhood center. Eventually, the women invited their husbands into the classes. This project was funded by an external source, and the agency was required to report to the funders about the outcomes of the project. Hogan-Garcia and Scheinberg (2000) summarize these outcomes thusly:

> By the end of the contract year, the agency had exceeded the expectations of funders with the project and the Comadres Project had spread the word about HIV prevention to friends, neighbors, and family members. The empowerment of disenfranchised women and men continued beyond the contract term. CCAP staff continued to meet with and follow this special group of friends. Three women went back to school, a group of the women formed a Spanish-speaking PTA group, and one went on to become a school board member. (p. 28)

In 2000 the agency served more than 12,000 clients, providing after-school recreational services, tutoring, academic enrichment programs, physical examinations, parenting education, conflict resolution, cultural-diversity training, school-based group counseling, a homeless shelter, drug abuse prevention, and child care training. This agency is an example of an effective collaboration that is committed to ensuring that the members of the community have a full voice in determining the nature of community services.

The projects that are a part of CCAP are based on a set of culturally competent practice principles, which have been described by Hogan-Garcia and Scheinberg (2000) and Hogan-Garcia (2003):

- Be willing to examine your assumptions and personal values.
- In an agency, bring together an ethnically diverse staff and board.
- Develop and maintain positive relationships with key people in the community.
- Ask community members about their perceptions of what is needed in the community.
- Bring community members and agency staff together in genuine dialogue.
- Design a program based on the community's definition of their needs.
- In implementing a program, be sensitive to the pace of the community.
- Advocate for the needs of the community and serve as a bridge between cultural groups.
- Translate the progress of the community in terms that the funders of the project will understand.

Based on the discussion of the CCAP project, respond to the following questions:

- Are you open to learning first-hand about other cultures?

- Would you value this kind of ongoing self-evaluation?
- Do you think ethnic diversity of staff members is necessary for a community agency to be successful?

✓ **The Case of Maribel.** Maribel is the director of a community clinic in an inner-city neighborhood. Her agency provides birth control counseling and funding for abortion for low-income women. As the time approaches for her to submit her request for financing to the state government, she is contacted by a local politician who is adamantly opposed to abortion. He informs her that if she requests funding for abortion he will do everything in his power not only to deny the money but also to reduce the overall funding for the agency. Faced with the prospect of radically reduced funds, Maribel omits her request for money for abortion services.

- In light of the threats that were made, did Maribel act in the best interest of her community? Can you see any justification for her action? What ethical concerns are raised by her decision?
- What if Maribel seemed to go along with the politician's request, but later on, when the funding for the other programs was acquired, she diverted some of the money for abortion services? Would this be ethical? Would Maribel be breaking the law?
- How ethically bound was Maribel to disclose the coercive attempts of the influential politician, even though it was only her word against his?
- What would you have done in her place?

✓ **The Case of Natalie.** Natalie is an intern with a community agency that provides counseling services to local elementary schools. She facilitates a group for children with behavioral problems. On one occasion the principal overheard one of the students reacting angrily. The principal assumed control of the group, got into a verbal exchange with the child, and suspended him from school. When Natalie appealed to her clinical director, he angrily told her: "Back off, and don't you dare challenge the principal." He let her know in no uncertain terms that if she were to take action against the principal the contract of providing counseling services to the school would be jeopardized, with the subsequent loss of funding to the clinic.

- What are the possible ethical considerations in this case?
- If you were Natalie, what would you do?
- If you were her supervisor, what would you say to her? What would you feel obligated to do, if anything?

Promoting Change in the Community

Homan (personal communication, January 20, 2005) poses a question that has significant implications for community work: Are you willing to honestly examine who owns the project or the change? From Homan's perspective, if we are just doing things we think are right *for* people, rather than the project really being theirs to take charge of, we may just be politely reasserting a form of social control. While some client/constituent groups do not have the immediate skills, or even the time to take care of every aspect of a change project, they can learn skills and receive support for their work, rather than receive a substitution for it. Thus the matter of "who owns" the project is an important ethical concern.

Homan (2004) emphasizes the notion that promoting community change is a broader issue than merely solving the problems of the community. He raises a series of questions that community workers need to address in their change efforts (p. 57):

- Is there an identified community? If so, who has defined it and how is it defined?
- Does the project build skills of community members? Can these skills be identified?
- Does the project produce new leaders and new *teachers*?
- Who owns the project? How is this seen? Who holds decision-making authority? If ownership is external, what processes are in place to transfer ownership to the members of the community?
- Does the project produce new community resources that can exist apart from the project or after the intended life of the project?
- Do the benefits or resources created by the project in turn create new benefits or resources?
- Which community capacities or assets will the project build upon? How will these be expanded by the project?
- Which community conditions does the project intend to change?

The answers to these questions can provide community workers with a framework for developing the capacity within a community to recognize conditions that need to be changed and the willingness and ability to take action to bring this change about.

Ways to Involve Yourself in the Community

Consider your responsibility to teach constituents to use the resources available to them in their communities. Here is a list of things you might do to link residents to the environment in which they live. Rate each of these activities, using the following code:

A = I would do this *routinely.*
B = I would do this *occasionally.*
C = I would do this *rarely.*

______ 1. I would work with agencies to determine which services need to be offered and how they might best be offered.

______ 2. I would familiarize myself with available community resources so that I could refer people to appropriate sources of further help.

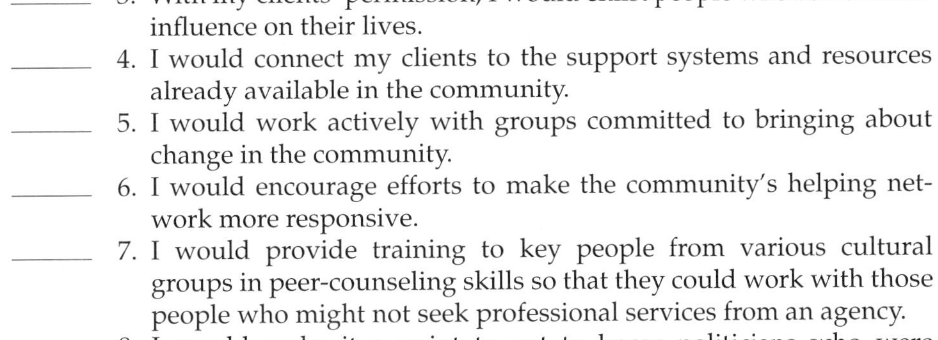

_____ 3. With my clients' permission, I would enlist people who had a direct influence on their lives.

_____ 4. I would connect my clients to the support systems and resources already available in the community.

_____ 5. I would work actively with groups committed to bringing about change in the community.

_____ 6. I would encourage efforts to make the community's helping network more responsive.

_____ 7. I would provide training to key people from various cultural groups in peer-counseling skills so that they could work with those people who might not seek professional services from an agency.

_____ 8. I would make it a point to get to know politicians who were actively involved in helping the community.

If you plan on going into one of the mental health professions, you are likely to spend some time working in a community agency setting, and you will be working with many different facets of the community. If you were to work in such a setting at this time, consider the following questions:

- How would you go about learning what it takes to become an effective agent for change in the community?
- What skills do you already have that can be applied to community change?
- What is the most essential skill you need to acquire?
- What fears or concerns do you have of working in the community?
- How would you translate your ideas into a practical set of strategies aimed at community change?
- How aware are you of your beliefs and attitudes toward the people you serve, and how might this affect the way you work?

Making a Difference in the Community

In his article, "Making a Difference," Rob Waters (2004) profiles the work of five community-oriented therapists who engaged in social activism. These five "citizen-therapists" exemplify people who are deeply connected to their own communities and who are actively working to promote change. Each of these therapists has taken a different path to change the community, yet each of them has been motivated by the question, "How can I make a difference?" As you read about their efforts, imagine yourself engaging in similar community work.

- Ramon Rojano is convinced that the direction the helping profession needs to take is for therapists to become active agents of social change. A psychiatrist who had worked primarily with rich Caucasians, Rojano shifted his focus and began working in a child guidance clinic with Latinos and African Americans. He quickly realized that relying on traditional psychotherapy approaches to deal with a family's psychological needs was pointless unless he addressed poverty, violence, and the social and economic crises that were part of the lives of these family members. Referring to his approach as "community family therapy," Rojano has shifted from the traditional role for which he was trained as a psychiatrist to an alternative role of bettering the mental health system for the poor.

- Diane Sollee is a leader in the marriage education movement. Part of her work has involved seminars to train people to become marriage educators, who then have the task of teaching basic communication skills to couples. To avoid becoming identified with any political faction, Sollee has refused to accept funding from anyone. The core of her work is to get couples the information and skills they need to succeed in their marriage and family life.
- Kenneth Hardy is a family therapist who over the years has developed projects in schools, churches, corporations, and the United States military to help groups deal with diversity issues. Hardy's goal is to help people acknowledge the reality of social injustice and the inequalities of race, gender, and social class in ways that people can develop a true understanding of diversity. In his professional work, Hardy has focused increasingly on those who are disenfranchised and disempowered.
- Jack Saul is the director of New York University's International Trauma Studies Program, which is committed to helping people survive disaster. In reflecting on the aftermath of 9/11, Saul contends that "collective suffering requires a collective response" (p. 40). In disaster situations, Saul believes that therapists need to think in broader terms and develop models for mobilizing a community's own resources for healing. He met with officials to set up Project Liberty, which was the commission established to distribute $100 million in mental health funds that Congress provided for recovery from the 9/11 disaster. Currently, Saul is devoting his energies toward developing community resources for healing 6,000 Liberian refugees living on Staten Island. He operates largely behind the scenes to help organize drop-in centers, job-placement programs, and family support programs that bring together various community leaders. Saul says, "The key thing in doing this kind of work is to bring your therapeutic skills to the community in a way that promotes the community's own capacities, without becoming too central" (p. 41).
- Barbara Lee, a graduate of the School of Social Welfare at the University of California at Berkeley, is now a member of Congress on Capitol Hill. Lee has learned that she is able to have the widest possible impact by exercising political power. Lee brings a clinician's perspective to bear on the running of her congressional office. She and her staff give major attention to social work in action by advocating for low-income people. Lee co-sponsored a bill that authorized AIDS relief to Africa that passed the House and Senate and was signed into law by President Bush in 2003. This achievement is but one example of what Lee means when she says, "I didn't go into politics to be part of the system, but to change the system, to shake it up and make things better" (p. 43).

These five social activists give testimony to the power of changing systems and helping communities in discovering their own resources for healing.

Working Within a System

One of the major challenges for counselors who work in the community is to learn how to make the system work for the clients they serve and, secondarily, work for themselves so that in the process they do not lose their ability to be effective with clients. Working in a system can put an added strain on the counselor due to the monumental amount of paperwork required to justify continued funding, high caseloads, and a multitude of policy directives. Another source of strain is the counselor's relationships with those who administer the agency or institution, who may have long forgotten the practicalities involved in providing direct services to clients. Conversely, practitioners who deal with clients directly may have little appreciation for the intricacies with which administrators must contend in managing and funding their programs. If communication and problem solving are inadequate, as they often are, tension and problems are inevitable. The ultimate challenge is to empower the community to address its own problems. This will be difficult if the system trying to effect change is itself impaired.

Case Management in a Community Setting

The emergence of case management as a dominant force in human-service delivery presents new ethical challenges. **Case management** involves planning and coordinating approaches to treatment. It is guided by the principles of fairness, accountability, collaboration, advocacy for individuals' needs, effective and efficient delivery of services, treatment of the whole person, and individual empowerment. True to this holistic stance, the overall goal of case management is to promote, restore, or maintain the independent functioning of clients in the least-restrictive community environment.

Because of the collaborative and holistic nature of case management, both within and between human-service agencies, the interdisciplinary approach plays a pivotal role in the provision of assessment, planning, resource information, monitoring, and evaluation of client services. Depending on the range and complexity of human services offered, interdisciplinary teams include professionals from many disciplines, each representing a service the consumer may need. However, the effectiveness of the interdisciplinary team approach is very much dependent on the professionalism, respect, and cooperation between team members. For instance, a team that is dominated by one discipline or one team member can be detrimental to human-service delivery. When team members lack professional skills and resource knowledge to make appropriate interventions, recommendations, and referrals, clients may be harmed. Time and efficiency considerations can also play a role in the careless exclusion of clients and their families from the interdisciplinary process deliberations, which is a failure to honor the principle of empowering the client. Similarly, in the interest of time and job security, the case manager may ignore client advocacy responsibilities, which raises a serious ethical issue.

Cooperation and collaboration between human-service agencies can be particularly challenging. Typically, each community agency has specific eligibility criteria (often state or federally mandated), a specific range of services, and a limited budget. Depending on the financial health of the agency budget, the eligibility criteria are interpreted in a less or more strict manner, forcing consideration of the principle of fairness as it is applied to agency applicants. The principle of fairness must also be considered with regard to cooperation between agencies in the provision of client services.

Nowhere today is the application of the case management system of human-service delivery more pronounced than in health maintenance organizations (HMOs). Although it is generally accepted that case management has provided accountability and a level of fairness to health care, many criticisms are raised. One criticism is that necessary health services are often denied by a case manager within the HMO organization. Furthermore, the HMO case manager is acting as a gatekeeper for the HMO corporation, rationing medicine to paying clients to promote and protect corporate profits. This also creates an ethical dilemma.

Consider these questions as they pertain to the ethical issues associated with case management as a way to deliver human services in a community agency:

- In delivering services, how does one balance staying within the budget with service to clients?
- Is it ethical to break rules (federal, state, agency) for the welfare of the individual client?
- Should I always consult with agency management when I see the necessity of breaking rules?
- Am I willing to advocate for client needs at the risk of losing my job?
- It can be efficient for client files to be accessible to all agency professional staff on the agency computer network. What risks, if any, are involved in this?
- In what kind of situations might client autonomy be honored more than professional codes or agency policies and procedures?
- Am I ethically bound to resign from my position as an agency worker if my work assignments are beyond my professional capabilities?
- Should I be a "whistle-blower" when agency management or staff engage in unethical or illegal behavior?
- Do I have an ethical obligation to challenge those systems that overload workers, which can result in superficial work?

The Challenge of Maintaining Integrity in an Agency Environment

Many professionals struggle with the issue of how to work within a system while retaining their integrity and vitality. Although working in an organization is oftentimes frustrating, counselors need to examine their attitude, which might be part of the problem. Blaming others does not effect change. Focusing on the things that can be changed fosters a sense of personal power that may allow for progress.

Practitioners need to evaluate the options they have in responding to unacceptable circumstances. Homan (2004) raises some thought-provoking questions in this regard:

- If you respond to the presence of disturbing social conditions within your midst by attempting to mainly soften the pain they cause, does this imply tolerance for these problems in the system?
- If you genuinely believe that your efforts make a difference, should you accept limitations on your efforts?
- To what degree is it your ethical responsibility to work toward shaping the system that shapes your practice?

Homan suggests that simply putting up with problems within a system is rarely gratifying and that workers gain professional satisfaction by actively taking steps to promote positive changes:

> I believe that you do have options for challenging the circumstances that lead to the problems you confront. And I believe that you have options for creating conditions that permit you to do effective work. In my experience, workers who have acted thoughtfully and purposefully to confront and resolve systemic problems have produced many positive results. (p. 77)

Recognizing the need for action is the first step toward responding to unacceptable circumstances. Once a problem has been identified, Homan suggests that you have four basic responses to choose from (p. 87):

- You can change your perception by identifying the situation as acceptable.
- You can leave the situation, either by emotionally withdrawing or by physically leaving.
- You can recognize the situation as unacceptable and then decide to adjust to the situation.
- You can identify the situation as unacceptable and do what you can to change it.

Each of these actions has consequences for both you and your clients. If you recognize that you do have choices in how you respond to unacceptable situations, you may be challenged to take action to change these circumstances. From an ethical perspective, you are expected to alert your employer to circumstances that may impair your ability to reach clients.

We support Homan's ideas of how to respond to problems in a system. We also need to recognize that sometimes a worker's physical and mental health may be at risk in a dysfunctional system. In such a case, the only viable option might be to withdraw from the system to prevent serious health problems or burnout.

By creating and participating in support groups, those who work in an agency might find ways to collectively address problems in the system of which they are a part. Sherman and Wenocur (1983) make a strong case for the value of support groups in agency settings. These groups create an internal subculture that provides some support in dealing with bureaucratic pressure. Workers alone would have difficulty changing large organizations, but when they unite, they have a greater opportunity for effecting change.

✓ **The Case of Toni.** For 19 years Toni has worked with women in recovery in a community agency that is funded by a grant. To prevent burnout, she and her co-workers organized a support group among the community workers in the agency. Her group consists of about 15 people, some of whom are case managers, treatment counselors, nurses, social workers, and supervisors. They meet at the agency during work hours twice a month for up to 2 hours. During these sessions the workers have opportunities to talk about difficult clients or stressful situations they are facing on the job or in their personal lives. Personal concerns sometimes have an impact on workers' abilities to function professionally, and members are able to use the support within the group as a way to deal with personal issues.

Unfortunately, because of cuts in many of the nonprofit grants, many of the benefits they previously had have been cut. Toni says,

> I have recently been hard hit by these cuts. The grant on which I have been working for the past 19 years was recently cut by 10%. To make ends meet in the organization, many employees have been laid off, which has resulted in greater workloads for those remaining. These cutbacks were especially felt in the counseling area. We have lost a treatment counselor as well as two social workers, one based at the intensive day treatment program and the other at a hospital-based clinic. All of us are feeling the increased stress resulting from these losses. We have been forced to let go of our bi-monthly stress reduction meetings that over the years have been so valuable to us. This has left me alone in the clinic and hospital area without backup. Being unable to have someone to consult with on a daily basis has greatly increased my stress level. I am quickly realizing how important our meetings were to the welfare of the organization, as well as to the clients. Exploring new ways to manage our work-related stress is a top priority for our agency now. (Toni Wallace, personal communication, December 23, 2004)

- If you worked for this agency, would you want to join this group?
- Do you think members of this group might have more power within the agency than workers who are not in the group?
- How would you cope with the cutbacks and the loss of a program you valued?
- How might you deal with the demands of an increased workload due to the layoffs?

Relationships Between Community Worker and Agency

The ethical violations in a community agency are more complex and difficult to resolve than violations pertaining to individual counseling. If a worker is not motivated, the system may tolerate this lack of motivation. If the system violates the rights of the client (community), then this is a real challenge to address. There is no easy solution to the problem of a system abusing clients, but clearly the people seeking help are vulnerable and need to be protected. Correcting such an abuse that may be systemwide demands the willingness of those involved in the system to practice aspirational ethics and take action.

To be an effective community helper, human service workers need to have the knowledge and skills necessary to effectively work in bureaucratic organizations *before* they assume professional employment (Sherman & Wenocur, 1983). In addition to their degrees, training, and professional competencies, they need to learn how to best deal with the rules and regulations of their agency. Typically they have little say in the formulation of agency policies, and furthermore, they are limited in what they can do by the agency's rules and regulations. The system may be so cumbersome and difficult for clients to work with that practitioners must assist clients in obtaining resources through lobbying, advocacy, referrals, and networking.

As a mental health practitioner, you need to decide how you will work within the system and how you can be most effective. Study an agency's philosophy before you accept a position, and determine whether the agency's norms, values, and expectations coincide with what you expect from the position. If you are not able to support the philosophy and policies of that agency, you are almost certain to experience conflicts, if not failure. It will be up to you to find your own answers to questions such as these:

- To what degree is my philosophy of helping compatible with the agency where I work?
- How can I meet the requirements of an institution and at the same time do what I most believe in?
- What can I do to bring about change in a particular system?
- Would I consider mobilizing clients to promote changes in the community? in my own agency?
- At what point does the price of attempting to work within an organized structure become too high?
- What special ethical obligations am I likely to face in working in a system?

Moving Toward Empowerment. We suggest you respond to the following questions to clarify your position on ways in which you could increase your chances of assuming power within the system:

- What would you do if the organization for which you worked instituted a policy to which you were opposed?
- What would you do if you believed strongly that certain changes needed to be made in your institution but your colleagues disagreed?
- How would you attempt to make contact with your colleagues if members of the staff seemed to work largely in isolation from one another?
- If the staff seemed to be divided by jealousies, hostilities, or unspoken conflicts, how would you intervene?
- What do you consider to be the ethics involved in staying with a job after you have done everything you can to bring about change, but to no avail?

Now let's look at some examples that illustrate issues discussed in this chapter. Try to imagine yourself in each of these situations, and ask yourself how you would deal with them.

✓ **The Case of Ronnie.** Ronnie, an African American student, moved with his family into a mostly White community and attends high school there. Almost immediately he becomes the butt of racial jokes and experiences social isolation. A teacher notices his isolation and sends him to the school counselor. It is evident to the counselor that Ronnie is being discriminated against, not only by many of the students but also by some of the faculty. The counselor has no reason to doubt the information provided by Ronnie because she is aware of racism in the school and in the community. She determines that it would be much more practical to help Ronnie learn to ignore the prejudice than to try to change the racist attitudes of the school and the community.

- How do you evaluate this counselor's decision? What are its ethical ramifications? Does she have an obligation to work to change community attitudes?
- What would you do in this situation?
- Does a school system have an ethical obligation to attempt to change attitudes of a community that discriminates against some of its citizens?
- What are the risks of not addressing the problem of racism?

Commentary. In this case, the counselor may be experiencing a conflict of values and may fear reprisals if she acts on values that are not shared by many in the community. She may want to do what is needed to promote the well-being of her client, yet she may be struggling with self-doubts and with anxiety about not being accepted by the faculty. If you were consulting with this counselor, what might you say to her?

✓ **The Case of Adriana.** Adriana works in a community mental health clinic, and most of her time is devoted to dealing with immediate crises. The more she works with people in crisis, the more she is convinced that the focus of her work should be on preventive programs designed to educate the public. Adriana comes to believe strongly that there would be far fewer clients in distress if people were effectively contacted and motivated to participate in growth-oriented educational programs. She develops detailed, logical, and convincing proposals for programs she would like to implement in the community, but they are consistently rejected by the director of her center. Because the clinic is partially funded by the government for the express purpose of crisis intervention, the director feels uneasy about approving any program that does not relate directly to this objective.

If you were in Adriana's place, what would you do? Which of the following courses of action would you be likely to take?

_____ 1. I would do what the director expected and complain that the bureaucratic structure inhibited imaginative programs.

_____ 2. I would continue to work toward a compromise and try to find some way to make room for my special project. I would work with the director until I convinced her to permit me to launch my program in some form.

_____ 3. If I could not do what I deemed important, I would look for another job.

_____ 4. I would involve clients in setting the direction for the proposal and providing the necessary support to secure approval.

_____ 5. I would examine the director's responses and try to incorporate them into my approach.

_____ 6. I would get several other staff members together, pool our resources, and look for ways to implement the program as a group.

_____ 7. With my director's approval, I would try to obtain a grant for a pilot program in the community.

Chapter Summary

The primary focus of this chapter has been on the importance of working in the community as a change agent. The community mental health orientation is one way to meet the increasing demand for a variety of services. Too often mental health professionals have been denied the opportunity to devise programs that address the diverse needs of the community. Over the past few years some alternatives to conventional therapy have arisen, creating new roles for counselors who work in a community agency setting. It is our position that it is ethically incumbent on the counselor to be aware of community resources as a way to more effectively address the client's needs.

You may be seeking a full-time career in a system. We think it is essential to consider how to make the system work *for* you and your clients rather than *against* you and your clients. As Homan (1999) puts it: "If you treat people as if they are allies, they are more likely to become allies; if you treat them as enemies, they are more likely to become enemies" (p. 141).

We challenge you to think of ways to accept the responsibility of working effectively in an organization and thus increasing your effectiveness as a professional. Finally, we ask you to reflect on the major causes of disillusionment that often accompany working in a system and to find creative ways to retain your vitality.

Authors' Concluding Commentary

We have raised some of the ethical and professional issues that are likely to be encountered in your counseling practice and have tried to stimulate you to think about your own guidelines for professional practice. If one fundamental question can serve to tie together all the issues we have discussed, it is this: "Who has the right to counsel another person?" This question can be the basis for self-examination whenever you have concerns about clients. At times you may be troubled and believe that you have no right to counsel others, perhaps because you are not doing in your own life what you are challenging your clients to do. Yet occasional self-doubt is far less damaging, in our view, than a failure to question. Complacency will stifle your growth as a practitioner; honest self-examination, although sometimes difficult, will make you a more effective helper.

Developing a sense of professional and ethical responsibility is a task that is never really finished. There are no final or universal answers to many of the questions we have posed. For ourselves, we hope we never reach the point where we think we have figured it all out and no longer need to reexamine our assumptions and practices. The issues raised in this book demand periodic reflection and an openness to change. We hope you will continue to give careful thought to your own values and ethics and that you will be willing to rethink your positions as you gain more experience. An interest in what you do and in the people you serve will most likely make you not only an ethical practitioner, but also an interesting one.

Suggested Activities

1. Retake the self-assessment at the end of Chapter 1, which surveys your attitudes about ethical and professional issues. Cover your initial answers when you complete the self-assessment, and compare your responses now to see whether your thinking has changed. In addition, circle the 10 questions that are most significant to you or that you are most interested in pursuing further. Bring these to class and discuss them in small groups. Write down a few of the most important things you have learned in this course and from this book. You might also write down some questions that remain unanswered for you. Exchange your ideas with other students.
2. In small groups explore specific ways of becoming involved in the community or using community resources to assist you in working with your clients.
3. Reflect on and discuss alternative roles human-service professionals might play when working in the community. Which of the following roles do you think you could assume as a community worker: (a) advocate, (b) change agent, (c) consultant, (d) adviser, (e) facilitator of indigenous support systems, or (f) facilitator of indigenous healing systems. In small groups discuss in which of these roles you would feel least comfortable functioning, and why. How could you learn to carry out professional roles in the community different from those in which you were trained?
4. An issue you may well face in your practice is how to get through the hesitation people have toward asking for professional assistance. Ask yourself how you should respond to clients who have questions such as these: "What will people think if they find out that I am coming for professional help?" "Shouldn't I really be able to solve my problems on my own? Isn't it a sign of weakness that I need others to help me?" "Will I really be able to resolve my problems by consulting you?" After you have thought through your own responses, share them in dyads or in small groups.
5. How aware are you of the resources that exist in your community? Would you know where to refer clients for special needs? Investigate a community

mental health center in your area and find the answers to questions such as these:

- Where would you send a family who needed help?
- Where would you send a family who has a child with a learning or developmental disability?
- What website resources would you recommend?
- What facilities are available to treat drug and alcohol abuse?
- Is crisis intervention available?
- Are health and medical services available at the center?
- What groups are offered?
- Is individual counseling available? for whom? at what fee? long-term? short-term?
- Where would you refer a couple seeking couples counseling?
- Are hot-line services available?
- What provisions are there for emergency situations?
- What do people have to do to qualify for help at the center?

6. Several students can interview a variety of professionals in the mental health field about the major problems they encounter in their institution. What barriers do they meet when they attempt to implement programs? How do they deal with obstacles? Compare the responses of experienced and inexperienced personnel without revealing the identities of the persons interviewed.

7. After recognizing that a problem exists within the organization for which you work, identify skills you would need to make the desired changes. How might you go about developing strategies for getting support from coworkers if you were interested in changing an agency?

8. Consider asking professionals how they view workers who organize and mobilize clients, particularly toward making changes in the agency in which the professional works.

9. Interview clients in an agency and get their perceptions of how community workers have involved them in changing the conditions they face.

10. Some websites offer useful information pertaining to topics addressed in this chapter. Choose several topics that interest you and check these resources to see what information is available.

- Welfare Information Network: www.welfareinfo.org
- The Web Counseling Site: http://home.nww.net/willcars/index.html
- Addiction: www.jointogether.org *or* www.atforum.com
- Multicultural Services: www.mc-memhr.org
- Child Welfare League of America: www.handsmt.org/cwla
- National Institute on Drug Abuse: www.nida.nih.gov
- Substance Abuse and Mental Health Services Administration: www.samhsa.gov
- Mental Retardation: www.thearc.org
- National Coalition for the Homeless: www.ari.net/hone/nch
- Homeless Population Resources: www.homeless.org

- Psychosocial Rehabilitation: www.ucpsychrehab.org
- Posttraumatic Stress Disorder: www.ncptsd.org
- Program for Assertive Community Treatment: www.nami.org/about/pactfact.html
- Crisis Counseling: www.crisiscounseling.com
- Suicide Crisis Intervention: www.mhsantuary.com
- Prevention: www.prevention.org
- Advocacy Institute: www.advocacy.com
- Law and Social Policy: www.clasp.org

InfoTrac® College Edition Resources

For additional readings, explore InfoTrac College Edition, our online library. Key words are listed in a form that enables the search engine to locate a wider range of articles in the online university library. Key words should be entered exactly as shown, including asterisks, "Wl," "W2," "AND," and other search engine tools. Go to http://www.infotrac-college.com and select these key word searches:

community W1 counsel*
community W1 mental W1 health
mental W1 health AND paraprofessional*
community W1 agency AND ethic*
direct W1 client W1 service*
direct W1 community W1 service*
change W1 agent AND community AND ethic*
case W1 management AND community AND ethic*

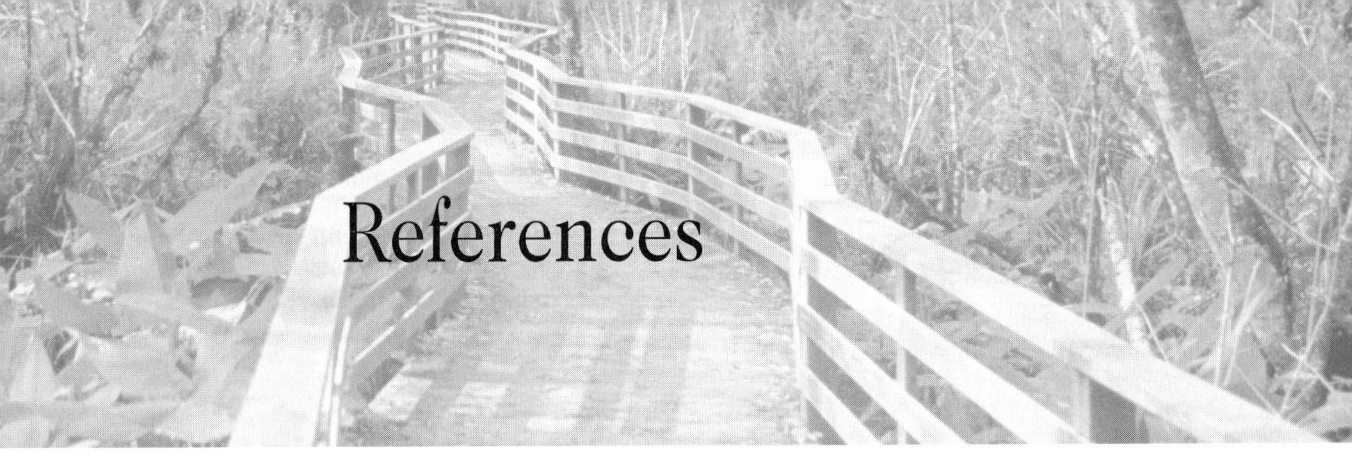

References

*Books and articles marked with an asterisk are suggested for further study.

Abeles, N., & Barlev, A. (1999). End of life decisions and assisted suicide. *Professional Psychology: Research and Practice, 30*(3), 229–234.

Acuff, C., Bennett, B. E., Bricklin, P. M., Canter, M. B., Knapp, S. J., Moldawsky, S., & Phelps, R. (1999). Considerations for ethical practice of managed care. *Professional Psychology: Research and Practice, 30*(6), 563–575.

Adair, J. G., Dushenko, T. W., & Lindsay, R. C. L. (1985). Ethical regulations and their impact on research practice. *American Psychologist, 40*(1), 59–72.

*Ahia, C. E., & Martin, D. (1993). *The danger-to-self-or-others exception to confidentiality.* Alexandria, VA: American Counseling Association.

*Albright, D. E., & Hazler, R. J. (1995). A right to die? Ethical dilemmas of euthanasia. *Counseling and Values, 39*(3), 177–189.

American Association for Marriage and Family Therapy. (2001). *AAMFT code of ethics.* Washington, DC: Author.

American Counseling Association. (2005). *Code of ethics.* Alexandria, VA: Author.

American Mental Health Counselors Association. (2000). *Code of ethics of the American Mental Health Counselors Association.* Alexandria, VA: Author.

American Psychiatric Association. (2000). *Diagnostic and statistical manual of mental disorders: Text revision* (4th ed.). Washington, DC: Author.

American Psychiatric Association. (2001). *The principles of medical ethics with annotations especially applicable to psychiatry.* Washington, DC: Author.

American Psychological Association. (1985). *White paper on duty to protect.* Washington, DC: Author.

American Psychological Association. (1992). *Ethical principles of psychologists and code of conduct.* Washington, DC: Author.

American Psychological Association. (1993). Guidelines for providers of psychological services to ethnic, linguistic, and culturally diverse populations. *American Psychologist, 48*(1), 45–48.

American Psychological Association, Division 44. (2000). Guidelines for psychotherapy with lesbian, gay, and bisexual clients. *American Psychologist, 55*(12), 1440–1451.

American Psychological Association. (2002). Ethical principles of psychologists and code of conduct. *American Psychologist, 57*(12), 1060–1073.

American Psychological Association. (2003a). Guidelines on multicultural education, training, research, practice, and organizational change for psychologists. *American Psychologist, 58*(5), 377–402.

American Psychological Association. (2003b). Report of the ethics committee, 2002. *American Psychologist, 58*(8), 650–657.

American School Counselor Association. (2004). *Ethical standards for school counselors.* Alexandria, VA: Author.

*Anderson, B. S. (1996). *The counselor and the law* (4th ed.). Alexandria, VA: American Counseling Association.

Anderson, J. R., & Barret, B. (Eds.). (2001). *Ethics in HIV-related psychotherapy: Clinical decision making in complex cases.* Washington, DC: American Psychological Association.

Anderson, S. K., & Kitchener, K. S. (1996). Nonromantic, nonsexual posttherapy relationships between psychologists and former clients: An exploratory study of critical incidents. *Professional Psychology: Research and Practice, 27*(1), 59–66.

*Anderson, S. K., & Kitchener, K. S. (1998). Nonsexual posttherapy relationships: A conceptual framework to assess ethical risks. *Professional Psychology: Research and Practice, 29*(1), 91–99.

*Anderson, S. K., & Middleton, V. A. (2005). *Explorations in privilege, oppression, and diversity.* Belmont, CA: Thomson Brooks/Cole.

*Aponte, H. J. (1994). How personal can training get? *Journal of Marital and Family Therapy, 20*(1), 3–15.

Arredondo, P. (1999). Multicultural counseling competencies as tools to address oppression and racism. *Journal of Counseling and Development, 77*(1), 102–108.

*Arredondo, P., Toporek, R., Brown, S., Jones, J., Locke, D., Sanchez, J., & Stadler, H. A. (1996). Operationalization of multicultural counseling competencies. *Journal of Multicultural Counseling and Development, 24*(1), 42–78.

*Arthur, G. L., & Swanson, C. D. (1993). *Confidentiality and privileged communication.* Alexandria, VA: American Counseling Association.

Association for Counselor Education and Supervision. (1993, Summer). Ethical guidelines for counseling supervisors. *ACES Spectrum, 53*(4), 3–8.

Association for Counselor Education and Supervision. (1995). Ethical guidelines for counseling supervisors. *Counselor Education and Supervision, 34*(3), 270–276.

Arthur, N., & Achenbach, K. (2002). Developing multicultural counseling competencies through experiential learning. *Counselor Education and Supervision, 42*(1), 2–14.

Association for Specialists in Group Work. (1998). Best practice guidelines. *Journal for Specialists in Group Work, 23*(3), 237–244.

Association for Specialists in Group Work. (1999). Principles for diversity-competent group workers. *Journal for Specialists in Group Work, 24*(1), 7–14.

Association for Specialists in Group Work. (2000). Professional standards for the training of group workers. *The Group Worker, 29*(3), 1–10.

*Atkinson, D. R. (2004). *Counseling American minorities* (6th ed.). Boston, MA: McGraw-Hill.

Atkinson, D. R., Thompson, C. E., & Grant, S. K. (1993). A three-dimensional model for counseling racial/ethnic minorities. *The Counseling Psychologist, 21*(2), 257–277.

Austad, C. S. (1996). *Is long-term psychotherapy unethical? Toward a social ethic in an era of managed care.* San Francisco, CA: Jossey-Bass.

Austin, K. M., Moline, M. M., & Williams, G. T. (1990). *Confronting malpractice: Legal and ethical dilemmas in psychotherapy.* Newbury Park, CA: Sage.

Axelson, J. A. (1999). *Counseling and development in a multicultural society* (3rd ed.). Pacific Grove, CA: Brooks/Cole.

*Baker, E. K. (2003). *Caring for ourselves: A therapist's guide to personal and professional well-being.* Washington, DC: American Psychological Association.

Barlow, S. H. (2004). A strategic three-year plan to teach beginning, intermediate, and advanced group skills. *Journal for Specialists in Group Work, 29*(1), 113–126.

Barlow, S. H., Fuhriman, A. J., & Burlingame, G. M. (2004). The history of group counseling and psychotherapy. In J. L. DeLucia-Waack, D. Gerrity, C. R. Kalodner, & M. T. Riva, (Eds), *Handbook of group counseling and psychotherapy* (pp. 3–22). Thousand Oaks, CA: Sage.

Barnett, J. E., & Hillard, D. (2001). Psychological distress and impairment: The availability, nature, and use of colleague assistance programs for psychologists. *Professional Psychology: Research and Practice, 32*(2), 205–210.

*Barret, B., & Logan, C. (2002). *Counseling gay men and lesbians: A practice primer.* Belmont, CA: Thomson Brooks/Cole.

Basham, A., & O'Connor, M. (2005). In C. S. Cashwell & J. S. Young, (Eds.). *Integrating spirituality and religion into counseling: A guide to competent practice* (pp. 143–167). Alexandria, VA: American Counseling Association.

Bednar, R. L., Bednar, S. C., Lambert, M. J., & Waite, D. R. (1991). *Psychotherapy with high-risk clients: Legal and professional standards.* Pacific Grove, CA: Brooks/Cole.

Behnke, S. (2005). Record-keeping under the new ethics code. *Monitor on Psychology, 36*(2), 72–73.

*Behnke, S., Preis, J. J., & Bates, R. T. (1998). *The essentials of California mental health law.* New York: Norton.

Belaire, C., Young, J. S., & Elder, A. (2005). Inclusion of religious behaviors and attitudes in counseling: Expectations of conservative Christians. *Counseling and Values, 49*(2), 82–94.

Bemak, F., & Chung, R. C-Y. (2004). Teaching multicultural group counseling: Perspectives by a new era. *Journal for Specialists in Group Work, 29*(1), 31–41.

Bemak, F., Epp, L. R., & Keys, S. G. (1999). Impaired graduate students: A process model of graduate program monitoring and intervention. *International Journal for the Advancement of Counselling, 21,* 19–30.

Benitez, B. R. (2004). Confidentiality and its exceptions. *The Therapist, 16*(4), 32–36.

Bennett, B. E., Bricklin, P. M., & VandeCreek, L. (1994). Response to Lazarus's "How certain boundaries and ethics diminish therapeutic effectiveness." *Ethics and Behavior, 4*(3), 263–266.

Bennett, B. E., Bryant, B. K., VandenBos, G. R., & Greenwood, A. (1990). *Professional liability and risk management.* Washington, DC: American Psychological Association.

Benningfield, A. B. (1994). The impaired therapist. In G. W. Brock (Ed.), *American Association for Marriage and Family Therapy ethics casebook* (pp. 131–139). Washington, DC: American Association for Marriage and Family Therapy.

Benson, H., with Stark, M. (1996). *Timeless healing: The power and biology of belief.* New York: Scribner.

Bergin, A. E. (1991). Values and religious issues in psychotherapy and mental health. *American Psychology, 46*(4), 393–403.

Bernard, J. M. (1994). Multicultural supervision: A reaction to Leong and Wagner, Cook, Priest, and Fukuyama. *Counselor Education and Supervision, 34*(2), 159–171.

*Bernard, J. M., & Goodyear, R. K. (2004). *Fundamentals of clinical supervision* (3rd ed.). Boston, MA: Allyn & Bacon.

Bersoff, D. N. (1996). The virtue of principle ethics. *The Counseling Psychologist, 24*(1), 86–91.

*Bersoff, D. N. (2003a). *Ethical conflicts in psychology* (3rd ed.). Washington, DC: American Psychological Association.

Bersoff, D. N. (2003b). HIPAA: Federal regulations of healthcare records. In D. N. Bersoff (Ed.), *Ethical conflicts in psychology* (3rd ed., pp. 526–528). Washington, DC: American Psychological Association.

*Beutler, L. E., & Malik, M. L. (2002). *Rethinking DSM: A psychological perspective.* Washington, DC: American Psychological Association.

Biaggio, M., Orchard, S., Larson, J., Petrino, K., & Mihara, R. (2003). Guidelines for gay/lesbian/bisexual affirmative educational practices in graduate psychology programs. *Professional Psychology: Research and Practice, 34*(5), 548–554.

Biaggio, M., Paget, T. L., & Chenoweth, M. S. (1997). A model for ethical management of faculty-student dual relationships. *Professional Psychology: Research and Practice, 28*(2), 184–189.

Birdsall, B., & Hubert, M. (2000, October). Ethical issues in school counseling. *Counseling Today,* pp. 30, 36.

Bishop, D. R., Avila-Juarbe, E., & Thumme, B. (2003). Recognizing spirituality as an important factor in counselor supervision. *Counseling and Values, 48*(1), 34–46.

Board of Curators of the University of Missouri v. Horowitz, 435 U.S. 78 (1978).

Boisvert, C. M., & Faust, D. (2003). Leading researchers' consensus on psychotherapy research findings: Implications for the teaching and conduct of psychotherapy. *Professional Psychology: Research and Practice, 34*(5), 508–513.

Bonger, B. (2002). *The suicidal patient: Clinical and legal standards of care* (2nd ed.) Washington, DC: American Psychological Association.

Borders, L. D. (1991). A systematic approach to peer group supervision. *Journal of Counseling and Development, 69*(3), 248–252.

Borys, D. S. (1994). Maintaining therapeutic boundaries: The motive is therapeutic effectiveness, not defensive practice. *Ethics and Behavior, 4*(3), 267–273.

Bouhoutsos, J., Holroyd, J., Lerman, H., Forer, B. R., & Greenberg, M. (1983). Sexual intimacy between psychotherapists and patients. *Professional Psychology: Research and Practice, 14*(2), 185–196.

Bowman, V. E., Hatley, L. D., & Bowman, R. (1995). Faculty-student relationships: The dual role controversy. *Counselor Education and Supervision, 24*(3), 232–242.

*Brabeck, M. M. (Ed.). (2000). *Practicing feminist ethics in psychology.* Washington, DC: American Psychological Association.

Brace, K. (1997). Ethical considerations in the development of counseling goals. In *The Hatherleigh guide to ethics in therapy* (pp. 17–35). New York: Hatherleigh Press.

Bradley Center v. Wessner, 250 Ga. 199, 296 S.E. 2d 693 (1982).

*Bradley, L. J., Kottler, J. A., & Lehrman-Waterman, D. (2001). Ethical issues in supervision. In L. J. Bradley & N. Ladany (Eds.), *Counselor supervision: Principles, process and practice* (3rd ed., pp. 342–360). Philadelphia, PA: Brunner-Routledge/Taylor & Francis Group.

Brawer, P. A., Handal, P. J., Fabricatore, A. N., Roberts, R., & Wajda-Johnston, V. A. (2002). Training and education in religion/spirituality within APA-accredited clinical psychology programs. *Professional Psychology: Research and Practice, 33*(2), 203–206.

*Brock, G. W. (Ed.). (1998). *Ethics casebook.* Washington, DC: American Association for Marriage and Family Therapy.

Broskowski, A. (1991). Current mental health care environments: Why managed care is necessary. *Professional Psychology: Research and Practice, 22*(1) 6–14.

Brown, C., & O'Brien, K. M. (1998). Understanding stress and burnout in shelter workers. *Professional Psychology: Research and Practice, 29*(4), 383–385.

Brown, L. S. (1994). Concrete boundaries and the problem of literal-mindedness: A response to Lazarus. *Ethics and Behavior, 4*(3), 275–281.

Bruff v. North Mississippi Health Services, Inc., 244 F.3d 495 (5th Cir. 2001).

Burian, B. K., & O'Conner Slimp, A. (2000). Social dual-role relationships during internship: A decision-making model. *Professional Psychology: Research and Practice, 31*(3), 332–338.

Burke, M. T., Hackney, H., Hudson, P., Miranti, J., Watts, G. A., & Epp, L. (1999). Sprituality, religion, and CACREP curriculum standards. *Journal of Counseling and Development, 77*(3), 251–257.

Burlingame, G. M., Fuhriman, A. J., & Johnson, J. (2004). Current status and future directions of group therapy research. In J. L. DeLucia-Waack, D. Gerrity, C. R. Kalodner, & M. T. Riva (Eds.), *Handbook of group counseling and psychotherapy* (pp. 651–660). Thousand Oaks, CA: Sage.

Calfee, B. E. (1997). Lawsuit prevention techniques. In *The Hatherleigh guide to ethics in therapy* (pp. 109–125). New York: Hatherleigh Press.

California Association of Marriage and Family Therapists. (1996a, March/April). Disciplinary actions. *The California Therapist, 8*(2), 18.

California Association of Marriage and Family Therapists. (1996b, May/June). Disciplinary actions. *The California Therapist, 8*(3), 25–26.

California Association of Marriage and Family Therapists. (1996c, July/August). Disciplinary actions. *The California Therapist, 8*(4), 34.

California Association of Marriage and Family Therapists. (2001, January/February). Disciplinary actions. *The California Therapist, 13*(1), 40.

California Association of Marriage and Family Therapists. (2004a, July/August). Disciplinary actions. *The Therapist, 16*(4), 5–6.

California Association of Marriage and Family Therapists. (2004b, July/August). Disciplinary actions. *The Therapist, 16*(4), 49.

California Association of Marriage and Family Therapists. (2004c, July/August). Disciplinary actions. *The Therapist, 16*(4), 50.

California Association of Marriage and Family Therapists. (2005, March/April). Disciplinary actions. *The Therapist, 17*(2), 50.

California Department of Consumer Affairs. (2004). *Professional therapy never includes sex* (pamphlet). Sacramento, CA: Author.

California Department of Consumer Affairs, Board of Psychology. (1999, May). Disciplinary actions. *Board of Psychology Update, 6,* 12–13.

Campbell, C. D., & Gordon, M. C. (2003). Acknowledging the inevitable: Understanding multiple relationships in rural practice. *Professional Psychology: Research and Practice, 34*(4), 430–434.

Canadian Association of Social Workers. (1994). *Code of ethics.* Ottawa: Author.

Canadian Counselling Association. (1999). *CCA code of ethics.* Ottawa: Author.

Canadian Psychological Association. (2000). *Canadian code of ethics for psychologists.* (3rd ed.). Ottawa: Author.

*Canter, M. B., Bennett, B. E., Jones, S. E., & Nagy, T. F. (1994). *Ethics for psychologists: A commentary on the APA ethics code.* Washington, DC: American Psychological Association.

Capuzzi, D. (2002). Legal and ethical challenges in counseling suicidal students. *Professional School Counseling, 6,* 36–45.

*Capuzzi, D. (Ed.). (2004). *Suicide across the life span: Implications for counselors.* Alexandria, VA: American Counseling Association.

Capuzzi, D., & Gross, D. R. (Eds.). (2000). *Youth at risk: A prevention resource for counselors, teachers, and parents* (3rd ed.). Alexandria, VA: American Counseling Association.

Cardemil, E. V., & Battle, C. L. (2003). Guess who's coming to therapy? Getting comfortable with conversations about race and ethnicity in psychotherapy. *Professional Psychology: Research and Practice, 34*(3), 278–286.

Carrier, J. W. (2004). Assessing suicidal risk. In D. Capuzzi (Ed.), *Suicide across the life span: Implications for counselors* (pp. 139–162). Alexandria, VA: American Counseling Association.

Carta-Falsa, J., & Anderson, L. (2001). A model of clinical/counseling supervision. *The California Therapist, 13*(2), 47–51.

*Cashwell, C. S., & Young, J. S. (2005). *Integrating spirituality and religion into counseling: A guide to competent practice.* Alexandria, VA: American Counseling Association.

Casto, C., Caldwell, C., & Salazar, C. F. (2005). Creating mentoring relationships between female faculty and students in counselor education: Guidelines for potential mentees and mentors. *Journal of Counseling and Development, 83*(3), 331–336.

Chang, T., & Yeh, C. J. (2003). Using online groups to provide support to Asian American men: Racial, cultural, gender, and treatment issues. *Professional Psychology: Research and Practice, 34*(6), 634–643.

Chauvin, J. C., & Remley, T. P. (1996). Responding to allegations of unethical conduct. *Journal of Counseling and Development, 74*(6), 563–568.

Christensen, T. M., & Kline, W. B. (2000). A qualitative investigation of the process of group supervision with group counselors. *Journal for Specialists in Group Work, 25*(4), 376–393.

Cobia, D. C., & Boes, S. R. (2000). Professional disclosure statements and formal plans for supervision: Two strategies for minimizing the risk of ethical conflicts in postmaster's supervision. *Journal of Counseling and Development, 78*(3), 293–296.

**Codes of Ethics for the Helping Professions* (3rd ed.). (2007). Belmont, CA: Thomson Brooks/Cole.

Cohen, E. D. (1997). Ethical standards in counseling sexually active clients with HIV. In *The Hatherleigh guide to ethics in therapy* (pp. 211–233). New York: Hatherleigh Press.

Cohen, R. (2004). *Clinical supervision: What to do and how to do it.* Belmont, CA: Thomson Brooks/Cole.

Commission on Rehabilitation Counselor Certification. (2001). *Code of professional ethics for rehabilitation counselors.* Rolling Meadows, IL: Author.

Committee on Professional Practice and Standards. (2003). Legal issues in the professional practice of psychology. *Professional Psychology: Research and Practice, 34*(6), 595–600.

Committee on Professional Practice and Standards, Board of Professional Affairs. (1993). Record keeping guidelines. *American Psychologist, 48,* 984–986.

Committee on Women in Psychology, American Psychological Association. (1989). If sex enters into the psychotherapy relationship. *Professional Psychology: Research and Practice, 20*(2), 112–115.

*Constantine, M. G. (1997). Facilitating multicultural competency in counseling supervision: Operationalizing a practical framework. In D. B. Pope-Davis & H. L. K. Coleman, (Eds.), *Multicultural counseling competencies: Assessment, education and training, and supervision* (pp. 310–324). Thousand Oaks, CA: Sage.

Constantine, M. G., Myers, L. J., Kindaichi, M., & Moore, J. L. (2004). Exploring indigenous mental health practices: The role of healers and helpers in promoting well-being in people of color. *Counseling and Values, 48*(2), 110–125.

Cook, D. A. (1994). Racial identity in supervision. *Counselor Education and Supervision, 34*(2), 132–141.

Cooper, C. C., & Gottlieb, M. C. (2000). Ethical issues with managed care: Challenges facing counseling psychology. *The Counseling Psychologist, 28*(2), 179–236.

*Corey, G. (2001). *The art of integrative counseling.* Pacific Grove, CA: Brooks/Cole.

Corey, G. (2004). *Theory and practice of group counseling* (6th ed.) and *Manual.* Pacific Grove, CA: Brooks/Cole.

Corey, G. (2005a). *Case approach to counseling and psychotherapy* (6th ed.). Belmont, CA: Thomson Brooks/Cole.

Corey, G. (2005b). *Theory and practice of counseling and psychotherapy* (7th ed.) and *Manual.* Belmont, CA: Thomson Brooks/Cole.

Corey, G., & Corey, M. (2006). *I never knew I had a choice* (8th ed.). Belmont, CA: Thomson Brooks/Cole.

Corey, G., Corey, M., & Callanan, P. (2005). An approach to teaching ethics courses in human services and counseling. *Counseling and Values, 49*(3), 193–207.

Corey, G., Corey, M., Callanan, P., & Russell, J. M. (2004). *Group techniques* (3rd ed.). Pacific Grove, CA: Brooks/Cole.

Corey, G., & Herlihy, B. (1993). Dual relationships: Associated risks and potential benefits. *Ethical Issues in Professional Counseling, 1*(1), 3–11.

Corey, G., & Herlihy, B. (2006a). Client rights and informed consent. In B. Herlihy & G. Corey (Eds.), ACA *ethical standards casebook* (6th ed.). Alexandria, VA: American Counseling Association.

Corey, G., & Herlihy, B. (2006b). Competence. In B. Herlihy & G. Corey (Eds.), *ACA ethical standards casebook* (6th ed.). Alexandria, VA: American Counseling Association.

Corey, G., & Herlihy, B. (1996). Dual/multiple relationships: Toward a consensus of thinking. In *The Hatherleigh guide to ethics in therapy* (pp. 183–194). New York: Hatherleigh Press.

Corey, G., Williams, G. T., & Moline, M. E. (1995). Ethical and legal issues in group counseling. *Ethics and Behavior, 5*(2), 161–183.

Corey, M., & Corey, G. (1993). Difficult group members—difficult group leaders. *New York State Association for Counseling and Development, 8*(2), 9–24.

*Corey, M., & Corey, G. (2006). *Groups: Process and practice* (7th ed.). Belmont, CA: Thomson Brooks/Cole.

Corsini, R., & Wedding, D. (2005). *Current psychotherapies* (7th ed.). Belmont, CA: Thomson Brooks/Cole.

Costa, L., & Altekruse, M. (1994). Duty-to-warn guidelines for mental health counselors. *Journal of Counseling and Development, 72*(4), 346–350.

Costanzo, M. (2004). *Psychology applied to law.* Belmont, CA: Thomson Wadsworth.

Coster, J. S., & Schwebel, M. (1997). Well-functioning in professional psychologists. *Professional Psychology: Research and Practice, 28*(1), 5–13.

Cottone, R. R. (2001). A social constructivism model of ethical decision making in counseling. *Journal of Counseling and Development, 79*(1), 39–45.

Cottone, R. R., & Claus, R. E. (2000). Ethical decision-making models: A review of the literature. *Journal of Counseling and Development, 78*(3), 275–283.

Cottone, R. R., & Tarvydas, V. M. (2003). *Ethical and professional issues in counseling* (2nd ed.). Upper Saddle River, NJ: Merrill/Prentice-Hall.

Council for Accreditation of Counseling and Related Educational Programs. (CACREP) (2001). *CACREP: The 2001 standards [Statement].* Alexandria, VA: Author.

Crawford, I., McLeod, A., Zamboni, B. D., & Jordan, M. B. (1999). Psychologists' attitudes toward gay and lesbian parenting. *Professional Psychology: Research and Practice, 30*(4), 394–401.

Crawford, R. L. (1994). *Avoiding counselor malpractice.* Alexandria, VA: American Counseling Association.

Crawford, R. (1999). Law and ethics: Comparisons and contrasts. In P. Stevens (Ed.), *Ethical casebook for the practice of marriage and family counseling* (pp. 17–39). Alexandria, VA: American Counseling Association.

Crespi, T. D., Fischetti, B. A., & Butler, S. K. (2001, January). Clinical supervision in the schools. *Counseling Today, 7*, 28, 34.

Cukrowicz, K. C., White, B. A., Reitzel, L. R., Burns, A. B., Driscoll, K. A., Kemper, T. S., & Joiner, T. E. (2005). Improved treatment outcome associated with the shift to empirically supported treatments in a graduate training clinic. *Professional Psychology: Research and Practice, 36*(3), 330–337.

Cummings, N. A. (1995). Impact of managed care on employment and training: A primer for survival. *Professional Psychology: Research and Practice, 26*(1), 10–15.

Custer, G. (1994, November) Can universities be liable for incompetent grads? *APA Monitor, 25*(11), 7.

Das, A. K. (1995). Rethinking multicultural counseling: Implications for counselor education. *Journal of Counseling and Development, 74*(1), 45–52.

Davis, J. W. (1981). Counselor licensure: Overskill? *Personnel and Guidance Journal, 60*(2), 83–85.

*Davis, S. R., & Meier, S. T. (2001). *The elements of managed care: A guide for helping professionals.* Pacific Grove, CA: Brooks/Cole.

Dearing, R. L., Maddux, J. E., & Tangney, J. P. (2005). Predictors of psychological help seeking in clinical and counseling psychology graduate students. *Professional Psychology: Research and Practice, 36*(3), 323–329.

DeBell, C., & Jones, R. D. (1997). Privileged communication at last? An overview of *Jaffee v. Redmond. Professional Psychology: Research and Practice, 28*(6), 559–566.

Deegear, J., & Lawson, D. M. (2003). The utility of empirically supported treatments. *Professional Psychology: Research and Practice, 34*(3), 271–277.

DeLeon, P. H., Giesting, B., & Kenkel, M. B. (2003). Community health centers: Exciting opportunities for the 21st century. *Professional Psychology: Research and Practice, 34*(6), 579–585.

*DeLucia-Waack, J. L., & Donigian, J. (2004). *The practice of multicultural group work: Visions and perspectives from the field.* Belmont, CA: Thomson Brooks/Cole.

DeMayo, R. A. (2000). Patients' sexual behavior and sexual harassment: A survey of clinical supervisors. *Professional Psychology: Research and Practice, 31*(6), 706–709.

De Vaney Olvey, C., Hogg, A., & Counts, W. (2002). Licensure requirements: Have we raised the bar too far? *Professional Psychology: Research and Practice, 33*(3), 323–329.

Deutsch, C. J. (1984). Self-reported sources of stress among psychotherapists. *Professional Psychology: Research and Practice, 15*(6), 833–845.

Diller, J. V. (2004). *Cultural diversity: A primer for the human services* (2nd ed.). Belmont, CA: Thomson Brooks/Cole.

Dineen, T. (2002). The psychotherapist and the quest for power: How boundaries have become an obsession. In A. A. Lazarus & O. Zur (Eds.), *Dual relationships and psychotherapy* (pp. 115–139.). New York: Springer.

Dittmann, M. (2003). Maintaining ethics in a rural setting. *Monitor on Psychology, 34*(6), 66.

DiVerde-Nushawg, N., & Walls, G. B. (1998). The implications of pager use for the therapeutic relationship in independent practice. *Professional Psychology: Research and Practice, 29*(4), 368–372.

Doss, B. D., Simpson, L. E., & Christensen, A. (2004). Why do couples seek marital therapy? *Professional Psychology: Research and Practice, 35*(6), 608–614.

Dougherty, A. M. (2005). *Psychological consultation and collaboration in schools and community settings* (4th ed.). Belmont, CA: Thomson Brooks/Cole.

Dougherty, J. L. (2005). Ethics in case conceptualization and diagnosis: Incorporating a medical model into the developmental counseling tradition. *Counseling and Values, 49*(2), 132–140.

Downs, L. (2003). A preliminary survey of relationships between counselor educators' ethics education and ensuing pedagogy and responses to attractions with counseling students. *Counseling and Values, 48*(1), 2–13.

Edwards, J. A., Dattilio, F. M., & Bromley, D. B. (2004). Developing evidence-based practice: The role of case-based research. *Professional Psychology: Research and Practice, 35*(6), 589–597.

Edwards, J. K., & Bess, J. M. (1998). Developing effectiveness in the therapeutic use of self. *Clinical Social Work Journal, 26*(1), 89–105.

Eisel v. Board of Education, 597 A.2d 447 (Md. 1991).

Egan, H., James, M., & Wagner, B. (2004). *Retiring well.* New York: Barnes & Noble.

Elman, N. S., & Forrest, L. (2004). Psychotherapy in the remediation of psychology trainees: Exploratory interviews with training directors. *Professional Psychology: Research and Practice, 35*(2), 123–130.

Emerson, S., & Markos, P. A. (1996). Signs and symptoms of the impaired counselor. *Journal of Humanistic Education and Development, 34,* 108–117.

Engels, D. W. (2004). *The professional counselor: Portfolio, competencies, performance guidelines, and assessment* (3rd ed.). Alexandria, VA: American Counseling Association.

Erickson, S. H. (1993). Ethics and confidentiality in AIDS counseling: A professional dilemma. *Journal of Mental Health Counseling, 15*(2), 118–131.

Evans, G. D., & Rey, J. (2001). In the echoes of gunfire: Practicing psychologists' responses to school violence. *Professional Psychology: Research and Practice, 32*(2), 157–164.

Evans, K. M. (2003). Including spirituality in multicultural counseling: Overcoming counselor resistance. In G. Roysircar, D. S. Sandhu, & V. E. Bibbins (Eds.), *Multicultural competencies: A guidebook of practices* (pp. 161–171). Alexandria, VA: Association for Multicultural Counseling and Development.

Ewing v. Goldstein, B163122, 2nd Dist. Div. 8. Cal. App. 4th (2004).

Ezell, M. (2001). *Advocacy in the human services.* Pacific Grove, CA: Brooks/Cole.

Fadiman, A. (1997). *The Spirit Catches You and You Fall Down.* New York: Farrar, Straus and Giroux.

Faiver, C., & Ingersoll, R. E. (2005). Knowing one's limits. In C. S. Cashwell & J. S. Young, (Eds.), *Integrating spirituality and religion into counseling: A guide to competent practice* (pp.169–183). Alexandria, VA: American Counseling Association.

Faiver, C., Ingersoll, R. E., O'Brien, E., & McNally, C. (2001). *Explorations in counseling and spirituality: Philosophical, practical, and personal reflections.* Pacific Grove, CA: Brooks/Cole.

Faiver, C. M., Eisengart, S., & Colonna, R. (2000). *The counselor intern's handbook* (2nd ed.). Pacific Grove, CA: Brooks/Cole.

Faiver, C. M., & O'Brien, E. M. (1993). Assessment of religious beliefs form. *Counseling and Values, 37*(3), 176–178.

Faiver, C. M., O'Brien, E. M., & Ingersoll, R. E. (2000). Religion, guilt, and mental health. *Journal of Counseling and Development, 78*(2), 155–161.

*Falender, C. A., & Shafranske, E. P. (2004). *Clinical supervision: A competency-based approach.* Washington, DC: American Psychological Association.

Fall, M., & Sutton, J. (2004). *Clinical supervision: A handbook for practitioners.* Boston, MA: Allyn & Bacon.

*Falvey, J. (2002). *Managing clinical supervision: Ethical and legal risk management.* Pacific Grove, CA: Brooks/Cole.

Farber, B. A. (1983a). Psychotherapists' perceptions of stressful patient behavior. *Professional Psychology: Research and Practice, 14*(5), 697–705.

Farber, B. A. (1983b). *Stress and burnout in the human service professions.* New York: Pergamon Press.

Farberman, R. K. (1997). Terminal illness and hastened death requests: The important role of the mental health professional. *Professional Psychology: Research and Practice, 28*(6), 544–547.

Fay, A. (2002). The case against boundaries in psychotherapy. In A. A. Lazarus & O. Zur (Eds.), *Dual relationships and psychotherapy* (pp. 146–166.). New York: Springer.

Feist, S. C. (1999). Practice and theory of professional supervision for mental health counselors. *Directions in Mental Health Counseling, 9*(9), 105–119.

Feminist Therapy Institute. (2000). *Feminist therapy code of ethics* (revised, 1999). San Francisco: Feminist Therapy Institute.

Ford, M. P., & Hendrick, S. S. (2003). Therapists' sexual values for self and clients: Implications for practice and training. *Professional Psychology: Research and Practice, 34*(1), 80–87.

Forester-Miller, H. (2006). Rural communities: Can dual relationships be avoided? In B. Herlihy & G. Corey (Eds.), *Boundary issues in counseling: Multiple roles and responsibilities* (2nd ed.). Alexandria, VA: American Counseling Association.

Forester-Miller, H., & Davis, T. E. (1995). *A practitioner's guide to ethical decision making.* Alexandria, VA: American Counseling Association.

*Forrest, L., Elman, N., Gizara, S., & Vacha-Haase, T. (1999). Trainee impairment: A review of identification, remediation, dismissal, and legal issues. *The Counseling Psychologist, 27*(5), 627–686.

Foster, R. P. (1998). The clinician's cultural countertransference: The psychodynamics of culturally competent practice. *Clinical Social Work Journal, 26*(3), 253–270.

Foster, S. (1996, January). The consequences of violating the "forbidden zone." *Counseling Today,* p. 24.

Foxhall, K. (2000). How will the rules on telehealth be written? *Monitor on Psychology, 31*(4), 38.

*Frame, M. W. (2003). *Integrating religion and spirituality into counseling: A comprehensive approach.* Pacific Grove, CA: Brooks/Cole.

Frame, M. W., & Williams, C. B. (2005). A model of ethical decision making from a multicultural perspective. *Counseling and Values, 49*(3), 165–179.

Frankel, A. S. (2000). Watch out for the third man death. *Board of Psychology Update,* 8, 2–3.

Freeny, M. (2001). Better than being there. *Psychotherapy Networker, 25*(2), 30–70.

Fremon, C. (1991, January 27). Love and death. *Los Angeles Times Magazine*, pp. 17–35.

Fujimura, L. E., Weis, D. M., & Cochran, J. R. (1985). Suicide: Dynamics and implications for counseling. *Journal of Counseling and Development, 63*(10), 612–615.

Fukuyama, M. A. (1994). Critical incidents in multicultural counseling: A phenomenological approach to supervision research. *Counselor Education and Supervision, 34*(2), 142–151.

Gabbard, G. O. (1994). Teetering on the precipice: A commentary on Lazarus's "How certain boundaries and ethics diminish therapeutic effectiveness." *Ethics and Behavior, 4*(3), 283–286.

Gabbard, G. O. (1995, April). What are boundaries in psychotherapy? *The Menninger Letter, 3*(4), 1–2.

Gabbard, G. O. (1996). Lessons to be learned from the study of sexual boundary violations. *American Journal of Psychotherapy, 50*(3), 311–322.

Gabbard, G. O. (2000). *Psychodynamic psychiatry in clinical practice* (3rd ed.). Washington, DC: American Psychiatric Press.

Garcia, J. G., Cartwright, B., Winston, S. M., & Borzuchowska, B. (2003). A transcultural integrative model for ethical decision making in counseling. *Journal of Counseling and Development, 81*(3), 268–277.

Gaubatz, M. D., & Vera, E. M. (2002). Do formalized gatekeeping procedures increase programs' follow-up with deficient trainees? *Counselor Education and Supervision, 41*(4), 294–305.

Gelso, C. J., & Carter, J. A. (1985). The relationship in counseling and psychotherapy: Components, consequences, and theoretical antecedents. *The Counseling Psychologist, 13*(2), 155–243.

Gehart, D. R., & Tuttle, A. R. (2003). *Theory-based treatment planning for marriage and family therapists: Integrating theory and practice.* Pacific Grove, CA: Thomson Brooks/Cole.

Genia, V. (1994). Secular psychotherapists and religious clients: Professional considerations and recommendations. *Journal of Counseling and Development, 72*(4), 395–398.

Getz, H. D. (1999). Assessment of clinical supervisor competencies. *Journal of Counseling and Development, 77*(4), 491–497.

Getz, J. G., & Protinsky, H. O. (1994). Training marriage and family counselors: A family-of-origin approach. *Counselor Education and Supervision, 33*(3), 183–200.

Gilroy, P. J., Carroll, L., & Murra, J. (2002). A preliminary survey of counseling psychologists' personal experiences with depression and treatment. *Professional Psychology: Research and Practice, 33*(4), 402–407.

Giordano, M. A., Altekruse, M. K., & Kern, C. W. (2000). *Supervisee's bill of rights.* Unpublished manuscript.

Gizara, S. S., & Forrest, L. (2004). Supervisors' experiences of trainee impairment and incompetence at APA-accredited internship sites. *Professional Psychology: Research and Practice, 35*(2), 131–140.

Glaberson, W. (2000, August 4). Judges dismiss civil suits in school killings. *The Times-Picayune,* p. A-4.

Gladding, S. T., Remley, T. P., & Huber, C. H. (2001). *Ethical, legal, and professional issues in the practice of marriage and family therapy* (3rd ed.) Upper Saddle River, NJ: Merrill/Prentice-Hall.

Glosoff, H. L., Corey, G., & Herlihy, B. (2006). Avoiding detrimental multiple relationships. In B. Herlihy & G. Corey, (Eds.), *ACA ethical standards casebook* (6th ed.). Alexandria, VA: American Counseling Association.

*Glosoff, H. L., Garcia, J., Herlihy, B., & Remley, T. P. (1999). Managed care: Ethical considerations for counselors. *Counseling and Values, 44*(1), 8–16.

*Glosoff, H. L., Herlihy, S. B., Herlihy, B., & Spence, E. B. (1997). Privileged communication in the psychologist-client relationship. *Professional Psychology: Research and Practice, 28*(6), 573–581.

*Glosoff, H. L., Herlihy, B., & Spence, E. B. (2000). Privileged communication in the counselor-client relationship. *Journal of Counseling and Development, 78*(4), 454–462.

Glosoff, H. L., & Pate, R. H. (2002). Privacy and confidentiality in school counseling. *Professional School Counseling, 6,* 20–27.

*Goldenberg, I., & Goldenberg, H. (2004). *Family therapy: An overview* (6th. ed.). Belmont, CA: Thomson Brooks/Cole.

Gray, L. A., & Harding, A. I. (1988). Confidentiality limits with clients who have the AIDS virus. *Journal of Counseling and Development, 66*(5), 219–223.

Green, J. B. (2003). *Introduction to family theory and therapy: Exploring an evolving field.* Belmont, CA: Thomson Brooks/Cole.

Greenhut, M. (1991, May/June). Professional networking: The downward spiral to "health." *The California Therapist,* pp. 47–48.

Greenspan, M. (1994). On professionalism. In C. Heyward (Ed.), *When boundaries betray us* (pp. 193–205). San Francisco: HarperCollins.

Greenspan, M. (2002). Out of bounds. In A. A. Lazarus & O. Zur (Eds.), *Dual relationships and psychotherapy* (pp. 425–431). New York: Springer.

Grimm, D. W. (1994). Therapist spiritual and religious values in psychotherapy. *Counseling and Values, 38*(3), 154–164.

*Grosso, F. C. (2002). *Complete applications of law and ethics: A workbook for California Marriage and Family Therapists.* Santa Barbara, CA: Author.

Guadalupe, K. L., & Lum, D. (2005). *Multidimensional contextual practice: Diversity and transcendence.* Belmont, CA: Thomson Brooks/Cole.

Guest, C. L., & Dooley, K. (1999). Supervisor malpractice: Liability to the supervisee in clinical supervision. *Counselor Education and Supervision, 38*(4), 269–279.

Gutheil, T. G. (1994). Discussion of Lazarus's "How certain boundaries and ethics diminish therapeutic effectiveness." *Ethics and Behavior, 4*(3), 295–298.

Gutheil, T. G., & Gabbard, G. O. (1993). The concept of boundaries in clinical practice: Theoretical and risk-management dimensions. *American Journal of Psychiatry, 150*(2), 188–196.

Guthmann, D., & Sandberg, K. A. (2002). Dual relationships in the deaf community: When dual relationships are unavoidable and essential. In A. A. Lazarus & O. Zur (Eds.), *Dual relationships and psychotherapy* (pp. 287–297). New York: Springer.

Guy, J. D. (2000). Holding the holding environment together: Self-psychology and psychotherapist care. *Professional Psychology: Research and Practice, 31*(3), 351–352.

Haas, L. J., & Cummings, N. A. (1991). Managed outpatient mental health plans: Clinical, ethical, and practical guidelines for participation. *Professional Psychology: Research and Practice, 22*(1), 45–51.

Hagedorn, W. B. (2005). Counselor self-awareness and self-exploration of religious and spiritual beliefs: Know thyself. In C. S. Cashwell & J. S. Young (Eds.), *Integrating spirituality and religion into counseling: A guide to competent practice* (pp. 63–84). Alexandria, VA: American Counseling Association.

Haley, W. E., Larson, D. G., Kasl-Godley, J., Neimeyer, R. A., & Kwilosz, D. M. (2003). Roles for psychologists in end-of-life care: Emerging models of practice. *Professional Psychology: Research and Practice, 34*(6), 626–633.

Hall, C. R., Dixon, W. A., & Mauzey, E. D. (2004). Spirituality and religion: Implications for counselors. *Journal of Counseling and Development, 82*(4), 504–507.

Hall, L. A. (1996). Bartering: A payment methodology whose time has come again or an unethical practice? *Family Therapy News, 27*(4), 7, 19.

Hamann, E. E. (1994). Clinicians and diagnosis: Ethical concerns and clinical competence. *Journal of Counseling and Development, 72*(3), 259–260.

Hamilton, J. C., & Spruill, J. (1999). Identifying and reducing risk factors related to trainee-client sexual misconduct. *Professional Psychology: Research and Practice, 30*(3), 318–327.

Hammel, G. A., Olkin, R., & Taube, D. O. (1996). Student-educator sex in clinical and counseling psychology doctoral training. *Professional Psychology: Research and Practice, 27*(1), 93–97.

Handelsman, M. M., Gottlieb, M. C., & Knapp, S. (2005). Training ethical psychologists: An acculturation model. *Professional Psychology: Research and Practice, 36*(1), 59–65.

Handerscheid, R. W., Henderson, M. J., & Chalk, M. (2002). Responding to HIPAA regulations: An update on electronic transaction and privacy requirements. *Family Therapy Magazine, 1*(3), 30–33.

Hanna, S. M., & Brown, J. H. (2004). *The practice of family therapy: Key elements across models* (3rd ed.). Belmont, CA: Thomson Brooks/Cole.

Hanson, S. L., Kerkhoff, T. R., & Bush, S. S. (2005). *Health care ethics for psychologists: A casebook.* Washington, DC: American Psychological Association.

Hardina, D. (2004). Guidelines for ethical practice in community organization. *Social Work, 49*(4), 595–604.

Harper, M. C., & Gill, C. S. (2005). Assessing the client's spiritual domain. In C. S. Cashwell & J. S. Young (Eds.), *Integrating spirituality and religion into counseling: A guide to competent practice* (pp. 31–62). Alexandria, VA: American Counseling Association.

Harrar, W. R., VandeCreek, L., & Knapp, S. (1990). Ethical and legal aspects of clinical supervision. *Professional Psychology: Research and Practice, 21*(1), 37–41.

Hathaway, W. L., Scott, S. Y., & Garver, S. A. (2004). Assessing religious/spiritual functioning: A neglected domain in clinical practice? *Professional Psychology: Research and Practice, 35*(1), 97–104.

Hatherleigh guide to ethics in therapy. (1997). New York: Hatherleigh Press.

*Haynes, R., Corey, G., & Moulton, P. (2003). *Clinical supervision in the helping professions: A practical guide.* Pacific Grove, CA: Brooks/Cole.

Hedlund v. Superior Court, 34 Cal. 3d 695, 669, P.2d 41 (1983).

Heiden, J. M. (1993). Preview-prevent: A training strategy to prevent counselor-client sexual relationships. *Counselor Education and Supervision, 33*(1), 53–60.

Hering, N. (2000). Managed care: Notes from the underground. *The California Therapist, 12*(4), 36–38.

Herlihy, B. (1996). When a colleague is impaired: The individual counselor's response. *Journal of Humanistic Education and Development, 34,* 118–127.

Herlihy, B., & Corey, G. (1994). Codes of ethics as catalysts for improving practice. *Ethical Issues in Professional Counseling, 2*(3), 2–12.

*Herlihy, B., & Corey, G. (Eds.). (2006a). *ACA Ethical standards casebook* (6th ed.). Alexandria, VA: American Counseling Association.

*Herlihy, B., & Corey, G. (2006b). *Boundary issues in counseling: Multiple roles and responsibilities* (2nd ed.). Alexandria, VA: American Counseling Association.

Herlihy, B., & Corey, G. (2006c). Confidentiality. In B. Herlihy & G. Corey (Eds.), *ACA ethical standards casebook* (6th ed.). Alexandria, VA: American Counseling Association.

Herlihy, B., & Corey, G. (2006d). Working with multiple clients. In B. Herlihy & G. Corey (Eds.), *ACA ethical standards casebook* (6th ed.). Alexandria, VA: American Counseling Association.

Herlihy, B., Gray, N., & McCollum, V. (2002). Legal and ethical issues in school counselor supervision. *Professional School Counseling, 6*(1), 55–60.

Herlihy, B., & Remley, T. P. (1995). Unified ethical standards: A challenge for professionalism. *Journal of Counseling and Development, 74*(2), 130–133.

Herlihy, B. R., & Watson, Z. E. P. (2004). Assisted suicide: Ethical issues. In D. Capuzzi (Ed.), *Suicide across the life span: Implications for counselors* (pp. 163–184). Alexandria, VA: American Counseling Association.

Hermann, M. A. (2001). *Legal issues in counseling: Incidence, preparation, and consultation.* Doctoral dissertation, University of New Orleans.

Hermann, M. A. (2002). A study of legal issues encountered by school counselors and their perceptions of their preparedness to respond to legal challenges. *Professional School Counseling, 6,* 12–19.

Hermann, M. A. (2006). Legal perspectives on dual relationships. In B. Herlihy & G. Corey (Eds.), *Boundary issues in counseling: Multiple roles and responsibilities* (2nd ed.). Alexandria, VA: American Counseling Association.

Hermann, M. A., & Finn, A. (2002). An ethical and legal perspective on the role of school counselors in preventing violence in schools. *Professional School Counseling, 6,* 46–54.

Hermann, M. A., & Herlihy, B. R. (in press). Legal and ethical implications of refusing to counsel homosexual clients. *Journal of Counseling and Development.*

Hermann, M. A., & Remley, T. P. (2000). Guns, violence, and schools: The results of school violence—litigation against educators and students shedding more constitutional rights at the school house gate. *Loyola Law Review, 46*(2), 389–439.

Hersch, L. (1995). Adapting to health care reform and managed care: Three strategies for survival and growth. *Professional Psychology: Research and Practice, 26*(1), 16–26.

*Hill, M., Glaser, K., & Harden, J. (1995). A feminist model for ethical decision making. In E. J. Rave & C. C. Larsen (Eds.), *Ethical decision making in therapy: Feminist perspectives* (pp. 18–37). New York: Guilford Press.

Hinnefeld, B., & Towers, K. D. (1996). Supreme Court ruling upholds psychotherapist-patient privilege. *Practitioner Focus, 9*(2), 4, 18.

Hoffman, M. A. (1991a). Counseling the HIV-infected client: A psychosocial model for assessment and intervention. *The Counseling Psychologist, 19*(4), 467–542.

Hoffman, M. A. (1991b). Training mental health counselors for the AIDS crisis. *Journal of Mental Health Counseling, 13*(2), 264–269.

Hogan-Garcia, M. (2003). *The four skills of cultural diversity competence: A process for understanding and practice* (2nd ed.). Belmont, CA: Thomson Brooks/Cole.

*Hogan-Garcia, M., & Scheinberg, C. (2000). Culturally competent practice principles for planned intervention in organizations and communities. *Practicing Anthropology, 22*(2), 27–30.

Holmes, J. (1996). Values in psychotherapy. *American Journal of Psychotherapy, 50*(3), 259–273.

Holub, E. A., & Lee, S. S. (1990). Therapists' use of nonerotic physical contact: Ethical concerns. *Professional Psychology: Research and Practice, 21*(2), 115–117.

Holzman, L. A., Searight, H. R., & Hughes, H. M. (1996). Clinical psychology graduate students and personal psychotherapy: Results of an exploratory study. *Professional Psychology: Research and Practice, 27*(1), 98–101.

Homan, M. (1999). *Rules of the game: Lessons from the field of community change.* Pacific Grove, CA: Brooks/Cole.

*Homan, M. (2004). *Promoting community change: Making it happen in the real world* (3rd ed.). Belmont, CA: Brooks/Cole-Wadsworth.

Hosie, T. W. (1995). Counseling specialties: A case of basic preparation rather than advanced specialization. *Journal of Counseling and Development, 74*(2), 177–180.

Housman, L. M., & Stake, J. E. (1999). The current state of sexual ethics training in clinical psychology: Issues of quantity, quality, and effectiveness. *Professional Psychology: Research and Practice, 30*(3), 302–311.

Humphreys, K., Winzelberg, A., & Klaw, E. (2000). Psychologists' ethical responsibilities in Internet-based groups: Issues, strategies, and a call for dialogue. *Professional Psychology: Research and Practice, 31*(5), 493–496.

Ibrahim, E. A., & Arredondo, R. M. (1990). Ethical issues in multicultural counseling. In B. Herlihy & L. B. Golden (Eds.), *AACD ethical standards casebook* (4th ed., pp. 137–145). Alexandria, VA: American Association for Counseling and Development.

Imber, S. D., Glanz, L. M., Elkin, I., Sotsky, S. M., Boyer, J. L., & Leber, W. R. (1986). Ethical issues in psychotherapy research: Problems in a collaborative clinical trials study. *American Psychologist, 41*(2), 137–146.

Ingraham, C. L. (2000). Consultation through a multicultural lens: Multicultural and cross-cultural consultation in schools. *School Psychology Review, 29,* 320–343.

International Association of Marriage and Family Counselors. (2002). Ethical code for International Association of Marriage and Family Counselors. *The Family Journal, 1,* 73–77.

Isaacs, M. L. (1997). The duty to warn and protect: *Tarasoff* and the elementary school counselor. *Elementary School Guidance and Counseling, 31,* 326–342.

Isaacs, M. L., & Stone, C. (1999). School counselors and confidentiality: Factors affecting professional choices. *Professional School Counseling, 2,* 258–266.

Itai, G., & McRae, C. (1994). Counseling older Japanese American clients: An overview and observations. *Journal of Counseling and Development, 72*(4), 373–377.

*Ivey, A. E., & Ivey, M. B. (1998). Reframing DSM-IV: Positive strategies from developmental counseling and therapy. *Journal of Counseling and Development, 76*(3), 334–350.

Ivey, A. E., & Ivey, M. B. (1999). Toward a developmental diagnostic and statistical manual: The vitality of a contextual framework. *Journal of Counseling and Development, 77*(4), 484–490.

*Ivey, A. E., & Ivey, M. B. (2007). *Intentional interviewing and counseling: Facilitating client development* *in a multicultural society* (6th ed.). Belmont, CA: Thomson Brooks/Cole.

Ivey, A. E., D'Andrea, M., Ivey, M. B., & Simek-Morgan, L. (2002). *Theories of counseling and psychotherapy: A multicultural perspective* (5th ed.). Boston: Allyn & Bacon.

Ivey, A. E., Ivey, M. B., Myers, J., & Sweeney, T. (2005). *Developmental counseling and therapy: Promoting wellness over the lifespan.* Boston: Lashaska Houghton Mifflin.

*Ivey, A. E., Pedersen, P. B., & Ivey, M. B. (2001). *Intentional group counseling: A microskills approach.* Pacific Grove, CA: Brooks/Cole.

Jablonski v. United States, 712 F.2d 391 (9th Cir. 1983).

Jackson, D. N., & Hayes, D. H. (1993). Multicultural issues in consultation. *Journal of Counseling and Development, 72*(2), 144–147.

Jackson, H., & Nuttall, R. L. (2001). A relationship between childhood sexual abuse and professional sexual misconduct. *Professional Psychology: Research and Practice, 32*(2), 200–204.

Jacob, S. (2002). Best practices in utilizing professional ethics. In A. Thomas and J. Grimes (Eds.), *Best practices in school psychology* (4th ed.), (pp. 77–87). Bethesda, MD: National Association of School Psychologists.

Jaffee v. Redmond, WL 315 841 (U.S. 1996).

*James, R. K., & Gilliland, B. E. (2005). *Crisis intervention strategies* (5th ed.). Belmont, CA: Thomson Brooks/Cole.

Jensen, D. G. (2003a). HIPAA: How to comply with the transaction standards. *The Therapist, 15*(4), 16–19.

Jensen, D. G. (2003b). HIPAA overview. *The Therapist, 15*(3), 26–27.

Jensen, D. G. (2003c). HIPAA: Overview of the security standards. *The Therapist, 15*(5), 22–24.

Jensen, D. G. (2003d). How to comply with the privacy rule. *The Therapist, 15*(3), 28–37.

Jensen, D. G. (2003e). To be or not to be a covered entity: That is the question. *The Therapist, 15*(2), 14–17.

Jensen, D. G. (2005). The two *Ewing* cases and *Tarasoff. The Therapist, 17*(2), 31–37.

Jensen, J. P., & Bergin, A. E. (1988). Mental health values of professional therapists: A national interdisciplinary survey. *Professional Psychology: Research and Practice, 19*(3), 290–297.

Johnson, D., & Johnson, S. (2003). *Real world treatment planning: A workbook about mental health documentation and reimbursement compliance issues.* Belmont, CA: Thomson Brooks/Cole.

Johnson, W. B., & Campbell, C. D. (2002). Character and fitness requirements for professional psychologists: Are there any? *Professional Psychology: Research and Practice, 33*(1), 46–53.

Johnson, W. B., & Campbell, C. D. (2004). Character and fitness requirements for professional psychologists: Training directors' perspectives. *Professional Psychology: Research and Practice, 35*(4), 405–411.

Johnson, W. B., Ralph, J., & Johnson, S. J. (2005). Managing multiple roles in embedded environments: The case of aircraft carrier psychology. *Professional Psychology: Research and Practice, 36*(1), 73–81.

Jordan, A. E., & Meara, N. M. (1990). Ethics and the professional practice of psychologists: The role of virtues and principles. *Professional Psychology: Research and Practice, 21*(2), 107–114.

Jourard, S. (1968). *Disclosing man to himself.* Princeton, NJ: Van Nostrand.

*Kain, C. D. (1996). *Positive HIV affirmative counseling.* Alexandria, VA: American Counseling Association.

Kalichman, S. C., & Craig, M. E. (1991). Professional psychologists' decisions to report suspected child abuse: Clinician and situation influences. *Professional Psychology: Research and Practice, 22*(1), 84–89.

Kaplan, D. M. (2000). Using an informed consent brochure to help establish a solid therapeutic relationship. In R. E. Watts (Ed.), *Techniques in marriage and family counseling: Volume One* (pp. 3–10). Alexandria, VA: American Counseling Association.

Karon, B. P. (1995). Provision of psychotherapy under managed health care: A growing crisis and national nightmare. *Professional Psychology: Research and Practice, 26*(1), 5–9.

Kelly, E. W. (1995a). Counselor values: A national survey. *Journal of Counseling and Development, 73*(6), 648–653.

Kelly, E. W. (1995b). *Spirituality and religion in counseling and psychotherapy.* Alexandria, VA: American Counseling Association.

Kennedy, J. (2003). Man of many roles. *Monitor on Psychology, 34*(6), 67.

Kennedy, P. F., Vandehey, M., Norman, W. B., & Diekhoff, G. M. (2003). Recommendations for risk-management practices. *Professional Psychology: Research and Practice, 34*(3), 309–311.

Kerl, S. B., Garcia, J. L., McCullough, S., & Maxwell, M. E. (2002). Systematic evaluation of professional performance: Legally supported procedure and process. *Counselor Education and Supervision, 41*(4), 321–334.

Kessler, L. E., & Waehler, C. A. (2005). Addressing multiple relationships between clients and therapists in lesbian, gay, bisexual, and transgender communities. *Professional Psychology: Research and Practice, 36*(1), 66–72.

King, K. A., Price, J. H., Telljohann, S. K., & Wahl, J. (1999). How confident do high school counselors feel in recognizing students at risk for suicide? *American Journal of Health Behavior, 23*, 457–467.

King, K. A., Price, J. H., Telljohann, S. K., & Wahl, J. (2000). Preventing adolescent suicide: Do high school counselors know the risk factors? *Professional School Counseling, 3*, 255–263.

Kirland, K., Kirkland, K. L., & Reaves, R. P. (2004). On the professional use of disciplinary data. *Professional Psychology: Research and Practice, 35*(2), 179–184.

Kiser, J. D. (1996). Counselors and the legalization of physician-assisted suicide. *Counseling and Values, 40*(2), 127–131.

Kiser, J. D., & Korpi, K. N. (1996). The need for ethical reasoning regarding physician-assisted suicide. *Counseling Today*, p. 28.

Kitchener, K. S. (1984). Intuition, critical evaluation and ethical principles: The foundation for ethical decisions in counseling psychology. *The Counseling Psychologist, 12*(3), 43–55.

*Kleespies, P. M. (2004). *Life and death decisions: Psychological and ethical considerations in end-of-life care.* Washington, DC: American Psychological Association.

Knapp, S., & Slattery, J. M. (2004). Professional boundaries in nontraditional settings. *Professional Psychology: Research and Practice, 35*(5), 553–558.

Knapp, S., & VandeCreek, L. (1982). *Tarasoff.* Five years later. *Professional Psychology, 13*(4), 511–516.

Knapp, S., & VandeCreek, L. (1990). Application of the duty to protect to HIV-positive patients. *Professional Psychology: Research and Practice, 21*(3), 161–166.

Knapp, S., & VandeCreek, L. (1997). *Jaffee v. Redmond:* The Supreme Court recognizes a psychotherapist-patient privilege in federal courts. *Professional Psychology: Research and Practice, 28*(6), 567–572.

Knapp, S., & VandeCreek, L. (2003a). *A guide to the 2002 revision of the American Psychological Association's ethics code.* Sarasota, FL: Professional Resource Press.

Knapp, S., & VandeCreek, L. (2003b). An overview of the major changes in the 2002 APA ethics code. *Professional Psychology: Research and Practice, 34*(3), 301–308.

Koocher, G. P., & Keith-Spiegel, P. (1998). *Ethics in psychology: Professional standards and cases* (2nd ed.). New York: Oxford University Press.

Koocher, G. P., & Morray, E. (2000). Regulation of telepsychology: A survey of state attorneys general. *Professional Psychology: Research and Practice, 31*(5), 503–508.

Kramen-Kahn, B., & Hansen, N. D. (1998). Rafting the rapids: Occupational hazards, rewards, and coping strategies of psychotherapists. *Professional Psychology: Research and Practice, 29*(2), 130–134.

Kramer, S. A. (1990). *Positive endings in psychotherapy: Bringing meaningful closure to therapeutic relationships.* San Francisco: Jossey-Bass.

Kratochwill,T. R., & Pittman, P. H. (2002). Expanding problem-solving consultation training: Prospects and frameworks. *Journal of Educational and Psychological Consultation, 13*(1&2), 69–95.

Kremer, T. G., & Gesten, E. L. (1998). Confidentiality limits of managed care and clients' willingness to self-disclose. *Professional Psychology: Research and Practice, 29*(6), 553–558.

Kress, V. E. W., Eriksen, K. P., Rayle, A. D., & Ford, S. J. W. (2005). The DSM-IV-TR and culture: Considerations for counselors. *Journal of Counseling and Development, 83*(1), 97–104.

Krieger, K. M., & Stockton, R. (2004). Technology and group leadership training: Teaching group counseling in an online environment. *Journal for Specialists in Group Work, 29*(4), 343–359.

*Ladany, N., Lehrman-Waterman, D., Molinaro, M., & Wolgast, B. (1999). Psychotherapy supervisor ethical practices: Adherence to guidelines, the supervisory working alliance, and supervisee satisfaction. *The Counseling Psychologist, 27*(3), 443–475.

Lamb, D. H., & Catanzaro, S. J. (1998). Sexual and nonsexual boundary violations involving psychologists, clients, supervisees, and students: Implications for professional practice. *Professional Psychology: Research and Practice, 29*(5), 498–503.

Lamb, D. H., Catanzaro, S. J., & Moorman, A. S. (2003). Psychologists reflect on their sexual relationships with clients, supervisees, and students: Occurrence, impact, rationales, and collegial intervention. *Professional Psychology: Research and Practice, 34*(1), 102–107.

Lamb, D. H., Clark, C., Drumheller, P., Frizzell, K., & Surrey, L. (1989). Applying *Tarasoff* to AIDS-related psychotherapy issues. *Professional Psychology: Research and Practice, 20*(1), 37–43.

Lamb, D. H., Cochran, D. J., & Jackson, V. R. (1991). Training and organizational issues associated with identifying and responding to intern impairment. *Professional Psychology: Research and Practice, 22,* 291–296.

Lambert, M. J., & Cattani-Thompson, K. (1996). Current findings regarding the effectiveness of counseling: Implications for practice. *Journal of Counseling and Development, 74*(6), 601–608.

La Roche, M. J., & Maxie, A. (2003). Ten considerations in addressing cultural differences in psychotherapy. *Professional Psychology: Research and Practice, 34*(2), 180–186.

Lasser, J. S., & Gottlieb, M. C. (2004). Treating patients distressed regarding their sexual orientation: Clinical and ethical alternatives. *Professional Psychology: Research and Practice, 35*(2), 194–200.

Laughran, W., & Bakken, G. M. (1984). The psychotherapist's responsibility toward third parties under current California law. *Western State University Law Review, 12*(1), 1–33.

Lawrence, G., & Kurpius, S. E. R. (2000). Legal and ethical issues involved when counseling minors in nonschool settings. *Journal of Counseling and Development, 78*(2), 130–136.

Lazarus, A. A. (1990). Can psychotherapists transcend the shackles of their training and superstitions? *Journal of Clinical Psychology, 4*(3), 351–358.

*Lazarus, A. A. (1994a). How certain boundaries and ethics diminish therapeutic effectiveness. *Ethics and Behavior, 4*(3), 255–261.

Lazarus, A. A. (1994b). The illusion of the therapist's power and the patient's fragility: My rejoinder. *Ethics and Behavior, 4*(3), 299–306.

Lazarus, A. A. (1998). How do you like these boundaries? *The Clinical Psychologist, 51*(1), 22–25.

Lazarus, A. A. (2000). Multimodal replenishment. *Professional Psychology: Research and Practice, 31*(1), 93–94.

Lazarus, A. A. (2001). Not all "dual relationships" are taboo: Some tend to enhance treatment outcomes. *The National Psychologist, 10*(1), 16.

Lazarus, A. A. (2005) Multimodal therapy. In R. J. Corsini & D. Wedding (Eds.), *Current psychotherapies* (7th ed.). Belmont, CA: Thomson Brooks/Cole.

*Lazarus, A. A., & Zur, O. (Eds.). (2002). *Dual relationships and psychotherapy.* New York: Springer.

Lee, C. C. (1997a). Cultural dynamics: Their importance in culturally responsive counseling. In C. C. Lee (Ed.), *Multicultural issues in counseling: New approaches to diversity* (pp. 15–30). Alexandria, VA: American Counseling Association.

Lee, C. C. (1997b). New approaches to diversity: Implications for professional counselor training and research. In C. C. Lee (Ed.), *Multicultural issues in counseling: New approaches to diversity* (pp. 353–360). Alexandria, VA: American Counseling Association.

Lee, C. C. (1997c). The promise and pitfalls of multicultural counseling. In C. C. Lee (Ed.), *Multicultural issues in counseling: New approaches to diversity* (pp. 3–13). Alexandria, VA: American Counseling Association.

Lee, C. C., & Ramsey, C. J. (2006). Multicultural counseling: A new paradigm for a new century (pp. 3–11). In C. C. Lee (Ed.), *Multicultural issues in counseling: New approaches to diversity* (3rd ed.). Alexandria, VA: American Counseling Association.

Lewis, G. J., Greenburg, S. L., & Hatch, D. B. (1988). Peer consultation groups for psychologists in private practice: A national survey. *Professional Psychology: Research and Practice, 19*(1), 81–86.

Leverett-Main, S. (2004). Program directors' perceptions of admission screening measures and indicators of student success. *Counselor Education and Supervision, 43*(3), 207–219.

*Lewis, J. A., Lewis, M. D., Daniels, J. A., & D'Andrea, M. J. (2003). *Community counseling: Empowerment strategies for a diverse society* (3rd ed.). Belmont, CA: Thomson Brooks/Cole.

Lindsey, R. I. (1984). Informed consent and deception in psychotherapy research: An ethical analysis. *The Counseling Psychologist, 12*(3), 79–86.

Lum, D. (1999). *Culturally competent practice: A framework for growth and action.* Pacific Grove, CA: Brooks/Cole.

*Lum, D. (2000). *Social work practice and people of color. A process-stage approach* (4th ed.). Pacific Grove, CA: Brooks/Cole.

Lumadue, C. A., & Duffey, T. H. (1999). The role of graduate programs as gatekeepers: A model for evaluating student counselor competence. *Counselor Education and Supervision, 39*(2), 101–109.

Mabe, A. R., & Rollin, S. A. (1986). The role of a code of ethical standards in counseling. *Journal of Counseling and Development, 64*(5), 294–297.

*MacCluskie, K. C., & Ingersoll, R. E. (2001). *Becoming a 21st century agency counselor: Personal and professional explorations.* Pacific Grove, CA: Brooks/Cole.

Maheu, M. M., & Gordon, B. L. (2000). Counseling and therapy on the Internet. *Professional Psychology: Research and Practice, 31*(5), 484–489.

Mahrer, A. R. (2000). How to use psychotherapy on, for and by oneself. *Professional Psychology: Research and Practice, 31*(2), 226–229.

Malley, P. B., & Reilly, E. P. (1999). *Legal and ethical dimensions for mental health professionals.* Philadelphia, PA: Accelerated Development (Taylor & Francis).

Mappes, D. C., Robb, G. P., & Engels, D. W. (1985). Conflicts between ethics and law in counseling and psychotherapy. *Journal of Counseling and Development, 64*(4), 246–252.

Margolin, G. (1982). Ethical and legal considerations in marital and family therapy. *American Psychologist, 37*(7), 788–801.

Markus, H. E., & King, D. A. (2003). A survey of group psychotherapy training during predoctoral psychology internship. *Professional Psychology: Research and Practice, 34*(2), 203–209.

*Maslach, C., & Leiter, M. P. (1997). *The truth about burnout.* San Francisco: Jossey-Bass.

McCabe, O. L. (2004). Crossing the quality chasm in behavioral health care: The role of evidence-based practice. *Professional Psychology: Research and Practice, 35*(6), 571–579.

McCarthy, P., Sugden, S., Koker, M., Lamendola, F., Maurer, S., & Renninger, S. (1995). A practical guide to informed consent in clinical supervision. *Counselor Education and Supervision, 35*(2), 130–138.

McGee, T. F. (2003). Observations on the retirement of professional psychologists. *Professional Psychology: Research and Practice, 34*(4), 388–395.

McGuire, J., Nieri, D., Abbott, D., Sheridan, K., & Fisher, R. (1995). Do *Tarasoff* principles apply in AIDS-related psychotherapy? Ethical decision making and the role of therapist homophobia and perceived client dangerousness. *Professional Psychology: Research and Practice, 26*(6), 608–611.

McMahon, M., & Simons, R. (2004). Supervision training for professional counselors: An exploratory study. *Counselor Education and Supervision, 43*(4), 301–309.

McMinn, M. R., Aikins, D. C., & Lish, R. A. (2003). Basic and advanced competence in collaborating with clergy. *Professional Psychology: Research and Practice, 34*(2), 197–202.

McMinn, M. R., Buchanan, T., Ellens, B. M., & Ryan, M. K. (1999). Technology, professional practice, and ethics: Survey findings and implications. *Professional Psychology: Research and Practice, 30*(2), 165–172.

McMinn, M. R., Chaddock, T. P., Edwards, L. C., Lim, B. R. K. B., & Campbell, C. D. (1998). Psychologists collaborating with the clergy. *Professional Psychology: Research and Practice, 29*(6), 564–570.

Meara, N. M., Schmidt, L. D., & Day, J. D. (1996). Principles and virtues: A foundation for ethical decisions, policies, and character. *The Counseling Psychologist, 24*(1), 4–77.

Melchert, T. P., & Patterson, M. M. (1999). Duty to warn and interventions with HIV-positive clients. *Professional Psychology: Research and Practice, 30*(2), 180–186.

Melton, G. B. (1988). Ethical and legal issues in AIDS-related practice. *American Psychologist, 43*(11), 941–947.

Merrill, T. S. (2003). Licensure anachronisms: Is it time for a change? *Professional Psychology: Research and Practice, 34*(5), 459–462.

Messer, S. B. (2004). Evidence-based practice: Beyond empirically supported treatment. *Professional Psychology: Research and Practice, 35*(6), 580–588.

Miars, R. (2000, November 10). *The evolution of ethical responsibility and legal liability in clinical instruction and supervision.* Presentation given at Western Association for Counselor Education and Supervision, Los Gatos, California.

Miller, G. (1999). The development of the spiritual focus in counseling and counselor education. *Journal of Counseling and Development, 77*(4), 498–501.

Miller, G. M., & Larrabee, M. J. (1995). Sexual intimacy in counselor education and supervision: A national survey. *Counselor Education and Supervision, 34*(4), 332–343.

Miller, I. J. (1996a). Ethical and liability issues concerning invisible rationing. *Professional Psychology: Research and Practice, 27*(6), 583–587.

Miller, I. J. (1996b). Managed health care is harmful to outpatient mental health services: A call for accountability. *Professional Psychology: Research and Practice, 27*(4), 349–363.

Miller, I. J. (1996c). Time-limited brief therapy has gone too far: The result is invisible rationing. *Professional Psychology: Research and Practice, 27*(6), 567–576.

Miller, I. J. (1996d). Some "short-term therapy values" are a formula for invisible rationing. *Professional Psychology: Research and Practice, 27*(6), 577–582.

Miller, W. R. (Ed.). (1999). *Integrating spirituality into treatment: Resources for practitioners.* Washington, DC: American Psychological Association.

Millner, V. S., & Hanks, R. B. (2002). Induced abortion: An ethical conundrum for counselors. *Journal of Counseling and Development, 80*(1), 57–63.

Miranti, J., & Burke, M. T. (1995). Spirituality: An integral component of the counseling process. In M. T. Burke & J. G. Miranti (Eds.), *Counseling: The spiritual dimension* (pp. 1–3). Alexandria, VA: American Counseling Association.

Mitchell, R. (2001). *Documentation in counseling records* (2nd ed.). Alexandria, VA: American Counseling Association.

Moleski, S. M., & Kiselica, M. S. (2005). Dual relationships: A continuum ranging from the destructive to the therapeutic. *Journal of Counseling and Development, 83*(1), 3–11.

Moline, M. E., Williams, G. T., & Austin, K. M. (1998). *Documenting psychotherapy: Essentials for mental health practitioners.* Thousand Oaks, CA: Sage.

Monahan, J. (1993). Limiting therapist exposure to *Tarasoff* liability: Guidelines for risk containment. *American Psychologist, 48*(4), 242–250.

Morrison, C. F. (1989). AIDS: Ethical implications for psychological intervention. *Professional Psychology: Research and Practice, 20*(3), 166–171.

Morrissey, M. (1996). Supreme Court extends confidentiality privilege. *Counseling Today,* pp. 1, 6, 10.

Muratori, M. C. (2001). Examining supervisor impairment from the counselor trainee's perspective. *Counselor Education and Supervision, 41*(1), 41–56.

Murphy, J. A., Rawlings, E. I., & Howe, S. R. (2002). A survey of clinical psychologists on treating lesbian, gay, and bisexual clients. *Professional Psychology: Research and Practice, 33*(2), 183–189.

Myers, J. E., Sweeney, T. J., & Witmer, J. M. (2000). The wheel of wellness counseling for wellness: A holistic model. *Journal of Counseling and Development, 78*(3), 251–266.

*Nagy, T. F. (2000). *Ethics in plain English: An illustrative casebook for psychologists.* Washington, DC: American Psychological Association.

*Nagy, T. F. (2005). *Ethics in plain English: An illustrative casebook for psychologists* (2nd ed.). Washington, DC: American Psychological Association.

National Association of Social Workers. (1994a). Client self-determination in end-of-life decisions. In *Social work speaks: NASW policy statements* (3rd ed., pp. 58–61). Washington, DC: Author.

National Association of Social Workers. (1994b). *Guidelines for clinical social work supervision.* Washington, DC: Author.

National Association of Social Workers. (1999). *Code of ethics.* Washington, DC: Author.

National Center on Elder Abuse. (2003). *The basics: Major types of elder abuse.* Washington, DC: Author.

National Organization for Human Services. (2000). Ethical standards of human service professionals. *Human Service Education, 20*(1), 61–68.

Neimeyer, R. A. (2000). Suicide and hastened death: Toward a training agenda for counseling psychology. *The Counseling Psychologist, 28*(4), 551–560.

Nessman, A., & Herndon, P. (2000, December). New Jersey settlement offers strong protections for psychologists. *Monitor on Psychology, 31*(11), 20–21.

Newhouse-Session, A. N. (2004). *Effects of personal counseling on the professional counselor in the delivery of clinical services.* Unpublished doctoral dissertation, Capella University.

Newman, J. L., Robinson-Kurpius, S. E., & Fuqua, D. R. (2002). Issues in the ethical practice of consulting psychology. In R. L. Lowman (Ed.), *Handbook of organizational consulting psychology: A comprehensive guide to theory, skills, and techniques* (pp. 733–758). San Francisco: Jossey-Bass.

Newman, R. (1996). Supreme Court affirms privilege. *APA Monitor, 27*(8), 44.

Newman, R., & Bricklin, P. M. (1991). Parameters of managed mental health care: Legal, ethical, and professional guidelines. *Professional Psychology: Research and Practice, 22*(1), 26–35.

Nichols, M. P., & Schwartz, R. C. (2004). *Family therapy: Concepts and methods* (6th ed.). Boston: Allyn & Bacon.

Nicolai, K. M., & Scott, N. A. (1994). Provision of confidentiality information and its relation to child abuse reporting. *Professional Psychology: Research and Practice, 25*(2), 154–160.

Olarte, S. W. (1997). Sexual boundary violations. In *The Hatherleigh guide to ethics in therapy* (pp. 195–209). New York: Hatherleigh Press.

*O'Laughlin, M. J. (2001). Dr. Strangelove: Therapist-client dual relationship bans and freedom of association, or how I learned to stop worrying and love my clients. *University of Missouri-Kansas City School of Law Review, 69*(30), 697–731.

Oliver, M. N. I., Bernstein, J. H., Anderson, K. G., Blashfield, R. K., & Roberts, M. C. (2004). An exploratory examination of student attitudes toward "impaired" peers in clinical psychology training programs. *Professional Psychology: Research and Practice, 35*(2), 141–147.

Orchin, I. (2004). Taking therapy outdoors: How to use nature to get tough cases unstuck. *Psychotherapy Networker, 28*(6), 27–28.

Orr, P. (1997). Psychology impaired? *Professional Psychology: Research and Practice, 28*(3), 293–296.

Osborn, C. J. (2004). Seven salutary suggestions for counselor stamina. *Journal of Counseling and Development, 82*(3), 319–328.

Overholser, J. C. (1991). The Socratic method as a technique in psychotherapy supervision. *Professional Psychology: Research and Practice, 22*(1), 68–74.

Page, B. J., Pietrzak, D. R., & Sutton, J. M. (2001). National survey of school counselor supervision. *Counselor Education and Supervision, 41*(2), 142–150.

Palmer, B. (2003). *Interpersonal skills for helping professionals: An interactive online guide.* Boston: Allyn & Bacon.

Paradise, L. V., & Siegelwaks, B. (1982). Ethical training for group leaders. *Journal for Specialists in Group Work, 7*(3), 162–166.

Parham, T. A. (Ed.). (2002). *Counseling persons of African descent: Raising the bar of practitioner competence*. Thousand Oaks, CA: Sage.

Parham, T. A., & Caldwell, L. D. (2006). Dual relationships revisited: An African centered imperative. In B. Herlihy & G. Corey (Eds.), *Boundary issues in counseling: Multiple roles and responsibilities* (2nd ed.). Alexandria, VA: American Counseling Association.

Parsons, R. D., & Kahn, W. J. (2005). *The school counselor as consultant: An integrated model for school-based consultation.* Belmont, CA: Thomson Brooks/Cole.

Patterson, C. H. (1985a). New light for counseling theory. *Journal of Counseling and Development, 63*(6), 349–350.

Patterson, C. H. (1985b). *The therapeutic relationship: Foundations for an eclectic psychotherapy.* Pacific Grove, CA: Brooks/Cole.

Patterson, C. H. (1996). Multicultural counseling: From diversity to universality. *Journal of Counseling and Development, 74*(3), 227–231.

Pedersen, P. (1991). Multiculturalism as a generic approach to counseling. *Journal of Counseling and Development, 70*(1), 6–12.

Pedersen, P. (1994). *A handbook for developing multicultural awareness* (2nd ed.). Alexandria, VA: American Counseling Association.

Pedersen, P. (1999). Training counselors to hear the self-talk of culturally different clients. *Directions in Mental Health Counseling, 9*(8), 91–102.

*Pedersen, P. (2000). *A handbook for developing multicultural awareness* (3rd ed.). Alexandria, VA: American Counseling Association.

Pedersen, P. (2003). Culturally biased assumptions in counseling psychology. *The Counseling Psychologist, 31*(4), 396–403.

Perlin, M. L. (1997). The "duty to protect" others from violence. In *The Hatherleigh guide to ethics in therapy* (pp. 127–146). New York: Hatherleigh Press.

Peruzzi, N., & Bongar, B. (1999). Assessing risk for completed suicide in patients with major depression: Psychologists' views of critical factors. *Professional Psychology: Research and Practice, 30*(6), 576–580.

Peterson, M. R. (1992). *At personal risk: Boundary violations in professional-client relationships.* New York: Norton.

Pipes, R. B., Holstein, J. E., & Aguirre, M. G. (2005). Examining the personal-professional distinction: Ethics codes and the difficulty of drawing a boundary. *American Psychologist, 60*(4), 325–334.

Polanski, P. (2000). Training supervisors at the master's level: Developmental consideration. *ACES Spectrum Newsletter, 61*(2), 3–5.

Polanski, P. (2003). Spirituality in supervision. *Counseling and Values, 47*(2), 131–141.

Pomerantz, A. M., & Handelsman, M. M. (2004). Informed consent revisited: An updated written question format. *Professional Psychology: Research and Practice, 35*(2), 201–205.

Pope, K. S. (1985a, April). Dual relationships: A violation of ethical, legal, and clinical standards. *California State Psychologist, 20*(3), 3–5.

Pope, K. S. (1985b, July/August). The suicidal client: Guidelines for assessment and treatment. *California State Psychologist, 20*(5), 3–7.

Pope, K. S. (1987). Preventing therapist-patient sexual intimacy: Therapy for a therapist at risk. *Professional Psychology: Research and Practice, 18*(6), 624–628.

Pope, K. S. (1994). *Sexual involvement with therapists.* Washington, DC: American Psychological Association.

Pope, K. S., Keith-Spiegel, P., & Tabachnick, B. G. (1986). Sexual attraction to clients: The human therapist and the (sometimes) inhuman training system. *American Psychologist, 41*(2), 147–158.

*Pope, K. S., Sonne, J. L., & Holroyd, J. (1993). *Sexual feelings in psychotherapy: Explorations for therapists and therapists-in-training.* Washington, DC: American Psychological Association.

Pope, K. S., & Tabachnick, B. G. (1994). Therapists as patients: A national survey of psychologists' experiences, problems, and beliefs. *Professional Psychology: Research and Practice, 25*(3), 247–258.

*Pope, K. S., & Vasquez, M. J. T. (1998). *Ethics in psychotherapy and counseling: A practical guide for psychologists* (2nd ed.). San Francisco: Jossey-Bass.

*Porter, N., & Vasquez, M. (1997). Covision: Feminist supervision, process, and collaboration. In J. Worell & N. G. Johnson (Eds.), *Shaping the future of feminist psychology: Education, research, and practice* (pp. 155–171). Washington, DC: American Psychological Association.

Powers, R. (2005). Counseling and spirituality: A historical review. *Counseling and Values, 49*(3), 217–225.

Priest, R. (1994). Minority supervisor and majority supervisee: Another perspective of clinical reality. *Counselor Education and Supervision, 34*(2), 152–158.

Rabasca, L. (2000a). Self-help sites: A blessing or a bane? *Monitor on Psychology, 31*(4), 28–30.

Rabasca, L. (2000b). Taking telehealth to the next step. *Monitor on Psychology, 31*(4), 36–37.

Rabinowitz, E. E. (1991). The male-to-male-embrace: Breaking the touch taboo in a men's therapy group. *Journal of Counseling and Development, 69*(6), 574–576.

Radeke, J. T., & Mahoney, M. J. (2000). Comparing the personal lives of psychotherapists and research psychologists. *Professional Psychology: Research and Practice, 31*(1), 82–84.

Reamer, F. G. (1998). *Ethical standards in social work: A review of the NASW Code of Ethics.* Washington, DC: NASW Press.

Reaves, R. P. (2003). *Avoiding liability in mental health practice.* Montgomery, AL: Association of State and Provincial Psychology Boards.

Remley, T. P. (1991). *Preparing for court appearances.* Alexandria, VA: American Association for Counseling and Development.

Remley, T. P. (1993). Consultation contracts. *Journal of Counseling and Development, 72*(2), 157–158.

Remley, T. P. (1995). A proposed alternative to the licensing of specialties in counseling. *Journal of Counseling and Development, 74*(2) 126–129.

Remley, T. P. (1996). The relationship between law and ethics. In B. Herlihy & G. Corey, (Eds.), *ACA ethical standards casebook* (5th ed., pp. 285–292). Alexandria, VA: American Counseling Association.

Remley, T. P. (2004). Suicide and the law. In D. Capuzzi (Ed.), *Suicide across the life span: Implications for counselors* (pp. 185–210). Alexandria, VA: American Counseling Association.

*Remley, T. P., & Herlihy, B. (2005). *Ethical, legal, and professional issues in counseling* (2nd ed.). Upper Saddle River, NJ: Merrill/Prentice-Hall.

Remley, T. P., & Hermann, M. A. (2000). Legal and ethical issues in school counseling. In J. Wittmer (Ed.), *Managing your school counseling program: K–12 developmental strategies* (pp. 314–329). Minneapolis, MN: Educational Media Corporation.

Remley, T. P., Hermann, M., & Huey, W. C. (2003). *Ethical and legal issues in school counseling* (2nd ed.). Alexandria, VA: American Counseling Association.

Remley, T. P., Hulse-Killacky, D., Christensen, T., Gibbs, K., Schaefer, P., Tanigoshi, H., Hermann, M., & Miller, J. (2002, October 18). *Dismissing graduate students for non-academic reasons.* Paper presented at the Association for Counselor Education and Supervision Convention, Park City, Utah.

Remley, T. P., & Sparkman, L. B. (1993). Student suicides: The counselor's limited legal liability. *The School Counselor, 40*, 164–169.

*Richards, P. S., & Bergin, A. E. (1997). *A spiritual strategy for counseling and psychotherapy.* Washington, DC: American Psychological Association.

*Richards, P. S., & Bergin, A. E. (Eds.). (2000). *Handbook of psychotherapy and religious diversity.* Washington, DC: American Psychological Association.

*Richards, P. S., & Bergin, A. E. (Eds.). (2004a). *Casebook for a spiritual strategy in counseling and psychotherapy.* Washington, DC: American Psychological Association.

*Richards, P. S., & Bergin, A. E. (Eds.). (2004b). *Theistic perspectives in psychotherapy: Conclusions and recommendations.* In P. S. Richards & A. E. Bergin (Eds.), *Casebook for a spiritual strategy in counseling and psychotherapy* (pp. 287–308). Washington, DC: American Psychological Association.

*Richards, P. S., & Bergin, A. E. (Eds.). (2004c). *A theistic spiritual strategy for psychotherapy.* In P. S. Richards & A. E. Bergin (Eds.), *Casebook for a spiritual strategy in counseling and psychotherapy* (pp. 3–32). Washington, DC: American Psychological Association.

Richards, P. S., Rector, J. M., & Tjeltveit, A. C. (1999). Values, spirituality, and psychotherapy. In W. R. Miller (Ed.), *Integrating spirituality into treatment: Resources for practitioners* (pp. 133–160). Washington, DC: American Psychological Association.

Richardson, T. Q., & Molinaro, K. L. (1996). White counselor self-awareness: A prerequisite for developing multicultural competence. *Journal of Counseling and Development, 74*(3), 238–242.

Ridley, C. R. (1989). Racism in counseling as an adversive behavioral process. In P. Pedersen, J. Draguns, W. Lormer, & J. Trimble (Eds.), *Counseling across cultures* (3rd ed., pp. 55–77). Honolulu: University of Hawaii Press.

Ridley, C. R. (2005). *Overcoming unintentional racism in counseling and therapy: A practitioner's guide to intentional intervention* (2nd ed.). Thousand Oaks, CA: Sage.

Ridley, C. R., Mendoza, D. W., & Kanitz, B. E. (1994). Multicultural training: Reexamination, operationalization, and integration. *The Counseling Psychologist, 22*(2), 227–289.

Riemersma, M. (2000). What about record keeping? *The California Therapist, 12*(5), 22–24.

Riemersma, M., & Leslie, R. S. (1999). Therapy/counseling over the Internet: Innovation or unnecessary risk? *The California Therapist, 11*(6), 33–36.

Ritterband, L. M., Gonder-Frederick, L. A., Cox, D. J., Clifton, A. D., West, R. W., & Borowitz, S. M. (2003). Internet interventions: In review, in use, and into the future. *Professional Psychology: Research and Practice, 34*(5), 527–534.

Rivas-Vasquez, R. A., Blais, M. A., Rey, G. J., & Rivas-Vazquez, A. A. (2001). A brief reminder about documenting the psychological consultation. *Professional Psychology: Research and Practice, 32*(2), 194–199.

Robiner, W. N., & Crew, D. P. (2000). Rightsizing the workforce of psychologists in health care: Trends from licensing boards, training programs, and managed care. *Professional Psychology: Research and Practice, 22,* 427–440.

Rodolfa, E., Ko, S. F., & Petersen, L. (2004). Psychology training directors' views of trainees' readiness to practice independently. *Professional Psychology: Research and Practice, 35*(4), 397–404.

Rogers, C. (1961). *On becoming a person.* Boston: Houghton Mifflin.

Rogers, C. (1980). *A way of being.* Boston: Houghton Mifflin.

Rogers, J. R., Gueulette, C. M., Abbey-Hines, J., Carney, J. V., & Werth, J. L. (2001). Rational suicide: An empirical investigation of counselor attitudes. *Journal of Counseling and Development, 79*(3), 365–372.

Rosenberg, J. I. (1999). Suicide prevention: An integrated training model using affective and action-based interventions. *Professional Psychology: Research and Practice, 30*(1), 83–87.

Rowley, W. J., & MacDonald, D. (2001). Counseling and the law: A cross-cultural perspective. *Journal of Counseling and Development, 79*(4), 422–429.

Roysircar, G. (2003). Counselor awareness of own assumptions, values, and biases. In G. Roysircar, P. Arredondo, J. N. Fuertes, J. G. Ponterotto, & R. L. Toporek (Eds.), *Multicultural counseling competencies 2003: Association for Multicultural Counseling and Development* (pp. 17–38). Alexandria, VA: American Counseling Association.

Roysircar, G. (2004). Cultural self-awareness assessment: Practice examples from psychology training. *Professional Psychology: Research and Practice, 35*(6), 658–666.

Roysircar, G., Arredondo, P., Fuertes, J. N., Ponterotto, J. G., & Toporek, R. L. (2003). *Multicultural counseling competencies 2003: Association for Multicultural Counseling and Development.* Alexandria, VA: American Counseling Association.

Roysircar, G., Sandhu, D. S., & Bibbins, V. E. (2003). *Multicultural competencies: A guidebook of practices.* Alexandria, VA: American Counseling Association.

Rubin, S. S. (2002). The multiple roles and relationships of ethical psychotherapy: Revising the ideal, the real, and the unethical. In A. A. Lazarus & O. Zur (Eds.), *Dual relationships and psychotherapy* (pp. 98–114.). New York: Springer.

Rupert, P. A., & Baird, K. A. (2004). Managed care and the independent practice of psychology. *Professional Psychology: Research and Practice, 35*(2), 185–193.

Rutter, P. (1989). *Sex in the forbidden zone.* Los Angeles: J. P. Tarcher.

Sales, B. D., & Folkman, S. (2000). *Ethics in research with human participants.* Washington, DC: American Psychological Association.

Sampson, J. P., Kolodinsky, R. W., & Greeno, B. P. (1997). Counseling on the information highway: Future possibilities and potential problems. *Journal of Counseling and Development, 75*(3), 203–212.

Samuel, S. E., & Gorton, G. E. (1998). National survey of psychology internship directors regarding education for prevention of psychologist-patient sexual exploitation. *Professional Psychology: Research and Practice, 29*(1), 86–90.

Sapienza, B. G., & Bugental, J. F. T. (2000). Keeping our instruments finely tuned: An existential-humanistic perspective. *Professional Psychology: Research and Practice, 31*(4), 458–460.

Schaffer, S. J. (1997). Don't be aloof about record-keeping; it may be your best liability coverage. *The National Psychologist, 6*(1), 21.

Schank, J. A., & Skovholt, T. M. (1997). Dual-relationship dilemmas of rural and small community psychologists. *Professional Psychology: Research and Practice, 28*(1), 44–49.

Scheflin, A. W. (2002). Are dual relationships antitherapeutic? In A. A. Lazarus & O. Zur (Eds.), *Dual relationships and psychotherapy* (pp. 257–269). New York: Springer.

Schreier, B., Davis, D., & Rodolfa, E. (2005). Diversity based psychology with lesbian, gay and bisexual patients: Clinical and training issues—Practical actions. *California Department of Consumer Affairs (Board of Psychology), 12,* 1–13.

Schwebel, M., & Coster, J. (1998). Well-functioning in professional psychologists: As program heads see it. *Professional Psychology: Research and Practice, 29,* 284–292.

Seligman, L. (2001). *Systems, strategies, and skills of counseling and psychotherapy.* Upper Saddle River, NJ: Merrill/Prentice-Hall.

Seppa, N. (1996, August). Supreme Court protects patient-therapist privilege. *APA Monitor, 27*(8), 39.

Shafranske, E. P., & Sperry, L. (2005a). Addressing the spiritual dimension in psychotherapy: Introduction and overview. In L. Sperry & E. P. Shafranske (Eds.), *Spiritually oriented psychotherapy* (pp. 11–29). Washington, DC: American Psychological Association.

Shafranske, E. P., & Sperry, L. (2005b). Future directions: Opportunities and challenges. In L. Sperry & E. P. Shafranske (Eds.), *Spiritually oriented psychotherapy* (pp. 351–354). Washington, DC: American Psychological Association.

Shapiro, D. E., & Schulman, C. E. (1996). Ethical and legal issues in e-mail therapy. *Ethics and Behavior, 6*, 107–124.

Shapiro, E. L., & Ginzberg, R. (2003). To accept or not to accept: Referrals and the maintenance of boundaries. *Professional Psychology: Research and Practice, 34*(3), 258–263.

Sharf, R. S. (2004). *Theories of psychotherapy and counseling: Concepts and cases* (3rd ed.). Pacific Grove, CA: Brooks/Cole.

Sherman, W. R., & Wenocur, S. (1983). Empowering public welfare workers through mutual support. *Social Work* (September/October), 375–379.

Sherry, R. (1991). Ethical issues in the conduct of supervision. *The Counseling Psychologist, 19*(4), 566–584.

Shore, K. (1996). Managed care: An alternative view. *Professional Psychology: Research and Practice, 27*(4), 323–324.

Shuffer v. Board of Trustees of California State University and Colleges, 67 Cal. App. 3d 208 (2nd Cir. 1977).

Shuman, D. W., & Foote, W. (1999). *Jaffee v. Redmond*'s impact: Life after the Supreme Court's recognition of a psychotherapist-patient privilege. *Professional Psychology: Research and Practice, 30*(5), 479–487.

Silverman, M. M. (2000). Rational suicide, hastened death, and self-destructive behaviors. *The Counseling Psychologist, 28*(4), 540–550.

Sinacore-Guinn, A. L. (1995). The diagnostic window: Culture- and gender-sensitive diagnosis and training. *Counselor Education and Supervision, 35*(1), 18–31.

*Skovholt, T. M. (2001). *The resilient practitioner: Burnout prevention and self-care strategies for counselors, therapists, teachers, and health professionals.* Boston: Allyn & Bacon.

Sleek, S. (1994, December). Ethical dilemmas plague rural practice. *APA Monitor*, 26–27.

Sleek, S. (1996, April). Ensuring accuracy in clinical decisions. *APA Monitor, 26*(4), 30.

Smith, D., & Fitzpatrick, M. (1995). Patient-therapist boundary issues: An integrative review of theory and research. *Professional Psychology: Research and Practice, 26*(5), 499–506.

Smith, R. L. (1999). Client confidentiality in marriage and family counseling. In P. Stevens (Ed.), *Ethical casebook for the practice of marriage and family counseling* (pp. 83–92). Alexandria, VA: American Counseling Association.

Smith, T. S., McGuire, J. M., Abbott, D. W, & Blau, B. I. (1991). Clinical ethical decision making: An investigation of the rationales used to justify doing less than one believes one should. *Professional Psychology: Research and Practice, 22*(3), 235–239.

Somberg, D. R., Stone, G. L., & Claiborn, C. D. (1993). Informed consent: Therapists' beliefs and practices. *Professional Psychology: Research and Practice, 24*(2), 153–159.

Sommers-Flanagan, J., & Sommers-Flanagan, R. (1995). Intake interviewing with suicidal patients: A systematic approach. *Professional Psychology: Research and Practice, 26*(1), 41–47.

Sperry, L., & Shafranske, E. P. (2005). (Eds.). *Spiritually oriented psychotherapy.* Washington, DC: American Psychological Association.

Stadler, H. A. (1986a). Making hard choices: Clarifying controversial ethical issues. *Counseling and Human Development, 19*(1), 1–10.

Stadler, H. A. (1986b). To counsel or not to counsel: The ethical dilemma of dual relationships. *Journal of Counseling and Human Service Professions, 1*(1), 134–140.

Stevens, P. (Ed.). (1999). *Ethical casebook for the practice of marriage and family counseling.* Alexandria, VA: American Counseling Association.

St. Germaine, J. (1993). Dual relationships: What's wrong with them? *American Counselor, 2*(3), 25–30.

Storm, C. L. (1994). Defensive supervision: Balancing ethical responsibility with vulnerability. In G. W. Brock (Ed.), *American Association for Marriage and Family Therapy ethics casebook* (pp. 173–190). Washington,

DC: American Association for Marriage and Family Therapy.

Strasburger, L. H., Jorgenson, L., & Sutherland, P. (1992). The prevention of psychotherapist sexual misconduct: Avoiding the slippery slope. *American Journal of Psychotherapy, 46*, 544–555.

Stromberg, C., & Dellinger, A. (1993, December). Malpractice and other professional liability. *The Psychologist's Legal Update.* Washington, DC: National Register of Health Service Providers in Psychology.

Stromberg, C., Schneider, J., & Joondeph, B. (1993, August). Dealing with potentially dangerous patients. *The Psychologist's Legal Update.* Washington, DC: National Register of Health Service Providers in Psychology.

Stromberg, C., and his colleagues in the Law Firm of Hogan & Hartson of Washington, DC. (1993, April). Privacy, confidentiality and privilege. *The Psychologist's Legal Update.* Washington, DC: National Register of Health Service Providers in Psychology.

Stone, C. (2002). Negligence in academic advising and abortion counseling: Courts rulings and implications. *Professional School Counseling, 6*, 28–35.

Stuart, R. B. (2004). Twelve practical suggestions for achieving multicultural competence. *Professional Psychology: Research and Practice, 35*(1), 3–9.

Sue, D. W. (2005). Racism and the conspiracy of silence: Presidential address. *The Counseling Psychologist, 33*(1), 100–114.

Sue, D. W. (2006). Multicultural perspectives on multiple relationships. In B. Herlihy & G. Corey (Eds.), *Boundary issues in counseling: Multiple roles and responsibilities* (2nd ed.). Alexandria, VA: American Counseling Association.

Sue, D. W., Arredondo, P., & McDavis, R. J. (1992). Multicultural counseling competencies and standards: A call to the profession. *Journal of Counseling and Development, 70*(4), 477–486.

Sue, D. W., Bernier, J. E., Durran, A., Feinberg, L., Pedersen, P., Smith, E. J., & Nuttall, E. V. (1982). Position paper: Cross-cultural counseling competencies. *The Counseling Psychologist, 10*(2), 45–52.

*Sue, D. W., Carter, R. T., and colleagues. (1998). *Multicultural counseling competencies: Individual and organizational development.* Thousand Oaks, CA: Sage.

*Sue, D. W., Ivey, A. E., & Pedersen, P. B. (1996). *A theory of multicultural counseling and therapy.* Pacific Grove, CA: Brooks/Cole.

Sue, D. W., & Sue, D. (1985). Asian Americans and Pacific Islanders. In P. Pedersen (Ed.), *Handbook of cross-cultural counseling and therapy* (pp. 141–146). Westport, CT: Greenwood Press.

*Sue, D. W., & Sue, D. (2003). *Counseling the culturally diverse: Theory and practice* (4th ed.). New York: Wiley.

Sulksy, L., & Smith, C. (2005). *Work stress.* Belmont, CA: Thomson Wadsworth.

Sumerel, M. B., & Borders, L. D. (1996). Addressing personal issues in supervision: Impact on counselors' experience level on various aspects of the supervisory relationship. *Counselor Education and Supervision, 35*(4), 268–286.

Summit on Spirituality. (1995, December). *Counseling Today*, p. 30.

Sutter, E., McPherson, R. H., & Geeseman, R. (2002). Contracting for supervision. *Professional Psychology: Research and Practice, 33*(5), 495-498.

Sweeney, T. J. (1995). Accreditation, credentialing, professionalization: The role of specialties. *Journal of Counseling and Development, 74*(2), 117–125.

Swenson, L. C. (1997). *Psychology and law for the helping professions.* Pacific Grove, CA: Brooks/Cole.

Szasz, T. (1986). The case against suicide prevention. *American Psychologist, 41*(7), 806–812.

Tarasoff v. Board of Regents of the University of California, 17 Cal. 3d 425, 551 (1976).

Thapar, v. Zezulka, 994 S. W. 2d 635 (Tex. 1999).

Thomas, J. L. (2002). Bartering. In A. A. Lazarus & O. Zur (Eds.), *Dual relationships and psychotherapy* (pp. 394–408). New York: Springer.

Thompson, V. L. S., Bazile, A., & Akbar, M. (2004). African Americans' perceptions of psychotherapy and psychotherapists. *Professional Psychology: Research and Practice, 35*(1), 19–26.

Tomm, K. (1993, January/February). The ethics of dual relationships. *The California Therapist*, pp. 7–19.

Totten, G., Lamb, D. H., & Reeder, G. D. (1990). *Tarasoff* and confidentiality in AIDS-related psychotherapy. *Professional Psychology: Research and Practice, 21*(3), 155–160.

Trull, T. J. (2005). *Clinical psychology* (7th ed.). Belmont, CA: Wadsworth/Thomson Learning.

Truscott, D., Evans, J., & Mansell, S. (1995). Outpatient psychotherapy with dangerous clients: A model for clinical decision making. *Psychology: Research and Practice, 26*(5), 484–490.

Twemlow, S. W. (1997). Exploitation of patients: Themes in the psychopathology of their therapists. *American Journal of Psychotherapy, 51*(3), 357–375.

Tymchuk, A. J. (1981). Ethical decision making and psychological treatment. *Journal of Psychiatric Treatment and Evaluation, 3*, 507–513.

United States Department of Health and Human Services. (2003). *Protecting the privacy of patients' health information*. Fact Sheet. Retrieved April 14, 2003, from http://www.hhs.gov/news/facts/privacy.html

Urofsky, R., & Sowa, C. (2004). Ethics education in CACREP-accredited counselor education programs. *Counseling and Values, 49*(1), 37–47.

Vacha-Haase, T., Davenport, D. S., & Kerewsky, S. D. (2004). Problematic students: Gatekeeping practices of academic professional psychology programs. *Professional Psychology: Research and Practice, 35*(2), 115–122.

VandeCreek, L., & Knapp, S. (1994). Ethical and legal issues. In F. M. Dattilio & A. Freeman (Eds.), *Cognitive-behavioral strategies in crisis intervention* (pp. 362–373). New York: Guilford Press.

VandeCreek, L., & Knapp, S. (2001). Tarasoff *and beyond: Legal and clinical considerations in the treatment of life-endangering patients* (3rd ed.). Sarasota, FL: Professional Resource Press.

VandenBos, G. R., & Williams, S. (2000). The Internet versus the telephone: What is telehealth, anyway? *Professional Psychology: Research and Practice, 31*(5), 490–492.

Vasquez, M. J. T. (1988). Counselor-client sexual contact: Implications for ethics training. *Journal of Counseling and Development, 67*(4), 238–241.

Vasquez, M. J. T. (1992). Psychologist as clinical supervisor: Promoting ethical practice. *Professional Psychology: Research and Practice, 23*(3), 196–202.

Vera, E. M., & Speight, S. L. (2003). Multicultural competence, social justice, and counseling psychology: Expanding our roles. *The Counseling Psychologist, 31*(3), 253–272.

*Vontress, C. E., Johnson, J. A., & Epp, L. R. (1999). *Cross-cultural counseling: A casebook.* Alexandria, VA: American Counseling Association.

Walden, S. L. (2006). Inclusion of the client's voice in ethical practice. In B. Herlihy & G. Corey (Eds.), *Boundary issues in counseling: Multiple roles and responsibilities* (2nd ed.). Alexandria, VA: American Counseling Association.

Walden, S. L., Herlihy, B., & Ashton, L. (2003). The evolution of ethics: Personal perspectives of ACA ethics committee chairs. *Journal of Counseling and Development, 81*(1), 106–110.

Waldo, S. L., & Malley, P. (1992). *Tarasoff* and its progeny: Implications for the school counselor. *The School Counselor, 40*, 46–54.

Walker, D. F., Gorsuch, R. L., & Tan, S. Y. (2004). Therapists' integration of religion and spirituality in counseling: A meta-analysis. *Counseling and Values, 49*(1), 69–80.

Walker, D. F., Gorsuch, R. L., & Tan, S. Y. (2005). Therapists' use of religious and spiritual interventions in Christian counseling: A preliminary report. *Counseling and Values, 49*(2), 107–119.

Wallace, W. A., & Hall, D. L. (1996). *Psychological consultation: Perspectives and applications.* Pacific Grove, CA: Brooks/Cole.

Wampold, B. E., & Bhati, K. S. (2004). Attending to the omissions: A historical examination of evidence-based practice movements. *Professional Psychology: Research and Practice, 35*(6), 563–570.

Warren, E. S. (2005). Future colleague or convenient friend: The ethics of mentorship. *Counseling and Values, 49*(2), 141–146.

Waters, R. (2004). Making a difference: Five therapists who've taken on the wider world. *Psychotherapy Networker, 28*(6), 32–43.

Watkins, C. E. (1985). Countertransference: Its impact on the counseling situation. *Journal of Counseling and Development, 63*(6), 356–359.

Webb, D. (2005). *The soul of counseling: A new model for understanding human experience.* Atascadero, CA: Impact Publishers.

*Weinrach, S. G., & Thomas, K. R. (1998). Diversity-sensitive counseling today: A postmodern clash of values. *Journal of Counseling and Development, 76*(2), 115–122.

Welfel, E. R. (2005). Accepting fallibility: A model for personal responsibility for nonegregious ethics infractions. *Counseling and Values, 49*(2), 120–131.

*Welfel, E. R. (2006). *Ethics in counseling and psychotherapy: Standards, research, and emerging issues* (3rd ed.). Belmont, CA: Thomson Brooks/Cole.

Werth, J. L., Jr. (1996). *Rational suicide? Implications for mental health professionals.* Washington, DC: Taylor & Francis.

Werth, J. L., Jr. (1999a). Mental health professionals and assisted death: Perceived ethical obligations and proposed guidelines for practice. *Ethics and Behavior, 9*(2), 159–183.

Werth, J. L., Jr. (1999b). The role of the mental health professional in helping significant others of persons who are assisted in death. *Death Studies, 23,* 239–255.

Werth, J. L., Jr. (1999c). When is a mental health professional competent to assess a person's decision to hasten death? *Ethics and Behavior, 9*(2), 141–157.

Werth, J. L., Jr. (2000). Recent developments in the debate over assisted death. In R. W. Maris, S. S. Canetto, J. L. McIntosh, & M. M. Silverman (Eds.), *Review of Suicidology* (pp. 255–276). New York: Guilford.

Werth, J. L, Jr., & Carney, J. (1994). Incorporating HIV-related issues into graduate student training. *Professional Psychology: Research and Practice, 25*(4), 458–465.

Werth, J. L., Jr., & Gordon, J. R. (2002). *Amicus curiae* brief for the United States Supreme Court on mental health issues associated with "physician-assisted suicide." *Journal of Counseling and Development, 80*(2), 160–172.

*Werth, J. L., Jr., & Holdwick, D. J. (2000). A primer on rational suicide and other forms of hastened death. *The Counseling Psychologist, 28*(4), 511–539.

Wheeler, N., & Bertram, B. (1994). Legal aspects of counseling: Avoiding lawsuits and legal problems. (Workshop material and video seminar). Alexandria, VA: American Counseling Association.

Whiston, S. C., & Emerson, S. (1989). Ethical implications for supervisors in counseling of trainees. *Counselor Education and Supervision, 28*(4), 318–325.

Wiederman, M. W., & Sansone, R. A. (1999). Sexuality training for professional psychologists: A national survey of training directors of doctoral programs and predoctoral internships. *Professional Psychology: Research and Practice, 30*(3), 312–317.

Williams, B. (2003). The worldview dimensions of individualism and collectivism: Implications for counseling. *Journal of Counseling and Development, 81*(3), 370–374.

Williams, M. H. (2000). Victimized by "victims": A taxonomy of antecedents of false complaints against psychologists. *Professional Psychology: Research and Practice, 31*(1), 75–81.

Wilson, F. R., Rapin, L. S., & Haley-Banez, L. (2004). How teaching group work can be guided by foundational documents: Best practice guidelines, diversity principles, training standards. *Journal for Specialists in Group Work, 29*(1), 19–29.

Wineburgh, M. (1998). Ethics, managed care, and outpatient psychotherapy. *Clinical Social Work Journal, 26*(4), 433–443.

*Woody, R. H. (1998). Bartering for psychological services. *Professional Psychology: Research and Practice, 29*(2), 174–178.

*Woody, R. H., & Woody, J. D. (2001). *Ethics in marriage and family therapy: Understanding the 2001 ethics code from the American Association for Marriage and Family Therapy.* Washington, DC: American Association for Marriage and Family Therapy.

Wrenn, C. G. (1962). The culturally encapsulated counselor. *Harvard Educational Review, 32,* 444–449.

Wrenn, C. G. (1985). Afterword: The culturally encapsulated counselor revisited. In P. Pedersen (Ed.), *Handbook of cross-cultural counseling and therapy* (pp. 323–329). Westport, CT: Greenwood Press.

Wright, J., Coley, S., & Corey, G. (1989, May). Challenges facing human services education today. *Journal of Counseling and Human Service Professions, 3*(2), 3–11.

Wubbolding, R. E. (2006). Case study: A suicidal teenager. In B. Herlihy & G. Corey (Eds.), *ACA ethical standards casebook* (6th ed.). Alexandria, VA: American Counseling Association.

Wyke v. Polk County School Board, 129 F. 3d 560 (11th Cir. 1997).

Wylie, M. S. (1995). Diagnosing for dollars? *The Family Therapy Networker, 19*(3), 22–69.

*Yalom, I., with Leszcz, M. (2005). *The theory and practice of group psychotherapy* (5th ed.). New York: Basic Books.

Yalom, I. (1998), *Lying on the couch: A novel.* New York: Perennial.

Yarhouse, M. A. (2003). Ethical issues in considering "religious impairment" in diagnosis. *Mental Health, Religion & Culture, 6,* 131–147.

Yarhouse, M. A., & Burkett, L. A. (2002). An inclusive response to LGB and conservative religious persons: The case of same-sex attraction and behavior. *Professional Psychology: Research and Practice, 33*(3), 235–241.

Yarhouse, M. A., & VanOrman, B. T. (1999). When psychologists work with religious clients: Applications of the general principles of ethical conduct. *Professional Psychology: Research and Practice, 30*(6), 557–562.

Younggren, J. N. (2000). Is managed care really just another unethical Model T? *The Counseling Psychologist, 28*(2), 253–262.

Younggren, J. N., & Gottlieb, M. C. (2004). Managing risk when contemplating multiple relationships. *Professional Psychology: Research and Practice, 35*(3), 255–260.

Zinnbauer, B. J., & Pargament, K. I. (2000). Working with the sacred: Four approaches to religious and spiritual issues in counseling. *Journal of Counseling and Development, 78*(2), 162–171.

Zur, O. (1994). Psychotherapists and their families: The effect of clinical practice on individuals and family dynamics. *Psychotherapy in Private Practice, 13*(1), 69–75.

Zur, O. (1999). The demonization of dual relationship: How prohibition on non-sexual dual relationships compromises effective therapy and keeps incompetent therapists in business. *Critical thinking about psychology series, monograph #2.* Oakland, CA: Independent Thinking Review.

Zur, O. (2000a). Going too far in the right direction: Reflections on the mythic ban of dual relationships. *The California Psychologist, 33*(4), 14–16.

Zur, O. (2000b). In celebration of dual relationships. *The Independent Practitioner, 20,* 97–100.

Zur, O. (2002a). How consensus regarding the prohibition of dual relationships has been contrived. In A. A. Lazarus & O. Zur (Eds.), *Dual relationships and psychotherapy* (pp. 449–462). New York: Springer.

Zur, O. (2002b). Out-of-office experience: When crossing office boundaries and engaging in dual relationships are clinically beneficial and ethically sound. In A. A. Lazarus & O. Zur (Eds.), *Dual relationships and psychotherapy* (pp. 88–97). New York: Springer.

Zur, O. (2005). Tarasoff *statute in California: An update.* Retrieved February 1, 2005, from http://www.drzur.com/tarasoff.html.

Zur, O., & Lazarus, A. A. (2002). Six arguments against dual relationships and their rebuttals. In A. A. Lazarus & O. Zur (Eds.), *Dual relationships and psychotherapy* (pp. 3–24). New York: Springer.

Credits

This page constitutes an extension of the copyright page. We have made every effort to trace the ownership of all copyrighted material and to secure permission from copyright holders. In the event of any question arising as to the use of any material, we will be pleased to make the necessary corrections in future printings. Thanks are due to the following authors, publishers, and agents for permission to use the material indicated.

Chapter 1.

7: Canadian Counselling Association (1999). CCA Code of Ethics. Reprinted with permission. **7:** National Association of Social Workers (1999). Code of Ethics. Washington, DC: Author. Copyright 1999, National Association of Social Workers, Inc. Used by permission. **10:** Commission on Rehabilitation Counselor Certification (2001). Code of Professional Ethics for Rehabilitation Counselors. Used by permission. **11:** Canadian Counselling Association (1999). CCA Code of Ethics. Reprinted with permission. **17:** American Counseling Association (2005). Code of Ethics. Alexandria, VA: Author. **17:** American Psychological Association (2004). Ethical principles of psychologists and code of conduct. American Psychologist, 57(12), 1060-1073. Copyright © 2004 by the American Psychological Association. **18:** American Counseling Association (2005). Code of Ethics. Alexandria, VA: Author. **18:** American Psychological Association (2004). Ethical principles of psychologists and code of conduct. American Psychologist, 57(12), 1060-1073. Copyright © 2004 by the American Psychological Association. **18:** National Association of Social Workers (1999). Code of Ethics. Washington, DC: Author. Copyright 1999, National Association of Social Workers, Inc. Used by permission. **19:** American Counseling Association (2005). Code of Ethics. Alexandria, VA: Author. **19:** American Psychological Association (2004). Ethical principles of psychologists and code of conduct. American Psychologist, 57(12), 1060-1073. Copyright © 2004 by the American Psychological Association. **24:** American Counseling Association (2005). Code of Ethics. Alexandria, VA: Author. **24:** American Counseling Association (2005). Code of Ethics. Alexandria, VA: Author. **24:** American Psychological Association (2004). Ethical principles of psychologists and code of conduct. American Psychologist, 57(12), 1060-1073. Copyright © 2004 by the American Psychological Association. **24:** National Association of Social Workers (1999). Code of Ethics. Washington, DC: Author. Copyright 1999, National Association of Social Workers, Inc. Used by permission. **24:** National Organization for Human Service Education (2000). Ethical Standards of Human Service Professionals.

Chapter 2.

40: Commission on Rehabilitation Counselor Certification (2001). Code of Professional Ethics for Rehabilitation Counselors. Used by permission. **41:** American Psychological Association (2004). Ethical principles of psychologists and code of conduct. American Psychologist, 57(12), 1060-1073. Copyright © 2004 by the American Psychological Association. **41:** American Psychological Association (2004). Ethical principles of psychologists and code of conduct. American Psychologist, 57(12), 1060-1073. Copyright © 2004 by the American Psychological Association. **46:** American Psychological Association (2004). Ethical principles of psychologists and code of conduct. American Psychologist, 57(12), 1060-1073. Copyright © 2004 by the American Psychological Association. **63:** American Association for Marriage and Family Therapy (2001). AAMFT Code of Ethics. Washington, DC: Author. **63:** American Counseling Association (2005). Code of Ethics. Alexandria, VA: Author. **63:** American Psychological Association (2004). Ethical principles of psychologists and code of conduct. American Psychologist, 57(12), 1060-1073. Copyright © 2004 by the American Psychological Association. **63:** National Association of Social Workers (1999). Code of Ethics. Washington, DC: Author. Copyright 1999, National Association of Social Workers, Inc. Used by permission. **64:** Canadian Assn. of Social Workers, 1994. **64:** Feminist Therapy Institute (2000). Feminist Therapy Code of Ethics (Revised, 1999). San Francisco: Feminist Therapy Institute. Copyright 2000, Feminist Therapy Institute, Inc. FTI, c/o Marcia Chappell, 912 Five Islands Road, Georgetown, Maine 04548; www.feministtherapyinstitute.org.

Chapter 3.

75: American Counseling Association (2005). Code of Ethics. Alexandria, VA: Author. **75:** American Psychological Association (2004). Ethical principles of psychologists and code of conduct. American Psychologist, 57(12), 1060-1073. Copyright © 2004 by the American Psychological Association. **75:** American School Counselor Association (2004). Ethical Standards for School Counselors. Alexandria, VA: Author. Used by permission. **102:** American Counseling Association (2005). Code of Ethics. Alexandria, VA: Author. **102:** American Counseling Association (2005). Code of Ethics. Alexandria, VA: Author. **102:** American Counseling Association (2005). Code of Ethics.

Chapter 4.

118: Feminist Therapy Institute (2000). Feminist Therapy Code of Ethics (Revised, 1999). San Francisco: Feminist Therapy Institute. Copyright 2000, Feminist Therapy Institute, Inc. FTI, c/o Marcia Chappell, 912 Five Islands Road, Georgetown, Maine 04548; www.feministtherapyinstitute.org. **119:** American Psychological Association (2004). Ethical principles of psychologists and code of conduct. American Psychologist, 57(12), 1060-1073. Copyright © 2004 by the American Psychological Association. **119:** Canadian Assn. of Social Workers, 1994. **119:** Canadian Counselling Association (1999). CCA Code of Ethics. Reprinted with permission. **119:** National Association of Social Workers (1999). Code of Ethics. Washington, DC: Author. Copyright 1999, National Association of Social Workers, Inc. Used by permission. **127:** American Psychological Association (2004). Ethical principles of psychologists and code of conduct. American Psychologist, 57(12), 1060-1073. Copyright © 2004 by the American Psychological Association.

Chapter 5.

155: American Counseling Association (2005). Code of Ethics. Alexandria, VA: Author. **155:** American Mental Health Counselors Association. **155:** American Psychological Association (2004). Ethical principles of psychologists and code of conduct. American Psychologist, 57(12), 1060-1073. Copyright © 2004 by the American Psychological Association. **155:** Feminist Therapy Institute (2000). Feminist Therapy Code of Ethics (Revised, 1999). San Francisco: Feminist Therapy Institute. Copyright 2000, Feminist Therapy Institute, Inc. FTI, c/o Marcia Chappell, 912 Five Islands Road, Georgetown, Maine 04548; www.feministtherapyinstitute.org. **155:** National Association of Social Workers (1999). Code of Ethics. Washington, DC: Author. Copyright 1999, National Association of Social Workers, Inc. Used by permission. **156:** International Association of Marriage and Family Counselors (2000). Ethical Standards. Used by permission. **162:** American Association for Marriage and Family Therapy (2001). AAMFT Code of Ethics. Washington, DC: Author. **162:** American Counseling Association (2005). Code of Ethics. Alexandria, VA: Author. **162:** American Psychological Association (2004). Ethical principles of psychologists and code of conduct. American Psychologist, 57(12), 1060-1073. Copyright © 2004 by the American Psychological Association. **162:** Commission on Rehabilitation Counselor Certification (2001). Code of Professional Ethics for Rehabilitation Counselors. Used by permission. **162:** National Association of Social Workers (1999). Code of Ethics. Washington, DC: Author. Copyright 1999, National Association of Social Workers, Inc. Used by permission. **164:** National Association of Social Workers (1999). Code of Ethics. Washington, DC: Author. Copyright 1999, National Association of Social Workers, Inc. Used by permission. **165:** American Counseling Association (2005). Code of Ethics. Alexandria, VA: Author. **165:** Canadian Counseling Association (1999). CCA Code of Ethics. Reprinted with permission. **166:** American Mental Health Counselors Association. **167:** National Association of Social Workers (1999). Code of Ethics. Washington, DC: Author. Copyright 1999, National Association of Social Workers, Inc. Used by permission. **171:** American Psychological Association (2004). Ethical principles of psychologists and code of conduct. American Psychologist, 57(12), 1060-1073. Copyright © 2004 by the American Psychological Association. **171:** Canadian Counseling Association (1999). CCA Code of Ethics. Reprinted with permission. **171:** National Association of Social Workers (1999). Code of Ethics. Washington, DC: Author. Copyright 1999, National Association of Social Workers, Inc. Used by permission. **173:** American School Counselor Association (2004). Ethical Standards for School Counselors. Alexandria, VA: Author. Used by permission. **175:** Canadian Counseling Association (1999). CCA Code of Ethics. Reprinted with permission. **181:** American Psychological Association (2004). Ethical principles of psychologists and code of conduct. American Psychologist, 57(12), 1060-1073. Copyright © 2004 by the American Psychological Association. **187:** American Counseling Association (2005). Code of Ethics. Alexandria, VA: Author. **188:** American School Counselor Association (2004). Ethical Standards for School Counselors. Alexandria, VA. Used by permission.

Chapter 6.

209: American Association for Marriage and Family Therapy (2001). AAMFT Code of Ethics. Washington, DC: Author. **209:** American Counseling Association (2005). Code of Ethics. Alexandria, VA: Author. **209:** American Mental Health Counselors Association. **209:** American Psychological Association (2004). Ethical principles of psychologists and code of conduct. American Psychologist, 57(12), 1060-1073. Copyright © 2004 by the American Psychological Association. **209:** American School Counselor Association (2004). Ethical Standards for School Counselors. Alexandria, VA: Author. Used by permission. **209:** Canadian Counseling Association (1999). CCA Code of Ethics. Reprinted with permission. **209:** National Association of Social Workers (1999). Code of Ethics. Washington, DC: Author. Copyright 1999, National Association of Social Workers, Inc. Used by permission. **210:** American Psychological Association (2004). Ethical principles of psychologists and code of conduct. American Psychologist, 57(12), 1060-1073. Copyright © 2004 by the American Psychological Association. **210:** International Association of Marriage and Family Counselors (2000). Ethical Standards. Used by permission. **213:** American Counseling Association (2005). Code of Ethics. Alexandria, VA: Author. **213:** American Psychological Association (2004). Ethical principles of psychologists and code of conduct. American Psychologist, 57(12), 1060-1073. Copyright © 2004 by the American Psychological Association. **213:** National Association of Social Workers (1999). Code of Ethics. Washington, DC: Author. Copyright 1999, National Association of Social Workers, Inc. Used by permission. **214:** American School Counselor Association (2004). Ethical Standards for School Counselors. Alexandria, VA: Author. Used by permission. **217:** American School Counselor Association (2004). Ethical Standards for School Counselors. Alexandria, VA: Author. Used by permission. **251:** American Counseling Association (2005). Code of Ethics. Alexandria, VA: Author. **252:** Commission on Rehabilitation Counselor Certification (2001). Code of Professional Ethics for Rehabilitation Counselors. Used by permission.

Chapter 7.

264: American Association for Marriage and Family Therapy (2001).

AAMFT Code of Ethics. Washington, DC: Author. **264:** American School Counselor Association (2004). Ethical Standards for School Counselors. Alexandria, VA: Author. Used by permission. **264:** Canadian Assn. of Social Workers, 1994. **264:** Feminist Therapy Institute (2000). Feminist Therapy Code of Ethics (Revised, 1999). San Francisco: Feminist Therapy Institute. Copyright 2000, Feminist Therapy Institute, Inc. FTI, c/o Marcia Chappell, 912 Five Islands Road, Georgetown, Maine 04548; www.feministtherapyinstitute.org. **264:** National Association of Social Workers (1999). Code of Ethics. Washington, DC: Author. Copyright 1999, National Association of Social Workers, Inc. Used by permission. **264:** National Organization for Human Service Education (2000). Ethical Standards of Human Service Professionals. **265:** American Counseling Association (2005). Code of Ethics. Alexandria, VA: Author. **265:** American Psychological Association (2004). Ethical principles of psychologists and code of conduct. American Psychologist, 57(12), 1060-1073. Copyright © 2004 by the American Psychological Association. **279:** American Counseling Association (2005). Code of Ethics. Alexandria, VA: Author. **279:** American Psychological Association (2004). Ethical principles of psychologists and code of conduct. American Psychologist, 57(12), 1060-1073. Copyright © 2004 by the American Psychological Association. **280:** American Association for Marriage and Family Therapy (2001). AAMFT Code of Ethics. Washington, DC: Author. **280:** National Association of Social Workers (1999). Code of Ethics. Washington, DC: Author. Copyright 1999, National Association of Social Workers, Inc. Used by permission. **285:** American Counseling Association (2005). Code of Ethics. Alexandria, VA: Author. **288:** Canadian Counseling Association (1999). CCA Code of Ethics. Reprinted with permission. **296:** American Association for Marriage and Family Therapy (2001). AAMFT Code of Ethics. Washington, DC: Author. **296:** American Counseling Association (2005). Code of Ethics. Alexandria, VA: Author. **296:** American Psychological Association (2004). Ethical principles of psychologists and code of conduct. American Psychologist, 57(12), 1060-1073. Copyright © 2004 by the American Psychological Association. **296:** Canadian Assn. of Social Workers, 1994. **296:** National Association of Social Workers (1999). Code of Ethics. Washington, DC: Author. Copyright 1999, National Association of Social Workers, Inc. Used by permission. **302:** American Counseling Association (2005). Code of Ethics. Alexandria, VA: Author. **302:** American Psychological Association (2004). Ethical principles of psychologists and code of conduct. American Psychologist, 57(12), 1060-1073. Copyright © 2004 by the American Psychological Association. **302:** Canadian Counseling Association (1999). CCA Code of Ethics. Reprinted with permission. **302:** Commission on Rehabilitation Counselor Certification (2001). Code of Professional Ethics for Rehabilitation Counselors. Used by permission. **302:** National Association of Social Workers (1999). Code of Ethics. Washington, DC: Author. Copyright 1999, National Association of Social Workers, Inc. Used by permission. **303:** American Association for Marriage and Family Therapy (2001). AAMFT Code of Ethics.

Chapter 8.

316: American Association for Marriage and Family Therapy (2001). AAMFT Code of Ethics. Washington, DC: Author. **316:** American Psychological Association (2004). Ethical principles of psychologists and code of conduct. American Psychologist, 57(12), 1060-1073. Copyright © 2004 by the American Psychological Association. **316:** American School Counselor Association (2004). Ethical Standards for School Counselors. Alexandria, VA: Author. Used by permission. **316:** Feminist Therapy Institute (2000). Feminist Therapy Code of Ethics (Revised, 1999). San Francisco: Feminist Therapy Institute. Copyright 2000, Feminist Therapy Institute, Inc. FTI, c/o Marcia Chappell, 912 Five Islands Road, Georgetown, Maine 04548; www.feministtherapyinstitute.org. **316:** International Association of Marriage and Family Counselors (2000). Ethical Standards. Used by permission. **316:** National Association of Social Workers (1999). Code of Ethics. Washington, DC: Author. Copyright 1999, National Association of Social Workers, Inc. Used by permission. **317:** American Counseling Association (2005). Code of Ethics. Alexandria, VA: Author. **317:** American Mental Health Counselors Association. **317:** Canadian Assn. of Social Workers, 1994. **317:** Canadian Counselling Association (1999). CCA Code of Ethics. Reprinted with permission. **318:** National Association of Social Workers (1999). Code of Ethics. Washington, DC: Author. Copyright 1999, National Association of Social Workers, Inc. Used by permission. **326:** American Counseling Association (2005). Code of Ethics. Alexandria, VA: Author. **326:** American Psychological Association (2004). Ethical principles of psychologists and code of conduct. American Psychologist, 57(12), 1060-1073. Copyright © 2004 by the American Psychological Association. **341:** American Association for Marriage and Family Therapy (2001). AAMFT Code of Ethics. Washington, DC: Author. **341:** American Counseling Association (2005). Code of Ethics. Alexandria, VA: Author. **341:** American Mental Health Counselors Association. **341:** American Psychological Association (2004). Ethical principles of psychologists and code of conduct. American Psychologist, 57(12), 1060-1073. Copyright © 2004 by the American Psychological Association. **341:** American School Counselor Association (2004). Ethical Standards for School Counselors. Alexandria, VA: Author. Used by permission. **341:** National Association of Social Workers (1999). Code of Ethics. Washington, DC: Author. Copyright 1999, National Association of Social Workers, Inc. Used by permission.

Chapter 9.

367: American Counseling Association (2005). Code of Ethics. Alexandria, VA: Author. **372:** American Counseling Association (2005). Code of Ethics. Alexandria, VA: Author. **374:** American Counseling Association (2005). Code of Ethics. Alexandria, VA: Author. **374:** Commission on Rehabilitation Counselor Certification (2001). Code of Professional Ethics for Rehabilitation Counselors. Used by permission. **375:** American Association for Marriage and Family

Therapy (2001). AAMFT Code of Ethics. Washington, DC. **375:** American Psychological Association (2004). Ethical principles of psychologists and code of conduct. American Psychologist, 57(12), 1060-1073. Copyright © 2004 by the American Psychological Association. **375:** International Association of Marriage and Family Counselors (2000). Ethical Standards. Used by permission. **375:** National Association of Social Workers (1999). Code of Ethics. Washington, DC: Author. Copyright 1999, National Association of Social Workers, Inc. Used by permission. **377:** American Counseling Association (2005). Code of Ethics. Alexandria, VA: Author. **379:** American Association for Marriage and Family Therapy (2001). AAMFT Code of Ethics. Washington, DC: Author. **379:** American Counseling Association (2005). Code of Ethics. Alexandria, VA: Author. **384:** National Association of Social Workers (1999). Code of Ethics. Washington, DC: Author. Copyright 1999, National Association of Social Workers, Inc. Used by permission.

Chapter 10.

413: American Counseling Association (2005). Code of Ethics. Alexandria, VA: Author. **413:** American Psychological Association (2004). Ethical principles of psychologists and code of conduct. American Psychologist, 57(12), 1060-1073. Copyright © 2004 by the American Psychological Association. **413:** Commission on Rehabilitation Counselor Certification (2001). Code of Professional Ethics for Rehabilitation Counselors. Used by permission. **415:** American Counseling Association (2005). Code of Ethics. Alexandria, VA: Author. **426:** American Psychological Association (2004). Ethical principles of psychologists and code of conduct. American Psychologist, 57(12), 1060-1073. Copyright © 2004 by the American Psychological Association. **427:** National Association of Social Workers (1999). Code of Ethics. Washington, DC: Author. Copyright 1999, National Association of Social Workers, Inc. Used by permission. **428:** American Psychological Association (2004). Ethical principles of psychologists and code of conduct. American Psychologist, 57(12), 1060-1073. Copyright © 2004 by the American Psychological Association. **430:** American Counseling Association (2005). Code of Ethics. Alexandria, VA.

Chapter 11.

439: American Association for Marriage and Family Therapy (2001). AAMFT Code of Ethics. Washington, DC. **445:** International Association of Marriage and Family Counselors (2000). Ethical Standards. Used by permission. **448:** International Association of Marriage and Family Counselors (2000). Ethical Standards. Used by permission. **454:** American Counseling Association (2005). Code of Ethics. Alexandria, VA.

Chapter 12.

470: American Counseling Association (2005). Code of Ethics. Alexandria, VA. **474:** American Counseling Association (2005). Code of Ethics. Alexandria, VA: Author. **474:** American Psychological Association (2004). Ethical principles of psychologists and code of conduct. American Psychologist, 57(12), 1060-1073. Copyright © 2004 by the American Psychological Association. **474:** American School Counselor Association (2004). Ethical Standards for School Counselors. Alexandria, VA: Author. Used by permission.

Chapter 13.

489: American School Counselor Association (2004). Ethical Standards for School Counselors. Alexandria, VA. Used by permission. **489:** Canadian Assn. of Social Workers, 1994. **489:** National Association of Social Workers (1999). Code of Ethics. Washington, DC. Copyright 1999, National Association of Social Workers, Inc. Used by permission. **489:** National Organization for Human Service Education (2000). Ethical Standards of Human Service Professionals. **490:** Feminist Therapy Institute (2000). Feminist Therapy Code of Ethics (Revised, 1999). San Francisco: Feminist Therapy Institute. Copyright 2000, Feminist Therapy Institute, Inc. FTI, c/o Marcia Chappell, 912 Five Islands Road, Georgetown, Maine 04548; www.feministtherapyinstitute.org.

Author Index

Subject Index

TO THE OWNER OF THIS BOOK:

We hope that you have found *Issues & Ethics in the Helping Professions,* Seventh Edition useful. So that this book can be improved in a future edition, would you take the time to complete this sheet and return it? Thank you.

School and address:____

Department:____

Instructor's name:____

1. What I like most about this book is:______________________________

2. What I like least about this book is:

3. My general reaction to this book is:

4. The name of the course in which I used this book is:

5. Were all of the chapters of the book assigned for you to read?________________

   If not, which ones weren't?______________________________

6. In the space below, or on a separate sheet of paper, please write specific suggestions for improving this book and anything else you'd care to share about your experience in using this book.

DO NOT STAPLE. PLEASE SEAL WITH TAPE.

FOLD HERE

NO POSTAGE NECESSARY IF MAILED IN THE UNITED STATES

BUSINESS REPLY MAIL

FIRST-CLASS MAIL PERMIT NO. 34 BELMONT CA

POSTAGE WILL BE PAID BY ADDRESSEE

Attn: Marquita Flemming, Counseling

BrooksCole/Thomson Learning
10 Davis Drive
Belmont, CA 94002-9801

FOLD HERE

OPTIONAL:

Your name:____ Date: _____________

May we quote you, either in promotion for *Issues & Ethics in the Helping Professions,* Seventh Edition, or in future publishing ventures?

Yes: ________________ No: __________

Sincerely yours,

Gerald Corey

Marianne Schneider Corey

Patrick Callanan